AF681943

booksonline

**Read this book online today:**

With SAP PRESS BooksOnline we offer you online access to knowledge from the leading SAP experts. Whether you use it as a beneficial supplement or as an alternative to the printed book, with SAP PRESS BooksOnline you can:

- Access your book anywhere, at any time. All you need is an Internet connection.
- Perform full text searches on your book and on the entire SAP PRESS library.
- Build your own personalized SAP library.

**The SAP PRESS customer advantage:**

Register this book today at *www.sap-press.com* and obtain exclusive free trial access to its online version. If you like it (and we think you will), you can choose to purchase permanent, unrestricted access to the online edition at a very special price!

**Here's how to get started:**

1. Visit *www.sap-press.com*.
2. Click on the link for SAP PRESS BooksOnline and login (or create an account).
3. Enter your free trial license key, shown below in the corner of the page.
4. Try out your online book with full, unrestricted access for a limited time!

Your personal free trial **license key** for this online book is: nvdx-t6by-g52f-sz7w

# ABAP™ Cookbook

SAP PRESS

SAP PRESS is a joint initiative of SAP and Galileo Press. The know-how offered by SAP specialists combined with the expertise of the Galileo Press publishing house offers the reader expert books in the field. SAP PRESS features first-hand information and expert advice, and provides useful skills for professional decision-making.

SAP PRESS offers a variety of books on technical and business related topics for the SAP user. For further information, please visit our website: *www.sap-press.com*.

James Wood
Object-Oriented Programming with ABAP Objects
2009, app. 400 pp.
978-1-59229-235-6

Christian Assig, Aldo Hermann Fobbe, Arno Niemietz
Object Services in ABAP
2010, app. 200 pp.
978-1-59229-339-1

Tobias Trapp
XML Data Exchange Using ABAP
2007, app. 150 pp.
978-1-59229-076-5

Thorsten Franz, Tobias Trapp
ABAP Objects: Application Development from Scratch
2008, app. 500 pp.
978-1-59229-211-0

James Wood

# ABAP™ Cookbook

## Programming Recipes for Everyday Solutions

Galileo Press

Bonn • Boston

Galileo Press is named after the Italian physicist, mathematician and philosopher Galileo Galilei (1564–1642). He is known as one of the founders of modern science and an advocate of our contemporary, heliocentric worldview. His words *Eppur se muove* (And yet it moves) have become legendary. The Galileo Press logo depicts Jupiter orbited by the four Galilean moons, which were discovered by Galileo in 1610.

**Editor** Stefan Proksch
**Developmental Editor** Kelly Grace Harris
**Copyeditor** Julie McNamee
**Cover Design** Graham Geary
**Photo Credit** iStockphoto.com/The-Tor
**Layout Design** Vera Brauner
**Production Editor** Kelly O'Callaghan
**Assistant Production Editor** Graham Geary
**Typesetting** Publishers' Design and Production Services, Inc.
**Printed and bound in** Canada

**ISBN 978-1-59229-326-1**

1st Edition 2010

**Library of Congress Cataloging-in-Publication Data**
Wood, James, 1978-
ABAP Cookbook: Programming Recipes for Everyday Solutions / James Wood.
p. cm.
Includes bibliographical references and index.
ISBN-13: 978-1-59229-326-1 (alk. paper)
ISBN-10: 1-59229-326-3 (alk. paper)
1. ABAP/4 (Computer program language) I. Title.
QA76.73.A12W66 2010
005.13'3—dc22 2010009054

# Contents at a Glance

# Contents

# Introduction

Unlike a lot of hard-core techies my age, I didn't grow up in front of a computer. Instead, I spent much of my formative years in the kitchen experimenting with all kinds of recipes. When I discovered programming later in life, I found that there were quite a few similarities between the two tasks. Consequently, I have made a habit of developing and collecting programming *recipes* over the years. This book is a collection of many of these recipes.

As a connoisseur of programming books, I must confess that I have mixed feelings about programming cookbooks. Frequently, I have purchased a cookbook to help me solve a particular problem and then filed it away on my bookshelf never to be used again. My goal with this book is to give you something more. Rather than simply showing you a solution in source code, I start from the ground up by describing problem context, solution alternatives, and the thought process that goes into the development of a solution. As you read through these chapters, I hope you'll pick up on useful tips and best practices that will help you become a better programmer.

## Target Group and Prerequisites

This book is intended for ABAP application developers that have some basic experience writing ABAP programs using the ABAP Development Workbench. Basic ABAP language concepts are not covered in this book, so if you haven't worked with ABAP before, then I recommend that you start off by reading *ABAP Objects – ABAP Programming in SAP NetWeaver* (SAP PRESS, 2007). In addition, as many of the newer features covered are based on the object-oriented extensions to ABAP, allow me to offer a shameless plug for my other book: *Object-Oriented Programming with ABAP Objects* (SAP PRESS, 2009).

Though many of the topics covered in this book extend beyond the context of ABAP (e.g., Web services, etc.), no preexisting background knowledge on these subjects is required. Here, introductions are provided to help you understand these concepts before applying them to ABAP-based solutions.

Some of the recipes considered are based on newer features to the SAP NetWeaver Application Server (SAP NetWeaver AS ABAP). Where appropriate, I point out these dependencies so you can determine whether the solution is relevant for your system.

To help you follow along with the examples demonstrated in the book, I've provided two source code bundles that you can install on your local SAP NetWeaver AS ABAP system:

- The first bundle includes a transport file that contains reusable library code that can be used in real-life development projects. Each of the development objects included in this bundle are prefixed using the /BOWDK/ namespace.
- The second bundle contains the example programs described throughout the course of the book. These programs are stored as plain text files, and so on.

Each of the source code bundles can be downloaded from the book's companion website at *www.sap-press.com* and *www.bowdarkconsulting.com/books/abapcookbook*.

Finally, if you don't have access to an SAP NetWeaver AS ABAP system, you can download a trial version from the SAP Developer Network at *www.sdn.sap.com*. From the SDN Community main page, select DOWNLOADS • SOFTWARE • SAP NETWEAVER MAIN RELEASES to find the version of the SAP NetWeaver AS ABAP that matches your preferred operating system. Each download package comes with a set of instructions to help you get started. The SAP Developer Network forums can also provide useful tips if you run into problems.

## Structure of the Book

One of my goals in writing this book was to make it *readable*. Frequently, cookbooks are positioned as reference manuals that you occasionally flip through to find a solution to a particular problem. While this book can be used in that capacity, we also hope that you will find each chapter to be an interesting read in and of itself.

For the most part, you'll find that each of the following chapters is self-contained. However, where appropriate, I refer to previous chapters so that you can see how certain technologies can be used together to implement more sophisticated solutions.

- **Chapter 1: String Processing Techniques**
  To begin, I look at some of the basic and advanced string processing capabilities available in ABAP. In particular, I focus your attention around the *regular expression* support added with release 7.0 of the SAP NetWeaver AS ABAP.
- **Chapter 2: Working with Numbers, Dates, and Bytes**
  In this chapter, I look at some of the lesser-known features of elementary data types provided in ABAP. Here, you'll see examples demonstrating the use of random number generators, advanced date/time calculations, and byte string manipulation.
- **Chapter 3: Dynamic and Reflective Programming**
  This chapter is all about the dynamic programming capabilities available in ABAP. Topics discussed here include field symbols, data references, and the *ABAP Runtime Type Services* (RTTS). Throughout the course of the discussion, I provide lots of practical examples that demonstrate how to use these features to develop generic solutions to common problems.
- **Chapter 4: ABAP and Unicode**
  If you've heard about Unicode but are unsure what it's all about, then this chapter is for you. The chapter begins by describing what Unicode is and how it relates to other character-encoding standards, such as ASCII. From there, I look at the impacts of Unicode support in SAP NetWeaver AS ABAP from an ABAP perspective. Finally, I conclude the discussion by showing you how to work with built-in system classes that can assist you in data conversion processes, and so on.
- **Chapter 5: Working with Files**
  This chapter shows you how to work with files in ABAP. Topics discussed include the ABAP file interface used to process files on the SAP NetWeaver AS ABAP host, frontend services used to process files on client workstations, ZIP file processing, and much more.
- **Chapter 6: Database Programming**
  Database programming is a fundamental task for any ABAP developer. This chapter goes beyond basic SQL programming to show you how to work with the *Persistence Service* framework provided with ABAP Object Services. Additional topics include text objects and external database access.
- **Chapter 7: Transactional Programming**
  In this chapter, I show you how to work with transactions in ABAP. In particular, I show you how to use the following features of SAP NetWeaver AS ABAP to implement reliable transactions:

- SAP Logical Units of Work
- The Transaction Service provided with ABAP Object Services
- The SAP Lock Concept
- Change documents

- **Chapter 8: XML Processing in ABAP**
  This chapter explores the XML processing capabilities of the ABAP programming language. I begin the discussion by showing you how to work with the iXML library integrated into the ABAP runtime environment. Then, I explain the concept of *XML transformations* using the XSLT and Simple Transformation languages.
- **Chapter 9: Web Programming with the ICF**
  In this chapter, I show you how to use the *Internet Connection Framework* (ICF) to develop programs that use the features of the Web. Here, I frame the discussion around the concept of *RESTful Web services* by demonstrating how to consume and provide these services using the ICF library. Along the way, I introduce you to basic Web technologies such as HTTP, URLs, and so on.
- **Chapter 10: Web Services**
  This chapter expands on Chapter 9 by showing you how to work with SOAP-based Web services using the ABAP *Web Service Framework*. I begin the discussion by introducing core Web service technologies such as SOAP, WSDL, and UDDI. Then, I show you how to use the Web Service Framework tools to Web service-enable existing development objects. Finally, I conclude the discussion by showing you how to develop *proxy objects* that simplify the way you consume Web services.
- **Chapter 11: Email Programming**
  In this chapter, I show you how to send and receive emails using the *Business Communication Services* (BCS) framework. After a brief introduction to email protocols, this chapter demonstrates some basic and advanced email processing scenarios using attachments, rich text email, and inbound processing rules.
- **Chapter 12: Security Programming**
  This chapter describes the creation of a holistic security model using ABAP-based technologies. The first part of this chapter discusses the *ABAP Authorization Concept*, showing you how your custom developments can be integrated with standard SAP security tools. From there, I branch out and look at ways of encrypting data, performing virus scans on incoming files, and protecting Web content using CAPTCHA.

- **Chapter 13: Logging and Tracing**
  In this chapter, I show you how to use the *Business Application Log* (BAL) to realize logging and tracing requirements in your custom ABAP programs. After introducing the core features of the BAL, this chapter considers the development of a custom BAL class-based library that expands upon the basic features of the BAL to implement configurable logging.
- **Chapter 14: Interacting with the Operating System**
  This chapter demonstrates the use of *external commands* that access features of the underlying SAP NetWeaver AS ABAP host operating system. After describing the basic architecture of the surrounding API, this chapter shows you how to create custom commands to execute scripts written in scripting languages such as Perl or Python.
- **Chapter 15: Interprocess Communication**
  This chapter introduces you to two basic methods of implementing interprocess communication in ABAP: data clusters and shared memory objects. Throughout the course of this chapter, I describe both of these features in the context of examples that demonstrate practical use cases.
- **Chapter 16: Parallel and Distributed Processing with RFCs**
  In this final chapter, I show you how to implement parallelized solutions using the RFC interface. Here, I explore the implementation of such solutions from the ground up. I also consider situations in which parallelized solutions are not practical and should be avoided.

## Conventions

This book contains many examples demonstrating syntax, functionality, and so on. To distinguish these sections, I use a font similar to the one used in many integrated development environments to improve code readability (see Listing I.1). As new syntax concepts are introduced, I highlight them using a bold listing font (i.e., the `PUBLIC SECTION` statement in Listing I.1).

```
CLASS lcl_test DEFINITION.
  PUBLIC SECTION.
    ...
ENDCLASS.
```

**Listing I.1** Code Syntax Format Example

Also, throughout the book, you'll find that we draw your attention to certain items using special icons in the margin area. These icons can be interpreted as follows:

**Tip:** This icon is used to point out important tips that you can use when working in a particular development area.

**Caution:** This icon is used as a caution flag to draw your attention to potential pitfalls and/or errors.

**Instructions:** This icon identifies a set of instructions that you can use when working on your own developments.

## Programming Style

While this book is positioned as a cookbook, it also endeavors to demonstrate best programming practices. Of course, having said that, there are certain situations where it makes sense to bend the rules a bit to emphasize a particular point or for the sake of brevity. Nevertheless, the following general programming conventions are used to develop the example programs demonstrated in the book:

- Wherever possible, object-oriented programming is used.
- Core functionality in example reports is encapsulated in local classes. This design approach allows us to focus on the structure of the code without having to dig through includes and/or Class Builder screens.
- Only the relevant portions of the code is displayed in the book. You can find the complete implementations in the provided source code bundles.

If you're interested in learning more about best practices for ABAP programming, I highly recommend *Official ABAP Programming Guidelines* (SAP PRESS, 2009).

## Acknowledgments

In many ways, this book is the culmination of years of reading, tinkering, and experimenting. During this journey, I have been fortunate to be surrounded by some great people who have helped me along my way.

First of all, I would like to thank my editor, Stefan Proksch, who was instrumental in getting this project off the ground. Without his help and guidance, this book would have remained a disorderly collection of recipes scribbled down in a notebook. Also, a special thanks to Kelly Harris who was instrumental in helping me through the copyediting process.

To Thorsten Franz, Tobias Trapp, John Pitlak, and Brian Orr, thank you for your useful feedback on some of the more troublesome topics in this book. Your comments helped shape the content of this book more than you know.

To the late Irene Berger, thank you for your love and support during this project. I always enjoyed watching the question marks formulate over your head as I tried to describe ABAP programming to you, and I am grateful for the time we had together.

To my son, Andersen, and my daughter, Paige, thank you for providing me with so much inspiration. A father couldn't ask for two better kids. I am very proud of you both.

And finally, to my wife Andrea, thank you for putting up with many late nights listening to me pound away at the keyboard. You are the best thing to ever happen to me, and I appreciate all the love and support you give me. There's no other person I would rather spend this journey through life with than you.

# PART I
# Appetizers

*Many chefs have fundamental ingredients that they use in many dishes. In the same way, string processing is a fundamental ingredient that can be found in almost every ABAP program. In this chapter, you'll learn about some basic and advanced string processing techniques that can be used to greatly simplify working with character data in programs.*

# 1 String Processing Techniques

Computers are designed from the ground up to work with numbers. In the early days of computing, this fundamental behavior aligned very closely with applications that were primarily concerned with crunching numbers. However, over the years, much of the emphasis in computing has shifted toward information processing. The emergence of the World Wide Web has ushered the world into the so-called *Information Age*. As you might guess, much of this information is captured as various forms of text.

In this chapter, you'll learn about some of the basic and advanced string processing capabilities available in ABAP. In particular, we show you how to use *regular expressions* to implement sophisticated text processing procedures using only a few lines of code. Along the way, we study the design of a custom string library (provided with the source code bundle for this book) that consolidates these features into an easy-to-use ABAP Objects class-based API.

## 1.1 ABAP Character Types

Before delving too far into specific string processing operations, it's important to first understand the built-in character data types that are integrated into the SAP NetWeaver AS ABAP kernel. Table 1.1 lists the predefined ABAP character types that you can use to define local data objects, interface parameters, and so on.

| Data Type | Length | Standard Length | Description |
|---|---|---|---|
| C | 1 to 65,535 characters | 1 character | A fixed-length text field that contains a string of alphanumeric characters. |
| N | 1 to 65,535 characters | 1 character | A fixed-length numeric text field that contains a string of numeric characters in the range 0-9. |
| STRING | Variable | Variable | A variable-length string of alphanumeric characters. The size of the data object at runtime is equal to the number of characters in the string object multiplied by the size of the internal representation of a single character. |
| D | 8 characters | N/A | A date field in the form YYYYMMDD. |
| T | 6 characters | N/A | A time field in the form HHMMSS. |

**Table 1.1** Predefined ABAP Character Types

Generally speaking, the choice of which predefined character type to use in a given situation is fairly straightforward. Typically, the choice comes down to speed versus flexibility. The STRING data type offers the most flexibility because it's a *variable-length* data type. Unfortunately, this flexibility comes with a price (albeit a small one) because an administrative header object is tasked with keeping track of the characters in memory behind the scenes. Therefore, if you already know that a particular data field will never exceed a certain length (perhaps because that's the way it's defined in the database), you should lean toward using the fixed-length character types (e.g., the C data type, etc.). However, if you know that you're going to be manipulating a string via concatenation, and so on, then you'll want to use the STRING type. As we develop our string library in Section 1.2, Designing a Custom String Library, we use the dynamic STRING data type to store the value of the character string in context.

As you'll see, by default, each of the built-in string processing statements supports the character types described in Table 1.1. It's also important to note that ABAP allows you to generically define character-based parameters and field symbols using the CLIKE and CSEQUENCE data types. The CLIKE type is compatible with each of the character types listed in Table 1.1. The CSEQUENCE type is compatible with types C and STRING. We use these generic types quite a bit as we develop our custom string library.

## 1.2 Designing a Custom String Library

In this section, we begin to introduce you to a custom string library that can be used to simplify various string processing tasks. If you've been programming in ABAP for a while, you might wonder why you would want to bother creating something like this when ABAP provides so much out-of-the-box functionality with built-in statements such as `CONCATENATE`, `SPLIT`, and so on. As we progress through this design, keep in mind that the goal here isn't to reinvent the wheel. Rather, we are looking at ways to encapsulate this core functionality into a set of services that are easy to use when solving common string processing problems.

### 1.2.1 Developing the API

When you think about it, a lot of string processing requirements tend to look the same. Ordinary string processing tasks include searching for patterns (and possibly replacing matches with some other character sequence), checking for equality or sort order, moving characters around, appending character sequences to the end of a string, and so on. ABAP provides support for these common tasks with the statements/functions listed in Table 1.2.

| Statement/ Function | Description |
|---|---|
| `FIND` | Statement used to search for patterns within strings. |
| `REPLACE` | Statement used to find a pattern within a string and replace it with a given substring. |
| `SHIFT` | Statement used to shift characters around within a string. |
| `CONCATENATE` | Statement used to concatenate one or more strings together into a single string. |
| `SPLIT` | Statement used to split (or *tokenize*) a string into a series of substrings using a delimiter sequence. For instance, when applied to the string X#Y#Z with a delimiter of #, `SPLIT` would return a table containing the substrings X, Y, and Z. |
| `TRANSLATE` | Statement used to translate a string to uppercase or lowercase. |
| `CONDENSE` | Statement used to remove redundant spaces from a string. |
| `STRLEN` | Function used to return the number of characters in the string. |

**Table 1.2** Basic String Processing Statements in ABAP

Frequently, these fundamental operations need to be combined in different ways to perform a particular task. For instance, imagine that you need to compare two strings in a case-insensitive manner. In this situation, several steps are required to carry out this comparison:

1. First, you need to copy the comparison strings into a couple of local data objects. The additional overhead here is necessary because both comparison strings must be modified to enable a case-insensitive comparison.
2. Next, after we've copied the comparison strings into local data objects, we need to translate both of these comparison strings to a common case using the `TRANSLATE` statement. This step ensures that an equality check using the `EQ` operator works in situations where we are performing a comparison between the strings "Abap" and "ABAP," or other similar situations.
3. Finally, we can test the equality of the two translated comparison strings using the `EQ` operator, per usual.

The simple report program `ZEQUALTEST` shown in Listing 1.1 shows how a subroutine called `ARE_STRINGS_EQUAL` can be created to compare two strings in a case-insensitive manner.

```
REPORT ZEQUALTEST.
TYPE-POOLS: abap.
PARAMETERS: p_str1 TYPE string,
            p_str2 TYPE string.
DATA: lv_equal_flag TYPE abap_bool.

START-OF-SELECTION.
  PERFORM are_strings_equal USING p_str1
                                  p_str2
                         CHANGING lv_equal_flag.

  IF lv_equal_flag EQ abap_true.
    WRITE: / 'Strings are equal.'.
  ELSE.
    WRITE: / 'Strings are not equal.'.
  ENDIF.

FORM are_strings_equal USING im_string1
                             im_string2
                    CHANGING ch_flag.
* Local Data Declarations:
  DATA: lv_string1 TYPE string,
```

```
        lv_string2 TYPE string.

* Copy strings over to locals so that we can translate them:
  lv_string1 = im_string1.
  lv_string2 = im_string2.

***** The following will not work *****
*  IF lv_string1 EQ lv_string2.
*    ch_flag = abap_true.
*  ELSE.
*    ch_flag = abap_false.
*  ENDIF.

* Instead, we have to translate the two strings to a common
* case before comparing for equality:
  TRANSLATE lv_string1 TO UPPER CASE.
  TRANSLATE lv_string2 TO UPPER CASE.

  IF lv_string1 EQ lv_string2.
    ch_flag = abap_true.
  ELSE.
    ch_flag = abap_false.
  ENDIF.
ENDFORM.
```

**Listing 1.1** Example of Case-Insensitive String Comparisons in ABAP

The subroutine ARE_STRINGS_EQUAL shown in Listing 1.1 does a fairly good job of encapsulating the case-insensitive comparison requirements. However, if you take that same logic and encapsulate it inside of a functional method in an ABAP Objects class, you can carry out the same comparison in a single line of code, as shown in Listing 1.2. This syntax demonstrates the power of functional methods in ABAP. The results of functional methods can be used as operands in conditional statements (e.g., IF or CASE), the LOOP statement, and so on. In this case, when a functional method operand is evaluated in an *expression*, the ABAP runtime environment invokes the function and evaluates its result in one fell swoop.

```
IF lr_str1->equals_ignore_case( lr_str2 ) EQ abap_true.
  WRITE: / 'Strings are equal.'.
ELSE.
  WRITE: / 'Strings are not equal.'.
ENDIF.
```

**Listing 1.2** Example of String Comparison Using Functional Methods

The EQUALS_IGNORE_CASE() method demonstrated in Listing 1.2 is a perfect example of the type of utility methods that we want to provide with our custom string library. Figure 1.1 contains a UML (Unified Modeling Language) class diagram that depicts the basic methods that we've implemented in our custom string library class called /BOWDK/CL_STRING. The UML is a modeling language that is used to model object-oriented software designs. Class diagrams show how classes within an object-oriented design are constructed.

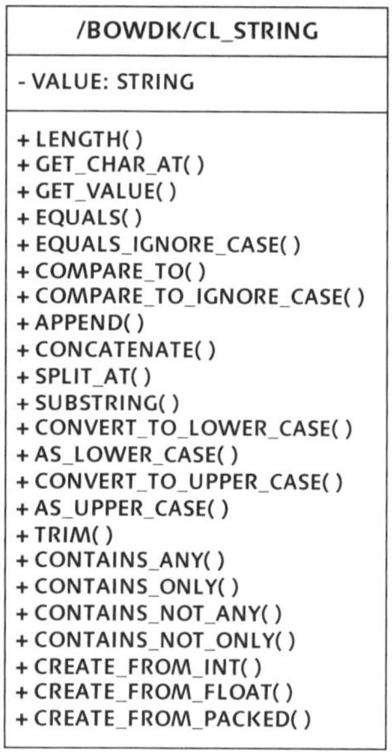


**Figure 1.1** UML Class Diagram for String Library

If you've worked with string libraries in other languages, you'll find that there are many commonalities between those implementations and the one portrayed in Figure 1.1. Internally, the /BOWDK/CL_STRING class uses a private attribute called VALUE to keep track of the actual string contents. To maximize flexibility, we assigned the variable-length STRING data type to the VALUE attribute. All of the methods shown in the bottom section of the class diagram operate on this internal data object to provide their various services. One set of methods that is conspicuously missing from the class diagram shown in Figure 1.1 provides various forms of find/replace functionality; we've purposefully delayed the definition of these methods until Section 1.3, Improving Productivity with Regular Expressions.

Right off the bat, you can probably guess how many of these methods might be implemented using basic string processing statements. Of course, some of these methods must also implement certain checks to make sure that important preconditions are met, and so on. In the next section, we begin fleshing out the implementation details of our custom string library class. If you've never written object-oriented code using ABAP Objects, you might want to read *Object-Oriented Programming with ABAP Objects* (SAP PRESS, 2009). However, one of the beauties of object-oriented programming is that you don't have to be an OO guru to use a class in your programs. Here, you need only create an object, and you'll then be able to access its services via method calls. Of course, this process is much easier if the class has an intuitive service interface.

### 1.2.2 Encapsulating Basic String Processing Statements

Classes in ABAP Objects are created and maintained in the Class Builder, which can be accessed via Transaction SE24. Figure 1.2 shows class /BOWDK/CL_STRING in the Class Editor perspective of the Class Builder.

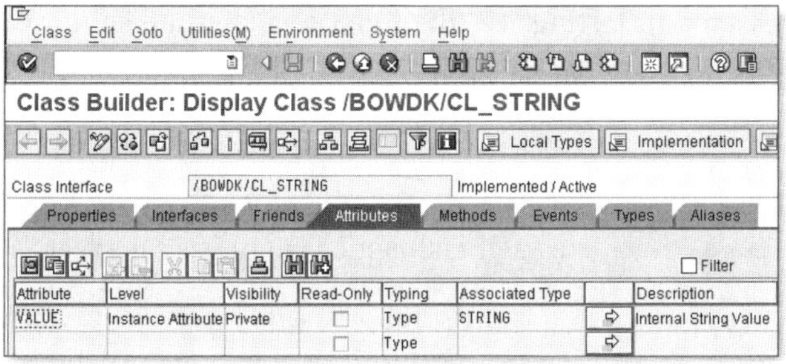


**Figure 1.2** Editing the String Library in the Class Builder

On the Attributes tab shown in Figure 1.2, you can see where we've defined a private instance attribute called VALUE that is of type STRING. This attribute is used to keep track of the string represented by class /BOWDK/CL_STRING. The use of the private visibility section ensures that the internal string can't be modified outside of the class. Instead, all modifications must occur via instance methods that define the behavior of the class.

Now that you have a feel for how the string library is organized, let's take a look at the implementation of the EQUALS_IGNORE_CASE() method originally described in Listing 1.2. Figure 1.3 shows the signature of this method. The first parameter, IM_STRING, represents the comparison string in this equality test and has the object reference type /BOWDK/CL_STRING. The result of the equality test is provided via a returning parameter of type ABAP_BOOL called RE_RESULT. In case you haven't worked with it before, the ABAP_BOOL data type is a Boolea' t'p' t'at has two possible values: true ('X') or false (SPACE).

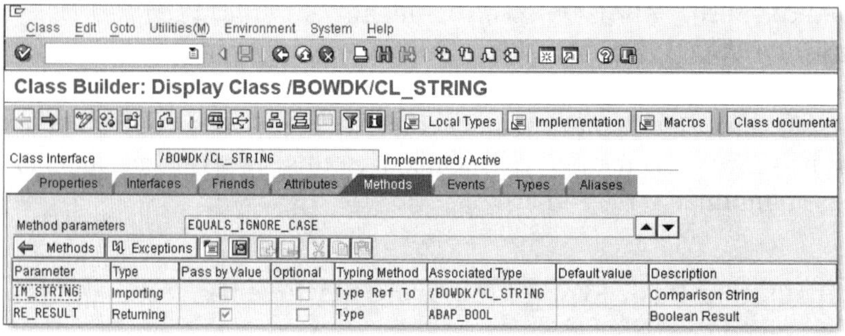


**Figure 1.3** Signature of Method EQUALS_IGNORE_CASE

As you can see in Listing 1.3, the implementation of the EQUALS_IGNORE_CASE() method is very similar to that of the subroutine ARE_STRINGS_EQUAL shown in Listing 1.1. However, as demonstrated in Listing 1.2, the functional method solution is much easier to use in logical expressions.

```
METHOD equals_ignore_case.
* Method-Local Data Declarations:
  DATA: lv_value1 TYPE string,
        lv_value2 TYPE string.

* Copy the values of both strings being compared:
  lv_value1 = me->value.
  lv_value2 = im_string->value.

* Translate both values to uppercase so that we can perform
* a case-insensitive comparison:
  TRANSLATE lv_value1 TO UPPER CASE.
  TRANSLATE lv_value2 TO UPPER CASE.

* Check to see if the two strings are equal
* lexicographically:
  IF lv_value1 EQ lv_value2.
    re_result = abap_true.
  ELSE.
    re_result = abap_false.
  ENDIF.
ENDMETHOD.
```

**Listing 1.3** Implementing Method EQUALS_IGNORE_CASE()

In addition to functional methods such as EQUALS_IGNORE_CASE(), class /BOWDK/CL_STRING also defines various methods that can be used to manipulate the value of the string itself. For example, Listing 1.4 shows the implementation of method TRIM(). This method is used to remove leading and training whitespace from a string object. We can achieve this using the SHIFT statement, as shown in Listing 1.4.

```
METHOD trim.
* Remove leading/trailing whitespace from the string:
  SHIFT me->value LEFT DELETING LEADING SPACE.
  SHIFT me->value RIGHT DELETING TRAILING SPACE.

* Return a reference to this updated string instance:
  re_string = me.
ENDMETHOD.
```

**Listing 1.4** Implementing Method TRIM( )

If you look carefully at the implementation of method TRIM() in Listing 1.4, you'll notice that a copy of the reference to the current object (i.e., the me self-reference) is assigned to the re_string returning parameter. At first, this kind of assignment might seem redundant because we clearly have a reference to the string object already; otherwise, we wouldn't have been able to invoke the method in the first place! However, there is a method to our madness because this assignment makes it possible to implement *chained method calls* in the future.

One of the long-term advantages of implementing a custom string library using ABAP Objects classes is the fact that SAP has made it known that there are plans in the works to support chained method calls in future releases of the SAP NetWeaver AS ABAP. If you're not familiar with this concept, the Java code excerpt in Listing 1.5 provides an example. Here, the code defines a reference variable called someString of type String. The String class defines methods called trim() and length(), among others. The trim() method returns a copy of the string with leading and trailing whitespace removed. Because this resultant copy is also a String object, it can be used as the target of the length() method that is chained onto the end of the method call expression. Thus, the length of the trimmed string (12) can be calculated in one fell swoop, as shown in Listing 1.5.

```
String someString = "   ABAP Objects   ";
int length = someString.trim().length();
```

**Listing 1.5** Example of Chained Method Calls in Java

The chained method call syntax shown in Listing 1.5 is very common in modern programming languages such as Java or .NET. One of the keys to being able to carry out something like this is to return a reference to an object in lieu of an elementary data object. This resultant object reference can then be used as the target of subsequent method calls.

## 1.3 Improving Productivity with Regular Expressions

As we saw in Section 1.2, Designing a Custom String Library, ABAP has always provided basic support for string processing via a series of built-in statements. These built-in statements make it easy to perform common operations such as case translation, string tokenization, concatenation, and so on. However, while these statements simplify certain tasks, they lack the expressiveness to implement more complex requirements. Without additional support, ABAP developers must resort to the creation of custom string processing algorithms in ABAP to satisfy these difficult requirements.

In other modern programming languages, such as .NET or Java, complex string processing tasks are often handled using *regular expressions*. A regular expression represents a *text pattern* that is described using a specialized pattern-based notation. Regular expressions (or regexes, with a hard *g* sound like "regular") are processed inside of a regular expression engine that can be implemented in many different ways. Beginning with release 7.0 of the SAP NetWeaver AS ABAP, ABAP now supports the use of POSIX-style regular expressions.[1] Underneath the hood, ABAP regular expression support is implemented using the *Boost Regex library* written in C++ by John Maddock. You can find out more information about the Boost Regex library online at *www.boost.org/doc/libs/1_39_0/libs/regex/doc/html/index.html*.

### 1.3.1 Understanding Regular Expressions

Even if you've never heard of regular expressions before, you're probably already familiar with the concept. For example, if you need to find a document somewhere

1 The term POSIX stands for "**P**ortable **O**perating **S**ystem **I**nterface for Uni**x**," a name given to a set of standards defined by the IEEE for defining the how operating systems are implemented. This includes the specification of regular expression support in common tools like grep, sed, awk, and emacs. This level of support is also provided in the Boost Regex Library.

on your computer, you might use your operating system's search engine to search within a particular directory for a document using the pattern `*.doc`. This pattern tells the search engine to look for any file whose name ends with `.doc`. The preceding asterisk is a wildcard (or *metacharacter*) that tells the search engine to match anything prior to the literal characters `.doc`. Similarly, the `?` metacharacter can be used to match a single character in a character sequence.

Collectively, the character sequence `*.doc` represents a pattern whose syntax is consistent with the syntax supported by the operating system's search engine. In this particular use case, the limited set of metacharacters available is sufficient to perform the required tasks. However, if we wanted to search for other types of text patterns, additional metacharacters would be required. Rather than reinventing the wheel each time, developers began recognizing the need for a generalized pattern language that would be expressive enough to support all kinds of text-processing requirements. The various dialects of this language are collectively referred to as *regular expressions*.

### 1.3.2 Regular Expression Syntax

Much like the file search example described earlier, regular expressions have a grammar that combines special metacharacters with literal characters to describe a text pattern. Table 1.3 describes some of the basic metacharacters supported in most regular expression engines.

| Group | Metacharacter Sequence | Description |
|---|---|---|
| Match a Single Character | `.` | Within a regex, this "dot" metacharacter is used to match any possible character. |
| | `[...]` | This metacharacter sequence is called a *character class*. Character classes are used to match any one character in the set of characters listed between the brackets. |
| | `[^...]` | This metacharacter sequence is referred to as a *negated character class*. Unlike normal character classes, negated character classes match any one character that is *not* listed in the set of characters between the brackets. Note that negated character classes must match *something* in order to work. |

**Table 1.3** Basic Regular Expression Metacharacters

| Group | Metacharacter Sequence | Description |
|---|---|---|
| | `\char` | This metacharacter sequence represents an *escape sequence*. To understand how escape sequences work, imagine that you want to match an IP address that is of the form 255.255.255.0. As you build your regex, you use the period character to match the boundaries between the octets in the address. However, without an escape sequence, the regex engine assumes that you're using the dot metacharacter and that you want to match *any* character rather than just a period. In this situation, you need to use the escape sequence `\.` to indicate that you want to match the literal period. |
| Quantifiers | `?` | The `?` metacharacter is a quantifier that can be used to indicate that the preceding token in the regular expression is optional. For example, the regex `colou?r` matches both colour and color. |
| | `*` | The `*` metacharacter is a quantifier that can be used to indicate that the preceding token in the regular expression can occur zero or more times. |
| | `+` | The `+` metacharacter is a quantifier that can be used to indicate that the preceding token in the regular expression can occur one or more times. |
| | `{Min, Max}` | The `{Min, Max}` metacharacter sequence works similarly to the other quantifiers. The primary difference is that the `Min` and `Max` values constrain the minimum and maximum number of times the preceding token can occur. |
| Match a Position | `^` | The `^` (or caret) metacharacter is used to match the position at the start of the line. |
| | `$` | The `$` metacharacter is used to match the position at the end of the line. |
| | `\<` | The `\<` metacharacter sequence matches the position at the start of a word. |
| | `\>` | The `\>` metacharacter sequence matches the position at the end of a word. |

**Table 1.3** Basic Regular Expression Metacharacters (Cont.)

| Group | Metacharacter Sequence | Description |
|---|---|---|
| | `\b` | The `\b` metacharacter sequence matches a word boundary (the start or end of a word). |
| | `\B` | The `\B` metacharacter sequence is a negated word boundary sequence. |
| | `(?=...)` | The `(?=...)` metacharacter sequence defines a *positive lookahead* sequence. Positive lookahead matches a position preceding the expression embedded between the `(?=` and `)` metacharacters. |
| | `(?!...)` | The `(?!...)` metacharacter sequence defines a *negative lookahead* sequence. Negative lookahead matches a position if the expression embedded between the `(?!` and `)` metacharacters doesn't match. |
| Common Shorthands | `\t` | The `\t` metacharacter sequence is shorthand for the tab character. |
| | `\n` | The `\n` metacharacter sequence is shorthand for the new line character. |
| | `\r` | The `\r` metacharacter sequence is shorthand for the carriage return character. |
| | `\s` | The `\s` metacharacter sequence is shorthand for any kind of whitespace character. |
| | `\S` | The `\S` metacharacter sequence is shorthand for any non-whitespace character. |
| | `\w` | The `\w` metacharacter sequence is shorthand for a word character (typically [a-zA-Z0-9_]). |
| | `\W` | The `\W` metacharacter sequence is shorthand for a non-word character (i.e., anything not `\w`). |
| | `\d` | The `\d` metacharacter sequence is shorthand for a digit character (i.e., [0-9]). |
| | `\D` | The `\D` metacharacter sequence is shorthand for a non-digit character (i.e., anything not `\d`). |

**Table 1.3** Basic Regular Expression Metacharacters (Cont.)

<table>
<tr><th>Group</th><th>Metacharacter Sequence</th><th>Description</th></tr>
<tr><td>Misc.</td><td>|</td><td>The | metacharacter is used to represent *alternation*. For example, to match different spellings of the name "Anderson," you could use alternation such as this: `(Anderson|Andersen)`. This would match "Anderson" or "Andersen."</td></tr>
<tr><td></td><td>(...)</td><td>Parentheses are used to limit the scope of alternation, provide grouping for quantifiers, and provide "captures" for backreferences.</td></tr>
<tr><td></td><td>\1, \2, etc.</td><td>When backreferences are used, the metacharacter sequences \1, \2, and so on refer to captured text matched earlier in the regex evaluation process.</td></tr>
<tr><td></td><td>(?:...)</td><td>The ?: metacharacter sequence, when embedded inside parentheses, can be used to limit the scope of alternation or provide grouping for quantifies. The matched texts in the ellipses aren't captured in backreferences.</td></tr>
</table>

**Table 1.3** Basic Regular Expression Metacharacters (Cont.)

After you understand how metacharacters work, you can begin to construct regular expressions to describe various text patterns. The following subsections provide several examples that show how to build regexes to match common text patterns frequently encountered in routine programming tasks. As we progress through the examples, we describe the use of some of the more common metacharacters available. Of course, the detailed treatment of each of the metacharacter sequences listed in Table 1.3 is outside the scope of this book. However, if you're interested in learning more about advanced concepts, we highly recommend Jeffrey Friedl's *Mastering Regular Expressions*, 3rd ed. (O'Reilly, 2006).

### Matching ABAP Variable Names

An ABAP variable name can contain standard ASCII letters (e.g., letters in the English alphabet: a-z or A-Z), numbers, and underscores. However, the first character in the variable name must be a letter. Given these requirements, let's look at how we would match an ABAP variable name using regular expressions. The regular expression shown in Listing 1.6 demonstrates one possible approach using character classes.

```
\b[a-zA-Z][_a-zA-Z0-9]*\b
```

**Listing 1.6** Regex to Match an ABAP Variable Name

Before we begin to dissect this regular expression, let's take a look back at the definition of a character class in Table 1.3. A character class can be used to match a single character by comparing it against all of the characters contained within a set of brackets (e.g., [...]). To simplify the creation of character classes, regular expression engines allow you to specify a range of characters using a dash (-). Thus, the range a-z describes every lowercase letter in the English alphabet, and so on.

Now that we understand character classes a little better, let's examine the regex shown in Listing 1.6 piece by piece. The first and last metacharacters \b are used to match a *word boundary*. This anchors our search to ensure that we don't match valid substrings inside of an invalid variable name, and so on. Next, we have a character class that is used to match a letter regardless of case. The second character class is a little more extensive; supporting an underscore character ( _ ), a letter, or a number. The use of the asterisk (*) quantifier after the character class implies that we want to match zero or more characters against the character class.

We could have also used the \w word character shorthand to match the characters in the variable name after the first one (see Listing 1.7). However, this would not have worked for the first character because \w matches letters, numbers, and the underscore. Also, notice how we've used the {Min,Max} quantifier after the \w sequence in the regex shown in Listing 1.7 to ensure that variable names don't exceed the 30-character limit defined within the ABAP programming language specification.

```
\b[a-zA-Z]\w{0,29}\b
```

**Listing 1.7** Using the Word Character Shorthand

### Searching for HTML Markup

The ubiquitous HTML is used in many different types of applications these days. The text-based nature of HTML makes regular expressions a natural fit for sifting through the mountains of information embedded within HTML markup. To demonstrate this, let's consider an example.

Imagine that you want to scan through an HTML document and formulate a table of contents. In HTML, you can define up to six levels of section headings using the `<h1>` to `<h6>` tags. Therefore, there are two things that you need to capture in your regular expression. First, you need to grab hold of the heading tag because this defines the level of indention within the table of contents (with `<h1>` being the leftmost, etc.). Next, you need to seize the actual heading text embedded within the heading tag. For instance, if you were scanning the markup `<h2>ABAP Character Types</h2>`, then the heading text would be "ABAP Character Types" (i.e., everything between the `<h2>` and `</h2>` tags).

Given what you know so far about regular expressions, you might be wondering how we could match more than one pattern in a piece of text. Fortunately, regular expressions make it very easy to capture subexpressions within a match by using *backreferences*. Backreferences can be created inside a regular expression by grouping subexpressions within parentheses. Regular expression engines that support backreferences see this grouping and know that they need to hold on to the matched text within the parentheses. The matched text can then be used later within the regular expression matching process or even after the expression has been evaluated completely. We'll explain how the latter works in Section 1.3.3, Using Regular Expressions in ABAP.

Getting back to the matter at hand, let's think about how we can use backreferences to satisfy our requirements. Listing 1.8 shows an example of a regular expression that matches any kind of HTML heading tag.

```
<([hH][1-6]).*>(.*)</\1>
```

**Listing 1.8** Extracting HTML Headings Using Backreferences

To understand how a regex engine evaluates the regex shown in Listing 1.8, let's consider each token in turn:

- The expression in Listing 1.8 begins with the literal < character, followed by the character classes `[hH]` and `[1-6]` that are used to match the heading tag itself. As you can see, these character classes are embedded within parentheses to designate the subexpression as a backreference. Because the parentheses are metacharacters, they aren't included in the match. In other words, if we wanted to match the literal expression `(<h1>)`, we would have to escape the parentheses using a pattern such as `\(<[hH][1-6]>\)`. However, because we only want to match the heading tag, we simply wrap it inside parentheses so that the regular expression engine hangs onto it.
- After the closing parenthesis, we combine the dot (.) metacharacter with the asterisk (*) quantifier to indicate that zero or more of *any* kind of character can

follow the heading tag. This ensures that we match heading tags that may have various optional attributes associated with them (e.g., <h1 id="MainHeader">). The use of the literal > character anchors the match to ensure that the heading tag is closed properly.

- Next, we combine the dot and asterisk metacharacters once again within parentheses to match the actual heading text. In other words, we want to match any kind of text embedded within the heading tag markup.
- Finally, we match the closing tag using </\1>. The only thing out of the ordinary here is the use of the \1 sequence within the closing tag. As you may recall from earlier, we mentioned that backreferences can be used later within the matching process. In this case, the \1 represents the subexpression captured within the first set of parentheses shown in Listing 1.8 (e.g., the h1, h2, etc.). This is preferable to using the generic [hH][1-6] again because we want to make sure that the closing heading tag matches the opening tag. Otherwise, we could match something like <h1>ABAP and Regular Expressions</h5>.

As you can see, backreferences can be very powerful. However, it's important not to abuse this power because it can slow the matching process down considerably. Most POSIX-style regular expression engines only support up to nine backreferences, but the ABAP-based implementation lifts this restriction. You can refer to these backreferences later in a regular expression using the sequences \1, \2, and so on.

### Parsing Delimited File Records

A frequent requirement on many SAP projects is to write an ABAP conversion program to upload data from some external data source into the system. Sometimes these files have a fixed-length record format; other times the records are delimited in some way (e.g., a comma-separated values, or CSV, file). In a perfect world, you could parse these records using the ABAP SPLIT statement, as shown in Listing 1.9.

```
SPLIT lv_record AT ',' INTO lt_tokens.
```

**Listing 1.9** Parsing a CSV Record Using the ABAP SPLIT Statement

However, let's imagine that the elements in the delimited file record may contain the delimited character in question. Here, each field must be further escaped by something else. Listing 1.10 shows an example of a delimited file record that represents a material master entry. As you can see, each field in the record is surrounded by double quotes. Within the double quotes, each element can contain the delimiter character in addition to other normal characters. The elements can also include double quotes, as long as they are escaped using the \ character.

```
"1622151-957","2\"x2\" Bolt, Aluminum","IN","OZ"
```

**Listing 1.10** Example CSV Record Using Double-Quoted Strings

Listing 1.11 shows a regular expression that can be used to match delimited file records like the one shown in Listing 1.10. This expression may seem a little more complex than some of the ones we've seen before, but if you think about it, it makes sense. First, we want to match the literal opening quote. Next, we use parentheses to capture the actual token within the parentheses. Within the parentheses, we are using the alternation operator (|),which is used to implement a sort of logical OR operation. In this case, we have two alternatives. The first alternative is a negated character class that instructs the engine not to match the literal \ or " character within the field. The next alternative says that it's okay to match any character that is preceded by the \ character (e.g., \"). Collectively, this expression tells the engine to match any character that isn't a closing " character, unless it's escaped using the sequence \". This gives us exactly what we want.

```
"([^\\"]|\\.)*"
```

**Listing 1.11** Parsing a Delimited File Record Using Regexes

Alternation can be very useful in building expressions where subexpressions have certain constraints. As the regular expression engine evaluates a delimited file record against the regex from Listing 1.11, it's free to continue the match process so long as any of the subexpressions combined via the | operator provide a match. You'll see alternation used extensively in regular expressions.

### Formatting URLs

A general requirement in many web/portal applications is to make sure that URLs are well formed. A common HTML validation problem with URLs occurs whenever an ampersand character (&) is used incorrectly.

For example, consider the URL shown in Listing 1.12. Here, the intent is to search the SAP PRESS website for books about ABAP written in English. However, the query string parameter (`&lang`) conflicts with the HTML entity reference for the *left pointing angle bracket* (or more commonly, the < character), yielding an invalid query string parameter of `<=en`. Although some browsers are smart enough to recover from these kinds of errors, it's a good practice to properly escape HTML entities in URLs, just to be safe.

```
http://www.sap-press.com/search.cfm?query=ABAP&lang=en
```

**Listing 1.12** URL Example with an Invalid HTML Entity Reference

To properly escape the URL shown in Listing 1.12, we need to replace any reference to & with the HTML entity reference `&`. However because the entity reference `&` also contains &, we must be careful not to mistakenly replace any properly escaped ampersands — because this would generate `&`. One way to achieve this with regular expressions is to use *lookahead*.

Lookahead is used to match a position within an expression. There are two types of lookahead: *positive lookahead* and *negative lookahead*.

- Positive lookahead peeks ahead in the text to see if its subexpression can match at a certain position.
- Similarly, negative lookahead checks to see if its subexpression does *not* match at a certain position.

If you're confused, don't worry, this concept is best explained with an example.

Looking at our URL validation example, we want to replace any occurrences of & with `&amp` if & isn't immediately followed by an `amp;`. To satisfy the second requirement, we can use negative lookahead to make sure that we don't match & if it's followed by `amp;`. Listing 1.13 shows an example of a regular expression that uses negative lookahead for this purpose.

```
&(?!amp;?)
```

**Listing 1.13** Regular Expression Example Using Lookahead

The regular expression in Listing 1.13 begins by matching the literal & character. Next, it uses the negative lookahead sequence `(?!...)` to set the boundaries where we want to match &. The expression inside the negative lookahead sequence is used to match the character sequence amp followed by an optional ; (hence the use of the `?` quantifier on the end). We'll see how this expression can be used in a find/replace operation in Section 1.3.3, Using Regular Expressions in ABAP.

The important thing to keep in mind with lookahead is that it's all about matching positions. In other words, you would use positive lookahead if you want to match the position that precedes a particular character sequence. Conversely, negative lookahead matches positions that aren't followed by a particular character sequence. If you find yourself confounded by the semantics of lookahead, go back and review the syntax described in Table 1.3.

### 1.3.3 Using Regular Expressions in ABAP

There are two ways to use regular expressions in an ABAP program.

- Beginning with release 7.0 of SAP NetWeaver AS ABAP, native regular expression support has been added to the `FIND` and `REPLACE` statements.
- Support for regular expressions is also provided via ABAP regular expression classes.

Whether you use the native `FIND` and `REPLACE` statements or the ABAP regular expression classes is mostly a matter of preference. However, as you'll learn, there are certain advantages to using the class-based approach. The following subsections show you how to work with regular expressions using both techniques.

#### Using Regular Expressions in the FIND and REPLACE Statements

If you've used the `FIND` or `REPLACE` statements in the past, you might recall that their basic syntax reads something like `FIND/REPLACE [pattern] IN [data object]...` where `[pattern]` refers to some text pattern within the given data object. Listing 1.14 shows how the syntax of the `FIND` statement has been expanded in release 7.0 of SAP NetWeaver AS ABAP to support the use of regular expressions. Here, the regular expression is provided after the `REGEX` addition, either as a literal string pattern or an instance of class `CL_ABAP_REGEX`.

```
FIND [{FIRST OCCURRENCE}|{ALL OCCURRENCES} OF]
  REGEX [{Regex Pattern}|{Instance of CL_ABAP_REGEX}]
  IN dobj [{Match Options}].
```

**Listing 1.14** Syntax Diagram for Regex Use in FIND Statement

To demonstrate the use of this syntax, let's consider how we would search for HTML headings using the regular expression example from Listing 1.8 with the `FIND` statement. Listing 1.15 shows a code snippet that conducts this search on the HTML markup contained in the `lv_html` string variable. The results of the search are stored in an internal table that has the table type `MATCH_RESULT_TAB`. This table contains useful information about match results, including the logical line in which a match was found, the offset index of the match within the data object being searched, and the length of the match, as well as any submatches (e.g., backreferences) within a given match instance. Figure 1.4 shows the definition of the

MATCH_RESULT line type used in the definition of the MATCH_RESULT_TAB table type in the ABAP Dictionary.

```
DATA: lv_html      TYPE string,
      lt_results   TYPE match_result_tab.
FIELD-SYMBOLS:
  <lfs_result>    LIKE LINE OF lt_results,
  <lfs_submatch> TYPE submatch_result.

lv_html =
  '<body><h1>Using Regular Expressions in ABAP</h1></body>'.

FIND ALL OCCURRENCES OF REGEX
  '<([hH][1-6]).*>(.*)</\1>'
  IN lv_html RESULTS lt_results.

LOOP AT lt_results ASSIGNING <lfs_result>.
  WRITE: / 'Found match at', <lfs_result>-offset,
           'length', <lfs_result>-length.
  LOOP AT <lfs_result>-submatches ASSIGNING <lfs_submatch>.
    WRITE: / 'Found submatch at', <lfs_submatch>-offset,
             'length', <lfs_submatch>-length.
  ENDLOOP.
ENDLOOP.
```

**Listing 1.15** Example Using Regexes in the FIND Statement

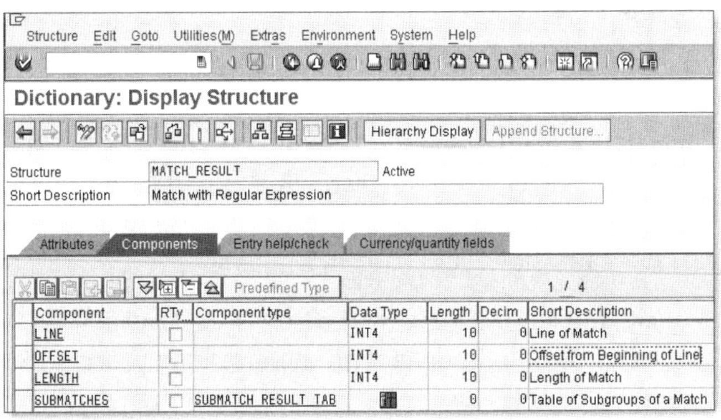


**Figure 1.4** ABAP Dictionary Structure MATCH_RESULT

The regex-related syntax changes for the REPLACE statement are very similar to the ones made to the FIND statement. Listing 1.16 shows the enhanced syntax diagram of the REPLACE statement.

```
REPLACE [{FIRST OCCURRENCE}|{ALL OCCURRENCES} OF]
  REGEX [{Regex Pattern}|{Instance of CL_ABAP_REGEX}]
  IN dobj WITH new [{Replacement Options}].
```

**Listing 1.16** Syntax Diagram for Regex Use in REPLACE Statement

The code snippet in Listing 1.17 shows how the sample regular expression from Listing 1.13 can be used in the REPLACE statement to replace all non-escaped occurrences of & within a URL with the HTML entity reference &.

```
DATA: lv_url     TYPE string,
      lv_html    TYPE string.

CONCATENATE
  'http://www.sap-press.com/search.cfm'
  '?query=ABAP&x=0&amp;y=0'
       INTO lv_url.
CONCATENATE '<a href="' lv_url '">Books About ABAP</a>'
       INTO lv_html.

WRITE: / lv_html.
REPLACE ALL OCCURRENCES OF REGEX
  '&(?!amp;?)' IN lv_html WITH '&amp;'.
WRITE: / lv_html.
```

**Listing 1.17** Example Using Regexes in the REPLACE Statement

### Using ABAP Regular Expression Classes

SAP provides two standard classes for working with regular expressions: CL_ABAP_REGEX and CL_ABAP_MATCHER. The class CL_ABAP_REGEX represents a precompiled regular expression. After an instance of CL_ABAP_REGEX is constructed, you can call method CREATE_MATCHER( ) to create a "matcher" object, which provides an interface to the regular expression engine. The relationship between these two classes is depicted in the UML class diagram shown in Figure 1.5.

As you can see in the UML class diagram in Figure 1.5, class CL_ABAP_MATCHER defines many methods that can be used to interact with the matching process. To get a feel for how these methods work, let's use the regular expression introduced in Listing 1.8 to build a program that extracts a table of contents from an HTML document. Listing 1.18 defines a simple report called ZREGEXDEMO that we use to accomplish this task.

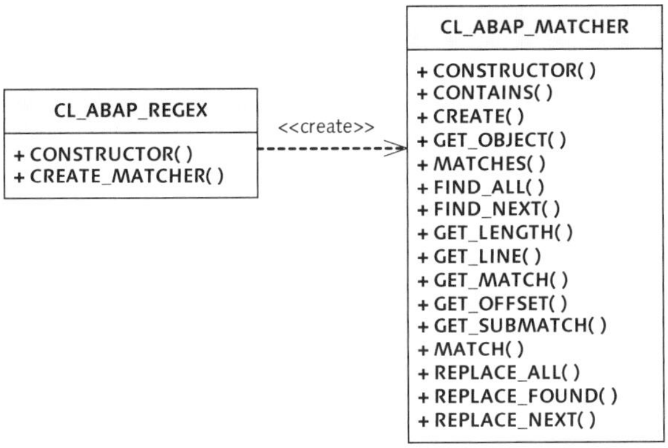


**Figure 1.5** UML Class Diagram for ABAP Regex Classes

```
REPORT zregexdemo.
TYPE-POOLS: abap.
DATA: lt_html        TYPE TABLE OF string,
      lo_pattern     TYPE REF TO cl_abap_regex,
      lo_matcher     TYPE REF TO cl_abap_matcher,
      ls_match       TYPE match_result,
      lv_header      TYPE string,
      lv_header_txt  TYPE string.
FIELD-SYMBOLS:
  <lfs_html> TYPE string,
  <lfs_sub>  TYPE submatch_result.

START-OF-SELECTION.
* Build the HTML document sample.
  APPEND '<html><head></head><body>' TO lt_html.
  APPEND '<H1>String Processing Techniques</H1>' TO lt_html.
  APPEND '<h2>ABAP Character Types</h2>' TO lt_html.
  APPEND '<H2>Developing a String Library</h2>' TO lt_html.
  APPEND '<h3>Designing the API</h3>' TO lt_html.
  APPEND '<h3>...</h3>' TO lt_html.
  APPEND '</body></html>' TO lt_html.

* Extract a table of contents from the HTML document:
  TRY.
*   Parse the regex pattern:
    CREATE OBJECT lo_pattern
      EXPORTING
        pattern     = '<([h][1-6]).*>(.*)</\1>'
        ignore_case = abap_true.
```

```
*   Create a matcher to search the example HTML document:
    lo_matcher =
      lo_pattern->create_matcher( table = lt_html ).

*   Add each match to the table of contents:
    WHILE lo_matcher->find_next( ) EQ abap_true.
*     Retrieve the next match found in the HTML document:
      ls_match = lo_matcher->get_match( ).
      READ TABLE lt_html INDEX ls_match-line
           ASSIGNING <lfs_html>.

*     Since we are using backreferences, the captured text
*     is actually stored in the submatch results:
      LOOP AT ls_match-submatches ASSIGNING <lfs_sub>.
        IF sy-tabix EQ 1.
          lv_header =
            <lfs_html>+<lfs_sub>-offset(<lfs_sub>-length).
        ELSEIF sy-tabix EQ 2.
          lv_header_txt =
            <lfs_html>+<lfs_sub>-offset(<lfs_sub>-length).
        ENDIF.
      ENDLOOP.

*     Output the table of contents record:
      CASE lv_header.
        WHEN 'H1' OR 'h1'.
          WRITE: / lv_header_txt.
        WHEN 'H2' OR 'h2'.
          WRITE: / '##', lv_header_txt.
        WHEN 'H3' OR 'h3'.
          WRITE: / '####', lv_header_txt.
      ENDCASE.
    ENDWHILE.
  CATCH cx_sy_regex.
    "Invalid regular expression pattern...
  CATCH cx_sy_matcher.
    "Problem generating matcher instance...
  ENDTRY.
```

**Listing 1.18** Working with ABAP Regex Classes

As you can see in Listing 1.18, the logic in the ZREGEXEX program is fairly straightforward. The regex processing begins with a TRY statement that is used to capture any exceptions that might be triggered during the matching process by the ABAP regex engine. In particular, the operations performed within the TRY block could trigger exceptions of type CX_SY_REGEX or CX_SY_MATCHER. Keep in mind that the FIND and REPLACE statements can also throw exceptions if the provided regex pattern is invalid, too complex, and so on. You can read more information about these errors in the ABAP Keyword Documentation for these statements.

Within the TRY block, we precompile our HTML header regex and assign the results to an object reference variable called lo_pattern. In a contrived example like this, precompiling the regex pattern doesn't add a whole lot of value. However, if you're evaluating the same expression over and over again (perhaps within a loop), there are some tremendous performance gains to be made by precompiling the regular expression ahead of time.

One additional thing you might have noticed in the CREATE OBJECT statement used to instantiate the regex is that we are passing a true value to the importing parameter IGNORE_CASE. This parameter instructs the regex engine to perform a case-insensitive matching process. This allowed us to avoid having to use a character class such as [hH] to match the HTML heading tag.

After the regex is precompiled, we call method CREATE_MATCHER( ) to create a matcher instance that evaluates the regex against the example HTML document stored in table lt_html. Next, we iterate through the matches inside of a WHILE loop that calls method FIND_NEXT( ) to determine if the matcher has additional matches in context. Within the loop, the current match is extracted via a call to method GET_MATCH( ). Because we are using backreferences in our regular expression, the text we're interested in is stored in *submatches* within the match. Therefore, for each match, we loop through the SUBMATCHES table to extract the heading and heading text. This information is used to output the table of contents report within a CASE statement.

In addition to the GET_MATCH( ) method introduced in Listing 1.18, there are also various other "getter" methods that you can use to query information about the current match. The other public instance methods provided in class CL_ABAP_MATCHER make it easy to perform replacements, retrieve a table of all matches (as we saw with the FIND statement in Listing 1.15), and perform a Boolean check to see if there are any matches within a text sequence. For more information about how these classes work, look at the context-based class/method documentation inside the Class Builder.

### Experimenting with DEMO_REGEX_TOY

As you get a feel for how regular expressions are constructed, you may want to try out expressions of your own to see how they work. Fortunately, SAP provides a very useful tool out of the box called the *Regex Toy*. To use this tool, follow these steps:

1. Start this tool by navigating to Transaction SE38 and executing the `DEMO_REGEX_TOY` report program. Figure 1.6 shows an example of this program running in a SAP GUI window. As you can see, the Input and Options boxes provide options to test a regex using the `FIND` and `REPLACE` statements.
2. Enter the sample text to test against in the Text text area. To perform the test, select the appropriate options, and enter the regex in the Regex input field.
3. After you type in the regex, press the [Enter] key to execute the test. The results show up in the Matches and Submatches sections at the bottom of the screen.

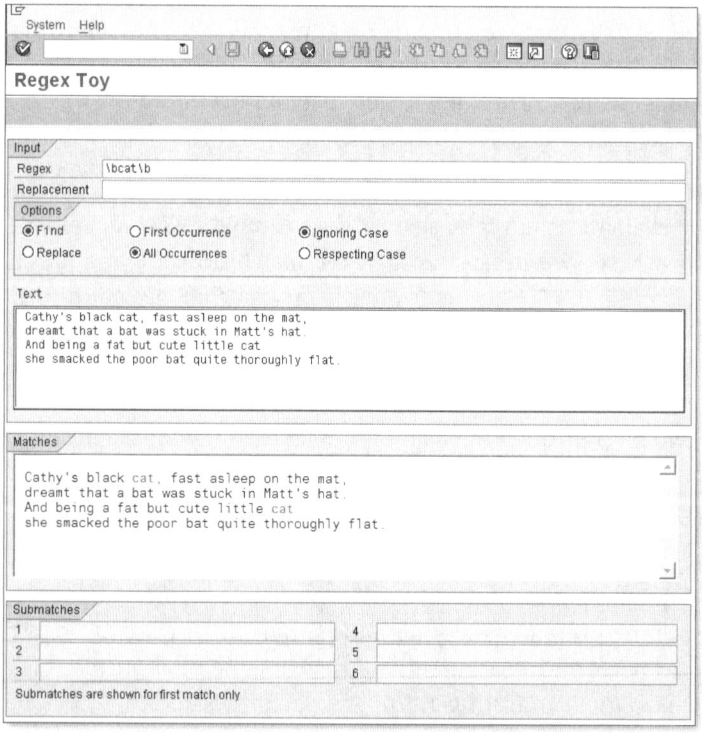


**Figure 1.6** Testing Regular Expressions Using the Regex Toy

We highly recommend that you use the Regex Toy tool to thoroughly test your regular expressions before you add them to your programs. That way, you can concentrate on building the logic in your program without having to worry about whether or not the regex works properly.

### 1.3.4 Integrating Regular Expression Support into the String Library

Now that you understand how to use regular expressions in your programs, let's go back and enhance our string library to provide search and replace functionality. The UML class diagram shown in Figure 1.7 shows some additional methods added to class /BOWDK/CL_STRING to implement this functionality.

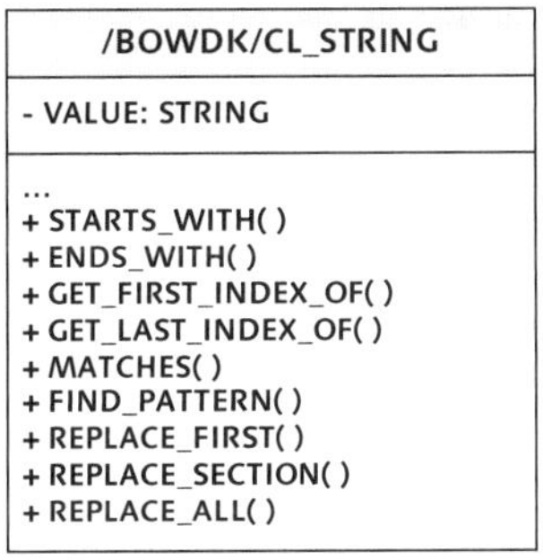


**Figure 1.7** Enhancing the String Library with Regular Expressions

Each of the methods shown in Figure 1.7 are described in further detail in Table 1.4. You can also find detailed documentation about these methods within the /BOWDK/CL_STRING class definition in the Class Builder tool.

| Method Name | Description |
|---|---|
| STARTS_WITH() | Used to determine if the string object begins with the provided text pattern |
| ENDS_WITH() | Used to determine if the string object ends with the provided text pattern |
| GET_FIRST_INDEX_OF() | Returns the index of the first occurrence of a pattern, or -1 if the pattern isn't found |
| GET_LAST_INDEX_OF() | Returns the index of the last occurrence of a pattern, or -1 if the pattern isn't found |

**Table 1.4** Regex Methods Provided in Class /BOWDK/CL_STRING

| Method Name | Description |
|---|---|
| MATCHES() | Returns a Boolean indicating whether or not the provided pattern has a match somewhere inside the string object |
| FIND_PATTERN() | Returns a match list that describes the location of every match of a given pattern within the string object |
| REPLACE_FIRST() | Replaces the first occurrence of a pattern within a string object and replaces it with another substring |
| REPLACE_SECTION() | Replaces a pattern within a section of the string object with another substring |
| REPLACE_ALL() | Replaces all occurrences of a particular pattern within the string object with another substring |

**Table 1.4** Regex Methods Provided in Class /BOWDK/CL_STRING (Cont.)

To give you a feel for how all this fits together in the code, let's look at how we might implement the STARTS_WITH() method. Figure 1.8 shows the signature of this method. The regex pattern is provided in importing parameter IM_PATTERN, which has the generic type CLIKE. There is also an optional Boolean parameter called IM_IGNORE_CASE that can be used to instruct the regex engine to conduct a case-insensitive search. The Boolean result of the operation is provided via returning parameter RE_RESULT. Once again, the use of the returning parameter here makes the STARTS_WITH() method a functional method, enabling it to be used inline in many different kinds of ABAP expressions.

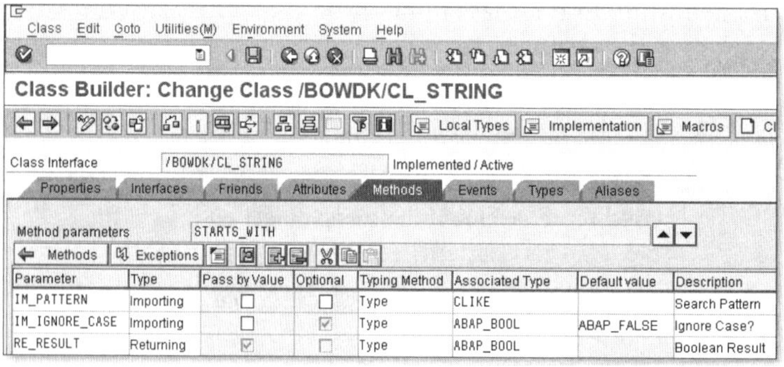


**Figure 1.8** Signature of the STARTS_WITH() Method

The actual implementation of the STARTS_WITH() method is shown in Listing 1.19. The logic here isn't terribly complicated. After some brief precondition checks, we construct the regular expression based on the provided pattern. Here, we are using the ^ and $ metacharacters to anchor the search to the entire contents of the string object on which STARTS_WITH() is operating. After the provided expression, we use the .* sequence to match everything in the string after the provided pattern.

```
METHOD starts_with.
* Method-Local Data Declarations:
  DATA: lv_pattern TYPE string,
        lo_regex   TYPE REF TO cl_abap_regex,
        lo_matcher TYPE REF TO cl_abap_matcher.

* Make sure the string is not empty:
  IF strlen( me->value ) EQ 0.
    re_result = abap_false.
    RETURN.
  ENDIF.

* Check to see if the string ends with the provided
* sequence:
  TRY.
*   Construct the regular expression needed to determine
*   if this string object begins with the provided string
*   value:
    CONCATENATE '^' im_pattern '.*$' INTO lv_pattern.
    CREATE OBJECT lo_regex
      EXPORTING
        pattern     = lv_pattern
        ignore_case = im_ignore_case.

*   Construct a matcher object to conduct the
*   match operation:
    lo_matcher =
      lo_regex->create_matcher( text = me->value ).

*   Test the results:
    re_result = lo_matcher->match( ).
  CATCH cx_sy_regex.
    re_result = abap_false.
  CATCH cx_sy_matcher.
    re_result = abap_false.
  ENDTRY.
ENDMETHOD.
```

**Listing 1.19** Implementation of the STARTS_WITH() Method

The other methods listed in Table 1.4 have similar implementations to the one shown in Listing 1.19. If you're interested in learning more about how the rest of these methods were implemented, take a look at the source code bundle for this book available online.

## 1.4 Summary

Hopefully by now you've come to appreciate the power of regular expressions. When combined with the rich set of string processing functions provided in ABAP, regular expressions allow you to deal with character strings at a much higher level of abstraction. The next chapter takes a look at some other basic ingredients available in ABAP.

*Although amateur cooks may hesitate to experiment with spices, accomplished chefs know how to use them to create the perfect dish. As an ABAP developer, the same can be said of certain data types. In this chapter, we show you how you can use some of these types to improve the quality of your programs.*

# 2 Working with Numbers, Dates, and Bytes

One of the nice things about working with an advanced programming language like ABAP is that you don't often have to worry about how that data is represented behind the scenes at the bits and bytes level; the language does such a good job of abstracting data that it becomes irrelevant. However, if you do come across a requirement that compels you to dig a little deeper, you'll find that ABAP also has excellent support for performing more advanced operations with elementary data types. In this chapter, we investigate some of these operations and show you techniques for using these features in your programs.

## 2.1 Numeric Operations

Whether it's keeping up with a loop index or calculating entries in a balance sheet, almost every ABAP program works with numbers on some level. Typically, whenever we perform operations on these numbers, we use basic arithmetic operators such as the + (addition), - (subtraction), * (multiplication), or / (division) operators. Occasionally, we might use the `MOD` operator to calculate the remainder of an integer division operation, or the ** operator to calculate the value of a number raised to the power of another. However, sometimes we need to perform more advanced calculations. If you're a mathematics guru, then perhaps you could come up with an algorithm to perform these advanced calculations using the basic arithmetic operators available in ABAP. For the rest of us mere mortals, ABAP provides an extensive set of mathematics tools that can be used to simplify these requirements. In the next two sections, we'll examine these tools and see how to use them in your programs.

### 2.1.1 ABAP Math Functions

ABAP provides many built-in math functions that you can use to develop advanced mathematical formulas as listed in Table 2.1. In many cases, these functions can be called using any of the built-in numeric data types in ABAP (e.g., the `I`, `F`, and `P` data types). However, some of these functions require the precision of the floating point data type (see Table 2.1 for more details). Because ABAP supports implicit type conversion between numeric types, you can easily cast non-floating point types into floating point types for use within these functions.

| Function | Supported Numeric Types | Description |
|---|---|---|
| `abs` | `(All)` | Calculates the absolute value of the provided argument. |
| `sign` | `(All)` | Determines the sign of the provided argument. If the sign is positive, the function returns 1; if it's negative, it returns -1; otherwise, it returns 0. |
| `ceil` | `(All)` | Calculates the smallest integer value that isn't smaller than the argument. |
| `floor` | `(All)` | Calculates the largest integer value that isn't larger than the argument. |
| `trunc` | `(All)` | Returns the integer part of the argument. |
| `frac` | `(All)` | Returns the fractional part of the argument. |
| `cos, sin, tan` | `F` | Implements the basic trigonometric functions. |
| `acos, asin, atan` | `F` | Implements the inverse trigonometric functions. |
| `cosh, sinh, tanh` | `F` | Implements the hyperbolic trigonometric functions. |
| `exp` | `F` | Implements the exponential function with a base e ≈ 2.7182818285. |
| `log` | `F` | Implements the natural logarithm function. |
| `log10` | `F` | Calculates a logarithm using base 10. |
| `sqrt` | `F` | Calculates the square root of a number. |

**Table 2.1** ABAP Math Functions

The report program ZMATHDEMO shown in Listing 2.1 contains examples of how to call the math functions listed in Table 2.1 in an ABAP program. The output of this program is displayed in Figure 2.1.

```
REPORT zmathdemo.

START-OF-SELECTION.
CONSTANTS: CO_PI TYPE f VALUE '3.14159265'.
DATA: lv_result TYPE p DECIMALS 2.

lv_result = abs( -3 ).
WRITE: / 'Absolute Value:      ', lv_result.

lv_result = sign( -12 ).
WRITE: / 'Sign:                ', lv_result.

lv_result = ceil( '4.7' ).
WRITE: / 'Ceiling:             ', lv_result.

lv_result = floor( '4.7' ).
WRITE: / 'Floor:               ', lv_result.

lv_result = trunc( '4.7' ).
WRITE: / 'Integer Part:        ', lv_result.

lv_result = frac( '4.7' ).
WRITE: / 'Fractional Part:     ', lv_result.

lv_result = sin( CO_PI ).
WRITE: / 'Sine of PI:          ', lv_result.

lv_result = cos( CO_PI ).
WRITE: / 'Cosine of PI:        ', lv_result.

lv_result = tan( CO_PI ).
WRITE: / 'Tangent of PI:       ', lv_result.

lv_result = exp( '2.3026' ).
WRITE: / 'Exponential Function:', lv_result.

lv_result = log( lv_result ).
WRITE: / 'Natural Logarithm:   ', lv_result.
```

```
lv_result = log10( '1000.0' ).
WRITE: / 'Log Base 10 of 1000: ', lv_result.

lv_result = log( 8 ) / log( 2 ).
WRITE: / 'Log Base 2 of 8:      ', lv_result.

lv_result = sqrt( '16.0' ).
WRITE: / 'Square Root:          ', lv_result.
```

**Listing 2.1** Working with ABAP Math Functions

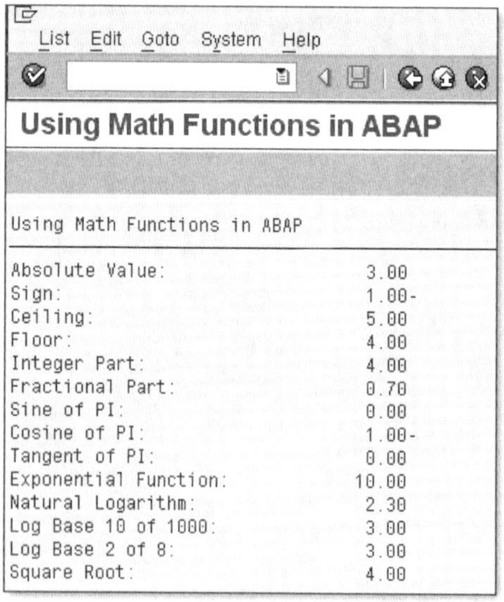


**Figure 2.1** Output Generated by Report ZMATHDEMO

The values of the function calls can be used as operands in more complex expressions. For example, in Listing 2.1, notice how we're calculating the value of `log( 8 )`. Here, we use the change of base formula `log( x ) / log( b )` (where `b` refers to the target base, and `x` refers to the value applied to the logarithm function) to derive the base 2 value. Collectively, these functions can be combined with typical math operators to devise some very complex mathematical formulas.

### 2.1.2 Generating Random Numbers

Computers live in a logical world where everything is supposed to make sense. Whereas this characteristic makes computers very good at automating many kinds of tasks, it can also make it somewhat difficult to model certain real-world phenomena. Often, we need to simulate *imperfection* in some form or another. One common method for achieving this is to produce randomized data using random number generators. Random numbers are commonly used in statistics, cryptography, and many kinds of scientific applications. They are also used in algorithm design to implement *fairness* and to simulate useful metaphors applied to the study of artificial intelligence (e.g., genetic algorithms with randomized mutations, etc.).

SAP provides random number generators for all of the built-in numeric data types via a series of ABAP Objects classes. These classes begin with the prefix `CL_ABAP_RANDOM` (e.g., `CL_ABAP_RANDOM_FLOAT`, `CL_ABAP_RANDOM_INT`, etc.). Though none of these classes inherit from the `CL_ABAP_RANDOM` base class, they do use its features behind the scenes using a common OO technique called *composition*. Composition basically implies that one class delegates certain functionality to an instance of another class. The UML class diagram shown in Figure 2.2 shows the basic structure of the provided random number generator classes.

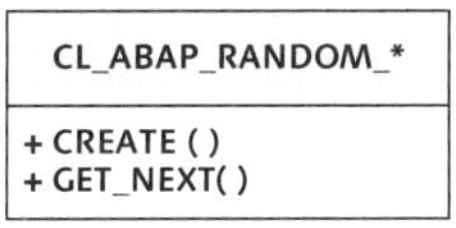


**Figure 2.2** Basic UML Class Diagram for Random Number Generators

Unlike most classes where you create an object using the `CREATE OBJECT` statement, instances of random number generators must be created via a call to a factory class method called `CREATE()`. The signature of the `CREATE()` method is shown in Figure 2.3. Here, you can see that the method defines an importing parameter called `SEED` that *seeds* the pseudo-random number generator algorithm that is used behind the scenes to generate the random numbers. In a pseudo-random number generator, random numbers are generated in sequence based on some calculation performed using the seed. Thus, a given seed value causes the random number generator to generate the same sequence of random numbers each time.

The `CREATE()` method for class `CL_ABAP_RANDOM_INT` also provides `MIN` and `MAX` parameters that can place limits around the random numbers that are generated (e.g., a range of 1-100, etc.). The returning `PRNG` parameter represents the generated random number generator instance. Once created, you can begin retrieving random numbers via a call to the `GET_NEXT()` instance method.

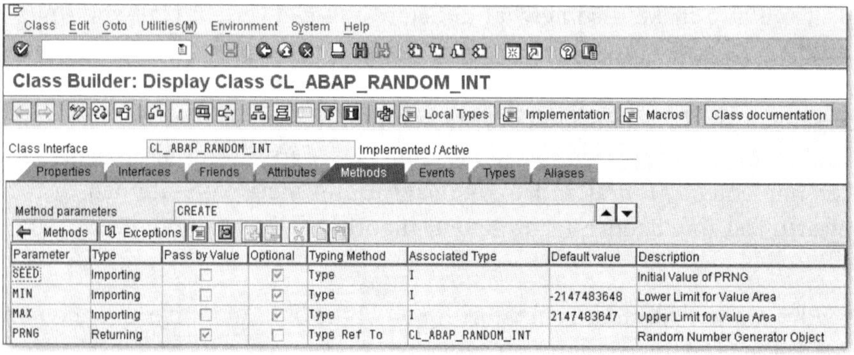


**Figure 2.3** Signature of Class Method CREATE()

To demonstrate how these random number generator classes work, let's consider an example program. Listing 2.2 contains a simple report program named ZSCRAMBLER that defines a local class called LCL_SCRAMBLER. The LCL_SCRAMBLER class includes an instance method SCRAMBLE() that can be used to randomly scramble around the characters in a string. This primitive implementation creates a random number generator to produce random numbers in the range of [0... {String Length}]. Perhaps the most complex part of the implementation is related to the fact that random number generators produce some duplicates along the way. Therefore, we have to make sure that we haven't used the randomly generated number previously to make sure that each character in the original string is copied into the new one.

```
REPORT zscrambler.

CLASS lcl_scrambler DEFINITION.
  PUBLIC SECTION.
    METHODS: scramble IMPORTING im_value TYPE clike
                      RETURNING VALUE(re_svalue) TYPE string
                      EXCEPTIONS cx_abap_random.

  PRIVATE SECTION.
    CONSTANTS: CO_SEED TYPE i VALUE 100.

    TYPES: BEGIN OF ty_index,
             index TYPE i,
           END OF ty_index.
ENDCLASS.

CLASS lcl_scrambler IMPLEMENTATION.
  METHOD scramble.
```

```
*   Method-Local Data Declarations:
    DATA: lv_length  TYPE i,
          lv_min     TYPE i VALUE 0,
          lv_max     TYPE i,
          lo_prng    TYPE REF TO cl_abap_random_int,
          lv_index   TYPE i,
          lt_indexes TYPE STANDARD TABLE OF ty_index.
    FIELD-SYMBOLS:
      <lfs_index> LIKE LINE OF lt_indexes.

*   Determine the length of the string as this sets the
*   bounds on the scramble routine:
    lv_length = strlen( im_value ).
    lv_max = lv_length - 1.

*   Create a random number generator to return random
*   numbers in the range of 1..{String Length}:
    CALL METHOD cl_abap_random_int=>create
      EXPORTING
        seed   = CO_SEED
        min    = lv_min
        max    = lv_max
      RECEIVING
        prng   = lo_prng.

*   Add the characters from the string in random order to
*   the result string:
    WHILE strlen( re_svalue ) LT lv_length.
      lv_index = lo_prng->get_next( ).
      READ TABLE lt_indexes TRANSPORTING NO FIELDS
            WITH KEY index = lv_index.
      IF sy-subrc EQ 0.
        CONTINUE.
      ENDIF.

      CONCATENATE re_svalue im_value+lv_index(1)
             INTO re_svalue.
      APPEND INITIAL LINE TO lt_indexes
             ASSIGNING <lfs_index>.
      <lfs_index>-index = lv_index.
    ENDWHILE.
  ENDMETHOD.
ENDCLASS.
```

```
START-OF-SELECTION.
* Local Data Declarations:
  DATA: lo_scrambler TYPE REF TO lcl_scrambler,
        lv_scrambled TYPE string.

* Use the scrambler to scramble around a word:
  CREATE OBJECT lo_scrambler.
  lv_scrambled = lo_scrambler->scramble( 'Andersen' ).
  WRITE: / lv_scrambled.
```

**Listing 2.2** Using Random Number Generators in ABAP

Obviously, a simple scrambler routine like the one shown in Listing 2.2 isn't production quality. Nevertheless, it does give you a glimpse of how you can use random number generators to implement some interesting algorithms. As a reader exercise, you might think about how you could use random number generators to implement an `UNSCRAMBLE()` method to unscramble strings generated from calls to method `SCRAMBLE()`.

## 2.2 Date and Time Processing

Online transaction processing (OLTP) systems such as the ones that make up the SAP Business Suite maintain quite a bit of time-sensitive data, so it's important that you understand how to work with the built-in date and time types provided in ABAP. In the following subsections, we discuss these types and explain how to use them to perform calculations and conversions.

### 2.2.1 Understanding ABAP Date and Time Types

ABAP provides two built-in types to work with dates and times: the `D` (date) data type and the `T` (time) data type. Both of these types are fixed-length character types that have the form `YYYYMMDD` and `HHMMSS`, respectively. In addition to these built-in types, the ABAP Dictionary types `TIMESTAMP` and `TIMESTAMPL` are being used more and more in many standard application tables, and so on, to store a timestamp in the UTC format.[1] Table 2.2 shows the basic date and time types available in ABAP.

---

1 The term "UTC" is an abbreviation for "Consolidated Universal Time," which is a time standard based on the International Atomic Time standard. UTC is roughly equivalent to the Greenwich Mean Time standard (or GMT) which refers to the mean solar time at the Royal Observatory in Greenwich, London. Collectively, these standards define a global time standard that can be used to convert a given time to local time, and vice versa.

| Data Type | Description |
|---|---|
| D | A built-in fixed-length date type of the form YYYYMMDD. For example, the value 20100913 represents the date September 13, 2010. |
| T | A built-in fixed-length time type of the form HHMMSS. For example, the value 102305 represents the time 10:23:05 AM. |
| TIMESTAMP (Type P - Length 8 No decimals) | An ABAP Dictionary type used to represent short timestamps in the form YYYYMMDDhhmmss. For example, the value 20100913102305 represents the date September 13, 2010 at 10:23:05 AM. |
| TIMESTAMPL (Type P - Length 11 Decimals 7) | An ABAP Dictionary type used to represent long timestamps in the form YYYYMMDDhhmmssmmmuuun. The additional digits mmmuuun represent fractions of a second. |

**Table 2.2** ABAP Date and Time Data Types

### 2.2.2 Date and Time Calculations

When you're working with dates, you often need to perform various calculations to compute the difference between two dates, make comparisons, or determine a valid date range. As we mentioned in Section 2.2.1, Understanding ABAP Date and Time Types, the built-in date and time types in ABAP are *character types*, not numeric types. Nevertheless, the ABAP runtime environment allows you to perform basic numeric operations on these types by implicitly converting them to numeric types behind the scenes.

The code excerpt shown in Listing 2.3 demonstrates how these calculations work. Initially, the variable lv_date is assigned the value of the current system date (e.g., the system field SY-DATUM). Next, we increment that date value by 30. In terms of a date calculation in ABAP, this implies that we're increasing the *day* component of the date object by 30 days. Here, note that the ABAP runtime environment is smart enough to *roll over* the date value whenever it reaches the end of a month, and so on. In other words, you can rely on the system to ensure that you don't calculate an invalid date value (e.g., 01/43/2011).

```
DATA: lv_date TYPE d.
lv_date = sy-datum.
WRITE: / 'Current Date:', lv_date MM/DD/YYYY.
```

```
lv_date = lv_date + 30.
WRITE: / 'Future Date:', lv_date MM/DD/YYYY.
```

**Listing 2.3** Performing Date Calculations in ABAP

Time calculations in ABAP work very similarly to the date calculations shown in Listing 2.3. With time calculations, the computation is based upon the *seconds* component of the time object. The code in Listing 2.4 shows how we can increment the current system time by 90 seconds using basic time arithmetic.

```
DATA: lv_time TYPE t.
lv_time = sy-uzeit.
WRITE /(60) lv_time USING EDIT MASK
  'The current time is __:__:__'.
lv_time = lv_time + 90.
WRITE /(60) lv_time USING EDIT MASK
  'A minute and a half from now it will be __:__:__'.
```

**Listing 2.4** Performing Time Calculations in ABAP

In addition to typical numeric calculations, you also have the option of working with date/time fields using normal character-based semantics. For instance, you can use the offset/length functionality to initialize date or time components. The code excerpt in Listing 2.5 demonstrates how you can adjust the date 02/13/2003 to 01/13/2003 using offset/length semantics.

```
DATA: lv_date TYPE d VALUE '20030213'.
WRITE: / lv_date MM/DD/YYYY.
lv_date+4(2) = '01'.
WRITE: / lv_date MM/DD/YYYY.
```

**Listing 2.5** Manipulating a Date Using Offset/Length Functionality

### 2.2.3 Working with Timestamps

If you've been working with some of the newer releases of the products in the SAP Business Suite, you may have encountered certain applications that use the `TIMESTAMP` or `TIMESTAMPL` data types to store time-sensitive data. As you can see in Table 2.2, these ABAP Dictionary types store timestamps with varying degrees of accuracy. Interestingly, though these types aren't built-in types like `D` or `T`, ABAP does provide some native support for them in the form of a couple of built-in statements. In addition, SAP also provides a system class called `CL_ABAP_TSTMP`, which can be used to simplify the process of working with timestamps. We investigate these features in the following subsections.

### Retrieving the Current Timestamp

You can retrieve the current system time and store it in a timestamp variable using the `GET TIME STAMP` statement whose syntax is demonstrated in Listing 2.6. The `GET TIME STAMP` statement stores the timestamp in a shorthand or longhand format depending upon the type of the timestamp data object used after the `FIELD` addition. The timestamp value is encoded using the UTC standard.

```
DATA: lv_tstamp_s TYPE timestamp,
      lv_tstamp_l TYPE timestampl.
GET TIME STAMP FIELD lv_tstamp_s.
WRITE: / 'Short Time Stamp:', lv_tstamp_s
  TIME ZONE sy-zonlo.
GET TIME STAMP FIELD lv_tstamp_l.
WRITE: / 'Long Time Stamp: ', lv_tstamp_l
  TIME ZONE sy-zonlo.
```

**Listing 2.6** Using the GET TIME STAMP Statement

Looking at the code excerpt in Listing 2.6, you can see that we're displaying the timestamp using the `TIME ZONE` addition of the `WRITE` statement. This addition formats the output of the timestamp according to the rules for the time zone specified. In Listing 2.6, we used the system field `SY-ZONLO` to display the *local time zone* configured in the user's preferences. However, we could have just as easily used a data object of type `TIMEZONE`, or even a hard-coded literal such as `'CST'`.

**Time Zones**

For a complete list of time zones configured in the system, have a look at the contents of ABAP Dictionary Table TTZZ.

### Converting Timestamps

You can convert a timestamp to a date/time data object and vice versa using the `CONVERT` statement in ABAP. Listing 2.7 shows the syntax used to convert a timestamp into data objects of type `D` and `T`. The `TIME ZONE` addition adjusts the UTC date/time value within the timestamp in accordance with a particular time zone. Additionally, the optional `DAYLIGHT SAVING TIME` addition can be used to determine whether or not the timestamp value happens to coincide with daylight savings time. If it does, the `lv_dst` variable has the value `'X'`; otherwise, it's blank.

This feature can be helpful in differentiating between timestamp values that lie within the transitional period between *summer time* and *winter time.*[2]

```
CONVERT TIME STAMP lv_tstamp TIME ZONE lv_tzone
   INTO [ DATE lv_date ] [ TIME lv_time ]
   [DAYLIGHT SAVING TIME lv_dst].
```

**Listing 2.7** Syntax of CONVERT TIME STAMP Statement

Listing 2.8 shows how the `CONVERT TIME STAMP` statement is used to convert the current system timestamp to date/time data objects using the local time zone.

```
TYPE-POOLS: abap.
DATA: lv_tstamp TYPE timestamp,
      lv_date   TYPE d,
      lv_time   TYPE t,
      lv_dst    TYPE abap_bool.

GET TIME STAMP FIELD lv_tstamp.
CONVERT TIME STAMP lv_tstamp TIME ZONE sy-zonlo
   INTO DATE lv_date TIME lv_time
   DAYLIGHT SAVING TIME lv_dst.

WRITE: / 'Today's date is:    ', lv_date MM/DD/YYYY.
WRITE: /(60) lv_time USING EDIT MASK
             'The current time is: __:__:__'.

IF lv_dst EQ abap_true.
  WRITE: / 'In daylight savings time...'.
ELSE.
  WRITE: / 'Not in daylight savings time...'.
ENDIF.
```

**Listing 2.8** Converting Timestamps to Date/Time Objects

To create a timestamp using a date/time object, you can use the syntax variant of the `CONVERT` statement shown in Listing 2.9. The date/time values are qualified using the `TIME ZONE` addition so that the appropriate offsets can be applied as the UTC timestamp is generated.

2 For a complete list of daylight savings time rules, have a look at the contents of the ABAP Dictionary table TTZDV.

```
CONVERT DATE lv_date
       [TIME lv_time [DAYLIGHT SAVING TIME lv_dst]]
   INTO TIME STAMP lv_tstamp TIME ZONE lv_tzone.
```

**Listing 2.9** Syntax of CONVERT DATE Statement

The code excerpt in Listing 2.10 shows how the `CONVERT DATE` statement can be used to generate a timestamp object from a date/time object.

```
TYPE-POOLS: abap.
DATA: lv_tstamp TYPE timestamp,
      lv_date   TYPE d,
      lv_time   TYPE t,
      lv_dst    TYPE abap_bool.

lv_date = sy-datum.
lv_time = sy-uzeit.

CONVERT DATE lv_date TIME lv_time
   INTO TIME STAMP lv_tstamp TIME ZONE sy-zonlo.

WRITE: / 'Time Stamp Value:', lv_tstamp TIME ZONE sy-zonlo.
```

**Listing 2.10** Creating a Timestamp from a Date/Time Object

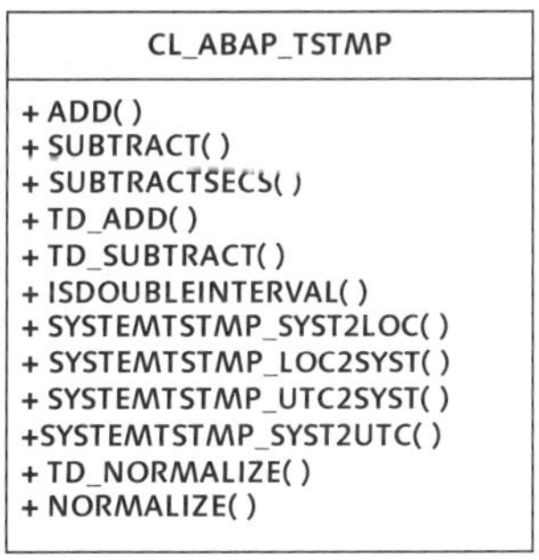


**Figure 2.4** UML Class Diagram for Class CL_ABAP_TSTMP

### Timestamp Operations Using System Class CL_ABAP_TSTMP

Unlike the native `D` and `T` types, the ABAP runtime environment doesn't have built-in functionality to perform calculations on timestamps (e.g., add or subtract, etc.). Instead, SAP provides a system class called `CL_ABAP_TSTMP` for this purpose. Figure 2.4 contains a UML class diagram that shows the publicly available methods provided in this class. As you would expect, there are various forms of `ADD()` and

SUBTRACT() methods to perform timestamp calculations. In addition, a series of conversion methods (e.g., SYSTEMTSTMP_SYST2LOC(), etc.) can be used to convert a timestamp to various time zones, a Boolean method called ISDOUBLEINTERVAL() can be used to determine if a timestamp is in daylight savings time, and a couple of methods can be used to *normalize* a timestamp. Here, normalization implies that an invalid time value such as 10:30:60 would be adjusted to the value 10:31:00.

In UML class diagram notation, methods that are underlined are defined as *class methods*. Class methods can be invoked without first creating an instance of the class in which they are defined, as evidenced in the code excerpt shown in Listing 2.11. Here, we're using the class method ADD() to add 75 seconds to the current system time.

```
DATA: lv_tstamp TYPE timestamp,
      lv_date   TYPE d,
      lv_time   TYPE t.

GET TIME STAMP FIELD lv_tstamp.
WRITE: / 'Time Stamp Value:', lv_tstamp TIME ZONE sy-zonlo.

TRY.
  CALL METHOD cl_abap_tstmp=>add
    EXPORTING
      tstmp   = lv_tstamp
      secs    = 75
    RECEIVING
      r_tstmp = lv_tstamp.
CATCH CX_PARAMETER_INVALID_RANGE.
CATCH CX_PARAMETER_INVALID_TYPE.
ENDTRY.

WRITE: / 'Time Stamp Value:', lv_tstamp TIME ZONE sy-zonlo.
```

**Listing 2.11** Working with Timestamps Using CL_ABAP_TSTMP

The call signatures of most of the other methods in class CL_ABAP_TSTMP are similar to the ADD() method demonstrated in Listing 2.11. For more details concerning the functionality of particular methods in this class, see the class/method documentation for this class in the Class Builder (Transaction SE24).

### 2.2.4 Calendar Operations

So far, our discussion on dates has focused on raw calculations and conversions.

However, many typical use cases in the business world require that we look at dates from a semantic point of view. For example, you might ask whether or not the date 1/13/2010 is a working day, or whether 4/4/2010 is a holiday. The answers to these kinds of questions require the use of a *calendar*. Fortunately, SAP provides a very robust set of calendaring features straight out of the box with SAP NetWeaver AS ABAP.

The SAP Calendar is maintained in a client-specific manner inside the SAP Customizing implementation guide (Transaction SPRO). Depending on how your system is set up, you might have a project-specific implementation guide. However, for the purposes of this discussion, we assume that you're using the default SAP Reference Implementation Guide (IMG). You can access this guide by clicking on the button labeled SAP Reference IMG on the initial screen of Transaction SPRO (see Figure 2.5).

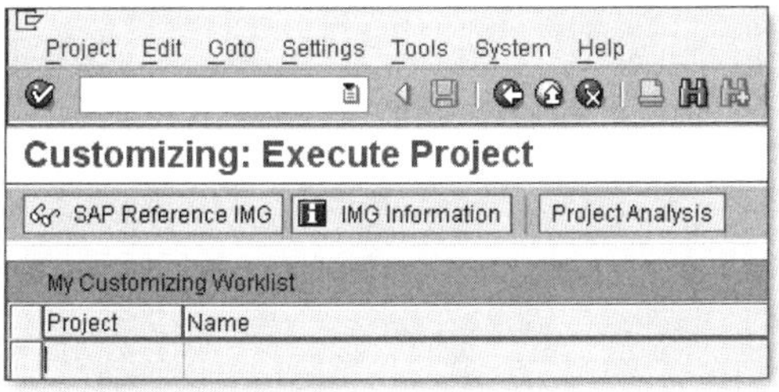


**Figure 2.5** Initial Screen of Transaction SPRO

Inside the SAP Reference IMG, you can find the SAP Calendar under the navigation path SAP NetWeaver • General Settings • Maintain Calendar (see Figure 2.6).

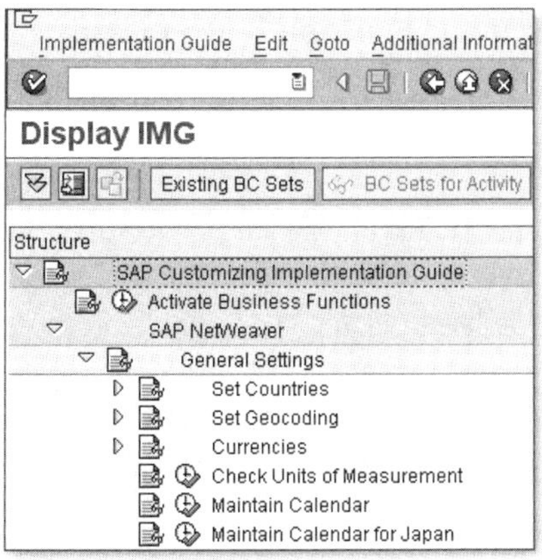


**Figure 2.6** Navigating to the SAP Calendar in the IMG

Figure 2.7 shows the main menu of the SAP Calendar transaction. From here, you can configure subobjects such as public holidays, holiday calendars, and factory calendars. By default, an SAP NetWeaver system comes preconfigured with some typical settings in these subareas. However, you're also free to create customized holidays and calendars as needed.

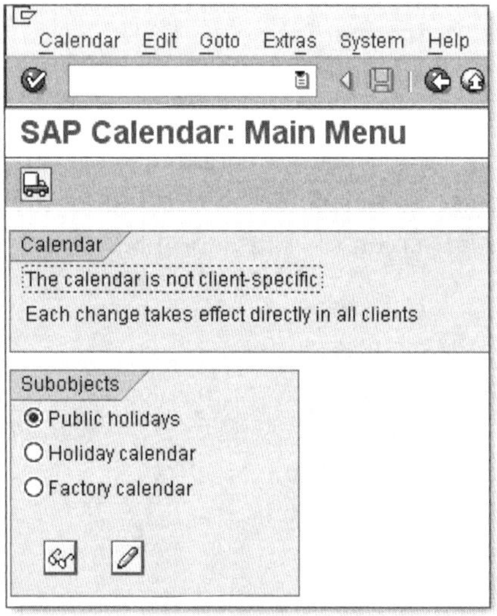


**Figure 2.7** Maintaining the SAP Calendar in the IMG

After the SAP Calendar is configured properly, you can use this data to perform various types of calculations. Table 2.3 shows some useful function modules that leverage this data to determine whether or not a given date is a working day, holiday, and so on. You can find out more information about these function modules in the documentation provided for each module in the Function Builder (Transaction SE37).

| Function Name | Description |
|---|---|
| DATE_COMPUTE_DAY | Computes the day of the week for a given date. Day values are calculated as 1 (Monday), 2 (Tuesday), and so on. |
| DATE_COMPUTE_DAY_ENHANCED | Computes the day of the week just like DATE_COMPUTE_DAY; also returns the day value as text (e.g., TUESDAY, etc.). |

**Table 2.3** Useful Date Functions in Function Group SCAL

| Function Name | Description |
|---|---|
| DATE_CONVERT_TO_FACTORYDATE | Calculates the factory date value for a given date. Also provides an indicator that confirms whether or not the given date is considered a working day according to the selected factory calendar. |
| DATE_GET_WEEK | Determines the week of the year for the given date. For example, the date 9/13/2010 would be the 37th week of the year 2010. |
| FACTORYDATE_CONVERT_TO_DATE | Converts a factory date value back into a date object. |
| HOLIDAY_CHECK_AND_GET_INFO | Tests to determine whether or not a given date is a holiday based on the configured holiday calendar. |
| WEEK_GET_FIRST_DAY | Calculates the first day of a given week. |

**Table 2.3** Useful Date Functions in Function Group SCAL (Cont.)

## 2.3 Bits and Bytes

Modern programming languages do such a tremendous job of abstracting the complexities of computer architectures that, these days, we seldom have any need to work at the bits and bytes level. However, with the advent of Unicode, it's becoming more important to understand how to work at this level because many external data sources encode their data using multi-byte encodings — as opposed to the single-byte code pages normally used in ABAP (e.g., ASCII, etc.). In addition, knowledge of this area can be quite handy in other applications, as you'll see in a moment.

### 2.3.1 Introduction to the Hexadecimal Type in ABAP

Normally, whenever we talk about the built-in native data types provided in the ABAP programming language, we focus our attention around the numeric and character data types. However, ABAP also provides a hexadecimal data type (X) that is used to represent individual bytes in memory. The values stored in the individual bytes are represented as two-digit hexadecimal numbers.

### Binary and Hexadecimal Numbers

If you have never worked with binary or hexadecimal numbers before, then a brief introduction is in order. A *byte* is a unit of measure for memory inside of a computer. Each byte is comprised of 8 bits. The term *bit* is an abbreviation for *binary digit*. A bit can have one of two logical values: `1` (or true) or `0` (or false). In terms of computer circuitry, bits that have the value `1` are turned *on*, while those that have the value `0` are turned *off*.

The binary (or base-2) number system represents numeric values using binary digits. Figure 2.8 shows an example of an 8-bit binary number whose decimal value is 170. As you can see, reading from right to left, the value of each bit is calculated by multiplying one or zero (i.e., the bit value) by two raised to the power of the current index (where indexes start at zero).

| $2^7$ | $2^6$ | $2^5$ | $2^4$ | $2^3$ | $2^2$ | $2^1$ | $2^0$ |
|---|---|---|---|---|---|---|---|
| 1 | 0 | 1 | 0 | 1 | 0 | 1 | 0 |

$$= (2^7 * 1) + (2^5 * 1) + (2^3 * 1) + (2^1 * 1)$$
$$= 170$$

**Figure 2.8** Example of an 8-Bit Binary Number

Binary numbers can be very difficult to work with if you're not a computer. Therefore, the values of bytes are often represented using the hexadecimal (or base-16) numbering system. Each hexadecimal digit is in the range [0123456789ABCDEF], where A = 10, B = 11, C = 12, and so on. Conveniently, each hexadecimal digit can hold any possible value of 4 bits (commonly called a *nibble*). Therefore, two hexadecimal digits can be used to represent a single byte of information in memory.

In addition to the fixed length `X` data type, ABAP also provides the `XSTRING` variable-length hexadecimal type, which is commonly used in various input/output (I/O) operations. Here, as is the case with the `C` and `STRING` data types described in Chapter 1, String Processing Techniques, there is a trade-off between performance and flexibility.

Now that you know a little bit about the hexadecimal type, let's take a look at the types of operations you can perform on data objects of this type. The following sections describe the built-in bitwise operators available in ABAP.

### 2.3.2 Reading and Writing Individual Bits

You can use the `GET BIT` and `SET BIT` statements to read and write individual bits of a hexadecimal data object. The general syntax of these statements is shown in Listing 2.12 and Listing 2.13, respectively.

```
GET BIT lv_index OF lv_hex INTO lv_bit.
```

**Listing 2.12** Syntax of GET BIT Statement

```
SET BIT lv_index OF lv_hex TO lv_bit.
```

**Listing 2.13** Syntax of SET BIT Statement

To demonstrate how these statements work, let's consider an example. Listing 2.14 contains a contrived piece of sample code that swaps the first byte of a two-byte hexadecimal data object with the last byte by manipulating individual bits internally. For good measure, we also shift the bits around one more time at the end of the code snippet, using the `SHIFT` statement in *byte mode*.

```
DATA: lv_hex(2)     TYPE x VALUE 'F00F',
      lv_front_idx TYPE i,
      lv_back_idx  TYPE i,
      lv_front_bit TYPE i,
      lv_back_bit  TYPE i.
WRITE: / lv_hex.
DO 8 TIMES.
  lv_front_idx = sy-index.
  lv_back_idx = lv_front_idx + 8.

  GET BIT lv_front_idx OF lv_hex INTO lv_front_bit.
  GET BIT lv_back_idx OF lv_hex INTO lv_back_bit.

  SET BIT lv_front_idx OF lv_hex TO lv_back_bit.
  SET BIT lv_back_idx OF lv_hex TO lv_front_bit.
ENDDO.
WRITE: / lv_hex.
SHIFT lv_hex BY 1 PLACES CIRCULAR IN BYTE MODE.
WRITE: / lv_hex.
```

**Listing 2.14** Reading and Writing Bits in ABAP

In and of itself, low-level bit manipulation isn't all that exciting. However, there are situations where it can be quite useful.

For example, let's imagine you're working on a problem where you need to work with arbitrarily large numbers that exceed the limits of the built-in ABAP numeric types. One way other modern programming languages, such as Java or .NET, get around this limitation is by developing a so-called numeric *wrapper class*. For instance, the `java.math.BigInteger` class provided with the Java 2 SDK is used to represent arbitrarily large integer values. Internally, bitwise operators are used to mimic the behavior of a normal primitive type represented in two's complement notation.[3] Because this implementation is open source, it wouldn't be too difficult to reverse-engineer an ABAP version of this class to suit your purposes.

### 2.3.3 Bitwise Logical Operators

In addition to the `GET BIT` and `SET BIT` statements, ABAP also provides a series of bitwise logical operators that can be used to build Boolean algebraic expressions. If you aren't familiar with Boolean algebra, there are many excellent resources available online — simply search for the term "Boolean Algebra," and you'll find a wealth of information. Of course, even if you have worked with Boolean operators before, you might need a bit of a refresher. Table 2.4 depicts a *truth table* that shows the values generated when applying the Boolean `AND`, `OR`, or `XOR` operators against the two bit values contained in Field A and Field B.

| Field A | Field B | AND | OR | XOR |
|---|---|---|---|---|
| 0 | 0 | 0 | 0 | 0 |
| 0 | 1 | 0 | 1 | 1 |
| 1 | 0 | 0 | 1 | 1 |
| 1 | 1 | 1 | 1 | 0 |

**Table 2.4** Truth Table for Boolean Operators

Table 2.5 shows the bitwise operators provided with the ABAP language. Just like normal arithmetic operators, the bitwise operators can be combined in complex expressions using parentheses, and so on.

3 The two's complement notation is a common system used to represent signed integers in computers.

| Bitwise Operator | Description |
|---|---|
| BIT-NOT | Unary operator that flips all of the bits in the hexadecimal number to the opposite value. For example, applying this operator to a hexadecimal number having the bit-level value 10101010 (e.g., 'AA') would yield 01010101. |
| BIT-AND | Binary operator that compares each field bit-by-bit using the Boolean AND operator. |
| BIT-XOR | Binary operator that compares each field bit-by-bit using the Boolean XOR (or *eXclusive OR*) operator. |
| BIT-OR | Binary operator that compares each field bit-by-bit using the Boolean OR operator. |

**Table 2.5** Bitwise Logical Operators in ABAP

To see the power of bitwise operators such as the ones listed in Table 2.5, it's useful to consider an example. Imagine that you are tasked with building a custom document management system. One of the requirements of this system is to be able to assign rights permissions to the individual documents maintained in the system. For the purposes of this simple example, let's assume that the possible permissions are *Create*, *Remove*, *Update*, and *Display*.

One way to store these assignments might be to create a database table that contained a series of *flag* columns to indicate whether or not a user had a particular permission for a given document. Unfortunately, there are a couple of problems with this approach. First of all, it requires that we create separate fields for each possible permission type. As the system grows, additional permission types require a modification to the database table. This phenomenon leads into the second problem — namely, space. In other words, each additional flag column adds another byte or two of storage to every row in the table. Of course, another option is to capture the permissions in separate rows. Still, either way you slice it, this can get expensive from a storage perspective.

Instead of creating a new flag column each time we want to add a new permission type to our system, what if we could figure out a way to store a bunch of Boolean flags in a single field? Naturally, the hexadecimal data type lends itself well to this kind of storage operation because it can be used as a type of *bit mask* to represent a large number of flags at the bit level. For example, a single byte bit mask could represent up to 28, or 256, possible values, leaving us plenty of room to grow. The values of the individual Boolean flags can then be set using bitwise operators. Collectively, the process of representing a series of flags at the bit level and manipulating those flags using bitwise operators is referred to as *bit masking*.

The code excerpt in Listing 2.15 demonstrates how bit masking works using the ABAP bitwise logical operators. To keep things simple, we've created an interface that contains constants to represent the possible permission values (e.g., CO_CREATE, etc.). These permission values are assigned to a display-only user using the BIT-OR operator, which effectively works like an addition operator in this case. We can then confirm whether or not the user has a given permission by applying the BIT-AND operator. Here, the result matches the permission constant bit-for-bit if the particular permission has been assigned. This can be confirmed by using the equality operator in an IF statement. In the example, the user has *Display* permissions but not *Create* permissions.

```
INTERFACE lif_permissions.
  CONSTANTS: CO_CREATE  TYPE x VALUE '01',
             CO_REMOVE  TYPE x VALUE '02',
             CO_UPDATE  TYPE x VALUE '04',
             CO_DISPLAY TYPE x VALUE '08'.
ENDINTERFACE.

DATA: lv_display_user TYPE x,
      lv_permission   TYPE x.

* Assign read-only access to a display user:
lv_display_user =
  lv_display_user BIT-OR lif_permissions=>CO_DISPLAY.

* Check the user's permissions:
lv_permission =
  lv_display_user BIT-AND lif_permissions=>CO_DISPLAY.
IF lv_permission EQ lif_permissions=>CO_DISPLAY.
  WRITE: / 'User has display only access.'.
ELSE.
  WRITE: / 'User does not have display access.'.
ENDIF.

lv_permission =
  lv_display_user BIT-AND lif_permissions=>CO_CREATE.
IF lv_permission EQ lif_permissions=>CO_CREATE.
  WRITE: / 'User can create documents.'.
```

```
ELSE.
  WRITE: / 'User is not authorized to create documents.'.
ENDIF.
```

**Listing 2.15** Mapping Permissions Using Bit Masking

As you can see, bit masking can be used as an effective compression technique. Other practical examples of bit masking include the storage of user preferences and set operations, which are described in an example in the online SAP Help Portal.

## 2.4 Summary

In this chapter, you learned about some advanced and perhaps lesser-known features of elementary data types in ABAP. During the course of this book, you'll see how some of these fundamental concepts provide the foundation for implementing new features in SAP NetWeaverAS ABAP, such as support for Unicode and XML processing. In the next chapter, we mix things up a bit and take a look at dynamic programming in ABAP.

*One of the characteristics of a good chef is the ability to improvise whenever the situation calls for it. In this chapter, we show you techniques for developing dynamic ABAP programs that are flexible enough to adapt to changes in their surrounding environment.*

# 3 Dynamic and Reflective Programming

One of the few things that you can plan for in the software development process is change; consequently, one of the measuring sticks of a good piece of software is its ability to adapt to change. One of the primary ways we deal with change as developers is to find what varies and encapsulate it.[1] Of course, without clairvoyance, it's very difficult to anticipate every possible way a piece of software will evolve. Nevertheless, we have a better chance of reacting to unexpected variations if we can gather information about the input source that triggered the change. In programming terms, this knowledge gathering process is referred to as *introspection* or *reflective programming*.

Although reflective programming techniques allow you to detect and investigate environmental changes within a program, they don't allow you to react to those changes. Here, you may need to dynamically define new data types, create data objects on demand, or even implement custom program logic. In this chapter, we look at the dynamic and reflective programming capabilities available in ABAP. These features support the creation of very powerful algorithms and are used in many areas of SAP.

## 3.1 Working with Field Symbols

Field symbols are often the source of much confusion (and consternation) for developers new to ABAP. In this section, we attempt to demystify the concept of

1 In his book *Design Patterns Explained: A New Perspective on Object-Oriented Design* (Addison-Wesley, 2005), Alan Shalloway uses the term "variability analysis" to describe this process.

field symbols by showing you ways to implement generic code and improve the performance in your programs.

### 3.1.1 What Is a Field Symbol?

Before we delve into syntax and usage concerns with field symbols, it's important to understand, conceptually, exactly what a field symbol is. Essentially, a field symbol is a *symbol* (or alias) that refers to a given *field* (i.e., data object) that is visible within the current program scope. If you've worked with other programming languages such as C/C++, you might be inclined to think that field symbols are a type of *pointer* in ABAP. However, that assumption is incorrect.

While the term "pointer" is often used to describe any type of reference variable, it more accurately refers to data objects that can be manipulated as a memory address. As such, pointers *indirectly* refer to a variable by storing that variable's address rather than its contents. To access or manipulate the contents of the variable a pointer points to, you must *de-reference* the pointer using a special de-reference operator. Figure 3.1 depicts the relationship among a data object, a pointer, and a field symbol.

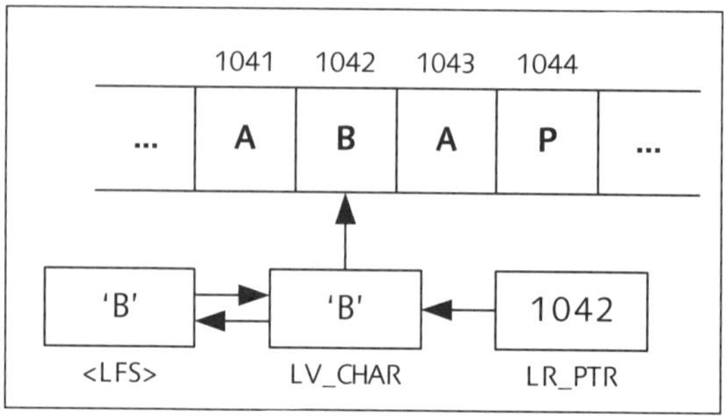


**Figure 3.1** Representation of Pointers and Field Symbols

Looking at the relationship diagram in Figure 3.1, you can see a set of contiguous bytes represented somewhere in memory (note that the address numbers are fictitious values used for demonstration purposes only). The three data objects positioned underneath this memory snapshot represent a character data object, a pointer, and a field symbol, respectively. As you can see, the character data object `LV_CHAR` is stored at address 1042 and has the value `'B'`. The `LR_PTR` data object is a pointer type that references `LV_CHAR`. Note that the contents of `LR_PTR` contain the *address* of `LV_CHAR` (e.g., 1042) rather than its value. To access the value of `LV_CHAR` using LR_PTR, a *de-referencing* operation must be used to tell the runtime environment to access the contents of memory address 1042. On the left side of Figure 3.1, you can see the relationship between a field symbol called <LFS> and LV_CHAR. In this case, <LFS> is strictly an alias for LV_CHAR; changes that are made to LV_CHAR are reflected in <LFS> and vice versa. No special operations are required to access the contents of LV_CHAR using <LFS>. Therefore, you can think of a field symbol as a kind of *permanently de-referenced pointer*.

### 3.1.2 Field Symbol Declarations

Field symbols are declared using the FIELD-SYMBOLS statement whose syntax is shown in Listing 3.1. Note the use of the angle brackets (e.g., < and >) in the definition of the field symbol name. These angle brackets are required for the ABAP runtime environment to differentiate between field symbols and regular data objects.

```
FIELD-SYMBOLS <fs> [TYPING].
```

**Listing 3.1** Syntax Diagram for Field Symbol Declarations

Field symbols can be declared in the global and local context of a report or module pool program. In the object-oriented (OO) context, field symbols can only be defined locally inside of a method implementation; which is to say that you can't define field symbols as attributes of a class or interface.

One advantage field symbols have over normal data objects is their ability to be typed *generically*. Generically typed field symbols inherit the attributes of the data object they point to whenever an assignment is made at runtime. Of course, field symbols can also be declared statically using a specific built-in or custom type. In this case, the data object aliased by the field symbol must be *compatible* with the declared type of the field symbol.

To demonstrate some of the various options for declaring field symbols, let's consider an example. The code excerpt in Listing 3.2 declares several field symbols using different typing methods. For the most part, these definitions are fairly straightforward:

- The field symbol <lfs_builtin_type> is defined using the built-in integer (I) type. Therefore, any attempt to assign a non-integer data object to <lfs_builtin_type> results in a syntax error.

- The <lfs_custom_type> field symbol is declared using the custom type ly_custom_type. We could have just as easily plugged in an ABAP Dictionary type here as well.
- Field symbol <lfs_generic_type> is defined using the generic type ANY. This implies that <lfs_generic_type> can effectively point to any type of data object at runtime.
- The <lfs_number_type> and <lfs_char_type> show how you can use some of the generic types allowed in the specification of interfaces for procedures, methods, and so on to declare generic field symbols.
- The declaration of <lfs_table_type> demonstrates how you can declare a field symbol that can point to any type of internal table. It's also possible to declare a field symbol using a custom table type or a table type defined in the ABAP Dictionary.
- In addition to the TYPE addition, you can also declare a field symbol using another data object as a reference, as evidenced in the declaration of <lfs_like_type>. Here, <lfs_like_type> is typed just like the structure variable ls_custom. Similarly, the field symbol <lfs_wa_type> is declared to be like the line type of internal table lt_custom (i.e., the custom ly_custom_type type).

```
TYPES: BEGIN OF ly_custom_type,
         column1 TYPE i,
         column2 TYPE string,
         column3 TYPE f,
       END OF ly_custom_type.

DATA: ls_custom TYPE ly_custom_type.
DATA: lt_custom TYPE STANDARD TABLE OF ly_custom_type.

FIELD-SYMBOLS:
  <lfs_builtin_type> TYPE i,
  <lfs_custom_type>  TYPE ly_custom_type,
  <lfs_generic_type> TYPE ANY,
  <lfs_number_type>  TYPE numeric,
  <lfs_char_type>    TYPE clike,
  <lfs_table_type>   TYPF ANY TABLE,
  <lfs_like_type>    LIKE ls_custom,
  <lfs_wa_type>      LIKE LINE OF lt_custom.
```

**Listing 3.2** Declaring Field Symbols Using Different Typing Methods

In a non-OO context, it's technically possible to declare a field symbol without any kind of type specification. However, this is considered poor practice because it causes confusion (and perhaps misuse). Therefore, you should always strive to specify a field symbol's type as fully as you can so that the compiler can help guide you in making sure that you use the field symbol properly.

### 3.1.3 Assigning Data Objects to Field Symbols

Initially, a field symbol isn't assigned to any data object. Therefore, to begin using a field symbol, you must use the `ASSIGN` statement to *bind* it to a data object; otherwise, an error occurs if you try to access the field symbol at runtime. The basic syntax of the `ASSIGN` statement is shown in Listing 3.3. This syntax assigns the data object `dobj` to the field symbol called `<fs>`. If the assignment is successful, the system field `SY-SUBRC` has the value `0`; otherwise, it has the value `4`.

```
ASSIGN dobj TO <fs>.
```

**Listing 3.3** Basic Syntax of the ASSIGN Statement

You can also determine whether or not a field symbol is assigned using the `IS ASSIGNED` logical expression demonstrated in Listing 3.4.

```
DATA: lv_name(10) TYPE c VALUE 'Paige Wood'.
FIELD-SYMBOLS: <lfs> TYPE string.

ASSIGN lv_name TO <lfs>.
IF <lfs> IS ASSIGNED.
  WRITE: / 'Field symbol value:', <lfs>.
ELSE.
  WRITE: / 'Field symbol is unassigned!'.
ENDIF.
```

**Listing 3.4** Checking Whether a Field Symbol Is Assigned

#### Static Field Symbol Assignments

The syntax for the `ASSIGN` statement shown in Listing 3.3 is an example of a *static assignment*. Here, the term "static" implies that we know the name of the field that we want to assign to the field symbol at compile time. Static assignments also support the use of offset/length specifications when performing assignments using character types. For example, Listing 3.5 shows how we can assign a substring of the `LV_NAME` data object to `<lfs>`.

```
DATA: lv_name(10) TYPE c VALUE 'Paige Wood'.
FIELD-SYMBOLS: <lfs> TYPE string.

ASSIGN lv_name+0(5) TO <lfs>.
WRITE: / <lfs>.
```

**Listing 3.5** Static Assignments Using Offset/Length Specifications

### Dynamic Field Symbol Assignments

Frequently, whenever you're developing generic algorithms, you may not know the name of the data objects that you want to alias at compile time. In these situations, you can use the dynamic variant of the `ASSIGN` statement as shown in Listing 3.6. Here, the use of parentheses around a character data object (or a string literal) causes the ABAP runtime environment to interpret the value of the character string as the name of the data object to be assigned to the field symbol. In Section 3.3, Introspection with ABAP Run Time Type Services, we'll explain how to use the ABAP Run Time Type Services (RTTS) to introspect simple and complex data objects to dynamically determine the names of data objects. These features are particularly useful whenever a module needs to dynamically process parameters that are passed around generically.

```
DATA: lv_field_name TYPE string VALUE 'LV_FIELD',
      lv_field TYPE i VALUE 50.
FIELD-SYMBOLS: <lfs> TYPE string.

ASSIGN (lv_field_name) TO <lfs>.
WRITE: / <lfs>.
```

**Listing 3.6** Assigning Field Symbols Dynamically

One thing to keep in mind is that the static and dynamic variants of the `ASSIGN` statement described in this section can also be applied to assignments between field symbols. For instance, Listing 3.7 demonstrates how field symbol <lfs_1> is assigned to field symbol <lfs_2>.

```
DATA: lv_field TYPE i VALUE 50.
FIELD-SYMBOLS: <lfs_1> TYPE i,
               <lfs_2> TYPE i.
ASSIGN lv_field TO <lfs_1>.
WRITE: 'Field Symbol #1:', <lfs_1>.
ASSIGN <lfs_1> TO <lfs_2>.
WRITE: 'Field Symbol #2:', <lfs_2>.
```

**Listing 3.7** Performing Assignments Between Field Symbols

### Working with Structures

So far, all of the field symbol assignment examples that we have seen have been based on elementary data types. Now, let's see what happens when we want to assign a structure to a field symbol. In Listing 3.8, we've assigned a structured data object named ls_flight to a field symbol called <lfs_flight>. As you can see, after the assignment is made, we're able to access components of the ls_flight structure via the <lfs_flight> field symbol using the structure component selector operator (-), per usual.

```
DATA: ls_flight TYPE sflight.
FIELD-SYMBOLS: <lfs_flight> LIKE ls_flight.

ls_flight-connid = '1825'.
ls_flight-seatsocc = 60.

ASSIGN ls_flight TO <lfs_flight>.
WRITE: / 'Flight', <lfs_flight>-connid, 'has',
         <lfs_flight>-seatsocc, 'currently filled.'.
```

**Listing 3.8** Assigning a Structure to a Field Symbol

In the example code contained in Listing 3.8, we used the field symbol in exactly the same way that we would have used the structure that it's aliasing. However, sometimes you may know little to nothing about the structure object you're working with. In these circumstances, you can use the ASSIGN COMPONENT statement to dynamically iterate over the components of a given structure. Listing 3.9 shows an example of this approach for the ls_flight structure defined in Listing 3.8. Here, we're using the DESCRIBE FIELD statement to determine the number of components within the structure dynamically. After we know how many components there are, we can iterate through each of them inside of a DO loop. In Listing 3.9, we're using the SY-INDEX system variable to define the index of each component.

```
DATA: ls_flight      TYPE sflight,
      lv_type        TYPE c,
      lv_components  TYPE i.

FIELD-SYMBOLS: <lfs_component> TYPE ANY.

ls_flight-connid = '1845'.
ls_flight-seatsocc = 60.

DESCRIBE FIELD ls_flight
```

```
    TYPE lv_type COMPONENTS lv_components.

DO lv_components TIMES.
  ASSIGN COMPONENT sy-index OF STRUCTURE ls_flight
      TO <lfs_component>.
  WRITE: / 'Component Value is:', <lfs_component>.
ENDDO.
```

**Listing 3.9** Assigning Components of Structures to a Field Symbol

In addition to the index-based approach shown in Listing 3.9, the `ASSIGN COMPONENT` statement also makes it possible to select a component using the component's name. In this variant, the component name is specified via a character data object, string literal, or even another field symbol.

### Working with Internal Tables

Field symbols can also be used to reference internal table variables. After an internal table is assigned to a field symbol, you can use that field symbol in `LOOP` statements, `READ` statements, and so on, just like you would reference a normal internal table variable. Perhaps the most powerful aspect of field symbol usage with internal tables is in the access of individual table rows using these kinds of statements.

Prior to the advent of ABAP Objects, many loops through an internal table looked something like the code excerpt shown in Listing 3.10. In this legacy syntax, `lt_itab` is an internal table that includes a *header line*, which is a sort of work area for table rows accessed via a `LOOP` or `READ` statement, and so on. In Listing 3.10, the code uses the header line to output the flight number for each flight record in the `lt_itab` table. Here, the context in which `lt_itab` is used determines whether or not we're referring to the internal table as a whole or just the header line. Over time, this approach caused quite a bit of confusion because a single name simultaneously referred to two different data objects. Therefore, the use of the `HEADER LINE` addition has been deprecated.

```
DATA: lt_itab TYPE sflight OCCURS 10 WITH HEADER LINE.
LOOP AT lt_itab.
  WRITE: 'Flight #', lt_itab-connid.
ENDLOOP.
```

**Listing 3.10** Legacy Internal Tables with Header Lines

These days, many developers implement a loop such as the one shown in Listing 3.10 using a defined work area as illustrated in Listing 3.11. However, there is a problem with this approach. In each iteration of the loop on table lt_flights, the current table line must be copied into the ls_flight work area. As you can imagine, this copy operation can get pretty expensive for large internal tables.

```
DATA: ls_flight  TYPE sflight,
      lt_flights TYPE STANDARD TABLE OF sflight.
LOOP AT lt_flights INTO ls_flight.
  WRITE: 'Flight #', ls_flight-connid.
ENDLOOP.
```

**Listing 3.11** Accessing Internal Tables Using a Defined Work Area

An effective way to improve the performance of these kinds of loops is to use field symbols. Listing 3.12 demonstrates the approach. Rather than copying the current line into a separate work area using the INTO addition of the LOOP statement, we simply assign the current line to a type-compatible field symbol using the ASSIGNING addition of the LOOP statement. This technique avoids the unnecessary copy operation by simply assigning a reference to the current line to the <lfs_flight> field symbol. After the assignment is made, we can use the <lfs_flight> field symbol just as we would use a header line or explicit work area.

```
DATA: lt_flights TYPE STANDARD TABLE OF sflight.
FIELD-SYMBOLS: <lfs_flight> LIKE LINE OF lt_flights.
LOOP AT lt_flights ASSIGNING <lfs_flight>.
  WRITE: 'Flight #', <lfs_flight>-connid.
ENDLOOP.
```

**Listing 3.12** Accessing Internal Tables Using Field Symbols

The approach demonstrated in Listing 3.12 is considered a best practice for accessing and manipulating individual rows of an internal table. There is also an ASSIGNING addition available with the READ TABLE statement. For more details, consult the ABAP Keyword Documentation.

### 3.1.4 Casting Data Objects During the Assignment Process

In each of the field symbol assignments demonstrated in Section 3.1.3, Assigning Data Objects to Field Symbols, the data objects and field symbols shared the same data type. ABAP also includes support for mixed data type assignments via the CASTING addition to the ASSIGN statement. The lone stipulation here is that the length and alignment of the data object being assigned must be *compatible* with the field symbol type. In other words, you can't use the CASTING addition to assign an internal table data object to an integer field symbol, for instance.

To demonstrate the use of the CASTING addition, let's consider an example. The code excerpt in Listing 3.13 defines a custom timestamp structure type called ly_timestamp. What we would like to do is take the current system timestamp and assign it to a field symbol that has the ly_timestamp type. This would allow us to access each of the components of the timestamp (e.g., YEAR, MONTH, etc.) individually in a structured data object. However, we can't assign a packed number to a structure of type ly_timestamp because their lengths differ. Therefore, we must first copy the contents of the raw timestamp into a character data object. This assignment causes an implicit cast, converting the packed number value into a character string. The length of the resultant character string matches the length of the ly_timestamp type, allowing us to perform our field symbol assignment using the lv_tstamp_txt data object.

```
TYPES: BEGIN OF ly_timestamp,
         year(4)    TYPE c,
         month(2)   TYPE c,
         day(2)     TYPE c,
         hour(2)    TYPE c,
         minutes(2) TYPE c,
         seconds(2) TYPE c,
       END OF ly_timestamp.

DATA: lv_tstamp_raw      TYPE timestamp,
      lv_tstamp_txt(14) TYPE c,
      lv_time            TYPE string.
FIELD-SYMBOLS: <lfs_timestamp> TYPE ly_timestamp,
               <lfs_generic>   TYPE ANY.

GET TIME STAMP FIELD lv_tstamp_raw.
* Note: The following statement is not allowed since
*       lv_tstamp_raw (being a packed number) is too
*       small for <lfs_timestamp>.
*ASSIGN lv_tstamp_raw TO <lfs_timestamp> CASTING.
lv_tstamp_txt = lv_tstamp_raw.
ASSIGN lv_tstamp_txt TO <lfs_timestamp> CASTING.

CONCATENATE <lfs_timestamp>-month '/'
            <lfs_timestamp>-day '/'
            <lfs_timestamp>-year '-'
```

```
          <lfs_timestamp>-hour ':'
          <lfs_timestamp>-minutes ':'
          <lfs_timestamp>-seconds
     INTO lv_time.
WRITE: lv_time.

ASSIGN lv_tstamp_txt TO <lfs_generic>
  CASTING TYPE ly_timestamp.
```

**Listing 3.13** Performing a Cast in a Field Symbol Assignment

Looking at the code in Listing 3.13, you'll notice that we actually perform two field symbol assignments: one to the fully typed <lfs_timestamp> and the other to the generically typed <lfs_generic>. In the assignment to <lfs_timestamp>, notice that the `CASTING` addition used in the assignment doesn't qualify the cast in any way. Here, type specification isn't needed because <lfs_timestamp> is fully typed. Conversely, type qualification *is* needed in the assignment to the generic field symbol <lfs_generic> if we want to be able to access the components of the timestamp encoded inside the contents of the `lv_tstamp_txt` data object. We can specify an explicit type in the casting operation using the syntax variants shown in Listing 3.14. We'll explain more about the `TYPE HANDLE` addition in Section 3.3, Introspection with ABAP Run Time Type Services.

```
ASSIGN dobj TO <fs>
  CASTING [ {TYPE type | (name)} |
            {LIKE dobj} |
            {TYPE HANDLE handle} ].
```

**Listing 3.14** Syntax Diagram of Casting Specifications

## 3.2 Reference Data Objects

As you learned in Section 3.1, Working with Field Symbols, a field symbol is technically not a pointer. Pointers in ABAP are realized in the form of *data references*. In the following subsections, we explore the concept of data references and look at how they can be used as containers for various kinds of data objects.

### 3.2.1 Declaring Data Reference Variables

Data references are stored in a special type of variable called a *data reference variable*. You can declare data reference variables in your programs using the syntax shown in Listing 3.15. Here, we have declared a data reference variable called `lr_dref`.

```
DATA: lr_dref TYPE REF TO DATA.
```

**Listing 3.15** General Syntax for Declaring Data Reference Variables

Now that you know how to declare a data reference variable, let's take a step back and think about what we've defined. Data reference variables can be used to store a reference to any kind of data object. To illustrate this process, consider the visual example provided in Figure 3.2. This graphic depicts the relationship between a data reference variable called `lr_dref` and an integer data object named `lv_value`. Initially, when we declare `lr_dref`, its value is initial; meaning that it doesn't point to anything. However, after we assign a reference to the `lv_value` data object into `lr_dref`, `lr_dref` *points* to the `lv_value` data object.

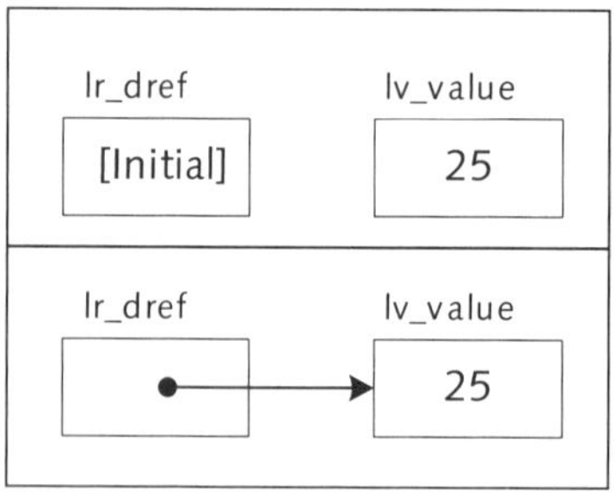


**Figure 3.2** Before and After View of a Data Reference Assignment

Unlike field symbols, `lr_dref` isn't an alias for `lv_value`. For instance, we can't simply use the `lr_dref` identifier to access the contents of `lv_value`. Instead, a data reference variable must be *de-referenced* to access the data object it points to. At first, this indirection may seem like a nuisance as compared to the relative ease of use of field symbols. Nevertheless, this indirection makes it possible to dynamically create data objects and reference them in a program at runtime. We'll see how to de-reference data references in Section 3.2.5, De-Referencing Data References.

In addition to the general data reference declaration syntax shown in Listing 3.15, it's also possible to declare data reference variables that are fully typed. For example, Listing 3.16 shows how to create a data reference variable named `lr_int_ref` that can only point to integer data objects.

```
DATA: lr_int_ref TYPE REF TO i.
```

**Listing 3.16** Declaring Fully Typed Data Reference Variables

### 3.2.2 Assigning References to Data Objects

To obtain a reference to a data object, you use the GET REFERENCE OF statement whose syntax is shown in Listing 3.17. This statement can be used to obtain references to data objects that are statically declared, data objects that are created dynamically, or even field symbols.

```
GET REFERENCE OF dobj INTO dref.
```

**Listing 3.17** Syntax Diagram of GET REFERENCE Statement

To see how reference assignments work, let's take a look at how the GET REFERENCE OF statement is used to obtain a reference to a data object at runtime. The example code in Listing 3.18 demonstrates how to obtain a reference to an integer data object called lv_dobj and store it in a data reference variable called lr_dref.

```
DATA: lv_dobj TYPE i VALUE 27,
      lr_dref TYPE REF TO DATA.
GET REFERENCE OF lv_dobj INTO lr_dref.
```

**Listing 3.18** Using the GET REFERENCE Statement

One important thing to be mindful of when acquiring data references is that a data reference can't point to data objects that pass out of scope, for example, the assignment of a local data object to a global data reference variable. Listing 3.19 contains a sample report called ZREFSCOPE that shows how this works. Here, we've defined a global data reference variable called gr_dref. Inside the procedure SOME_PROCEDURE, a reference to the local variable lv_counter is stored in gr_dref using the GET REFERENCE OF statement. The problem is that the data object lv_counter becomes invalid as soon as the SOME_PROCEDURE procedure completes. Therefore, code that is depending on the gr_dref data reference being bound after the call to SOME_PROCEDURE fails because the data reference has the initial value.

```
REPORT zrefscope.
DATA: gr_dref TYPE REF TO DATA.
FIELD-SYMBOLS:
  <lfs_counter> TYPE ANY.

START-OF-SELECTION.
  IF gr_dref IS INITIAL.
```

```
    WRITE: / 'Not bound initially.'.
  ENDIF.

  PERFORM some_procedure.

  IF gr_dref IS INITIAL.
    WRITE: / 'Data reference is not bound.'.
  ELSE.
    WRITE: / 'Still bound!'.
  ENDIF.

  ASSIGN gr_dref->* TO <lfs_counter>.
  IF sy-subrc EQ 0.
    WRITE: / 'Counter is:', <lfs_counter>.
  ELSE.
    WRITE: / 'Where's my counter???''.
  ENDIF.

FORM some_procedure.
* Local Data Declarations:
  DATA: lv_counter TYPE i VALUE 5.

* Place a reference to lv_counter in gr_dref:
  GET REFERENCE OF lv_counter INTO gr_dref.

* The reference to lv_counter passes out of scope here...
ENDFORM.
```

**Listing 3.19** Avoiding Scoping Issues with Data References

### 3.2.3 Dynamic Data Object Creation

One of the most powerful features of data reference objects is their ability to point to *any* type of data object. This functionality extends beyond statically defined data objects to include support for data objects that are created dynamically by the ABAP runtime environment. To create a data object dynamically, you must use the `CREATE DATA` statement whose syntax is shown in Listing 3.20. As you can see, the typing syntax used to create data objects dynamically is almost identical to that used to declare normal variables in ABAP. The primary difference is the `TYPE HANDLE` addition, which is covered in Section 3.3, Introspection with ABAP Run Time Type Services.

```
CREATE DATA dref TYPE (TABLE OF) type | (typename).
CREATE DATA dref TYPE REF TO type | (typename).
CREATE DATA dref LIKE field.
CREATE DATA dref TYPE HANDLE type_object.
```

**Listing 3.20** Syntax Diagram of CREATE DATA Statement

The code excerpt in Listing 3.21 demonstrates how you can use the `CREATE DATA` statement to dynamically create a data object of type `STRING`. At runtime, this dynamically created data object can only be accessed via the `lr_dref` data reference variable. We'll see how to achieve this in Section 3.2.5, De-Referencing Data References.

```
DATA: lr_dref TYPE REF TO DATA.
CREATE DATA lr_dref TYPE string.
```

**Listing 3.21** Creating Data Objects Dynamically at Runtime

Now that you understand the basic syntax of the `CREATE DATA` statement, let's take a moment to consider what it is used for and what happens behind the scenes when you issue this statement. Most of the time, you know the type and number of data objects that your program needs ahead of time. However, occasionally you may encounter a requirement in which you don't know how many data objects are needed until runtime. Modern runtime environments such as the ABAP runtime environment help solve this problem by maintaining a special area of memory called a *heap*. A heap is essentially a large pool of memory that is typically allocated on a first-come, first-serve basis. The `CREATE DATA` statement submits a request to the ABAP runtime environment to carve out a chunk of memory that can be used to store a data object of a particular type (namely, the type declared using the `TYPE` addition of the `CREATE DATA` statement). If enough memory is available, the ABAP runtime environment allocates the necessary space, returns a reference to that space, and stores it in the specified target data reference variable. After the operation is completed, the dynamically allocated memory area can only be referenced programmatically via the data reference variable. If this reference is deleted, the dynamic data object is orphaned and is eventually cleaned up by the ABAP runtime environment.

It's worth mentioning that unlike other pointer implementations (e.g., C or C++), you can't access the *contents* of a data reference variable in your programs. In other words, you can't manipulate the memory address of the reference, and so on. This is a safety precaution that saves developers from themselves (and others) by avoiding unprotected access to memory addresses. Such measures are particularly important whenever data objects are allocated off of a shared memory heap. Pointers are powerful, but they can also be dangerous, so it's important to have as much built-in protection as possible.

### 3.2.4 Performing Assignments Using Data Reference Variables

Just like other variables in ABAP, you can perform assignments between data reference variables. Listing 3.22 shows how you can use the assignment operator (=) or the MOVE statement to copy a data reference to another data reference variable. Here, it's important to keep in mind that you're copying a *pointer* to a data object, and not the data object itself (a concept often described using the term *reference semantics*). For example, the assignment shown in Listing 3.22 causes both lr_dref1 and lr_dref2 to point at the same data object — namely, the one pointed to by lr_dref1 when the assignment is made.

```
DATA: lv_dobj  TYPE string VALUE 'Paige',
      lr_dref1 TYPE REF TO DATA,
      lr_dref2 TYPE REF TO DATA.

* Obtain a reference to the lv_dobj data object:
GET REFERENCE OF lv_dobj INTO lr_dref1.

* Perform the data reference variable assignment:
lr_dref2 = lr_dref1.     "Or...
MOVE lr_dref1 TO lr_dref2.
```

**Listing 3.22** Data Reference Variable Assignments

### 3.2.5 De-Referencing Data References

The process of accessing the data object pointed to by a data reference variable is referred to as a *de-referencing* operation. Whenever we de-reference a data reference variable, we're telling the ABAP runtime environment that we want to access the data object to which the data reference variable points, rather than the data reference itself. You can de-reference data references using the de-referencing operator (->*) as demonstrated in the sample code shown in Listing 3.23.

```
DATA: lr_dref    TYPE REF TO i,
      lv_counter TYPE i.

CREATE DATA lr_dref.
lr_dref->* = 25.
WRITE: / lr_dref->*.
```

```
lv_counter = lr_dref->*.
WRITE: / lv_counter.
```

**Listing 3.23** De-Referencing a Data Reference Variable

In Listing 3.23, notice that the de-referenced `lr_dref` reference can be used both as an "lvalue" and an "rvalue."[2] This is made possible by the fact that the `lr_dref` data reference is fully specified. Had we declared `lr_dref` generically (e.g., using the `TYPE REF TO DATA` specification), then the code in Listing 3.23 would have produced a syntax error. This is because generically typed data references must be de-referenced into a field symbol before they can be accessed in a program. This process is demonstrated in the example code shown in Listing 3.24.

```
DATA: lr_dref TYPE REF TO DATA.
FIELD-SYMBOLS: <lfs_value> TYPE ANY.

CREATE DATA lr_dref TYPE i.

ASSIGN lr_dref->* TO <lfs_value>.
<lfs_value> = 25.
WRITE: / <lfs_value>.
```

**Listing 3.24** De-Referencing Generically Typed Data References

Notice that we declared the `<lfs_value>` field symbol generically in Listing 3.24. In this case, the field symbol adopts the type of the data object it's assigned (e.g., the integer data object created in the `CREATE DATA` statement). We could have just as easily defined the `<lfs_value>` field symbol as an integer. The point is that assignment statements involving data references behave just like normal assignment statements involving regular data objects. This implies that we can use the `CASTING` addition during an assignment, and so on.

The process of working with de-referenced structured data objects is a little bit different from what we have seen for other data types. These subtle differences are best explained with an example. The code excerpt in Listing 3.25 copies a reference to a structured data object of type `SFLIGHT` into the `lr_flight` data reference. To de-reference individual components of that structure, we must use a

2 If you're not familiar with these terms, an "lvalue" is a value that has an address and can be assigned in an assignment statement. An "rvalue" *could be* an "lvalue," but it could also be a literal value (e.g. 'ABAP') that can't be used as the target of an assignment statement.

special variant of the de-referencing operator (->comp). Of course, to de-reference the structure as a whole, we would still use the normal de-referencing operator (->*), per usual.

```
DATA: ls_flight TYPE sflight,
      lr_flight TYPE REF TO sflight.

ls_flight-connid = '2157'.
GET REFERENCE OF ls_flight INTO lr_flight.
WRITE: 'Flight Number:', lr_flight->connid.
```

**Listing 3.25** De-Referencing Structure Components (Part 1)

If the data reference pointing to the structure is generically typed, you have to assign both the structure and the individual components to a field symbol, as shown in Listing 3.26. Here, once again, we're using a DO loop to iterate over each of the components in the structure generically.

```
DATA: ls_flight TYPE sflight,
      lr_flight TYPE REF TO DATA,
      lv_type   TYPE c,
      lv_fields TYPE i.
FIELD-SYMBOLS: <lfs_flight> TYPE sflight,
               <lfs_comp>   TYPE ANY.

ls_flight-carrid = 'AA'.
ls_flight-connid = '2157'.
GET REFERENCE OF ls_flight INTO lr_flight.

ASSIGN lr_flight->* TO <lfs_flight>.
DESCRIBE FIELD <lfs_flight>
    TYPE lv_type COMPONENTS lv_fields.
DO lv_fields TIMES.
  ASSIGN COMPONENT sy-index OF STRUCTURE <lfs_flight>
      TO <lfs_comp>.
  WRITE: / <lfs_comp>.
ENDDO.
```

**Listing 3.26** De-Referencing Structure Components (Part 2)

## 3.3 Introspection with ABAP Run Time Type Services

In the previous two sections, you learned how to use field symbols and data references to implement some fairly generic program logic. However, up to this point, all of the samples that we have considered have assumed that we're working with a particular data type. But what if we don't know the data type that we're going to be working with ahead of time? After all, to be truly generic, we need to have the ability to look up and introspect information about data types and data objects at runtime. Fortunately, ABAP provides this kind of functionality via the ABAP Run Time Type Services (RTTS) API.

### 3.3.1 ABAP RTTS System Classes

The core functionality of the RTTS API is implemented in the form of a series of ABAP Objects classes. Figure 3.3 depicts a UML class diagram that illustrates the RTTS class hierarchy. As you can see, the root of the RTTS class hierarchy is the abstract class `CL_ABAP_TYPEDESCR`. Each of the concrete subclasses underneath `CL_ABAP_TYPEDESCR` in the class hierarchy corresponds with types defined in the ABAP type hierarchy (e.g., elementary data types, structure data types, class types, etc.).

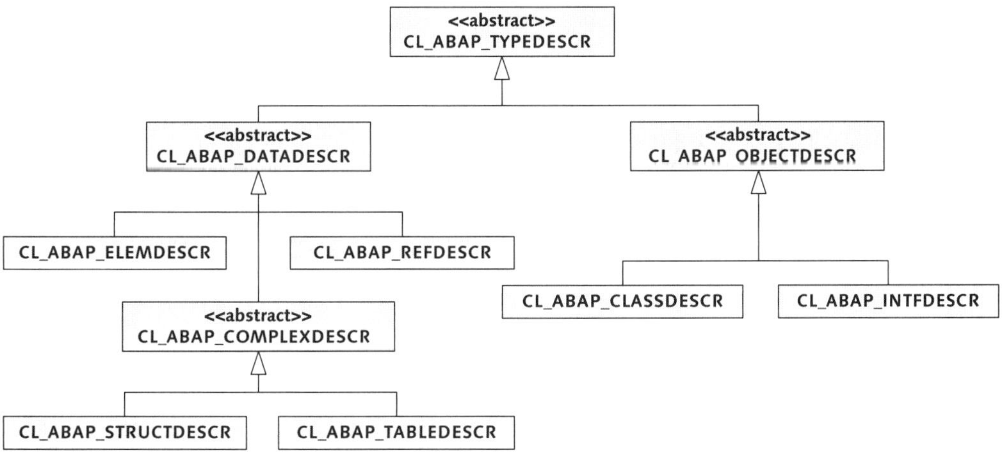


**Figure 3.3** UML Class Diagram of RTTS Class Hierarchy

To appreciate the power of the RTTS, it's helpful to consider the services that they provide. The UML class diagram in Figure 3.4 shows the public methods available in the abstract root class `CL_ABAP_TYPEDESCR` (and inherited in the RTTS subclasses shown in Figure 3.3). Because class `CL_ABAP_TYPEDESCR` is defined as an abstract class, you can't create instances of this class directly. Nevertheless, you can think of `CL_ABAP_TYPEDESCR` as a sort of abstract factory class that provides quite a bit of useful functionality that is applied in the various concrete subclasses. Among the features made available in class `CL_ABAP_TYPEDESCR` is a series of factory class methods that can be used to create instances of concrete type objects using either a preexisting data object, the name of an ABAP data type, an object reference, or a data reference. The names of these class methods begin with the prefix `DESCRIBE_BY_`. In a moment, we'll explain how to use these methods to create instances of concrete type objects. After an instance of a type object is created, you can use the provided instance methods to find out more information about the type in question. For example, the method `IS_DDIC_TYPE()` can tell you whether or not a data type is an ABAP Dictionary type.

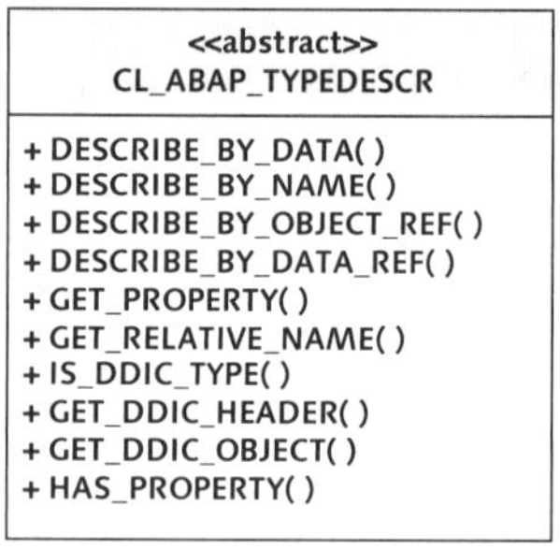


**Figure 3.4** UML Class Diagram for Class CL_ABAP_TYPEDESCR

Each subclass in the RTTS class hierarchy defines its own set of instance methods that provide additional type-specific information. For instance, class `CL_ABAP_TABLEDESCR` provides a method called `GET_TABLE_LINE_TYPE()` that returns information about the line type of the internal table that is being introspected.

### 3.3.2 Working with Type Objects

In addition to the useful type information that they provide, instances of RTTS classes can also be used to represent a particular data type when creating a data object dynamically or casting a data object that is being assigned to a field symbol. You can tap into this functionality using the `TYPE HANDLE` addition described in Section 3.1.4, Casting Data Objects During the Assignment Process, and Section 3.2.3, Dynamic Data Object Creation, respectively. The code excerpt in Listing

3.27 shows how an RTTS type object can be used to create a data object and dereference it into a field symbol.

```
DATA: lr_fname_ref  TYPE REF TO DATA,
      lo_fname_type TYPE REF TO cl_abap_elemdescr.
FIELD-SYMBOLS:
  <lfs_fname> TYPE ANY.

lo_fname_type ?=
  cl_abap_typedescr=>describe_by_name( 'AD_NAMEFIR' ).

CREATE DATA lr_fname_ref TYPE HANDLE lo_fname_type.

ASSIGN lr_fname_ref->* TO <lfs_fname>
  CASTING TYPE HANDLE lo_fname_type.

<lfs_fname> = 'Andersen'.
WRITE: 'First Name is:', <lfs_fname>.
```

**Listing 3.27** Creating Data Objects Using Type Handles

Let's examine the example code from Listing 3.27 step by step:

1. First, we begin by creating an elementary type object using the static method `DESCRIBE_BY_NAME()` of class `CL_ABAP_TYPEDESCR`. Here, we're using the `AD_NAMEFIR` data element from the ABAP Dictionary as a reference to define a "first name" type object. When assigning the type object to the `lo_fname_type` object reference variable, notice that we're using the casting operator (?=) to perform a *widening cast*. If you look carefully, you'll notice that `lo_fname_type` is defined as an object reference variable of type `CL_ABAP_ELEMDESCR`. This widening cast is necessary because of the following:
   - Because class `CL_ABAP_TYPEDESCR` is abstract, we can't create an instance of it directly.
   - The `TYPE HANDLE` addition only supports the specification of type objects that have the static type `CL_ABAP_DATADESCR` or one of its subclasses. Because the `AD_NAMEFIR` data element is defined as an elementary type, we chose to define our type object using the `CL_ABAP_ELEMDESCR` type. Had we wanted to define a complete "person" data object, we might have used the ABAP Dictionary type `ADRP` and the RTTS subclass `CL_ABAP_STRUCTDESCR`.
2. After we have our type object, we can use the `TYPE HANDLE` addition of the `CREATE DATA` statement to create a data object of this type. Here, the ABAP runtime

environment uses the information in the type handle object as a guide for constructing the requested data object dynamically.

3. To do something useful with our generated data reference, we must de-reference it. Here, we're de-referencing it into a generically defined field symbol called <lfs_fname> using the CASTING addition of the ASSIGN statement. The use of the CASTING addition ensures that the <lfs_fname> field symbol takes on the dynamic type specified in our lo_fname_type type object.
4. After the assignment is made, we can use the field symbol just like a regular data object of type AD_NAMEFIR, as evidenced in the WRITE statement.

### 3.3.3 Defining Custom Data Types Dynamically

The DESCRIBE_BY... factory methods described in Section 3.3.1, ABAP RTTS System Classes, are useful if you have some kind of reference type or data object to work off of. But what if you need to create a custom type from scratch on the fly? In these cases, you can use the creational methods defined in the concrete RTTS type classes to dynamically create a new type. For example, instead of using the ABAP Dictionary type AD_NAMEFIR as a reference to define our "first name" type object in Listing 3.27, we could have used the class method GET_C() of class CL_ABAP_ELEMDESCR, as shown in Listing 3.28.

```
DATA: lr_fname_ref  TYPE REF TO DATA,
      lo_fname_type TYPE REF TO cl_abap_elemdescr.
FIELD-SYMBOLS:
  <lfs_fname> TYPE ANY.

lo_fname_type = cl_abap_elemdescr=>get_c( 40 ).
CREATE DATA lr_fname_ref TYPE HANDLE lo_fname_type.
```

**Listing 3.28** Creating a Custom Elementary Type

Listing 3.29 shows how to create a custom structure type using the CREATE() factory method of class CL_ABAP_STRUCTDESCR. Here, the components of the structure type are specified as entries in an internal table parameter called P_COMPONENTS. Typically, you need only specify the name and type of the component. However, there are also parameters that help you to specify an include structure — see the online help documentation in the Class Builder for more details. After the structure type object is created, we can use it to create data objects, per usual, as evidenced in the example code from Listing 3.29.

```
DATA: lt_components TYPE
          cl_abap_structdescr=>component_table,
      lo_name_type  TYPE REF TO cl_abap_structdescr,
      lr_name_ref   TYPE REF TO DATA,
      lv_type       TYPE c,
      lv_components TYPE i.

FIELD-SYMBOLS:
  <lfs_component> LIKE LINE OF lt_components,
  <lfs_name>      TYPE ANY,
  <lfs_field>     TYPE ANY.

* Define the components of our custom name type:
APPEND INITIAL LINE TO lt_components
  ASSIGNING <lfs_component>.
<lfs_component>-name = 'FIRST_NAME'.
<lfs_component>-type = cl_abap_elemdescr=>get_c( 40 ).

APPEND INITIAL LINE TO lt_components
  ASSIGNING <lfs_component>.
<lfs_component>-name = 'MIDDLE_INITIAL'.
<lfs_component>-type = cl_abap_elemdescr=>get_c( 1 ).

APPEND INITIAL LINE TO lt_components
  ASSIGNING <lfs_component>.
<lfs_component>-name = 'LAST_NAME'.
<lfs_component>-type = cl_abap_elemdescr=>get_c( 40 ).

* Create the new structure type:
lo_name_type = cl_abap_structdescr=>create( lt_components ).

* Create a new name structure:
CREATE DATA lr_name_ref TYPE HANDLE lo_name_type.

* De-reference the name structure reference:
ASSIGN lr_name_ref->* TO <lfs_name>
  CASTING TYPE HANDLE lo_name_type.

* Assign values to the name structure components:
DESCRIBE FIELD <lfs_name>
    TYPE lv_type COMPONENTS lv_components.

DO lv_components TIMES.
```

```
    ASSIGN COMPONENT sy-index
        OF STRUCTURE <lfs_name> TO <lfs_field>.

    CASE sy-index.
      WHEN 1.
        <lfs_field> = 'Paige'.
      WHEN 2.
        <lfs_field> = 'A'.
      WHEN 3.
        <lfs_field> = 'Wood'.
    ENDCASE.
ENDDO.
```

**Listing 3.29** Creating a Custom Structure Type

### 3.3.4 Case Study: RTTS Usage in the ALV Object Model

Sometimes, when learning a new technology, it's helpful to see how that technology is used in everyday life. Even if you're just getting your first exposure to the RTTS API, you've likely encountered it at various points in your programming tasks. One common place where you see the RTTS used is in the SAP List Viewer (or ALV). In the past, one of the prerequisites for working with ALV was the generation of a *field catalog* that was used to define the columns of the two-dimensional grid (e.g., column names, data types, etc.). Figure 3.5 shows an example of an ALV grid display in the Data Browser (Transaction SE16).

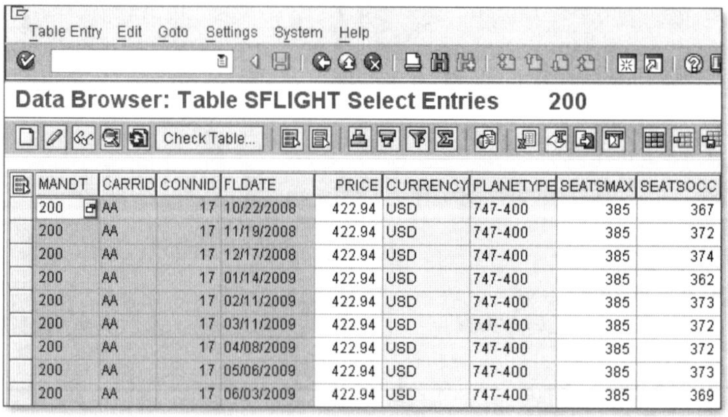


**Figure 3.5** Example of ALV Grid Display in the Data Browser

Beginning with the SAP NetWeaver 2004 release of the AS ABAP, the ALV API has been consolidated into a class-based model called the *ALV Object Model*. One of the primary benefits of working with this model is that you no longer have to specify a field catalog to display a table in an ALV grid. Instead, you simply pass an internal table as a parameter to a factory method defined in one of the main ALV classes, and the framework takes care of the rest. Given what you've seen already with the RTTS API, you can probably guess how the framework is able to perform this task. Nevertheless, let's take a look under the hood and see what's going on.

For the purposes of our discussion, let's assume that we're using the core CL_SALV_TABLE class to build a simple two-dimensional grid. The following task flow provides a high-level overview of the steps taken by this class to dynamically generate a field catalog at runtime:

1. To create an instance of class CL_SALV_TABLE, you must invoke the factory method appropriately named FACTORY(). In addition to some various display parameters, this class method has a changing parameter called T_TABLE that is used to specify the internal table that you want to display in the grid. Internally, the FACTORY() method creates an instance of the ALV grid and then binds the data table via a call to instance method SET_DATA().
2. Inside method SET_DATA(), a reference to the T_TABLE parameter is stored in a data reference attribute called R_TABLE. This data reference variable is then passed along with an object reference variable of type CL_SALV_COLUMNS to a generic class method called DESCRIBE_TABLE() in class CL_SALV_DATA_DESCR. This method performs the magic of deriving the columns that are displayed in the grid
3. To derive the metadata of a row in the internal table, method DESCRIBE_TABLE() first de-references the imported table reference (i.e., R_TABLE) into a field symbol and then creates a data object that has the line type of that table. This dynamically generated data object can then be used as a reference type in a call to method DESCRIBE_BY_DATA_REF() of class CL_ABAP_STRUCTDESCR. This sequence of steps is illustrated in the code excerpt shown in Listing 3.30.

```
ASSIGN r_table->* TO <table>.
CREATE DATA r_data LIKE LINE OF <table>.

r_tabdescr ?=
  cl_abap_structdescr=>describe_by_data_ref( r_data ).
```

**Listing 3.30** Building a Field Catalog Using RTTS

4. After the type object r_tabdescr is derived, the properties of the internal table line type can be introspected via a series of calls to the instance methods provided by class CL_ABAP_STRUCTDESCR, as evidenced in the implementation of helper method READ_STRUCTDESCR() of class CL_SALV_DATA_DESCR. These properties can be used to formulate the field catalog realized in the R_COLUMNS object reference parameter.

We hope by now you can see the power of the RTTS API in building generic and flexible programs. The integration of the RTTS API in the ALV Object Model has made it possible to implement ALV reports using a fraction of the code that was required in the past. Other applications of the RTTS API include the BSP HTMLB and Web Dynpro frameworks as well as the ABAP proxy runtime integrated with the SAP NetWeaver Process Integration (SAP NetWeaver PI) solution.

## 3.4 Dynamic Program Generation

In rare circumstances, you might encounter a situation where you need to dynamically create some program logic on the fly. In these cases, ABAP allows you to create subroutine pools and report programs dynamically. These generated objects can then be invoked using the same call syntax used to execute statically defined ABAP Repository objects.

### 3.4.1 Creating a Subroutine Pool

The process of creating a subroutine pool dynamically is fairly straightforward. First, you build up the source code in an internal table, and then you use that source code to create the subroutine pool via the GENERATE SUBROUTINE POOL statement. The report program ZSUBPOOLDEMO in Listing 3.31 shows how this works.

```
REPORT zsubpooldemo.
START-OF-SELECTION.

DATA: lt_source_code TYPE TABLE OF string,
      lv_program     TYPE string.

* Build the source code for the subroutine pool:
APPEND 'PROGRAM zmysubpool.' TO lt_source_code.
APPEND 'FORM dynamicsub.' TO lt_source_code.
APPEND 'WRITE: / ''Dynamic code goes here...''.'
    TO lt_source_code.
APPEND 'ENDFORM.' TO lt_source_code.
```

```
* Generate the subroutine pool:
GENERATE SUBROUTINE POOL lt_source_code
    NAME lv_program.
WRITE: / 'Generated program name:', lv_program.

* Call the dynamically generated subroutine:
WRITE: / 'Some static code...'.
PERFORM dynamicsub IN PROGRAM (lv_program).
WRITE: / 'More static code...'.
```

**Listing 3.31** Dynamically Generating a Subroutine Pool

The report program ZSUBPOOLDEMO in Listing 3.31 creates a subroutine called DYNAMICSUB in the subroutine pool ZMYSUBPOOL. The subroutine pool is then generated using the GENERATE SUBROUTINE POOL statement. If you execute the code, you'll see that the generated program name stored in variable lv_program is an internally generated name created by the ABAP runtime environment. The generated program name allows us to access the program via the PERFORM subroutine IN PROGRAM statement.

One important thing to note with dynamically generated subroutine pools is that they are *transient*. In other words, you won't find a subroutine pool with that name in the ABAP Repository. The subroutine pool is only accessible within the internal session of the program that created it.

### 3.4.2 Creating a Report Program

The process of creating a report program dynamically is very similar to the one used to create a subroutine pool. The primary difference is the use of the INSERT REPORT statement in lieu of the GENERATE SUBROUTINE POOL statement. The report program ZREPORTDEMO in Listing 3.32 demonstrates how this works.

```
REPORT zreportdemo.
START-OF-SELECTION.

CONSTANTS: CO_REPORT_NAME TYPE program VALUE 'ZDYNREPT'.
DATA: lt_source_code TYPE TABLE OF string.

* Build the source code for the subroutine pool:
APPEND 'PROGRAM zdynrept.' TO lt_source_code.
APPEND 'WRITE: / ''Dynamic report code here...''.'
    TO lt_source_code.
```

```
* Generate and invoke the report program:
INSERT REPORT CO_REPORT_NAME FROM lt_source_code.
IF sy-subrc EQ 0.
  SUBMIT (CO_REPORT_NAME) AND RETURN.
ELSE.
  WRITE: / 'The report could not be created.'.
ENDIF.
```

**Listing 3.32** Dynamically Creating a Report Program

A very important thing to keep in mind when dynamically creating report programs is that these report programs *are* created as ABAP Repository objects. Among other things, this implies that you could accidentally overwrite an existing report program if you're not careful to check the name beforehand.

### 3.4.3 Drawbacks to Dynamic Program Generation

The dynamic program creation techniques shown in this section are powerful and can be dangerous if not used properly. Some of the drawbacks to using these approaches include the following:

- Slow performance due to the need for compilation of dynamically generated code
- Potential for overwriting existing report programs via the `INSERT REPORT` statement
- Possibility for uncatchable runtime errors due to syntax errors in the dynamically generated code
- Cumbersome and often error-prone generation of the program code

As such, these techniques should be saved as a last-ditch method for implementing a particular requirement.

## 3.5 Summary

As you've seen, dynamic programming can be used to develop highly flexible solutions. In particular, the use of reference types and dynamic type introspection makes it easy to convert a piece of throwaway code into a self-contained module that is easy to reuse. In the next chapter, we investigate the native support for Unicode introduced in release 6.10 of SAP NetWeaver AS ABAP.

*There's nothing more frustrating than reading through a recipe and having to perform conversions between different measurement standards. In the field of computer science, it's equally wearisome to process character data that is encoded using different encoding schemes. In this chapter, we show you how Unicode is leveling the playing field so that computers can work with one universal standard when processing character data.*

# 4 ABAP and Unicode

Human beings are wonderfully adept at thinking in terms of abstract concepts such as languages, grammar, and alphabets. Unfortunately, computers lack the capability for this kind of creative expression. Therefore, for computers to be able to work with text, specific rules must be established to define mundane details such as what makes up a character. These rules are typically collectively referred to as a *character-encoding system*.

In this chapter, we introduce you to the Unicode character-encoding system and describe the impacts of Unicode support in many areas of ABAP development. Once you're familiar with these basic concepts, we teach you how to *think* in Unicode. Finally, we conclude our discussion by showing you how a series of utility classes provided by SAP can be used to work with individual Unicode characters, perform conversions between data encoded using different encoding systems, and more.

## 4.1 Introduction to Character Codes and Unicode

Internally, computers represent all kinds of data in the binary format. As such, there is no way for a computer to physically store character data directly. To get around this basic limitation, early software researchers devised character-encoding systems that assigned a discrete numeric value to a given character. On the surface, such a solution seems relatively straightforward. However, almost 50 years later, the concept of character-encoding remains a hotly contested subject among software engineers. In this section, we show you how Unicode is standardizing the way that characters are represented in computers.

### 4.1.1 Understanding Character-Encoding Systems

As we mentioned earlier, a character-encoding system assigns a discrete numeric value (called a *code point*) to each character within a given set of characters. This set of characters is referred to as the encoding system's *character set*. Frequently, you'll hear the term *code page* used when describing the table that maps the characters in an encoding system's character set to their assigned code point values.

Table 4.1 contains an excerpt from the ASCII[1] code page, showing the code point values for the English letters A-D. Of course, code pages map more than just letters; they also map punctuation marks, numeric characters, symbols, control characters, and so on. If you're interested in seeing a comprehensive list of characters defined in the ASCII character set, perform a keyword search online using the phrase "ASCII table."

| Character | Hex Value | Decimal Value | Binary Value |
|---|---|---|---|
| ... | ... | ... | ... |
| A | 41 | 65 | 0100 0001 |
| B | 42 | 66 | 0100 0010 |
| C | 43 | 67 | 0100 0011 |
| D | 44 | 68 | 0100 0100 |
| ... | ... | ... | ... |

**Table 4.1** Sample Excerpt from the ASCII Code Page

Now that you have a feel for how code pages are organized, let's think about the implications of all this from a storage perspective. Each character in an encoding scheme's character set is represented in memory using its assigned code point value encoded in binary. Therefore, the letter A is represented with the value "0100 0001," as shown in Table 4.1. In this case, only a single byte of memory is required to store the letter A (e.g., 8 bits = 1 byte). Indeed, a single byte of memory can represent 28, or 256, different code points. Of course, as the character set grows, so

1 ASCII stands for American Standard Code for Information Interchange. The ASCII standard was formally published as ISO/IEC 646 in 1972.

also does the amount of memory needed to represent the individual characters — a concept we revisit in Section 4.1.3, What Is Unicode?

### 4.1.2 Limitations of Early Character-encoding Systems

One of the earliest character-encoding systems to gain widespread use was the ASCII standard. Being developed in the United States, ASCII was based on the ordering of the English alphabet. Initially, ASCII was intended to be part of an international standard that shared common characters while reserving specific ranges of code points for language-specific characters. However, while acceptance of this international standard took longer than expected, the ASCII standard emerged as a worldwide standard almost by default.

The original ASCII standard defined 128 characters that could be represented using 7 bits. Over time, additional standards emerged that expanded on ASCII to define character-encodings for other languages besides English — the most successful of which was the ISO/IEC 8859 standard. The ISO/IEC 8859 standard defined an 8-bit encoding scheme that was split up into various parts: ISO 8859-1 for Western European languages, ISO 8859-2 for Central European languages, and so on.

As more and more encoding systems were introduced, developers began to encounter complex interoperability problems. For example, what if a file generated on an IBM mainframe system (which uses the EBCDIC[2] standard) needs to be processed on a PC system using the ASCII standard? Like the story of the Tower of Babel, character-encoding systems confounded developers to the point that data exchange was nearly impossible. Clearly, a better solution was needed, and that solution was Unicode.

### 4.1.3 What Is Unicode?

Like ASCII and EBCDIC before it, Unicode is a character-encoding system. What sets Unicode apart is that it was built from the ground up to support almost all of the known writing systems in the world. As such, Unicode has a massive character set (more than 100,000 characters at the time this book is being written) that assigns discrete values to pretty much every character imaginable.

2 EBCDIC stands for Extended Binary Coded Decimal Interchange Code, an 8-bit character-encoding system developed by IBM in the 1960s.

One of the primary challenges with implementing a universal character set such as Unicode is figuring out how to store every possible code point efficiently. Indeed, some Unicode characters have assigned code point values that are so large that it requires up to 4 bytes of memory to represent them. The common solution to this problem has been to employ a *variable-length character-encoding scheme*. The term "variable" here implies that a reduced number of bytes are required to represent certain frequently used code points. For example, to simplify the conversion process, the first 256 code points in the Unicode standard were taken directly from the 8-bit ISO 8859-1 standard. Variable-length character-encodings can take advantage of this fact by storing ASCII characters in a single byte, for example. Table 4.2 describes the common character-encodings used in Unicode.

| Character-encoding | Description |
|---|---|
| UTF-8 | Variable-length encoding that encodes each character in the Unicode standard using 1-4 bytes. Only 1 byte is required to represent ASCII characters. |
| UTF-16 | Variable-length encoding that encodes each character in the Unicode standard using either 2 or 4 bytes. Most of the Unicode characters identified thus far fall into the *Basic Multilingual Plane* (BMP). Each of the characters in the BMP can be represented using 2 bytes. Therefore, most of the time, UTF-16 only requires 2 bytes to represent a character. However, characters outside of the BMP are represented using *surrogate pairs* that split a code point value over 4 bytes. |
| UTF-32 | Fixed-length encoding that encodes each character of the Unicode standard using exactly 4 bytes. Though technically easier to work with, UTF-32 is rarely used because of its massive storage requirements. |

**Table 4.2** Character-Encodings for Unicode

One aspect of the Unicode standard that is often ignored is the fact that it extends its focus beyond simple encoding concerns to tackle more complex issues such as classification, character relationships, and so on. These features make it easier to identify the uppercase equivalent for a character, determine whether or not a given character is a punctuation mark, and so on. In the past, developers often resorted to the error-prone approach of hard-coding this information into their programs. Today, modern languages such as .NET and Java are integrating these aspects of character-encoding systems into string and character types so that developers have a standard way of performing these tasks.

### 4.1.4 Unicode Support in SAP Systems

In the not-so-distant past, language support in an SAP system was a very tricky proposition. During that time, characters from the set of languages supported by SAP were encoded using single-byte encoding schemes (e.g., ASCII or EBCDIC) or double-byte encoding schemes (e.g., SJIS for Japanese or BIG5 for traditional Chinese). As described in Section 4.1.2, Limitations of Early Character-encoding Systems, there were all kinds of compatibility issues associated with the exchange of data between these disparate character sets. Recognizing these limitations, SAP elected to tackle the daunting task of integrating native Unicode support into the ABAP runtime environment. The fruits of this development effort were first realized with release 6.10 of SAP NetWeaver AS ABAP.

To a large degree, this major addition to the architecture of SAP NetWeaver AS ABAP flew in under the radar for many developers who didn't really see any noticeable difference in the majority of their everyday programming tasks. This seamless transition was a result of a carefully laid out development plan that specified the following goals:

1. Maintain backward compatibility with non-Unicode systems.
2. Keep ABAP language changes to a minimum to reduce the effort involved in converting non-Unicode systems/programs.
3. Make it easy to exchange data between Unicode and non-Unicode systems.

In recent years, Unicode support has gone from an optional installation task to a mandatory one; in fact, as of the year 2007, all new SAP products must be installed using Unicode. If you want to learn more about Unicode installations, technical underpinnings, and so on, we highly recommend *Unicode in SAP Systems* (SAP PRESS, 2007).

## 4.2 Developing Unicode-Enabled Programs in ABAP

One of SAP's primary design goals during the Unicode integration process was to minimize the impacts to the ABAP programming language as much as possible. However, despite SAP's best efforts to shield developers from character-encoding issues, there are certain situations where you need to understand what is going on from a Unicode perspective. In this section, we teach you how to recognize these circumstances so that you can leverage special language extensions designed to deal with these occurrences.

### 4.2.1 Overview of Unicode-Related Changes to ABAP

Generally speaking, the impacts of the switch to Unicode from an ABAP perspective are limited to statements that make assumptions about the internal length of a character. In the past, such statements always assumed that the length of a single character was 1 byte. However, in a Unicode system, these suppositions don't hold true. These days, for instance, Unicode-enabled SAP systems are installed by default using the UTF-16 encoding scheme. This implies that the byte size of an individual character in a Unicode system can be either 2 bytes or 4 bytes.

#### Definition of Character Types in Unicode Systems

The complexity of variable-length encoding schemes such as UTF-8 and UTF-16 forced SAP to make some hard decisions regarding language constructs that had loose requirements around what a character data type actually looks like. In the end, it was decided that such vagaries should be deprecated and that only the following types should be treated as character data types:

- `C`
- `N`
- `D`
- `T`
- `STRING`

For the most part, these character data types can be used in string processing statements without restrictions. However, to reduce ambiguity in certain situations, many of these statements now allow you to specify a *processing mode* that determines whether or not character-based processing or byte-based processing should be used. For example, Listing 4.1 shows how the `IN BYTE MODE` addition can be used to calculate the length of a character data object in bytes. In this case, the ABAP Dictionary type `AD_NAMEFIR` is specified as `CHAR(40)`, which means that the size of the `LV_NAME` data object in bytes is 40 * 2 = 80.

```
DATA: lv_name     TYPE ad_namefir VALUE 'Paige',
      lv_byte_len TYPE i.
DESCRIBE FIELD lv_name LENGTH lv_byte_len
      IN BYTE MODE.
```

**Listing 4.1** Specifying Byte Processing Mode

Listing 4.2 shows how the same DESCRIBE FIELD statement can be processed in character mode using the IN CHARACTER MODE addition. In this case, the calculated length of the LV_NAME data object is 40 characters, as you would expect.

```
DATA: lv_name     TYPE ad_namefir VALUE 'Paige',
      lv_char_len TYPE i.
DESCRIBE FIELD lv_name LENGTH lv_char_len
      IN CHARACTER MODE.
```

**Listing 4.2** Specifying Character Processing Mode

In addition to the elementary character types described previously, flat structures that only contain components of type C, N, D, or T can also be used where elementary character types are expected in certain situations (e.g., in a WRITE statement, etc.). Such structures can in turn contain substructures as long as the components of the substructure are also of type C, N, D, or T.

### Impacts to Structure Operations

Another subtle impact of Unicode support in the ABAP runtime environment is that the alignment of complex data objects such as structures is different in a Unicode-enabled system as opposed to a non-Unicode system. These layout changes are best described using an example. Consider the custom LS_STRUCT1 structure defined in Listing 4.3. The LS_STRUCT1 structure type defines a couple of components as well as a substructure called LS_STRUCT2. Because each of the components defined in LS_STRUCT1 has been defined statically (i.e., without variable-length types such as the STRING type), you might expect that the byte layout of this structure in memory would be contiguous. However, if you look carefully at Figure 4.1, you'll see that this assumption is incorrect. In a Unicode system, each character data object must be positioned at a memory address that is divisible by 2 or 4. Furthermore, data types such as the I data type, object reference types, and so on. also require special alignments in memory. Therefore, structures containing these types of components are padded internally using special *alignment bytes*. For instance, in Figure 4.1, alignment bytes are used to align structure LS_STRUCT1, character data object C, and integer data object D.

```
BEGIN OF ls_struct1,
  a(1) TYPE x,
  BEGIN OF ls_struct2,
    b(1)  TYPE x,
    c(10) TYPE c,
  END OF ls_struct2,
```

```
  d TYPE i,
END OF ls_struct1.
```

**Listing 4.3** Understanding the Layout of Structured Types

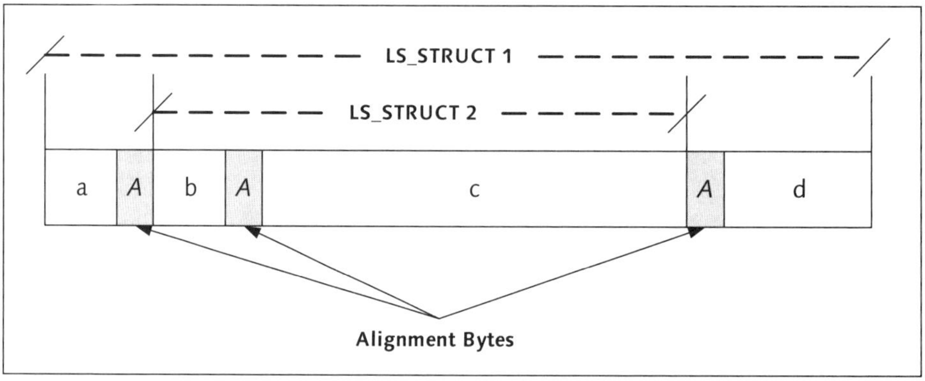


**Figure 4.1** Alignment of Structures in a Unicode System

These alignment changes make assignments and comparisons between incompatible structures impossible in Unicode systems. For instance, in a non-Unicode system, the code excerpt shown in Listing 4.4 would work because a character could fit inside a single byte. However, in a Unicode system, such an assignment causes the ABAP syntax check to complain that the two structure objects aren't compatible.

```
DATA:
  BEGIN OF ls_struct1,
    a(1) TYPE c,
    b(1) TYPE x,
  END OF ls_struct1,

  BEGIN OF ls_struct2,
    a(1) TYPE c,
    b(1) TYPE c,
  END OF ls_struct2.

ls_struct1 = ls_struct2.
```

**Listing 4.4** Incompatible Assignments Between Structure Types

### Other Changes

The Unicode-related changes described in this section represent some of the basic adjustments that must be made to work with character data objects in a Unicode system. As you get more comfortable with Unicode, we highly recommend that you read through the ABAP Keyword Documentation to learn about other minor syntax changes that have been incorporated into various ABAP statements. Further information can also be found online in the SAP Help Portal at *http://help.sap.com*.

## 4.2.2 Thinking in Unicode

As we mentioned at the beginning of this section, SAP strove to make the adoption of Unicode in SAP NetWeaver AS ABAP as transparent as possible from a development perspective. Therefore, in many ways, you have to work pretty hard to introduce Unicode-related problems into your ABAP programs. However because the Unicode conversion process allowed SAP to go back and clean up certain syntax elements with ambiguous usage rules, there are particular programming practices that should be avoided in the Unicode context. For the most part, the changes here are quite intuitive as long as you maintain some perspective.

### Avoiding the Use of Structured Fields as Character Types

In non-Unicode systems, there is an implicit rule that makes it possible for any flat structure type to be used where character types are expected. With Unicode systems, this rule has been constrained to only support the use of flat structures whose components only consist of character types. Still, generally speaking, it's better to avoid using structured types for these purposes altogether. For example, consider the code excerpt shown in Listing 4.5. Here, we've defined a flat structured field called LS_STRUCTURE that only contains character types as its components. Technically, we can access this structure field using offset/length specifications, as we have done in the WRITE statement that outputs the current month value embedded within the structure. However, if we decide to go back and add in an integer component directly before FIELD2, the offset-based access causes a syntax error because the length of the character type start of the structure has been reduced to 10 characters (e.g., the length of the FIELD1 component).

```
DATA: BEGIN OF ls_structure,
        field1(10) TYPE c,
        field2     TYPE d,
        field3     TYPE t,
      END OF ls_structure.
```

```
ls_structure-field1 = 'Andersen'.
ls_structure-field2 = sy-datum.
ls_structure-field3 = sy-uzeit.

WRITE: / 'Month is: ', ls_structure+14(2).
```

**Listing 4.5** Offset/Length-Based Access to Flat Structures

The bottom line is that offset/length-based access to structured fields is a poor programming practice that should be avoided regardless of whether the system is a Unicode system. Not only will the avoidance of such practices make your code more clear, but it will also guarantee that you won't run into Unicode-related access issues down the road.

#### Preventing Elusive Errors in Structure Operations

In Section 4.2.1, Overview of Unicode-Related Changes to ABAP, we learned about the changes to the alignment of structures in Unicode systems. These alignment modifications make the process of performing assignments and comparisons between structures much more dicey than they were in the past. Generally speaking, structure types are compatible as long as they have the same type and length. However, the possibility for implicit and explicit type conversions makes the compatibility lines much more blurry. For example, consider the assignment shown in Listing 4.6. Here, we're assigning a structured type to an elementary character type. This is allowed because the collective size of the structure fields FIELD1 and FIELD2 matches the size of the LV_TARGET data object. However, if the LS_STRUCTURE type changes in incompatible ways, then the assignment is no longer allowed between these two types.

```
DATA: lv_target(10) TYPE c,
      BEGIN OF ls_structure,
        field1(8) TYPE c,
        field2(2) TYPE n,
        field3    TYPE i,
        field4    TYPE f,
      END OF ls_structure.

lv_target = ls_structure.
```

**Listing 4.6** Mixed Type Assignments in the Unicode Context

As a rule, assignments between incompatible structure types should be avoided in the Unicode context. Instead, it's preferable to process these structure types component-wise to guarantee compatibility. For more complex scenarios, such logic should be encapsulated inside an ABAP Objects class that defines methods that control the assignment/comparison process.

One step that you can take to maintain compatibility for structure types defined in the ABAP Dictionary is to specify an *enhancement category*. This setting is maintained in the ABAP Dictionary (Transaction SE11) by selecting EXTRAS • ENHANCEMENT CATEGORY in the menu bar. Figure 4.2 shows the dialog screen enhancement category maintenance screen for the BAPIRET2 type. From a Unicode perspective, the selection of the Can Be Enhanced (Character-Type) or Cannot Be Enhanced options makes sure that if the structure type is enhanced, it's only enhanced to include additional character types.

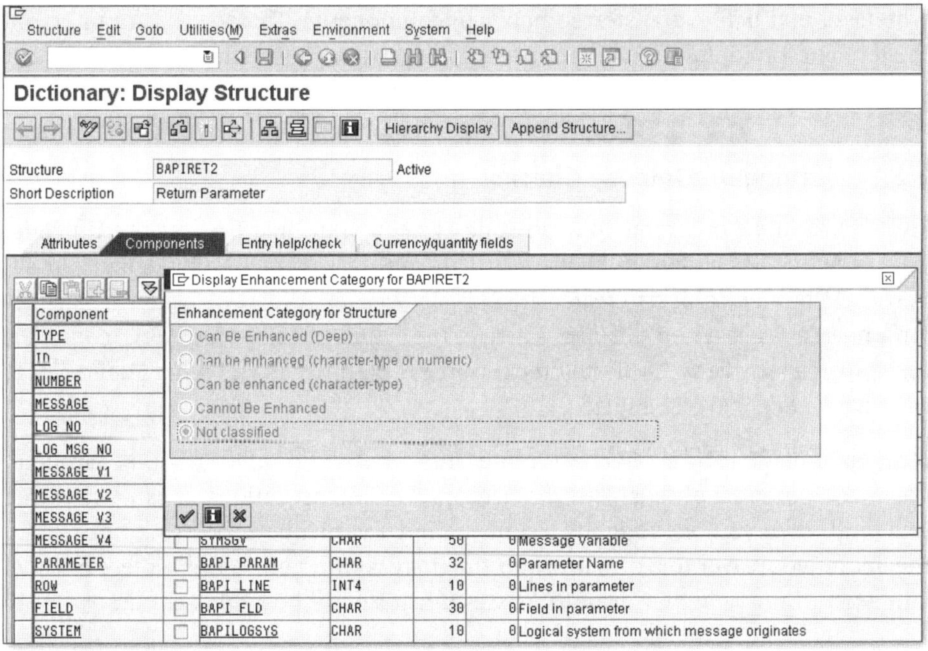


**Figure 4.2** Enhancement Category for ABAP Dictionary Structures

**Thinking Outside of the Box**

Besides ABAP-specific Unicode concerns, it's also important that you maintain a global perspective when interfacing with components/services outside of SAP NetWeaver AS ABAP. For example, if you're writing some kind of conversion program that processes a text file, you need to take the encoding scheme of that file into account whenever you read it. Similarly, if you're generating a file in your ABAP program, you need to think about how you want to encode it so that other systems can process it. We explain more about these Unicode-related impacts in Chapter 5, Working with Files.

Other examples of areas of the system impacted by Unicode include the RFC interface (described in Chapter 16, Parallel and Distributed Processing with RFCs), the Internet Communication Framework (described in Chapter 9, Web Programming with the ICF), web-based programming in general, the output of text data in ABAP lists, and so on. A good rule of thumb here is to always put on your Unicode hat whenever text data is transferred between components. That way, you can be on the lookout for configuration options/language extensions which ensure that data is transferred reliably in and out of the SAP system.

### 4.2.3 Turning on Unicode Checks

To execute ABAP programs in a Unicode system, you must first set the Unicode Checks Active flag shown in Figure 4.3. This setting is turned on by default for all new development objects created in SAP NetWeaver AS ABAP systems, starting with release 6.10. When this flag is active, the syntax check of the ABAP compiler carefully inspects each ABAP statement to see if there are places where deprecated syntax elements have been used.

If all else fails, the Unicode check represents a powerful safety net that can help you avoid potential pitfalls with character processing operations. It can also come in handy when you're struggling to understand a particular processing rule. Here, the definitive answer to a puzzling question may come from testing a piece of code and determining whether or not it passes muster with the syntax check.

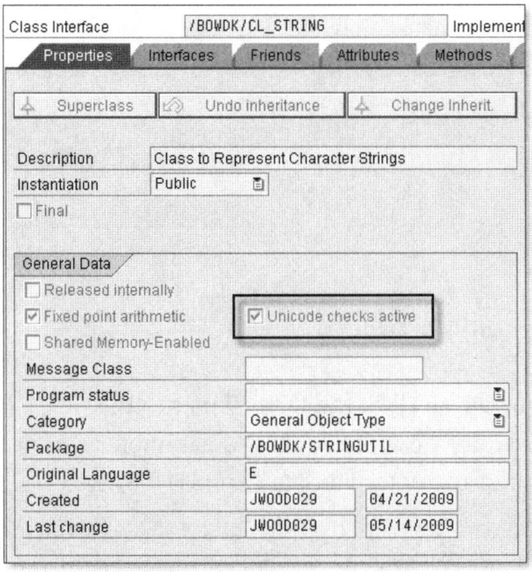


**Figure 4.3** Turning on the Unicode Check in the ABAP Workbench

## 4.3 Working with Unicode System Classes

Besides the Unicode-specific changes added to the ABAP language specification, SAP has also provided a series of system classes that can be used to make it easier to work with Unicode data. In this section, we look at the services these classes have to offer and show you how to use them to perform common tasks.

### 4.3.1 Converting External Data into ABAP Data Objects

Given the various types of encoding schemes employed by enterprise systems these days, it's important to have a toolset that can be used to reliably convert external data into ABAP data objects. Fortunately, SAP provides the system class `CL_ABAP_CONV_IN_CE` for this purpose. The UML class diagram depicted in Figure 4.4 shows the basic components of this class.

Before we dive into API-specific details of class `CL_ABAP_CONV_IN_CE`, it's helpful to see how it can be used to perform a simple conversion. The `ZCONVDEMO_IN` report program shown in Listing 4.7 converts a small chunk of binary data (e.g., the constant `CO_EXTERNAL_DATA`) into a `STRING` data object. The conversion process consists of two steps:

| CL_ABAP_CONV_IN_CE |
|---|
| + CREATE( )<br>+ UCCP( )<br>+ UCCPI( )<br>+ CONVERT( )<br>+ CONVERT_STRUC( )<br>+ GET_BUFFER( )<br>+ READ( )<br>+ RESET( )<br>+ SET_REPLACEMENT( )<br>+ SKIP_C( )<br>+ SKIP_X( ) |

**Figure 4.4** UML Class Diagram for CL_ABAP_CONV_IN_CE

1. First, we obtain a converter reference via a call to the factory method `CREATE()` of class `CL_ABAP_CONV_IN_CE`. Here, notice how the `ENCODING` parameter can be used to specify the encoding scheme of the external data (e.g., UTF-8, etc.).
2. After we have our converter reference, we can use the `CONVERT()` instance method to convert the data into an ABAP data object. Because the exporting parameter `DATA` is defined using the generic `SIMPLE` type, we can assign the conversion result to any elementary type, including type `STRING`, as you can see in Listing 4.7.

```
REPORT zconvdemo_in.
CLASS lcl_converter DEFINITION.
  PUBLIC SECTION.
    CLASS-METHODS:
      convert_to_internal.

  PRIVATE SECTION.
    CONSTANTS:
      CO_EXTERNAL_DATA(16) TYPE x
        VALUE '4142415020616E6420556E69636F6465'.
ENDCLASS.

CLASS lcl_converter IMPLEMENTATION.
  METHOD convert_to_internal.
*   Method-Local Data Declarations:
    DATA: lo_conv   TYPE REF TO cl_abap_conv_in_ce,
          lv_result TYPE string.

*   Convert from external format to internal format:
    TRY.
      WRITE: / 'Original Message:', CO_EXTERNAL_DATA.
```

```
*     Create an instance of class CL_ABAP_CONV_IN_CE:
      lo_conv =
        cl_abap_conv_in_ce=>create( encoding = 'UTF-8' ).

*     Call method CONVERT() to perform the conversion:
      CALL METHOD lo_conv->convert
        EXPORTING
          input = CO_EXTERNAL_DATA
        IMPORTING
          data  = lv_result.

*     Where LV_RESULT = "ABAP and Unicode"...
      WRITE: / 'Translated message:', lv_result.
    CATCH cx_parameter_invalid_range.
    CATCH cx_sy_codepage_converter_init.
    CATCH cx_sy_conversion_codepage.
    CATCH cx_parameter_invalid_type.
    ENDTRY.
  ENDMETHOD.
ENDCLASS.

START-OF-SELECTION.
  CALL METHOD lcl_converter=>convert_to_internal( ).
```

**Listing 4.7** Converting External Data into ABAP Data Objects

When you execute the code in Listing 4.7, you'll find that the converted message stored in LV_RESULT is the string "ABAP and Unicode." If you look carefully at the raw data in CO_EXTERNAL_DATA, you can see each Unicode character encoded using their assigned hexadecimal value. For example, the first two digits in CO_EXTERNAL_DATA are 41; the exact same value assigned to the letter "A" in Table 4.1. Similarly, the next two digits match the assigned value of letter "B," and so on.

Given the fact that we were able to perform a data conversion using only the CREATE() and CONVERT() methods of class CL_ABAP_CONV_IN_CE, you might be wondering what the other instance methods are for. For the most part, these additional methods support a stream-based processing model. In the stream-based model, a set of bytes are placed inside the converter instance's buffer via the INPUT parameter of method CREATE(). From here, the contents of the buffer are converted in pieces via calls to method READ(). At any time, the contents of the buffer can be read using the GET_BUFFER() method or refreshed using the RESET() method. You can also use the `SKIP_C()` and `SKIP_X()` methods to move the read position forward a given number of characters or bytes.

In either processing model, you can specify a default *replacement character* that the converter can use as a substitute for characters that can't be represented in an ABAP character object. This replacement character can be defined whenever the converter is first created (using the `REPLACEMENT` parameter of method `CREATE()`) or via a call to method `SET_REPLACEMENT()`.

So far, we've only described how to perform conversions using elementary ABAP data types. However, it's also possible to convert external data into flat structures using the `CONVERT_STRUC()` method. The primary difference here is that the converter must also be provided with metadata about the layout and organization of the structure type being converted. This metadata is represented in the form of an instance of class `CL_ABAP_VIEW_OFFLEN`. You can see examples of this type of conversion in the class documentation available in the Class Builder for class `CL_ABAP_CONV_IN_CE`.

### 4.3.2 Converting ABAP Data Objects into External Data Formats

To convert ABAP data objects into various external data formats, you use the analog of the `CL_ABAP_CONV_IN_CE` class: class `CL_ABAP_CONV_OUT_CE`. As you can see in the UML class diagram shown in Figure 4.5, the APIs of these two classes are quite similar.

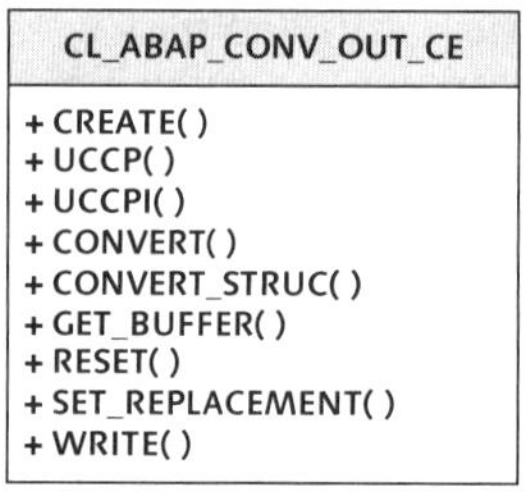


**Figure 4.5** UML Class Diagram for CL_ABAP_CONV_OUT_CE

The report program `ZCONVDEMO_OUT` shows how class `CL_ABAP_CONV_OUT_CE` can be used to convert the string "ABAP and Unicode" into a UTF-8 encoded byte sequence (see Listing 4.8).

```
REPORT zconvdemo_out.
CLASS lcl_converter DEFINITION.
```

```
  PUBLIC SECTION.
    CLASS-METHODS:
      convert_to_external.

  PRIVATE SECTION.
    CONSTANTS:
      CO_INTERNAL_DATA TYPE string
        VALUE 'ABAP and Unicode'.
ENDCLASS.

CLASS lcl_converter IMPLEMENTATION.
  METHOD convert_to_external.
*   Local Data Declarations:
    DATA: lo_conv   TYPE REF TO cl_abap_conv_out_ce,
          lv_buffer TYPE xstring.

    TRY.
      WRITE: / 'Original message:', CO_INTERNAL_DATA.

*     Create an instance of class CL_ABAP_CONV_OUT_CE:
      lo_conv =
        cl_abap_conv_out_ce=>create( encoding = 'UTF-8' ).

*     Perform the conversion:
      CALL METHOD lo_conv->convert
        EXPORTING
          data   = CO_INTERNAL_DATA
        IMPORTING
          buffer = lv_buffer.

*     Output the converted data:
      WRITE: / 'Converted data:', lv_buffer.
    CATCH cx_parameter_invalid_range.
    CATCH cx_sy_codepage_converter_init.
    CATCH cx_sy_conversion_codepage.
    CATCH cx_parameter_invalid_type.
    ENDTRY.
  ENDMETHOD.
ENDCLASS.

START-OF-SELECTION.
  CALL METHOD lcl_converter=>convert_to_external( ).
```

**Listing 4.8** Converting ABAP Data Objects into External Formats

Much like class CL_ABAP_CONV_IN_CE, class CL_ABAP_CONV_OUT_CE also supports a stream-based processing model. Here, you can append ABAP data objects to the internal buffer using the WRITE() method. You can then get the concatenated results via a call to method GET_BUFFER(). The converter can be reset at any time with the RESET() method.

### 4.3.3 Converting Between External Formats

Occasionally, you may find yourself caught in the middle between two different encoding schemes. For example, imagine that you're writing a program that maps an input file encoded in UTF-8 to an output file encoded using ISO 8859-1. In these situations, you can use class CL_ABAP_CONV_X2X_CE to perform the necessary data conversions. Figure 4.6 shows the UML class diagram for class CL_ABAP_CONV_X2X_CE.

| CL_ABAP_CONV_X2X_CE |
|---|
| + CREATE( )<br>+ CONVERT_C( )<br>+ COVNERT_D( )<br>+ CONVERT_F( )<br>+ CONVERT_I( )<br>+ CONVERT_INT2( )<br>+ CONVERT_N( )<br>+ CONVERT_P( )<br>+ CONVERT_T( )<br>+ CONVERT_X( )<br>+ GET_IN_BUFFER( )<br>+ GET_OUT_BUFFER( )<br>+ RESET( )<br>+ SET_REPLACEMENT( )<br>+ SKIP_C( )<br>+ SKIP_X( )<br>+ WRITE( ) |

**Figure 4.6** UML Class Diagram for CL_ABAP_CONV_X2X_CE

The ZCONVDEMO_INOUT report program shown in Listing 4.9 demonstrates how class CL_ABAP_CONV_X2X_CE can be used to translate a piece of text encoded using UTF-8 into the ISO 8859-1 encoding scheme. The transformation process is carried out as follows:

1. First, we take the sample text and encode it as a UTF-8 byte sequence using class CL_ABAP_CONV_OUT_CE.
2. Next, we use the CREATE() factory method of class CL_ABAP_CONV_X2X_CE to create an instance of the converter. As you can see, we've specified the input encoding as UTF-8 and the output encoding as 1100. In this case, 1100 refers to

the SAP code page for the ISO 8859-1 encoding system. You can see a comprehensive list of installed code pages in the system using Transaction SCP.

3. Before we can actually perform the conversion, we need to calculate the number of characters represented by the UTF-8 byte stream. Here, we can use the `STRLEN()` function to calculate the number of *logical* characters in the input string. However, because the input stream could very well contain characters in the surrogate area (e.g., the German o-umlaut, etc.), it's important that we pad this value to avoid truncation. In the example code, we're multiplying the number of logical characters by the size of the internal representation of a character in the system. You'll learn more about this in Section 4.3.4, Useful Character Utilities.
4. After we determine the number of characters that need to be converted, we can perform the conversion using method `CONVERT_C()` of class `CL_ABAP_CONV_X2X_CE`.
5. Lastly, we convert the results back into an ABAP `STRING` data object so that we can verify that the characters were translated correctly.

```
REPORT zconvdemo_inout.
CLASS lcl_converter DEFINITION.
  PUBLIC SECTION.
    CLASS-METHODS:
      convert_utf8_to_iso88591.
ENDCLASS.

CLASS lcl_converter IMPLEMENTATION.
  METHOD convert_utf8_to_iso88591.
*   Method-Local Data Declarations:
    DATA:
      lv_utf8_string TYPE string,
      lv_strlen      TYPE i,
      lo_conv_out    TYPE REF TO cl_abap_conv_out_ce,
      lv_utf8_buffer TYPE xstring,
      lo_conv_x2x    TYPE REF TO cl_abap_conv_x2x_ce,
      lv_8859_buffer TYPE xstring,
      lo_conv_in     TYPE REF TO cl_abap_conv_in_ce,
      lv_8859_string TYPE string.

*   Create some sample UTF-8 encoded data:
    CONCATENATE 'Lösungen für die täglichen Aufgaben'
                'der ABAP-Programmierung'
```

```
        INTO lv_utf8_string SEPARATED BY SPACE.
    WRITE: / 'String as UTF-8:', 23 lv_utf8_string.

*   Convert the UTF-8 data to ISO-88591:
    TRY.
*     Create an instance of class CL_ABAP_CONV_OUT_CE:
      lo_conv_out =
        cl_abap_conv_out_ce=>create( encoding = 'UTF-8' ).

*     Convert the input data into a UTF-8 byte sequence:
      CALL METHOD lo_conv_out->convert
        EXPORTING
          data   = lv_utf8_string
        IMPORTING
          buffer = lv_utf8_buffer.

*     Create an instance of class CL_ABAP_CONV_X2X_CE:
      lo_conv_x2x =
        cl_abap_conv_x2x_ce=>create(
          in_encoding = 'UTF-8'
          out_encoding = '1100' "SAP Code Page ISO 8859-1
          input = lv_utf8_buffer ).

*     Perform the conversion to the output format;
*     First, we need to calculate the length of the UTF-8
*     string in characters; Since function STRLEN() only
*     returns a logical character count, we need to multiply
*     this value by the internal size of a character in the
*     system in order to avoid truncation.
      lv_strlen = strlen( lv_utf8_string ).
      lv_strlen =
        lv_strlen * cl_abap_char_utilities=>charsize.

      lo_conv_x2x->convert_c( lv_strlen ).
      lv_8859_buffer = lo_conv_x2x->get_out_buffer( ).

*     Now, convert the data in the external format back into
*     a STRING data object:
      lo_conv_in =
        cl_abap_conv_in_ce=>create( encoding = '1100' ).

      CALL METHOD lo_conv_in->convert
        EXPORTING
```

```
          input = lv_8859_buffer
        IMPORTING
          data  = lv_8859_string.

*     Output the converted data:
      WRITE: / 'String as ISO 8859-1:', lv_8859_string.
    CATCH cx_parameter_invalid_range.
    CATCH cx_sy_codepage_converter_init.
    CATCH cx_sy_conversion_codepage.
    CATCH cx_parameter_invalid_type.
    ENDTRY.
  ENDMETHOD.
ENDCLASS.

START-OF-SELECTION.
  CALL METHOD lcl_converter=>convert_utf8_to_iso88591( ).
```

**Listing 4.9** Converting Between Different Encoding Schemes

We should point out that class CL_ABAP_CONV_X2X_CE can also be used to convert numeric data between different number formats. For more details about this conversion process, consult the class documentation for this class in the Class Builder transaction.

### 4.3.4 Useful Character Utilities

Whenever you work with Unicode data, there are times when you need to deal with individual characters. For example, imagine that you're writing a Business Server Page (BSP) application that has a form containing free-form text stored in an HTML <textarea> input field. When this form is submitted, you want to extract that text and store it in a format that is consistent with the one the user used when he filled out the form (e.g., with the proper line breaks, etc.). However, because the contents of the text area are concatenated together inside of a STRING data object, you must split the text into pieces at each line break. To do so, you need a way to represent the "Carriage Return" and "Line Feed" characters in Unicode.

Fortunately, SAP has provided a utility class called CL_ABAP_CHAR_UTILITIES that defines a constant field named CR_LF that contains this value. Figure 4.7 contains a UML class diagram that illustrates some of the other useful constants defined by this class. As you can see, CL_ABAP_CHAR_UTILITIES also defines a method called GET_SIMPLE_SPACES_FOR_CUR_CP() that provides a concatenated list of all of the simple space characters for the current system code page.

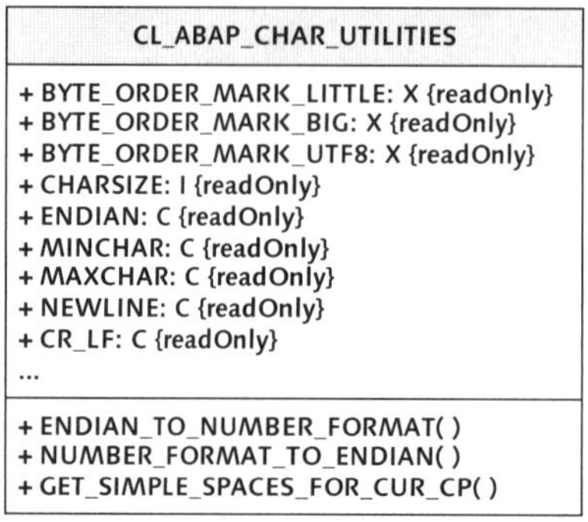


**Figure 4.7** UML Class Diagram for CL_ABAP_CHAR_UTILITIES

Though class `CL_ABAP_CHAR_UTILITIES` provides quite a few useful constants that represent common Unicode characters, you may sometimes stumble across a requirement where you need to deal with characters that are more obscure. In these situations, you can use the `UCCP()` and `UCCPI()` methods of classes `CL_ABAP_CONV_OUT_CE` and `CL_ABAP_CONV_IN_CE` to convert an ABAP character into a Unicode code point value, and vice versa. The code excerpt in Listing 4.10 shows how we're using the `UCCP()` method of class `CL_ABAP_CONV_OUT_CE` to derive the Unicode code point value assigned to the English letter "A" (U+0041). We can then convert this code point value back into an ABAP character using the `UCCP()` method of class `CL_ABAP_CONV_IN_CE`.

```
DATA: lv_char       TYPE c,
      lv_code_point TYPE syhex02.
lv_code_point = cl_abap_conv_out_ce=>uccp( 'A' ).
lv_char = cl_abap_conv_in_ce=>uccp( lv_code_point ).
IF lv_char EQ 'A'.
  WRITE: / 'Code point conversion worked.'.
ENDIF.
```

**Listing 4.10** Converting Unicode Characters and Code Points

The `UCCPI()` methods of classes `CL_ABAP_CONV_OUT_CE` and `CL_ABAP_CONV_IN_CE` work just like their `UCCP()` counterparts. The only difference is that the Unicode code point value is represented as a decimal integer value as opposed to a hexadecimal one.

## 4.4 Summary

Support for Unicode is a welcome addition to SAP NetWeaver AS ABAP. As the enterprise landscape evolves into a *service-oriented architecture*, the need for openness and standardization is perhaps more important than ever before. We'll see evidence of this as we discuss interface technologies, and so on. – an investigation that begins in the next chapter, in which we consider file-processing techniques in ABAP.

# PART II
# Main Courses

*No matter how complicated the recipe, food connoisseurs only care about one thing: the finished product. Similarly, as software engineers, the quality of our work is measured by the usefulness of the output it generates. Because one of the most common types of output generated by computers comes in the form of files, this chapter shows you how to work with files in ABAP.*

# 5 Working with Files

In the database-centric world that is SAP, it isn't uncommon to hear someone on a project utter the phrase "just stick it in a Z-table" whenever the subject of data storage comes up. However, there are times when database storage is simply not practical. For instance, what if we need to transport some data outside of the SAP landscape? One option here might be to store the data in a file and then transport that file to its target destination using the File Transfer Protocol (FTP). Indeed, there are many use cases where a file-based approach makes a lot of sense.

In this chapter, we explore the various file-processing capabilities available in ABAP. Along the way, we investigate the impacts of Unicode support in ABAP as it relates to file processing. Finally, we conclude our discussion by showing you how to use the SAPFTP library provided by SAP to transmit files over the network using FTP.

## 5.1 File Processing on the Application Server

The ABAP programming language offers extensive support for file processing, which enables ABAP programs to access the file systems of the application server host as well as the frontend workstation. In this section, we focus our attention on file processing on the application server, showing you how to use the built-in file-processing statements provided in ABAP. We consider file-processing techniques on the frontend workstation in Section 5.5, File Processing on the Presentation Server.

### 5.1.1 Understanding the ABAP File Interface

You can create and manipulate files on an SAP NetWeaver AS ABAP application server host using the *ABAP file interface*. The ABAP file interface is implemented in the form of a series of built-in statements that perform basic file I/O operations. As you'll soon see, each of these statements works with an abstraction called a *dataset*. You can think of a dataset as a kind of file handle that binds I/O operations to a particular file. This distinction is important because it's possible to have multiple files open simultaneously within an ABAP program.

In the upcoming subsections, we investigate the ABAP file interface from a nuts-and-bolts perspective. This introduction provides you with the foundation necessary to work with files in your ABAP programs.

#### The OPEN DATASET Statement

To open a file in ABAP, you use the `OPEN DATASET` statement whose basic syntax is shown in Listing 5.1. Here, the name of the file is specified in the `dataset` variable, which is a character-type data object (i.e., type `STRING`, etc.). The file name stored in `dataset` is platform-specific based on the underlying operating system running the SAP NetWeaver AS ABAP. Therefore, it's important to always use fully qualified file names in `dataset` (i.e., a file name that is specified with a complete directory path such as */home/sapfiles/somefile.txt*) because the default directory varies from system to system.[1]

```
OPEN DATASET dataset
 FOR [INPUT | OUTPUT | APPENDING | UPDATE]
  IN [TEXT MODE {options} | BINARY MODE] {options}].
```

**Listing 5.1** Basic Syntax of the OPEN DATASET Statement

The `FOR` addition to the `OPEN DATASET` statement determines whether or not you want to *read*, *write*, or *update* a file. Obviously, the behavior of the `OPEN DATASET` statement varies depending upon the access mode that gets selected here. For example, if the `FOR OUTPUT` addition is chosen, one of two things happens:

- If the file specified in `dataset` doesn't exist already, then the `OPEN DATASET` statement creates it.
- Otherwise, any previous content in the file is overwritten.

1 The default directory is configured in the profile parameter `DIR_HOME`. You can determine the value of this parameter in your system by looking at Transaction RZ11.

This same behavior is also produced with the `FOR APPENDING` addition. However, if an attempt is made to open a non-existing file using the `FOR INPUT` or `FOR UPDATE` additions, the `OPEN DATASET` statement produces an error. You'll see how to deal with these errors in a moment.

As you open a file using the `OPEN DATASET` statement, you also need to specify a *storage mode* that determines how the ABAP file interface interprets the contents of the file. Generally speaking, you have one of two options to choose from here: `TEXT MODE` or `BINARY MODE`. If you're unsure as to which option you should use, see the following boxed section entitled "Text Files Versus Binary Files: What's the Difference?" We'll also investigate certain Unicode-related aspects to working with text files in Section 5.2, Working with Unicode.

**Text Files versus Binary Files: What's the Difference?**

When it comes to file processing, many developers are often confused about the difference between plain text files and binary files. Amid all this confusion, it can be difficult to choose the right tool to process a given type of file.

Strictly speaking, all files are technically binary files at heart (i.e., a collection of 1s and 0s). To make sense of all this binary data, programmers develop *file formats* that describe how the binary data is structured within the file. For example, the Rich Text Format (RTF) is a file format that can be used to develop *rich text documents* (i.e., documents containing text that is formatted using particular types of fonts, etc.). As such, RTF files contain plain text data as well as *markup* that describes how that text is formatted when it's output to the screen, the printer, and so on.

So, what exactly is the difference between text files and binary files? Well, based on the preceding definition — nothing. Technically, the contents of a text file are stored as a series of 1s and 0s just like any other binary file. The question is, how do we represent plain text content as a series of bytes? The solution to this problem is to use a *character-encoding system*.

As you learned in Chapter 4, ABAP and Unicode, a character-encoding system assigns numeric values to a set of characters that make up the encoding system's character set. For example, in the ASCII encoding scheme, the English letter "A" is assigned the decimal value 65 (or the binary equivalent "0100 0001"). These numeric values make it possible to represent character data in a binary format. In addition to the plain character data, character-encoding systems also define a series of control characters that demarcate positions in a text object (e.g., carriage returns, line feeds, etc.). Collectively, these control characters are interspersed with printable characters to represent the contents of a text file. When a text file is saved, each character within it is substituted with its assigned binary value as it is written to disk.

The just mentioned ASCII standard is among the oldest and most popular encoding schemes used to create text files. As such, developers sometimes mistakenly use the terms "plain text files" and "ASCII files" synonymously. However, to be precise, an ASCII file is just one of many different types of plain text files. Indeed, these days, many plain text files are being encoded using the UTF-8 standard — a variable-length encoding for Unicode.

Given the various types of encodings available, the ABAP file interface needs to know the encoding scheme of a text file to be able to process it as text — otherwise, it's just a senseless blob of binary data. If the encoding scheme is known, the text data can easily be converted to/from ABAP character data objects and processed accordingly.

The results of the `OPEN DATASET` statement can be determined by examining the value of the `SY-SUBRC` system status variable. If the file was opened successfully, `SY-SUBRC` has the value 0; otherwise, it has the value 8. You can extract additional information about an error by using the `MESSAGE` addition of the `OPEN DATASET` statement, as shown in the code excerpt in Listing 5.2. Here, an error occurs because an invalid (empty) dataset was specified. Of course, the contents of the actual error message produced vary from operating system to operating system.

```
DATA lv_message TYPE string.

OPEN DATASET '' FOR INPUT IN TEXT MODE MESSAGE lv_message.
IF sy-subrc EQ 8.
  MESSAGE lv_message TYPE 'E'.
ENDIF.
```

**Listing 5.2** Capturing Error Information When Opening a File

One thing to be mindful of when using the `OPEN DATASET` statement is the fact that it can trigger certain class-based exceptions at runtime. For example, if there is insufficient access to the dataset in question, an exception of type `CX_SY_FILE_AUTHORITY` is thrown. Therefore, it's always a good idea to enclose the `OPEN DATASET` statement inside of a `TRY` statement. For a comprehensive list of possible exceptions that can be raised, perform a keyword search on the `OPEN DATASET` statement in the ABAP Keyword Documentation.

### The TRANSFER Statement

To write data to a file, you use the `TRANSFER` statement. The syntax of the `TRANSFER` statement is shown in Listing 5.3. The semantics of this statement are fairly intuitive. Here, we're *transferring* the contents of the data object `dobj` to the open dataset object. The data object can be an elementary or flat structure type.[2] After the transfer operation, the file pointer is moved forward to point at the position immediately following the data that was just added to the file.

```
TRANSFER dobj TO dataset
  [LENGTH length]
  [NO END OF LINE].
```

**Listing 5.3** Syntax Diagram of the TRANSFER Statement

The LENGTH addition allows you to only copy a portion of the source data object over to the dataset. For instance, if we were writing to a text file and dobj was a STRING object, the LENGTH addition could be used to only transfer the first 20 characters of the string to the dataset. Similarly, the LENGTH addition can be used to limit the number of bytes written to a binary file.

The NO END OF LINE addition is used when processing a file in text mode. This addition can be used to omit the default end-of-line separator when writing a line to a text file.

As is the case with any I/O operation, exceptions can occur when data is written to a file. Consequently, the TRANSFER statement does trigger a series of catchable class-based exceptions. For more information about these exception types, perform a keyword search on the TRANSFER statement in the ABAP Keyword Documentation.

### The READ DATASET Statement

You can read the contents of a file using the READ DATASET statement. This statement expects the target data object to be either an elementary data type or a flat structure type. Listing 5.4 shows the syntax diagram of the READ DATASET statement.

```
READ DATASET dataset INTO dobj
  [MAXIMUM LENGTH mlen]
  [ACTUAL LENGTH alen].
```

**Listing 5.4** Syntax Diagram for the READ DATASET Statement

2 The term *flat structure type* refers to structure types that only contain components that are defined using fixed-length elementary types (which means that the variable-length STRING and XSTRING types are excluded).

The MAXIMUM LENGTH addition allows you to specify the maximum number of characters or bytes that you want to read from the dataset at a time. The ACTUAL LENGTH addition can be used to determine the number of characters or bytes that are actually read from the dataset during a READ DATASET operation.

Much like the TRANSFER statement used to write data to files, the READ DATASET statement can also produce catchable class-based I/O exceptions. For more information about these exception types, perform a keyword search on the READ DATASET statement in the ABAP Keyword Documentation.

### The CLOSE DATASET Statement

To close a file, you use the analog of the OPEN DATASET statement: the CLOSE DATASET statement. The syntax of the CLOSE DATASET statement is shown in Listing 5.5.

```
CLOSE DATASET dataset.
```

**Listing 5.5** Syntax Diagram for the CLOSE DATASET Statement

Much like the OPEN DATASET statement, the results of the CLOSE DATASET statement can be evaluated using the SY-SUBRC system status variable. The CLOSE DATASET statement can also trigger a catchable class-based exception of type CX_SY_FILE_CLOSE. This exception occurs if the system encounters an I/O error when it tries to flush any remaining buffered data that is waiting to be written to the file before it's closed.

### The DELETE DATASET Statement

If you need to delete a file, you can do so using the DELETE DATASET statement as shown in Listing 5.6. If the delete operation is successful, the SY-SUBRC system status variable will have the value 0; otherwise, it will have the value 4.

```
DELETE DATASET dataset.
```

**Listing 5.6** Syntax Diagram for the DELETE DATASET Statement

In the event that there aren't sufficient authorizations for deleting the dataset in question, the DELETE DATASET statement triggers an exception of type CX_SY_FILE_AUTHORITY. Similarly, if the dataset can't be opened for deletion, an exception of type CX_SY_FILE_OPEN is raised.

### 5.1.2 Case Study: Processing Files with the ABAP File Interface

Now that you have a better understanding of the ABAP file interface and the statements that make up its API, let's consider some common file-processing use cases and see how to implement them in ABAP. The following subsections demonstrate how to create, read, and update files in ABAP.

#### Creating Files with the ABAP File Interface

Regardless of the programming language, the steps involved in creating a file are pretty much the same.

1. First, you determine the name of the file you want to create and the directory in which the file is stored.
2. Next, you open up that file in output mode.
3. Once the file is opened, you can begin writing data to it.
4. Finally, after all of the data has been written to the file, you close it.

To demonstrate how these basic steps correspond with the ABAP file interface, let's consider the sample report program called ZCREATEFILEDEMO in Listing 5.7. This program generates a plain text file using the file name specified in the P_FILE selection screen parameter.

```
REPORT zcreatefiledemo.
CLASS lcl_file_manager DEFINITION.
  PUBLIC SECTION.
    CLASS-METHODS:
      create_file IMPORTING im_file TYPE string.

  PRIVATE SECTION.
    TYPES: BEGIN OF ty_record,
             id_number  TYPE numc4,
             first_name TYPE ad_namefir,
             last_name  TYPE ad_namelas,
           END OF ty_record.
ENDCLASS.

CLASS lcl_file_manager IMPLEMENTATION.
  METHOD create_file.
*   Method-Local Data Declarations:
    DATA: lv_message TYPE string,
          ls_record  TYPE ty_record.
```

```
*   Create a new text file and return a dataset that can be
*   used as a handle for writing to the file:
    OPEN DATASET im_file FOR OUTPUT
      IN TEXT MODE ENCODING UTF-8
      WITH BYTE-ORDER MARK
      WITH SMART LINEFEED
      MESSAGE lv_message.

*   Check the results:
    IF sy-subrc NE 0.
      MESSAGE lv_message TYPE 'I'.
      RETURN.
    ENDIF.

*   Output a couple of records to the file:
    ls_record-id_number  = '0001'.
    ls_record-first_name = 'Andersen'.
    ls_record-last_name  = 'Wood'.
    TRANSFER ls_record TO im_file.

    ls_record-id_number  = '0003'.
    ls_record-first_name = 'Paige'.
    ls_record-last_name  = 'Wood'.
    TRANSFER ls_record TO im_file.

*   Always be sure to close the file:
    CLOSE DATASET im_file.
    WRITE: / 'File', im_file, 'created successfully'.
  ENDMETHOD.
ENDCLASS.

PARAMETERS:
  p_file TYPE string LOWER CASE OBLIGATORY.

START-OF-SELECTION.
  CALL METHOD lcl_file_manager=>create_file( p_file ).
```

**Listing 5.7** Creating a Plain Text File in ABAP

As you can see in Listing 5.7, the heavy lifting in the ZCREATEFILEDEMO report program is carried out by the CREATE_FILE method of class LCL_FILE_MANAGER. This method performs the following steps:

1. First, it creates a new file using the OPEN DATASET statement with the FOR OUTPUT addition. The name of the file is specified using the P_FILE selection screen parameter. Here, the directory path specified in the P_FILE parameter exists somewhere on the SAP NetWeaver AS ABAP host where this report program will run. In Section 5.3, Logical Files and Directories, we show you how to work with logical files and directories that abstract away the tedious details of working with OS-specific directory structures.
2. Assuming the file is opened successfully, the CREATE_FILE method then writes some data records to it using the TRANSFER statement. Because the dataset was opened in text mode, we must use character data objects to output data to the file. Here, we're using a custom flat structure type called TY_RECORD to write records to the file.
3. Finally, after all of the records are written to the file, the file is closed using the CLOSE DATASET statement.

If you look carefully at the OPEN DATASET statement in Listing 5.7, you'll notice that we used a couple of optional additions to specify the way that we want to format the contents of the text file that we're creating. The ENCODING UTF-8 addition indicates that we're using the UTF-8 encoding scheme. You'll learn more about this option in Section 5.2, Working with Unicode. The WITH SMART LINEFEED addition causes the end-of-line marker to be output according to the underlying operating system of the SAP NetWeaver AS ABAP host (e.g., "CRLF" for MS Windows, "CR" for UNIX, etc.). For more information about these options, as well as some legacy syntax variants, perform a keyword search on the OPEN DATASET statement in the ABAP Keyword Documentation.

### Reading Files with the ABAP File Interface

As you learned in Section 5.1.1, Understanding the ABAP File Interface, you can read data from files using the READ DATASET statement. This process is demonstrated in the report program ZREADFILEDEMO contained in Listing 5.8.

```
REPORT zreadfiledemo.
CLASS lcl_file_manager DEFINITION.
  PUBLIC SECTION.
    CLASS-METHODS:
      read_file IMPORTING im_file TYPE string.

  PRIVATE SECTION.
    TYPES: BEGIN OF ty_record,
```

```
              id_number  TYPE numc4,
              first_name TYPE ad_namefir,
              last_name  TYPE ad_namelas,
            END OF ty_record.
ENDCLASS.

CLASS lcl_file_manager IMPLEMENTATION.
  METHOD read_file.
*   Method-Local Data Declarations:
    DATA: lv_message TYPE string,
          ls_record  TYPE ty_record,
          lv_chars   TYPE i.

*   Open up a text file and return a dataset that can be
*   used as a handle for writing to the file:
    OPEN DATASET im_file FOR INPUT
      IN TEXT MODE ENCODING UTF-8
      MESSAGE lv_message.

*   Check the results:
    IF sy-subrc NE 0.
      MESSAGE lv_message TYPE 'I'.
      RETURN.
    ENDIF.

*   Read the contents of the file and display the results
*   in the standard list:
    DO.
      READ DATASET im_file INTO ls_record
        ACTUAL LENGTH lv_chars.
      IF sy-subrc EQ 0.
        WRITE: / ls_record.
        WRITE: / 'Number of characters read:', lv_chars.
        SKIP.
      ELSE.
        EXIT.
      ENDIF.
    ENDDO.

*   Always be sure to close the file:
    CLOSE DATASET im_file.
  ENDMETHOD.                 " METHOD read_file
ENDCLASS.
```

```
PARAMETERS:
  p_file TYPE string LOWER CASE OBLIGATORY.

START-OF-SELECTION.
  CALL METHOD lcl_file_manager=>read_file( p_file ).
```

**Listing 5.8** Reading Files in ABAP

Looking carefully at the code in Listing 5.8, let's consider how the input file is being read step by step:

1. Inside the `READ_FILE` method, the target dataset is opened using the `OPEN DATASET` statement. Here, we're using the access mode `FOR INPUT` to specify that we want to read from the file. For the purposes of this demonstration, let's assume that we're using the same plain text file generated in the `ZCREATEFILEDEMO` report from Listing 5.7.
2. After the file is opened, the data records are read sequentially in a `DO` loop using the `READ DATASET` statement. If the read operation is successful, we output the record to the report list. In addition, we're also outputting the number of characters read in the `READ DATASET` operation. This value is calculated using the `ACTUAL LENGTH` addition, as shown in Listing 5.8.
3. When the end of the file is reached, the subsequent `READ DATASET` statement fails. We can detect this occurrence by evaluating the value of the `SY-SUBRC` system status variable. If `SY-SUBRC` has a value other than 0, then our work is done, and we can exit the `DO` loop using the `EXIT` statement.
4. Finally, it's always important to remember to close the file using the `CLOSE DATASET` statement.

### Updating Files with the ABAP File Interface

For the most part, the process for updating a file is almost identical to that of creating a file. The primary difference is the use of the `FOR APPENDING` or `FOR UPDATE` access modes in lieu of the `FOR OUTPUT` access mode used to create a file initially. Here, it's important to understand the behavior of each of these access modes:

- The use of the `FOR APPENDING` addition causes the file pointer to be positioned at the end of the file whenever it's opened. Therefore, any data written to the file using the `TRANSFER` statement is written *after* any existing data records.

- The use of the FOR UPDATE addition causes the file pointer to be positioned at the beginning of the file. Therefore, unless the file pointer is repositioned beforehand, any data written to the file using the TRANSFER statement overwrites the existing content within the file.

In certain situations, you may not want to begin updating a file at the beginning or ending positions. For example, if you wanted to append a record to an ordered list, you would want to position the file cursor at the proper index before writing out the record. In these circumstances, you can advance the file pointer in one of two ways:

- The file pointer can be set explicitly using the SET DATASET statement.
- The READ DATASET statement can be used to advance the file pointer forward line by line until you reach the position in the file that you want to edit.

Comparatively speaking, the SET DATASET statement gives you much more flexibility when positioning the file pointer, allowing you to advance it to a particular byte position within the file. Listing 5.9 shows the basic syntax of the SET DATASET statement.

```
SET DATASET dataset
  [POSITION {position}|{END OF FILE}].
```

**Listing 5.9** Syntax Diagram of the SET DATASET Statement

In addition to the SET DATASET statement, the ABAP file interface also provides the analog GET DATASET statement that can be used to determine the current position of the file pointer. The basic syntax of the GET DATASET statement is shown in Listing 5.10.

```
GET DATASET dataset POSITION position.
```

**Listing 5.10** Syntax Diagram of the GET DATASET Statement

The report program ZUPDATEFILEDEMO in Listing 5.11 shows how the update access mode can be used to update the plain text file created via the report program ZCREATEFILEDEMO from Listing 5.7. Here, we're updating the second record in the file and then appending a new record onto the end of the file. As you can see, we're advancing the file pointer to the beginning of the second record using the READ DATASET statement. For demonstration purposes, we're also using the GET DATASET statement to determine the actual byte position of the file pointer after the READ DATASET statement is completed. After the file pointer is positioned in the right spot, we can update the file using the TRANSFER statement, per usual.

```
REPORT zupdatefiledemo.
CLASS lcl_file_manager DEFINITION.
  PUBLIC SECTION.
    CLASS-METHODS:
      update_file IMPORTING im_file TYPE string.

  PRIVATE SECTION.
    TYPES: BEGIN OF ty_record,
             id_number  TYPE numc4,
             first_name TYPE ad_namefir,
             last_name  TYPE ad_namelas,
           END OF ty_record.
ENDCLASS.

CLASS lcl_file_manager IMPLEMENTATION.
  METHOD update_file.
*   Method-Local Data Declarations:
    DATA: lv_message TYPE string,
          ls_record  TYPE ty_record,
          lv_pointer TYPE i.

*   Open up a text file and return a dataset that can be
*   used as a handle for updating the file:
    OPEN DATASET im_file FOR UPDATE
      IN TEXT MODE ENCODING UTF-8
      WITH SMART LINEFEED
      MESSAGE lv_message.

*   Check the results:
    IF sy-subrc NE 0.
      MESSAGE lv_message TYPE 'I'.
      RETURN.
    ENDIF.

*   Read the first record in the file to advance the file
*   pointer to the second record:
    READ DATASET im_file INTO ls_record.
    GET DATASET im_file POSITION lv_pointer.
    WRITE: / 'Current position after read:', lv_pointer.

*   Overwrite the existing data record with a new one:
    ls_record-id_number  = '0002'.
    ls_record-first_name = 'Andrea'.
```

```
    ls_record-last_name  = 'Wood'.
    TRANSFER ls_record TO im_file.

*   Add another record to the end of the file:
    ls_record-id_number  = '0003'.
    ls_record-first_name = 'Paige'.
    ls_record-last_name  = 'Wood'.
    TRANSFER ls_record TO im_file.

*   Always be sure to close the file:
    CLOSE DATASET im_file.
  ENDMETHOD.                  " METHOD update_file
ENDCLASS.

PARAMETERS:
  p_file TYPE string LOWER CASE OBLIGATORY.

START-OF-SELECTION.
* Update a file using the ABAP file interface:
  CALL METHOD lcl_file_manager=>update_file( p_file ).
```

**Listing 5.11** Updating Files in ABAP

## 5.2 Working with Unicode

SAP applications frequently need to exchange data with external systems that may or may not use the same character-encoding scheme. As you learned in Chapter 4, ABAP and Unicode, SAP has made it much easier to bridge these potential communication gaps by providing Unicode support in the ABAP programming language. While SAP endeavored to make its Unicode support as transparent as possible to the ABAP developer, there are still circumstances where you need to take on a more active role in defining how the system will work with character data. This is particularly true when it comes to processing text files that could be encoded using many different encoding schemes. In this section, we examine areas of the ABAP file interface where you need to put your Unicode hat on to make sure that you're processing text files correctly. We also look at a system class that you can use to gather information about the encoding of a text file before you attempt to process it.

### 5.2.1 Changes to the OPEN DATASET Statement to Support Unicode

Beginning with the arrival of Unicode support in SAP NetWeaver AS ABAP 6.10, the `OPEN DATASET` statement was modified to require the specification of an encoding scheme if a file is opened in text mode. Listing 5.12 shows the syntax additions that you can choose from to identify the encoding scheme used to process a text file.

```
OPEN DATASET dataset
 FOR [INPUT | OUTPUT | APPENDING | UPDATE]
  IN TEXT MODE
  ENCODING {DEFAULT |
           UTF-8 [{SKIPPING|WITH} BYTE ORDER MARK] |
           NON-UNICODE}.
```

**Listing 5.12** Specifying the Encoding Scheme for Text Files

Let's consider each of these encoding options from Listing 5.12 in turn:

- The `DEFAULT` addition causes the file to be handled using the UTF-8 encoding scheme in Unicode systems and the default code page in non-Unicode systems.
- The `UTF-8` addition selects the UTF-8 encoding scheme. Here, you have the option of specifying how you want to handle the byte-order mark (BOM) at the beginning of the file. A BOM is a special Unicode code point that defines the *endianness* (or byte order) of the content that follows in the file.
- The `NON-UNICODE` addition is used to select a non-Unicode code page in Unicode systems or the default code page in non-Unicode systems.

These days, most programming environments use the UTF-8 encoding scheme by default. Therefore, unless there's a compelling reason to specify another encoding scheme, it's a good idea to specifically select the UTF-8 scheme using the `ENCODING UTF-8` addition.

### 5.2.2 Using Class CL_ABAP_FILE_UTILITIES

In addition to the built-in Unicode support integrated into the statements that make up the ABAP file interface, SAP also provides a very useful utility class called `CL_ABAP_FILE_UTILITIES` that you can use to determine the encoding scheme of a given file. Figure 5.1 contains a UML class diagram that shows the public class methods provided by this class.

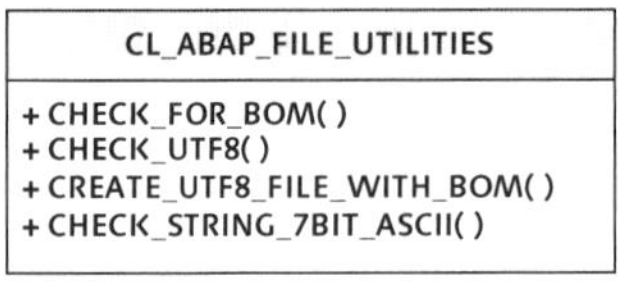


**Figure 5.1** UML Class Diagram for Class CL_ABAP_FILE_UTILITIES

Table 5.1 describes the functionality of each of the methods listed in Figure 5.1 in more detail. You can also learn more about this class by reading the class documentation available in the Class Builder.

| Method Name | Description |
|---|---|
| `CHECK_FOR_BOM()` | This method checks whether a file begins with a BOM. |
| `CHECK_UTF8()` | This method determines whether a file is encoded using UTF-8. The `MAX_KB` parameter can be used to limit the total number of kilobytes scanned during the evaluation process. |
| `CREATE_UTF8_FILE_WITH_BOM()` | This method creates an empty UTF-8 file beginning with a BOM. |
| `CHECK_STRING_7BIT_ASCII()` | This method determines whether a string contains only ASCII characters. |

**Table 5.1** Description of Methods in Class CL_ABAP_FILE_UTILITIES

## 5.3 Logical Files and Directories

In the code examples demonstrated in Section 5.1, File Processing on the Application Server, we defined our datasets using selection screen parameters that required us to specify a fully qualified file path. While this sort of approach worked for the purposes of a simple demonstration, it can be cumbersome to work with in a productive environment. Ideally, we want to decouple our programs from the underlying directory structure of the host operating system so that the two can vary independently. For example, if a QA system needs to be migrated from a Windows environment to a UNIX environment, then that change should be transparent to the programs running on that system. Fortunately, SAP provides an API that makes it very easy to abstract physical directory paths and file names into logical ones.

### 5.3.1 Defining Logical Directory Paths and Files in Transaction FILE

The basis of the logical file API is a view cluster called `FILENAME` that consolidates a series of maintenance tables together to define mappings between logical and physical directory paths and file names. You can edit these relationships in Transaction FILE. When you initially execute Transaction FILE, you're prompted with the dialog box shown in Figure 5.2. This prompt is there to advise you that objects maintained in Transaction FILE are *cross-client* configuration objects. Therefore, if you change a logical file path in client 200, that change is also reflected in client 400, and so on.

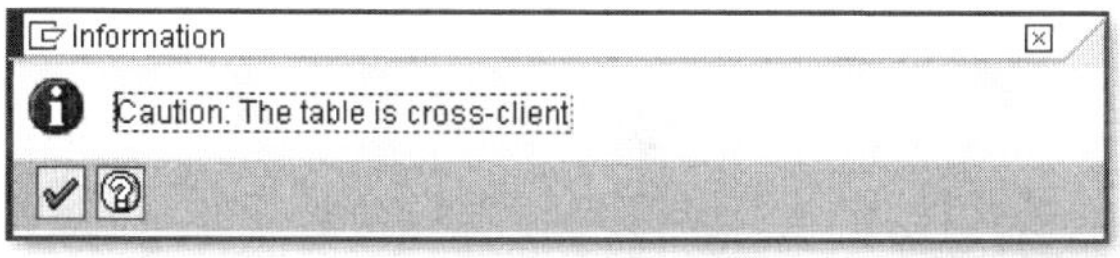


**Figure 5.2** Prompt Showing Logical File Paths Are Cross-Client

Figure 5.3 shows the initial screen of Transaction FILE. Within this transaction, you can create *logical file paths* and *logical file names* and assign them to physical directory paths and file names.

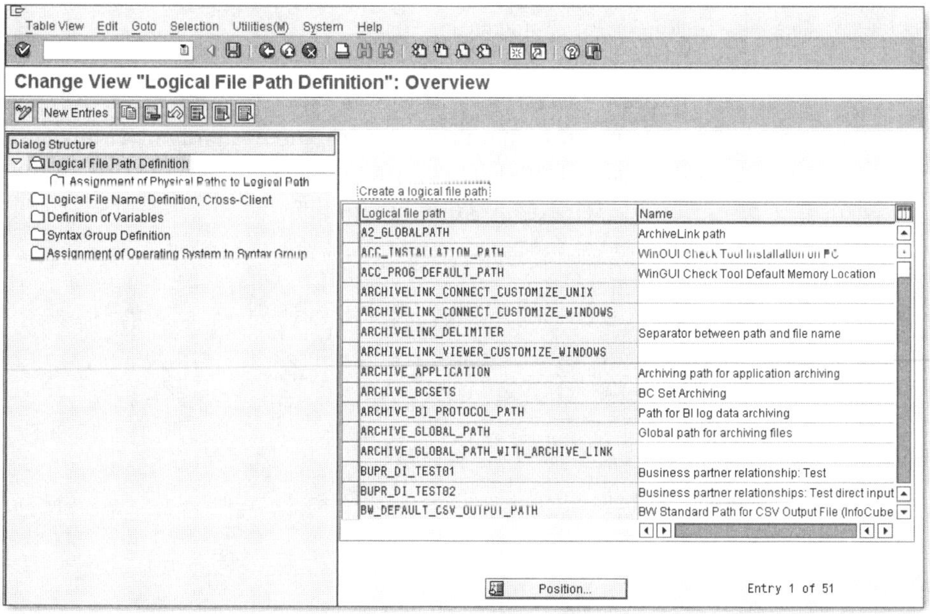


**Figure 5.3** Initial View of Transaction FILE

To understand the purpose/positioning of logical file paths and file names, it's useful to see how they are configured. This process begins with the definition of a logical file path. The steps required to create a logical file path in Transaction FILE are as follows:

1. When you first open Transaction FILE, the node Logical File Path Definition will be selected within the Dialog Structure on the left side of the screen (see Figure 5.3). To create a new logical file path, click the New Entries button in the toolbar. This brings up the Create a Logical File Path editor view shown in Figure 5.4. The logical file path should be named using a customer namespace. When you save your changes, you're prompted for a transport request.

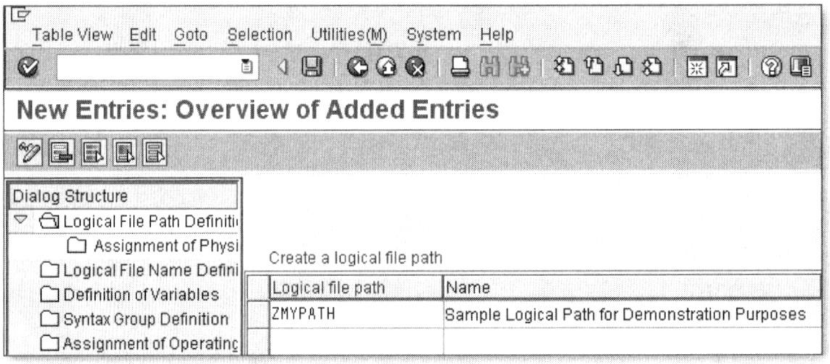


**Figure 5.4** Creating a Logical File Path in Transaction FILE

2. After the logical file path is created, you can assign a physical path to it by selecting your logical path and then double-clicking the Assignment of Physical Paths to Logical Paths node in the Dialog Structure tree on the left side of the screen. This brings up the screen shown in Figure 5.5.

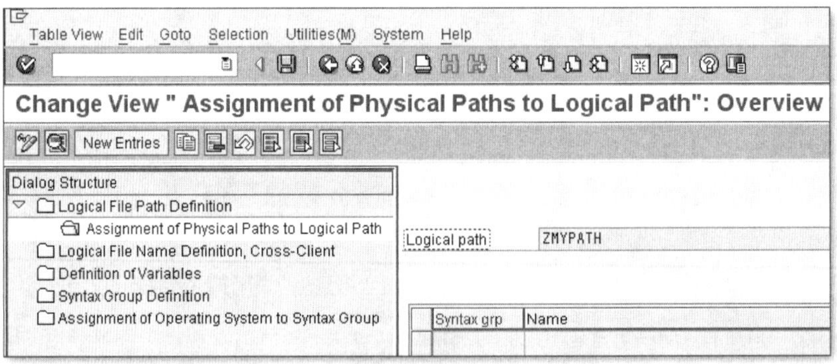


**Figure 5.5** Assigning a Physical Path to a Logical Path — Part 1

3. To create a new entry, click on the New Entries button in the toolbar to switch the editor to edit mode. Figure 5.6 shows what this view looks like when we create a physical path assignment for the logical path `ZMYPATH`.

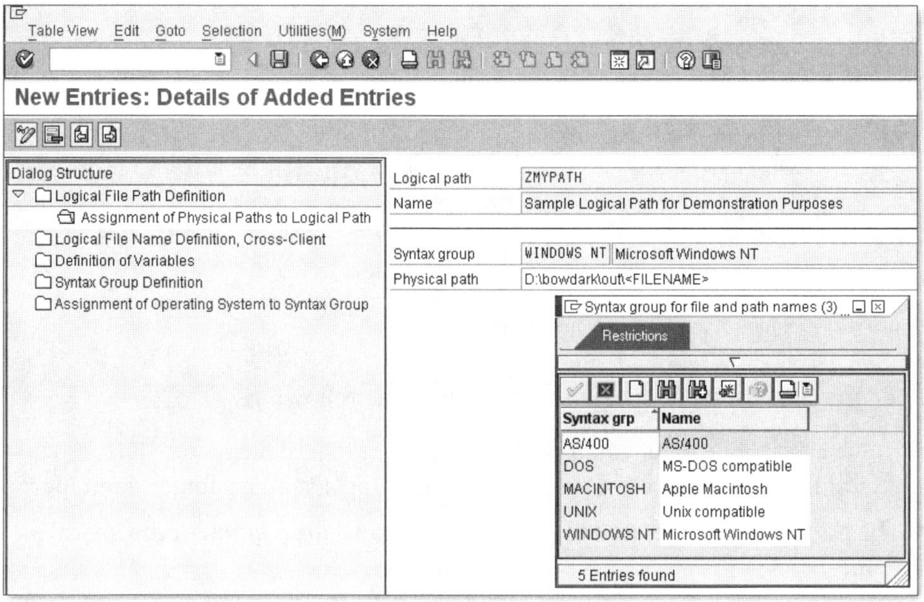


**Figure 5.6** Assigning a Physical Path to a Logical Path — Part 2

4. Here, you need to specify a physical directory path on the underlying SAP NetWeaver AS ABAP host. Looking carefully at Figure 5.6, you can see that we've appended a placeholder token called `<FILENAME>` to the end of the physical path location. This placeholder will be used to concatenate a file name to the directory path at runtime.
5. In addition to the configuration of the physical path, you must also select a *syntax group* that describes the syntax of the directory path. As you can see in Figure 5.6, you can choose from various operating system flavors when assigning a syntax group to the entry.
6. Finally, be sure to save your changes by clicking on the Save button.

After you finish creating a logical file path, you can begin defining logical file names that are associated with that path by double-clicking on the Logical File Name Definition, Cross-Client node in the Dialog Structure on the left side of the screen. This opens the logical file editor. To create a new entry, click on the New Entries button in the toolbar. This brings up the input mask shown in Figure 5.7.

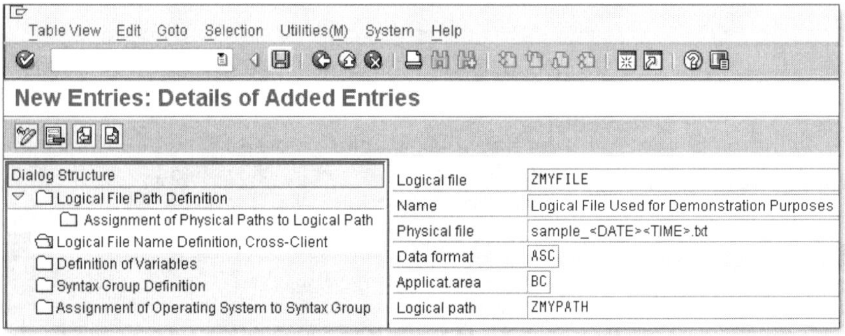


**Figure 5.7** Defining a Logical File Name in Transaction FILE

To define a logical file name, you must specify the following:

- In the Logical File field, you must enter a unique logical file name. Here, as with logical file paths, you must prefix the name using a valid customer namespace.
- The Name field can be used to provide an optional description of the logical file name.
- In the Physical file field, you specify the physical file name that you want to generate for the logical file at runtime. Here, you have the option of entering special placeholder variables that are replaced with parameter values at runtime when the file name is generated. For example, in Figure 5.7, the physical file name is using the `<DATE>` and `<TIME>` variables to add a timestamp onto the end of the file name. For a comprehensive list of options to choose from, place your cursor in the Physical File field, and press the F1 key to bring up the context-sensitive help documentation.
- In the Data Format field, you can specify the type of the file you're working with. You can use the F4 value help to guide your selection process.
- The Application Area field is used to assign the logical file to a particular application area within the system (see Transaction SE81 for more details).
- Finally, in the Logical Path field, you must assign the logical file name to a logical path. In Figure 5.7, for example, we've assigned the `ZMYFILE` logical file name to the `ZMYPATH` logical directory path created earlier.

### 5.3.2 Working with the Logical File API

After you've created a logical directory path and file name, you can work with those abstractions in your programs using the API functions provided in function group SFIL. These functions are described in Table 5.2. Additional documentation can be found in the Function Module Documentation available in the Function Builder (Transaction SE37).

| Function Name | Description |
|---|---|
| FILE_GET_NAME | This function derives a fully qualified file name using a logical file name configured in Transaction FILE. |
| FILE_GET_NAME_AND_LOGICAL_PATH | This function works just like FILE_GET_NAME but also returns the name of logical paths associated with the logical file. |
| FILE_GET_NAME_USING_PATH | This function derives a fully qualified file name dynamically using a logical directory path and a file name. |

**Table 5.2** API Functions of Function Group SFIL

The API functions listed in Table 5.2 are very straightforward to use. To demonstrate this, let's revise the ZCREATEFILEDEMO report to use a logical file name in lieu of a hard-coded one. The ZCREATEFILEDEMO2 report shown in Listing 5.13 is almost identical to the one we reviewed in Listing 5.7. However, if you look carefully at the bolded section, you can see where we derive the dataset name at runtime via a call to function FILE_GET_NAME.

```
REPORT zcreatefiledemo2.
CLASS lcl_file_manager DEFINITION.
  PUBLIC SECTION.
    CLASS-METHODS:
      create_file IMPORTING im_logical_file
                      TYPE filename-fileintern.

  PRIVATE SECTION.
    TYPES: BEGIN OF ty_record,
             id_number  TYPE numc4,
             first_name TYPE ad_namefir,
             last_name  TYPE ad_namelas,
           END OF ty_record.
ENDCLASS.
```

```
CLASS lcl_file_manager IMPLEMENTATION.
  METHOD create_file.
*   Method-Local Data Declarations:
    DATA: lv_dataset TYPE string,
          lv_message TYPE string,
          ls_record  TYPE ty_record.

*   Derive the physical file name for the provided
*   logical file:
    CALL FUNCTION 'FILE_GET_NAME'
      EXPORTING
        logical_filename = im_logical_file
      IMPORTING
        file_name        = lv_dataset
      EXCEPTIONS
        file_not_found   = 1
        others           = 2.

    IF sy-subrc NE 0.
      MESSAGE 'Invalid logical file name!' TYPE 'I'.
      RETURN.
    ENDIF.

*   Create a new text file and return a dataset that can be
*   used as a handle for writing to the file:
    OPEN DATASET lv_dataset FOR OUTPUT
      IN TEXT MODE ENCODING UTF-8
      WITH BYTE-ORDER MARK
      WITH SMART LINEFEED
      MESSAGE lv_message.

*   Check the results:
    IF sy-subrc NE 0.
      MESSAGE lv_message TYPE 'I'.
      RETURN.
    ENDIF.

*   Output a couple of records to the file:
    ls_record-id_number  = '0001'.
    ls_record-first_name = 'Andersen'.
    ls_record-last_name  = 'Wood'.
    TRANSFER ls_record TO lv_dataset.
```

```
    ls_record-id_number  = '0003'.
    ls_record-first_name = 'Paige'.
    ls_record-last_name  = 'Wood'.
    TRANSFER ls_record TO lv_dataset.

*   Always be sure to close the file:
    CLOSE DATASET lv_dataset.
    WRITE: / 'File', lv_dataset, 'created successfully'.
  ENDMETHOD.
ENDCLASS.

PARAMETERS:
  p_file TYPE filename-fileintern DEFAULT 'ZMYFILE'
         OBLIGATORY.

START-OF-SELECTION.
  CALL METHOD lcl_file_manager=>create_file( p_file ).
```

**Listing 5.13** Using Logical File Names to Derive a Dataset

In the example code shown in Listing 5.13, we're using the logical file name ZMYFILE to derive our dataset name. As you may recall from Section 5.3.1, Defining Logical Directory Paths and Files in Transaction FILE, we defined this logical file name using the pattern sample_<DATE><TIME>.txt. At runtime, function FILE_GET_NAME replaces the <DATE> and <TIME> placeholder variables with the system date and time, yielding a file name such as sample_20090619095443.txt. This derived file name is then concatenated with the physical directory associated with the logical directory path that is mapped to the logical file name to generate a fully qualified file name.

The usage scenarios for the other function modules in function group SFIL are very similar to that of FILE_GET_NAME. Collectively, this API greatly simplifies the process of defining and working with logical directory paths and file names so that programs can remain as system-independent as possible.

## 5.4 File Compression with ZIP Archives

One of the troubling aspects of working with files is that, if you're not careful, you can accumulate a lot of them. And, if some of those files happen to be fairly large, you may find that you're starting to run out of available disk space sooner rather than later. One common technique for dealing with these kinds of problems is to compress the files together in an *archive file*.

The ZIP file format defines the structure of an archive file that contains one or more files that may or may not be compressed to reduce the overall file size. Internally, the compression algorithms can be pretty complex. Fortunately, ABAP provides a series of system classes that makes it very easy to create and work with ZIP files.

### 5.4.1 The ABAP ZIP File API

The primary interface into the ABAP ZIP file-processing framework is the `CL_ABAP_ZIP` class. Figure 5.8 shows the URL class diagram for class `CL_ABAP_ZIP`.

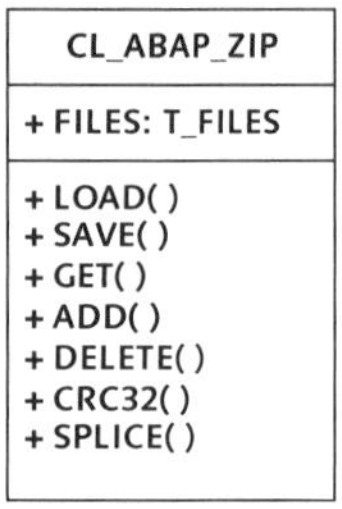


**Figure 5.8** UML Class Diagram for CL_ABAP_ZIP

If you aren't very familiar with the ZIP file format or haven't worked with ZIP files programmatically before, then some explanation is probably in order. Table 5.3 provides a more in-depth description of each of the methods defined in class `CL_ABAP_ZIP`. In the following sections, we'll see how to use these methods to perform some common ZIP file-processing tasks.

| Method Name | Description |
|---|---|
| `LOAD()` | This instance method loads a ZIP archive into context. |
| `SAVE()` | This instance method extracts the raw binary content of the ZIP archive (as an `XSTRING` data object) so that the archive file can be stored externally. |
| `GET()` | This instance method reads a file from the ZIP archive, returning the contents of the file as an `XSTRING` binary payload. |
| `ADD()` | This instance method adds a file to the ZIP archive. |

**Table 5.3** Description of Methods in Class CL_ABAP_ZIP

| Method Name | Description |
|---|---|
| DELETE() | This instance method removes a file from the ZIP archive. |
| CRC32() | This class method calculates a CRC-32 checksum that is used to make sure that file data isn't corrupted when it's decompressed, and so on. |
| SPLICE() | This class method *splices* a ZIP file apart to extract metadata about the individual file entries. This metadata can then be used as a key to read the individual files. |

**Table 5.3** Description of Methods in Class CL_ABAP_ZIP (Cont.)

### 5.4.2 Creating a ZIP File

To demonstrate the process of creating a ZIP file using the CL_ABAP_ZIP class, let's consider an example. Imagine that we want to zip up some files stored in the logical directory ZMYPATH created in Section 5.3.1, Defining Logical Directory Paths and Files in Transaction FILE. The steps required to carry out this task are as follows:

1. First, we need to come up with a list of the files in the specified logical directory path that we want to add to the ZIP archive.
2. Next, we need to read the contents of those files into an internal table keyed by the file name. Here, even if the file happens to be a plain text file, the file must be read in binary mode because ZIP files store their constituent files in binary format.
3. Then, we create an instance of class CL_ABAP_ZIP using the CREATE OBJECT statement.
4. After the CL_ABAP_ZIP instance is created, we can add entries to the ZIP archive using the ADD() method. The ADD() method defines two importing parameters called NAME and CONTENT that are used to specify the file's name and binary payload, respectively.
5. After all of the files have been added to the ZIP file, we can extract its binary payload via a call to the SAVE() method. This payload is captured in the form of an XSTRING data object. Because some of the files could be large, it's always best to convert this payload into a series of smaller *chunks* so that we can transfer the content to the target ZIP file using smaller I/O operations. This can be achieved via a call to standard function module SCMS_XSTRING_TO_BINARY.

6. Finally, we can create the target ZIP file by opening the file for output in binary mode and copying the ZIP file chunks to the file using the TRANSFER statement.

A complete implementation of this logic can be found in the sample report program ZCREATEZIPFILE, in the source code bundle for this book available online. However, if you're eager to see how these steps are implemented in the code, Listing 5.14 contains the relevant excerpts from report ZCREATEZIPFILE so that you can see what's going on.

```
REPORT zcreatezipfile.
CLASS lcl_compressor DEFINITION.
  PUBLIC SECTION.
    CLASS-METHODS:
      archive_directory
        IMPORTING im_path     TYPE filename-pathintern
                  im_zip_file TYPE string.

  PRIVATE SECTION.
    CLASS-DATA:
      physical_path TYPE char40,
      files TYPE STANDARD TABLE OF rsfillst.

    CLASS-METHODS:
      get_directory_files IMPORTING im_path
                                 TYPE filename-pathintern
                              RAISING cx_sy_file_io,
      compress_files IMPORTING im_zip_file TYPE string
                         RAISING cx_sy_file_io,
      read_directory_file IMPORTING im_file TYPE rsfillst
                            EXPORTING ex_contents TYPE xstring
                              RAISING cx_sy_file_io.
ENDCLASS.

CLASS lcl_compressor IMPLEMENTATION.
  METHOD archive_directory.
*   Method-Local Data Declarations:
    DATA: lo_exception TYPE REF TO cx_sy_file_io,
          lv_message   TYPE string.

    TRY.
*     First, we need to determine the files that we want
*     to archive:
```

```
      get_directory_files( im_path ).

*     Then, we can go ahead and compress the files into
*     a ZIP archive:
      compress_files( im_zip_file ).
    CATCH cx_sy_file_io INTO lo_exception.
      lv_message = lo_exception->get_text( ).
      MESSAGE lv_message TYPE 'I'.
    ENDTRY.
  ENDMETHOD.                    " METHOD archive_directory

  METHOD get_directory_files.
    ...
  ENDMETHOD.                    " METHOD get_directory_files

  METHOD compress_files.
*   Method-Local Data Declarations:
    DATA: lo_zip         TYPE REF TO cl_abap_zip,
          lv_name        TYPE string,
          lv_content     TYPE xstring,
          lv_zip_content TYPE xstring,
          lv_dataset     TYPE string,
          lt_zip_payload TYPE STANDARD TABLE OF x255.
    FIELD-SYMBOLS:
      <lfs_file> LIKE LINE OF files,
      <lfs_zip_chunk> LIKE LINE OF lt_zip_payload.

*   Create an instance of the ZIP library utility:
    CREATE OBJECT lo_zip.

*   Add each of the selected files to the ZIP archive:
    LOOP AT files ASSIGNING <lfs_file>.
*     Read the raw contents of the selected file:
      CALL METHOD read_directory_file
        EXPORTING
          im_file     = <lfs_file>
        IMPORTING
          ex_contents = lv_content.

*     Add the file to the ZIP archive:
      lv_name = <lfs_file>-name.

      CALL METHOD lo_zip->add
```

```
        EXPORTING
          name    = lv_name
          content = lv_content.
    ENDLOOP.

*   Extract the raw ZIP content into a binary payload:
    lv_zip_content = lo_zip->save( ).

*   Convert the ZIP byte string into binary chunks:
    CALL FUNCTION 'SCMS_XSTRING_TO_BINARY'
      EXPORTING
        buffer     = lv_zip_content
      TABLES
        binary_tab = lt_zip_payload.

*   Now create the physical ZIP file:
    CONCATENATE physical_path im_zip_file INTO lv_dataset.
    OPEN DATASET lv_dataset FOR OUTPUT IN BINARY MODE.
    IF sy-subrc NE 0.
      RAISE EXCEPTION TYPE cx_sy_file_io
        EXPORTING
          errorcode = sy-subrc
          errortext = 'Could not create ZIP file!'.
    ENDIF.

    LOOP AT lt_zip_payload ASSIGNING <lfs_zip_chunk>.
      TRANSFER <lfs_zip_chunk> TO lv_dataset.
    ENDLOOP.

    CLOSE DATASET lv_dataset.
  ENDMETHOD.                    " METHOD compress_files

  METHOD read_directory_file.
    ...
  ENDMETHOD.                    " METHOD read_directory_file
ENDCLASS.

PARAMETERS:
  p_path TYPE pathintern DEFAULT 'ZMYPATH' OBLIGATORY,
  p_zip  TYPE string LOWER CASE DEFAULT 'archive.zip'
                   OBLIGATORY.

START-OF-SELECTION.
```

```
  "Zip up all the files in the selected directory:
  CALL METHOD lcl_compressor=>archive_directory
    EXPORTING
      im_path     = p_path
      im_zip_file = p_zip.
```

**Listing 5.14** Creating a ZIP File Using Class CL_ABAP_ZIP

### 5.4.3 Reading a ZIP File

Now that you have a feel for how ZIP files are put together, let's look at how we would unpack an archive using the CL_ABAP_ZIP class:

1. First, the raw binary contents of the ZIP file must be read into context. This can be accomplished using the ABAP file interface, per usual.
2. Next, we must load the raw binary contents of the ZIP file into a new instance of class CL_ABAP_ZIP. The load process is performed by the LOAD() instance method.
3. After the contents are loaded into the ZIP file instance, we can iterate through each of the embedded files using the metadata stored in the public, read-only FILES attribute of class CL_ABAP_ZIP. This metadata provides, among other things, the names of the embedded files. These file names can be used as a key in a call to instance method GET() to retrieve the raw contents of an embedded file. The raw contents are returned in the form of an XSTRING data object.
4. Once again, we need to split up the raw payload into manageable chunks using the function module SCMS_XSTRING_TO_BINARY.
5. Finally, we can output the binary payload of the file using the ABAP file interface.

In the source code bundle available online, we've provided a complete implementation of this logic in a report program called ZREADZIPFILE. The code excerpt in Listing 5.15 hits on some of the high points of this program so that you can get a feel for how the API calls work.

```
REPORT zreadzipfile.
CLASS lcl_zip_utils DEFINITION.
  PUBLIC SECTION.
    CLASS-METHODS:
      unzip_file
        IMPORTING im_path TYPE filename-pathintern
```

```
                    im_zip  TYPE string.

  PRIVATE SECTION.
    CLASS-DATA:
      physical_path TYPE string.

    CLASS-METHODS:
      get_physical_path
        IMPORTING im_path TYPE filename-pathintern
          RAISING cx_sy_file_io,
      read_zip_file
        IMPORTING im_zip     TYPE string
        EXPORTING ex_payload TYPE xstring
          RAISING cx_sy_file_io,
      write_file
        IMPORTING im_file    TYPE string
                  im_payload TYPE xstring
          RAISING cx_sy_file_io.
ENDCLASS.

CLASS lcl_zip_utils IMPLEMENTATION.
  METHOD unzip_file.
*   Method-Local Data Declarations:
    DATA: lv_payload     TYPE xstring,
          lo_zip         TYPE REF TO cl_abap_zip,
          lv_message     TYPE string,
          lo_exception   TYPE REF TO cx_sy_file_io.
    FIELD-SYMBOLS:
      <lfs_file> TYPE cl_abap_zip=>t_file.

*   Unpack the selected ZIP file in its own directory:
    TRY.
*     Determine the physical directory path for the file:
      get_physical_path( im_path ).

*     Read the contents of the ZIP file into context:
      CALL METHOD read_zip_file
        EXPORTING
          im_zip     = im_zip
        IMPORTING
          ex_payload = lv_payload.

*     Load the contents of the ZIP file into an instance
```

```
*     of class CL_ABAP_ZIP:
      CREATE OBJECT lo_zip.

      CALL METHOD lo_zip->load
        EXPORTING
          zip             = lv_payload
        EXCEPTIONS
          zip_parse_error = 1
          others          = 2.

      IF sy-subrc NE 0.
        RAISE EXCEPTION TYPE cx_sy_file_io
          EXPORTING
            errorcode = sy-subrc
            errortext = 'The ZIP file could not be loaded.'.
      ENDIF.

*     Extract each embedded file in the ZIP archive:
      LOOP AT lo_zip->files ASSIGNING <lfs_file>.
*       Get the next file in the ZIP archive:
        CLEAR lv_payload.

        CALL METHOD lo_zip->get
          EXPORTING
            name                     = <lfs_file>-name
          IMPORTING
            content                  = lv_payload
          EXCEPTIONS
            zip_index_error          = 1
            zip_decompression_error  = 2
            others                   = 3.

        IF sy-subrc NE 0.
          CONCATENATE 'Could not read file' <lfs_file>-name
                 INTO lv_message SEPARATED BY space.
          RAISE EXCEPTION TYPE cx_sy_file_io
            EXPORTING
              errorcode = sy-subrc
              errortext = lv_message.
        ENDIF.

*       Output the decompressed file in the current
*       directory:
```

```
        CALL METHOD write_file
          EXPORTING
            im_file = <lfs_file>-name
            im_payload = lv_payload.
      ENDLOOP.
    CATCH cx_sy_file_io INTO lo_exception.
      lv_message = lo_exception->get_text( ).
      MESSAGE lv_message TYPE 'I'.
      RETURN.
    ENDTRY.
  ENDMETHOD.                    " METHOD unzip_file

  METHOD get_physical_path.
    ...
  ENDMETHOD.                    " METHOD get_physical_path

  METHOD read_zip_file.
    ...
  ENDMETHOD.                    " METHOD read_zip_file

  METHOD write_file.
    ...
  ENDMETHOD.                    " METHOD write_file
ENDCLASS.

PARAMETERS:
  p_path TYPE filename-pathintern DEFAULT 'ZMYPATH'
              OBLIGATORY,
  p_zip  TYPE string DEFAULT 'archive.zip' LOWER CASE
              OBLIGATORY.

START-OF-SELECTION.
* Unpack the selected ZIP archive file:
  CALL METHOD lcl_zip_utils=>unzip_file
    EXPORTING
      im_path = p_path
      im_zip  = p_zip.
```

**Listing 5.15** Unpacking a ZIP File Using Class CL_ABAP_ZIP

## 5.5 File Processing on the Presentation Server

Normally, whenever we work with files in ABAP, we're dealing with files that reside on some directory that is accessible on SAP NetWeaver AS ABAP host. However, sometimes we run into situations where we need to either upload or download a file from/to the SAP GUI presentation tier client. This remote transport is made possible using the RFC protocol.

In the past, file transfer between the application and presentation tiers was achieved using various function modules defined in the `GRAP` function group. However, as of SAP NetWeaver AS ABAP 6.10, these function modules have been deprecated in favor of an ABAP Objects class called `CL_GUI_FRONTEND_SERVICES`. In the following subsections, we introduce you to some of the services provided by this class and show you how to use them to upload and download files from/to the presentation tier.

### 5.5.1 Interacting with the SAP GUI via CL_GUI_FRONTEND_SERVICES

Class `CL_GUI_FRONTEND_SERVICES` provides many useful methods for interfacing with the SAP GUI frontend. Figure 5.9 contains a UML class diagram that shows some of the methods that can be used to work with files and directories on the frontend client. You can find out more information about these methods in the class documentation available for this class in the Class Builder.

| CL_GUI_FRONTEND_SERVICES |
| --- |
| ...<br>+ DIRECTORY_BROWSE( )<br>+ DIRECTORY_CREATE( )<br>+ DIRECTORY_DELETE( )<br>+ DIRECTORY_EXIST( )<br>+ DIRECTORY_LIST_FILES( )<br>+ FILE_COPY( )<br>+ FILE_DELETE( )<br>+ FILE_EXIST( )<br>+ FILE_GET_ATTRIBUTES( )<br>+ FILE_GET_SIZE( )<br>+ FILE_OPEN_DIALOG( )<br>+ FILE_SAVE_DIALOG( )<br>+ GET_DESKTOP_DIRECTORY( )<br>+ GET_FILE_SEPARATOR( )<br>+ GUI_DOWNLOAD( )<br>+ GUI_UPLOAD( )<br>... |

**Figure 5.9** UML Class Diagram of CL_GUI_FRONTEND_SERVICES

### 5.5.2 Downloading a File

To download a file to the SAP GUI frontend, you can use the class method `GUI_DOWNLOAD()` of class `CL_GUI_FRONTEND_SERVICES`. To invoke this method, you must specify a target file name as well as an internal table that contains the contents of the file that is being downloaded. In addition, this method also defines various other parameters that you can use to specify how the file is output, and so on.

Because an ABAP program running on a remote application server doesn't know much about the SAP GUI client it's servicing, the file name used in the call to method `GUI_DOWNLOAD()` is normally specified by the user. You can simplify this selection process for the user using the method `FILE_SAVE_DIALOG()` of class `CL_GUI_FRONTEND_SERVICES`. This class method displays a Save As dialog box, as shown in Figure 5.10. Users can then navigate within this dialog box to locate the target directory where they want to store the file.

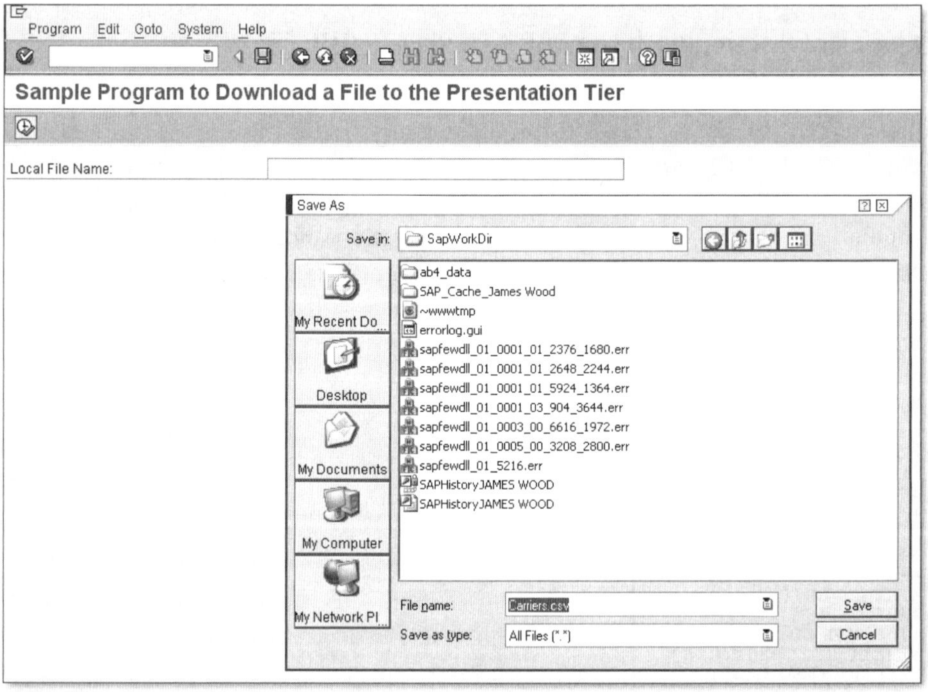


**Figure 5.10** Displaying a Save As Dialog Box in the SAP GUI

The report program `ZDOWNLOADFILE` presented in Listing 5.16 shows how the service methods of class `CL_GUI_FRONTEND_SERVICES` can be used to download a file to a user's local machine. In this simple example, we're generating a comma-separated values (CSV) file containing the records in the SCARR database table. Users can select the name of the file they want to create by using the F4 Value Help attached to the selection screen parameter p_file. Here, we're using the AT SELECTION-SCREEN ON VALUE-REQUEST event module as a trigger for calling a static method that leverages the previously mentioned FILE_SAVE_DIALOG() method of class CL_GUI_FRONTEND_SERVICES to display a Save As dialog box. After the local file name is selected, we can extract the data and download it via a call to method GUI_DOWNLOAD().

```
REPORT zdownloadfile.
CLASS lcl_file_manager DEFINITION.
  PUBLIC SECTION.
    CLASS-METHODS:
      get_local_filename CHANGING ch_file TYPE string,
      download_file IMPORTING im_file TYPE string.

  PRIVATE SECTION.
    CLASS-DATA:
      carriers_csv TYPE string_table.

    CLASS-METHODS:
      get_carriers.
ENDCLASS.

CLASS lcl_file_manager IMPLEMENTATION.
  METHOD get_local_filename.
*   Method-Local Data Declarations:
    DATA: lv_filename    TYPE string,
          lv_path        TYPE string,
          lv_fullpath    TYPE string,
          lv_user_action TYPE i.

*   Present the user with a dialog box that he can use
*   to select the name of the file he wants to create:
    CALL METHOD cl_gui_frontend_services=>file_save_dialog
      EXPORTING
        default_extension    = 'csv'
        file_filter          = '.csv'
      CHANGING
        filename             = lv_filename
        path                 = lv_path
```

```
        fullpath              = lv_fullpath
        user_action           = lv_user_action
      EXCEPTIONS
        cntl_error            = 1
        error_no_gui          = 2
        not_supported_by_gui  = 3
        others                = 4.

    IF sy-subrc EQ 0.
      IF lv_user_action NE
           cl_gui_frontend_services=>action_cancel.
        ch_file = lv_fullpath.
      ENDIF.
    ELSE.
      MESSAGE 'Could not determine target filename!'
         TYPE 'I'.
      RETURN.
    ENDIF.
  ENDMETHOD.                  " METHOD get_local_filename

  METHOD download_file.
*   Build the sample CSV file:
    get_carriers( ).

*   Download the file to the frontend:
    CALL METHOD cl_gui_frontend_services=>gui_download
      EXPORTING
        filename                = im_file
      CHANGING
        data_tab                = carriers_csv
      EXCEPTIONS
        file_write_error        = 1
        ...
        others                  = 24.

    IF sy-subrc NE 0.
      MESSAGE 'Could not download file!' TYPE 'I'.
      RETURN.
    ENDIF.
  ENDMETHOD.                  " METHOD download_file

  METHOD get_carriers.
    ...
```

```
  ENDMETHOD.                    " METHOD get_carriers
ENDCLASS.

PARAMETERS:
  p_file TYPE string OBLIGATORY.

AT SELECTION-SCREEN ON VALUE-REQUEST FOR p_file.
* Show a dialog box to allow the user to select a file:
  CALL METHOD lcl_file_manager=>get_local_filename
    CHANGING
      ch_file = p_file.

START-OF-SELECTION.
  CALL METHOD lcl_file_manager=>download_file( p_file ).
```

**Listing 5.16** Downloading a File to the Frontend

### 5.5.3 Uploading a File

The process of uploading a file from the SAP GUI client is very similar to the one used to download a file. Here, however, we must use the `FILE_OPEN_DIALOG()` to select the source input file and the `GUI_UPLOAD()` method to upload the file. Listing 5.17 shows how these methods are used in a simple report program called `ZUPLOADFILE`. This report program can be used to upload the CSV file created via program `ZDOWNLOADFILE` and display its contents in an ABAP list.

```
REPORT zuploadfile.
CLASS lcl_file_manager DEFINITION.
  PUBLIC SECTION.
    CLASS-METHODS:
      get_local_filename CHANGING ch_file TYPE string,
      upload_file IMPORTING im_file TYPE string.
ENDCLASS.

CLASS lcl_file_manager IMPLEMENTATION.
  METHOD get_local_filename.
*   Method-Local Data Declarations:
    DATA: lt_files       TYPE filetable,
          lv_retcode     TYPE i,
          lv_user_action TYPE i.
    FIELD-SYMBOLS:
      <lfs_file> LIKE LINE OF lt_files.
```

```
*   Present the user with a dialog box to select the name
*   of the file he wants to upload:
    CALL METHOD cl_gui_frontend_services=>file_open_dialog
      EXPORTING
        default_extension       = 'csv'
        file_filter             = '.csv'
      CHANGING
        file_table              = lt_files
        rc                      = lv_retcode
        user_action             = lv_user_action
      EXCEPTIONS
        file_open_dialog_failed = 1
        cntl_error              = 2
        error_no_gui            = 3
        not_supported_by_gui    = 4
        others                  = 5.

    IF sy-subrc EQ 0.
      IF lv_user_action NE
           cl_gui_frontend_services=>action_cancel.
        READ TABLE lt_files INDEX 1 ASSIGNING <lfs_file>.
        IF sy-subrc EQ 0.
          ch_file = <lfs_file>-filename.
        ENDIF.
      ENDIF.
    ELSE.
      MESSAGE 'Could not determine target filename!'
         TYPE 'I'.
      RETURN.
    ENDIF.
  ENDMETHOD.                    " METHOD get_local_filename

  METHOD upload_file.
*   Method-Local Data Declarations:
    DATA: lt_file_payload TYPE string_table.
    FIELD-SYMBOLS:
      <lfs_file_record> LIKE LINE OF lt_file_payload.

*   Upload the file from the frontend:
    CALL METHOD cl_gui_frontend_services=>gui_upload
      EXPORTING
        filename                = im_file
      CHANGING
```

```
        data_tab                   = lt_file_payload
      EXCEPTIONS
        file_open_error            = 1
        ...
        others                     = 19.

*   Display the file records in an ABAP list:
    LOOP AT lt_file_payload ASSIGNING <lfs_file_record>.
      WRITE: / <lfs_file_record>.
    ENDLOOP.
  ENDMETHOD.                    " METHOD upload_file
ENDCLASS.

PARAMETERS:
  p_file TYPE string OBLIGATORY.

AT SELECTION-SCREEN ON VALUE-REQUEST FOR p_file.
* Show a dialog box to allow the user to select a file:
  CALL METHOD lcl_file_manager=>get_local_filename
    CHANGING
      ch_file = p_file.

START-OF-SELECTION.
* Upload the file from the frontend:
  CALL METHOD lcl_file_manager=>upload_file( p_file ).
```

**Listing 5.17** Uploading a File from the Frontend

## 5.6 Transmitting Files Using FTP

The File Transfer Protocol (FTP) is a network protocol built on top of TCP/IP that makes it possible for two host machines to transfer files back and forth over the network. FTP is frequently used to implement *application-to-application* (A2A) or *business-to-business* (B2B) integration scenarios. In this section, we look at a custom ABAP Objects class that can be used to execute FTP commands in your ABAP programs.

### 5.6.1 Introducing the SAPFTP Library

SAP provides an FTP client library out of the box called SAPFTP. This client library is implemented in two parts:

- The raw connectivity is realized in the form of an executable file called SAPFTP. This program is installed on the SAP NetWeaver AS ABAP host. In addition, it's also installed as part of a SAP GUI client installation.
- The ABAP program interface is implemented in the form of a series of remote-enabled function modules in the function group SFTP. These function modules access the SAPFTP executable via RFC to connect to an FTP host and execute various commands. Some of the more prominent function modules in the SFTP function group are described in Table 5.4.

| Function Module | Description |
|---|---|
| FTP_CONNECT | Used to connect to an FTP host; returns a handle that is used to bind subsequent commands to the session. |
| FTP_COMMAND | Used to execute an FTP command on the FTP host. For a complete list of supported FTP commands on an FTP host, you can execute the help command. |
| FTP_R3_TO_CLIENT | Used to transfer a file down to the frontend. |
| FTP_CLIENT_TO_R3 | Used to upload a file from the frontend. |
| FTP_R3_TO_SERVER | Used to upload a file to the FTP host. |
| FTP_SERVER_TO_R3 | Used to download a file from the FTP host. |
| FTP_DISCONNECT | Used to disconnect from an FTP host. |

**Table 5.4** SAPFTP Modules Available in Function Group SFTP

To set up the SAPFTP client library on your system, you need to create a couple of RFC destinations. Fortunately, SAP provides a program called RSFTP005 that can be used to automate this task. This program creates two RFC destinations: SAPFTP for invoking the RFC library on the SAP GUI frontend, and SAPFTPA for invoking the RFC library on the SAP NetWeaver AS ABAP host. Figure 5.11 shows the automatically generated SAPFTP destination. The only difference in the SAPFTPA destination is that the Activation Type is set to Start on Application Server in lieu of the Start on Front-End Work Station option shown in Figure 5.11. After the RFC destinations are set up, you can test the FTP library using the report program RSFTP002 in package SFTP.

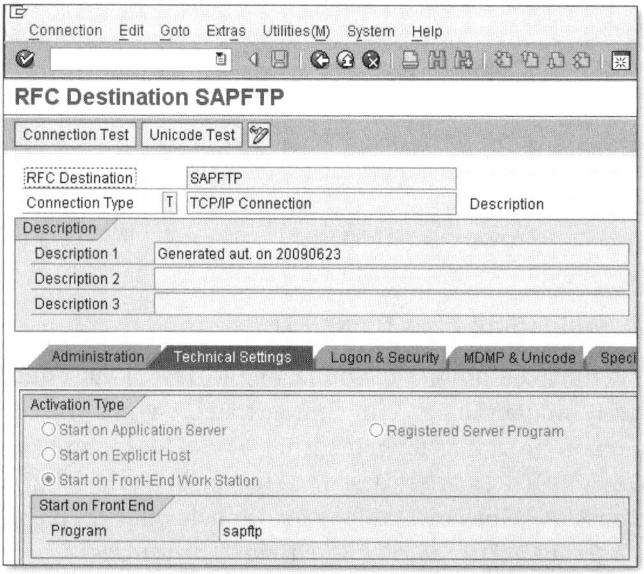


**Figure 5.11** Automatically Generated RFC Destination SAPFTP

The SAPFTP library implements FTP according to the RFC 959 specification. By default, it doesn't support secure communication (e.g., sFTP, etc.). However, it's possible to achieve secure FTP communication using the *Secure Socket Shell* (SSH) protocol. For more information on this technique, refer to SAP Note 795131.

### 5.6.2 Wrapping the SAPFTP Library in an ABAP Objects Class

To simplify the process of working with the SAPFTP library, we've created a custom ABAP Objects class called `/BOWDK/CL_FTP_CLIENT` in the source code bundle available for this book. This class abstracts away certain complexities of the `SFTP` function group and also takes care of some of the more mundane connection housekeeping tasks behind the scenes. To maximize portability, we're using the `SAPFTPA` RFC destination internally to provide the FTP connectivity.

Figure 5.12 shows the UML class diagram for class `/BOWDK/CL_FTP_CLIENT`. For the most part, the public instance methods mirror the core function modules described in Table 5.4. In addition, we've also included some utility methods that make it easy to upload/download files to/from the FTP host. We'll see how to use this class in Section 5.6.3, Uploading and Downloading Files Using FTP.

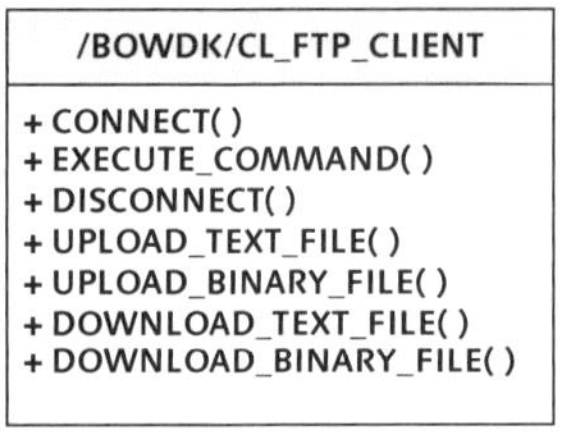


**Figure 5.12** UML Class Diagram for Class /BOWDK/CL_FTP_CLIENT

### 5.6.3 Uploading and Downloading Files Using FTP

After the SAPFTP library is set up, the process of connecting to an FTP host and issuing commands is relatively straightforward. To demonstrate how this works, let's consider the ZFTPDEMO report program shown in Listing 5.18. This report program leverages the /BOWDK/CL_FTP_CLIENT class described in Section 5.6.2, Wrapping the SAPFTP Library in an ABAP Objects Class to upload and download a plain text file from an FTP host. To test this class, we've created a local driver class called LCL_FTP_SERVICE that defines methods to connect to the FTP host, upload and download a plain text file, and then close the connection. As you can see, most of these methods can raise exceptions of type /BOWDK/CX_FTP_EXCEPTION. This custom exception class encapsulates the various types of exceptions that could occur during an FTP session (e.g., communication failure, etc.).

```
REPORT zftpdemo.
CLASS lcl_ftp_service DEFINITION.
  PUBLIC SECTION.
    CLASS-METHODS:
      process_file IMPORTING im_ftp_host TYPE csequence
                             im_user     TYPE csequence
                             im_password TYPE csequence.

    METHODS:
      constructor IMPORTING im_ftp_host TYPE csequence
                            im_user     TYPE csequence
                            im_password TYPE csequence
                  RAISING /bowdk/cx_ftp_exception,
      upload_file RAISING /bowdk/cx_ftp_exception,
      download_file RAISING /bowdk/cx_ftp_exception,
      disconnect.

  PRIVATE SECTION.
    DATA: ftp_client TYPE REF TO /bowdk/cl_ftp_client.
```

```
ENDCLASS.

CLASS lcl_ftp_service IMPLEMENTATION.
  METHOD process_file.
    "Method-Local Data Declarations:
    DATA: lo_ftp_service TYPE REF TO lcl_ftp_service,
          lo_ftp_ex      TYPE REF
                           TO /bowdk/cx_ftp_exception.

    TRY.
      "Create an instance of the local FTP client proxy
      "class:
      CREATE OBJECT lo_ftp_service
        EXPORTING
          im_ftp_host = im_ftp_host
          im_user     = im_user
          im_password = im_password.

      "Upload a plain text file to the FTP host:
      lo_ftp_service->upload_file( ).

      "Download the same file off the FTP host:
      lo_ftp_service->download_file( ).

      "Disconnect from the FTP host:
      lo_ftp_service->disconnect( ).
    CATCH /bowdk/cx_ftp_exception INTO lo_ftp_ex.
      MESSAGE lo_ftp_ex TYPE 'I'.
    ENDTRY.
  ENDMETHOD.                    " METHOD process_file

  METHOD constructor.
*   Method-Local Data Declarations:
    DATA: lv_password TYPE char40.

*   Create an instance of the FTP client:
    CREATE OBJECT ftp_client.

*   Connect to the FTP client:
    lv_password = im_password.

    CALL METHOD ftp_client->connect
      EXPORTING
```

```
        im_ftp_host = im_ftp_host
        im_user     = im_user
      CHANGING
        ch_password = lv_password.
  ENDMETHOD.                   " METHOD constructor

  METHOD upload_file.
*   Local Data Declarations:
    DATA: lt_text_file TYPE /bowdk/tt_textfile.
    FIELD-SYMBOLS:
      <lfs_file_line> LIKE LINE OF lt_text_file.

*   Create a plain text file:
    APPEND INITIAL LINE TO lt_text_file
      ASSIGNING <lfs_file_line>.
    <lfs_file_line>-line = 'ABAP FTP Demo'.

*   Upload the text file to the default directory on
*   the FTP host:
    CALL METHOD ftp_client->upload_text_file
      EXPORTING
        im_filename     = 'ftptest.txt'
        im_file_payload = lt_text_file.
  ENDMETHOD.                   " METHOD upload_file

  METHOD download_file.
*   Local Data Declarations:
    DATA: lt_text_file TYPE /bowdk/tt_textfile.
    FIELD-SYMBOLS:
      <lfs_file_line> LIKE LINE OF lt_text_file.

*   Download the plain text file off the FTP host:
    CALL METHOD ftp_client->download_text_file
      EXPORTING
        im_filename = 'ftptest.txt'
      RECEIVING
        re_file     = lt_text_file.

*   Display the file contents in a list:
    LOOP AT lt_text_file ASSIGNING <lfs_file_line>.
      WRITE: / <lfs_file_line>-line.
    ENDLOOP.
  ENDMETHOD.                   " METHOD download_file
```

```
  METHOD disconnect.
*   Disconnect from the FTP client:
    ftp_client->disconnect( ).
  ENDMETHOD.                    " METHOD disconnect
ENDCLASS.

PARAMETERS:
  p_ftp(60) TYPE c LOWER CASE,
  p_usr(30) TYPE c LOWER CASE,
  p_pwd(30) TYPE c LOWER CASE.

START-OF-SELECTION.
  "Process a file using the FTP client library:
  lcl_ftp_service=>process_file(
    im_ftp_host = p_ftp
    im_user     = p_usr
    im_password = p_pwd ).
```

**Listing 5.18** Executing FTP Commands in an ABAP Program

### 5.6.4 Implementation Details

Now that you have a feel for how to use the /BOWDK/CL_FTP_CLIENT class, let's look at how some of its methods are implemented behind the scenes. Listing 5.19 shows the implementation of instance method CONNECT(). This method leverages the FTP_CONNECT function to establish a connection to the target FTP host.

```
METHOD connect.
* Method Local Data Declarations:
  DATA: lv_ftp_host TYPE string.

* Scramble the password before sending it over the wire:
  CALL METHOD me->scramble_password
    CHANGING
      ch_password = ch_password.

* Try to connect to the target FTP host:
  CALL FUNCTION 'FTP_CONNECT'
    EXPORTING
      user             = im_user
      password         = ch_password
      host             = im_ftp_host
```

```
      rfc_destination = co_rfc_destination
    IMPORTING
      handle          = me->session_handle
    EXCEPTIONS
      not_connected   = 1
      others          = 2.

* Check the results:
  IF sy-subrc NE 0.
    lv_ftp_host = im_ftp_host.

    RAISE EXCEPTION TYPE /bowdk/cx_ftp_exception
      EXPORTING
        textid   =
          /bowdk/cx_ftp_exception=>co_connection_error
        ftp_host = lv_ftp_host.
  ENDIF.
ENDMETHOD.
```

**Listing 5.19** Implementing Method CONNECT()

As soon as a connection is established, we can issue FTP commands using method EXECUTE_COMMAND() or the utility upload/download methods described in Section 5.6.2, Wrapping the SAPFTP Library in an ABAP Objects Class. Listing 5.20 shows how the UPLOAD_TEXT_FILE() method is implemented. Here, you'll notice that we're encapsulating several FTP commands (e.g., set passive on and ascii) together to simplify the process of uploading a text file to the FTP host. The heavy lifting is performed by the RFC module FTP_R3_TO_SERVER. As you might expect, the other upload/download utility methods are implemented in much the same way as method UPLOAD_TEXT_FILE().

```
METHOD upload_text_file.
* Method-Local Data Declarations:
  DATA: lv_ftp_command TYPE string.

* Set the passive mode - as necessary:
  IF im_passive_mode EQ abap_true.
    me->execute_command( 'set passive on' ).
  ENDIF.

* Turn on the ASCII transfer mode:
  me->execute_command( 'ascii' ).
```

```
* Try to upload the file:
  CALL FUNCTION 'FTP_R3_TO_SERVER'
    EXPORTING
      handle         = me->session_handle
      fname          = im_filename
      character_mode = 'X'
    TABLES
      text           = im_file_payload
    EXCEPTIONS
      tcpip_error    = 1
      command_error  = 2
      data_error     = 3
      others         = 4.

* Check the results:
  CASE sy-subrc.
    WHEN 0.
      RETURN.
    WHEN 1.
      RAISE EXCEPTION TYPE /bowdk/cx_ftp_exception
        EXPORTING
          textid =
            /bowdk/cx_ftp_exception=>co_communication_error.
    WHEN 2.
      lv_ftp_command = 'put'.

      RAISE EXCEPTION TYPE /bowdk/cx_ftp_exception
        EXPORTING
          textid =
            /bowdk/cx_ftp_exception=>co_invalid_command
          ftp_command = lv_ftp_command.
    WHEN OTHERS.
      RAISE EXCEPTION TYPE /bowdk/cx_ftp_exception
        EXPORTING
          textid = /bowdk/cx_ftp_exception=>co_data_error.
  ENDCASE.
ENDMETHOD.
```

**Listing 5.20** Implementing Method UPLOAD_TEXT_FILE()

After we're finished executing commands with the FTP host, we need to close down the connection using RFC function `FTP_DISCONNECT`. Listing 5.21 shows how we've encapsulated this function call with some other housecleaning steps to make sure that the connection is closed down gracefully.

```
METHOD disconnect.
* Disconnect from the FTP host:
  CALL FUNCTION 'FTP_DISCONNECT'
    EXPORTING
      HANDLE = me->session_handle.

* Close the associated RFC connection:
  CALL FUNCTION 'RFC_CONNECTION_CLOSE'
    EXPORTING
      destination = co_rfc_destination
    EXCEPTIONS
      others = 1.

* Reset the internally managed session handle:
  CLEAR me->session_handle.
ENDMETHOD.
```

**Listing 5.21** Implementing Method DISCONNECT()

For more information about the implementation of other methods defined in class `/BOWDK/CL_FTP_CLIENT`, consult the class documentation available in the Class Builder.

## 5.7 Summary

While perhaps not as glamorous as newer interface technologies such as Web services, the fact remains that certain development scenarios are most efficiently handled using a file-based approach. Therefore, it's important that you understand all of the file-processing capabilities of SAP NetWeaver AS ABAP so that you can select the right tool for the job. In the next chapter, we look at another option for persistence in SAP NetWeaver AS ABAP when we consider database programming techniques.

*If you've spent much time around a cook, then you know how particular they can be about where things go in the kitchen. Everything has a place, and space is maximized as much as possible. In this chapter, we look at ways to use the ABAP database interface to store business objects in the database efficiently and effectively.*

# 6 Database Programming

One of the many benefits of working with a 4GL programming language such as ABAP is that the runtime environment relieves you of having to worry about low-level database connection details, database-specific SQL syntax, and so on. These features provide ABAP developers with the freedom to concentrate on application-level concerns, armed with the confidence that comes from knowing that they can access any table in the system database with only a few lines of Open SQL code. In fact, this abstraction was one of the cornerstones of the highly successful SAP R/3 system.

However, as SAP software has evolved over the years, developers have begun to look for ways to provide additional layers of abstraction around business data to maintain flexibility. One such abstraction is the object-relational mapping services provided by the ABAP Object Services framework. In this chapter, we show you how to use this framework to model database entities using ABAP Objects classes that don't contain a single line of hand-written SQL. We also investigate methods for storing text data and integrating data from external databases.

## 6.1 Object-Relational Mapping and Persistence

Prior to the advent of ABAP Objects, when procedural ABAP reigned supreme, the abstraction provided by Open SQL was sufficient for persisting data because the procedural programming paradigm has very little to say about how data is modeled internally. However, the natural impedance[1] that exists between the object-

1 The use of the term *impedance* for describing this phenomenon was coined by Scott Ambler in his book *Agile Database Technologies* (Wiley, 2003).

oriented and relational paradigms is much more palpable. A common workaround for bridging the gaps between these two disparate models is to use an *object-relational mapping* (ORM) tool. In this section, we introduce the concept of ORM tools and look at how the Persistence Service of the ABAP Object Services framework can be used to develop *persistent objects*.

### 6.1.1 Positioning of Object-Relational Mapping Tools

Before we delve into the details of the ABAP Object Services framework and the Persistence Service, it's important to understand the concepts from which it was derived. The ABAP Object Services framework was introduced in SAP NetWeaver AS ABAP 6.10 as an ABAP-based implementation of an ORM framework. ORM frameworks are used to encapsulate persistence details inside persistent classes by *mapping* a persistence data model onto an object-oriented data model. Conceptually, there's nothing magical about persistent classes; behind the scenes, SQL statements still have to be issued to interact with a database, and so on. However, the difference here is that the ORM framework takes care of these details so you don't have to.

There are several benefits to be gained by using ORM tools:

- First and foremost, they reduce the amount of program code you have to write to implement persistent classes.
- Secondly, you work with persistent objects in the exact same way that you use transient objects. This transparency frees you from having to worry about persistence issues, allowing you to focus your design around a pure object model.
- Finally, the encapsulation of persistence details inside of a framework provides the opportunity to improve performance through caching, lazy initialization techniques, and so on.

### 6.1.2 Persistence Service Overview

The lifecycle of an instance of an ABAP Objects class begins when it's created with the `CREATE OBJECT` statement and ends when there are no longer any references to it in a program (at which time it's marked for deletion and eventually removed by the garbage collector). In the meantime, data may be stored inside an object's attributes, but this data is only preserved if an explicit effort is made to *persist* it. As such, instances of ABAP Objects classes are considered to be *transient* in nature.

Most of the time, we persist the state of business objects using a relational database. After the data is stored, we can re-create the object later by issuing SQL queries to extract the relevant data and re-populate its attributes. As we mentioned previously, ORM frameworks such as the Persistence Service can be used to automate these tasks so that a class doesn't become obscured by SQL-related concerns, and so on. Figure 6.1 shows the layer of abstraction that the Persistence Service provides between an ABAP Objects class and the database.

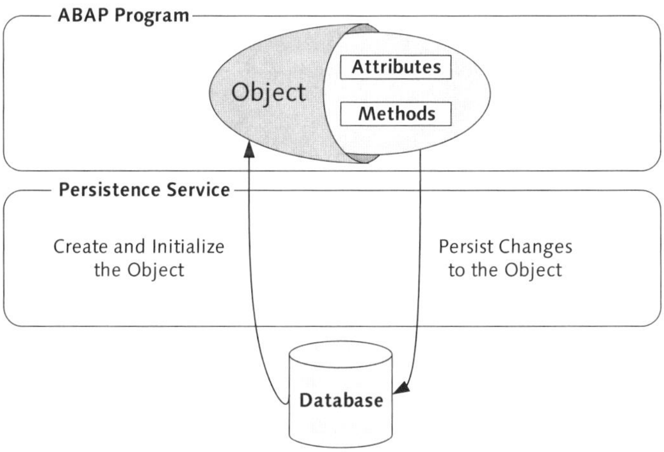


**Figure 6.1** The Lifecycle of a Persistent Object

There is nothing fundamentally different between a persistent class and a normal ABAP Objects class. In other words, instances of persistent classes are still transient in nature. However, when managed by the Persistence Service, these transient objects *behave* like persistent objects within an ABAP program. For example, as you can see in Figure 6.1, the Persistence Service extracts data from the underlying SAP NetWeaver AS ABAP database and initializes a persistent object on behalf of an ABAP program. Similarly, the Persistence Service brokers the persistence of changes made to those objects from within the program. You'll learn more about the relationship between a persistent object and the Persistence Service in the upcoming sections.

To work with the Persistence Service, you must define *persistent classes* in the Class Builder tool. In addition to the creation of the persistent class itself, the Class Builder also generates a couple of *agent classes* that encapsulate most of the ORM-related details outside of the persistent class. The UML class diagram shown in

Figure 6.2 depicts the relationships among a persistent class, its agent classes, and core interfaces that make up the Persistence Service framework.

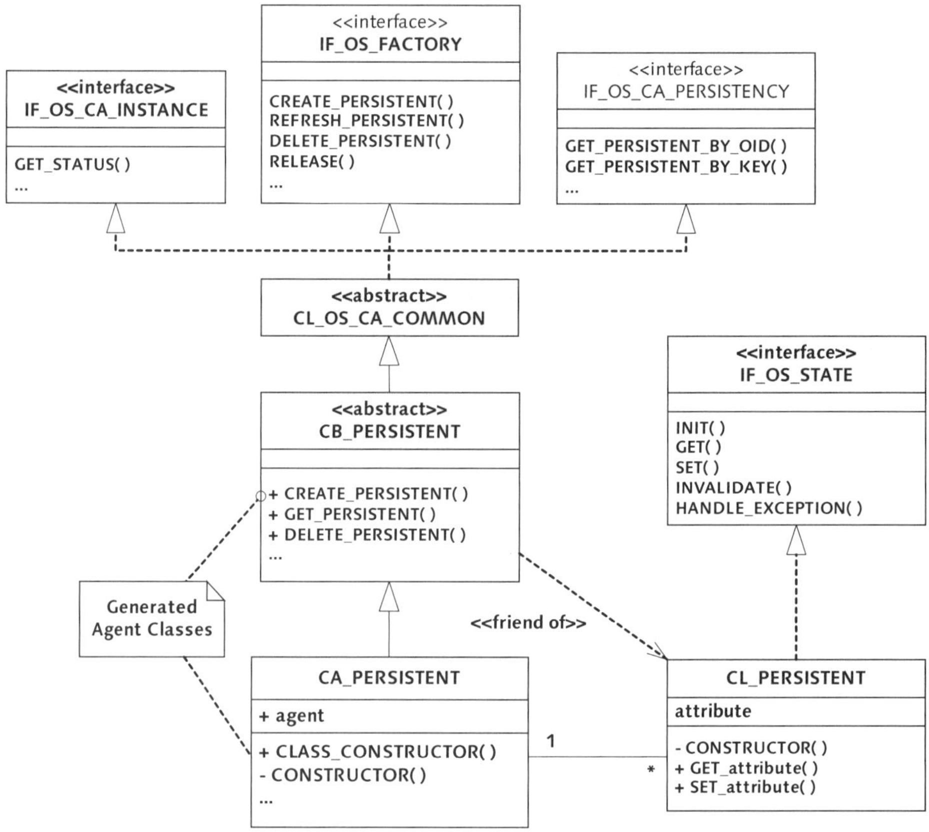


**Figure 6.2** UML Class Diagram of a Persistent Class

At first, the relationship between a persistent class and its agent classes may seem a little bit convoluted. If you look carefully at the UML class diagram in Figure 6.2, you can see that the CB_PERSISTENT agent class is defined as an *abstract class*. If you're not familiar with the concept of abstract classes, you can think of them as a kind of *template* for deriving subclasses. In the context of the Persistence Service, the abstract agent class defines all of the low-level interaction details between persistent objects and the Persistence Service. The CA_PERSISTENT subclass inherits this functionality to define a concrete agent class that *manages* instances of the CL_PERSISTENT class. For this reason, instances of persistent classes are often referred to as *managed objects*.

When you learn how to create persistent classes in Section 6.2, Developing Persistent Classes, you'll see that the Class Builder automatically adjusts the instantiation context of a persistent class to the *protected context*. This implies that you can't directly create an instance of a persistent class using the `CREATE OBJECT` statement. Instead, you must instantiate persistent objects using factory methods defined in its concrete agent class (i.e., class `CA_PERSISTENT`). These methods are able to exploit the friendship relationship defined between the base agent class and the persistent class to create an instance of the persistent class (refer to Figure 6.2). Of course, they also take care of various housekeeping details such as registering the persistent object with the Persistence Service framework, loading data from the database into context, and so on.

After you get past all of the indirection, you'll find that persistent objects are quite easy to work with. Looking back at the UML class diagram from Figure 6.2, you can see that attributes represented by the persistent class are exposed via *setter* and *getter* methods. This makes it very easy to manipulate persistent objects programmatically. We give examples of this in Section 6.3, Working with Persistent Objects.

### 6.1.3 Mapping Concepts

For the Persistence Service to translate between an object model and the underlying persistence layer, a *mapping* must be defined within the persistent class. Table 6.1 shows the three different types of mapping strategies that you can employ with your persistent classes. These mapping types provide you with the flexibility to tap into preexisting relational data models or generate new data models from scratch. However, keep in mind that you must be able to represent these models using ABAP Dictionary objects. These ABAP Dictionary objects must exist *before* you try to create a mapping in the Class Builder; the ORM tools provided by SAP do not generate these objects automatically.

| Mapping Type | Description |
|---|---|
| By Business Key | Can be used to map an existing table in the ABAP Dictionary that has a semantic primary key. For example, the business key for standard table `BUT000` is the `PARTNER` field. |
| By Instance-GUID | Used to map tables that have a primary key that consists of a single field of type `OS_GUID`. Here, the term *GUID* refers to a system-generated *Globally Unique Identifier*. |

**Table 6.1** Persistence Mapping Types

| Mapping Type | Description |
|---|---|
| By Instance-GUID and Business Key | This mapping type combines both techniques. In this case, the target table has a semantic primary key as well as a non-key field of type OS_GUID that is defined as part of a unique secondary index. The combination of these keys makes it possible to access a persistent object by a business key or an instance-GUID. |

**Table 6.1** Persistence Mapping Types (Cont.)

Normally, your persistence map will be based on one or more relational database tables. However, keep in mind that the Persistence Service also supports other storage media such as files, and so on. Irrespective of the underlying storage medium, you must use an ABAP Dictionary object (i.e., a table, view, or structure) as the basis for your mapping. The following list describes how various ABAP Dictionary objects can be used to help you create your persistence maps:

- **Single-table mapping**
  Most of the time, you'll map the attributes of your persistent class to a single ABAP Dictionary table. Here, you must map all of the fields from the table to attributes in the persistent class. Of course, sometimes you may not want to map all of the fields of a given table to your persistent class. In these situations, you can create a view that contains a subset of fields that you want to map and then use the view to build your persistence mapping.
- **Multiple-table mapping**
  You can also map multiple tables onto a single persistent class. The only requirement here is that each table shares the exact same primary key. At runtime, the Persistence Service is smart enough to connect the relevant attributes used in the mapping with their associated tables so that the object data is correctly distributed across each of the tables.
- **Structure mappings**
  For more complex mappings, you can also use structure types. Structure types are typically used to implement persistence mapping to files, and so on. However, they can also be used to map persistent classes that have a *one-to-many* relationship to another persistent class type (e.g., a sales order and its line items). Of course, because structure types do not refer to an actual database table, the ORM tool won't generate the code to persist the data. Instead, you must implement your own logic for storing the persistent data in persistent classes mapped from a structure.

## 6.2 Developing Persistent Classes

Now that you're familiar with the technical underpinnings of the Persistence Service, let's turn our attention to the creation of persistent classes in the ABAP Workbench. As a framework to guide our discussion, let's imagine that we've been tasked with developing a data model for an online bookstore application. To keep things simple, we limit the scope of our development to the entities depicted in the E-R (entity-relationship) diagram shown in Figure 6.3. Here, we've defined three basic entities:

- A table called `ZTCA_BOOKS` that stores some basic information about a book (e.g., its ISBN number, title, publisher, etc.)
- A table called `ZTCA_PUBLISHERS` that maintains information about book publishers
- A table called `ZTCA_AUTHORS` that keeps track of authors in the system

In addition, we've defined a link table called `ZTCA_BOOKAUTHORS` that describes the many-to-many relationship between tables `ZTCA_BOOKS` and `ZTCA_AUTHORS`. This relationship is necessary because an author can write many books, and a book might be written by multiple authors. (We explain how to implement this complex relationship in Section 6.4, Modeling Complex Relationships.)

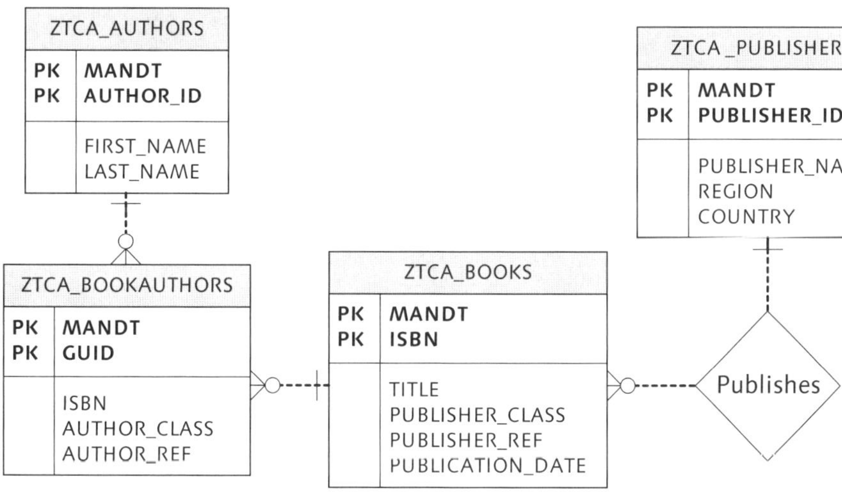


**Figure 6.3** Entity-Relationship Diagram for the Bookstore Data Model

Using the data model depicted in Figure 6.3, we've defined our persistent class model according to the UML class diagram shown in Figure 6.4. As you can see, there isn't necessarily a one-to-one correspondence between the attributes of the database tables and the persistent classes. We'll see why this is as we progress through the example.

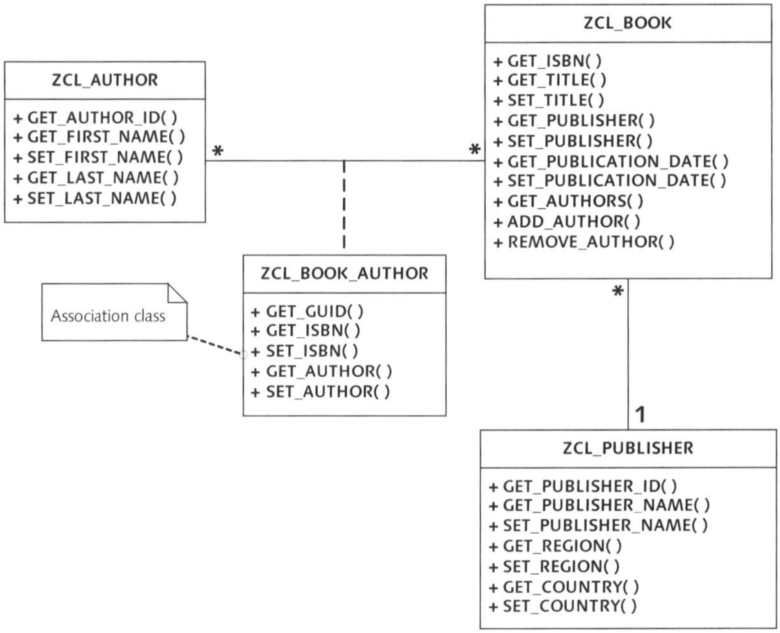


**Figure 6.4** UML Class Diagram of Bookstore Persistent Class Model

### 6.2.1 Creating Persistent Classes in the Class Builder

At this point, we're ready to start developing our persistent classes. To begin, we create the `ZCL_BOOK` persistent class depicted in Figure 6.4.

1. To create a persistent class, open the Class Builder (Transaction SE24), and click on the Create button. Alternatively, you can create a new class in the Object Navigator (Transaction SE80) by right-clicking on a package in the Repository Browser perspective and selecting the menu option CREATE • CLASS LIBRARY • CLASS.
2. In the Create Class dialog box that appears, fill out the class name, description, and so on, just as you would for a normal class. However, the thing that sets a

persistent class apart from regular classes is the selection of the Persistent Class radio button in the Class Type box (see Figure 6.5). After you confirm your entries, click on the Save button to save your changes.

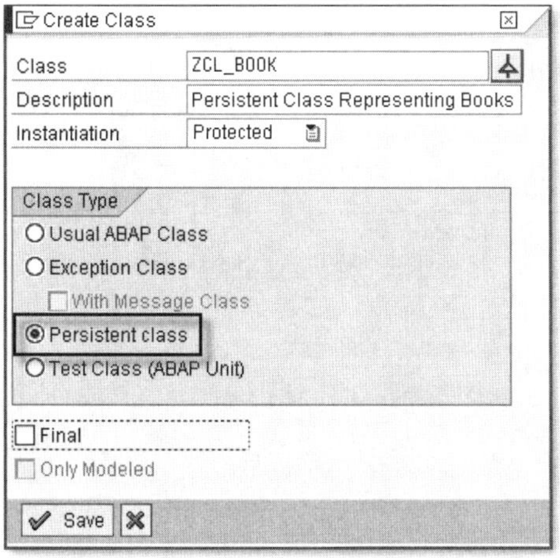

**Figure 6.5** Creating a Persistent Class — Part 1

3. After you confirm your changes, you're taken to the Class Editor perspective shown in Figure 6.6. As you can see, the Class Builder automatically defined an implementation relationship to interface IF_OS_STATE.

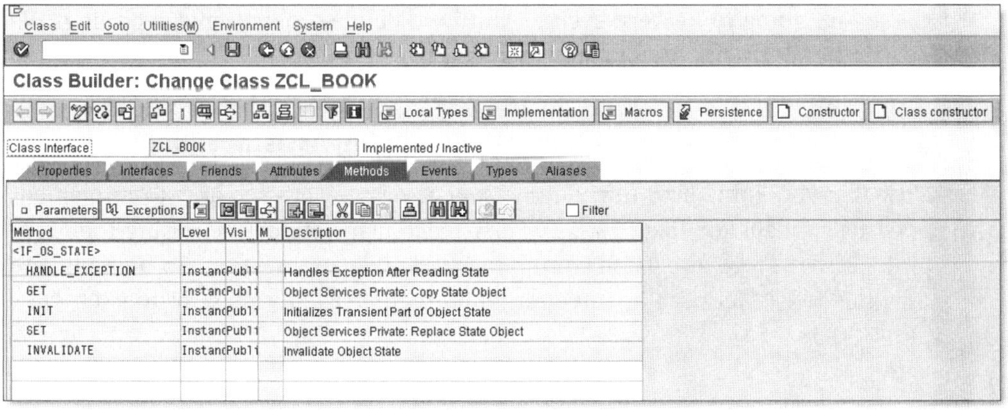

**Figure 6.6** Creating a Persistent Class — Part 2

4. If you look carefully, you'll also notice that the Class Builder also created the agent classes ZCB_BOOK and ZCA_BOOK (see Figure 6.7).

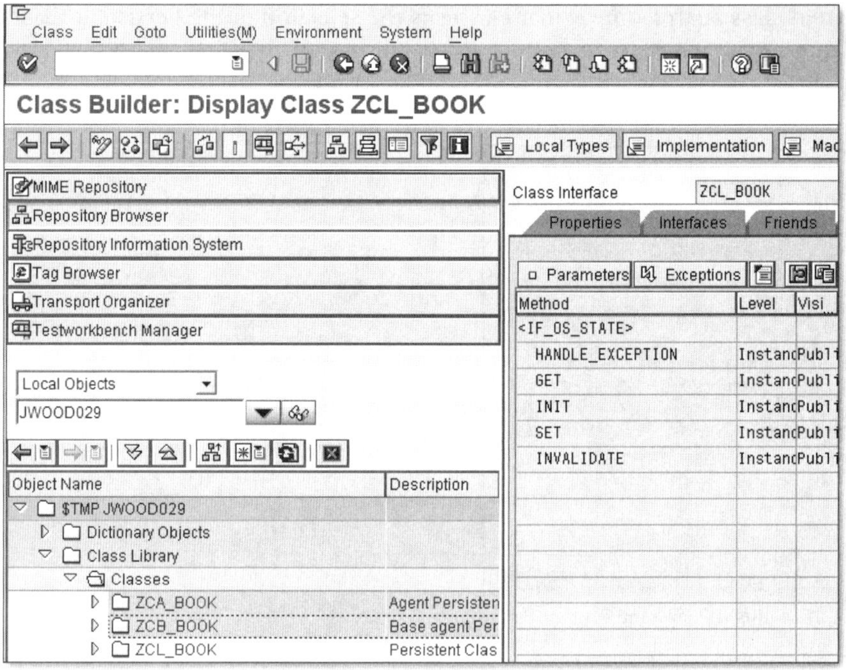


Figure 6.7 Creating a Persistent Class — Part 3

The other classes depicted in the UML diagram from Figure 6.4 can be created in exactly the same way as class ZCL_BOOK was created. Of course, none of these classes are going to be very exciting until we define a persistence mapping. We explain how to define these mappings next.

### 6.2.2 Defining Mappings Using the Mapping Assistant Tool

Now that you know how to create persistent classes, let's see how to implement persistence maps for these classes. Persistence maps are defined using the Mapping Assistant tool integrated into the Class Builder transaction. To demonstrate how this works, let's see how we can build the persistence map for the ZCL_PUBLISHER class.

1. Open the ZCL_PUBLISHER class in the Class Builder, and click on the Persistence button in the Class Editor (refer to Figure 6.6). This takes you to the Mapping Assistant screen shown in Figure 6.8. The first time you enter this tool for a persistent class, you're prompted to select a table/structure/view from the ABAP Dictionary that will be used as the basis of the mapping. For example, with the ZCL_PUBLISHER class, we've chosen the ZTCA_PUBLISHERS table (see Figure 6.8).

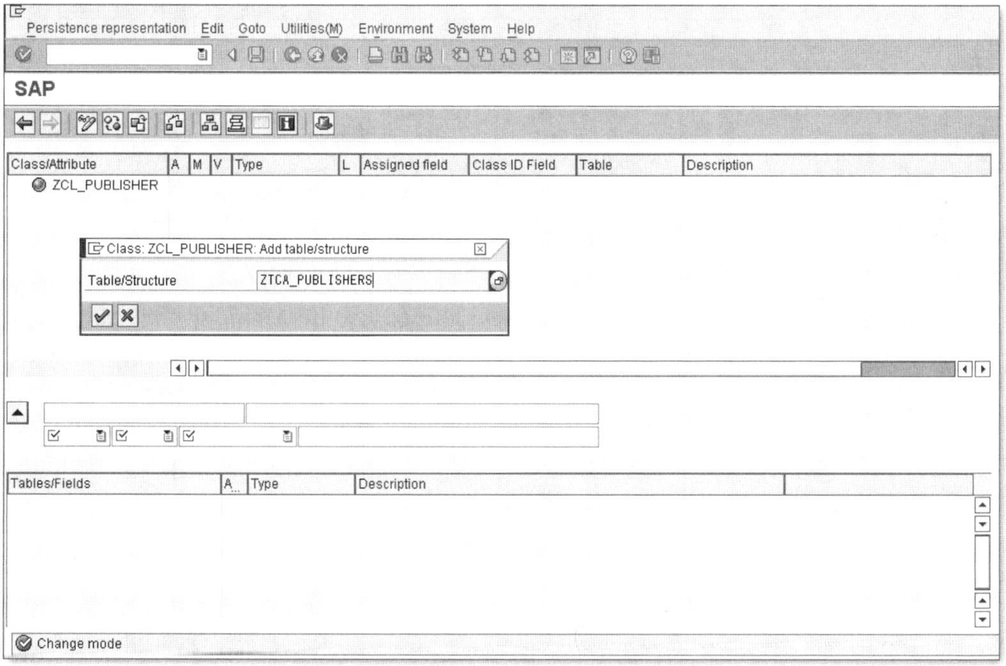


**Figure 6.8** Initial Screen of the Mapping Assistant Tool

2. As soon as you select your source ABAP Dictionary object, the bottom half of the Mapping Assistant is populated with a list of attributes that can be mapped to the persistent class (see Figure 6.9). To map an attribute, simply double-click it, and it's loaded into the editing area in the middle of the screen. Here, you can assign a name, description, visibility, accessibility, and assignment type for a given attribute.

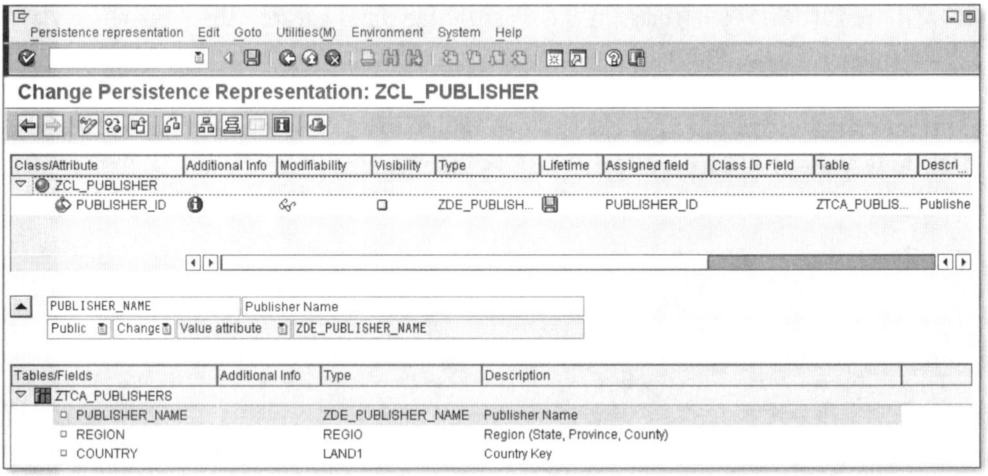


**Figure 6.9** Mapping Attributes in the Mapping Assistant Tool

3. In most cases, the default properties defined by the Mapping Assistant for a given attribute are correct. Of course, you may decide to restrict access to a particular field by customizing its visibility and accessibility properties. Also, you may need to modify the assignment type for certain fields. Table 6.2 provides a description of the assignment types that you can configure for a given attribute. We'll explore some of the more advanced assignment types as we define relationships between our persistent classes.

| Assignment Type | Meaning |
|---|---|
| Business Key | Derived by the Mapping Assistant for primary key fields of an ABAP Dictionary table that has a semantic primary key. You can't change this particular assignment type. |
| GUID | Derived by the Mapping Assistant for the primary key field of an ABAP Dictionary table that has a GUID-based primary key. You can't change this particular assignment type. |
| Value Attribute | Used to define non-key attributes of a given ABAP Dictionary object. |
| Class Identifier | Used in conjunction with another table/structure field to uniquely identify an object reference. The table/structure field must be of type `OS_GUID`. |
| Object Reference | Used in conjunction with another table/structure field to uniquely identify an object reference. The table/structure field must be of type `OS_GUID`. |

**Table 6.2** Persistent Attribute Assignment Types

4. After you've mapped all of the relevant attributes onto the persistent class, you can save your changes by clicking on the Save button in the Mapping Assistant toolbar. You can then click on the Back button to return to the Class Editor. As you can see in Figure 6.10, getter and setter methods are generated for each of the selected attributes according to the configuration settings specified in the Mapping Assistant tool.

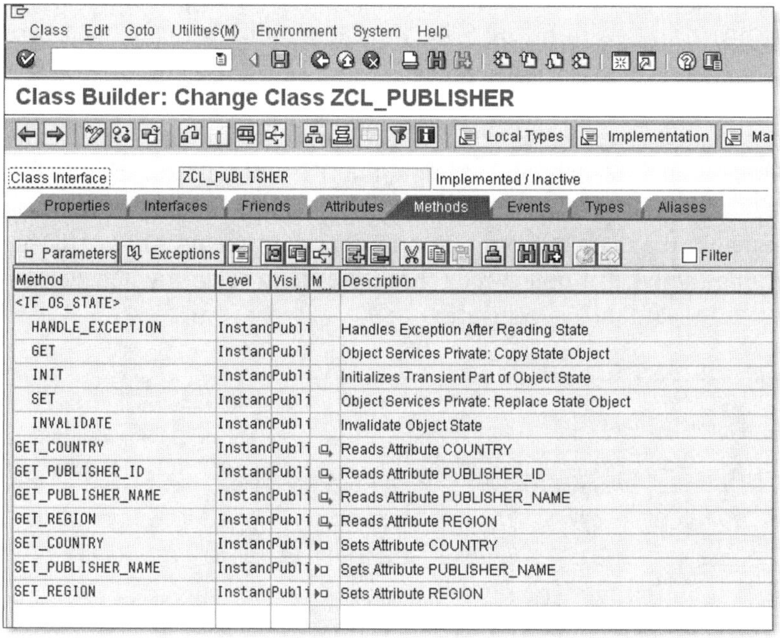

**Figure 6.10** Getter and Setter Methods for ZCL_PUBLISHER

5. When you activate your changes, you're asked whether or not you also want to activate the class actor (see Figure 6.11). This prompt is basically a warning advising that the mapping changes are going to be reflected in the class actor(s). In almost all cases, you should choose the option to go ahead and activate the class actor.

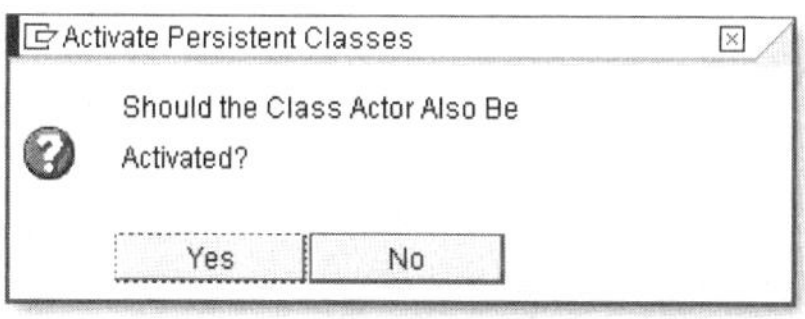


**Figure 6.11** Activating the Class Actor for a Persistent Class

The persistence mapping demonstrated for class ZCL_PUBLISHER showed you how to map simple value attributes. Here, we show you how to create a foreign key relationship to another persistent class by defining an *object reference attribute*. As a basis for our discussion, we model the relationship between the ZCL_BOOK and ZCL_PUBLISHER persistent classes. This relationship allows us to determine information about the publisher who produced a particular book.

To define an object reference attribute, you must specify two things: a *class identifier* and an *object reference key*. In Figure 6.12, you can see that we've defined two fields in table ZTCA_BOOKS for this purpose: PUBLISHER_CLASS and PUBLISHER_REF. Both of these fields have been assigned the OS_GUID type. At runtime, whenever an assignment is made between a book and a publisher, the publisher key value is stored in the PUBLISHER_REF field. In addition, the GUID of class ZCL_PUBLISHER is stored in the PUBLISHER_CLASS field. This GUID is generated implicitly for every global class created in the Class Builder. The Persistence Service uses the GUID as a key to determine the type of object reference it needs to rebuild whenever an instance of class ZCL_PUBLISHER is generated.

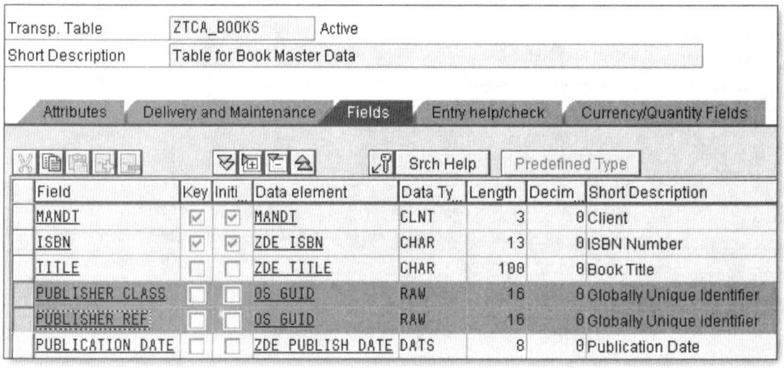


| Field | Key | Initi | Data element | Data Ty | Length | Decim | Short Description |
|---|---|---|---|---|---|---|---|
| MANDT | ☑ | ☑ | MANDT | CLNT | 3 | 0 | Client |
| ISBN | ☑ | ☑ | ZDE_ISBN | CHAR | 13 | 0 | ISBN Number |
| TITLE | ☐ | ☐ | ZDE_TITLE | CHAR | 100 | 0 | Book Title |
| PUBLISHER_CLASS | ☐ | ☐ | OS_GUID | RAW | 16 | 0 | Globally Unique Identifier |
| PUBLISHER_REF | ☐ | ☐ | OS_GUID | RAW | 16 | 0 | Globally Unique Identifier |
| PUBLICATION_DATE | ☐ | ☐ | ZDE_PUBLISH_DATE | DATS | 8 | 0 | Publication Date |

**Figure 6.12** ABAP Dictionary Table ZTCA_BOOKS

Even though an object reference must be mapped to two fields at the database layer, there is only one attribute defined in the persistent class. In Figure 6.13, you can see how we're mapping the PUBLISHER_CLASS field from table ZTCA_BOOKS. For this field, we've selected the Class Identifier assignment type. Also, notice that we've changed the name of the attribute to PUBLISHER.

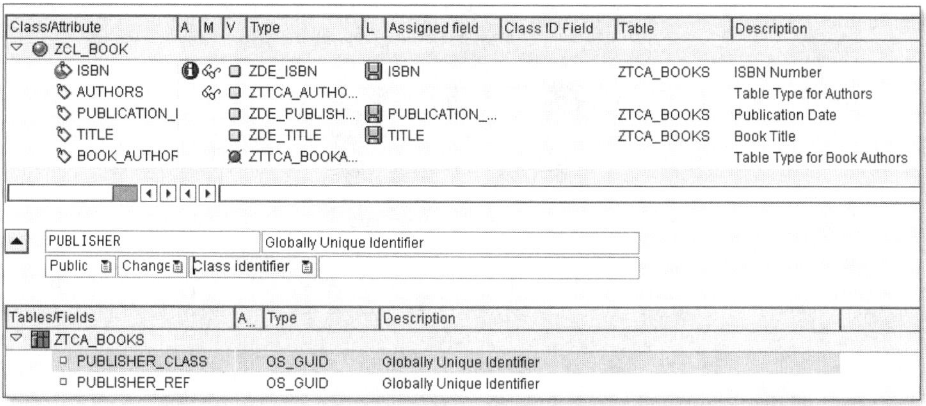


**Figure 6.13** Defining a Foreign Key Relationship — Part 1

As soon as the PUBLISHER attribute is created, we can bind the PUBLISHER_REF field to it to complete the object reference attribute definition. Figure 6.14 shows how we're mapping the PUBLISHER_REF field. In this case, we've selected the Object Reference assignment type and specified the class type ZCL_PUBLISHER.

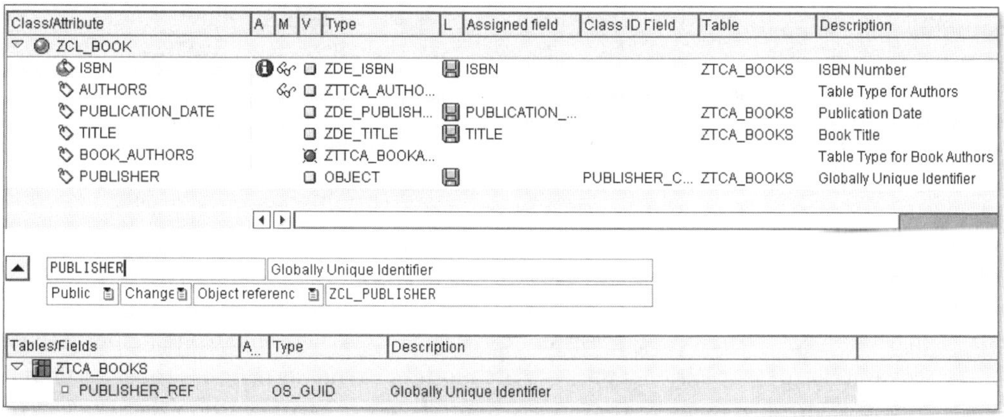


**Figure 6.14** Defining a Foreign Key Relationship — Part 2

After the mapping is complete, getter and setter methods for the PUBLISHER attribute are automatically generated in the ZCL_BOOK class (see Figure 6.15). As you can see in Figure 6.16, the signature of these methods is defined using object references of type ZCL_PUBLISHER. This implies that we can bind an instance of class ZCL_PUBLISHER to class ZCL_BOOK by simply passing that instance as a parameter to method SET_PUBLISHER().

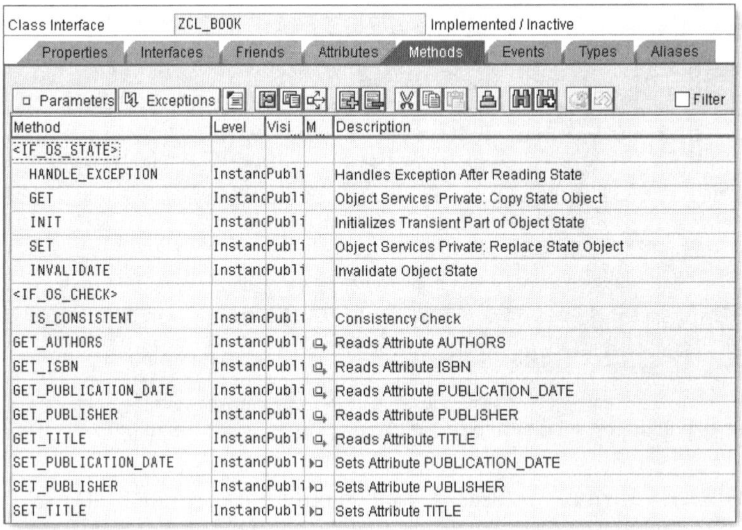


**Figure 6.15** Getter and Setter Methods for Publisher Object Reference

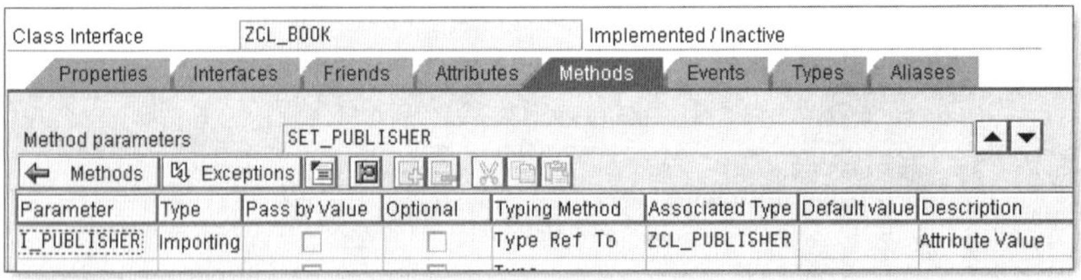


**Figure 6.16** Signature of Method SET_PUBLISHER()

## 6.3 Working with Persistent Objects

In Section 6.2, Developing Persistent Classes, you learned how to create persistent classes to represent various types of data models. In this section, we show you how to work with instances of those persistent classes in your ABAP programs. First, we familiarize you with the architecture of class agent API, used to interact with your persistent objects. From there, we demonstrate how to perform basic CRUD (*Create, Remove, Update, and Display*) operations with persistent objects. Finally, we conclude our discussion by showing you how to use the Query Service to perform advanced searches for persistent objects in the database.

### 6.3.1 Understanding the Class Agent API

Looking back at the UML class diagram in Figure 6.2, you can see the inheritance tree for the class agent of a persistent class. The parent classes/interfaces for this agent class make up the API that you'll use to access and manipulate persistent objects. For the most part, the names of these methods are pretty self-explanatory (i.e., you use the `CREATE_PERSISTENT()` method to create a persistent object, etc.). Of course, the generation of some of the methods defined in the base agent class varies depending on the mapping type you chose to implement in your persistent class. For example, the base agent class doesn't define the `GET_PERSISTENT()` and `DELETE_PERSISTENT()` methods if the persistent classes aren't managed using business keys. Conversely, if a persistent class is managed by business keys, these methods are defined with a signature that statically matches the mapped key types. For instance, notice how the signature of the `GET_PERSISTENT()` method of agent class `ZCA_BOOK` matches the primary key of table `ZTCA_BOOKS` (i.e., the `ISBN` field) in Figure 6.17.

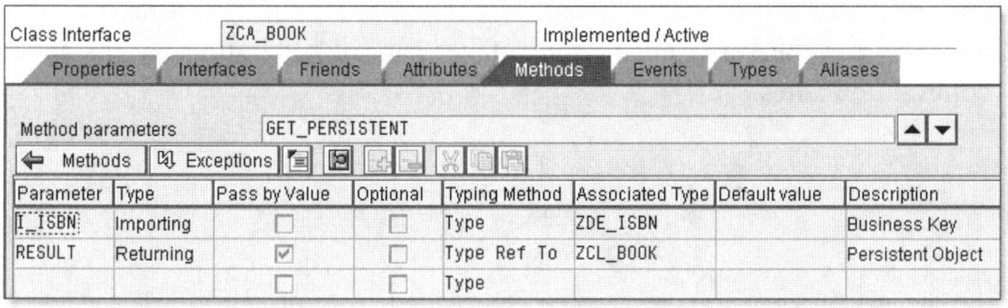


**Figure 6.17** Signature of Method GET_PERSISTENT()

You can find out more information about the class agent API methods in the SAP NetWeaver Library documentation available online at *http://help.sap.com*. Here, each method is described at length in the section entitled *Components of the Persistence Service*. You'll also see usage examples for some of the more common methods in the upcoming sections.

### 6.3.2 Performing Typical CRUD Operations

In this section, we show you how to perform some typical CRUD operations with persistent objects. These operations mirror the familiar OPEN SQL statements `INSERT`, `SELECT`, `UPDATE`, and `DELETE` in terms of functionality. However, from a usability perspective, you'll find that the API is purely object-oriented.

As you learned in Section 6.3.1, Understanding the Class Agent API, the class agent defines various methods that can be used to process persistent objects. Therefore, the first step for processing persistent objects is to obtain a reference to the class agent. This can be achieved by accessing the static AGENT attribute that is publicly available in every agent class. The AGENT attribute is initialized in the CLASS_CONSTRUCTOR() method of the agent class, so it's always available before any client tries to access it. Also, because the instantiation context of the agent class is set as private, only one instance of the agent class is ever created at runtime. As such, the agent is patterned as a *singleton.*[2]

### Creating Persistent Objects

To create a persistent object, use the CREATE_PERSISTENT() method of the agent class. This method is generated in accordance with the persistence map, defining parameters that directly align with the underlying ABAP Dictionary object. For example, Figure 6.18 shows the signature of the CREATE_PERSISTENT() method for agent class ZCA_AUTHOR. In this case, there isn't a primary key parameter because the mapping type of the ZCL_AUTHOR class is defined as *By Instance GUID*. At runtime, we'll see that the Persistence Service takes care of generating the instance GUID behind the scenes.

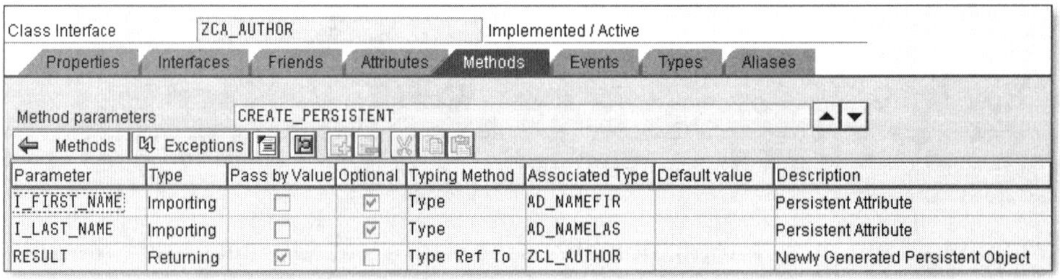


| Parameter | Type | Pass by Value | Optional | Typing Method | Associated Type | Default value | Description |
|---|---|---|---|---|---|---|---|
| I_FIRST_NAME | Importing | ☐ | ☑ | Type | AD_NAMEFIR | | Persistent Attribute |
| I_LAST_NAME | Importing | ☐ | ☑ | Type | AD_NAMELAS | | Persistent Attribute |
| RESULT | Returning | ☑ | ☐ | Type Ref To | ZCL_AUTHOR | | Newly Generated Persistent Object |

**Figure 6.18** Signature of Method CREATE_PERSISTENT()

The code excerpt from Listing 6.1 shows how we can create an author persistent object using the CREATE_PERSISTENT() method of agent class ZCA_AUTHOR. Notice how we've wrapped this call inside of a TRY statement because the CREATE_PERSISTENT() method can potentially raise exceptions of type CX_OS_OBJECT_EXISTING. After the CREATE_PERSISTENT() method executes, we issue the COMMIT WORK statement to commit the changes. Had we omitted this here, the persistent object

2 The term *singleton* refers to a design pattern in which instantiation is controlled to limit the number of objects created at a time (typically for performance reasons).

would not have been persisted in the database. In Chapter 7, Transactional Programming, we show you how you can use the *Transaction Service* to manage your transactions in an object-oriented context.

```
DATA: author TYPE REF TO zcl_author,
      os_ex  TYPE REF TO cx_os_object_existing.

TRY.
  CALL METHOD zca_author=>agent->create_persistent
    EXPORTING
      i_first_name = 'Thorsten'
      i_last_name  = 'Franz'
    RECEIVING
      result       = author.

  COMMIT WORK.
CATCH cx_os_object_existing INTO os_ex.
  "Exception handling goes here...
ENDTRY.
```

**Listing 6.1** Creating a Persistent Object

Figure 6.19 shows the author object persisted in the database. As you can see, the `AUTHOR_ID` field has been assigned a GUID value by the Persistence Service. This GUID was generated via the standard function module `GUID_CREATE`. You can also use this function to generate GUIDs for your own purposes whenever you need to generate a unique identifier.

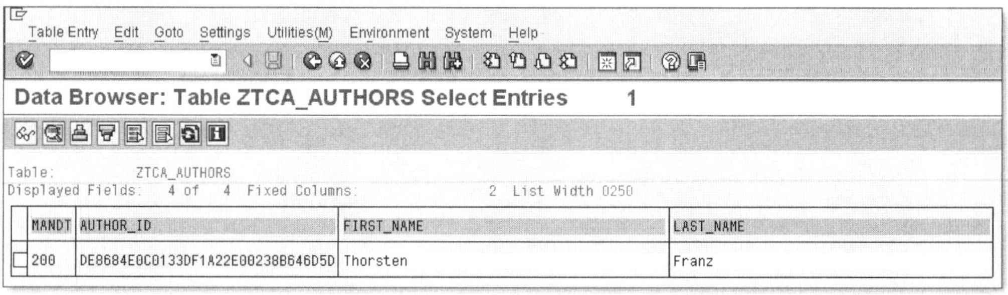


**Figure 6.19** Persistent Object Stored in the Database

### Reading Persistent Objects

If a persistent class is defined with a mapping type that uses a business key, we can use the generated `GET_PERSISTENT()` method to read persistent objects of that class from the database. Listing 6.2 shows how we can look up a particular book using its ISBN number. After we have an instance of the persistent object in context, we can use its getter methods to obtain information about it (e.g., its title, publication date, etc.).

```
DATA: book  TYPE REF TO zcl_book,
      title TYPE zde_title,
      os_ex TYPE REF TO cx_os_object_not_found.

TRY.
  book =
    zca_book=>agent->get_persistent( '9781592292356' ).

  title = book->get_title( ).
  WRITE: / 'Title is:', title.
CATCH cx_os_object_not_found INTO os_ex.
  "Exception handling goes here...
ENDTRY.
```

**Listing 6.2** Reading a Persistent Object from the Database

### Updating Persistent Objects

After you have a persistent object in context, you can update its attributes using the various setter methods generated for the relevant persistent class. This not only applies to elementary attributes but also to object references. For example, in Listing 6.3, we're assigning a publisher persistent object to an instance of class ZCL_BOOK using its SET_PUBLISHER() method. After the relevant attributes have been changed, we can persist our changes using the COMMIT WORK statement.

```
DATA: publisher      TYPE REF TO zcl_publisher,
      book           TYPE REF TO zcl_book,
      os_exist_ex    TYPE REF TO cx_os_object_existing,
      os_notfound_ex TYPE REF TO cx_os_object_not_found.

TRY.
* Create a publisher object:
  CALL METHOD zca_publisher=>agent->create_persistent
    EXPORTING
      i_publisher_name = 'Galileo Press, Inc.'
      i_region         = 'MA'
      i_country        = 'US'
    RECEIVING
      result           = publisher.
```

```
* Look up a book using its ISBN number:
  book =
    zca_book=>agent->get_persistent( '9781592292356' ).

* Assign a publisher to the book:
  book->set_publisher( publisher ).

* Commit the changes:
  COMMIT WORK.
CATCH cx_os_object_existing INTO os_exist_ex.
  "Exception handling goes here...
CATCH cx_os_object_not_found INTO os_notfound_ex.
  "Exception handling goes here...
ENDTRY.
```

**Listing 6.3** Updating a Persistent Object

### Deleting Persistent Objects

You can delete a persistent object using the `DELETE_PERSISTENT()` method defined in interface `IF_OS_FACTORY`. Looking back at the UML class diagram from Figure 6.2, you can see that class actors implement this interface implicitly. Listing 6.4 provides an example that demonstrates how to delete a book object using the `DELETE_PERSISTENT()` method.

```
DATA: book            TYPE REF TO zcl_book,
      os_notexist_ex  TYPE REF TO cx_os_object_not_existing,
      os_notfound_ex TYPE REF TO cx_os_object_not_found.

TRY.
* Look up a book using its ISBN number:
  book =
    zca_book=>agent->get_persistent( '9781592292356' ).

* Delete the book:
  zca_book=>agent->if_os_factory~delete_persistent( book ).

* Commit the changes:
  COMMIT WORK.
CATCH cx_os_object_not_found INTO os_notfound_ex.
  "Exception handling goes here...
CATCH cx_os_object_not_existing INTO os_notexist_ex.
  "Exception handling goes here...
ENDTRY.
```

**Listing 6.4** Deleting a Persistent Object

### 6.3.3 Querying Persistent Objects with the Query Service

In Section 6.3.2, Performing Typical CRUD Operations, you learned how to use the `GET_PERSISTENT()` method of a class agent to read a persistent object from the database. While this method can be useful in certain situations, it definitely has its limitations:

- The method is only generated for persistent classes that are mapped using a business key.
- The method can only be used to return a single instance of a persistent object.

For all but the simplest applications, you need to have the capability to perform more advanced queries. Fortunately, SAP provides another service within the ABAP Object Services framework that offers this functionality, the *Query Service*.

To understand how to work with the Query Service, let's consider an example. The sample report program `ZQUERY_DEMO` contained in Listing 6.5 demonstrates how to implement a query that can be used to search for book objects whose publication date falls within a certain date range.

```
REPORT zquery_demo.
CLASS lcl_query_demo DEFINITION.
  PUBLIC SECTION.
    CLASS-METHODS:
      search_books IMPORTING im_from_date TYPE datum
                             im_to_date TYPE datum.
ENDCLASS.

CLASS lcl_query_demo IMPLEMENTATION.
  METHOD search_books.
    "Local Data Declarations:
    DATA: lo_query_mgr TYPE REF TO if_os_query_manager,
          lo_query     TYPE REF TO if_os_query,
          lv_filter    TYPE string,
          lo_agent     TYPE REF TO if_os_ca_persistency,
          lt_books     TYPE osreftab,
          lo_book      TYPE REF TO zcl_book,
          lv_title     TYPE string.
    FIELD-SYMBOLS:
      <lfs_book> LIKE LINE OF lt_books.

    "Obtain a reference to the OS query manager:
    lo_query_mgr = cl_os_system=>get_query_manager( ).
```

```
    "Build a query object:
    IF im_to_date IS INITIAL.
      lv_filter = 'PUBLICATION_DATE >= PAR1'.
    ELSE.
      CONCATENATE 'PUBLICATION_DATE >= PAR1' 'AND'
                  'PUBLICATION_DATE <= PAR2'
             INTO lv_filter
        SEPARATED BY SPACE.
    ENDIF.

    lo_query =
      lo_query_mgr->create_query(
        i_filter = lv_filter ).

    "Execute the query:
    lo_agent = zca_book=>agent.
    lt_books =
      lo_agent->get_persistent_by_query(
        i_query = lo_query
        i_par1  = im_from_date
        i_par2  = im_to_date ).

    "Output the results:
    LOOP AT lt_books ASSIGNING <lfs_book>.
      lo_book ?= <lfs_book>.
      lv_title = lo_book->get_title( ).
      WRITE: / lv_title.
    ENDLOOP.
  ENDMETHOD.                    " METHOD search_books
ENDCLASS.

PARAMETERS:
  p_frdate TYPE datum,
  p_todate TYPE datum.

START-OF-SELECTION.
  "Execute a book query:
  lcl_query_demo=>search_books(
    im_from_date = p_frdate
    im_to_date = p_todate ).
```

**Listing 6.5** Searching for Persistent Objects with the Query Service

Now that you've had a chance to browse through the example code in Listing 6.5, let's take a closer look at what's going on at each step in the query process:

1. Before you can interact with the Query Service, you must obtain a reference to a *query manager* object. This object implements the IF_OS_QUERY_MANAGER interface and can be obtained via a call to the static GET_QUERY_MANAGER( ) method of class CL_OS_SYSTEM.
2. The query manager is used to create instances of *queries*. You can create an instance of a query using the CREATE_QUERY( ) method defined in interface IF_OS_QUERY_MANAGER( ). Looking at Listing 6.5, you can see that we're passing a *filter* to this method. This filter is analogous to the WHERE clause in a SELECT statement. You can find a comprehensive guide describing the syntax variants supported for these filters in the SAP Library documentation available online at *http://help.sap.com*.
3. After the query object is generated, you're ready to proceed with the lookup operation. As you can see in Listing 6.5, this is still driven by the target object's agent class using the IF_OS_CA_PERSISTENCY~GET_PERSISTENT_BY_QUERY( ) method. Here, you must pass in the query object and any optional parameters so that the framework can build a SQL query to execute behind the scenes.
4. The results of the query are returned in an internal table of type OSREFTAB (like the LT_BOOKS table in Listing 6.5). Because the line type of the OSREFTAB table is the generic base class OBJECT, we must perform a *widening cast* to access the actual persistent objects returned by the Query Service.
5. Finally, after the widening cast operation is performed, the persistent objects can be accessed as they are usually.

This example should help you understand how to use the Query Service to look up instances of persistent objects. You'll see another practical example of its usage in Section 6.4, Modeling Complex Relationships. You can also find a wealth of information in the SAP library documentation available online at *http://help.sap.com*.

## 6.4 Modeling Complex Relationships

At this point, the persistent class model introduced in Section 6.2, Developing Persistent Classes is almost complete. However, one thing that we still have not addressed is the many-to-many relationship between a particular book and its collaborating authors. In this case, we can't map the two entities directly. Instead, we must use the association class ZCL_BOOK_AUTHOR (and its corresponding table ZTCA_BOOKAUTHORS) to correlate a book with one or more authors.

### 6.4.1 Defining Custom Attributes

To unite the ZCL_BOOK and ZCL_AUTHOR entities, we must perform the following steps:

1. First, we need to develop the persistency map for the association class ZCL_BOOK_AUTHOR. This class is mapped using the *by instance-GUID* mapping type (i.e., a GUID is generated as the primary key for each instance persisted in the database). In addition, looking back at the UML class diagram from Figure 6.4, you can see that this class also defines two foreign key attributes called ISBN and AUTHOR:
   - The ISBN attribute is a value attribute that maps the ISBN of the book represented in the linkage relationship.
   - The AUTHOR attribute is an object reference attribute that refers to an instance of class ZCL_AUTHOR. As such, it's mapped in the exact same way that the PUBLISHER attribute was mapped for class ZCL_BOOK in Section 6.2.2, Defining Mappings Using the Mapping Assistant Tool.
2. After the persistency map is completed for class ZCL_BOOK_AUTHOR, we can use this persistent class to bind instances of collaborating authors with a specific book. However, this functionality isn't implemented automatically by the Persistence Service. Instead, we must define a custom AUTHORS attribute in class ZCL_BOOK and provide implementations for the corresponding getter and setter methods. We must also take ownership of the initialization process for this custom AUTHORS attribute in class ZCL_BOOK.

Now that you have a feel for how the book-author relationship is organized, let's look at how the AUTHORS attribute is defined in class ZCL_BOOK. This process begins with the definition of a new table type in the ABAP Dictionary, like the one shown in Figure 6.20. We can then define the AUTHORS attribute in class ZCL_BOOK using the custom table type, as shown in Figure 6.21.

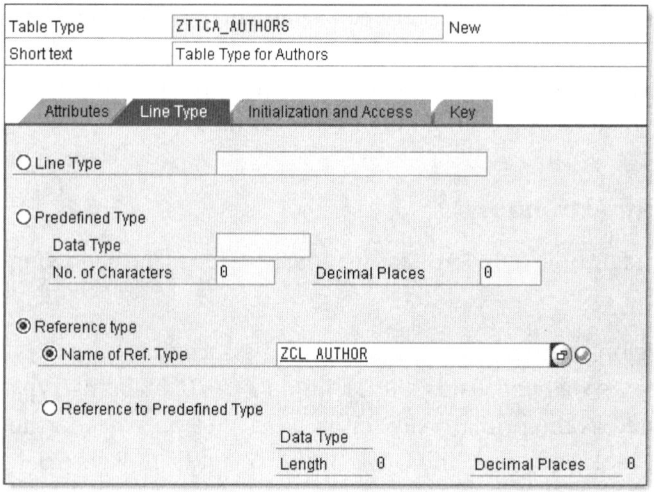


Figure 6.20 Defining a Table Type for Author Objects

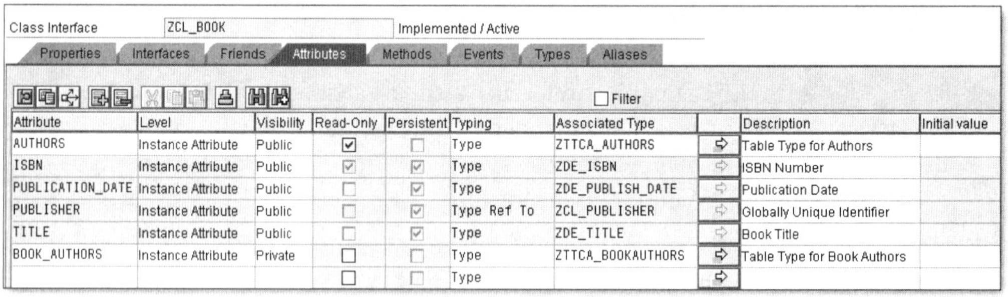


Figure 6.21 Defining the AUTHORS Table Attribute

Even though the AUTHORS attribute doesn't have the Persistent flag checked (i.e., it wasn't generated via the Mapping Assistant tool), you'll notice that the Class Builder generates getter and setter methods for it anyway. In this case, because we defined the attribute as READ-ONLY, the Class Builder only generates a getter method for the AUTHORS attribute (see Figure 6.22).

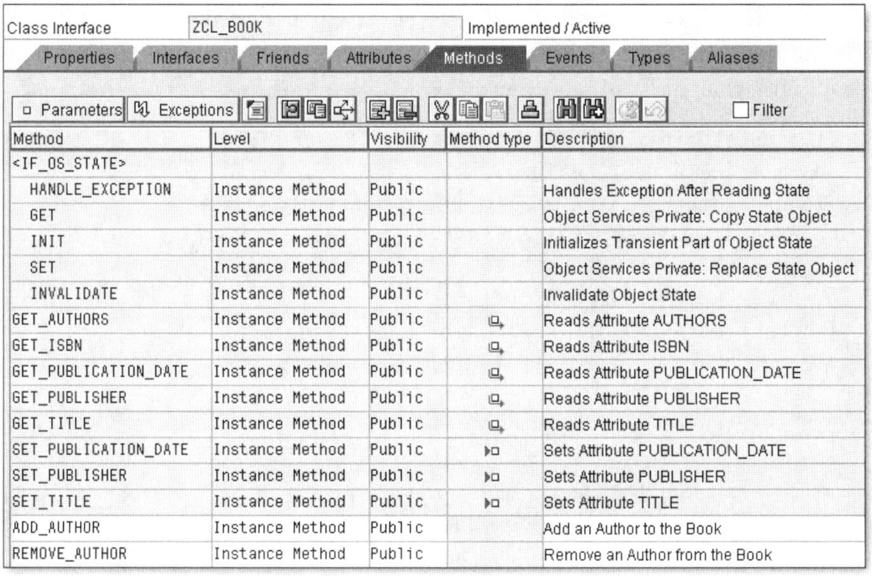


| Method | Level | Visibility | Method type | Description |
|---|---|---|---|---|
| <IF_OS_STATE> | | | | |
| HANDLE_EXCEPTION | Instance Method | Public | | Handles Exception After Reading State |
| GET | Instance Method | Public | | Object Services Private: Copy State Object |
| INIT | Instance Method | Public | | Initializes Transient Part of Object State |
| SET | Instance Method | Public | | Object Services Private: Replace State Object |
| INVALIDATE | Instance Method | Public | | Invalidate Object State |
| GET_AUTHORS | Instance Method | Public | | Reads Attribute AUTHORS |
| GET_ISBN | Instance Method | Public | | Reads Attribute ISBN |
| GET_PUBLICATION_DATE | Instance Method | Public | | Reads Attribute PUBLICATION_DATE |
| GET_PUBLISHER | Instance Method | Public | | Reads Attribute PUBLISHER |
| GET_TITLE | Instance Method | Public | | Reads Attribute TITLE |
| SET_PUBLICATION_DATE | Instance Method | Public | | Sets Attribute PUBLICATION_DATE |
| SET_PUBLISHER | Instance Method | Public | | Sets Attribute PUBLISHER |
| SET_TITLE | Instance Method | Public | | Sets Attribute TITLE |
| ADD_AUTHOR | Instance Method | Public | | Add an Author to the Book |
| REMOVE_AUTHOR | Instance Method | Public | | Remove an Author from the Book |

**Figure 6.22** Getter and Setter Methods for Custom Attributes

## 6.4.2 Filling in the Gaps

As you saw in Section 6.4.1, Defining Custom Attributes, the Class Builder automatically generates getter and setter methods for custom attributes, such as the AUTHORS attribute in class ZCL_BOOK. This allows clients of the ZCL_BOOK class to obtain a list of the authors that are assigned to a book by calling the GET_AUTHORS() method. Of course, because there is no persistency mapping for this custom attribute, the resultant list of authors is empty unless we fill it beforehand. We can perform this task using the INIT() callback method defined in the IF_OS_STATE interface implemented by persistent classes.

The IF_OS_STATE~INIT() method is called by the Persistence Service *after* the persistent attributes of a persistent class have been filled but *before* the object is turned over to the client. Consequently, the IF_OS_STATE~INIT() method is a very convenient place for implementing additional initialization logic for a persistent class.

Listing 6.6 provides an example implementation of the IF_OS_STATE~INIT() method. This method is using the Query Service to look up instances of ZCL_BOOK_AUTHOR whose ISBN attribute matches the ISBN of the book object in question. If one or more matches are found, the resultant ZCL_AUTHOR objects are stored in context in the AUTHORS table attribute. Also, note that we're also caching the book-author association class instances in the BOOK_AUTHORS table attribute. As you'll see in just a moment, this cached information comes in handy for maintaining this relationship internally.

```
METHOD if_os_state~init.
  "Method-Local Data Declarations:
  DATA: lo_query_mgr    TYPE REF TO if_os_query_manager,
        lo_query        TYPE REF TO if_os_query,
        lo_agent        TYPE REF TO if_os_ca_persistency,
        lt_book_authors TYPE osreftab,
        lo_book_author  TYPE REF TO zcl_book_author,
        lo_author       TYPE REF TO zcl_author.
  FIELD-SYMBOLS:
    <lfs_book_author> LIKE LINE OF lt_book_authors.

  "Obtain a reference to the OS query manager:
  lo_query_mgr = cl_os_system=>get_query_manager( ).

  "Build a query object to look up the authors:
  lo_query =
    lo_query_mgr->create_query( i_filter = 'ISBN = PAR1' ).

  "Execute the query:
  lo_agent = zca_book_author=>agent.
  lt_book_authors =
    lo_agent->get_persistent_by_query(
      i_query = lo_query
      i_par1  = me->isbn ).

  "Copy the query results into context:
  LOOP AT lt_book_authors ASSIGNING <lfs_book_author>.
    "Cache the association record to simplify
    "maintenance:
    lo_book_author ?= <lfs_book_author>.
    APPEND lo_book_author TO me->book_authors.

    "Store the author record in the AUTHORS persistent
    "attribute:
    lo_author = lo_book_author->get_author( ).
    APPEND lo_author TO me->authors.
  ENDLOOP.
ENDMETHOD.
```

**Listing 6.6** Initializing the Relationship in the INIT() Method

If you recall from Section 6.4.1, Defining Custom Attributes, we elected to define the AUTHORS attribute as a read-only attribute. Had we defined this as a regular attribute, the Class Builder would have generated a SET_AUTHORS() method in much the same way that setter methods are defined for regular object reference attributes. However, while this would allow clients to store a set of author objects in context, it would not automatically address that these author objects must be properly linked with a book for the relationship(s) to be persistent.

Rather than force users to maintain this relationship outside of the ZCL_BOOK class, we elected to implement a couple of helper methods to maintain the relationship: ADD_AUTHOR() and REMOVE_AUTHOR(). These methods enable clients to add/remove authors from a book directly without having to keep track of authors externally.

Listing 6.7 shows the implementation of method ADD_AUTHOR(). This method receives an instance of ZCL_AUTHOR in an importing parameter called IM_AUTHOR. Within this method, we're creating an instance of class ZCL_BOOK_AUTHOR to implement the linkage in the database. After the linkage is created, we also append the IM_AUTHOR parameter to the AUTHORS table attribute so that the persistent object remains in sync with the database. We're also caching the generated ZCL_BOOK_AUTHOR instance in the BOOK_AUTHORS table attribute so that we can keep track of the relationship internally.

```
METHOD add_author.
  "Method-Local Data Declarations:
  DATA: lo_author_agent TYPE REF TO if_os_ca_service,
        lv_author_guid  TYPE os_guid,
        lo_temp_author  TYPE REF to zcl_author,
        lv_temp_guid    TYPE os_guid,
        lo_book_author  TYPE REF TO zcl_book_author.
  FIELD-SYMBOLS:
    <lfs_book_author> LIKE LINE OF me->book_authors.

  "Determine the GUID of the author object being proposed:
  lo_author_agent = zca_author=>agent.
  lv_author_guid =
    lo_author_agent->get_oid_by_ref( im_author ).

  "Check to see if the author is already assigned
  "to the book:
  LOOP AT me->book_authors ASSIGNING <lfs_book_author>.
    lo_temp_author = <lfs_book_author>->get_author( ).
    lv_temp_guid =
```

```
      lo_author_agent->get_oid_by_ref( lo_temp_author ).

    IF lv_author_guid EQ lv_temp_guid.
      RAISE EXCEPTION TYPE cx_os_object_existing
        EXPORTING
          object = <lfs_book_author>.
    ENDIF.
  ENDLOOP.

  "If it is not, then we can go ahead and create
  "the relationship:
  lo_book_author =
    zca_book_author=>agent->create_persistent(
      i_isbn   = me->isbn
      i_author = im_author ).

  "And then cache the results:
  APPEND im_author TO me->authors.
  APPEND lo_book_author TO me->book_authors.
ENDMETHOD.
```

**Listing 6.7** Implementation of Method ADD_AUTHOR()

Because we're caching the book-author relationship data in the BOOK_AUTHORS table attribute, the implementation of method REMOVE_AUTHOR() is relatively straightforward:

1. First, we need to determine the GUID value of the IM_AUTHOR importing parameter because this is the key used to locate the corresponding book-author record. For this task, we can use the GET_OID_BY_REF() method of the IF_OS_CA_SERVICE interface that gets implemented by the ZCA_AUTHOR agent class.
2. After we have the author key in hand, we can loop through each of the book-author records to see if there's an entry that matches the author's GUID value.
3. If a match is found, we need to delete the selected book-author record using the DELETE_PERSISTENT() method demonstrated in Section 6.3.2, Performing Typical CRUD Operations.
4. Then, we need to remove the cache entries for the author record so that those tables remain up to date.

Listing 6.8 shows a sample implementation of the REMOVE_AUTHOR() method.

```
METHOD remove_author.
  "Method-Local Data Declarations:
  DATA: lo_author_agent TYPE REF TO if_os_ca_service,
        lv_author_guid  TYPE os_guid,
        lo_temp_author  TYPE REF to zcl_author,
        lv_temp_guid    TYPE os_guid,
        lo_assoc_agent  TYPE REF TO if_os_factory.
  FIELD-SYMBOLS:
    <lfs_book_author> LIKE LINE OF me->book_authors,
    <lfs_author>      LIKE LINE OF me->authors.

  "Determine the GUID of the author object being proposed:
  lo_author_agent = zca_author=>agent.
  lv_author_guid =
    lo_author_agent->get_oid_by_ref( im_author ).

  "Check to see if the author is assigned to the book:
  LOOP AT me->book_authors ASSIGNING <lfs_book_author>.
    lo_temp_author = <lfs_book_author>->get_author( ).
    lv_temp_guid =
      lo_author_agent->get_oid_by_ref( lo_temp_author ).

    "If it is, remove it:
    IF lv_author_guid EQ lv_temp_guid.
      "First from the database layer:
      lo_assoc_agent = zca_book_author=>agent.
      lo_assoc_agent->delete_persistent(
        <lfs_book_author> ).

      "And then from the cache:
      DELETE me->book_authors.

      LOOP AT me->authors ASSIGNING <lfs_author>.
        lv_temp_guid =
          lo_author_agent->get_oid_by_ref( <lfs_author> ).
        IF lv_temp_guid EQ lv_author_guid.
          DELETE me->authors.
        ENDIF.
      ENDLOOP.
    ENDIF.
  ENDLOOP.
ENDMETHOD.
```

**Listing 6.8** Implementation of Method REMOVE AUTHOR()

For the purposes of this demonstration, we elected to cache the book-author relationship data inside of the `ZCL_BOOK` instances. In this case, the use of the cache was justified because we're only dealing with a handful of `ZCL_AUTHOR` instances that are relatively small in size. However, if we were implementing such a relationship with sales order line items, we wouldn't want to implement the relationship this way. Instead, we would prefer to load this information on demand using the Query Service.

In general, it's important that you consider the nature of the data you're modeling so that you don't introduce unnecessary overhead at runtime. When in doubt, it's probably better to avoid caching data that might not be required.

## 6.5 Storing Text with Text Objects

Frequently, whenever we create a data model, we need to come up with a way to store long text data. For example, a purchase order data model needs to incorporate various types of long text to capture notes, instructions, and so on. Many business objects in the SAP Business Suite use SAPscript text objects to encapsulate long text information. Therefore, it's useful to understand how to work with these objects. In this section, we introduce you to SAPscript text objects and show you how to use their corresponding API functions. We conclude our discussion by showing you how new features of SAP NetWeaver AS ABAP can be used to store long text objects directly in the database.

### 6.5.1 Defining Text Objects

Before you can begin interacting with the SAPscript text object API, you must first define a *text object*. A text object defines a category for SAPscript texts, separating business partner text data from material text data, and so on. For a given text object, you can also define text IDs that further categorize a given piece of text. We'll see how to create both of these constructs in this section.

SAPscript text objects are created in Transaction SE75. To create a new text object, perform the following steps:

1. Select the Text Objects and IDs radio button in the SAPscript Control Tables group box, and click on the Change button (see Figure 6.23).

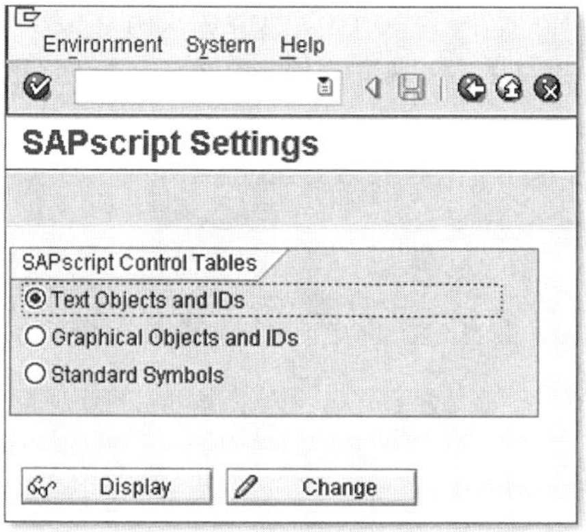


**Figure 6.23** Initial Screen of the SAPscript Settings Editor

2. A prompt appears advising you that the settings you change are reflected across all of the clients in the system (see Figure 6.24).

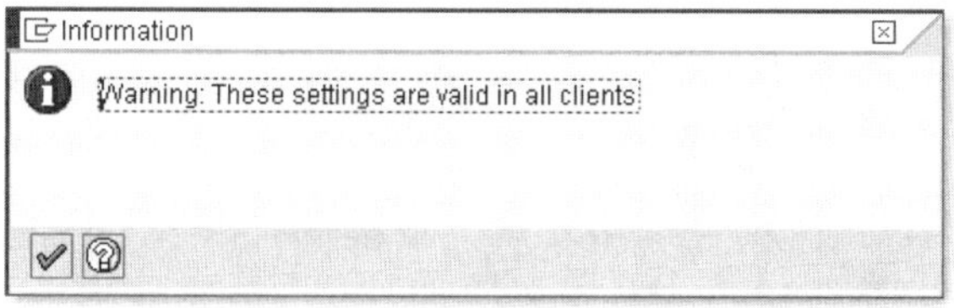


**Figure 6.24** Cross-Client Prompt for SAPscript Objects

3. After you've confirmed the cross-client prompt shown in Figure 6.24, you're taken to the Change Text Objects editor screen shown in Figure 6.25. Click the Create button to create a new text object.
4. In the Create Object dialog box that pops up, define a name for the text object as well as a description. In the example shown in Figure 6.26, we've defined a text object called `ZBOOK` that can be used to store long text data for the bookstore data model considered throughout the course of this chapter. Here, notice that the text object name begins with the familiar `Z` prefix to denote that the text object is to be created in the customer namespace. In addition to the name, you also can specify a save mode for the text object in the Save Mode group box. Normally, you'll want to select the Update save mode option to improve performance. You'll learn more about what this means in Chapter 7, Transactional Programming. Most of the settings in the Editor group box directly pertain to

SAPscript and aren't required unless the text data is to be displayed in a SAP-script form. However, it's important to specify a line width because this setting determines how text is broken up into *chunks* when it's saved to the database. You'll see evidence of this in Section 6.5.2, Using the Text Object API.

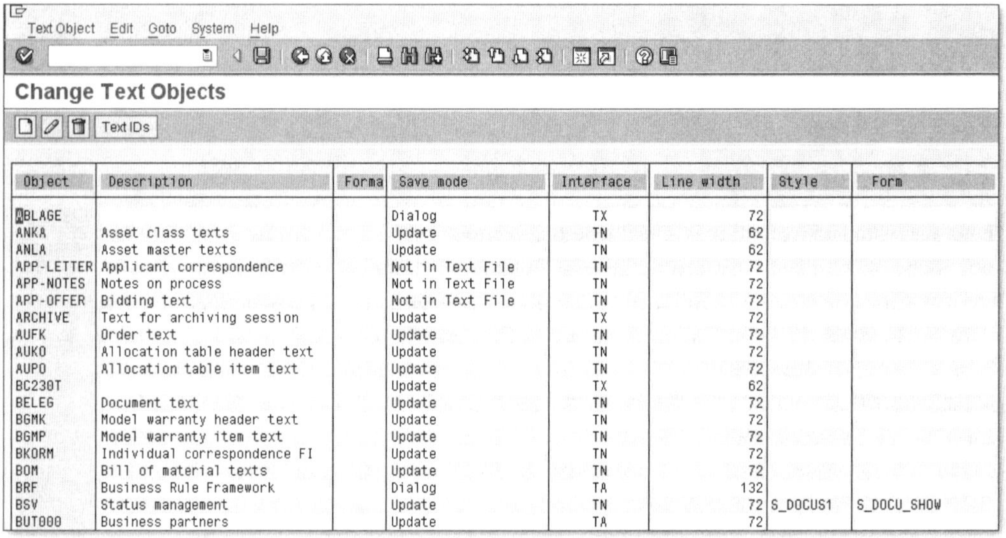


| Object | Description | Forma | Save mode | Interface | Line width | Style | Form |
|---|---|---|---|---|---|---|---|
| ABLAGE | | | Dialog | TX | 72 | | |
| ANKA | Asset class texts | | Update | TN | 62 | | |
| ANLA | Asset master texts | | Update | TN | 62 | | |
| APP-LETTER | Applicant correspondence | | Not in Text File | TN | 72 | | |
| APP-NOTES | Notes on process | | Not in Text File | TN | 72 | | |
| APP-OFFER | Bidding text | | Not in Text File | TN | 72 | | |
| ARCHIVE | Text for archiving session | | Update | TX | 72 | | |
| AUFK | Order text | | Update | TN | 72 | | |
| AUKO | Allocation table header text | | Update | TN | 72 | | |
| AUPO | Allocation table item text | | Update | TN | 72 | | |
| BC230T | | | Update | TX | 62 | | |
| BELEG | Document text | | Update | TN | 72 | | |
| BGMK | Model warranty header text | | Update | TN | 72 | | |
| BGMP | Model warranty item text | | Update | TN | 72 | | |
| BKORM | Individual correspondence FI | | Update | TN | 72 | | |
| BOM | Bill of material texts | | Update | TN | 72 | | |
| BRF | Business Rule Framework | | Dialog | TA | 132 | | |
| BSV | Status management | | Update | TN | 72 | S_DOCUS1 | S_DOCU_SHOW |
| BUT000 | Business partners | | Update | TA | 72 | | |

**Figure 6.25** Change Text Objects Editor Screen

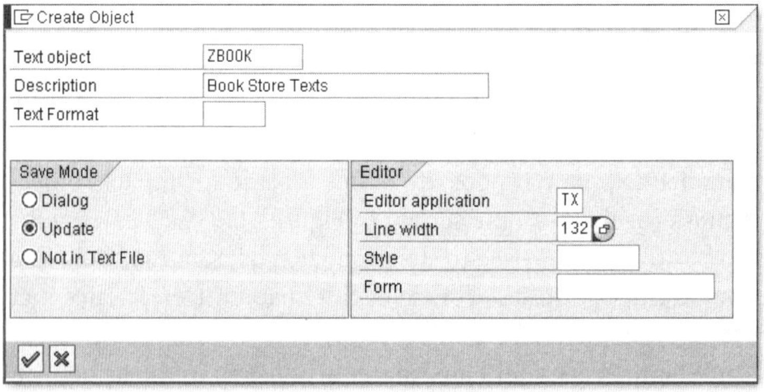


**Figure 6.26** Creating a Text Object

5. After you're satisfied with your settings, press the [Enter] key to confirm your entry, and click the Save button to save your changes.

As we mentioned earlier, a text object can be subdivided by specific text IDs. For instance, in our ZBOOK text object example, we might want to create text IDs that differentiate among long text descriptions for a given book, comments made about a book by various readers, and so on. To define text IDs for a given text object, perform the following steps:

1. Place your cursor on the text object in the Change Text Objects editor screen, and click the Text IDs button. This brings up the Change Text IDs screen shown in Figure 6.27.

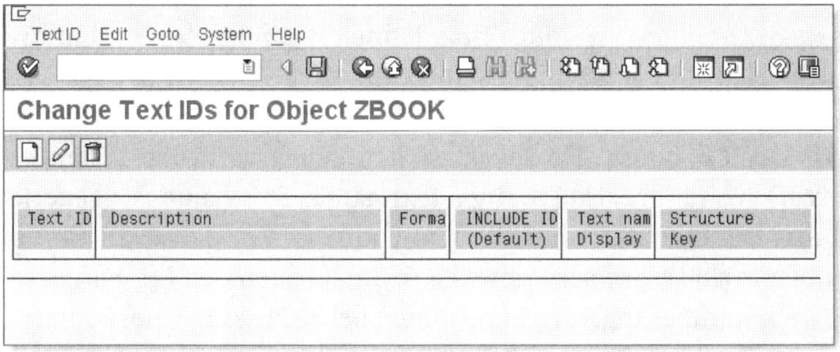


**Figure 6.27** Change Text IDs Screen

2. Click the Create button. This brings up the Create ID dialog box shown in Figure 6.28. Here, we have defined a text ID called ZLTX to capture a long text description for a given book in the book data model.

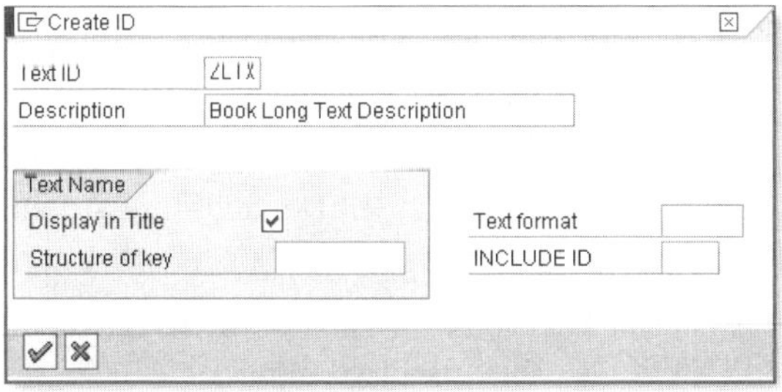


**Figure 6.28** Creating a Text ID

3. After you've confirmed your selection, press the Enter key to confirm your changes, and then click the Save button to save the text object.

### 6.5.2 Using the Text Object API

Now that you understand how text objects are created, let's see how you can use them in practical applications. In this section, we introduce you to the SAPscript text object API, showing you the functions you need to perform CRUD operations with text objects. As the basis for our discussion, we look at how to store a long text description for a book using the ZBOOK text object described in Section 6.5.1, Defining Text Objects.

#### Saving Text with the SAVE_TEXT Function

Before we can create a text object, we must first define certain header-level information that uniquely identifies a specific instance of a text object in the system. As you might expect, part of this key is the text object itself as well as any text IDs associated with the text object. However, to distinguish particular instances of a text object/text ID, you must also specify a text name. This name is a generic 70-character field that can contain pretty much any kind of key. For example, to identify instances of purchase order item texts, SAP concatenates the purchase order number and item number together in the name field. Other business objects use GUIDs, and so on. The final component in the text object key is the language of the text. This component allows you to define multiple translations for the same text object instance.

After you define the text object key, you can save instances of the text object using the SAVE_TEXT function. Listing 6.9 demonstrates how this function is used to save a long text description of a book that has the ISBN 978-1-59229-235-6. The header information for the text object is populated in a structure of type THEAD (i.e., the SAPscript Text Header table).

The long text itself must be split apart and stored in an internal table whose line type is TLINE (see Figure 6.29). As you can see, besides the TDLINE field that stores the raw text data, the TLINE structure also defines a field called TDFORMAT that can be used to define paragraph formatting for the embedded text. You can learn more about these options by reading the documentation for data element TDFORMAT.

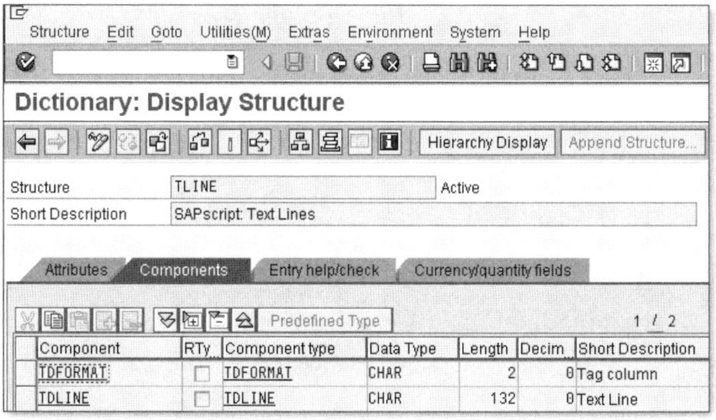


**Figure 6.29** ABAP Dictionary Structure TLINE

```
DATA: ls_header TYPE thead,
      lv_text   TYPE string,
      lt_lines  TYPE tline_tab.

* Populate the text header details for the ZBOOK
* text object:
  ls_header-tdobject = 'ZBOOK'.
  ls_header-tdid     = 'ZLTX'.
  ls_header-tdname   = '9781592292356'.
  ls_header-tdspras  = sy-langu.

* Create a long-text description for a book using a sample
* excerpt of text:
  CONCATENATE
    'Object-Oriented Programming with ABAP Objects'
    'If you're an ABAP application developer with basic'
    'ABAP programming skills, this book will teach you how'
    'to think about writing ABAP software from an object-'
    'oriented (OO) point of view, and prepare you to work'
    'with many of the exciting ABAP-based technologies in'
    'ABAP Objects (Release 7.0).'
         INTO lv_text
    SEPARATED BY cl_abap_char_utilities=>cr_lf.

* Convert the string to SAPscript lines using the
* /BOWDK/CL_SAPSCRIPT_UTILS class available with the
* source code bundle for this book:
  lt_lines =
```

```
    /bowdk/cl_sapscript_utils=>convert_string_to_sapscript(
      lv_text ).

* Save the text object:
  CALL FUNCTION 'SAVE_TEXT'
    EXPORTING
      header          = ls_header
      insert          = 'X'
    TABLES
      lines           = lt_lines
    EXCEPTIONS
      id              = 1
      language        = 2
      name            = 3
      object          = 4
      others          = 5.

  IF sy-subrc EQ 0.
    COMMIT WORK.
  ELSE.
    "Error handling goes here...
  ENDIF.
```

**Listing 6.9** Saving a Text Object with Function SAVE_TEXT

To simplify the process of converting normal ABAP character data objects into the SAPscript line format, we're using a custom utility class called /BOWDK/CL_SAPSCRIPT_UTILS. This class defines a static method called CONVERT_STRING_TO_SAPSCRIPT() that applies a "chunking" algorithm to split the text apart and also takes line breaks into account, and so on. The source code for this class is included in the source code bundle for this book available online.

If the call to SAVE_TEXT is successful, we can then commit our changes to the database using the COMMIT WORK statement. If you look closely at Figure 6.26, you can see where we have specified the Save Mode of the ZBOOK text object as Update. This implies that the text object is saved in an update task that is triggered by the COMMIT WORK statement. We explain more about how this works in Chapter 7, Transaction Processing.

Looking at the call to SAVE_TEXT in Listing 6.9, you can see that we have configured the INSERT parameter to indicate that the text object instance is new. Had we omitted this parameter, the system would have checked to see if the text object instance already existed, and, if necessary, updated it. As such, the SAVE_TEXT function can also be used to update text object instances as needed.

### Reading Text with the READ_TEXT Function

To read a text object into context, you use the READ_TEXT function. Listing 6.10 shows how READ_TEXT can be used to read the text object created by the example code in Listing 6.9. As you can see, this function uses the same key information that SAVE_TEXT uses to identify the text in the database.

```
DATA: ls_header TYPE thead,
      lt_lines  TYPE tline_tab.

* Define the text object metadata:
  ls_header-tdobject = 'ZBOOK'.
  ls_header-tdid     = 'ZLTX'.
  ls_header-tdname   = '9781592292356'.
  ls_header-tdspras  = sy-langu.

* Read the contents of the text object in the database:
  CALL FUNCTION 'READ_TEXT'
    EXPORTING
      id                      = ls_header-tdid
      language                = ls_header-tdspras
      name                    = ls_header-tdname
      object                  = ls_header-tdobject
    TABLES
      lines                   = lt_lines
    EXCEPTIONS
      id                      = 1
      language                = 2
      name                    = 3
      not_found               = 4
      object                  = 5
      reference_check         = 6
      wrong_access_to_archive = 7
      others                  = 8.

  IF sy-subrc NE 0.
    "Error handling goes here...
  ENDIF.
```

**Listing 6.10** Reading Texts with Function READ_TEXT

### Deleting Text with the DELETE_TEXT Function

You can delete text object instances using the DELETE_TEXT function. Listing 6.11 shows how we're deleting the text object instance created in the previous sections using DELETE_TEXT. Here, just like the SAVE_TEXT function, we must apply a COMMIT WORK statement to commit our changes to the database.

```
DATA: ls_header TYPE thead,
      lt_lines  TYPE tline_tab.

* Define the text object metadata:
  ls_header-tdobject = 'ZBOOK'.
  ls_header-tdid     = 'ZLTX'.
  ls_header-tdname   = '9781592292356'.
  ls_header-tdspras  = sy-langu.

* Delete the text object from the database:
  CALL FUNCTION 'DELETE_TEXT'
    EXPORTING
      id              = ls_header-tdid
      language        = ls_header-tdspras
      name            = ls_header-tdname
      object          = ls_header-tdobject
    EXCEPTIONS
      not_found       = 1
      others          = 2.

  IF sy-subrc EQ 0.
    COMMIT WORK.
  ELSE.
    "Error handling goes here...
  ENDIF.
```

**Listing 6.11** Deleting Text with Function DELETE_TEXT

## 6.5.3 Alternatives to Working with Text Objects

Beginning with SAP NetWeaver AS ABAP 6.10, SAP has provided support for character large database objects (*CLOBS*) and binary large database objects (*BLOBS*) in ABAP Dictionary tables. This functionality makes it easy to store long texts and/or MIME objects in the database without having to first break them apart into unwieldy chunks. For example, in Figure 6.30, we have defined a table called ZTCA_BOOKTEXT to store a long text description for the bookstore example considered throughout the course of this chapter. We can store a long text description for a given book in the `DESCRIPTION` field regardless of the size of the descriptive text.

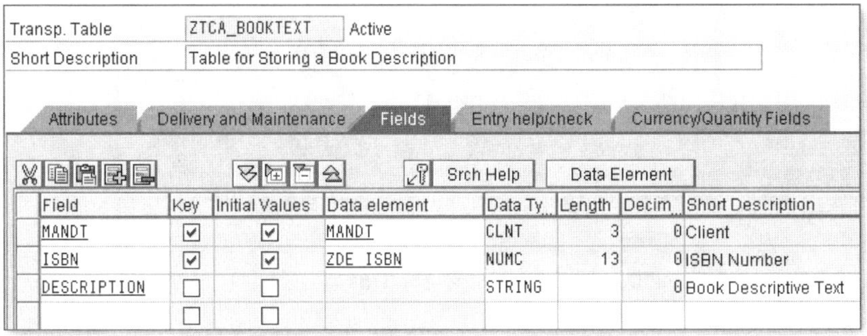


**Figure 6.30** Using the STRING Data Type in an ABAP Dictionary Table

Over time, large database objects eventually replace text objects as the standard way for storing long text data. In fact, the forthcoming release of the Locators and Streams API in SAP NetWeaver AS ABAP 7.02 will make the process of working with these objects even more powerful. You can learn more about the Locators and Streams API online at *www.sdn.sap.com*. Here, you can search for Thomas Jung's e-book entitled *Locators and Streams in ABAP 7.02*.

## 6.6 Connecting to External Databases

Occasionally, you may stumble across a requirement where you need to access data from an external database in an ABAP program. For example, imagine that a mid-sized company is replacing a home-grown database-driven solution with SAP ERP. Rather than forcing legacy developers to generate extracts of the data to import into SAP, it can be more cost-effective to simply configure a connection to that database and pull the data in directly. In this section, we show you how to create these external connections and execute Native SQL commands against them.

### 6.6.1 Configuring a Database Connection

To access an external database, you must configure a database connection in Transaction DBCO.[3] Figure 6.31 shows the initial screen of this transaction. As you can

3 Note: The configuration of external database connections is normally a Basis team activity, so make sure you get approval before trying this out on your own.

see, this transaction initially contains only connection details about the default SAP NetWeaver AS ABAP database connection.

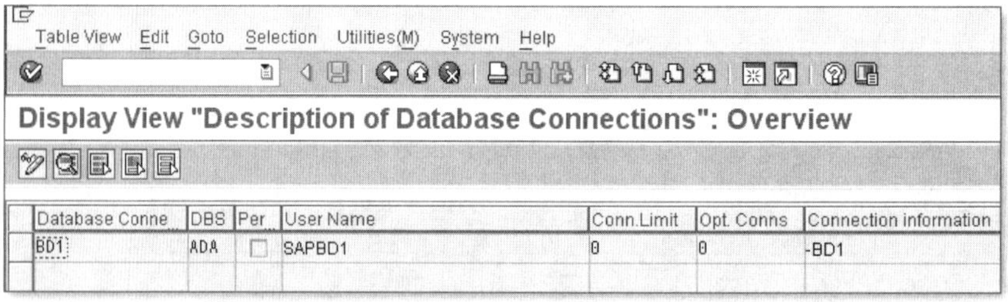


**Figure 6.31** Overview of External Database Connections in DBCO

To create a new connection in Transaction DBCO, you must perform the following steps:

1. Click the Change → Display button to get into edit mode, and then select the New Entries button.

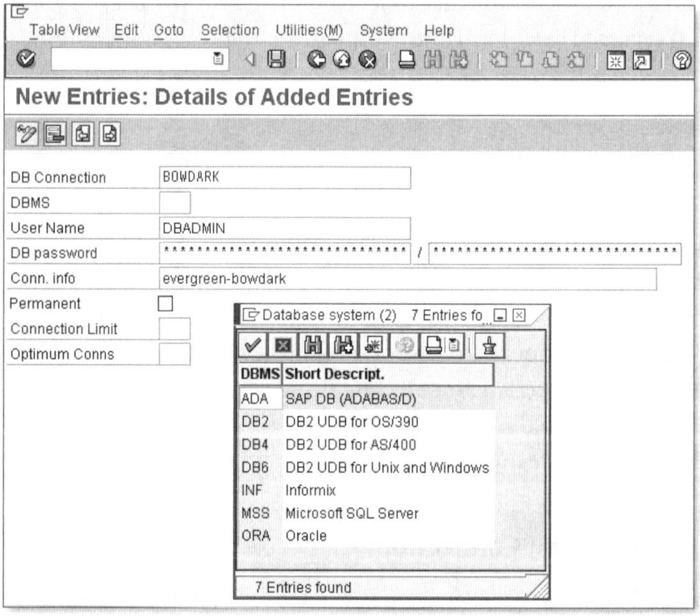


**Figure 6.32** Creating a Database Connection

2. In the New Entries: Details of Added Entries input mask (see Figure 6.32), you must specify the following information:

- **DB Connection:** The database connection name
- **DBMS:** The database system type (which must be supported by SAP)
- **User Name:** The database user account used to connect
- **DB Password:** The password of the database user account
- **Conn. Info:** Database-specific connection information[4]

3. When you're satisfied with your changes, click the Save button to save your changes.

### 6.6.2 Accessing the External Database

In keeping with our bookstore example, let's see how we would extract book information out of an external database table. For the purposes of this demonstration, we use the database connection defined in Section 6.6.1, Configuring a Database Connection, to connect to a custom SAP MaxDB instance called BOWDARK. Within this instance, there is a custom schema named BOOKSTORE that has a table called BOOKS. Figure 6.33 exhibits the fields defined in the BOOKS table, and Figure 6.34 shows some sample data loaded into the table.

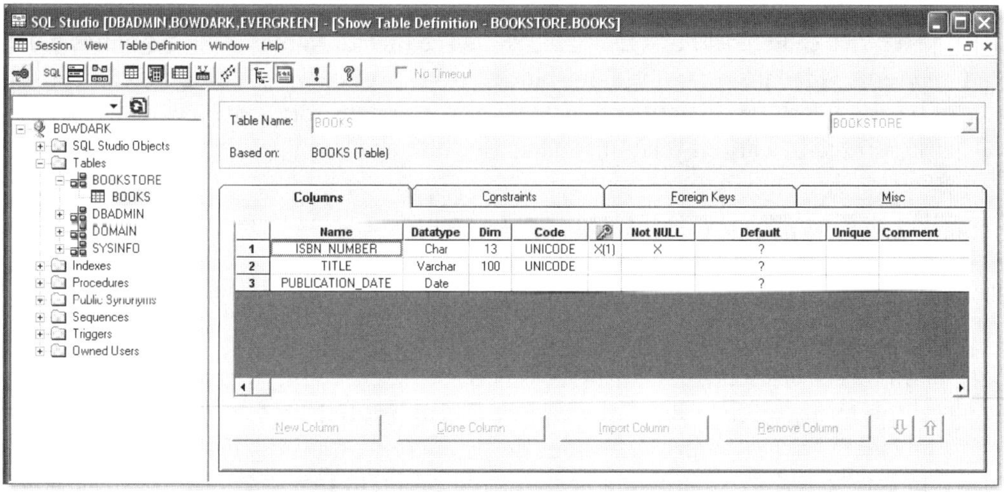


**Figure 6.33** Database Schema for Table BOOKSTORE.BOOKS

4 To find reference information about how to connect to your particular database, see SAP Note 323151.

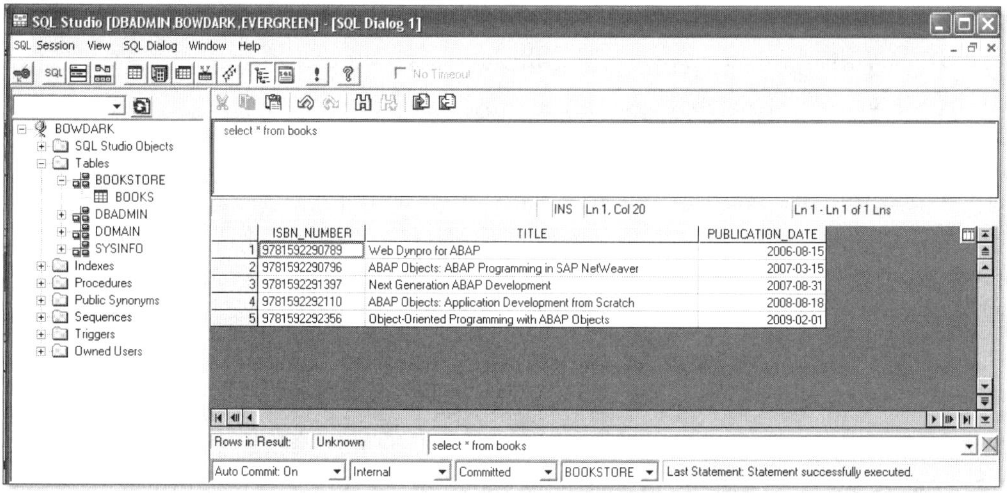


**Figure 6.34** Target Entries in the BOOKSTORE.BOOKS Table

By default, an ABAP program only maintains an implicit connection to the underlying SAP NetWeaver AS ABAP database. Therefore, to access an external database, you must first open a connection using the `CONNECT` statement whose syntax is shown in Listing 6.12. As you can see, this statement must be surrounded by an `EXEC SQL` code block. In a moment, you'll see that all Native SQL commands must be embedded inside an `EXEC SQL` block. This is necessary because the ABAP syntax check can't be expected to validate all of the various forms of Native SQL syntax supported by various relational database systems.

```
EXEC SQL.
  CONNECT TO dbs [AS con]
ENDEXEC.
```

**Listing 6.12** Syntax Diagram for the CONNECT Statement

After a connection is established, you can begin executing Native SQL commands to perform various CRUD operations, execute stored procedures, and so on. To illustrate how this works, consider the example report program `ZDBCONDEMO` listed in Listing 6.13. This program opens a connection to the `BOWDARK` database schema and performs a `SELECT` statement on the `BOOKS` table. Let's walk through this program to see what is happening at each step:

1. First, we open a connection to `BOWDARK` using the `CONNECT` statement. If there is an error, we need to handle it accordingly.

2. Next, we open a database cursor using the `OPEN dbcur` statement. In this case, the database cursor enables the exchange of result set data from the external database into the ABAP program context.
3. After the cursor is established, we can extract the entries from the result set into an internal table row by row using a `DO` loop. At each iteration of the loop, we obtain the current row data using the `FETCH NEXT` statement.
4. After all of the entries have been read, we close the database cursor using the `CLOSE` statement.
5. Then we close the external database connection using the `DISCONNECT` statement.
6. Finally, we loop through the extracted entries and output them to an ABAP list. Figure 6.35 shows the results.

```
REPORT zdbcondemo.
CLASS lcl_db_manager DEFINITION.
  PUBLIC SECTION.
    CLASS-METHODS:
      main.

    METHODS:
      constructor IMPORTING im_conn_name
                       TYPE dbcon_name,
      connect RAISING cx_sy_native_sql_error,
      get_books RAISING cx_sy_sql_error,
      disconnect.

  PRIVATE SECTION.
    TYPES: BEGIN OF ty_book,
             isbn_number      TYPE zde_isbn,
             title            TYPE zde_title,
             publication_date TYPE zde_publish_date,
           END OF ty_book.

    DATA: connection_name TYPE dbcon_name.
ENDCLASS.

CLASS lcl_db_manager IMPLEMENTATION.
  METHOD main.
    "Method-Local Data Declarations:
```

```
    DATA: lo_db_manager TYPE REF TO lcl_db_manager.

    TRY.
      "Create an instance of the database manager:
      CREATE OBJECT lo_db_manager
        EXPORTING
          im_conn_name = 'BOWDARK'.

      "Try to connect to the database:
      lo_db_manager->connect( ).

      "Read the set of books in the external database:
      lo_db_manager->get_books( ).

      "Disconnect from the database:
      lo_db_manager->disconnect( ).
    CATCH cx_root.
      "Exception handling goes here...
    ENDTRY.
  ENDMETHOD.

  METHOD constructor.
    "Store the connection name in context:
    me->connection_name = im_conn_name.
  ENDMETHOD.                 " METHOD construtor

  METHOD connect.
    "Try to connect to the database:
    EXEC SQL.
      CONNECT TO :me->connection_name
    ENDEXEC.

    IF sy-subrc NE 0.
      "Error handling goes here...
    ENDIF.
  ENDMETHOD.                 " METHOD connect

  METHOD get_books.
    "Method-Local Data Declarations:
    DATA: ls_book  TYPE ty_book,
          lt_books TYPE STANDARD TABLE OF ty_book.
    FIELD-SYMBOLS:
```

```
    <lfs_book> LIKE LINE OF lt_books.

  "Create a cursor to iterate over the books in the
  "BOOKSTORE schema's BOOKS table:
  EXEC SQL.
    OPEN dbcur
     FOR SELECT ISBN_NUMBER,
                TITLE,
                PUBLICATION_DATE
          FROM BOOKSTORE.BOOKS
  ENDEXEC.

  "Iterate over each of the book records:
  DO.
    EXEC SQL.
      FETCH NEXT dbcur
       INTO :ls_book-isbn_number,
            :ls_book-title,
            :ls_book-publication_date
    ENDEXEC.

    IF sy-subrc EQ 0.
      APPEND ls_book TO lt_books.
    ELSE.
      EXIT.
    ENDIF.
  ENDDO.

  "Close the cursor:
  EXEC SQL.
    CLOSE dbcur
  ENDEXEC.

  "Display the results:
  LOOP AT lt_books ASSIGNING <lfs_book>.
    WRITE: / <lfs_book>-isbn_number.
    WRITE: / <lfs_book>-title.
    WRITE: / <lfs_book>-publication_date.
    SKIP.
  ENDLOOP.
ENDMETHOD.                  " METHOD get_books
```

```
  METHOD disconnect.
    EXEC SQL.
      DISCONNECT :me->connection_name
    ENDEXEC.
  ENDMETHOD.                    " METHOD disconnect
ENDCLASS.

START-OF-SELECTION.
  lcl_db_manager=>main( ).
```

**Listing 6.13** Accessing an External Database Table in ABAP

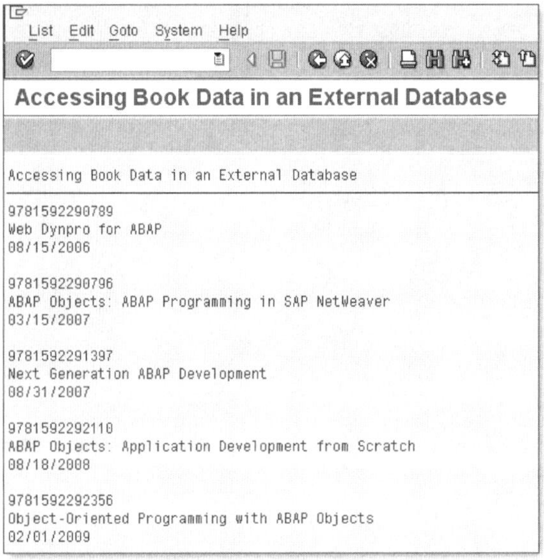


**Figure 6.35** Results of Program ZDBCONDEMO

## 6.6.3 Further Reading

You now should have an understanding of how to work with external databases. Of course, a short tutorial like this one can't address all of the possible scenarios that might come into play for a real project. Fortunately, the ABAP Keyword Documentation provides quite a bit of useful information to show you how to perform various other tasks using the Native SQL interface. To access this information, simply search using the phrase "Native SQL."

## 6.7 Summary

In many ways, this chapter barely scratches the surface of all of the available database programming options available in an advanced 4GL language such as ABAP. Entire books could be written about the Open SQL interface and its surrounding capabilities, but we had to draw the line somewhere. If you're interested in learning more about ABAP Object Services, we recommend that you check out *Object Services in ABAP* (SAP PRESS, 2010). In fact, we continue on that very topic in the next chapter, when we talk about transactional programming techniques in ABAP.

*Computer programs, like recipes, must be executed in an organized fashion to produce reliable results. Of course, there are times when everything doesn't run so smoothly. In these situations, programs must react to anomalous conditions and restore the system to a consistent state. In this chapter, we explore options for implementing dependable transactions in ABAP.*

# 7 Transactional Programming

Companies depend on online transaction processing (OLTP) systems such as SAP to guarantee that their day-to-day business operations run smoothly. Therefore, it's important that each transaction executed in the system be carried out completely and consistently each time without interruption. After all, given the investment involved, there's a lot at stake in even the simplest of ABAP programs.

Following best software engineering practices can go a long way toward making sure that ABAP programs perform as expected. However, there are certain environmental issues that are outside the control of every programmer. For example, what if there is a problem with the underlying SAP NetWeaver AS ABAP database? Or, what happens if two or more users try to access the same data record simultaneously? Fortunately, SAP provides many resources that can assist you in dealing with these problems. In this chapter, we explore these resources and see how they can be used to build robust transactions.

## 7.1 Introduction to the ACID Transaction Model

Before we begin looking at specific transactional services provided by SAP NetWeaver AS ABAP, it's important to establish some guidelines for what constitutes a successful transaction. One common method of describing these properties is the *ACID model*. The term "ACID" is an acronym that refers to four properties that every transaction must maintain to be successful. Table 7.1 describes each of these properties in detail.

| Transaction Property | Description |
|---|---|
| Atomic | Each transaction must execute completely or not at all. In other words, a transaction represents a set of steps that are *indivisible*. |
| Consistent | A transaction must leave the underlying data store (i.e., the SAP NetWeaver AS ABAP database, etc.) in a consistent state. |
| Isolated | Transactions must be allowed to execute without any interference. |
| Durable | Changes made by a transaction must not be lost if the system crashes. |

**Table 7.1** Properties of the ACID Transaction Model

A classic example used to illustrate the ACID model is a transfer of funds from one bank account to another. For instance, let's imagine that a customer wants to transfer $500 from his savings account to his checking account. In addition to the normal business rules (i.e., determining that there is enough money in the savings account, etc.), we also need to ensure the following:

1. The debit/credit operations must execute completely, or not at all. For instance, if the debit operation works, but the credit operation fails, then the customer loses $500. This isn't good for customer service.
2. At the end of the transaction, the balances on the customer's checking and savings account should be in a consistent state.
3. If there are multiple users on the account (i.e., a spouse, etc.), the transfer operation must be executed in isolation. Otherwise, the transaction might allow two or more users to transfer more money than is actually available in the savings account, and so on.
4. The changes made to the accounts must be persisted even in the event of a system crash. In addition to the actual account records, this also implies that a log of the transaction must be recorded.

Implementing these kinds of requirements in a distributed system such as SAP isn't a trivial task. In the upcoming sections, we explain how the different transactional services provided out of the box with SAP NetWeaver AS ABAP can be used to implement the ACID model for transaction processing.

## 7.2 Transaction Processing with SAP LUWs

As we mentioned earlier, there are various external factors that can jeopardize the integrity of a transaction. Despite that these circumstances are outside of your control as a programmer, they can't simply be ignored. Instead, you must detect these occurrences and react accordingly. For example, in the bank account transfer scenario, if the debit operation is successful, and the credit operation fails, you need to *roll back* the entire transaction to leave the system in a consistent state. In transaction processing terms, you need an *atomic commit protocol*.

In an atomic commit protocol, various changes to transactional resources are grouped together as a single operation that can either be committed or rolled back as a single unit. These operations are collectively referred to as a *logical unit of work* (LUW). In this section, we introduce you to the SAP LUW concept and show you how you can bundle database changes together so that business objects are updated completely and correctly.

### 7.2.1 Introduction to SAP Logical Units of Work

When you hear the term "LUW," it's frequently being talked about in the context of database programming. In this case, the LUW refers to a group of related SQL statements that make up a transaction in the database. Figure 7.1 shows the lifecycle of a database LUW starting at the point in which the transaction begins and ending with either a transaction commit or rollback. At the beginning of the transaction, the database is in a consistent state. Within the scope of the transaction, various SQL statements alter the state of the database tables grouped in the database LUW. However, in the transactional concept, these changes aren't applied immediately. Instead, they are committed together when all of the requisite transaction steps are completed. Of course, at any point along the way, an error may occur that causes the entire transaction to be rolled back (see Figure 7.1).

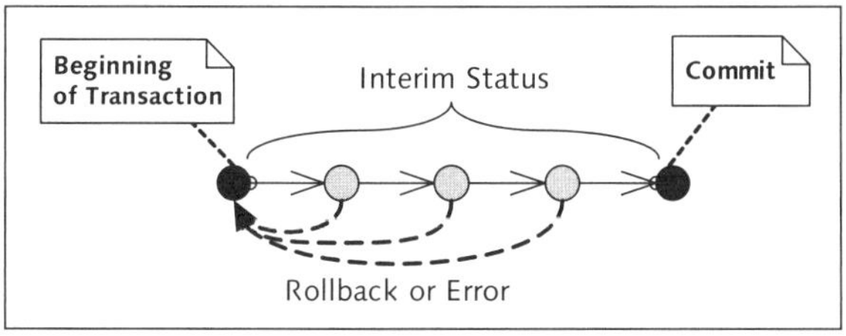


**Figure 7.1** Lifecyle of a Database Transaction

Though database LUWs are a very important part of any transaction-processing concept, they aren't sufficient to implement all of the transaction-processing requirements of a sophisticated three-tier system such as SAP. To see why, let's consider a simple Dynpro program that is used to update a series of normalized database tables. However, before we do so, we first need to take a step back and understand how dialog work processes are allocated for Dynpro programs.

### Managing Dialog Resources

SAP NetWeaver AS ABAP was designed from the ground up to be a *preemptive multitasking system*. This complex term basically implies that the application server *preempts* idle programs in favor of other user requests to maximize resources (namely, dialog processes). At the point of preemption, a context switch is performed, and the program state is *rolled out* to the user's *user session* in the shared memory of the application server. When the next dialog step is scheduled to run by the ABAP dispatcher, it's quite possible that a separate dialog process gets selected to process the request; at which time the program state is *rolled in* from the user's user session. Figure 7.2 illustrates the basic architecture of SAP NetWeaver AS ABAP.

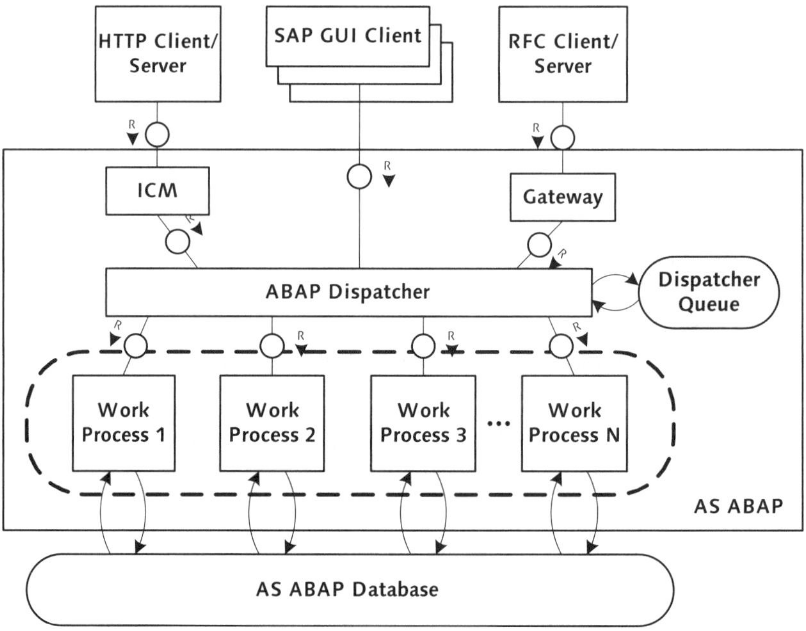


**Figure 7.2** Basic Architecture of SAP NetWeaver AS ABAP

In addition to dealing with program state, and so on, a dialog process also maintains a connection to the underlying SAP NetWeaver AS ABAP database. This connection operates in a kind of "pseudo-autocommit" mode in which database LUWs are implicitly committed at the end of each dialog step. These implicit commits are necessary because the dialog process may get reassigned to a different program when it's selected to process another user request by the ABAP dispatcher process. Of course, explicit LUWs can also be demarcated using the `COMMIT WORK` statement or `DB_COMMIT` function module.

### Dealing with Implicit Database Commits

Now that you understand how dialog processes are allocated to support incoming user requests, let's think about how our example Dynpro program might be affected by this architecture. As a frame of reference for our discussion, consider the progression of dialog steps depicted in Figure 7.3.

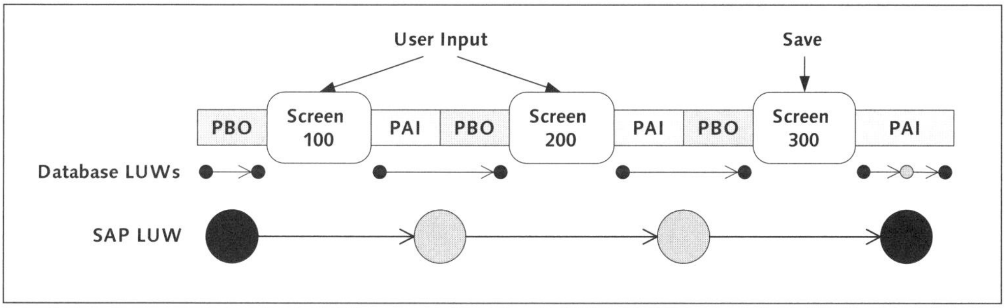


**Figure 7.3** Relationship Between Dialog Steps and Database LUWs

In ABAP dialog programming, a screen has two distinct event types that are processed by the application server:

- **Process before output (PBO) event**
  The PBO event is fired before a screen is rendered on the user's SAP GUI frontend, allowing input fields to be initialized, and so on. After the screen is initialized, a context switch occurs, and the dialog process that executed the PBO event is reclaimed to support other user requests.
- **Process after input (PAI) event**
  When a user has finished inputting his data on the screen, he can trigger the PAI event (by clicking a button, etc.) to have the application server process the input. This request is captured by the ABAP dispatcher process (refer to Figure

7.2) and then eventually handed off to a dialog process. This dialog process executes the PAI event of the current screen and the PBO event of the next screen. After the next screen is initialized, another context switch occurs, and the cycle starts all over again for another user request.

The execution of the PAI and PBO events between two screens is collectively referred to as a *dialog step*. As you saw in Figure 7.3, each dialog step has a database LUW associated with it. This database LUW is implicitly committed whenever the context switch occurs at the end of the dialog step. In terms of a long-running transaction with many dialog steps, this can be problematic; any Open SQL command that is executed within a dialog step is implicitly committed during a context switch.

Looking back at the screen-processing sequence of our example program in Figure 7.3, let's suppose that the user enters some data on Screens 100 and 200 that gets added to the database in the intermediate dialog steps. Now, imagine that the user clicks on the Save button on Screen 300 to complete the transaction. What happens if the final insert operation fails? Because each database LUW within the previous dialog steps was committed implicitly, those records have already been written to the database. Suffice it to say that it's not realistic to implement custom logic to delete these changes after the fact. Also, because implicit commits of database LUWs are also triggered by RFCs, `WAIT` statements, and so on, we can't simply chalk this up to a special dialog programming use case. Clearly, a better solution is needed.

### Expanding the Scope of LUWs

To address the kinds of problems associated with implicit database LUWs, SAP devised a broader LUW concept referred to as an *SAP LUW*. In the SAP LUW concept, each of the Open SQL statements executed in the dialog steps illustrated in Figure 7.3 are bundled together and written to a log table called `VBLOG`, which keeps track of the LUW. When the transaction is complete, it can be committed using the `COMMIT WORK` statement. This statement causes the entries buffered in the log table to be copied over to their target tables by a special work process in SAP NetWeaver AS ABAP called the *update work process* (sometimes referred to as the *update task*). We'll explain more about the update task in the upcoming sections.

The use of the intermediate log table also makes it possible to roll back a transaction using the `ROLLBACK WORK` statement. In this case, the entries in the log table are simply discarded, and the database remains in a consistent state.

By now you should understand how SAP LUWs work at a high level. However, you're probably wondering how Open SQL statements get bundled in an SAP LUW in the first place. Next, we show you how to develop custom function modules/subroutines to achieve this type of bundling. Also, in Section 7.3, Working with the Transaction Service, we demonstrate how persistent objects can be enrolled in SAP LUWs.

### 7.2.2 Bundling Database Changes in Update Function Modules

One way to bundle database changes together inside an SAP LUW is to create an *update function module*. Update function modules are maintained in the Function Builder (Transaction SE37), just like any normal function module. The only difference is that update modules have a different *processing type* than normal function modules. Figure 7.4 shows how we have selected the Update Module processing type for a function in the Function Builder. After we select this option, the Function Builder takes care of the rest.

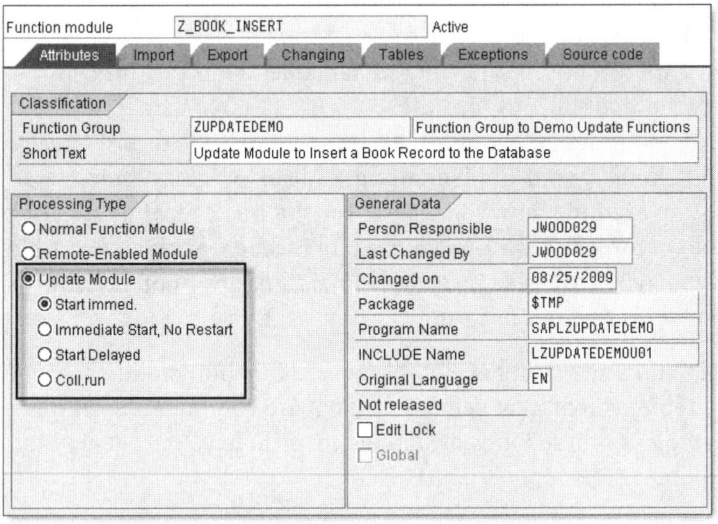


**Figure 7.4** Selecting the Update Module Processing Type

When you select the Update Module processing type, you have several different processing options to choose from. Though Table 7.2 describes these processing options in detail, you should normally choose the Start Immed. option.

| Processing Type | Description |
|---|---|
| Start Immediately | Causes the update module to be processed immediately by the update task whenever the transaction is committed via a COMMIT WORK statement. Because the module is processed by the update task, the dialog process that triggered the update doesn't wait for the module to finish. |
| Immediate Start, No Restart | Behaves just like the START IMMEDIATELY processing option, except that the module can't be reprocessed in Transaction SM13 (more on this in Section 7.2.5, Dealing with Exceptions in the Update Task). |
| Start Delayed | Causes the update module to be processed in the update task as a low-priority item. This might be used to write statistical data, and so on. |
| Collective Run | Internal option that should only be used by SAP. |

**Table 7.2** Update Module Processing Types

Listing 7.1 contains a sample update function called Z_BOOK_INSERT that adds a book record to the ZTCA_BOOKS table described in Chapter 6, Database Programming. As you can see, there's nothing terribly remarkable about this function; it simply tries to insert the book record into the ZTCA_BOOKS table using the Open SQL INSERT statement and raises an exception in the event that the record already exists. As a rule, you should avoid implementing a lot of program logic inside of update modules. For example, any validations on the book record passed to Z_BOOK_INSERT should occur *before* the update module is called. Sticking with this approach will help you avoid complex error-handling scenarios (more on this in Section 7.2.5, Dealing with Exceptions in the Update Task).

Another thing to keep in mind when developing update function modules is that you can't execute statements that may generate a database commit either implicitly or explicitly. Examples of these kinds of statements include COMMIT WORK, CALL TRANSACTION, and so on.

```
FUNCTION Z_BOOK_INSERT.
*"----------------------------------------------------------
*"*"Update Function Module:
*"
*"*"Local Interface:
*"  IMPORTING
*"     VALUE(IM_BOOK) TYPE  ZTCA_BOOKS
*"  EXCEPTIONS
```

```
*"      DUPLICATE_BOOK
*"----------------------------------------------------------
* Try to insert the record into the table:
  INSERT ztca_books FROM im_book.
  IF sy-subrc NE 0.
*   ISBN & already exists in the book database!
    MESSAGE E001(ZCA_BOOKSTORE)
       WITH im_book-isbn
      RAISING duplicate_book.
  ENDIF.
ENDFUNCTION.                    " Function Z_BOOK_INSERT
```

**Listing 7.1** Example Update Module to Add a Book to the Database

To invoke the `Z_BOOK_INSERT` module using the update task, you must use the `IN UPDATE TASK` addition of the `CALL FUNCTION` statement. The code excerpt shown in Listing 7.2 demonstrates how to do this. Here, notice how we're using the `COMMIT WORK` statement to commit the transaction. Prior to this statement, we can call as many update functions as we like; their changes simply remain queued up in the `VBLOG` table.

```
DATA: ls_book TYPE ztca_books.
ls_book-isbn = '9781592292356'.
ls_book-title =
  'Object-Oriented Programming with ABAP Objects'.
ls_book-publication_date = '20090201'.

CALL FUNCTION 'Z_BOOK_INSERT'
     IN UPDATE TASK
  EXPORTING
    im_book = ls_book
  EXCEPTIONS
    others  = 1.

COMMIT WORK.
```

**Listing 7.2** Calling an Update Function Module Asynchronously

When the `COMMIT WORK` statement in Listing 7.2 executes, the `Z_BOOK_INSERT` function is executed *asynchronously* in the update task. This implies that the calling process can move on to process other requests, and so on. In some scenarios, you may want to wait for the database changes to be committed before proceeding. In these situations, you can use the `AND WAIT` addition of the `COMMIT WORK` statement to cause the current work process to wait until the high-priority update modules are finished processing. Listing 7.3 demonstrates the syntax of the AND WAIT addition.

```
DATA: ls_book TYPE ztca_books.
ls_book-isbn = '9781592292356'.
ls_book-title =
  'Object-Oriented Programming with ABAP Objects'.
ls_book-publication_date = '20090201'.

CALL FUNCTION 'Z_BOOK_INSERT'
     IN UPDATE TASK
  EXPORTING
    im_book = ls_book
  EXCEPTIONS
    others  = 1.

COMMIT WORK AND WAIT.
```

**Listing 7.3** Calling an Update Function Module Synchronously

If you look carefully at the code in Listing 7.2 and Listing 7.3, you'll see that we haven't included any kind of exception-handling code after the call to Z_BOOK_INSERT. As you might have guessed already, this is because the update module is processed separately in the update task. In Section 7.2.5, Dealing with Exceptions in the Update Task, we'll show you how to handle exceptions that occur within the update task.

### 7.2.3 Bundling Database Changes in Subroutines

An alternative to creating update modules is to bundle database changes together in subroutines. These subroutines are registered using the ON COMMIT addition to the PERFORM statement as shown in Listing 7.4. Here, the syntax is fairly straightforward: The requested subroutine is registered to be executed whenever a transaction is committed using the COMMIT WORK statement.

```
PERFORM subroutine
     ON { {COMMIT [LEVEL idx]} | ROLLBACK }.
```

**Listing 7.4** Syntax Diagram for PERFORM ON COMMIT Statement

Looking closely at the syntax diagram in Listing 7.4, you can see that there is no mechanism for passing parameters to update subroutines. Instead, these modules must obtain their data through external data sources (e.g., ABAP memory, etc.). Given this limitation, subroutines executed within a COMMIT WORK are typically best suited to performing administrative or cleanup tasks rather than database updates. In fact, update subroutines are often called within update modules for this very purpose. In this case, the update subroutines are executed in the update task after all of the update modules have finished running.

The sample report program ZUPDATE_DEMO listed in Listing 7.5 demonstrates how to register an update subroutine using the PERFORM ON COMMIT statement. In terms of the overall call sequence, update subroutines are executed in their respective work process *before* update function modules are kicked off in the update task. Because they run in their respective work process, update subroutines have a major performance advantage over update modules: They don't have to incur the overhead of logging changes to table VBLOG.

```
REPORT zupdate_demo.
START-OF-SELECTION.
  PERFORM insert_book ON COMMIT.
  COMMIT WORK.

FORM insert_book.
* Local Data Declarations:
  DATA: ls_book TYPE ztca_books.

  ls_book-isbn = '9781592292356'.
  ls_book-title =
    'Object-Oriented Programming with ABAP Objects'.
  ls_book-publication_date = '20090201'.

* Try to insert the record into the table:
  INSERT ztca_books FROM ls_book.
  IF sy-subrc NE 0.
*   ISBN & already exists in the book database!
    MESSAGE E001(ZCA_BOOKSTORE)
       WITH ls_book-isbn
      RAISING duplicate_book.
  ENDIF.
ENDFORM.
```

**Listing 7.5** Bundling Database Updates Using a Subroutine

As you can see in the syntax diagram shown earlier in Listing 7.4, there are a couple of other syntax additions that can be applied to the PERFORM statement:

- The `LEVEL` addition is used to control the execution sequence of the update subroutines at runtime. Normally, update subroutines are executed in the order they are registered. However, when the `PERFORM ON COMMIT` statement is executed with the `LEVEL` addition, the provided integer value can be used to influence this sequencing.
- The `ON ROLLBACK` addition causes the update subroutine to be executed whenever the `ROLLBACK WORK` statement is executed. Such subroutines are normally used to clean up after a transaction.

Just like update modules, update subroutines can't execute statements that can perform database commits. For more information about update subroutines, perform a keyword search on the term "PERFORM ON" in the ABAP Keyword Documentation.

### 7.2.4 Performing Local Updates

In some situations, the overhead associated with queuing up an SAP LUW in the `VBLOG` table isn't really necessary. For instance, if you run a program in the background, you don't have to worry about implicit database commits via context switches. However, you still want to have the ability to enroll a series of Open SQL statements inside an SAP LUW. This can be achieved using the `SET UPDATE TASK LOCAL` statement.

The `SET UPDATE TASK LOCAL` statement switches on a local update mode in the current work process. When this mode is turned on, calls to update function modules are queued up in the ABAP memory as opposed to the `VBLOG` table. Whenever the `COMMIT WORK` statement is executed, the update functions are synchronously performed in the current work process. The code excerpt in Listing 7.6 demonstrates the call sequence necessary to execute update functions in the local update mode.

```
SET UPDATE TASK LOCAL.
...
CALL FUNCTION ... IN UPDATE TASK.
CALL FUNCTION ... IN UPDATE TASK.
CALL FUNCTION ... IN UPDATE TASK.
...
COMMIT WORK.
```

**Listing 7.6** Turning on the Local Update Mode in a Work Process

One thing to keep in mind with the local update mode is that it's always deactivated at the beginning of an SAP LUW. Thus, if you wanted to process another transaction in local update mode after the `COMMIT WORK` statement from Listing 7.6, you would have to execute the `SET UPDATE TASK LOCAL` statement again.

### 7.2.5 Dealing with Exceptions in the Update Task

Update functions running in the update task are cut off from their calling programs. In fact, it's possible that the update task may not get around to executing an asynchronous update until *after* the calling program is already completed. Consequently, the error-handling options available to you inside of an update function module are pretty limited. For instance, in Listing 7.1 earlier in this chapter, we're simply outputting an error message if the insert operation fails. At this point, you might be wondering where that message went — rest assured that it's not simply lost in the ether; rather, it's stored inside the *update request log*.

You can access the update request log by executing Transaction SM13. Figure 7.5 shows the initial screen of Transaction SM13. Here, you can enter various selection criteria (the user that would have initiated the request, the date/time range in which the request was created, its status, etc.) and search for update requests in the log.

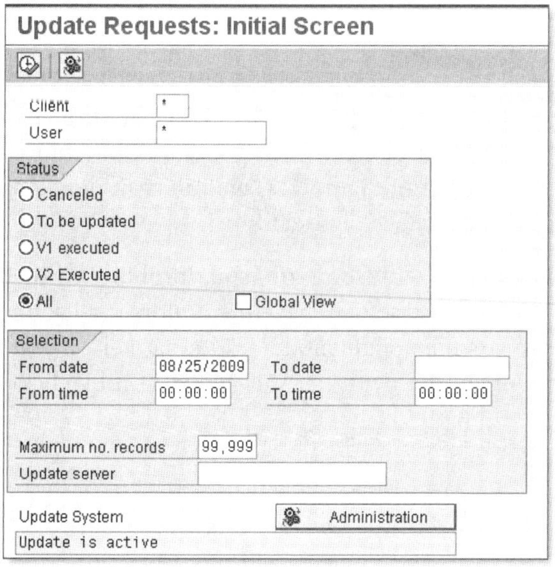


**Figure 7.5** Initial Screen of Transaction SM13

If there are entries in the log for the given selection criteria, they are displayed in the results screen shown in Figure 7.6. You can double-click a particular entry to see details about the update module associated with the update request (see Figure 7.7).

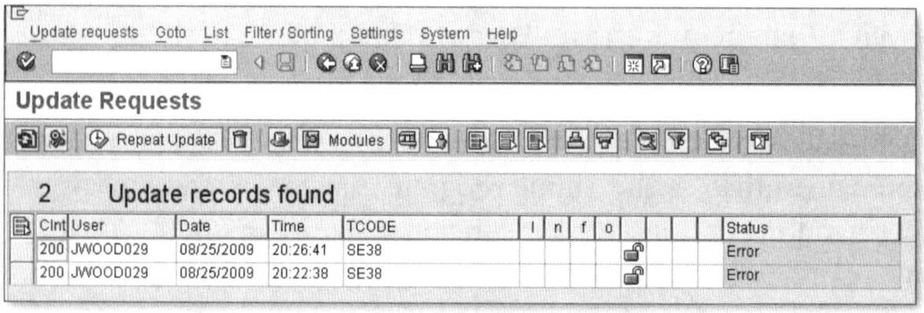


**Figure 7.6** Viewing Update Requests in the Log — Part 1

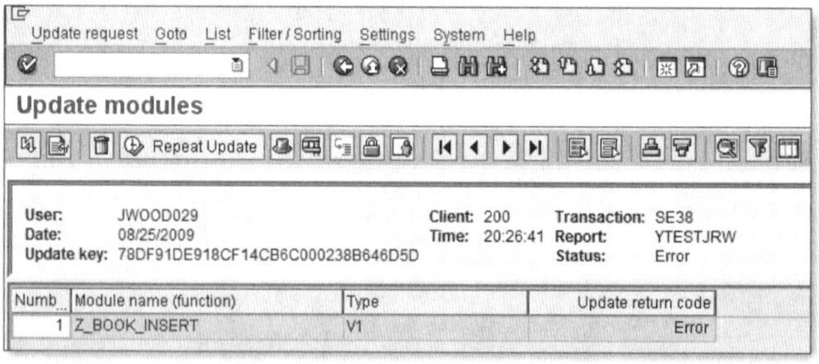


**Figure 7.7** Viewing Update Requests in the Log — Part 2

In Figure 7.7, you can see that the update module `Z_BOOK_INSERT` has an error status. This is because we executed the sample code from Listing 7.2 multiple times. If we double-click the update module record in Figure 7.7, we can read detailed information about the root cause of the error (see Figure 7.8).

Occasionally, an update module might fail because of an actual problem in the database (e.g., disk space issues, etc.). In this case, you have the option of clicking on the Repeat Update button to reprocess the update module. Alternatively, if you know that the update is definitely in error, then you can simply delete it by clicking on the Delete Record button.

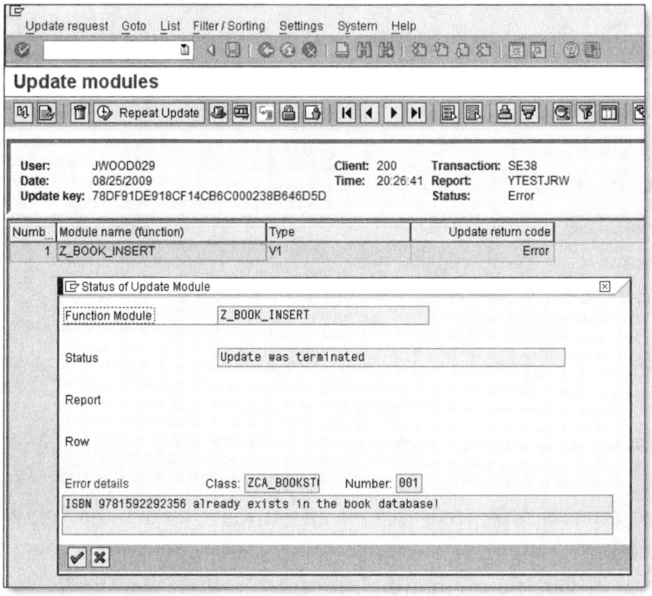


**Figure 7.8** Viewing Update Requests in the Log — Part 3

Whenever an update error occurs, an express message is also created and displayed for the user in the SAP GUI frontend (see Figure 7.9) and stored in the user's Business Workplace inbox (see Figure 7.10).

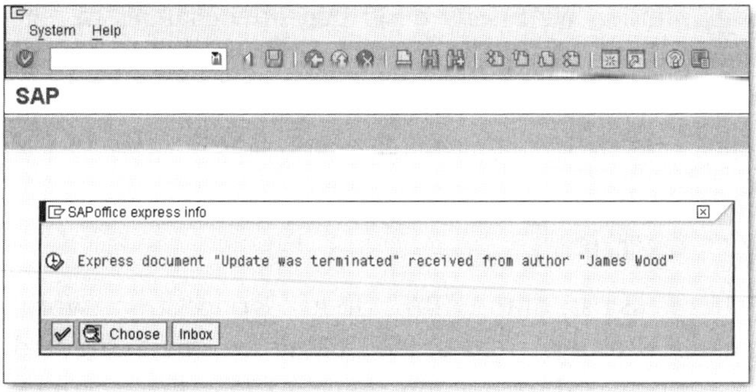


**Figure 7.9** SAPoffice Express Message for an Update Error

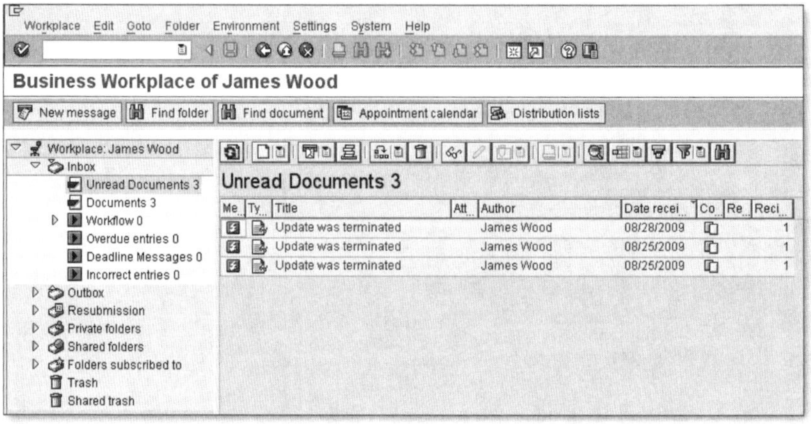


**Figure 7.10** Update Error Messages in the Business Workplace

Despite the fact that the update log keeps track of any update errors that may occur, it should not be used as a safety net. As we mentioned earlier, it's a good practice to validate data extensively before handing it off to an update module. As a rule, update errors should only occur in rare situations where there are technical issues with the system.

## 7.3 Working with the Transaction Service

In Chapter 6, Database Programming, we briefly described how changes to persistent objects are committed to the database using the `COMMIT WORK` statement. In this section, we expand on these concepts by showing you how to use the *Transaction Service* to manage changes to persistent objects inside of an SAP LUW.

### 7.3.1 Transaction Service Overview

The Transaction Service is offered as part of the ABAP Object Services framework; it allows you to manage changes to persistent objects using an object-oriented transaction concept. This object-oriented transaction concept is purely an abstraction of the Transaction Service; behind the scenes, the Transaction Service works in conjunction with the Persistence Service to enroll changes to persistent objects in an SAP LUW, per usual. However, much like the Persistence Service abstracts away the details of executing SQL commands, the Transaction Service hides the low-level aspects of working with SAP LUWs. In particular, it takes care of bundling changes inside of an update function module so that you don't have to break out of the object-oriented mindset when you need to manage persistent objects in a transactional context.

Figure 7.11 contains a UML class diagram that depicts the core components of the Transaction Service. Much like we saw with the architecture of the Persistence Service in Chapter 6, Database Programming, the Transaction Service also makes heavy use of interfaces to maintain flexibility. The core interface that represents a transaction is the `IF_OS_TRANSACTION` interface. Looking at the UML class diagram in Figure 7.11, you can see that this interface defines methods to start a transaction, end a transaction, undo a transaction, and so on. You'll learn more about these methods as you see some code examples in the upcoming sections.

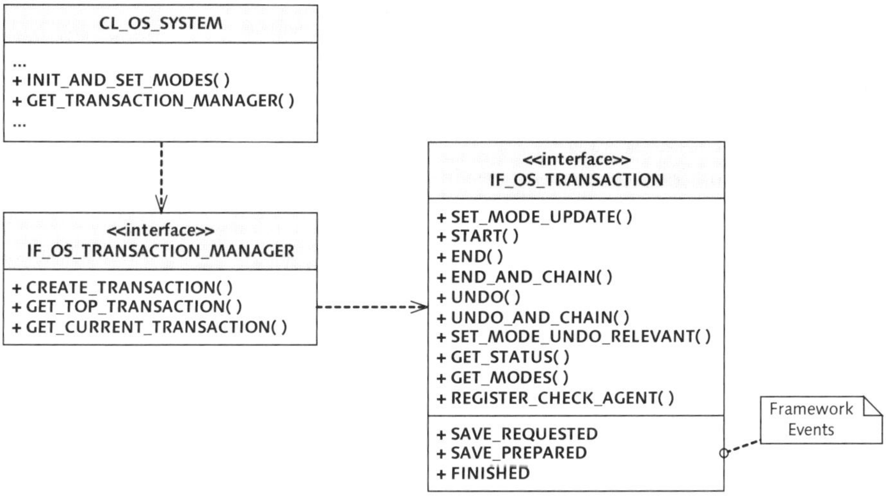


**Figure 7.11** UML Class Diagram of Transaction Service Components

Object-oriented transactions are managed by a *transaction manager* that is represented by the `IF_OS_TRANSACTION_MANAGER` interface. You can obtain a reference to an object that implements this interface by calling the static factory method `GET_TRANSACTION_MANAGER()` of class `CL_OS_SYSTEM`.

### 7.3.2 Understanding Transaction Modes

When you work with the Transaction Service, you need to specify a *transaction mode*. This mode defines the behavior of transactions in the context of the underlying SAP LUW. Table 7.3 shows the transaction modes that you can choose from when configuring the transaction manager.

| Transaction Mode | Description |
|---|---|
| Compatibility mode (Default) | In compatibility mode, you must execute the COMMIT WORK statement explicitly. You select this mode when you want to mix in persistent objects within the context of a preexisting transaction that is using update function modules, and so on. |
| Object-oriented mode | In object-oriented mode, you commit transactions by calling the END() or END_AND_CHAIN() methods of the IF_OS_TRANSACTION object. These methods trigger the COMMIT WORK behind the scenes. You aren't allowed to execute a COMMIT WORK statement within the scope of a transaction that is in object-oriented mode. |

**Table 7.3** Transaction Modes of the Transaction Service

In addition to a transaction mode, you must also select an *update mode* that defines how the Transaction Service performs the update whenever a transaction is committed. As you can see in Table 7.4, these options are directly related to the SAP LUW statements described in Section 7.2, Transaction Processing with SAP LUWs.

| Update Mode | Description |
|---|---|
| Direct {OSCON_DMODE_DIRECT} | This mode is analogous to executing the SET UPDATE TASK LOCAL statement prior to the creation of the transaction. |
| Asynchronous update task (Default) {OSCON_DMODE_UPDATE_TASK} | In this mode, the Transaction Service bundles the changes in an update function module that gets processed asynchronously in the update task. |
| Local {OSCON_DMODE_LOCAL} | This mode is analogous to executing the SET UPDATE TASK LOCAL statement prior to the creation of the transaction. |
| Synchronous update task {OSCON_DMODE_UPDATE_TASK_SYNC} | This mode behaves like the asynchronous update task update mode except that the Transaction Service uses the AND WAIT addition of the COMMIT WORK statement to execute the update synchronously. |

**Table 7.4** Update Modes of the Transaction Service

You can configure the transaction mode and update mode for the Transaction Service using the static method INIT_AND_SET_MODES() of class CL_OS_SYSTEM. Figure 7.12 shows the signature of this method and its two importing parameters: I_EXTERNAL_COMMIT and I_UPDATE_MODE. These parameters are used as follows:

- The I_EXTERNAL_COMMIT parameter is used to configure the transaction mode. As you can see, the default value of this parameter is set to OSCON_TRUE. This implies that the default transaction mode is *compatibility mode*. If you want to work in the object-oriented transaction mode, you must pass in a value of OSCON_FALSE here.
- The I_UPDATE_MODE parameter allows you to specify the type of update mode that you want to work with. Table 7.4 shows you the constant names that you can specify to configure each of the available update mode options.

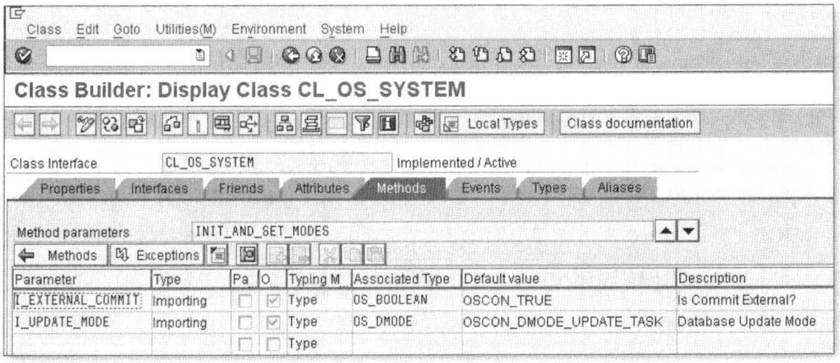


**Figure 7.12** Signature of Method INIT_AND_SET_MODES()

You must execute the INIT_AND_SET_MODES() method before you access the Persistence Service; otherwise, it raises an unchecked exception of type CX_OS_SYSTEM. Therefore, if you're going to explicitly initialize the Transaction Service using the INIT_AND_SET_MODES() method, we recommend that you do so in the LOAD-OF-PROGRAM event, a class constructor, and so on. That way, you can be sure that the Transaction Service is properly initialized before any attempts are made to access it.

If you don't explicitly configure a transaction mode and update mode, the Transaction Service implicitly initializes itself to operate in compatibility mode using the asynchronous update task. We saw evidence of this in Chapter 6, Database Programming, when we demonstrated how to commit changes to persistent objects.

Another option for configuring the transaction mode of the Transaction Service is to create an *object-oriented transaction* in Transaction SE93. In this case, you specify the desired transaction and update modes within the transaction itself. At runtime, whenever a user executes the object-oriented transaction, the runtime environment implicitly calls the `CL_OS_SYSTEM=>INIT_AND_SET_MODES()` method behind the scenes, based upon the selected values. To configure the transaction mode for an object-oriented transaction, perform the following steps:

1. Open Transaction SE93 and enter a transaction code in the Transaction Code field. Then click on the Create button (see Figure 7.13).

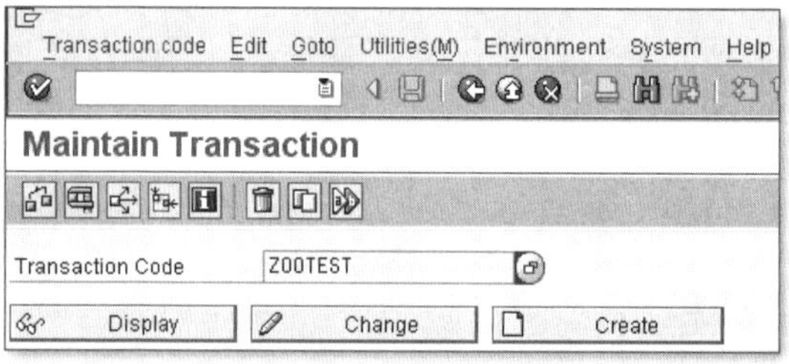


**Figure 7.13** Creating an Object-Oriented Transaction — Part 1

2. In the Create Transaction dialog box that pops up, enter a short text description for the transaction, and select the Method of a Class (OO Transaction) radio button in the Start Object group box (see Figure 7.14). Press Enter to confirm your selections.

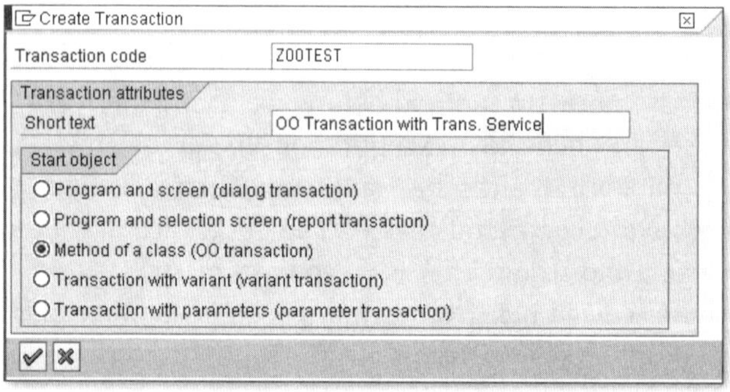


**Figure 7.14** Creating an Object-Oriented Transaction — Part 2

3. If you look carefully at the Create Object Transaction screen shown in Figure 7.15, you can see that there's a checkbox entitled OO Transaction Model that you can select to specify the object-oriented transaction mode. When this checkbox is selected, you also can configure an update mode in the Update Mode group box (see Figure 7.15).

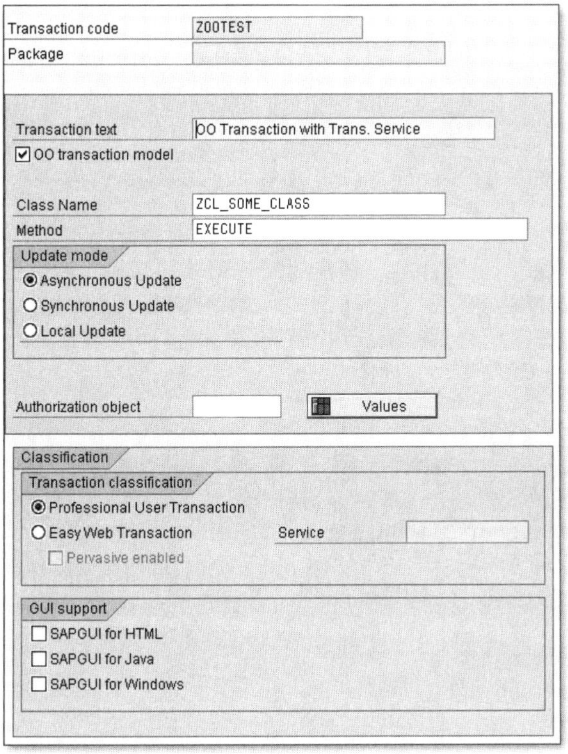


**Figure 7.15** Creating an Object-Oriented Transaction — Part 3

### 7.3.3 Processing Transactions in Object-Oriented Mode

Now that you understand the components that make up the Transaction Service, let's see how we can use this service to execute an object-oriented transaction. As a basis for our discussion, consider the ZTRANS_DEMO example program shown in Listing 7.7. This program is leveraging the persistent objects that we created in Chapter 6, Database Programming, to create a new book. As you can see, the heavy lifting is being performed by a local class called LCL_TRANSACTION_DEMO.

Before we start digging into the transaction code, notice how we're calling the static method INIT_AND_SET_MODES( ) of class CL_OS_SYSTEM in the class constructor of LCL_TRANSACTION_DEMO to explicitly turn on the object-oriented transaction mode in the Transaction Service. By calling this method in the class constructor, we're assured that there won't be any potential initialization errors later on.

```
REPORT ztrans_demo.
CLASS lcl_transaction_demo DEFINITION.
  PUBLIC SECTION.
```

```
    CLASS-METHODS:
      class_constructor,
      create_book.

    METHODS:
      handle_save_requested FOR EVENT save_requested
                             OF if_os_transaction,
      handle_save_prepared  FOR EVENT save_prepared
                             OF if_os_transaction,
      handle_finished       FOR EVENT finished
                             OF if_os_transaction
                            IMPORTING status.
ENDCLASS.

CLASS lcl_transaction_demo IMPLEMENTATION.
  METHOD class_constructor.
*   Initialize the Transaction Service to use the
*   object-oriented transaction mode:
    CALL METHOD cl_os_system=>init_and_set_modes
      EXPORTING
        i_external_commit = oscon_false
        i_update_mode     = oscon_dmode_update_task.
  ENDMETHOD.

  METHOD create_book.
    "Method-Local Data Declarations:
    DATA: lo_trans_svc TYPE REF
                         TO lcl_transaction_demo,
          lo_trans_mgr TYPE REF
                         TO if_os_transaction_manager,
          lo_trans     TYPE REF
                         TO if_os_transaction,
          lo_author1   TYPE REF
                         TO zcl_author,
          lo_author2   TYPE REF
                         TO zcl_author,
          lo_publisher TYPE REF
                         TO zcl_publisher,
          lo_book      TYPE REF
                         TO zcl_book.

    "Instantiate the test driver class:
    CREATE OBJECT lo_trans_svc.
```

```
*   Obtain a reference to the transaction manager:
    lo_trans_mgr =
      cl_os_system=>get_transaction_manager( ).

*   Create a top-level transaction:
    lo_trans = lo_trans_mgr->create_transaction( ).

*   Register event handlers for the transaction:
    SET HANDLER lo_trans_svc->handle_save_requested
            FOR lo_trans.
    SET HANDLER lo_trans_svc->handle_save_prepared
            FOR lo_trans.
    SET HANDLER lo_trans_svc->handle_finished
            FOR lo_trans.

    TRY.
      "Start the transaction:
      lo_trans->start( ).

      "Create a publisher for the book:
      CALL METHOD zca_publisher=>agent->create_persistent
        EXPORTING
          i_country        = 'US'
          i_publisher_name = 'Galileo Press, Inc.'
          i_region         = 'MA'
        RECEIVING
          result           = lo_publisher.

      "Create the book authors:
      CALL METHOD zca_author=>agent->create_persistent
        EXPORTING
          i_first_name = 'Horst'
          i_last_name  = 'Keller'
        RECEIVING
          result       = lo_author1.

      CALL METHOD zca_author=>agent->create_persistent
        EXPORTING
          i_first_name = 'Sascha'
          i_last_name  = 'Krüger'
        RECEIVING
          result       = lo_author2.
```

```
      "Now, create the book:
      CALL METHOD zca_book=>agent->create_persistent
        EXPORTING
          i_isbn             = '9781592290796'
          i_publication_date = '20070315'
          i_publisher        = lo_publisher
          i_title            =
            'ABAP Objects: ABAP Programming in NetWeaver'
        RECEIVING
          result             = lo_book.

      "Assign the authors to the book:
      lo_book->add_author( lo_author1 ).
      lo_book->add_author( lo_author2 ).

*     Commit the transaction:
      lo_trans->end( ).
    CATCH cx_root.
    ENDTRY.
  ENDMETHOD.

  METHOD handle_save_requested.
    WRITE: /
      'Save requested, perform any last-minute updates...'.
  ENDMETHOD.

  METHOD handle_save_prepared.
    WRITE: /
      'Save prepared, COMMIT WORK happens next...'.
  ENDMETHOD.

  METHOD handle_finished.
    IF status EQ OSCON_TSTATUS_FIN_SUCCESS.
      WRITE: / 'Transaction processed successfully.'.
    ENDIF.
  ENDMETHOD.
ENDCLASS.

START-OF-SELECTION.
* Hand the main processing off to the local demo class:
  lcl_transaction_demo=>create_book( ).
```

**Listing 7.7** Working with Object-Oriented Transactions

In method CREATE_BOOK(), you can see the transaction processing code highlighted in boldface font. Generally speaking, the order of operations for processing an object-oriented transaction is as follows:

1. First, you need to call the static method GET_TRANSACTION_MANAGER() of class CL_OS_SYSTEM to obtain a reference to the transaction manager.
2. After you have a reference to the transaction manager, you can call method CREATE_TRANSACTION() to create a top-level transaction object.
3. To start the transaction, invoke the START() method on the transaction object.
4. After the transaction is started, begin making changes to persistent objects, per usual. For instance, in Listing 7.7, we're creating book, author, and publisher persistent objects using the CREATE_PERSISTENT() method of their respective class agents.
5. If an error occurs along the way, the transaction can be rolled back by executing the UNDO() method on the transaction object.
6. Otherwise, after all of the transaction steps have been completed, you can call the END() method on the transaction to commit the changes to the persistent objects. After the transaction is committed, the persistent objects will be invalidated. Alternatively, you can call the END_AND_CHAIN() method to commit the transaction and then start a new transaction in the same context. In this case, the persistent objects aren't invalidated.

### Working with Subtransactions

In the example code shown in Listing 7.7, we're only working with a single *top-level* transaction. We emphasize the term "top-level" here to indicate that it's possible to divide a transaction into *subtransactions*. Here, you might want to bundle together a series of steps as a subtransaction within the scope of a larger transaction, and so on.

The process of creating a subtransaction is identical to the one used to create a top-level transaction: You simply call the transaction manager method CREATE_TRANSACTION(). The only difference is that the subtransaction executes inside the scope of the top-level transaction. The code excerpt in Listing 7.8 shows how this works.

```
DATA: lo_trans_mgr TYPE REF TO if_os_transaction_manager,
      lo_top_trans TYPE REF TO if_os_transaction,
      lo_sub_trans TYPE REF TO if_os_transaction.
```

```
* Obtain a reference to the transaction manager:
  lo_trans_mgr =
    cl_os_system=>get_transaction_manager( ).

* Create the top-level transaction:
  lo_top_trans = lo_trans_mgr->create_transaction( ).

* Start the top-level transaction:
  lo_top_trans->start( ).

*   Create the subtransaction:
    lo_sub_trans = lr_trans_mgr->create_transaction( ).

*   Start the subtransaction:
    lo_sub_trans->begin( ).

*   Subtransaction LUW goes here...

*   Commit the subtransaction (no COMMIT WORK yet):
    lo_sub_trans->end( ).

* Commit the top-level transaction:
  lo_top_trans->end( ).
```

**Listing 7.8** Working with Subtransactions

From a programming perspective, you treat a subtransaction just like any other normal transaction. You can commit the subtransaction using the `END()` method, roll it back using the `UNDO()` method, and so on. Of course, the scope of these changes is limited to the subtransaction. This implies that calling the `END()` method on a subtransaction doesn't cause the Transaction Service to commit the changes. Instead, these changes remain queued up to be committed whenever the top-level transaction is committed.

### Listening for Transaction Events

Another thing you might have noticed while looking at the code in Listing 7.7 is that we've registered a series of *event handler methods* on the top-level transaction. These event handlers allow you to be notified of important milestones during the commit process. Table 7.5 describes these events in greater detail.

| Event Name | Description |
|---|---|
| SAVE_REQUESTED | This event is raised whenever the END() method is executed on the transaction right before the class agents start transferring changes to the persistent objects to update records or transfer tables.<br>This event can be useful if you need to adjust the persistent attributes of your persistent class before it's saved (e.g., copying transient attribute values over, etc.). |
| SAVE_PREPARED | This event is raised after the class agents have transferred changes to persistent objects to update records or transfer tables and the framework is ready to execute the COMMIT WORK statement.<br>If you're using a persistence layer other than the SAP NetWeaver AS ABAP database, then you might use this event to coordinate the writing of the persistent object data to the underlying persistence layer. |
| FINISHED | This event is triggered when the transaction is completed. The STATUS parameter can be used to determine whether the operation was successful. |

**Table 7.5** Events of Interface IF_OS_TRANSACTION

### 7.3.4 Performing Consistency Checks with Check Agents

By the time we decide to commit a transaction, each of the relevant transactional resources *should* be in a consistent state. However, it never hurts to have an additional checkpoint to make sure that nothing slips through the cracks. That's why the Transaction Service allows you to register a *check agent* with a transaction to perform a consistency check before the transaction is committed.

To register a check agent with a transaction, you simply call method REGISTER_CHECK_AGENT() on the transaction object. This method expects an instance of a class that implements the IF_OS_CHECK interface. Interface IF_OS_CHECK defines a single method called IS_CONSISTENT(). Figure 7.16 shows the signature of the IS_CONSISTENT() method. As you can see, this method simply returns a Boolean result parameter that tells the framework whether the transactional resources are in a consistent state.

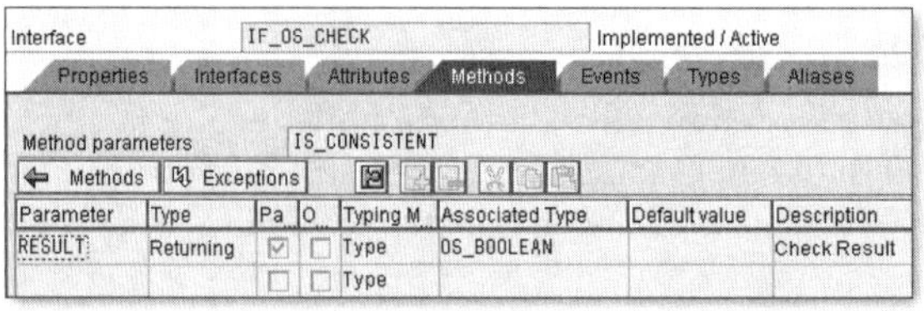


**Figure 7.16** Signature of Method IS_CONSISTENT( )

To demonstrate how check agents work, let's enhance the transaction code from Listing 7.7 to perform a consistency check on a book before committing a transaction. In this case, the `ZCL_BOOK` class is a logical candidate for implementing the `IF_OS_CHECK` interface because it should know whether or not a particular book is valid. Figure 7.17 shows how we've implemented the `IF_OS_CHECK` interface in class `ZCL_BOOK`.

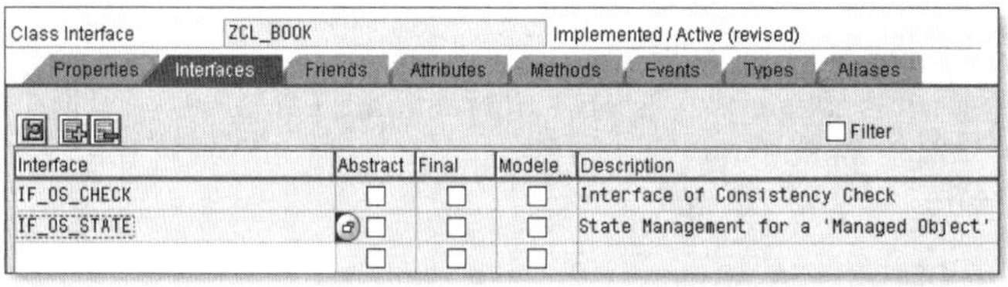


**Figure 7.17** Implementing Interface IF_OS_CHECK

Listing 7.9 shows a sample implementation of the `IF_OS_CHECK~IS_CONSISTENT()` method. Here, we're simply checking to make sure that a book has at least one author associated with it.

```
METHOD if_os_check~is_consistent.
* Make sure the book has at least one author:
  IF lines( me->authors ) GT 0.
    result = oscon_true.
  ELSE.
    result = oscon_false.
  ENDIF.
ENDMETHOD.
```

**Listing 7.9** Implementing Method IS_CONSISTENT()

Now that we have our check agent class, let's see how we can use it to validate the transaction used to create a book. Listing 7.10 contains a modified version of the `CREATE_BOOK()` method from class `LCL_TRANSACTION_DEMO` in Listing 7.7. Here, we have commented out the calls to method `ADD_AUTHOR()` so that our newly created book doesn't have an author assigned to it when we go to commit the transaction.

Looking at the code in Listing 7.10, you can see that we're passing a ZCL_BOOK instance to the REGISTER_CHECK_AGENT() method right before we call method END() on the transaction object. At runtime, this causes the Transaction Service to execute the IF_OS_CHECK~IS_CONSISTENT() method on the ZCL_BOOK instance before committing the transaction. As you would expect, this method returns false in this case because we have purposefully commented out the section of the code that assigns authors to the book. Consequently, the Transaction Service raises an exception of type CX_OS_CHECK_AGENT_FAILED to alert the client that the transactional resources are in an inconsistent state.

```
METHOD create_book.
  TRY.
    ...
    CALL METHOD zca_book=>agent->create_persistent
      EXPORTING
        i_isbn             = '9781592290796'
        i_publication_date = '20070315'
        i_publisher        = lo_publisher
        i_title            =
          'ABAP Objects: ABAP Programming in NetWeaver'
      RECEIVING
        result             = lo_book.

*   Assign the authors to the book:
    "lo_book->add_author( lo_author1 ).
    "lo_book->add_author( lo_author2 ).

*   Register a check agent with the transaction:
    lo_trans->register_check_agent( lo_book ).

*   Commit the transaction:
    lo_trans->end( ).
  CATCH cx_os_check_agent_failed.
    "Deal with check agent errors here...
  CATCH cx_root.
  ENDTRY.
ENDMETHOD.
```

**Listing 7.10** Working with Check Agents

For complex transactions, it's a good idea to use check agents as a final validation gate before committing a transaction. In the simple book creation example considered in this section, it made sense to implement the `IF_OS_CHECK` interface in class `ZCL_BOOK`. However, normally you'll want to create a separate check agent that implements all of the relevant validations independently of any particular transactional resource.

## 7.4 Implementing Locking with the Enqueue Service

As you learned in Section 7.1, Introduction to the ACID Transaction Model, transactions must be executed in isolation to avoid potentially catastrophic data corruption issues, and so on. One way to guarantee isolation in transactions is to ensure that critical resources remain *locked* throughout the course of the transaction. In this way, a transaction can be executed in a vacuum without having to worry about external tampering. In this section, we introduce you to the *SAP Lock Concept* and show you how to use lock objects to implement logical locking of transactional resources.

### 7.4.1 Introduction to the SAP Lock Concept

Normally, whenever we talk about transactional resources in ABAP, we're talking about records in ABAP Dictionary tables. Given this, you might be wondering why a custom locking concept is needed because modern relational database management systems (RDBMS) have sophisticated locking mechanisms available out of the box. The short answer to this question centers on the *scope* and *duration* of the lock.

As you may recall from Section 7.1, Introduction to the ACID Transaction Model, an SAP LUW may span multiple dialog steps (and consequently, multiple database LUWs). Because RDBMS locking concepts are tightly integrated into the database LUW concept, they are insufficient for implementing locking for transactions encapsulated inside of an SAP LUW. Consequently, SAP introduced its own custom locking scheme known as the *SAP Lock Concept*.

The SAP Lock Concept is based on a core service provided as part of the central instance in an ABAP system: the enqueue server. The enqueue server (or *lock server*) keeps track of lock requests in a centralized lock table. Work processes on SAP NetWeaver AS ABAP instances can access the enqueue server via a standard API. In Section 7.4.3, Programming with Locks, we'll explain how to interact with this API to lock and unlock objects. However, before we do so, we must first learn about *lock objects*.

### 7.4.2 Defining Lock Objects

A lock object is an ABAP Dictionary object that represents a kind of logical lock for one or more tables. To understand how lock objects work, it's useful to see how they are defined. To demonstrate this, let's look at how we would create a lock object for the ZTCA_BOOKS table described in Chapter 6, Database Programming.

1. Lock objects are created in the ABAP Dictionary. To create a lock object, navigate to Transaction SE11, and select the Lock Object radio button. Then, enter a name for the lock object, and click on the Create button. Figure 7.18 shows how we're creating a new lock object called EZLCK_BOOKS.[1]

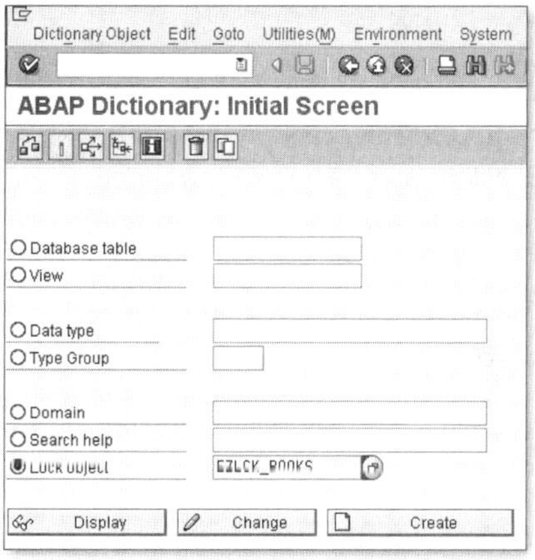


**Figure 7.18** Creating a Lock Object — Part 1

2. In the Maintain Lock Object perspective, you need to provide a description for the lock object in the Short Description field.
3. Then, on the Tables tab, you must select a primary table for the lock object. In this case, we want to choose the ZTCA_BOOKS table (see Figure 7.19).

1 Lock object names are prefixed with an "E". If you try to create something like "ZLCK_BOOKS," the ABAP Dictionary editor will issue a warning and prompt you for an access key even though you're using the normal "Z" prefix for the customer namespace.

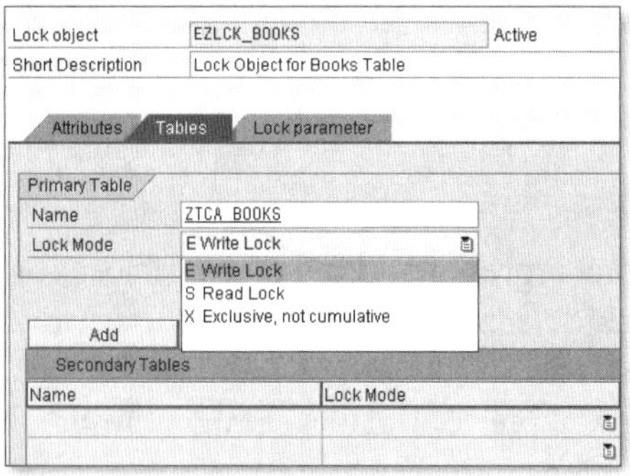


**Figure 7.19** Creating a Lock Object — Part 2

4. After you specify a primary table name, you must select a lock mode in the Lock Mode dropdown list shown in Figure 7.19. Table 7.6 describes the available lock modes in more detail.

| Type of Lock | Lock Mode | Meaning |
|---|---|---|
| Exclusive | E | This kind of lock protects the locked object against any other kind of lock request. The lock owner can reset the lock as needed. In other words, this lock type supports *lock accumulation* for a lock owner. |
| Shared | S | This kind of lock enables a kind of *read-only* access for an object. Multiple users can have a shared lock on the same object simultaneously; however, requests for exclusive locks are denied when shared locks exist for an object. |
| Exclusive (but not cumulative) | X | This kind of lock is similar to the exclusive lock, except that the owner can't accumulate additional locks after the lock is created. |

**Table 7.6** Lock Modes for Lock Objects

5. On the Lock Parameter tab, you view the lock parameters chosen for the lock object. These parameters are selected based upon the primary key of the selected primary table (see Figure 7.20).
6. Finally, you can save and activate your lock object by clicking on the Activate button (see Figure 7.20).

Lock objects like `EZLCK_BOOKS` behave similarly to database lock objects in the sense that they only lock records in a particular database table (in this case, `ZTCA_BOOKS`).

However, lock objects are capable of managing records in multiple tables as long as those tables maintain foreign key relationships that adhere to certain rules. You can learn more about these rules in the SAP Library documentation available online at *http://help.sap.com*. Search for "Lock Objects."

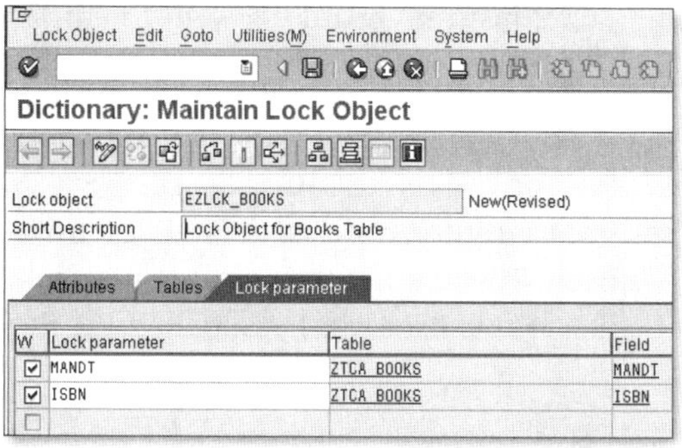


**Figure 7.20** Creating a Lock Object — Part 3

## 7.4.3 Programming with Locks

Now that you know how to create lock objects, you might be wondering how you use them to program locks in your ABAP programs. When you activate a lock object, the system generates two function modules behind the scenes: an *enqueue module* and a *dequeue module*. You can determine the names of these modules for your lock object by selecting GOTO • LOCK MODULES in the menu bar of the ABAP Dictionary. Figure 7.21 shows the generated lock modules for the EZLCK_BOOKS lock object.

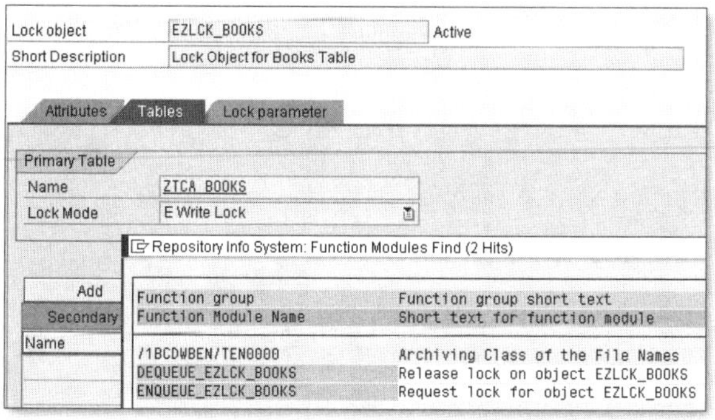


**Figure 7.21** Viewing Generated Lock Modules in Transaction SE11

To create a lock for a particular object, you call the ENQUEUE_{Lock Object} function; to delete a lock, you call the analog DEQUEUE_{Lock Object} function. The sample report program ZLOCKDEMO shown in Listing 7.11 demonstrates how to call these modules for the EZLCK_BOOKS lock object. In both cases, the key for the lock/unlock operation is the ISBN of the book in question. This is important because we don't want to lock the entire table; just the record we want to edit in a transaction.

Looking at the code in Listing 7.11, you'll notice that we've implemented some logic to test the results of a lock request after the call to the ENQUEUE_EZLCK_BOOKS function module. If this function passes back a return code value of 1, then we know that a *foreign lock* exception has occurred. This implies that another user currently has possession of the lock. The name of this user can be obtained via the system message variable SY-MSGV1.

```
REPORT zlockdemo.
PARAMETERS:
  p_isbn TYPE ztca_books-isbn.

START-OF-SELECTION.
* Try to lock the selected book:
  CALL FUNCTION 'ENQUEUE_EZLCK_BOOKS'
    EXPORTING
      isbn           = p_isbn
    EXCEPTIONS
      foreign_lock   = 1
      system_failure = 2
      others         = 3.

* Test the results:
  CASE sy-subrc.
    WHEN 0.
      WRITE: / 'Lock obtained successfully.'.
    WHEN 1.
      WRITE: / 'The book with ISBN #', p_isbn,
               'is locked by user', sy-msgv1.
    WHEN OTHERS.
      WRITE: / 'Could not obtain lock for ISBN #', p_isbn.
  ENDCASE.

* Execute the transaction to update the book here...
```

```
* Unlock the book as soon as we are done with it:
  CALL FUNCTION 'DEQUEUE_EZLCK_BOOKS'
    EXPORTING
      isbn = p_isbn.
```

**Listing 7.11** Programming with Enqueue/Dequeue Functions

### 7.4.4 Integration with the SAP Update System

As you might expect, the SAP Lock Concept is tightly integrated with the SAP update system. Collectively, these two features of SAP NetWeaver AS ABAP provide for highly sophisticated transaction processing capabilities. For the most part, these two services interoperate harmoniously. However, one thing you have to be mindful of when working with these two services is that the ownership of the lock can be become blurry if you're not careful.

Each `ENQUEUE_{Lock Object}` function module defines a parameter called `_SCOPE` that determines the owner of the lock. Table 7.7 describes the types of values that you can specify for the `_SCOPE` parameter. By default, the `_SCOPE` parameter is configured with a value of `2`.

| Scope Value | Description |
|---|---|
| 1 | This value implies that the lock belongs to the dialog owner that created the lock. The lock can be removed explicitly via a call to the corresponding dequeue function, or implicitly at the end of the transaction. |
| 2 | This value implies that the lock belongs to the update task. In this case, the lock is implicitly removed by the update task after all of the update function modules are completed. The lock can also be removed by the `ROLLBACK WORK` statement. |
| 3 | This value implies that the lock is mutually owned by the dialog owner and the update owner. In this case, the lock is removed when the last of the two owners releases the lock (typically the update task). |

**Table 7.7** Scope Values for a Lock Object

### 7.4.5 Lock Administration

Occasionally, you may run into a situation where a lock isn't removed correctly due to a program error, and so on. In these cases, you can manage locks directly via Transaction SM12. Figure 7.22 shows the initial screen of this transaction.

Here, you can enter the relevant lock parameters and click the List button to see the current entries.

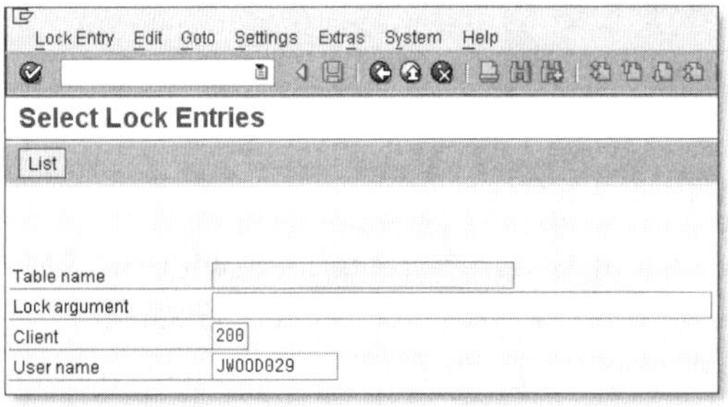


**Figure 7.22** Initial Screen of Transaction SM12

Figure 7.23 shows the Lock Entry List screen from which you can manage individual lock entries. In the rare case that you need to remove a lock directly, you can do so by selecting the lock entry and clicking on the Delete button.

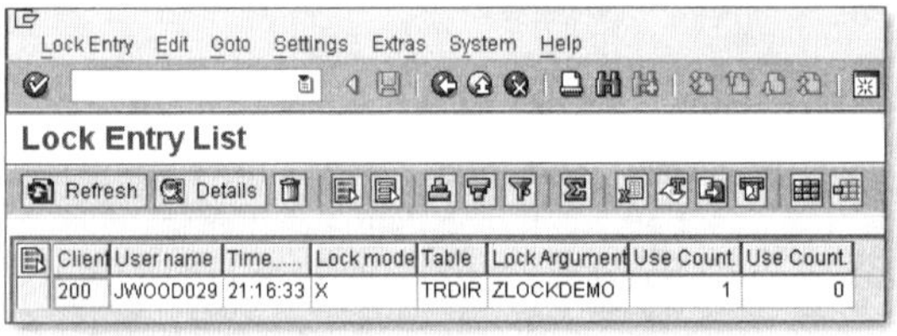


**Figure 7.23** Managing Lock Entries in Transaction SM12

Due to the potentially dangerous side effects associated with direct maintenance of lock entries, access to Transaction SM12 should be granted with caution. Few users ever have access to this transaction in a productive environment.

## 7.5 Tracking Changes with Change Documents

In a perfect world, every transaction would execute without a hitch. However, because we don't live in a perfect world, we must brace ourselves for the eventuality that some kind of error is going to occur. And when it does, we need to be able to react accordingly. In these situations, it's vitally important that we have an audit trail of changes so that we can retrace the steps carried out by the transaction and figure out what went wrong. SAP lets you track this kind of information using *change documents*. In this section, we introduce you to the concept of change document objects and show you how they can be used to track changes in transactions.

### 7.5.1 What Are Change Documents?

A change document is a special kind of log entry that records changes to business objects in the system. These log entries include a header record that provides audit trail information such as who made the change, when the change was made, and so on. They also contain individual line items that track record deletions, changes to fields, and more. In Section 7.5.4, Programming with Change Documents, we'll see that this information can be accessed via a common API.

Change documents are registered independently from the actual database changes using a *change document object*. A change document object provides a logical grouping of the tables that make up a business object. For example, the standard change document object `ORDER` encapsulates changes made to tables related to networks and production orders in an SAP ERP system (i.e., `AUFK`, `AFKO`, `AFPO`, etc.). This grouping gives rise to an API that makes it easy to track changes at the business object level rather than in individual tables.

### 7.5.2 Creating Change Document Objects

As you learned in the previous section, change documents are created using change document objects. In this section, we show you how to create change document objects. As a basis for our discussion, we demonstrate how to create a change document object for the `ZTCA_PUBLISHERS` table introduced in Chapter 6, Database Programming.

1. Change document objects are maintained in Transaction SCDO. Figure 7.24 shows the overview screen of the change document object editor. As you can see, there are many change document objects provided as part of the standard installation.
2. To create a new change document object, click on the Create button on the overview screen (see Figure 7.24). This opens up a dialog box where you must enter a name for the change document object. Here, you also have the option of specifying a custom namespace as needed (see Figure 7.25). Click the Continue button to proceed.

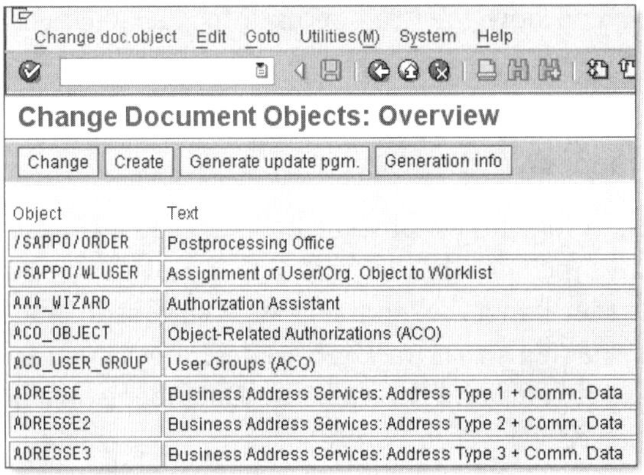


**Figure 7.24** Overview Screen of Transaction SCDO

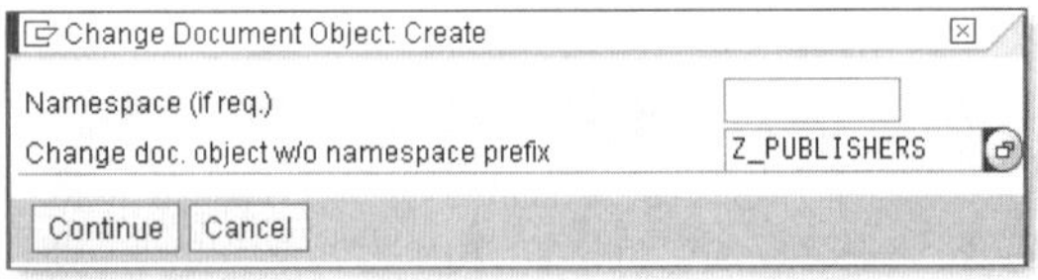


**Figure 7.25** Creating a Change Document Object — Part 1

3. Figure 7.26 shows the subsequent input mask that pops up during the change document object creation process. On this screen, provide the following information:
   - In the Name of Table column, select the ABAP Dictionary table(s) that you want to track as part of your change document object. For instance, in Figure 7.26, we have selected the `ZTCA_PUBLISHERS` table.
   - In the Copy as Internal Tab. column, select whether or not you want to pass in changes to a particular table in the form of an internal table. This option is used to track line item information for a business object, and so on.
   - The Doc. for Individual Fields at Delete column is used to identify whether or not you want to track record deletions on a field-by-field basis. Otherwise, only a single change document item is created to track the deletion occurrence.
   - The Name of Ref. tab. column refers to the name of the reference table used to define currency/unit fields in the table.
   - In the Name of Old Field String column, you can enter an alternative structure for passing in change records to the change document object.

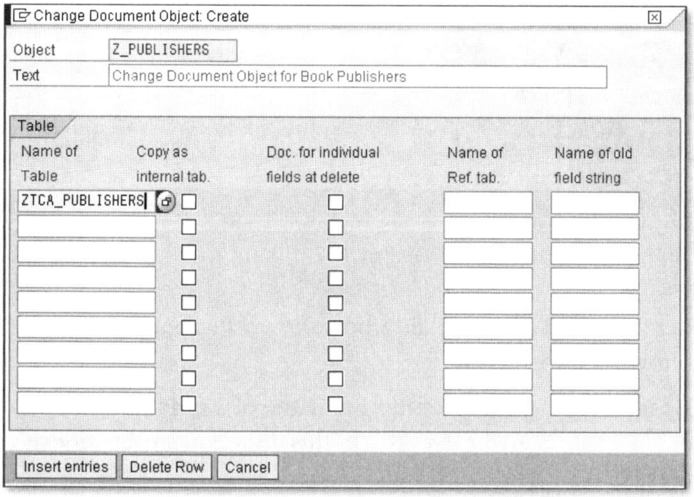


**Figure 7.26** Creating a Change Document Object — Part 2

4. After you've entered all of the tables that you want to track with the change document object, you can click on the Insert Entries button to confirm your changes (see Figure 7.26).
5. This brings you back to the overview screen shown in Figure 7.27. Here, you can click the Back button to complete the creation of the change document object. At this point, you're prompted to save your changes.

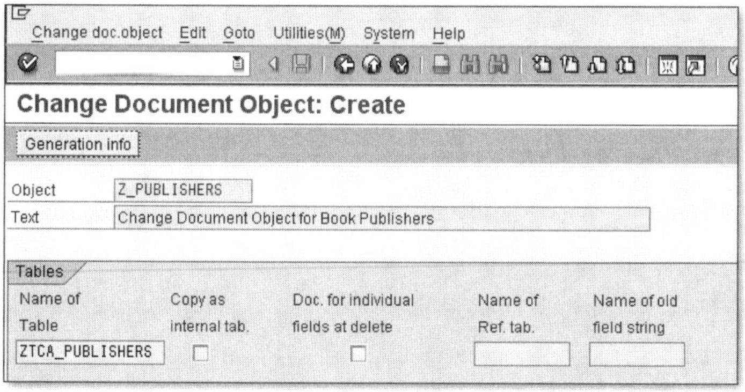


**Figure 7.27** Creating a Change Document Object — Part 3

6. After the change document is initially saved, you can generate the change document object update program module by clicking on the Generate Update Pgm. button shown in Figure 7.28.

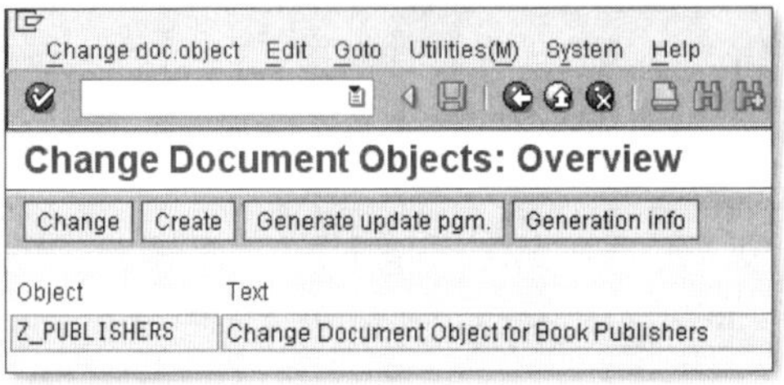


**Figure 7.28** Generating the Update Program Module — Part 1

7. In the ensuing Generate Update Pgm. dialog box shown in Figure 7.29, you must provide the following information:
   - In the Function Group field, you must enter the name of a function group in which the update module is to be stored. If this function group doesn't already exist, it is created.
   - The Fun. Mod. Structure Prefix field is used to define a prefix for generated transfer structures used to build the function module interface. This prefix is only used for internal table parameters.
   - The Error Message ID and Error Number fields refer to the message class/ number that you want the update module to use when issuing error messages. The default selections here are usually appropriate.
   - In the Processing Type group box, you have the option of determining how the change document object is saved. Normally, you want to keep the default Delayed Update setting here.

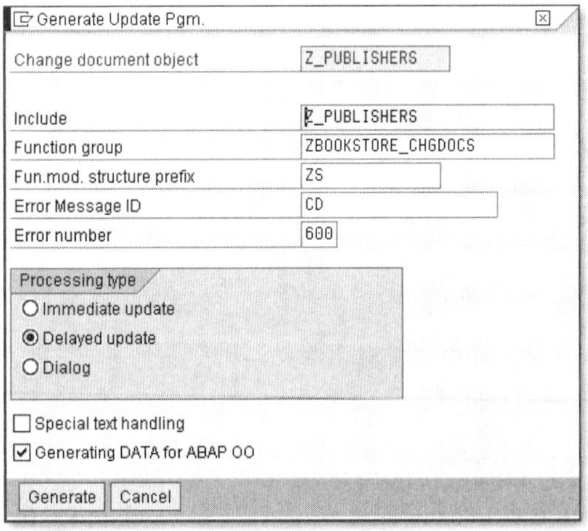


**Figure 7.29** Generating the Update Program Module — Part 2

- The Special Text Handling checkbox can be used to log long text changes, as needed.
- The Generating DATA for ABAP OO checkbox causes the declaration of the data to be transferred to use the `DATA` statement in lieu of the legacy `TABLES` statement. For more information about this option, see SAP Note 402805.

8. When you're satisfied with your entries, you can click on the Generate button to generate the update module (see Figure 7.29). Figure 7.30 shows the results of this generation process.

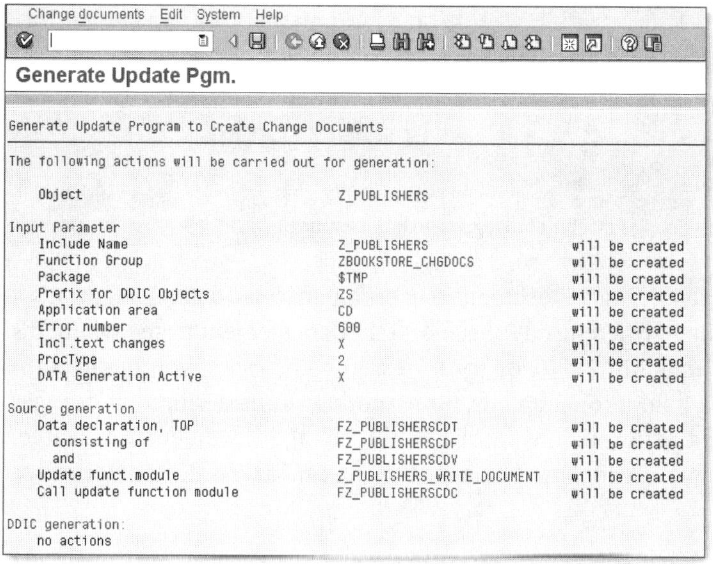


**Figure 7.30** Results of the Update Module Generation Process

Looking at the update module generation results in Figure 7.30, you can see that an update function module called `Z_PUBLISHERS_WRITE_DOCUMENT` was created. In Section 7.5.4, Programming with Change Documents, we explain how to use this function module to create change documents. However, before we do so, we need to briefly segue into another important topic when it comes to change document objects: How do you determine change-relevant fields?

### 7.5.3 Configuring Change-Relevant Fields

When you track changes to database records with change documents, there are certain fields that you probably don't want to keep track of. Therefore, by default, no field in a database table is marked as change relevant. Instead, you must explicitly declare your intentions to track changes to a field by marking the Change Document flag on that field's corresponding data element. Figure 7.31 shows how we've set this flag for the ZDE_PUBLISHER_NAME data element in the ABAP Dictionary (Transaction SE11).

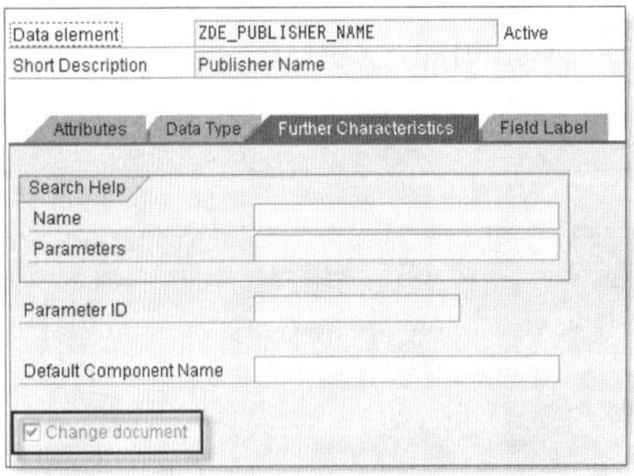


**Figure 7.31** Marking the Change Document Flag for a Data Element

Before you turn on the Change Document flag on a particular data element, it's a good idea to perform a "where-used" check on that data element to see where it's used elsewhere in other ABAP Dictionary tables. In some cases, you might want to track changes to a field in one table but not another. Considering that changes to a field are tracked as a separate record in the change document item table, turning this flag on for a widely used data element can have huge performance implications.

### 7.5.4 Programming with Change Documents

To demonstrate how to work with change document update modules, let's consider an example. The sample report ZCHGDOC_DEMO in Listing 7.12 contains a local class that is updating the region/country of the ZCL_PUBLISHER persistent object. Within the scope of this update process, we have included a call to the update module Z_PUBLISHERS_WRITE_DOCUMENT to track the changes. In this contrived example, we can assume that we're updating the publisher instance for "Galileo Press," and that a change document was generated when the publisher instance was first created.

For the most part, the code in class LCL_CHGDOC_DEMO should look familiar; we're using the Query Service to look up a ZCL_PUBLISHER persistent object and then updating it in compatibility mode. However, during this update process, we're also tracking the changes to the `REGION` and `COUNTRY` fields in data objects that have the structure type `ZTCA_PUBLISHERS`. Prior to committing the transaction, we pass this information to the `Z_PUBLISHERS_WRITE_DOCUMENT` module, which logs the changes. These changes are committed in the V2 update task whenever the `COMMIT WORK` statement is executed.

```
REPORT zchgdoc_demo.
CLASS lcl_chgdoc_demo DEFINITION.
  PUBLIC SECTION.
    CLASS-METHODS: main.
    METHODS:
      constructor IMPORTING im_publisher_name
                       TYPE zde_publisher_name
                  RAISING cx_os_object_not_found,
      change_publisher IMPORTING im_region TYPE regio
                                 im_country TYPE land1.

  PRIVATE SECTION.
    DATA: agent     TYPE REF TO zca_publisher,
          publisher TYPE REF TO zcl_publisher.
ENDCLASS.

CLASS lcl_chgdoc_demo IMPLEMENTATION.
  METHOD main.
*   Method-Local Data Declarations:
    DATA: lo_chgdoc_demo TYPE REF TO lcl_chgdoc_demo.

*   Process the change document demonstration:
    TRY.
*     Create an instance of the test driver class:
      CREATE OBJECT lo_chgdoc_demo
        EXPORTING
          im_publisher_name = 'Galileo Press%'.

*     Change the selected publisher record:
      lo_chgdoc_demo->change_publisher(
        im_region = '05'
        im_country = 'DE' ).
    CATCH cx_root.
      "Exception handling goes here...
    ENDTRY.
  ENDMETHOD.
```

```
  METHOD constructor.
*   Method-Local Data Declarations:
    DATA: lo_query_mgr  TYPE REF TO if_os_query_manager,
          lo_query      TYPE REF TO if_os_query,
          lt_publishers TYPE osreftab.
    FIELD-SYMBOLS:
      <lfs_publisher> LIKE LINE OF lt_publishers.

*   Build a query to look up the selected publisher:
    lo_query_mgr = cl_os_system=>get_query_manager( ).
    lo_query =
      lo_query_mgr->create_query(
        i_filter = 'PUBLISHER_NAME LIKE PAR1' ).

*   Obtain a reference to the selected publisher:
    agent = zca_publisher=>agent.
    lt_publishers =
      agent->if_os_ca_persistency~get_persistent_by_query(
        i_query = lo_query
        i_par1  = im_publisher_name ).
    READ TABLE lt_publishers INDEX 1
     ASSIGNING <lfs_publisher>.
    IF sy-subrc EQ 0.
      me->publisher ?= <lfs_publisher>.
    ELSE.
      RAISE EXCEPTION TYPE cx_os_object_not_found.
    ENDIF.
  ENDMETHOD.

  METHOD change_publisher.
*   Method-Local Data Declarations:
    DATA: lv_object_id     TYPE cdhdr-objectid,
          ls_new_publisher TYPE ztca_publishers,
          ls_old_publisher TYPE ztca_publishers.

*   Here, we want to change the location information on
*   selected publisher:
    TRY.
*     Copy the current values over to the change document
*     update record:
      ls_old_publisher-publisher_id =
        agent->if_os_ca_service~get_oid_by_ref( publisher ).
      ls_old_publisher-publisher_name =
```

```
          publisher->get_publisher_name( ).
        ls_old_publisher-region = publisher->get_region( ).
        ls_old_publisher-country = publisher->get_country( ).

        ls_new_publisher = ls_old_publisher.

*       Update the publisher persistent attributes:
        me->publisher->set_region( im_region ).
        me->publisher->set_country( im_country ).

        ls_new_publisher-region = publisher->get_region( ).
        ls_new_publisher-country = publisher->get_country( ).

*       Invoke the change document update module:
        lv_object_id = ls_old_publisher-publisher_id.

        CALL FUNCTION 'Z_PUBLISHERS_WRITE_DOCUMENT'
          EXPORTING
            objectid            = lv_object_id
            tcode               = sy-tcode
            utime               = sy-uzeit
            udate               = sy-datum
            username            = sy-uname
            n_ztca_publishers   = ls_new_publisher
            o_ztca_publishers   = ls_old_publisher
            upd_ztca_publishers = 'U'.

*       Commit the changes:
        COMMIT WORK.
      CATCH cx_root.
      ENDTRY.
  ENDMETHOD.
ENDCLASS.

START-OF-SELECTION.
* Delegate the core functionality to the test driver class:
  lcl_chgdoc_demo=>main( ).
```

**Listing 7.12** Working with Change Document Update Modules

To verify that the change documents were actually written to the database, we can look at the ABAP Dictionary tables CDHDR and CDPOS, respectively. For example,

Figure 7.32 and Figure 7.33 contain examples of change document records created by the ZCHGDOC_DEMO program contained in Listing 7.12.

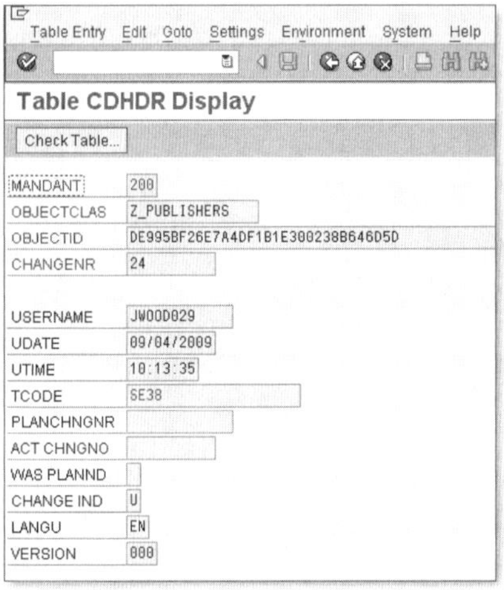


**Figure 7.32** Viewing Change Documents in Table CDHDR

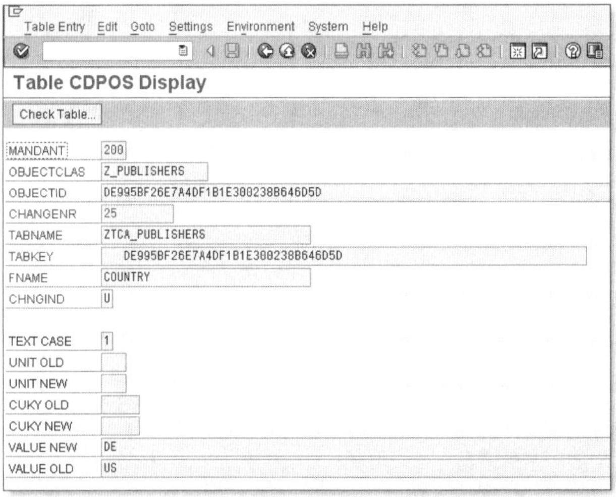


**Figure 7.33** Viewing Change Documents in Table CDPOS

We can also re-read the change document(s) using the standard function module CHANGEDOCUMENT_READ. For more information about how to use this API module, read the Function Module Documentation for this function in the Function Builder transaction.

## 7.6 Summary

This chapter covered a lot of ground quickly, demonstrating quite a few different techniques that you can use to create reliable transactions. When used properly, these methods can go a long way toward ensuring that programs gracefully react to unforeseen pitfalls. In the next chapter, we take a look at XML processing functionality available in ABAP.

# PART III
# Meals to Go

*To share recipes with one another, chefs must agree on a standard for quantifying measurements, and so on. Similarly, computer programmers must reach agreement on the structure of messages that are exchanged. As a meta-markup language used to define structured documents, XML has quickly become the "lingua franca" for information exchange in the IT industry. In this chapter, we explain how to work with XML using ABAP-based technologies.*

# 8 XML Processing in ABAP

In Chapter 5, Working with Files, you learned that software engineers organize the contents of files by defining *file types*. Here, a developer is free to arrange the layout of the file in any way he sees fit. However, when it comes to data exchange, this freedom comes with a price. To be able to work with a particular file type, you must have intimate knowledge of how that file is structured. With literally millions of file types to choose from, it's simply not feasible to reliably transfer data between systems without some form of standardization.

Since the late 1990s, the *Extensible Markup Language* (XML) has emerged as the de facto standard for defining the exchange of structured data over the Internet. In addition, its use has also proliferated into various other application domains, including content management, system configuration, and web development. Given the widespread adoption rate of XML-based technology, it's vital that you understand how to work with XML. Therefore, in this chapter, we show you how to use some of the various tools that make it easy to process XML using ABAP.

## 8.1 Introduction to XML

Before you can begin to appreciate the power of XML, it's important to first understand exactly what it is and what it isn't. When you get right down to it, XML is simply a standard that can be used to structure and organize various types of data. At first, this may seem underwhelming because XML doesn't really *do anything* in and of itself. However, its power lies in the types of applications it makes possible.

Like any good standard, XML has helped guide software vendors toward developing many useful tools that have made it much easier to solve some very complex problems. The following sections provide an introduction to XML and its syntax.

### 8.1.1 What Is XML?

XML is a standard endorsed by the W3C[1] that can be used to define the format of text-based documents. As such, XML is classified as a *meta-markup language*. If you aren't familiar with the concept of markup languages, then this definition requires some explanation. A *markup language* is used to *mark up* a document with instructions that define how its content is organized, formatted, and so on. For example, the *Hypertext Markup Language* (HTML) uses special annotations called *tags* to specify the layout of content in a web browser. Figure 8.1 shows an example of some HTML markup. Here, you can see that HTML tags are defined using angle brackets (i.e., the < and > characters). These tags give semantic meaning to the content within the document. For instance, the `<head>` tag defines the *heading* of the HTML document, and the `<body>` tag outlines its *body*.

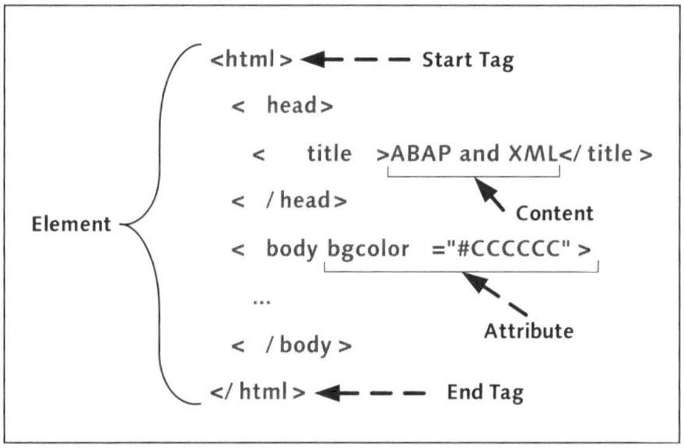


**Figure 8.1** Example of HTML Markup

Markup languages such as HTML have a predefined set of tags that can be used to structure a document in a certain way. Conversely, a meta-markup language such as XML doesn't define any particular markup. Rather, it describes a syntax that can be used to specify the creation of *other* markup languages such as XHTML, MathML, and so on. This is why XML is considered to be a *meta-markup language*.

1 W3C stands for *World Wide Web Consortium*. You can find out more about the W3C online at *www.w3.org*.

To facilitate the creation of various types of markup languages, the XML standard was designed to be extremely flexible. This flexibility allows you to customize the format of a document so that *form follows function*. In other words, because the XML standard has very little to say about the elements and content of a document, you don't have to try and bend an application data model to fit within the confines of some ill-fitting standard. Instead, you can define the document format using domain-specific terms that help to make the document *self-describing*. This characteristic of XML makes XML documents much easier to read and interpret for both humans and computers alike.

Much of the beauty of XML lies in its simplicity. Rather than defining a complex or proprietary binary file format, the designers of the XML standard defined an open, text-based format that provides support for multiple languages using Unicode. The openness of the XML standard simplifies the process of exchanging information between heterogeneous systems. This is perhaps best evidenced by the recent explosion of Web service technologies that use XML to define protocols for message exchange, and so on. You'll get a chance to get hands on with these technologies in Chapter 10, Web Services.

### 8.1.2 XML Syntax

Like HTML, XML is a derivative of the *Standard Generalized Markup Language* (SGML). Therefore, the syntax of XML markup is very similar to the HTML syntax shown earlier in Figure 8.1. However, unlike HTML, you aren't constrained to a finite number of tags such as `<table>`, `<div>`, and so on. Instead, you're free to define the tags (or *elements*) you need to best describe the data you're trying to characterize. For example, in Listing 8.1, we've defined an XML document that represents a set of business partners in a SAP ERP system. As you can see, the elements in this document have names that intuitively describe various attributes of a business partner (e.g., `<PartnerId>`, `<Name>`, etc.).

```
<?xml version="1.0" encoding="UTF-8"?>
<BusinessPartners>
  <BusinessPartner type="2">
    <PartnerId>1234567890</PartnerId>
    <Name>Bowdark Consulting, Inc.</Name>
    <CreationDate>2006-02-01</CreationDate>
  </BusinessPartner>
</BusinessPartners>
```

**Listing 8.1** Representing Business Partners Using XML

Surprisingly, there are relatively few syntax rules that you have to follow when creating XML documents. In the following subsections, we consider these rules by looking at the various components that make up an XML document. Everything else is just whitespace; something XML processors ignore.

### Elements

The content of an XML document is organized into a series of *elements*. An XML document must define a *root element* (or *document element*) that is the parent to all other elements. For example, in the XML document shown in Listing 8.1, the `<BusinessPartners>` element is the root element; all of the other elements defined within the document are *child elements* of the `<BusinessPartners>` element.

Listing 8.2 shows the basic syntax of an XML element. Here, just like HTML tags, an element is escaped using the angle bracket characters (i.e., the < and > characters). Everything between the element tags represents the body (or *content*) of the element. Here, you can embed additional elements such as the `<PartnerId>`, `<Name>`, and `<CreationDate>` elements nested underneath the `<BusinessPartner>` element in Listing 8.1, simple text, or both.

```
<element_name [attribute_name="attribute_value"...]>
   <!-- Element Content -->
</element_name>
```

**Listing 8.2** Basic Syntax for Defining an XML Element

Every element in XML must have an opening tag and a corresponding closing tag to be valid. The lone exception to this rule is the *empty element* whose syntax is shown in Listing 8.3.

```
<element_name [attribute_name="attribute_value"...] />
```

**Listing 8.3** Basic Syntax for Defining Empty Elements in XML

Within the angle brackets, an element must be named according to the following set of rules:

- An element name can consist of letters, numbers, and other characters.
- An element name can't contain any spaces.
- An element name can't begin with a number or punctuation character.
- An element name can't begin with the letters "xml" (i.e. "XML," "Xml," etc.).

Keep in mind that XML is case-sensitive, so the element names `<BUSINESSPARTNER>` and `<businesspartner>` aren't the same. Typical convention is to define element names using *CamelCase notation*. Here, the first letter in each word within a compound word is capitalized, such as `<BusinessPartner>`.

### Attributes

When processing XML documents, it's often helpful to access certain characteristics of an element in a format that is easy to read and work with. For example, in the business partner example from Listing 8.1, notice that the `<BusinessPartner>` element also contains a name-value pair that identifies the business partner *type*. This name-value pair is referred to as an *attribute* in XML. Listing 8.4 shows the syntax that you use to define an attribute for a given element. Here, each attribute must be given a name that is unique within the given element, as well as a value. Attribute values are surrounded by single quotes (') or double quotes ("). Technically, there are no limits with regards to the number of attributes you can define for a given element; however, a general rule of thumb is to keep the amount of attributes down to a manageable number (usually no more than four or five).

```
<element_name attribute_name="attribute_value"...>
```

**Listing 8.4** Basic Syntax for Defining an Attribute in XML

Generally speaking, there is no hard and fast rule that you can use to determine when to use an attribute instead of a child element. For instance, in the business partner example from Listing 8.1, we could have just as easily defined a child element called `<Type>` to capture the information stored in the `type` attribute. In many respects, this is merely a matter of preference. However, attributes do offer some advantages in certain situations. For example, if the business partner document shown in Listing 8.1 contained many business partners, we could use the `type` attribute in a query to find all business partners of a particular type. You'll see an example of this in Section 8.3, Transforming XML Using XSLT.

### Processing Instructions

Normally, most XML documents begin with an optional XML declaration that specifies the version of XML used to create the document as well as the character-encoding scheme of the document. An XML declaration is an example of an *XML processing instruction*. Processing instructions are used to provide information about the XML document to the applications that are processing them. As such, they are not part of the actual document content. Processing instructions begin and end with the character sequences (<?) and (?>), respectively. Listing 8.5 demonstrates this syntax with an XML declaration instruction.

```
<?xml version="1.0" encoding="UTF-8"?>
```

**Listing 8.5** An Example of a Processing Instruction in XML

### Comments

Unlike various types of binary message types, XML documents purely consist of text. This means that people can easily read XML documents. Of course, while XML documents are intended to be self-describing, it never hurts to pass along some additional information to the reader. This information can be captured in the form of a comment. Listing 8.6 shows the syntax used to define a comment in XML. The comment text within the (<!--) and (-->) characters can span multiple lines as needed. At runtime, the XML processor ignores the comments.

```
<!-- Comment Text -->
```

**Listing 8.6** Defining Comments in XML

### Entity References

As you've seen, certain characters have a special meaning in XML. For instance, the angle bracket characters (< and >) are used to mark the boundaries of an element. In some cases, however, we may need to embed these special characters somewhere inside the text content of the XML document. For example, consider the XML markup used to describe a material shown in Listing 8.7. In the `<LongDescription>` element, notice that the < character is used to specify certain tolerances for the material. As you might expect, the system complains whenever you try to process this document because it can't match a closing tag with each opening element tag.

```
<Material id="12345">
  <Description>Bolt</Description>
  <LongDescription>
    If hole positional tolerance < 0.03...
  </LongDescription>
</Material>
```

**Listing 8.7** Example Showing Special Character Issues with XML

To avoid the kinds of errors shown in Listing 8.7, you must *escape* special characters in XML using *entity references*. Table 8.1 shows the predefined entity references in XML. To correct the processing error from Listing 8.7, you must replace the <

character with the < entity reference. As you process XML, it's good to get into the habit of applying a conversion routine to plain text content that is being added to an XML document to escape special characters with entity references.

| Special Character | Entity Reference | Description |
|---|---|---|
| < | < | Less Than |
| > | > | Greater Than |
| & | & | Ampersand |
| ' | ' | Apostrophe |
| " | " | Quotation Mark |

**Table 8.1** Predefined Entity References in XML

### 8.1.3 Defining XML Documents Using XML Schema

Much of the HTML markup published on the Web doesn't conform to HTML syntax rules. Consequently, manufacturers of modern web browsers have been forced to integrate clever logic into their applications to interpret *broken HTML*. Such intelligence is made possible due to the fixed nature of HTML markup. Here, a browser can make educated guesses about what is missing based on opening tags, sequence, and so on. Unfortunately, the same sort of processing logic can't be applied to XML documents because their markup is unknown to the XML processor. Therefore, XML processors strictly enforce XML syntax rules. XML documents that follow the syntax rules described in Section 8.1.2, XML Syntax, are considered to be *well formed*.

Defining well-formed XML is a first step in enabling the exchange of XML data between systems. However, for another system to interpret a message, that system must also know how the document is organized. This descriptive information is captured in the form of an *XML schema* document. Here, the term "schema" refers to the format or outline of the content within an XML document. Schema languages are used to place *constraints* on documents to make sure that they are *valid* according to an agreed-on standard. For example, many industry sectors are using XML schema languages to define standard formats for various common EDI document types (e.g., invoices, sales orders, etc.).

Two of the more popular languages used to define XML schemas are the *Document Type Definition* (DTD) and *XML Schema* languages. Due to its more advanced capabilities, the XML Schema language has surpassed the DTD language as the standard for defining XML schemas. Though the description of the syntax of XML Schema documents is outside the scope of this book, a sample schema for the business partner document from Listing 8.1 is shown in Listing 8.8.

```
<?xml version="1.0" encoding="UTF-8"?>
<xsd:schema xmlns:xsd="http://www.w3.org/2001/XMLSchema"
            xmlns:tns="http://www.sap-press.com"
            targetNamespace="http://www.sap-press.com">
  <!-- Definition of "BusinessPartners" root element" -->
  <xsd:complexType name="BusinessPartners">
    <xsd:sequence>
      <!-- Definition of "BusinessPartner" element;
           Can occur many times -->
      <xsd:element name="BusinessPartner"
                   maxOccurs="unbounded">
        <xsd:complexType>
          <!-- Definition of child elements of
               "BusinessPartner" -->
          <xsd:sequence>
            <xsd:element name="PartnerId"
                         type="xsd:string" />
            <xsd:element name="Name" type="xsd:string" />
            <xsd:element name="CreationDate"
                         type="xsd:date" />
          </xsd:sequence>

          <!-- Definition of "Type" attribute -->
          <xsd:attribute name="Type" use="required">
            <xsd:simpleType>
              <xsd:restriction base="xsd:int">
                <!-- Person -->
                <xsd:enumeration value="1" />
                <!-- Organization -->
                <xsd:enumeration value="2" />
                <!-- Group -->
                <xsd:enumeration value="3" />
              </xsd:restriction>
            </xsd:simpleType>
          </xsd:attribute>
        </xsd:complexType>
      </xsd:element>
    </xsd:sequence>
  </xsd:complexType>
</xsd:schema>
```

**Listing 8.8** An XML Schema for Defining Business Partners in XML

Though XML Schema documents are produced in human-readable XML, they are normally input into specialized XML processing tools that can be used to validate documents or bind XML content to native programming language data objects. For more information about XML Schema and its uses, check out *www.w3.org/XML/Schema*.

## 8.2 Parsing XML with the iXML Library

Before you can begin processing an XML document in an ABAP program, you must first *parse* it. In this context, *parse* implies much more than just reading the raw content of an XML document into a character data object. XML documents have a distinct grammar, which means that their content can and should be organized according to that grammatical structure. Fortunately, this complex task can be performed quite easily using an XML parser.

SAP integrated an XML 1.0-compliant parser into the ABAP runtime environment beginning with release 4.6C of the Basis kernel (which was the predecessor of SAP NetWeaver AS ABAP). This parser, along with the ABAP Objects-based API that can be used to interface with it, makes up the *iXML library*. The iXML library allows you to process XML documents using the *Simple API for XML* (SAX) or *Document Object Model* (DOM) processing models. In addition, the iXML library also provides tools that make it easy to render output to various output types, and so on.

In the following sections, you'll learn how the iXML library is structured and see how it can be used to process XML documents. As a practical example, we apply these techniques toward the creation of an XML mapping program that can be used to develop an interface using SAP NetWeaver Process Integration (SAP NetWeaver PI).

### 8.2.1 Introducing the iXML Library API

The core of the iXML library is implemented using the C++ programming language, which has better support for raw stream-based I/O than ABAP. This implies that the ABAP portion of the iXML library is implemented using kernel methods[2] inside of an ABAP Objects class called `CL_IXML`. To minimize dependencies between this low-level functionality and the iXML library API, SAP developed a series of interfaces that provide an abstraction on top of an XML parser. This indi-

2 SAP uses kernel methods internally to call kernel functions implemented in C or C++.

rection makes it possible for SAP to swap out parser implementations down the road without impacting preexisting programs that use the iXML API. Figure 8.2 contains a UML class diagram that depicts the relationships between the various interfaces defined in the iXML library.

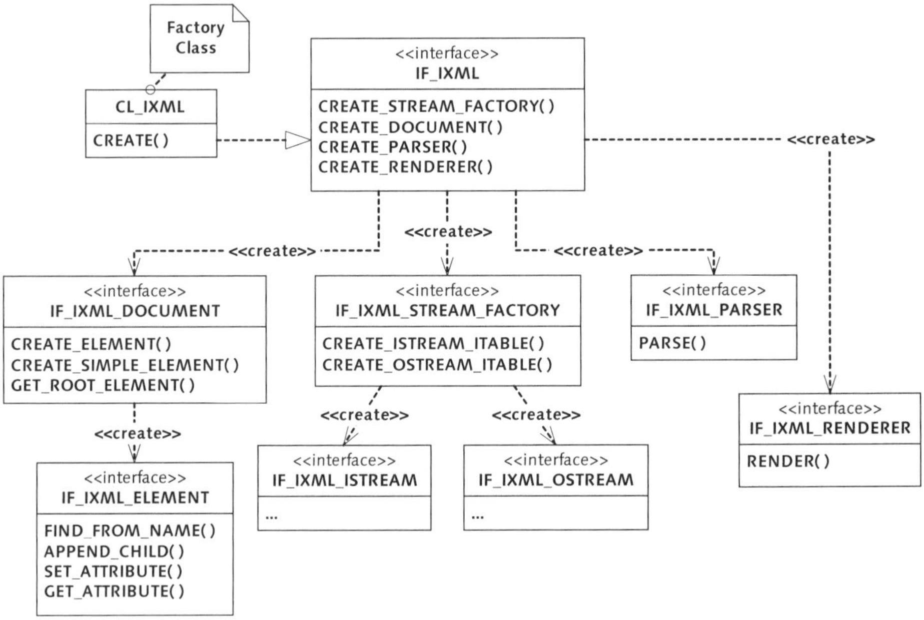


**Figure 8.2** UML Class Diagram for Core iXML Classes and Interfaces

As we mentioned earlier, the entry point into the iXML library is the `CL_IXML` class. This class contains a public factory class method called `CREATE()` that can be used to return an instance of a class that implements the `IF_IXML` interface. The `IF_IXML` interface defines a series of instance methods that return references to objects that you can use to parse an XML document, create a new XML document from scratch, or serialize a document to various output types. In Section 8.2.2, Working with DOM, you'll see how to use these objects to process XML according to the *Document Object Model* (DOM).

### 8.2.2 Working with DOM

In computer science, one of the most effective ways of representing hierarchical data is to store it in a tree-like data structure. Recognizing this, the W3C patterned its Document Object Model (DOM) after the tree data structure. As such, not only does the DOM describe how an XML document should be stored in memory, but it also defines common tree operations such as node traversal, searching, and manipulation of items within the tree (i.e., *grafting* and *pruning*).

Beginning with the root element, each element within an XML document is represented as a *node* within the tree model. Each node defines operations for accessing and manipulating child elements, attributes, and text content. It's also possible to perform context-based searches through child elements from a particular node within the tree.

To introduce you to the DOM implementation provided in the iXML library, let's consider an example. Listing 8.9 contains a report program called ZDOMDEMO that creates an XML document containing business partners like the one shown in Listing 8.1. The core functionality of this program is implemented in the local class LCL_DOM_PROCESSOR.

Before we delve into the implementation details of the methods defined in class LCL_DOM_PROCESSOR, let's glance ahead and look at the attributes it defines:

- The class attribute ixml_factory is an interface reference variable of type IF_IXML. We've named this attribute ixml_factory because it acts as a factory for creating references to various components within the iXML library. Because this object is defined as a singleton[3] inside the factory class CL_IXML, we've defined this attribute as a *static attribute* so that each instance of class LCL_DOM_PROCESSOR can share a single copy of it.
- The partners_doc instance attribute provides a reference to the DOM-based XML document that we're going to create as part of this demonstration. DOM-based documents are represented in the iXML library using the IF_IXML_DOCUMENT interface.
- The partners_node instance attribute stores a reference to the root element of the XML document (i.e., <BusinessPartners>). DOM elements in the iXML library are represented using the IF_IXML_ELEMENT interface.

```
REPORT zdomdemo.
CLASS lcl_dom_processor DEFINITION.
  PUBLIC SECTION.
    CLASS-METHODS:
      class_constructor,
```

3 The term *singleton* refers to objects that are created using the Singleton design pattern. This design pattern guarantees that only one instance of an object can exist at a time.

```
      main.

    METHODS:
      constructor,
      add_partner IMPORTING im_id   TYPE string
                            im_type TYPE i
                            im_name TYPE string
                            im_date TYPE d,
      show_document.

  PRIVATE SECTION.
    CLASS-DATA: ixml_factory TYPE REF TO if_ixml.

    DATA:
      partners_doc  TYPE REF TO if_ixml_document,
      partners_node TYPE REF TO if_ixml_element.
ENDCLASS.

CLASS lcl_dom_processor IMPLEMENTATION.
  METHOD class_constructor.
*   Retrieve a reference to the iXML factory:
    ixml_factory = cl_ixml=>create( ).
  ENDMETHOD.

  METHOD constructor.
*   Create a new DOM-based XML document:
    partners_doc = ixml_factory->create_document( ).

*   Create the root "BusinessPartners" element:
    partners_node =
      partners_doc->create_simple_element(
        name = 'BusinessPartners'
        parent = partners_doc ).
  ENDMETHOD.

  METHOD main.
*   Method-Local Data Declarations:
    DATA: lo_dom_processor TYPE REF TO lcl_dom_processor.

*   Create an instance of the test driver class:
    CREATE OBJECT lo_dom_processor.

*   Add a couple of partners to the list:
```

```
    lo_dom_processor->add_partner(
      im_id = '12345'
      im_type = 2
      im_name = 'Bowdark Consulting, Inc.'
      im_date = '20060201' ).

    lo_dom_processor->add_partner(
      im_id   = '23456'
      im_type = 2
      im_name = 'Simple Joys Photography'
      im_date = '20090615' ).

*   Display the resultant XML document on the screen:
    lo_dom_processor->show_document( ).
  ENDMETHOD.

  METHOD add_partner.
*   Method-Local Data Declarations:
    DATA: lo_partner_node  TYPE REF TO if_ixml_element,
          lv_type          TYPE string,
          lv_creation_date TYPE string.

*   Copy the parameters into string format:
    lv_type = im_type.
    CONCATENATE im_date+0(4) im_date+4(2) im_date+6(2)
           INTO lv_creation_date SEPARATED BY '-'.

*   Create a BusinessPartner node:
    lo_partner_node =
      partners_doc->create_simple_element(
        name = 'BusinessPartner'
        parent = partners_node ).

*   Set the "type" attribute on the BusinessPartner:
    lo_partner_node->set_attribute(
      name = 'Type'
      value = lv_type ).

*   Fill in the remaining information for the partner:
    partners_doc->create_simple_element(
      name = 'PartnerId'
      value = im_id
      parent = lo_partner_node ).
```

```
  partners_doc->create_simple_element(
   name = 'Name'
   value = im_name
   parent = lo_partner_node ).

  partners_doc->create_simple_element(
   name = 'CreationDate'
   value = lv_creation_date
   parent = lo_partner_node ).
 ENDMETHOD.

 METHOD show_document.
*  Display the XML document on the screen:
  CALL FUNCTION 'SDIXML_DOM_TO_SCREEN'
   EXPORTING
    document    = partners_doc
   EXCEPTIONS
    no_document = 1
    others      = 2.
 ENDMETHOD.
ENDCLASS.

START-OF-SELECTION.
 lcl_dom_processor=>main( ).
```

**Listing 8.9** Creating an XML Document Using DOM

Now that you've had a chance to digest the code in Listing 8.9, let's go back and examine each of the iXML library API calls in greater detail.

1. The first step is performed inside the `CLASS_CONSTRUCTOR()` method of class `LCL_DOM_PROCESSOR`. Here, we use the `CREATE()` factory method of the `CL_IXML` class to obtain a reference to the iXML library. Therefore, any instance of class `LCL_DOM_PROCESSOR` has all of the tools it needs to create XML documents before a programmer ever gets his hands on it.
2. Next, inside the `CONSTRUCTOR()` method of class `LCL_DOM_PROCESSOR`, we invoke the `CREATE_DOCUMENT()` method of the `ixml_factory` factory object to create a brand new DOM-based XML document and store its reference in the `partners_doc` instance attribute.
3. After the `partners_doc` attribute is initialized, we need to create the root `<BusinessPartners>` element. As you can see in Listing 8.9, we're using the `CREATE_`

SIMPLE_ELEMENT_NS() instance method of interface IF_IXML_DOCUMENT for this purpose. This method will generate the root element and return a reference to it in the form of an object reference that implements the IF_IXML_ELEMENT interface.

4. After the root element is defined, the process of creating the various elements inside the document is pretty much the same. Here, we simply use the CREATE_SIMPLE_ELEMENT_NS() method to create new elements and place them at the appropriate level in the hierarchy.
5. As you can see in the implementation of method ADD_PARTNER() in Listing 8.9, we're also defining the Type attribute using the SET_ATTRIBUTE_NS() method defined in interface IF_IXML_ELEMENT.
6. Finally, after the document is fully constructed, the ZDOMDEMO report program calls the helper method SHOW_DOCUMENT() to display the resultant XML document in a browser window. This helper method used the SDIXML_DOM_TO_SCREEN function module behind the scenes to render the XML output.

At this point, you should have a pretty good feel for how to create DOM-based XML documents using the iXML library. Therefore, let's move on and expand our horizons by learning how to parse and render these documents for more practical purposes. In the next section, you'll apply the concepts you've learned toward the creation of an ABAP-based XML mapping program that can be used to implement an interface scenario on the middleware platform of SAP NetWeaver PI.

### 8.2.3 Case Study: Developing XML Mapping Programs in ABAP

SAP NetWeaver Process Integration (SAP NetWeaver PI) is an enterprise application integration (EAI) tool that can be used to build cross-system business processes. With a wide array of adapters available out of the box, SAP NetWeaver PI can facilitate communication with many kinds of systems. As such, SAP NetWeaver PI can assume the role of "hub" in a hub-and-spoke architecture, brokering communication between disparate systems by defining sender/receiver endpoints known as *message interfaces*.

A message interface has an associated *message type* that defines the schema of the message being exchanged. Because SAP NetWeaver PI messages are based on XML, these schemas are naturally described using the XML Schema language introduced in Section 8.1.3, Defining XML Documents Using XML Schema. Most of the time, the message type of a sender interface is different from that of the receiver interface. Therefore, one of the most basic SAP NetWeaver PI development tasks is to create XML mapping programs. Here, you can choose from several kinds of development environments to create your mapping program:

- For developers who prefer not to get their hands dirty with XML, SAP NetWeaver PI provides a graphical mapping tool that can be used to implement basic mapping operations.
- Java developers can develop custom mapping programs using the Java programming language.
- Developers comfortable developing XML transformations using the XSLT language can develop an XSLT stylesheet and deploy it on either the SAP NetWeaver AS ABAP or SAP NetWeaver AS Java stacks.
- ABAP developers can develop custom mapping programs using the iXML library.

ABAP-based SAP NetWeaver PI mapping programs are implemented in the form of an ABAP Objects class. Internally, this class can use the iXML library to implement the XML mapping logic. To demonstrate how all this fits together, let's consider a mapping program that transforms the business partners XML document shown earlier in Listing 8.1 into the vendors document shown in Listing 8.10.

```
<?xml version="1.0" encoding="UTF-8"?>
<Vendors>
  <Vendor>
    <VendorNumber>1234567890</VendorNumber>
    <VendorName>Bowdark Consulting, Inc.</VendorName>
    <DateCreated>2006-02-01</DateCreated>
  </Vendor>
</Vendors>
```

**Listing 8.10** Target XML Document for SAP NetWeaver PI Mapping Program

To begin, we create a normal ABAP Objects class called `ZCL_PI_MAPPING_DEMO`. For this class to work inside the SAP NetWeaver PI mapping framework, it must implement the `IF_MAPPING` interface of package `SAI_MAPPING` as shown in Figure 8.3.

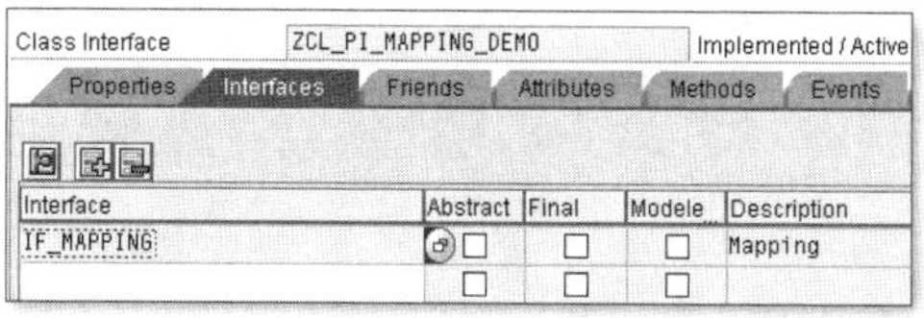


**Figure 8.3** Implementing the IF_MAPPING Interface

After you implement the IF_MAPPING interface, you can see that a new instance method called EXECUTE() has been added to the class' public interface. Figure 8.4 shows the signature of the IF_MAPPING~EXECUTE() method. For the purposes of this demonstration, we're primarily interested in the SOURCE and RESULT parameters, both of which are defined using the XSTRING data type. The use of the XSTRING data type implies that the source XML document will be received in the form of a stream of bytes. Similarly, after we've built the target vendors document, we have to *serialize* the result into an XSTRING data object.

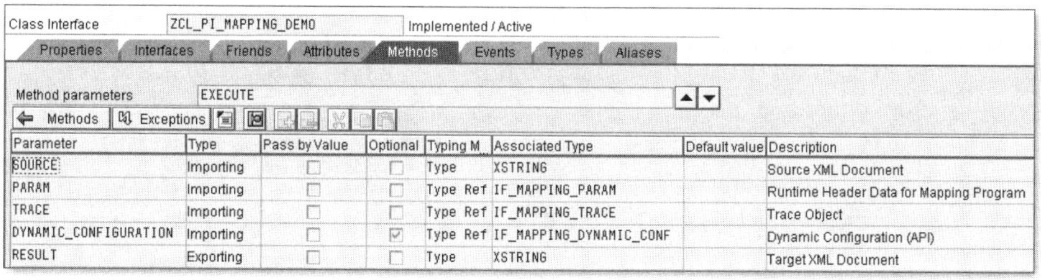


**Figure 8.4** Signature of Method IF_MAPPING~EXECUTE()

Listing 8.11 shows the implementation of the IF_MAPPING~EXECUTE() method. As you scan through the code, you'll notice that we're mapping the target XML document using the same API calls we used in Listing 8.9. However, before we can map the target vendor document, we must first *parse* the source business partner document so that we can extract the relevant data points using the DOM API. We investigate the parsing process in detail in a moment.

```
METHOD if_mapping~execute.
* Method-Local Data Declarations:
  DATA: lo_ixml_factory
          TYPE REF TO if_ixml,
        lo_stream_factory
          TYPE REF TO if_ixml_stream_factory,
        lo_istream
          TYPE REF TO if_ixml_istream,
```

```
        lo_parser
          TYPE REF TO if_ixml_parser,
        lo_source_doc
          TYPE REF TO if_ixml_document.

  DATA: lo_partners_elem
          TYPE REF TO if_ixml_element,
        lo_id_elem
          TYPE REF TO if_ixml_element,
        lo_name_elem
          TYPE REF TO if_ixml_element,
        lo_date_elem
          TYPE REF TO if_ixml_element.

  DATA: lv_vendor_no    TYPE string,
        lv_vendor_name  TYPE string,
        lv_date_created TYPE string.

  DATA: lo_target_doc
          TYPE REF TO if_ixml_document,
        lo_vendors_elem
          TYPE REF TO if_ixml_element,
        lo_vendor_elem
          TYPE REF TO if_ixml_element.

  DATA: lo_ostream
          TYPE REF TO if_ixml_ostream,
        lo_renderer
          TYPE REF TO if_ixml_renderer.

* Obtain a reference to the iXML factory object:
  lo_ixml_factory = cl_ixml=>create( ).

* Use the iXML factory to obtain a reference to the
* XML stream factory:
  lo_stream_factory =
    lo_ixml_factory->create_stream_factory( ).

* Pipe the source XML document onto an input stream:
  lo_istream =
    lo_stream_factory->create_istream_xstring( source ).

* Parse the source XML document:
```

```
  lo_source_doc =
    lo_ixml_factory->create_document( ).

  lo_parser =
    lo_ixml_factory->create_parser(
      stream_factory = lo_stream_factory
      istream        = lo_istream
      document       = lo_source_doc ).

  lo_parser->parse( ).

* Copy the relevant information from the source document:
  lo_partners_elem = l_source_doc->get_root_element( ).

  lo_id_elem =
    lo_partners_elem->find_from_name_ns(
      name = 'PartnerId' ).
  lv_vendor_no = lo_id_elem->get_value( ).

  lo_name_elem =
    lo_partners_elem->find_from_name_ns (
      name = 'Name' ).
  lv_vendor_name = lo_name_elem->get_value( ).

  lo_date_elem =
    lo_partners_elem->find_from_name_ns (
      name = 'CreationDate' ).
  lv_date_created = lo_date_elem->get_value( ).

* Now create the target document:
  lr_target_doc = lo_ixml_factory->create_document( ).

  lo_vendors_elem =
    lo_target_doc->create_simple_element_ns (
      name = 'Vendors'
      parent = lo_target_doc ).

  lo_vendor_elem =
    lo_target_doc->create_simple_element_ns (
      name = 'Vendor'
      parent = lo_vendors_elem ).

  lo_target_doc->create_simple_element_ns (
```

```
    name = 'VendorNumber'
    value = lv_vendor_no
    parent = lo_vendor_elem ).

  lo_target_doc->create_simple_element_ns (
    name = 'VendorName'
    value = lv_vendor_name
    parent = lo_vendor_elem ).

  lo_target_doc->create_simple_element_ns (
    name = 'DateCreated'
    value = lv_date_created
    parent = lo_vendor_elem ).

* Create an output stream to serialize the document:
  lo_ostream =
    lo_stream_factory->create_ostream_xstring( result ).

* Now, render the document to the output stream:
  lo_renderer =
    lo_ixml_factory->create_renderer(
      ostream  = lo_ostream
      document = lo_target_doc ).

  lo_renderer->render( ).
ENDMETHOD.                        " METHOD execute
```

**Listing 8.11** Implementing an ABAP Mapping Program Using iXML

Now that you've had a chance to digest the mapping code a little bit, let's take it apart and see what's going on underneath the hood:

1. Before we can even think about mapping XML, we first need to convert the incoming SOURCE parameter into a format that we can work with. Looking back at the signature of method IF_MAPPING~EXECUTE() in Figure 8.4, you can see that this parameter is defined as a byte string (i.e., type XSTRING). However, the PARSE() method of interface IF_IXML_PARSER is designed to work with an *input stream* (i.e., an object that implements the IF_IXML_ISTREAM interface). Therefore, our first step in the mapping process is to convert the raw contents of the SOURCE parameter into an input stream using an XML stream factory (based on interface IF_IXML_STREAM_FACTORY). We can use the CREATE_ISTREAM_XSTRING() method for this purpose.

2. Ultimately, the objective of the parsing process is to convert the raw XML stream into a DOM-based document. Therefore, before we actually parse the input document, we must create an instance of a DOM-based XML document and store a reference to it in the LO_SOURCE_DOC object reference variable.
3. The actual parsing process is controlled by an object that implements the IF_IXML_PARSER interface. A reference to the iXML parser can be obtained via the iXML factory method CREATE_PARSER(). Here, we pass the iXML library a reference to the input stream that we want to parse, as well as the target DOM-based document that will store the results. To parse the source document, we simply call the PARSE() method on the parser instance. Were this a production-worthy mapping program, we would implement some detailed exception-handling code after the PARSE() method to describe any errors that might have occurred during the parsing process. You can find detailed examples of such exception-handling code in the SAP Library documentation available online at *http://help.sap.com*. Here, perform a keyword search on the phrase "iXML ABAP Objects Jumpstart."
4. After the source document is parsed, we can extract the relevant information from it by invoking the GET_ROOT_ELEMENT() method on the LO_SOURCE_DOC object reference and then traversing the DOM-based tree using the FIND_FROM_NAME_NS() method defined in the IF_IXML_ELEMENT interface. When we locate the desired source elements, we can extract their values into string data objects using the GET_VALUE() method defined in the IF_IXML_ELEMENT interface.
5. After the relevant information has been extracted from the source document, we can build the target document using the same API methods described in Section 8.2.2, Working with DOM.
6. Finally, after the target document has been completely built out, we need to serialize it out to a byte string. To do so, we must use a *renderer object* that is an instance of an object that implements the IF_IXML_RENDERER interface. To create a renderer object, we must pass a reference to the DOM-based document to be serialized, as well as an *output stream* to serialize the document to. Here, the output stream is an object that implements the IF_IXML_OSTREAM interface. As you can see in Listing 8.11, we're generating an output stream for the RESULT byte string using the CREATE_OSTREAM_XSTRING() method defined in interface IF_IXML_STREAM_FACTORY. The actual rendering operation is performed by the RENDER() method of interface IF_IXML_RENDERER.

If you have an SAP NetWeaver PI instance that you can play with, you can test out this example code by developing a basic interface scenario. Alternatively, you might try to build a test driver program using the iXML library to simulate the execution of the mapping program via the SAP NetWeaver PI mapping engine.

### 8.2.4 Next Steps

By now you should have a feel for how to use the iXML library API to process XML documents. For a more thorough treatment of the iXML library as a whole, you can perform a keyword search using the term "iXML" in the SAP Help Portal available online at *http://help.sap.com*. Here, you can also find documentation that shows you how to parse an XML document event-based (i.e., using a SAX-like API), work with advanced node traversal operations, and so on.

In addition to the online help documentation, SAP also provides quite a bit of sample code in the `SIXML_TEST` package. Finally, we highly recommend Tobias Trapp's *XML Data Exchange Using ABAP* (SAP PRESS, 2006) as a general reference for all ABAP-based XML technologies.

## 8.3 Transforming XML Using XSLT

XML processing models such as DOM make it very easy to scan through and manipulate an XML document. However, if you need to copy the content of one XML document into another one that has a different schema, the process is somewhat tedious — as evidenced in Section 8.2.3, Case Study: Developing XML Mapping Programs in ABAP. The primary challenge here is that you have to account for the creation of all XML content when, in reality, only a fraction of the content is dynamic in nature. Ideally, it would be much more efficient if we could use a *template* to define the bulk of the static content and then weave in the dynamic content at runtime. Recognizing the need for a more economical development model, the W3C defined the *Extensible Stylesheet Language Transformations* (XSLT) language for this purpose.

In this section, we introduce you to the XSLT language and show you how to create and execute XSLT mapping programs in ABAP. Given the breadth of the XSLT language specification, it's not realistic for us to present a thorough treatment of XSLT here. Instead, we provide a basic introduction that you can use as a foundation for more advanced study. Two excellent resources are *XSLT Quickly* (Manning Publications, 2001) and *XML Data Exchange Using ABAP* (SAP PRESS, 2006).

### 8.3.1 What Is XSLT?

Initially, XSLT was positioned as a language that could be used to simplify the creation of HTML markup. Over time, it has evolved into a general-purpose language that can be used to perform all kinds of transformations. Regardless of the source and target content types, the process is essentially the same: an XSLT processor uses an XML document called a *stylesheet* as a template for transforming a source data object into a target data object. Here, even though the process is described as a *transformation*, the source data object isn't changed. Rather, its contents are used as a data source for building the target data object. Figure 8.5 illustrates this process as it relates to the transformation of XML documents.

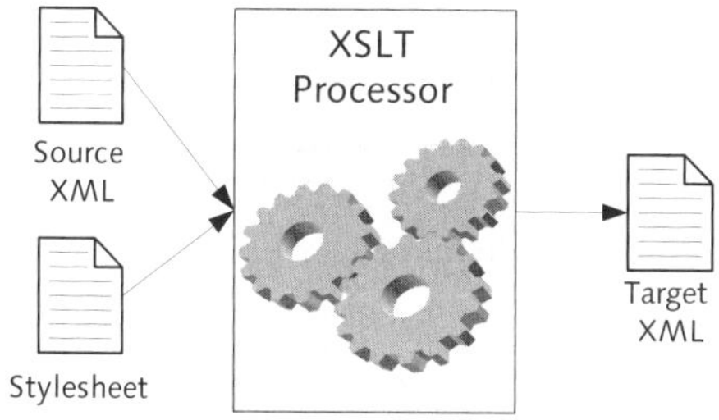


**Figure 8.5** Processing Model for an XSLT Processor

Unlike many conventional programming languages, XSLT uses a *declarative approach* that defines how the XSLT processor should handle particular nodes within the source data object. In XSLT parlance, these processing instructions are called *template rules*. A template rule blends static content with various types of functional expressions to build portions of the target data object. Collectively, an XSLT stylesheet combines these template rules together to define the transformation logic that the XSLT processor should apply toward the creation of the target data object. Next we explain how all of this fits together as we examine the structure of an XSLT stylesheet.

### 8.3.2 Anatomy of an XSLT Stylesheet

An XSLT stylesheet is an XML document whose vocabulary is defined by the W3C.[4] The root element of a stylesheet document can be either `<xsl:transform>` or `<xsl:stylesheet>`; use of one element versus the other is mostly a matter of

4 You can read the official XSLT specification online at *www.w3.org/TR/xslt*.

preference. Notice that both of these elements are prefixed using xsl. This prefix refers to a distinct *XML namespace* defined by the XSLT specification: *www.w3.org/1999/XSL/Transform*. XML namespaces are used to define unique names for elements or attributes in an XML document (much like namespaces in ABAP). The XSLT specification requires that all XSLT instructions be defined using the xsl namespace so that XSLT processors can recognize these elements at runtime. Listing 8.12 shows how the xsl namespace is defined in an XSLT stylesheet.

```
<xsl:transform version="1.0"
  xmlns:xsl="http://www.w3.org/1999/XSL/Transform"
  xmlns:sap="http://www.sap.com/sapxsl">
```

**Listing 8.12** Defining XML Namespaces

XSLT stylesheets are comprised of a series of template rules. Each template rule is designed to match a *pattern* in the source XML document. Match patterns are defined using a specialized XML query language called *XPath*. XPath expressions define a *location path* that is separated by slashes (/) into a series of *location steps*. According to the XPath specification,[5] a location step can be broken up into three parts:

- **Axes**
  Axes are used to orient the search toward a particular node direction within the XML tree structure. XPath defines many axes such as *child*, *parent*, *ancestor*, *descendant*, and so on. In XSLT, if no axis is selected explicitly, an XSLT processor assumes that the default child axis should be used.

- **Node Tests**
  Node tests identify the node (or nodes) to search for within the selected axis.

- **Predicates**
  Predicates are optional components that can be used to filter search results based upon the results of a logical expression. Predicates are used in much the same way that WHERE clauses are used in SQL.

Figure 8.6 shows an example of a location step used to find any descendant <BusinessPartner> elements whose type attribute has the value '2.'

5 You can read the official XPath specification online at *www.w3.org/TR/xpath*.

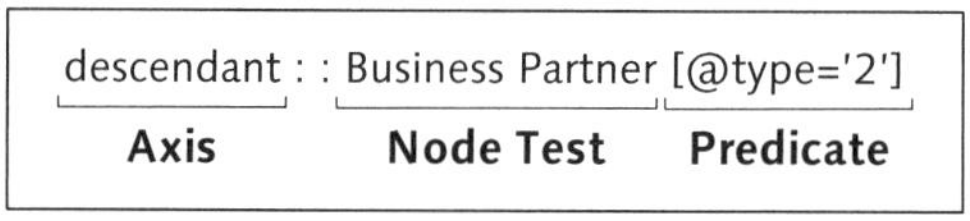


**Figure 8.6** Defining XPath Location Steps

When the XSLT processor finds a match for the specified query expression, the contents of a template rule are evaluated and added to the result tree. The contents of an XSLT template can include literal result elements as well as specialized XSLT instructions that can be used to copy data from the source document, define conditional processing logic, and so on. Like everything else in an XSLT stylesheet, these instructions are also specified using XML. Figure 8.7 shows how all of these pieces fit together inside of an XSLT stylesheet.

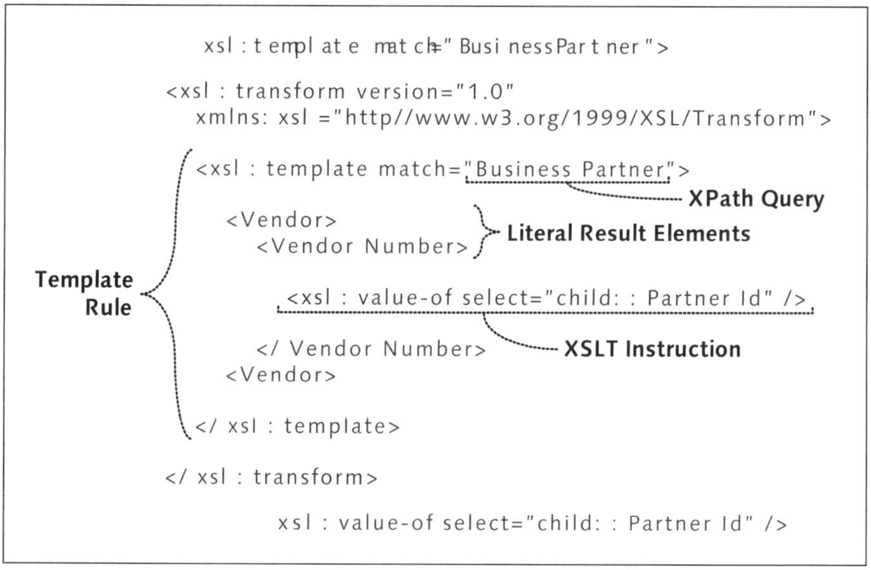


**Figure 8.7** Anatomy of an XSLT Stylesheet

As we mentioned earlier, XSLT is a *declarative language*. Therefore, you don't see any top-down logical flow in an XSLT stylesheet like you would in a procedural program. The starting execution point of an XSLT stylesheet is determined by the first template match found by the XSLT processor as it evaluates a given source document. From there, additional content is recursively added to the result tree as other matches are found for the remaining template rules in the stylesheet.

### 8.3.3 Integrating XSLT with ABAP

XSLT support was integrated into the ABAP runtime environment beginning with SAP NetWeaver AS ABAP 6.10. For the most part, SAP's implementation conforms to the XSLT 1.0 specification; however, because there are subtle differences in the SAP implementation, it's highly recommended that you read over the *SAP XSLT Processor Reference* available in the SAP Library documentation online at *http://help.sap.com*. This reference guide also provides detailed documentation about certain useful proprietary extensions integrated into the SAP XSLT processor.

### 8.3.4 Creating XSLT Stylesheets

XSLT programs are created as repository objects using the Object Navigator tool (Transaction SE80). To create an XSLT program, perform the following steps:

1. Open the Object Navigator, and select the Package option on the left side in the object list selection list box. Right-click and then choose the context menu option CREATE • OTHER (1) • TRANSFORMATION (see Figure 8.8).

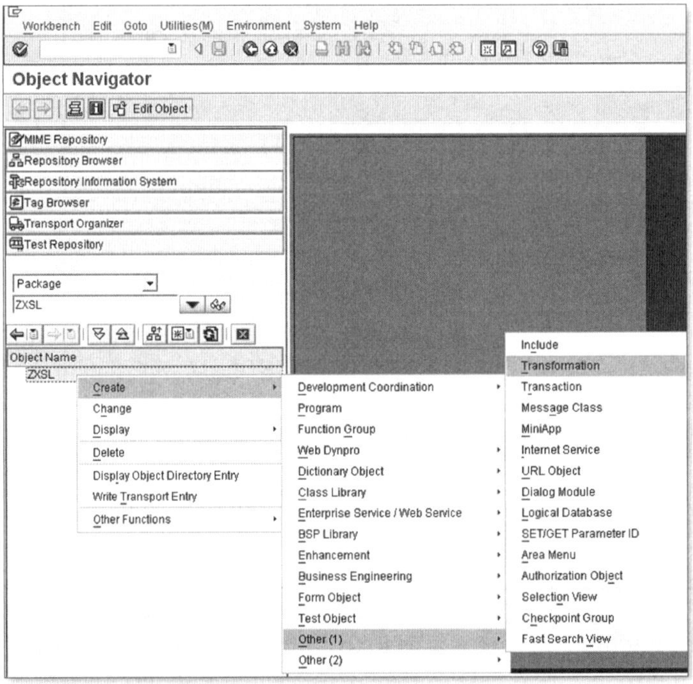


**Figure 8.8** Creating an XSLT Program — Part 1

2. In the Create Transformation dialog box shown in Figure 8.9, specify the name of the XSLT program, a description of its purpose, and the transformation type (which, in this case, is always XSLT Program). Press [Enter] to confirm your selections.

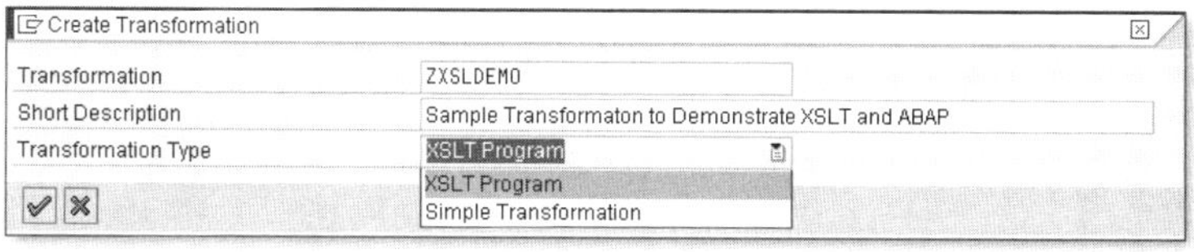


**Figure 8.9** Creating an XSLT Program — Part 2

After an XSLT program is created, you can edit it in the Transformation Editor tool integrated into the ABAP Workbench (see Figure 8.10). The Transformation Editor provides several useful tools to assist you in the development of XSLT programs, including a debugger, test tool, and a tag library that can be used to drag-and-drop XSLT instructions into the XSLT stylesheet.

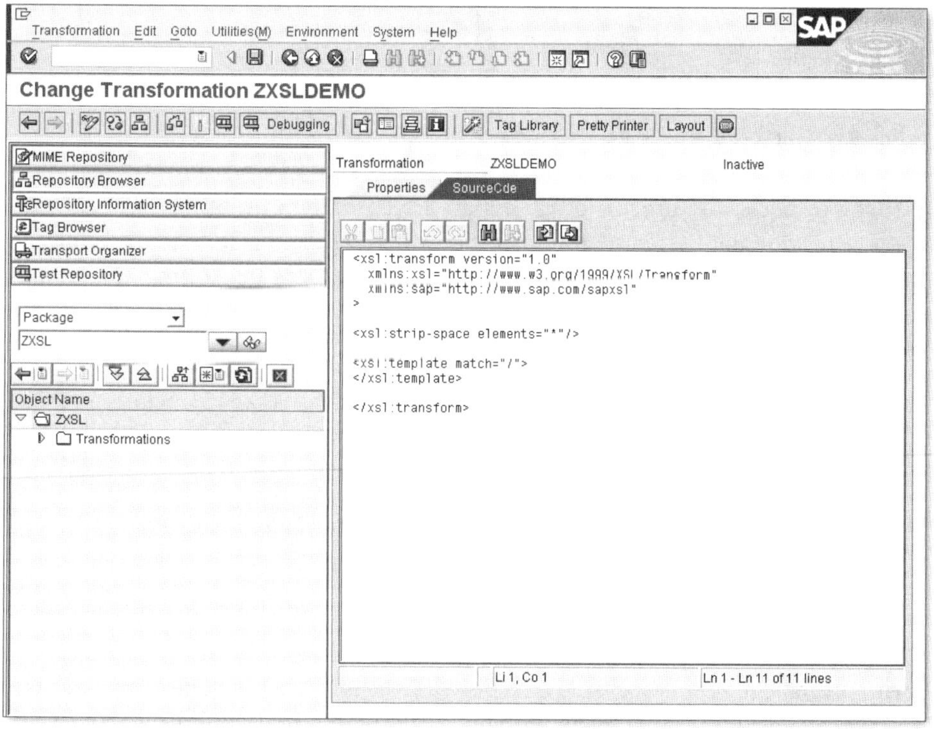


**Figure 8.10** Editing XSLT Programs in the Object Navigator

### 8.3.5 Processing XSLT Programs in ABAP

You can execute XSLT programs from ABAP using the CALL TRANSFORMATION statement. This statement can be used to perform the following types of transformations:

- XML to XML
- XML to ABAP
- ABAP to XML
- ABAP to ABAP

Given the breadth of functionality supported by the CALL TRANSFORMATION statement, the complete syntax diagram for this statement is very complex. However, for the purposes of our discussion, we focus our attention on the syntax involved in performing XML-to-XML transformations, as shown in Listing 8.13. We consider some of the other transformation types in Sections 8.3.7, Serialization of ABAP Data Objects Using asXML, and 8.4, Simple Transformation, respectively.

```
CALL TRANSFORMATION {trans|(name)}
  [PARAMETERS {p1 = e1 p2 = e2 ...}|(ptab)]
  SOURCE XML sxml
  RESULT XML rxml.
```

**Listing 8.13** Syntax of the CALL TRANSFORMATION Statement

In many respects, the process of calling an XSLT program using the CALL TRANSFORMATION statement is very similar in nature to a call to a function module or method. Here, as you would expect, the primary input is the source XML document, and the generated output is the resultant XML document created by the XSLT processor.

As you can see in Listing 8.13, you can specify the source XML document using the SOURCE XML addition. The source XML document can have one of the following forms:

- A data object of type STRING or XSTRING (or a standard table with a flat character line type)
- An interface reference variable of type IF_IXML_ISTREAM (as described in Section 8.2.1, Introducing the iXML Library API)
- An interface reference variable of type IF_IXML_NODE, which points to an iXML node set (see the iXML library reference in the SAP Library online at *http://help.sap.com*)

Similarly, the TARGET XML addition is used to specify the target XML document that can be returned in one of the following forms:

- A data object of type STRING or XSTRING (or a standard table with a flat character line type)
- An interface reference variable of type IF_IXML_OSTREAM (as described in Section 8.2.1, Introducing the iXML Library API)
- An interface reference variable of type IF_IXML_DOCUMENT (as described in Section 8.2.1, Introducing the iXML Library API)

It's also possible to pass in parameters (i.e., ABAP data objects) to the stylesheet using the PARAMETERS addition. Parameters can be used in various ways inside the stylesheet. One way that parameters are used is to pass in an instance of an ABAP Objects class that can then be used to invoke methods in the ABAP context. The XSLT processor also supports calls to ABAP function modules. These calls are made possible using special proprietary extensions integrated into the SAP XSLT processor and the custom XSLT instructions sap:call-external and sap:external-function, respectively.

The CALL TRANSFORMATION statement can trigger various types of catchable exceptions at runtime. For instance, if an error is detected in the XSLT processor, an exception of type CX_SY_XSLT_RUNTIME_ERROR is raised. Each of these exception types inherit from the CX_TRANSFORMATION_ERROR exception class, so you can use this type as a catch-all for any kind of exception that is raised. For more information about the types of exceptions that can be raised by the CALL TRANSFORMATION statement, consult the ABAP Keyword Documentation.

### 8.3.6 Case Study: Transforming Business Partners with XSLT

Now that you have a feel for how XSLT is integrated into the ABAP runtime environment, let's see how we can re-implement the business partner-to-vendor mapping program introduced in Section 8.2.3, Case Study: Developing XML Mapping Programs in ABAP, using XSLT. The first step here is to create an XSLT program in the Object Navigator (Transaction SE80), as described in Section 8.3.3, Integrating XSLT with ABAP.

Listing 8.14 shows the XSLT stylesheet code used to perform the transformation. This stylesheet contains a single template rule that matches the <BusinessPartners> root element of the source business partner document. When the XSLT processor finds this match, it will then apply the embedded template content to the output tree.

The embedded template content begins with the literal result element `<Vendors>`, which is the root element of the vendor document. Underneath the document element, we need to copy each business partner into a `<Vendor>` child element. As you can see, we're accomplishing this using the `<xsl:for-each>` instruction. The `select` attribute of the `<xsl:for-each>` instruction let's you specify an XPath query to select the elements that you want to iterate through in a loop. In this case, we're selecting child `<BusinessPartner>` elements whose `type` attribute is equal to '`2`'.

The relevant data for each vendor is copied over from the business partner in context using the `<xsl:value-of>` command. Here, once again, an XPath query selects the relevant element that we want to copy from. Because the selected elements are simple elements, the text content of these elements is copied over to the target document.

```
<xsl:transform version="1.0"
  xmlns:xsl="http://www.w3.org/1999/XSL/Transform"
  xmlns:sap="http://www.sap.com/sapxsl">
  <!-- Main template used to match root "BusinessPartners"
       element. -->
  <xsl:template match="BusinessPartners">
    <!-- Notice the use of literal result elements like
         "Vendors", etc. -->
    <Vendors>
      <!-- The XSLT "for-each" instruction implements a loop
           through each occurrence of the "BusinessPartner"
           child element of the root "BusinessPartners"
           element. -->
      <xsl:for-each select="BusinessPartner[@type='2']">
        <Vendor>
          <!-- The values of the source data objects are
               copied to the target using the XSLT
               "value-of" instruction. -->
          <VendorNumber>
            <xsl:value-of select="PartnerId" />
          </VendorNumber>
          <VendorName>
            <xsl:value-of select="Name" />
          </VendorName>
          <DateCreated>
            <xsl:value-of select="CreationDate" />
```

```
          </DateCreated>
        </Vendor>
      </xsl:for-each>
    </Vendors>
  </xsl:template>
</xsl:transform>
```

**Listing 8.14** Transforming Business Partners Using XSLT

We can use the XSLT Tester tool integrated into the ABAP Workbench to test the XSLT program contained in Listing 8.14. To open up this tool, press the [F8] key while in the Transformation Editor (or select TRANSFORMATION • TEST in the menu bar) as shown earlier in Figure 8.10. Inside the testing tool, you can test the stylesheet against a sample XML source file. The output of the transformation can be displayed online or saved as a file on your local machine (see Figure 8.11).

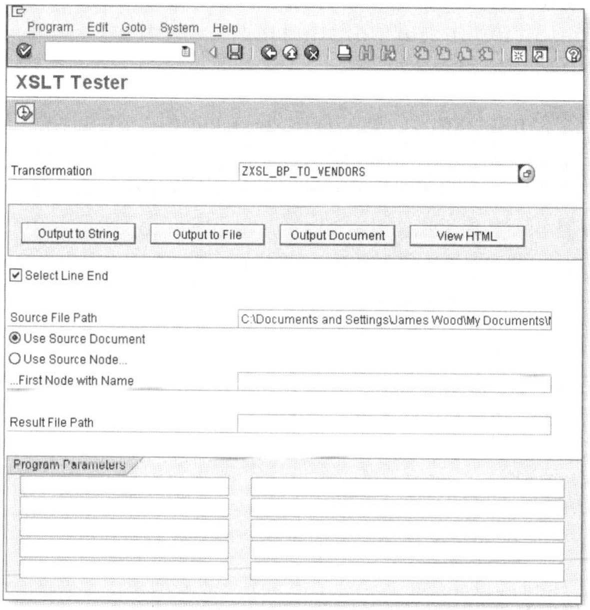


**Figure 8.11** Testing Stylesheets Using the XSLT Tester Tool

Figure 8.12 shows the resultant XML document derived using the sample XML from Listing 8.1. When you're satisfied with the results, you can integrate the stylesheet into your ABAP applications using the `CALL TRANSFORMATION` statement.

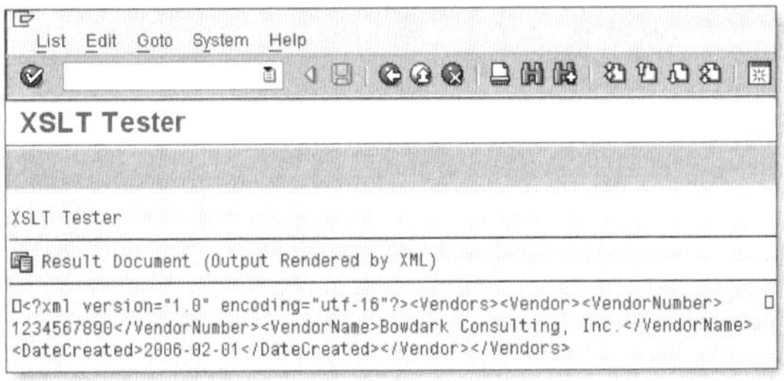


**Figure 8.12** Sample Output from XSLT Tester Tool

### 8.3.7 Serialization of ABAP Data Objects Using asXML

XSLT processors define default behavior that determines how the processor should handle empty stylesheets, certain types of data, and so on. In the case of SAP's implementation, this functionality has been extended to support the serialization of ABAP data objects into a canonical XML representation referred to as *ABAP Serialization XML* (asXML). You can tap into this functionality using the standard `ID` XSLT program provided by SAP.

Listing 8.15 shows how the `ID` XSLT program can be used to transform a structured data object (i.e., `LS_PARTNER`) into an XML document. As you can see, we're still invoking the XSLT program using the `CALL TRANSFORMATION` statement. However, if you look closely, you'll notice that we're using the `SOURCE` addition to specify the `LS_PARTNER` structure in lieu of the normal `SOURCE XML` addition. Figure 8.13 shows the resultant XML document containing the serialized data object.

```
DATA: BEGIN OF ls_partner,
        partner_id TYPE bu_partner,
        type       TYPE bu_type,
        address    TYPE adrc,
      END OF ls_partner.
DATA: lo_xml_factory  TYPE REF TO if_ixml,
      lo_partners_doc TYPE REF TO if_ixml_document.

ls_partner-partner_id    = '1234567890'.
ls_partner-type          = '2'.
ls_partner-address-name1 = 'Bowdark Consulting, Inc.'.

lo_xml_factory = cl_ixml=>create( ).
lo_partners_doc = lo_xml_factory->create_document( ).

CALL TRANSFORMATION id
```

```
SOURCE BusinessPartner = ls_partner
RESULT XML lr_partners_doc.

CALL FUNCTION 'SDIXML_DOM_TO_SCREEN'
  EXPORTING
    document     = lo_partners_doc
  EXCEPTIONS
    no_document = 1
    others      = 2.
```

**Listing 8.15** Transforming ABAP Data Objects to XML

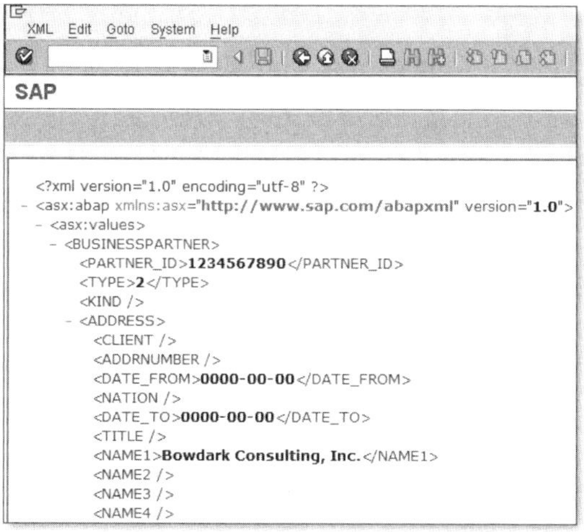


**Figure 8.13** Sample Excerpt of Generated asXML

The ID transformation demonstrated in Listing 8.15 can be used to serialize elementary data objects, structures, internal tables, and data references. In addition, it can be used to serialize ABAP Objects classes that implement the IF_SERIALIZABLE_OBJECT interface. The IF_SERIALIZABLE_OBJECT interface is considered to be a *tag interface* in the sense that it doesn't define any components that augment the public interface of implementing classes. Nevertheless, its presence signifies to the ABAP runtime environment that instances of implementing classes can be serialized.

To demonstrate how serialization works for ABAP Objects classes, let's consider an example. Figure 8.14 depicts a custom class called ZCL_SERIALIZABLE_PARTNER that implements the IF_SERIALIZABLE_OBJECT interface. The ZCL_SERIALIZABLE_PARTNER class defines instance attributes that represent various aspects of a business partner (see Figure 8.15).

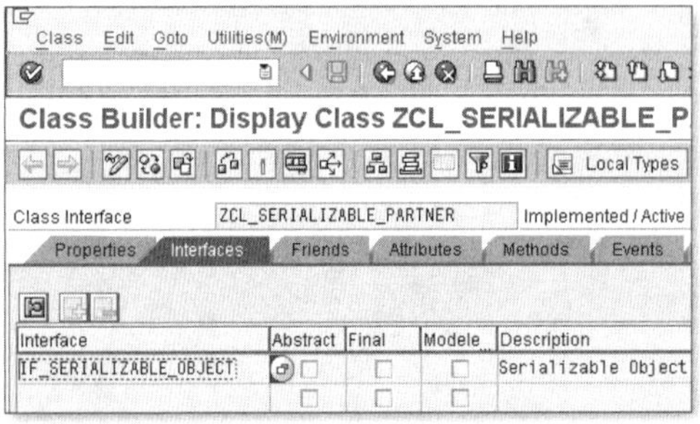


**Figure 8.14** Defining a Serializable Class in ABAP — Part 1

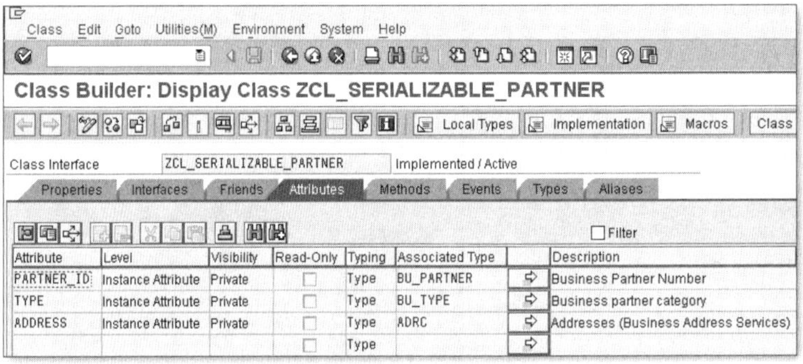


**Figure 8.15** Defining a Serializable Class in ABAP — Part 2

To keep things simple, we assume that the attributes illustrated in Figure 8.15 are initialized inside the `CONSTRUCTOR()` method. Beyond that, there's nothing else that we need to do to the `ZCL_SERIALIZABLE_PARTNER` class to serialize it. As you can see in the code excerpt shown in Listing 8.16, the actual serialization process for an ABAP Objects class is the same as the one we used to serialize a normal structured data object in Listing 8.15. Figure 8.16 shows the asXML generated by the identity transformation.

```
DATA: lo_partner TYPE REF TO zcl_serializable_partner,
      lo_ixml    TYPE REF TO if_ixml,
      lo_result  TYPE REF TO if_ixml_document.

CREATE OBJECT lo_partner.

lo_ixml = cl_ixml=>create( ).
lo_result = lo_ixml->create_document( ).

CALL TRANSFORMATION id
```

```
  SOURCE BusinessPartner = lo_partner
  RESULT XML lo_result.

CALL FUNCTION 'SDIXML_DOM_TO_SCREEN'
  EXPORTING
    document     = lo_result
  EXCEPTIONS
    no_document = 1
    others      = 2.
```

**Listing 8.16** Serializing Instances of ABAP Objects Classes

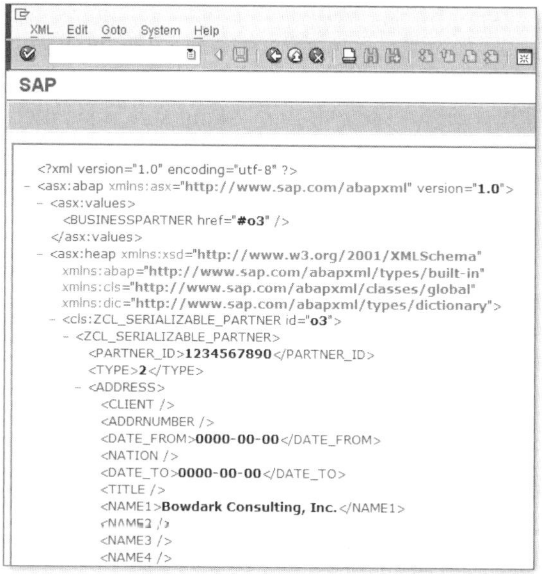


**Figure 8.16** Sample Excerpt of asXML for an ABAP Objects Class

## 8.4 Simple Transformation

The ABAP-XML serialization techniques demonstrated in Section 8.3.7, Serialization of ABAP Data Objects Using asXML, can be used to generate XML in situations where there is no predefined schema. As such, while canonical XML representations such as asXML can be useful in serialization scenarios, they aren't meant to be used in the general setting. After all, most of the time, the XML you create will need to conform to a specific schema type.

Technically, it's possible to perform these types of transformations using XSLT programs. However, such programs can be tedious to write because it's difficult to address ABAP data using XSLT. Recognizing this, SAP elected to create a new language that could be used to simplify the transformation of ABAP data to XML and vice versa. This new language is called *Simple Transformation*.

### 8.4.1 What Is Simple Transformation?

Simple Transformation (ST) is a proprietary language created by SAP to simplify transformations between ABAP data objects and XML. Like XSLT, ST uses a declarative approach, encoding program logic inside template rules using XML. However, the similarities pretty much stop there. Whereas XSLT is a general-purpose language that can be used to perform many kinds of transformations, ST only allows you to transform ABAP data objects into XML (serialization) and XML into ABAP data objects (deserialization). Due to this limited scope, the ST language is smaller and much easier to learn than XSLT.

### 8.4.2 Anatomy of a Simple Transformation Program

Given what you already know about XSLT, you'll find the syntax of an ST program to be quite intuitive. Figure 8.17 contains a diagram that depicts the layout of an ST program. The root element of an ST program is the `<tt:transform>` element, which has the assigned namespace URI `http://www.sap.com/transformation-templates`. By convention, this namespace is prefixed using `tt`.

The core processing logic of an ST program is defined within *templates*. Much like template rules in XSLT, templates contain literal XML result elements as well as ST commands that define how ABAP data is serialized/deserialized at runtime. When defining the `<tt:transform>` element, you have the option of specifying a *main template* using the `template` attribute. This is the first template executed when the ST program is run. If a main template isn't explicitly declared, there must be a default unnamed template defined somewhere within the ST program.

Besides the definition of a main template, ST programs can also specify other core elements, including the following:

- Data roots that represent the ABAP data objects bound to this ST program
- Parameters that can be passed into the ST program via the `PARAMETERS` addition of the `CALL TRANSFORMATION` statement
- Variables that are used as counters, placeholders, and so on

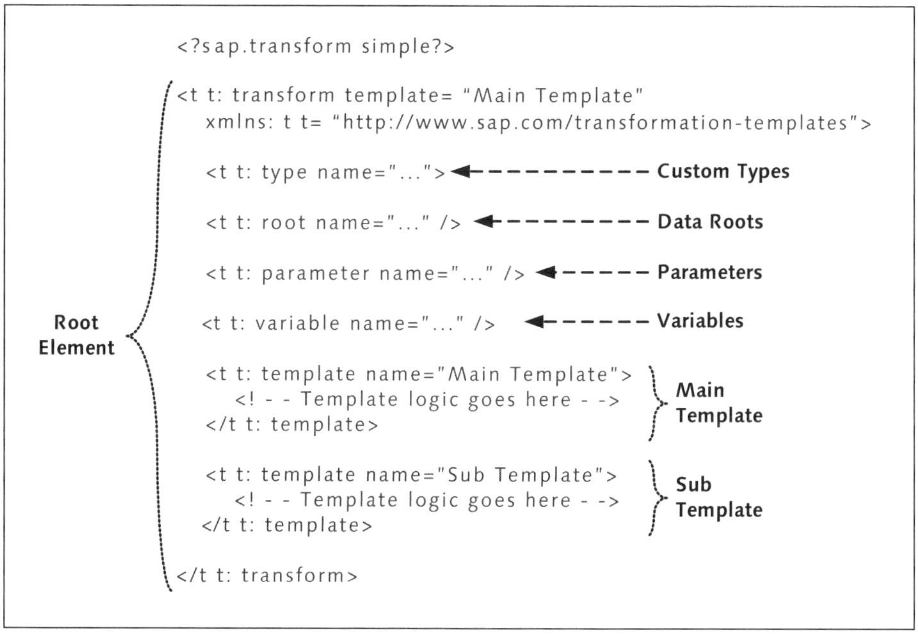


**Figure 8.17** Anatomy of an ST Program

- Custom data type declarations that are used to define data roots, parameters, and variables
- Subtemplates that can be used to implement modularization within the ST program

We'll learn more about some of these elements in the upcoming sections.

### 8.4.3 Learning Simple Transformation Syntax

In this section, we learn about some basic syntax that can be used to build simple ST programs. For a more comprehensive coverage of the ST language, we recommend that you read through the language documentation available in the SAP Library online (search for "Simple Transformation").

#### ABAP Data Binding

As we mentioned earlier, one of the major advantages ST programs have over XSLT programs lies in their ability to easily address ABAP data. The basis for this simplified addressing scheme is the definition of a special binding between the ST program and the calling ABAP context. These bindings are referred to as *data roots* and are defined using the `<tt:root>` element.

Listing 8.17 shows the syntax used to define a data root. Besides the obligatory name, you can also specify an optional data type for a given data root. Here, you can select from built-in elementary types, custom types defined using the `<tt:type>` element, ABAP Dictionary types, and so on. If a data root refers to an internal table, then you can specify the line type using the `line-type` addition shown in Listing 8.17.

```
<tt:root name="..." [[line-]type="..."
                     [length="..."]
                     [decimals="..."]] />
```

**Listing 8.17** Syntax Diagram for Defining Data Roots

The sample ST program shown in Listing 8.18 demonstrates how data roots can be defined within an ST program. In this program, we've defined two data roots called `X` and `Y` using the native `STRING` data type. Within the `Main` template, we're referencing these data roots using the `<tt:value>` command. This command causes the value of the data roots to be written to the resultant XML document during serialization, and the contents of the `<X>` and `<Y>` elements to be copied to these data roots during deserialization.

```
<?sap.transform simple?>
<tt:transform template="Main"
    xmlns:tt="http://www.sap.com/transformation-templates">
  <tt:root name="X" type="STRING" />
  <tt:root name="Y" type="STRING" />

  <tt:template name="Main">
    <RootTest>
      <X><tt:value ref="X" /></X>
      <Y><tt:value ref="Y" /></Y>
    </RootTest>
  </tt:template>
</tt:transform>
```

**Listing 8.18** Working with Data Roots in an ST Program

The code excerpt shown in Listing 8.19 demonstrates how you can use the sample ST program from Listing 8.18 to serialize and deserialize ABAP data objects. Here, notice how the data root names are used in the `SOURCE` and `RESULT` additions of the CALL TRANSFORMATION statement to bind the ABAP data objects to the ST programs.

```
DATA: lv_x1  TYPE string VALUE 'ABAP',
      lv_x2  TYPE string,
      lv_y1  TYPE string VALUE 'XML',
      lv_y2  TYPE string,
      lv_xml TYPE string.

CALL TRANSFORMATION zst_root_test
  SOURCE x = lv_x1
         y = lv_y1
  RESULT XML lv_xml.

WRITE: / lv_xml.
SKIP.

CALL TRANSFORMATION zst_root_test
  SOURCE XML lv_xml
  RESULT x = lv_x2
         y = lv_y2.

WRITE: / 'X =', lv_x2.
WRITE: / 'Y =', lv_y2.
```

**Listing 8.19** Binding Data Roots in ST Programs at Runtime

The term "data root" connotes the idea that ABAP data objects bound to an ST program are organized into tree-like data structures that branch outward from the data root definition. This arrangement makes it possible to traverse through a data root that is defined using a structure or table type and address each of its subnodes. Listing 8.20 shows the syntax used to address subnodes within a data root.

```
root_name.node1.node2. ... .noden
```

**Listing 8.20** Syntax for Addressing Subnodes in a Data Root

During the node traversal process, the address scope narrows from a global context to a local one. For example, consider the sample code shown earlier in Listing 8.18. Here, we're referencing the X and Y data roots directly without qualification. However, imagine that we've added a third data root called Z that is defined using a structure type that contains child components called X and Y. Now, the names X and Y can be ambiguous depending upon the context. You can bypass such vagaries using the syntax shown in Listing 8.21. In this case, the preceding dot (.) operator tells the ST runtime environment that the expression refers to a fully qualified node path.

```
.root_name.node1.node2. ... .noden
```

**Listing 8.21** Syntax for Explicitly Referencing a Data Root

### Flow Control

As we mentioned earlier, execution of an ST program begins with the processing of the designated main template. Within this template, literal XML content is interspersed with ST commands that address ABAP data objects, perform calculations, and so on. Of course, to implement real-world requirements, you need to organize these commands using flow control logic such as conditionals (i.e., an `IF` statement), loops, and so on. Table 8.2 shows the basic flow control commands provided in the ST language.

| ST Flow Control Command | Functionality |
| --- | --- |
| `<tt:skip>` | Allows you to skip over optional XML elements during the deserialization process. |
| `<tt:cond>` | Designates parts of the ST program that should only be executed if certain prerequisites are met (e.g., an `IF` statement in ABAP). Normally, the `<tt:cond>` command is embedded within `<tt:switch>` and `<tt:group>` commands. |
| `<tt:cond-var>` | Similar to the `<tt:cond>` command, allows you to evaluate variables (e.g., variables defined using the `<tt:variable>` or `<tt:parameter>` elements) to determine how data contents are read/written. Note that the `<tt:cond-var>` command can't affect data flow like the `<tt:cond>` command. |
| `<tt:switch>` | Like a `CASE` statement in ABAP, allows you to select from a series of conditional cases. The cases are defined using the `<tt:cond>` element. |
| `<tt:switch-var>` | Similar to the `<tt:switch>` command, allows you to evaluate variables (e.g., variables defined using the `<tt:variable>` or `<tt:parameter>` elements) to determine how data contents are read/written. Note that the `<tt:switch-var>` command can't affect data flow like the `<tt:switch>` command. |

**Table 8.2** ST Flow Control Commands

| ST Flow Control Command | Functionality |
| --- | --- |
| `<tt:group>` | Groups related elements together regardless of sequence. For example, the `<tt:group>` command could be used to process the following XML documents:<br>`<X><X1/><X2/></X>`<br>`<X><X2/><X1/></X>` |
| `<tt:loop>` | Iterates over a set of elements like the `LOOP` statement in ABAP. The data root type used in the statement must have an internal table type. |

**Table 8.2** ST Flow Control Commands (Cont.)

Among the many benefits of using ST is that you can build ST programs that are *symmetrical*. In other words, the same ST program can be used to serialize and deserialize ABAP data objects encoded in a particular XML schema. Of course, to make this work, you may sometimes need to compartmentalize serialization-specific or deserialization-specific logic into different sections. This can be accomplished using the `<tt:serialize>` and `<tt:deserialize>` commands. Listing 8.22 shows how these commands can be used to separate serialization-specific logic from deserialization-specific logic.

```
<tt:transform
  xmlns:tt="http://www.sap.com/transformation-templates">
  <tt:template>
    <tt:serialize>
      <!-- Serialization-specific content goes here -->
    </tt:serialize>

    <tt:deserialize>
      <!-- Deserialization-specific content goes here-->
    </tt:deserialize>
  </tt:template>
</tt:transform>
```

**Listing 8.22** Defining the Transformation Direction in ST Programs

It's also possible to specify the transformation direction within ST flow control statements. For example, you could have a `<tt:cond>` command that is only evaluated during serialization, and so on. For more information about these direction-specific additions, consult the ST language reference available online in the SAP Library documentation.

### 8.4.4 Creating Simple Transformation Programs

You create ST programs in the Object Navigator (Transaction SE80). To create a new ST program, perform the following steps:

1. Open the Object Navigator, and select the Package option on the left side in the object list selection list box. Then right-click and choose the context menu option CREATE • OTHER (1) • TRANSFORMATION (see Figure 8.18).

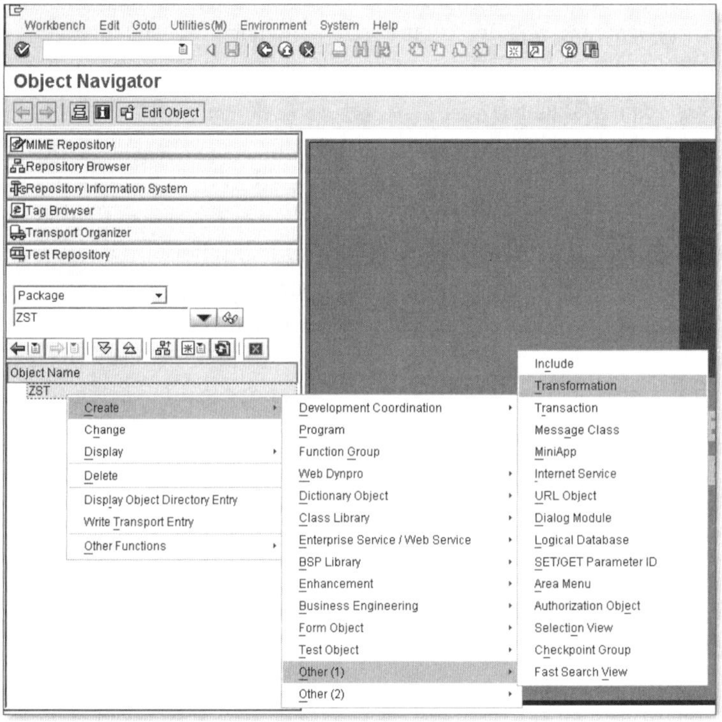


**Figure 8.18** Creating an ST Program — Part 1

2. In the Create Transformation dialog box shown in Figure 8.19, specify the name of the ST program, a description of its purpose, and the transformation type (which, in this case, is always Simple Transformation). Finally, press the Enter key to confirm your selections.

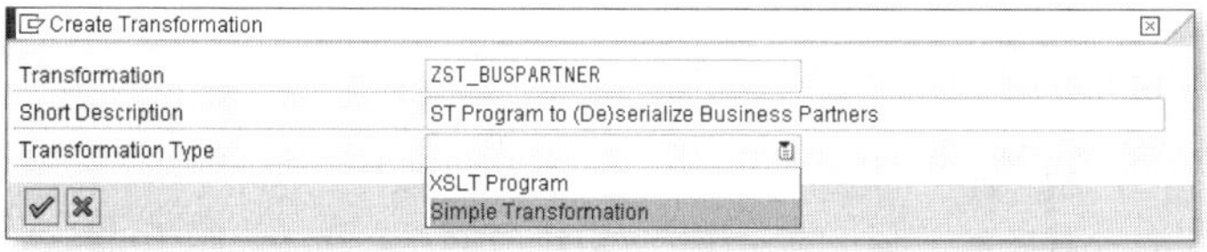


**Figure 8.19** Creating an ST Program — Part 2

After the ST program is created, you can edit it in the Transformation Editor tool integrated into the ABAP Workbench (see Figure 8.20). The Transformation Editor provides several useful tools to assist you in the development of ST programs.

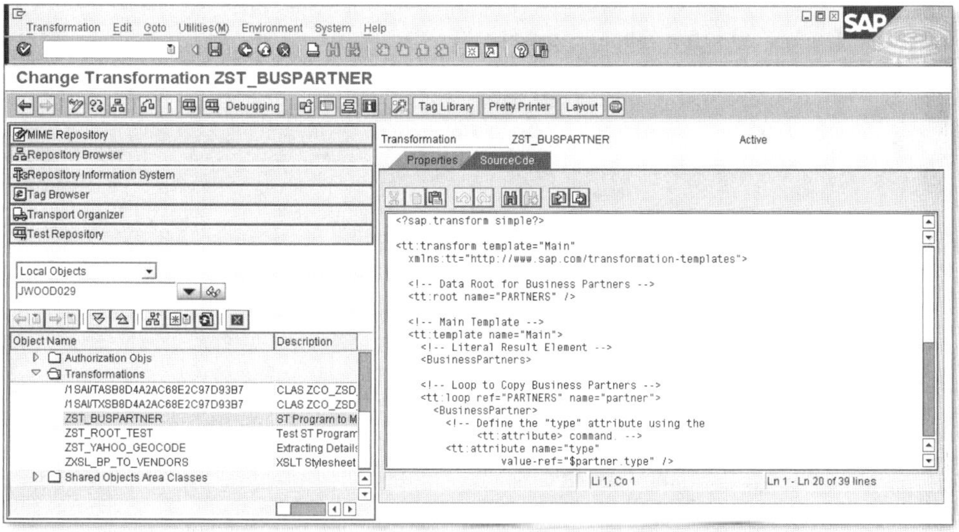


**Figure 8.20** Maintaining ST Programs in the ABAP Workbench

## 8.4.5 Case Study: Transforming Business Partners with ST

Now that you have a feel for the elements that make up an ST program, let's see how these pieces fit together using the business partner example document considered throughout the course of this chapter (refer to Listing 8.1). Listing 8.23 contains an example ST program that is designed to work with business partner data. This ST program can be used to serialize an internal table of business partner data into XML and vice versa.

```
<?sap.transform simple?>
<tt:transform template="Main"
  xmlns:tt="http://www.sap.com/transformation-templates">
```

```
  <!-- Data Root for Business Partners -->
  <tt:root name="PARTNERS" />

  <!-- Main Template -->
  <tt:template name="Main">
    <!-- Literal Result Element -->
    <BusinessPartners>

    <!-- Loop to Copy Business Partners -->
    <tt:loop ref="PARTNERS" name="partner">
      <BusinessPartner>
        <!-- Define the "type" attribute using the
             <tt:attribute> command. -->
        <tt:attribute name="type"
                 value-ref="$partner.type" />
        <!-- Copy the elementary values using the
             <tt:value> command. -->
        <PartnerId>
          <tt:value ref="$partner.partner_id" />
        </PartnerId>
        <Name>
          <tt:value ref="$partner.name" />
        </Name>
        <CreationDate>
          <tt:value ref="$partner.creation_date" />
        </CreationDate>
      </BusinessPartner>
    </tt:loop>

    </BusinessPartners>
  </tt:template>
</tt:transform>
```

**Listing 8.23** Transforming Business Partners Using an ST Program

The business partner data processed by the ST program in Listing 8.23 is represented in the data root called PARTNERS. In the data root declaration, notice that we haven't specified a particular type. Generally speaking, a type declaration is optional because the ST runtime environment doesn't need it to bind ABAP data object(s). Listing 8.24 shows how an internal table containing partner information could be defined to work with the ST program from Listing 8.23.

```
TYPES:
  BEGIN OF ty_partner,
    partner_id    TYPE bu_partner,
    type          TYPE bu_type,
    name          TYPE bu_nameor1,
    creation_date TYPE d,
  END OF ty_partner,
  ty_partners_tab TYPE STANDARD TABLE OF ty_partner.
DATA:
  partners_tab TYPE ty_partners_tab.
```

**Listing 8.24** Defining the Internal Table Used as the Data Root

Within the `Main` template, we've combined literal XML elements with ST commands to describe the transformation process. The bulk of this logic is embedded within a `<tt:loop>` command that iterates over each of the business partner records in the `PARTNERS` data root. For simplification purposes, we're using the `name` attribute of the `<tt:loop>` command to assign a name to the `PARTNERS` subnode within the context of the loop. We can refer to this subnode inside the loop using the reference name `$partner`.

Inside the loop, we're building out each `<BusinessPartner>` element by specifying child element data with the `<tt:value>` command. This command allows you to output the value of the node assigned to the `ref` attribute.

For each `<BusinessPartner>` element, we also need to specify the `type` attribute. This can be accomplished using the `<tt:attribute>` command. As you can see, this command allows you to specify the name of an attribute using the `name` attribute and the value with the `value-ref` attribute. In the `value-ref` attribute assignment, we can plug in the address of a data root/node, variable, parameter, and so on.

## 8.5 Summary

In this chapter, you learned some of the basics of XML processing in ABAP. In the upcoming chapters, we apply these fundamental concepts toward the development of several different types of applications. In fact, we get a jump-start on this in the next chapter, when we discuss web programming and RESTful Web services.

*"The Web as I envisaged it, we have not seen it yet. The future is still so much bigger than the past." (Tim Berners-Lee, Inventor of the World Wide Web)*

# 9 Web Programming with the ICF

For many developers who didn't grow up with the World Wide Web, the concepts of web programming can seem complex and intimidating. Ironically, much of this confusion stems from various abstractions and frameworks that are built on top of the Web in an effort to make web development easier. Nevertheless, at its core, the Web is a simple and ubiquitous platform that can be used to develop all kinds of distributed applications.

Normally, whenever you hear people converse about web programming, they are talking about developing applications for the *human web*; a web in which human users access interactive applications via some kind of browser device. Examples of such applications include websites built on Business Server Pages (BSP) or Web Dynpro for ABAP (WDA) technologies, and so on. Although these types of applications make up the majority of the applications deployed on the Web, they aren't its only inhabitants. Recently, a new breed of service-based applications has emerged, unlocking some of the Web's untapped potential as a platform for developing distributed applications. These services make up the *programmable web*; a web in which software clients access and manipulate resources programmatically.

In this chapter, we show you how to use the *Internet Communication Framework* (ICF) to interact with the programmable web. Along the way, we introduce you to fundamental technologies of the Web such as HTTP. Understanding these core concepts will help you untangle the mysteries of the Web and harness its power in your own developments.

## 9.1 HTTP Overview

To program for the Web, you must first understand how to work with its primary application-level protocol: the *Hypertext Transfer Protocol* (HTTP). HTTP defines the rules that determine how clients and servers interact with one another over the Internet. From a functional perspective, HTTP is a *document-based protocol* in which HTTP clients and servers communicate by sending documents back and forth in a request/reply fashion. Figure 9.1 illustrates this request/reply message chain for a series of web clients submitting various requests to a web server.

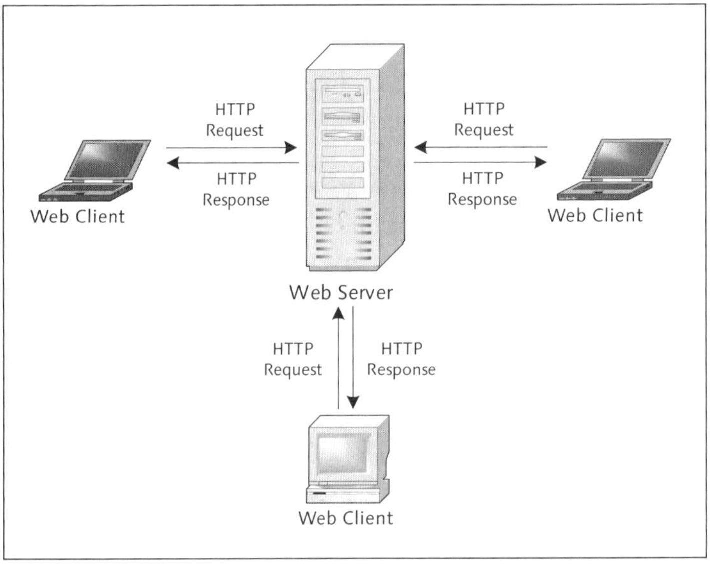


**Figure 9.1** HTTP Request/Response Cycle

For the most part, HTTP is a simple protocol to work with. HTTP clients submit requests, and HTTP server programs process those requests. Everything that goes on beyond the scope of the document exchange is left up to the application developers. In this section, we introduce you to some of the key components of HTTP. When you understand these basic concepts, you'll be ready to start developing your own HTTP-based applications.

### 9.1.1 Working with the Uniform Interface

HTTP is designed to work with *resources*. Here, the term *resource* could be used to describe a physical document such as a PDF file, a dynamically generated list of stock quotes, or even some kind of service offering. Given the fact that HTTP supports such a broad range of resource types, you might expect there to be many complex rules that define how to work with particular kinds of resources. However, in an effort to keep things simple, the designers of HTTP elected to define interactions with resources at an abstract level, deferring complex resource-specific details to server-side implementations. In HTTP parlance, resource interactions are described using a predefined set of action verbs referred to as *HTTP methods*. Table 9.1 describes some of the more common methods defined in the HTTP specification. You can find a comprehensive list of supported methods in the HTTP specification available online at *www.w3.org/Protocols/rfc2616/rfc2616-sec9.html*.

| HTTP Method | Description |
|---|---|
| GET | The GET method is used to retrieve a representation of the resource identified by a given URL. Whenever you open your web browser and navigate to a given URL, your browser is normally executing a GET method behind the scenes to load the requested page. |
| HEAD | The HEAD method is almost identical to the GET method in that it retrieves information about a resource identified by a given URL. However, unlike the GET method, the HEAD method doesn't return an entity body. The HEAD method can be useful in situations where you want to find out some basic information about a resource without having to download it in its entirety. |
| PUT | As the name implies, the PUT method *puts* (or stores) a resource on the server and associates it with a particular URL. |
| POST | The POST method can be used in two different ways:<br>In an ideal world, the POST method is used to create *subordinate resources* underneath a given URL. For example, consider a blog site. An author might create a blog entry at a particular URL using the PUT method. As readers come along and comment on the blog entry, they are creating subordinate resources underneath that blog entry. At the time of submission, the user may or may not know what the target URL should be. Therefore, the comment is *posted* underneath the top-level blog resource.<br>The other, more nebulous use of POST involves the general passing of data to some kind of data-handling process. In this latter case, the developer often isn't really addressing a particular type of resource. Rather, he is simply using POST as a way of pushing some data over the Web and letting some server program figure out what to do with it. |
| DELETE | The DELETE method is used to remove a resource located at a given URL. |

**Table 9.1** Common HTTP Request Methods

### 9.1.2 Addressability and URLs

As we mentioned in Section 9.1.1, Working with the Uniform Interface, HTTP server programs provide access to *resources*. However, to be able to access a resource, we must be able to uniquely identify it. In the context of HTTP, resources are identified by URLs. Even if you're not all that familiar with web programming, you've probably encountered many URLs during the course of your routine web browsing. For example, if you wanted to find out more about this book, you might open up your web browser and type in the URL *http://www.sap-press.com*. From here, you might click on hyperlinks to navigate around the website in search of particular bits of information. Each of these hyperlinks points to a particular resource. For instance, the URL *http://www.sap-press.com/product.cfm?product=H3000* refers to the book *Object-Oriented Programming with ABAP Objects* (SAP PRESS, 2009).

**Figure 9.2** Elements of URL Syntax

Figure 9.2 illustrates the basic elements of a URL. As you can see, a URL is made up of the following components:

- The first element in a URL is the *protocol specifier*. This element defines the protocol used to access the resource. In the case of HTTP, you'll see either "http" or "https" here, depending upon whether or not SSL encryption technology is being used on top of HTTP.
- Next, we need to identify the *host name* of the computer that is hosting the service. This could be a local intranet host such as the *evergreen.home* host name shown in Figure 9.2, or an Internet host such as *www.bowdarkconsulting.com*. Technically speaking, you could also interpose an IP address here, but for the purposes of our discussion, we'll assume the use of host names.
- In some cases, we may also need to specify the *port* for the HTTP service. Ports are used to associate requests with a particular program that is executing on the target host. Such designation might be necessary because a given host might be running multiple networked applications simultaneously. However, most of the time, there is only one instance of a web server running on a host, and it binds to the default port 80. Therefore, most web browsers assume that this is the port you want to access unless you instruct them otherwise by specifying a

port in the URL. For example, in Figure 9.2, we've specified port 8000 (the default HTTP port for the ICM in the SAP NetWeaver AS ABAP).

- Following the port specification is the *path* to the resource being accessed. The form of this resource path is similar to the path you would use to navigate to a file on your personal computer.
- The last element depicted is the optional *query string*. A URL query string can be made up of multiple parameters that provide additional *scoping information* about a particular resource. For instance, in Figure 9.2, the URL query string defines a parameter called "sap-client" that defines the client number of the target SAP instance in which we want to access the resource.

When you break a URL down like this, you can see the various elements of HTTP at work. Underneath the hood, HTTP uses TCP/IP as its *transport protocol*. Thus, the host name and port information provide the underlying TCP/IP layer with the information it needs to connect to the remote server host. After a connection is established, an HTTP request message can be submitted. Here, the path and query string information in the URL tell the web server how to route the incoming request internally so that it can be processed by a particular handler module.

### 9.1.3 Understanding the HTTP Message Format

Throughout the course of this chapter, we've described the mechanics of HTTP messaging using abstract terms such as "document" or "resource." While such terms are adequate for describing messaging semantics at a high level, it's nevertheless helpful to see how HTTP messages are formatted from a technical perspective. For this reason, let's look at the format of HTTP request and response messages at the nuts-and-bolts level.

Listing 9.1 contains the `GET` request generated by a specific web browser whenever the URL *http://www.sap-press.com is opened*. The first line of this request informs the web server that the client wants to access the *root resource* (i.e., the resource at path "/"). This first line also specifies the version of HTTP being used (i.e., version 1.1). Each of the entries underneath this initial line represent *HTTP header fields*. As you can see, HTTP header fields provide additional information about the request such as the types of documents the client accepts, the preferred language/encoding, and so on. In addition to these standard HTTP header fields, you can also pass along your own custom fields. Of course, whether or not they are actually used is up to the target web server implementation.

```
GET / HTTP/1.1
Host: www.sap-press.com
User-Agent: Mozilla/5.0 (Windows; U; Windows NT 5.1...
Accept: text/html,application/xhtml+xml,application/xml...
Accept-Language: en-us,en;q=0.5
Accept-Encoding: gzip,deflate
Accept-Charset: ISO-8859-1,utf-8;q=0.7,*;q=0.7
Keep-Alive: 300
Connection: keep-alive
```

**Listing 9.1** An HTTP GET Request

If we had submitted a PUT or POST request, then our request message would have also contained a *request entity body*. Request entity bodies are the documents that go inside of an HTTP request envelope. Here, you can stick just about any kind of document in the envelope. For example, if we were uploading a PDF document to a web server, the contents of that PDF document would go in the request entity body.

The response to an HTTP GET request like the one demonstrated in Listing 9.1 is shown in Listing 9.2. Here, the first line in the response contains an HTTP response code that indicates whether or not the request was successful. Then, much like the request message, the response message contains various response header fields that tell you when the response was generated, the content type of the response message, and so on. Underneath the response headers is the *response entity body*. In this example, the response document is encoded in HTML. However, it could have been an image file, a PDF file, and so on.

```
HTTP/1.1 200 OK
Connection: close
Date: Fri, 06 Nov 2009 02:49:07 GMT
Server: Microsoft-IIS/6.0
X-Powered-By: ASP.NET
Content-Type: text/html; charset=UTF-8

<html>
<head>
  <title>SAP PRESS</title>
...
```

**Listing 9.2** A Response to an HTTP GET Request

As you can see, after you peel back all of the layers, there's nothing terribly complex about web programming with HTTP from a technical perspective. Of course, while dealing with HTTP messages at this level can be informative, it's also quite tedious. To be productive in your web development, you need a good library that simplifies the way that you work with HTTP. Fortunately, ABAP developers have access to such a library, and it's called the ICF.

## 9.2 Introduction to the ICF

Prior to release 6.10, SAP NetWeaver AS ABAP was a fairly closed system in terms of its accessibility to the outside world. In the self-contained environment that was R/3, such limitations could be easily overcome with RFC-enabled connectors/middleware. However, when the World Wide Web exploded onto the scene in the late 1990s, SAP redesigned its application server to include native web support to keep pace with the rest of the IT world. Thus, the Basis kernel was enhanced to include a new component called the *Internet Communication Manager* (ICM) and the SAP Web Application Server (SAP Web AS) ABAP was born (later replaced with SAP NetWeaver AS ABAP).

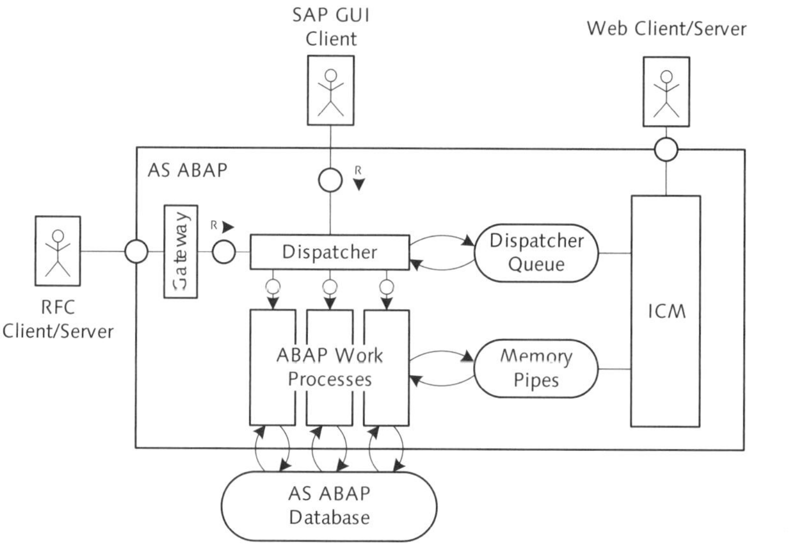


**Figure 9.3** Architecture of the SAP NetWeaver AS ABAP from Release 6.10 Onward

Figure 9.3 shows the positioning of the ICM within an SAP NetWeaver AS ABAP instance. As the name suggests, the ICM enables connectivity between SAP NetWeaver AS ABAP and the outside world using Internet-based technologies such as HTTP. This connectivity extends in both directions; in other words, the ICM can be used to host a website or develop an HTTP client for the programmable web.

Though a detailed discussion about the architecture of the ICM is outside the scope of this book, suffice it to say that it's a very sophisticated piece of software that provides robust support for web programming in ABAP.

As an ABAP developer, you don't interact directly with the ICM. Instead, SAP has provided an abstraction called the *Internet Communication Framework* (ICF) that simplifies the way that you handle and submit HTTP requests. In the upcoming sections, we dig deeper into the ICF and look at all of the services it provides.

## 9.3 Developing an HTTP Client Program

Now that you're familiar with the mechanics of HTTP and have a basic understanding of the positioning of the ICF, let's try getting our hands dirty by developing an HTTP client program that accesses a Web service. These days, there are many publicly available Web services online to choose from, so rather than going through some kind of contrived example, let's take a look at a real Web service provided by Yahoo! Inc. called the *Geocoding Web Service*. The Geocoding Web Service can be used to find the specific latitude and longitude for a given address.[1]

**RESTful Web Services**

Throughout the course of this chapter, we've routinely referred to various types of HTTP server programs as *Web services*. Based upon what you may have heard about Web services, you might find our use of this term odd. This is no doubt due to the fact that there is so much misinformation out there proclaiming that a Web service isn't a Web service unless it's implemented using the SOAP protocol. However, technically speaking, a Web service is defined by the W3C as "...a software system designed to support interoperable machine-to-machine interaction over a network...." As you can see, this generic definition has very little to say about how the service itself is implemented.

Recently, many developers frustrated by the complexities of SOAP-based Web services have begun to hearken back to basic principles outlined by the designers of the Web. Generally speaking, these principles can be summed up in one phrase: *Representational State Transfer* (or REST). The term *REST* was coined by Roy Fielding in a Ph.D. dissertation entitled *Architectural Styles and the Design of Network-Based Software Architectures*. Coincidentally, Roy Fielding also happened to be one of the major contributors to the design of HTTP. Therefore, not surprisingly, many of the basic principles of REST align very closely with the semantics of HTTP.

1 For more information about the Geocoding API, check out *http://developer.yahoo.com/maps/rest/V1/geocode.html*. Here, you'll need to register for a developer ID that is used to access the service.

From a conceptual perspective, "RESTful" Web services are *resource-oriented*. In other words, RESTful Web services manipulate and provide access to *resources*. The semantics for these operations are defined via the standard HTTP interface. For example, if you want to obtain a representation of a resource, you submit an HTTP `GET` request to the service. Similarly, if you want to create a new resource, you would submit an HTTP `PUT` request to a specific URL with the representation of the resource in the HTTP request entity body.

RESTful Web services are designed to be easy to use and can be a welcomed alternative to SOAP-based Web services in certain situations. This is particularly the case in legacy development environments that don't provide a SOAP toolkit but do offer an HTTP library. If you're interested in learning more about RESTful Web services, I highly recommend the book *RESTful Web Services* (O'Reilly, 2007).

### 9.3.1 Defining the Service Call

The Geocoding Web Service is a *RESTful Web service*. Therefore, to access the Geocoding API, we need to construct an HTTP `GET` request to the URL *http://local.yahooapis.com/MapsService/V1/geocode*. Additional scoping information about the target address is provided in the form of URL query string parameters. Table 9.2 outlines the parameters that we'll be using to conduct our search.

| Query String Parameter | Description |
|---|---|
| `appid` | To access the Maps service, you must register as a developer with Yahoo!. During this registration process, you're provided with an application ID that allows you to access their services. |
| `street` | The street address you want to locate. |
| `city` | The name of the city in which the address is located. |
| `state` | The name of the state in which the address is located. |
| `zip` | The postal code for the target address. |

**Table 9.2** URL Query String Parameters for the Geocoding Web Service

Before we set out to write any code, we need to formulate a plan. Our requirements for accessing the Geocoding API are as follows:

1. First, we need to construct a URL that includes all of the appropriate query string parameters. These parameters need to be *URL encoded* so that there are

no illegal characters in the URL. We discuss URL encoding in more detail a little bit later.

2. After the service URL is constructed, we use the ICF client API to connect to the service and issue an HTTP `GET` request.
3. The results from the Geocoding Web Service are returned in the form of an XML document. This document must be parsed to extract the latitude and longitude values.

Though most of these concepts should seem familiar by now, you still need to how to implement these requirements in ABAP. So, without further adieu, let's take a look at the ICF client API.

### 9.3.2 Working with the ICF Client API

The ICF API, like many of the standard APIs we've considered thus far in this book, is an object-oriented API based heavily on interfaces. The UML class diagram in Figure 9.4 highlights the core classes and interfaces that you need to develop an HTTP client program. As you might expect, the entry point into this API is the `IF_HTTP_CLIENT` interface that represents an HTTP client instance. You can create client instances using the static `CREATE` methods defined in the concrete `CL_HTTP_CLIENT` class.

After a client instance is created, you can use it to build and submit an HTTP request as follows:

1. First, to build the HTTP request message, you must use the `REQUEST` instance attribute available in the HTTP client instance. The `REQUEST` attribute is defined using the interface type `IF_HTTP_REQUEST`. The `IF_HTTP_REQUEST` interface provides methods that allow you to define the request method (i.e., `GET` or `POST`), set HTTP header fields, and so on.
2. After the HTTP request message is constructed, you can submit it using the `SEND()` method of the HTTP client instance.
3. If you look carefully at the signature of the `SEND()` method in interface `IF_HTTP_CLIENT`, you'll notice that it doesn't provide any returning parameters. Therefore, to retrieve the HTTP response message, you must call the `RECEIVE()` method on the HTTP client instance.

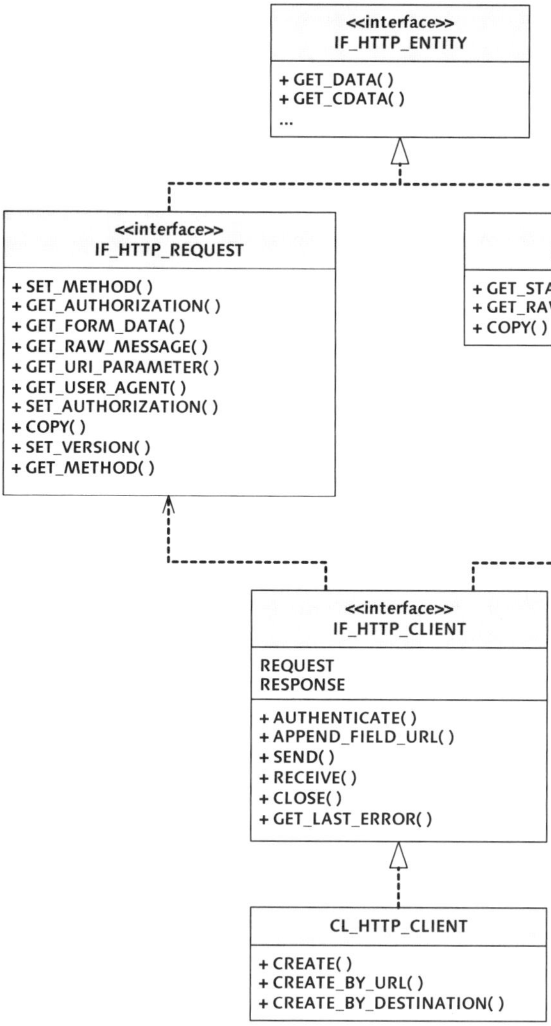


**Figure 9.4** UML Class Diagram for ICF Client API

4. After the `RECEIVE()` call completes, you can access the HTTP response message via the `RESPONSE` attribute of the HTTP client instance, which is of interface type `IF_HTTP_RESPONSE`.

5. Finally, when you're finished with the HTTP client connection, you can close it using the `CLOSE()` method of the HTTP client instance.

### 9.3.3 Putting It All Together

At this point, we're ready to begin developing our HTTP client. The report program ZICF_CLIENT_DEMO depicted in Listing 9.3 contains the bulk of the code required to access the Yahoo! Geocoding Web Service. Here, we've implemented a local class called LCL_MAP_SERVICE that defines a method called GET_POSITION() to perform the search.

```
REPORT zicf_client_demo.
CLASS lcx_icf_exception DEFINITION
      INHERITING FROM cx_dynamic_check.
ENDCLASS.

CLASS lcl_map_service DEFINITION.
  PUBLIC SECTION.
    CLASS-METHODS:
      main IMPORTING im_appid  TYPE string
                     im_street TYPE string
                     im_city   TYPE string
                     im_state  TYPE string
                     im_zip    TYPE string.

    METHODS:
      constructor IMPORTING im_appid TYPE string,
      get_position
        IMPORTING im_street    TYPE string
                  im_city      TYPE string
                  im_state     TYPE string
                  im_zip       TYPE string
        EXPORTING ex_latitude  TYPE string
                  ex_longitude TYPE string
          RAISING lcx_icf_exception.

  PRIVATE SECTION.
    CONSTANTS:
      CO_SERVICE_HOST TYPE string
         VALUE 'local.yahooapis.com',
      CO_SERVICE_PATH TYPE string
         VALUE '/MapsService/V1/geocode'.

    DATA: application_id TYPE string.

    METHODS:
      build_uri
```

```
        IMPORTING im_street    TYPE string
                  im_city      TYPE string
                  im_state     TYPE string
                  im_zip       TYPE string
        RETURNING VALUE(re_uri) TYPE string,

      parse_results
        IMPORTING im_results   TYPE string
         CHANGING ch_latitude  TYPE string
                  ch_longitude TYPE string
          RAISING cx_transformation_error.
ENDCLASS.

CLASS lcl_map_service IMPLEMENTATION.
  METHOD main.
*   Method-Local Data Declarations:
    DATA: lo_map_service TYPE REF TO lcl_map_service,
          lo_icf_ex      TYPE REF TO lcx_icf_exception,
          lv_latitude    TYPE string,
          lv_longitude   TYPE string.

*   Process the ICF request:
    TRY.
*     Create an instance of the map service:
      CREATE OBJECT lo_map_service
        EXPORTING
          im_appid = im_appid.

*     Retrieve the position of the requested address:
      CALL METHOD lo_map_service->get_position
        EXPORTING
          im_street    = im_street
          im_city      = im_city
          im_state     = im_state
          im_zip       = im_zip
        IMPORTING
          ex_latitude  = lv_latitude
          ex_longitude = lv_longitude.

*     Display the results:
      WRITE: / 'Latitude is:', lv_latitude.
      WRITE: / 'Longitude is:', lv_longitude.
    CATCH lcx_icf_exception INTO lo_icf_ex.
```

```
      "Exception handling goes here...
    ENDTRY.
  ENDMETHOD.                    " METHOD main

  METHOD constructor.
    me->application_id = im_appid.
  ENDMETHOD.                    " METHOD constructor

  METHOD get_position.
*   Method-Local Data Declarations:
    DATA: lo_http_client TYPE REF TO if_http_client,
          lv_uri         TYPE string,
          lv_results     TYPE string.

*   Create an instance of the HTTP client:
    CALL METHOD cl_http_client=>create
      EXPORTING
        host               = CO_SERVICE_HOST
      IMPORTING
        client             = lo_http_client
      EXCEPTIONS
        argument_not_found = 1
        plugin_not_active  = 2
        internal_error     = 3
        others             = 4.

    IF sy-subrc NE 0.
      RAISE EXCEPTION TYPE lcx_icf_exception.
    ENDIF.

*   Select the HTTP GET method:
    lo_http_client->request->set_method(
      if_http_request=>co_request_method_get ).

*   Build and configure the request URI:
    lv_uri =
      build_uri( im_street = im_street
                 im_city = im_city
                 im_state = im_state
                 im_zip = im_zip ).

    cl_http_utility=>set_request_uri(
      request = lo_http_client->request
```

```
        uri = lv_uri ).

*   Submit the request:
    CALL METHOD lo_http_client->send
      EXCEPTIONS
        http_communication_failure = 1
        http_invalid_state         = 2
        http_processing_failed     = 3
        http_invalid_timeout       = 4
        others                     = 5.

    IF sy-subrc NE 0.
      RAISE EXCEPTION TYPE lcx_icf_exception.
    ENDIF.

*   Receive the results:
    CALL METHOD lo_http_client->receive
      EXCEPTIONS
        http_communication_failure = 1
        http_invalid_state         = 2
        http_processing_failed     = 3
        others                     = 4.

    IF sy-subrc EQ 0.
      lv_results =
        lo_http_client->response->get_cdata( ).
    ELSE.
      RAISE EXCEPTION TYPE lcx_icf_exception.
    ENDIF.

*   Parse the results:
    CALL METHOD parse_results
      EXPORTING
        im_results   = lv_results
      CHANGING
        ch_latitude  = ex_latitude
        ch_longitude = ex_longitude.

*   Always remember to close the connection:
    lo_http_client->close( ).
  ENDMETHOD.                    " METHOD get_position

  METHOD build_uri.
```

```
    ...
  ENDMETHOD.                    " METHOD build_uri

  METHOD parse_results.
    ...
  ENDMETHOD.                    " METHOD parse_results
ENDCLASS.

PARAMETERS:
  p_appid  TYPE string LOWER CASE,
  p_street TYPE string LOWER CASE,
  p_city   TYPE string LOWER CASE,
  p_state  TYPE string LOWER CASE,
  p_zip    TYPE string LOWER CASE.

START-OF-SELECTION.
  CALL METHOD lcl_map_service=>main
    EXPORTING
      im_appid  = p_appid
      im_street = p_street
      im_city   = p_city
      im_state  = p_state
      im_zip    = p_zip.
```

**Listing 9.3** An ICF Client Accessing the Yahoo! Geocoding Service

As you can see in Listing 9.3, the logic within the `GET_POSITION()` method is closely aligned with the requirements set forth at the beginning of this section:

1. First, we create an instance of an ICF HTTP client using the static `CREATE()` method of class `CL_HTTP_CLIENT`.
2. Next, we configure the HTTP request by specifying the HTTP method (`GET` in this case) and the request URI. We'll take a closer look at the URI generation process in a moment.
3. After the request is built, we submit the request using the `SEND()` method of the ICF client instance.
4. Assuming everything works okay, we extract the results using the `RECEIVE()` method of the ICF client instance. Then, we forward the XML response to a private helper method called `PARSE_RESULTS()`. This method uses the iXML library described in Chapter 8, XML Processing in ABAP. For brevity's sake, we've omitted this implementation in the book. However, you can find a full implementation of this method in the source code bundle available online.

5. Finally, we close the HTTP connection using the `CLOSE()` method of the ICF client instance.

For the most part, the code outlined in Listing 9.3 is pretty straightforward. However, one item that we've glossed over up until now is the generation of the request URI. Listing 9.4 shows the implementation of the `BUILD_URI()` method. Here, we're essentially concatenating URL query string parameters together based on the user's input. However, one thing to note here is that certain query string parameters have to be *escaped*. For example, URLs can't contain spaces, so we can't pass along a query string parameter like this: "city=Fort Worth". Instead, we must pass the query string parameter as "city=Fort+Worth". Rather than building this logic from scratch, you can use the `IF_HTTP_UTILITY~ESCAPE_URL()` method of class `CL_HTTP_UTILITY` to encode query string parameters.

```
METHOD build_uri.
* Method-Local Data Declarations:
  DATA: lv_street TYPE string,
        lv_city   TYPE string.

  CONCATENATE CO_SERVICE_PATH
              '?appid='
              me->application_id
         INTO re_uri.

  IF NOT im_street IS INITIAL.
    lv_street =
      cl_http_utility=>if_http_utility~escape_url(
        unescaped = im_street ).

    CONCATENATE re_uri '&street=' lv_street
           INTO re uri
  ENDIF.

  IF NOT im_city IS INITIAL.
    lv_city =
      cl_http_utility=>if_http_utility~escape_url(
        unescaped = im_city ).

    CONCATENATF re_uri '&city-' lv_city
           INTO re_uri.
  ENDIF.

  IF NOT im_state IS INITIAL.
```

```
    CONCATENATE re_uri '&state=' im_state
           INTO re_uri.
  ENDIF.

  IF NOT im_zip IS INITIAL.
    CONCATENATE re_uri '&zip=' im_zip
           INTO re_uri.
  ENDIF.
ENDMETHOD.
```

**Listing 9.4** Building the URL for the Yahoo! Geocoding Service

Figure 9.5 shows the selection screen for the `ZICF_CLIENT_DEMO` report. Here, we've filled in the street address for the SAP office located in Irving, TX. According to Yahoo!, this office is located at the point (32.892617, -96.942624), as shown in Figure 9.6.

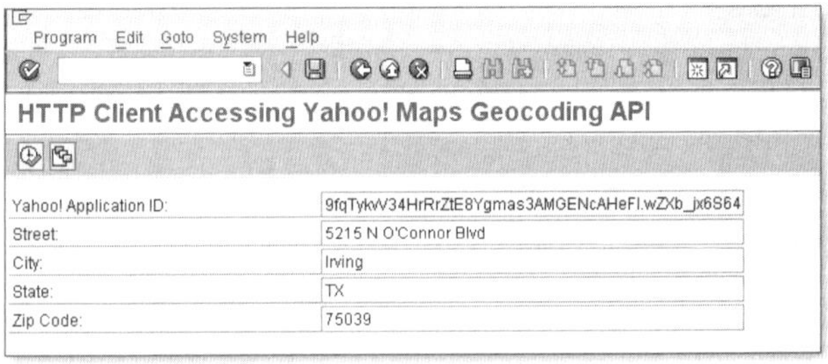


**Figure 9.5** Selection Screen for the ZICF_CLIENT_DEMO Report

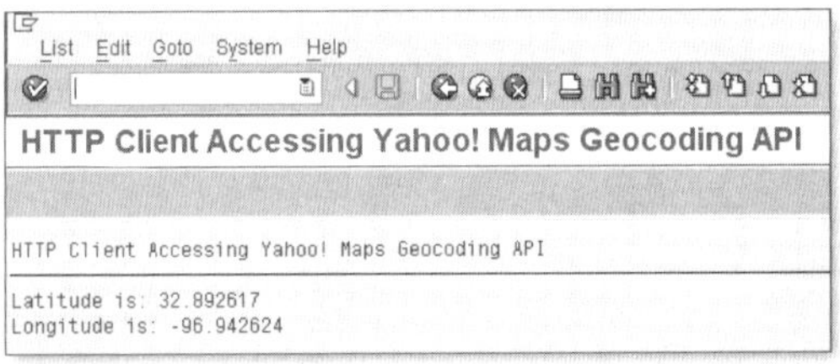


**Figure 9.6** Results of the ZICF_CLIENT_DEMO Report Program

## 9.4 Implementing ICF Handler Modules

In this section, we switch gears and show you how to use the ICF to implement server-side scenarios. As a basis for our discussion, we explore the creation of a

RESTful Web service that can be used to look up flight information in the familiar flight data model that comes out of the box with an SAP NetWeaver installation.

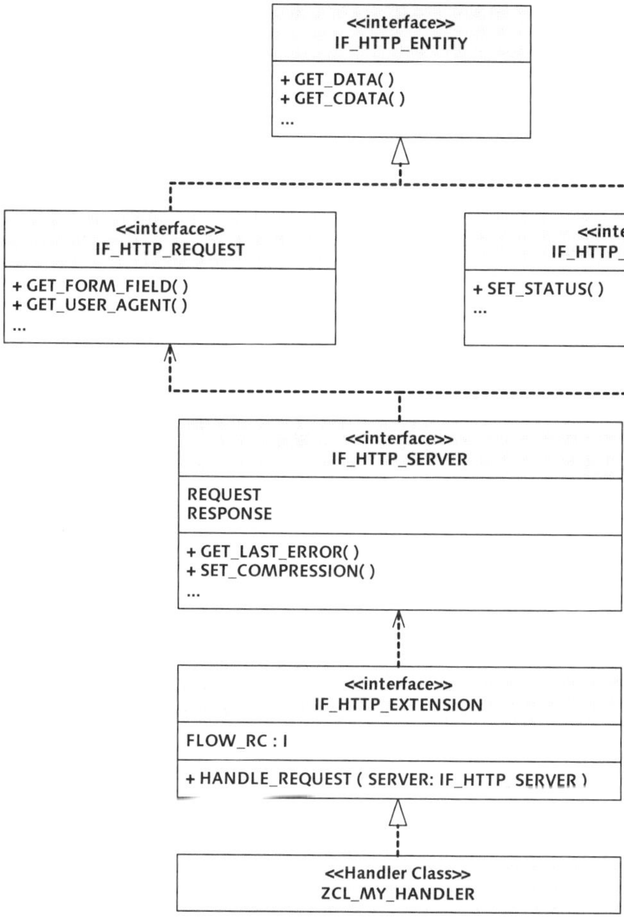


**Figure 9.7** UML Class Diagram for ICF Server-Side API

### 9.4.1 Working with the ICF Server-Side API

Before we get started working on our ICF service implementation, it's helpful to take a look at the classes and interfaces that play a key role in the processing of an HTTP request. The UML class diagram shown in Figure 9.7 depicts these classes and interfaces, as well as their relationships to other components within the framework. From a programming perspective, the entry point into this framework is the

IF_HTTP_EXTENSION interface. This interface defines the structure of handler classes that plug into the ICF service framework. You can think of these handler classes as user exits that you can configure within the ICF to handle requests to particular URLs. We'll see how to configure these URLs in Section 9.4.2, Creating an ICF Service Node.

As you can see in Figure 9.7, the IF_HTTP_EXTENSION interface defines a method called HANDLE_REQUEST(). Handler classes that implement the IF_HTTP_EXTENSION interface provide implementations of this method containing the logic necessary to process an HTTP request. To fulfill this task, the ICF provides a parameter called SERVER that contains an object reference that implements the IF_HTTP_SERVER interface. The SERVER parameter provides access to the HTTP request and response via its instance attributes REQUEST and RESPONSE, respectively. We'll show you how to use these attributes to process an HTTP request in Section 9.4.3, Developing an ICF Handler Class.

### 9.4.2 Creating an ICF Service Node

As we mentioned in Section 9.4.1, Working with the ICF Server-Side API, ICF handler classes handle HTTP requests issued to particular URLs. Of course, the ICF isn't clairvoyant; if you want a particular handler to process a given HTTP request, you must define an *ICF service node*. ICF service nodes are maintained in Transaction SICF.

Figure 9.8 shows the initial screen of Transaction SICF. As you can see, this initial screen provides a selection screen that can be used to narrow a search to specific ICF service nodes. For now, let's take a look at the entire list so that you can see how things are organized. To access the entire list of service nodes, click on the Execute button.

Figure 9.9 shows the maintenance screen for ICF services in Transaction SICF. Here, you can see that the service hierarchy is broken up into *virtual hosts* and *services*:

- **Virtual hosts**
  A virtual host is a specialized node that gets bound to a particular HTTP port defined within the ICM. Most of the time, you'll work with the "default_host" virtual host that gets set up out of the box during the installation process. This

virtual host is normally bound to the default HTTP port for the SAP NetWeaver AS ABAP.[2]

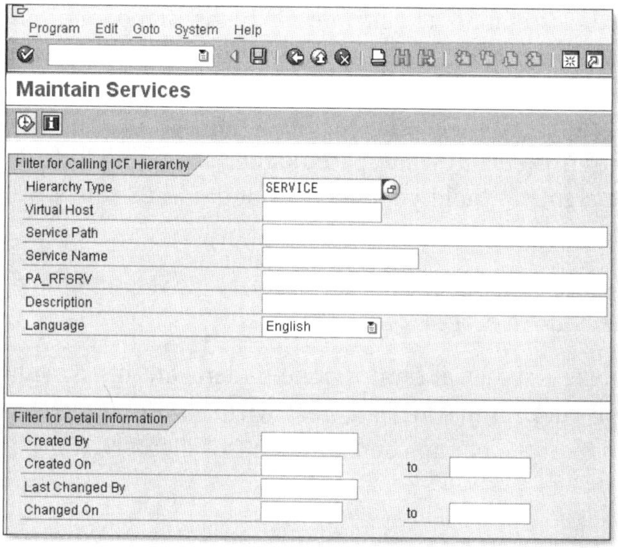

**Figure 9.8** Initial Screen of Transaction SICF

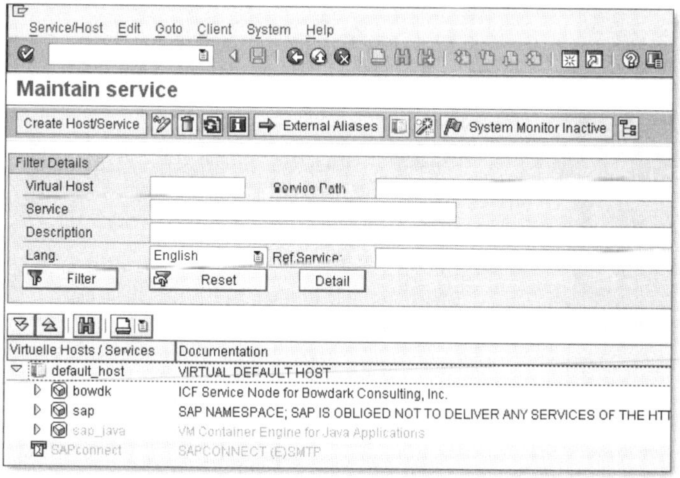

**Figure 9.9** Maintaining ICF Service Nodes

2 The default HTTP port for the SAP NetWeaver AS ABAP is an 8000 series port where the last two digits represent the system number of the SAP NetWeaver AS ABAP system.

- **Services**
  Underneath a virtual host is a series of services that can be nested arbitrarily deep. However, keep in mind that each service level represents a *path variable* in a URL, so you'll want to be careful not to generate a URL that is too long and unwieldy. As you can see in Figure 9.9, SAP provides a default service node called "sap" that comes with many prebuilt services. Because SAP frequently adds new services to this offering, it's recommended that you don't build your custom services underneath this default namespace. Rather, if you have a customer namespace, it's preferable to build your services underneath your own namespace to avoid collisions down the road.

Getting back to our RESTful service example, let's take a look at the steps required to configure a custom service node to process service requests:

1. First of all, we need to create a top-level service node underneath the default virtual host. To do so, right-click on the "default_host" virtual host, and select the New Sub-Element option in the popup context menu (see Figure 9.10).

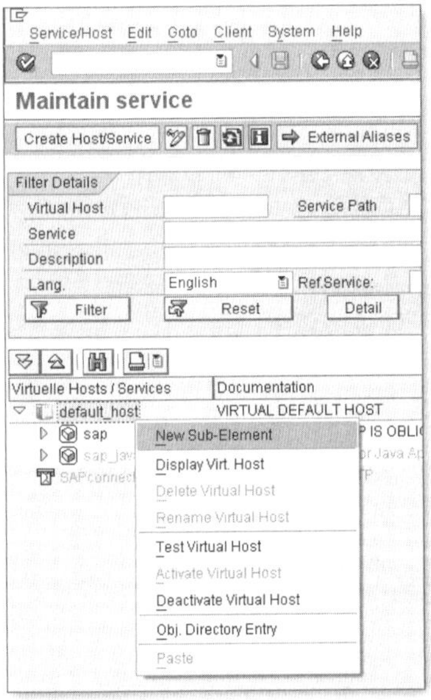


**Figure 9.10** Creating an ICF Service Node — Part 1

2. Before you're allowed to create the service node, you're prompted with a message like the one shown in Figure 9.11. This message basically reiterates SAP's preference that top-level nodes be created underneath a customer namespace.

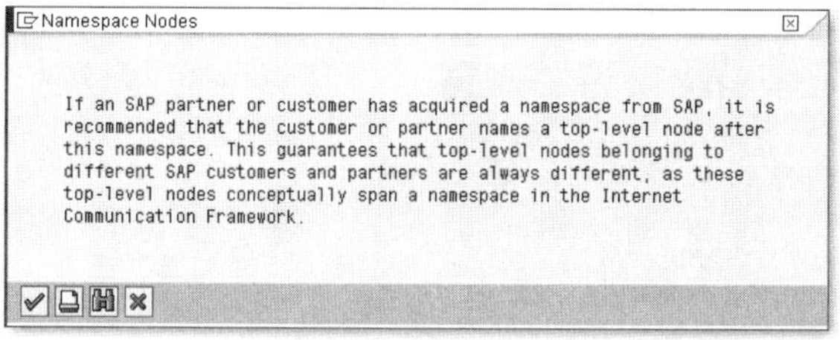


**Figure 9.11** Namespace Warning Issued in Transaction SICF

3. After you confirm the namespace warning in Figure 9.11, you're routed to the Create a Service Element dialog box shown in Figure 9.12. Here, define the service element using a customer namespace. You can press the Enter key to confirm your selection.

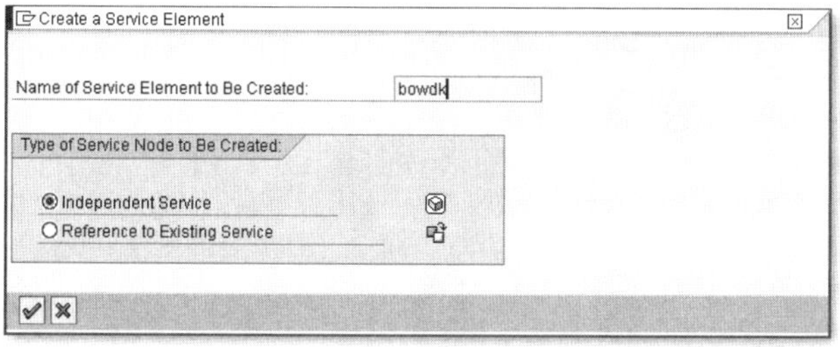


**Figure 9.12** Creating an ICF Service Node — Part 2

4. After the service element is created, you can edit it in the Create/Change a Service screen shown in Figure 9.13. Here, you can enter a short text description of the service and configure some basic service options.
5. Because external HTTP clients will be able to access the system through your ICF service node, you must determine how these clients will authenticate themselves with your service. In most scenarios, clients will authenticate using *basic authentication*. Basic authentication uses user name/password semantics to log a client on to the system. For the purposes of our RESTful Web service example, we want *any* user to be able to access the service. Therefore, on the Logon Data tab shown in Figure 9.14, we've plugged in an anonymous service account called `ANONYMOUS`. All incoming HTTP requests will be processed using this account; allowing clients to access the service without having to authenticate themselves beforehand.

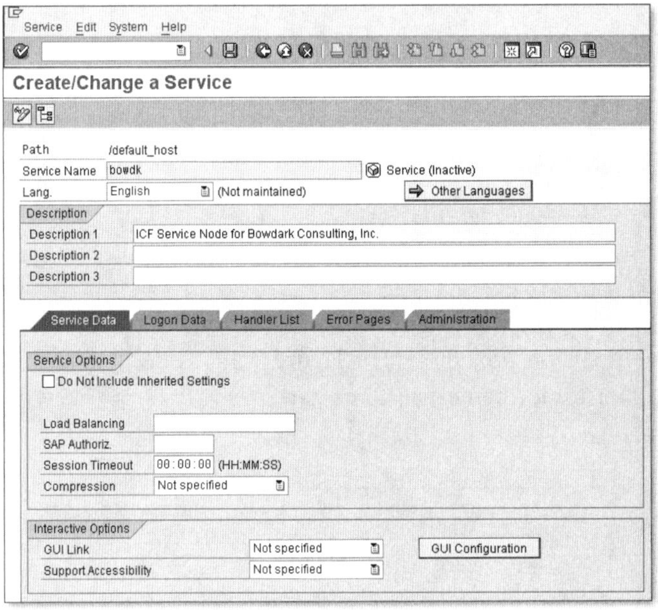


Figure 9.13 Creating an ICF Service Node — Part 3

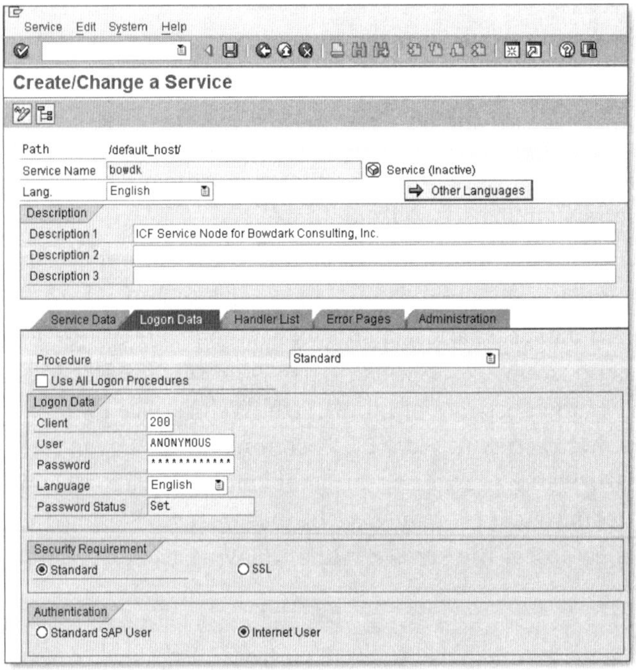


Figure 9.14 Creating an ICF Service Node — Part 4

6. At this point, we're ready to save our service. To do so, click on the Save button in the application toolbar. When you save your changes, you're presented with a warning like the one shown in Figure 9.15. This warning message indicates that the service can't yet be accessed because there is no handler class configured for the service. At this level of the hierarchy, this is actually what we want. We'll define specific functionality farther down in the hierarchy.

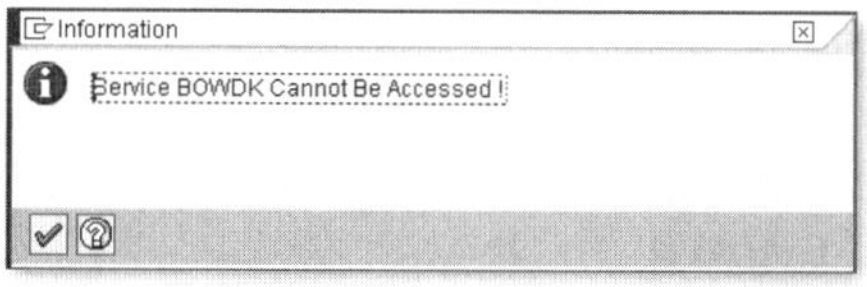


**Figure 9.15** Creating an ICF Service Node — Part 5

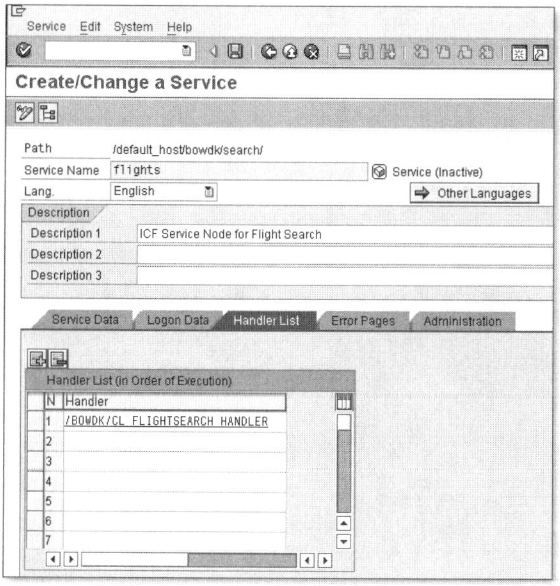


**Figure 9.16** Creating an ICF Service Node — Part 6

7. As soon as the root service node is created, you can begin building custom services underneath your namespace. With the flight search service, we want to define a hierarchy of "/search/flights." The process of creating these lower-level nodes is the same as the one used to create the root-level node. However, after we get down to the "flights" node, we need to plug in a *handler class*. As you can see in Figure 9.16, we've created a class called /BOWDK/CL_FLIGHTSEARCH_HANDLER for

this purpose. This class implements the IF_HTTP_EXTENSION interface described in Section 9.4.1, Working with the ICF Server-Side API. We'll see how this class is implemented in Section 9.4.3, Developing an ICF Handler Class.

8. Finally, after the "flights" service node has been saved, we're ready to activate our changes. To do so, right-click on the "flights" node, and select the Activate Service menu option in the popup context menu (see Figure 9.17). This step is important because ICF service nodes can only be accessed if they are activated.

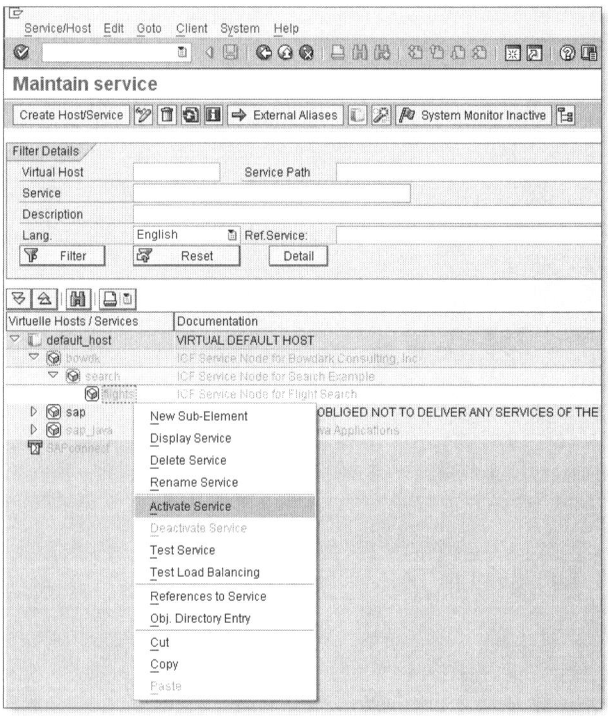


**Figure 9.17** Creating an ICF Service Node — Part 7

### 9.4.3 Developing an ICF Handler Class

At this point, we're finally ready to implement our ICF handler class. Listing 9.5 shows the implementation of the IF_HTTP_EXTENSION~HANDLE_REQUEST() method for class /BOWDK/CL_FLIGHTSEARCH_HANDLER. The basic logic involved in implementing this handler method is quite simple:

1. First, we extract the relevant flight request parameters from the URL query string. Here, we can use the GET_FORM_FIELD() method of the IF_HTTP_REQUEST interface (accessible via the SERVER->REQUEST attribute) to access these variables.
2. Next, we look up the requested flight details using the standard BAPI_FLIGHT_GETDETAIL BAPI function.
3. Before we pass back the results to the HTTP client, we need to encode them in a format that is web friendly. These days, that format is usually XML. So, we need to include a step in there to transform the BAPI results into XML. For this, we use the Simple Transformation language, as introduced in Chapter 8, XML Processing in ABAP. You can see how the /BOWDK/ST_FLIGHT_DETAILS transformation program is implemented by looking at the source code bundle available online.
4. Finally, we need to fill out the HTTP response code and entity body with the results of the query. For the purposes of this simple example, we haven't implemented much in the way of error handling. However, if this were a real service, we would want to be sure and pass back detailed error information in our response message. For a list of standard HTTP response codes, check out *www.w3.org/Protocols/rfc2616/rfc2616-sec10.html.*

```
METHOD if_http_extension~handle_request.
* Method-Local Data Declarations:
  DATA: lv_airline_id  TYPE s_carr_id,
        lv_flight_no   TYPE s_conn_id,
        lv_flight_date TYPE s_date,
        ls_flight_info TYPE bapisfldat,
        lv_flight_xml  TYPE string,
        lo_xml_ex
          TYPE REF TO cx_transformation_error,
        lv_fault_msg   TYPE string.

* Extract the search parameters out of the
* HTTP request:
  lv_airline_id =
    server->request->get_form_field(
      name = 'AIRLINE' ).
```

```
  lv_flight_no =
    server->request->get_form_field(
      name = 'NUMBER' ).

  lv_flight_date =
    server->request->get_form_field(
      name = 'DATE' ).

* Use a standard BAPI to lookup the flight details:
  CALL FUNCTION 'BAPI_FLIGHT_GETDETAIL'
    EXPORTING
      airlineid    = lv_airline_id
      connectionid = lv_flight_no
      flightdate   = lv_flight_date
    IMPORTING
      flight_data  = ls_flight_info.

* Transmit the results back to the client:
  TRY.
*   Transform the results into XML using
*   Simple Transformation:
    CALL TRANSFORMATION /bowdk/st_flight_details
      SOURCE flight_details = ls_flight_info
      RESULT XML lv_flight_xml.

*   Set the HTTP status code:
    if_http_extension~flow_rc =
      if_http_extension=>co_flow_ok.
    CALL METHOD server->response->set_status
      EXPORTING
        code   = 200
        reason = 'OK'.

*   Output the results in the HTTP response
*   entity body:
    CALL METHOD server->response->if_http_entity~set_cdata
      EXPORTING
        data = lv_flight_xml.
  CATCH cx_transformation_error INTO lo_xml_ex.
    lv_fault_msg = lo_xml_ex->get_text( ).
```

```
*    Set the HTTP status code:
     if_http_extension~flow_rc =
       if_http_extension=>co_flow_error.
     CALL METHOD server->response->set_status
       EXPORTING
         code   = 500
         reason = lv_fault_msg.
  ENDTRY.
ENDMETHOD.
```

**Listing 9.5** Implementing an ICF Handler Class

Looking at the code in Listing 9.5, you can see that the basic logic required to process an HTTP request isn't all that complicated. For the most part, you simply look at the HTTP request, determine a course of action, and then generate an HTTP response. Such simplicity gives rise to more advanced frameworks such as BSPs or Web Dynpro for ABAP. Indeed, if you look at the service node at "/sap/bc/bsp," you can see that the BSP runtime environment is driven by a handler class called CL_HTTP_EXT_BSP (see Figure 9.18). Similarly, the Web Dynpro runtime environment is defined by a handler class called CL_WDR_MAIN_TASK.

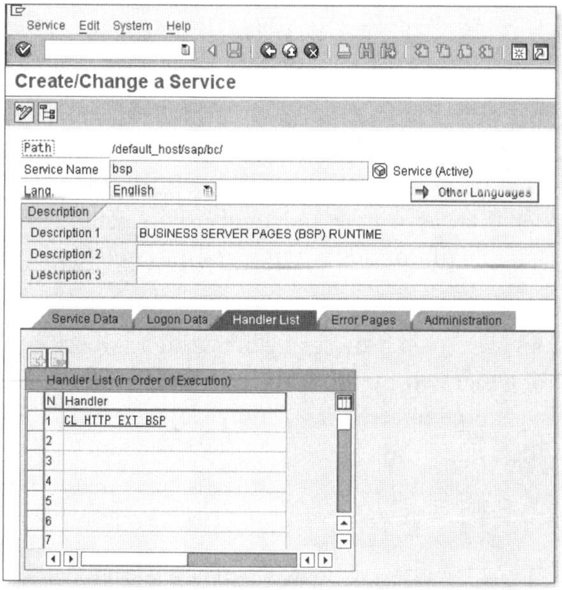


**Figure 9.18** Handler List for BSP Runtime Environment

If you look carefully at the Handler List tab in Figure 9.18, you can see that it's possible to plug in multiple handler classes for a particular service node. This functionality makes it possible to process HTTP requests using the *Chain of Command* design pattern. However, for this to work, individual handler classes need a way of responding to the ICF so that it can know whether or not it should proceed with processing a given request. This information is captured in the form of a return code attribute called `FLOW_RC` that is defined in the `IF_HTTP_EXTENSION` interface. Though it's not strictly required, it's a good practice to always fill in this value so that the framework knows whether or not your handler method was successful.

### 9.4.4 Testing the ICF Service Node

After you've finished developing your ICF handler class, you have several options for testing it. Perhaps the easiest way to test your code is to set an external breakpoint in the `IF_HTTP_EXTENSION~HANDLE_REQUEST()` method so that you can trace through the program flow in the ABAP Debugger. You can set external breakpoints in your method code by clicking on the Set/Delete External Breakpoint button in the Class Builder (see Figure 9.19). After the breakpoint is set, the ABAP Debugger fires up whenever you access the service via its configured URL. For my local server, the URL to access this service looks like this: *http://evergreen.home:8000/bowdk/search/flights?airline=AA&number=0017&date=20081022*. Of course, this URL varies based on the underlying host name/port of your SAP NetWeaver AS ABAP instance.

Unfortunately, anonymous services like the flight search service we've created in this section are difficult to debug. This is because the service executes using the "ANONYMOUS" user account rather than your own personal user account. For these types of services, you have a couple of options when it comes to testing:

- Because the flight search is based on a simple HTTP `GET` request, you can actually test the service directly in your local web browser by browsing to the target URL. Figure 9.20 shows the XML generated by the service in the Mozilla Firefox browser. Here, you can view the generated XML source by selecting the View • Page Source menu option.

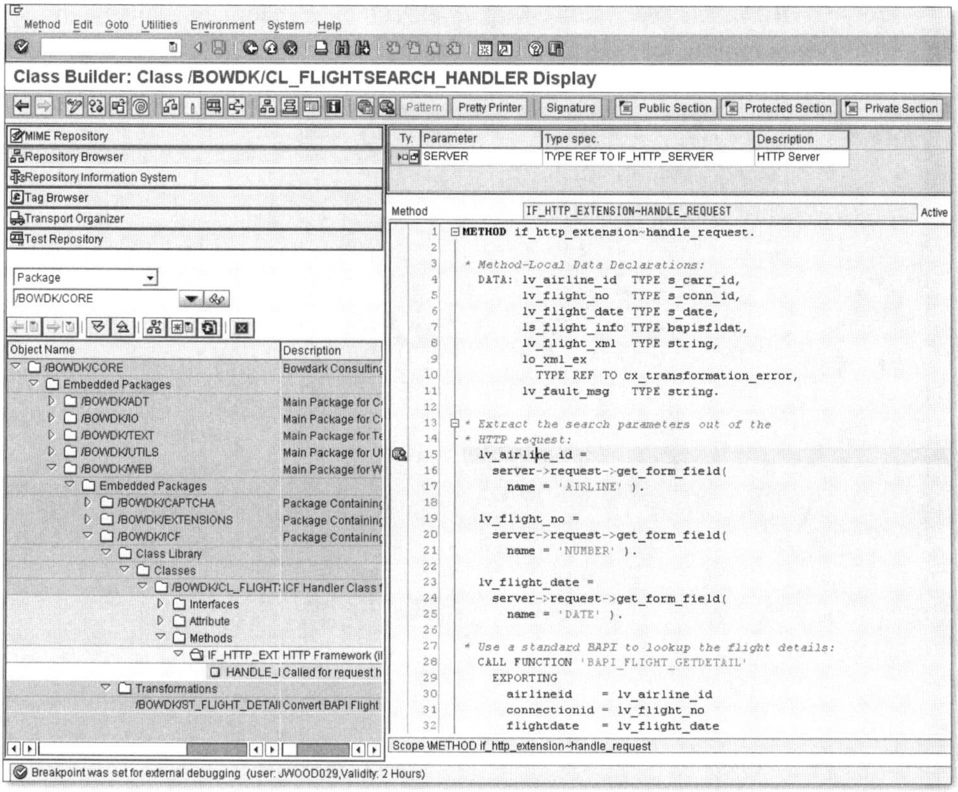

**Figure 9.19** Debugging ICF Handler Classes

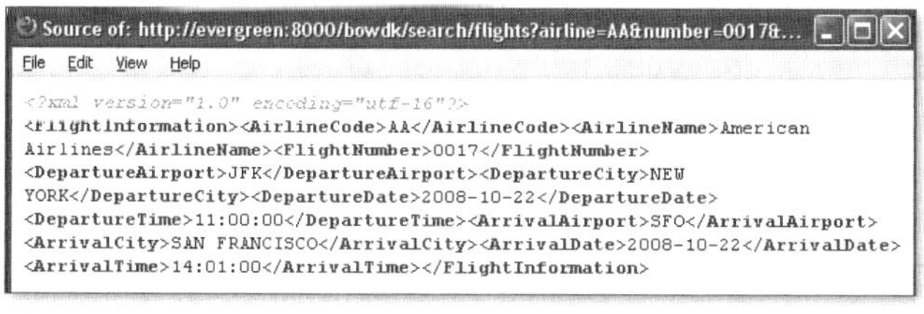

**Figure 9.20** Viewing the XML Source in Mozilla Firefox

- The other alternative is to create a simple REST client program that accesses the service directly. This client could be written in ABAP (like the one demonstrated in Section 9.3, Developing an HTTP Client Program), or in some other language. Figure 9.21 shows an example of a client written using the Adobe Flex framework and deployed using the Adobe AIR runtime environment. The source code for this client along with an executable version are available in the source code bundle for this book available online.

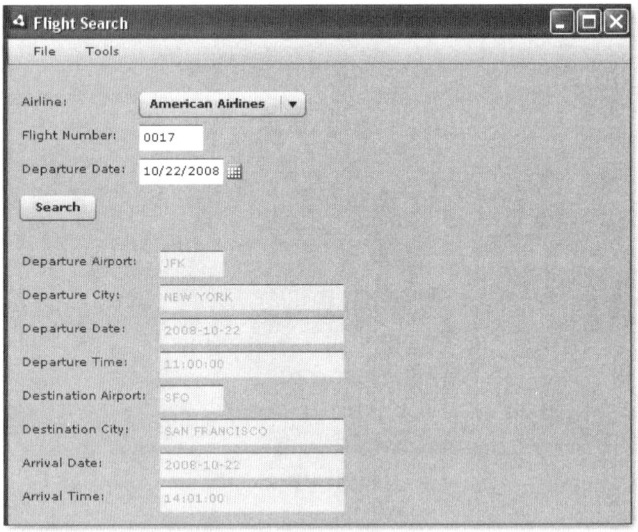


**Figure 9.21** An Adobe AIR REST Client

## 9.5 Summary

This chapter demonstrated some of the core capabilities made available with the introduction of the ICF. As you learned, these features make it possible to directly tap into the power of the Web. However, most of the time, you'll prefer to harness this functionality at a higher level of abstraction. In the next chapter, we show you how the Web Service Framework allows you to develop SOAP-based Web services without having to worry about lower-level HTTP transport issues.

*When the cupboard is bare, a chef must get creative and come up with new recipes using the ingredients on hand. In today's tough economic climate, companies are looking at ways of applying these same principles to cut costs. In this chapter, we show you how Web services can be used to get the most out of existing solutions and easily tap into new ones.*

# 10 Web Services

In Chapter 9, Web Programming with the ICF, we showed you how to build distributed applications using web-based technologies. These distributed applications were implemented in two parts: a client program and a server program. As you may recall, we frequently referred to the server-side portion of these applications as *services*. We even introduced you to a particular type of service architecture when we developed some examples based on the RESTful Web service model.

Our emphasis on a service-based design hasn't been by accident. These days, it's becoming increasingly important for companies to leverage their existing IT infrastructures toward the development of component-based composite applications. This architectural approach is referred to as a *service-oriented architecture* (SOA). Web services represent the building blocks of SOA, enabling all kinds of disparate applications both inside and outside of the enterprise to participate in collaborative processes.

In this chapter, we show you how to work with the Web Service Framework provided with SAP NetWeaver AS ABAP. As you'll soon see, this framework makes it possible to both consume and expose Web services from an ABAP context. After you learn how to work with this framework, you can use it to transform your existing SAP infrastructure into an SOA.

## 10.1 Web Service Overview

Generally speaking, the meaning of the term *Web service* is pretty open ended. For instance, the W3C defines a Web service as "...a software system designed to support interoperable machine-to-machine interaction over a network...." However, most of the time, whenever people talk about Web services, they are talking about Web services based on SOAP.

In this section, we introduce you to SOAP and some of the surrounding technologies that are used to interact with SOAP-based Web services. However, before we do so, it may be useful to look at another definition of Web services given by Michael Papazoglou in his book *Web Services: Principles and Technology* (Pearson Education Limited, 2008): "A Web service is a self-describing, self-contained software module available via a network, such as the Internet, which completes tasks, solves problems, or conducts transactions on behalf of a user or application." As we progress through our discussion on Web services, this definition should help you understand the positioning of specific tools within the Web services technology stack.

### 10.1.1 Introduction to SOAP

When you get past all of the hype, Web services are about facilitating inter-process communication (IPC). As such, despite the fact that they have enabled interoperability on an unprecedented scale, they aren't all that different conceptually from other IPC technologies such as a remote procedure call (RPC), remote function call (RFC), or remote method invocation (RMI). In fact, much of the modern Web service infrastructure has its roots in these legacy technologies. This is particularly the case when it comes to SOAP.

When the SOAP recommendation was originally submitted to the W3C, the term "SOAP" was an acronym for *simple object access protocol.* While this acronym has been removed in subsequent releases of the specification, it still gives us a feel for the positioning of SOAP as a type of *distributed object communication protocol.* In other words, it's a messaging protocol that enables Web service clients and Web service providers to communicate with one another in a structured manner over a network such as the Internet.

One of the things that sets SOAP apart from previous messaging protocols is that it uses XML as its message format. The use of an open technology such as XML facilitates language/platform independence, enabling all kinds of disparate applications to communicate with one another. Perhaps more importantly, the ubiquitous nature of XML means that SOAP clients and service providers don't have a *symmetrical requirement* like legacy applications did using technologies such as the *Common Object Request Broker Architecture* (or CORBA). Here, both ends of the communication would require the use of a common library that defines a mapping between a generic *interface description language* (IDL) and native data types. There is no such requirement with SOAP.

Figure 10.1 shows the structure of a SOAP message. As you can see, the root element of a SOAP message is the `<Envelope>` element. Within a SOAP envelope, you have an optional `<Header>` element and a mandatory `<Body>` element; everything else is left up to the application. For example, in Figure 10.1, the SOAP body contains a representation of a call to a method named `CreatePurchaseOrder`. However, instead of arranging the data in the form of a method call, we could have just as easily passed the purchase order data in document-style format similar to the one used in *Intermediate Documents* (IDocs).

```
<soap: Envelope
  xmlns: soap=" http://www.w3.org/2003/05/soap-envelope">
  <! - -
    The SOAP header contains optional application-specific
    information such as authentication tokens, etc.
   - ->
  <soap: Header>

  </ soap: Header>

  <! - -
    The SOAP body contains the actual message in RPC or
    document style format
   - ->
  <soap: Body>
    <Create Purchase Order>
      <POHeader>
        <PONumber>1234567890</ PONumber>
        <CreationDate>2010-01-13</ CreationDate>
      </ POHeader>
      <POItems>
        <POItem>
          <POItem>00010</ POItem>
          <Product>345623421</ Product>
        </ POItem>
      </ POItems>
    </ CreatePurchaseOrder>
  </ soap: Body>
</ soap: Envelope>
```

**Figure 10.1** Structure of a SOAP Message

Normally, SOAP uses HTTP as its transport layer protocol. However, it's technically possible to use other types of transport protocols, such as SMTP or FTP instead of HTTP. When HTTP is used as the transport layer protocol, the SOAP envelope is embedded as the request entity body of an HTTP POST request and submitted to a service provider. The target service provider then receives and decodes the message so that it can be processed by some kind of backend application module. For synchronous Web services, the results of the operation are returned in the entity body of the HTTP response message. This message flow is depicted in Figure 10.2. We'll see examples of this flow in Sections 10.2, Providing Web Services, and 10.3, Consuming Web Services.

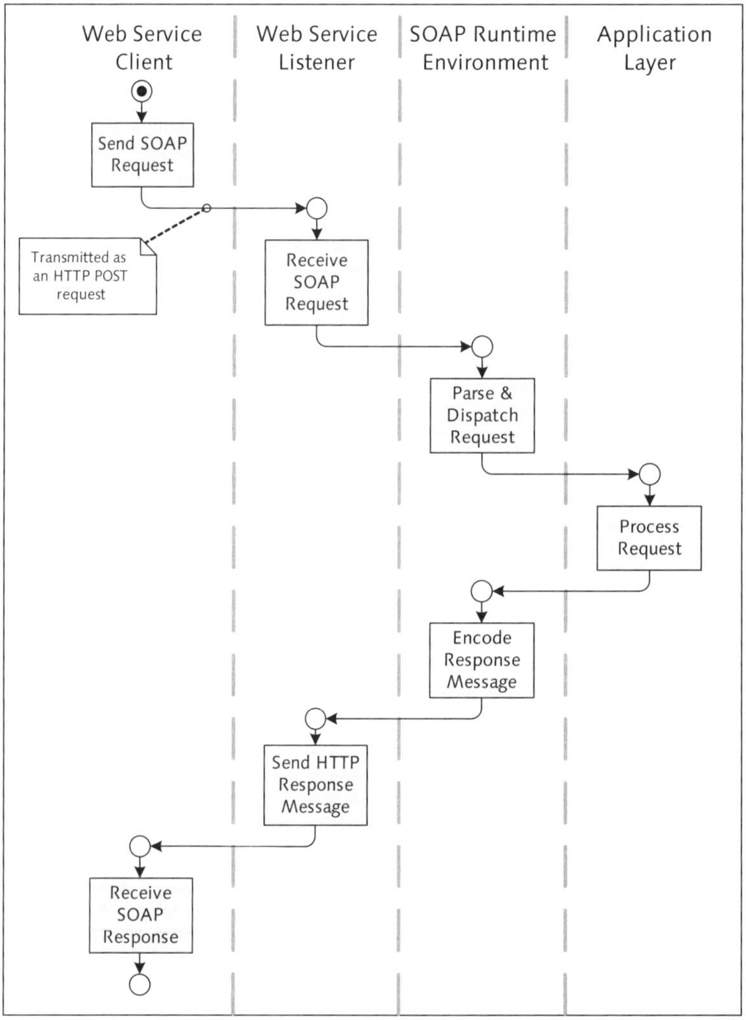


**Figure 10.2** Transmitting a SOAP Request over HTTP

### 10.1.2 Describing SOAP-Based Services with WSDL

As you learned in Section 10.1.1, Introduction to SOAP, SOAP doesn't have much to say about the functional characteristics of a Web service. Although this freedom gives service providers tremendous flexibility when it comes to designing Web services, it also presents a gap in the sense that clients need some form of documentation to consume a particular Web service. For example, how does a client know what the format of a SOAP request/response should look like for a given service? While such information could be captured in written form in an interface design document, it's advantageous to describe the interface in a standard, machine-readable format that can be used by Web service clients to generate *proxy objects*. We'll have a chance to look at proxy objects in more detail in Section 10.3, Consuming Web Services. For now, suffice it to say that proxies make it much easier for clients to consume Web services.

SOAP Web services are described using an XML-based service description language called the *Web Services Description Language* (WSDL). A WSDL document consists of various elements that define the operations supported by a Web service, the messages that are exchanged, and so on. As you might expect, the type declarations for the messages are defined using the XML Schema language introduced in Chapter 8, XML Processing in ABAP.

The information captured in a WSDL document makes a Web service *self-describing*. In other words, Web service clients can use the contents of a WSDL document to figure out how to build SOAP request messages, determine where messages should be sent, and so on.

Although you'll be interacting with WSDL quite a bit throughout the course of your Web service development, you'll rarely (if ever) have to develop the WSDL documents yourself. Instead, Web services toolkits like the ABAP Web Service Framework will take care of generating the WSDL for you. We'll see an example of a generated WSDL document in Section 10.2, Providing Web Services.

### 10.1.3 Web Service Discovery with UDDI

Developing Web services is a necessary first step toward implementing an SOA. However, your development efforts are wasted if no one within the organization uses these Web services in their own developments. Of course, you could try to advertise the existence of these services, but the effectiveness of your campaign is subject to the attention spans of developers that are often narrowly focused on other tasks.

A more effective way to get the word out about Web services is to publish them in a publicly available service registry. That way, developers can come and browse for services on demand. The *Universal Description, Discovery, and Integration* (UDDI) specification defines a standard for implementing these service registries.

Figure 10.3 shows how a UDDI service registry unites a Web service consumer with a Web service provider. As you can see, the description and discovery process takes place in three steps:

1. First, a Web service provider creates a Web service and publishes the WSDL to the UDDI service registry.
2. Next, a Web service consumer comes along looking for a particular kind of Web service and browses through the UDDI registry looking for a match. After a match is found, the consumer can then download the provider's WSDL file and generate a Web service proxy.
3. Finally, at runtime, the Web service proxy is used to broker SOAP-based communications between the Web service client and the target Web service.

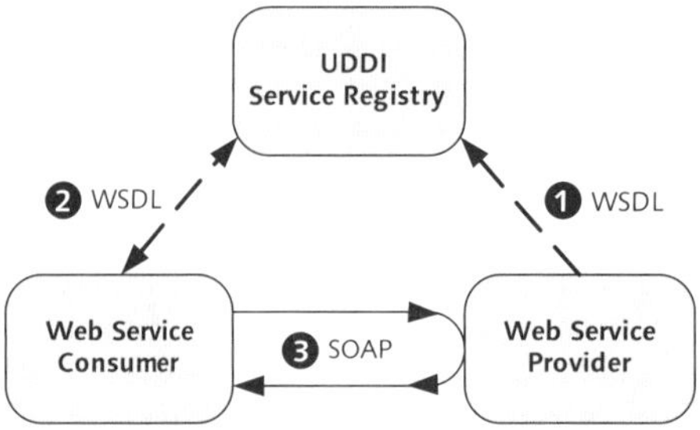


**Figure 10.3** Web Service Description and Discovery Cycle

Beginning with NetWeaver 7.1, SAP has delivered a UDDI-compliant registry called *Enterprise Services Repository (ES Repository) and Services Registry*. Because we're more interested in developing Web services from an ABAP perspective, we won't consider the ES Repository further here. However, if you're interested in learning more about the ES Repository, check out *www.sdn.sap.com/irj/sdn/nw-esr*.

## 10.2 Providing Web Services

The ABAP Web Service Framework makes it possible to design Web service providers using two different approaches:

- **Inside-out**
  In this scenario, preexisting ABAP objects (namely RFC-enabled function modules) are used as the basis for generating the service provider.
- **Outside-in**
  In this scenario, a service interface defined in the ES Repository is used to generate the skeleton of the service provider. The actual implementation code must be developed after the fact.

For the purposes of this book, we concentrate our focus on the inside-out approach. This approach makes it possible to Web service-enable preexisting RFC functions, BAPIs, and so on. It also makes it easy to develop new Web services from scratch based on custom RFC-enabled function modules. However, if you have an instance of SAP NetWeaver Process Integration (SAP NetWeaver PI) in your landscape, then you may want to take a look at all of the value-added features it can provide in an outside-in-based scenario.

### 10.2.1 Creating Service Definitions

To develop a Web service provider in the ABAP Web Service Framework, you must create a *service definition*. Service definitions can be created in the ABAP Workbench with the help of the Service Wizard. To demonstrate how to create service definitions using the Service Wizard, let's look at how you would Web service-enable a simple BAPI such as `BAPI_FLIGHT_GETDETAIL`:

1. You can start the Service Wizard inside the Object Navigator (Transaction SE80) by right-clicking a package and selecting the CREATE • ENTERPRISE SERVICE context menu option (see Figure 10.4).
2. The first step in the Service Wizard gives you an opportunity to determine the type of object you want to create. To create service providers, you select the Service Provider radio button (see Figure 10.5).
3. Next, you need to determine the approach that you want to take to develop the service provider. Because we're defining a Web service around the BAPI module `BAPI_FLIGHT_GETDETAIL`, we've selected the Existing ABAP Objects (Inside Out) radio button here (see Figure 10.6).

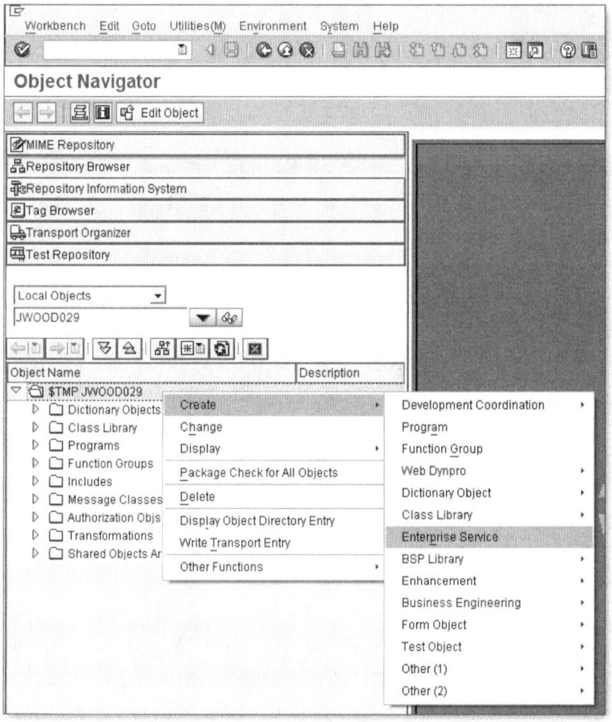


**Figure 10.4** Invoking the Service Wizard in Transaction SE80

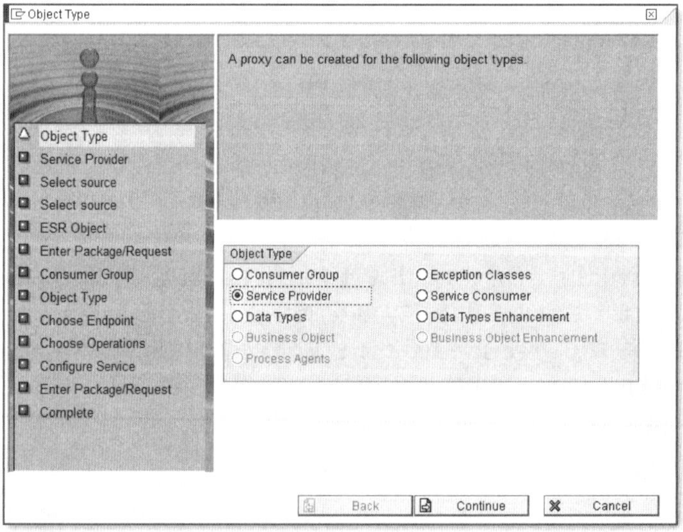


**Figure 10.5** Creating a Service Definition — Part 1

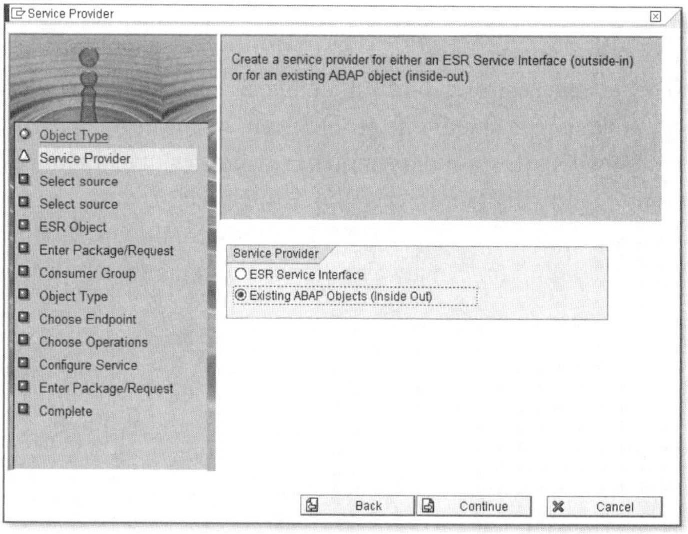


**Figure 10.6** Creating a Service Definition — Part 2

4. After you determine the approach you want to take to generate your service provider, provide a name and short text description for your service definition (see Figure 10.7). You also need to select the appropriate Endpoint Type (i.e., Function Module, etc.).

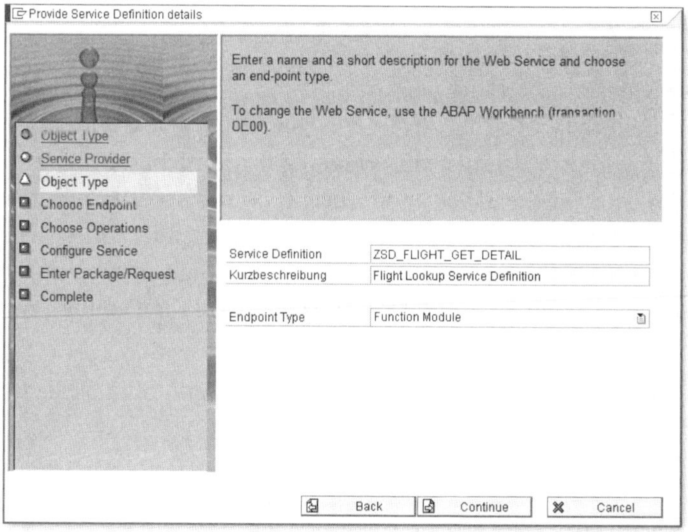


**Figure 10.7** Creating a Service Definition — Part 3

5. The next screen allows you to select the name of the function module you want to use to implement your endpoint. If you look closely at Figure 10.8, you can see that we've also selected the Mapping der Namen checkbox. While this text field apparently didn't make it into the English translation, its meaning is fairly straightforward. Essentially, its selection determines how you want to map the names of function module parameters into the WSDL interface. In most cases, you'll want to at least start with name mapping. Then, if you're unhappy with the derived ABAP-centric names, you can always change them later.

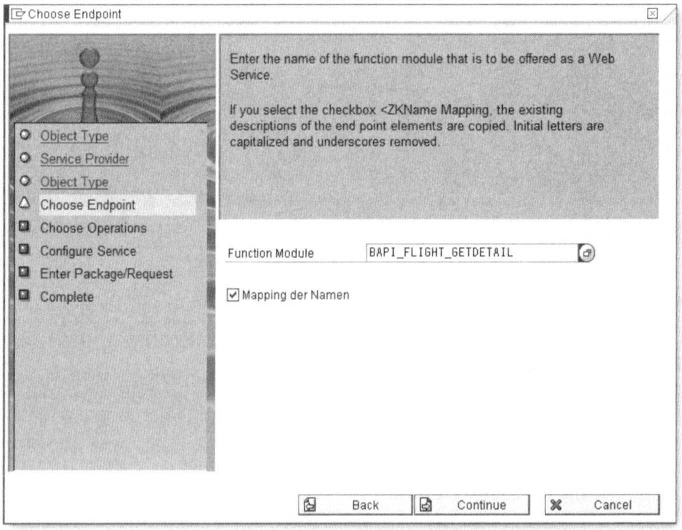


**Figure 10.8** Creating a Service Definition — Part 4

6. The screen shown in Figure 10.9 allows you to configure some basic runtime settings for the service, such as the SOAP application type and security profile. These default settings are only meant to serve as a baseline and can be customized and overridden at runtime as necessary. However, to do so, you must deploy the service to the runtime environment by clicking on the Deploy Service checkbox shown in Figure 10.9.

7. Before you can complete the service definition, you must assign it to a package and transport request (see Figure 10.10).

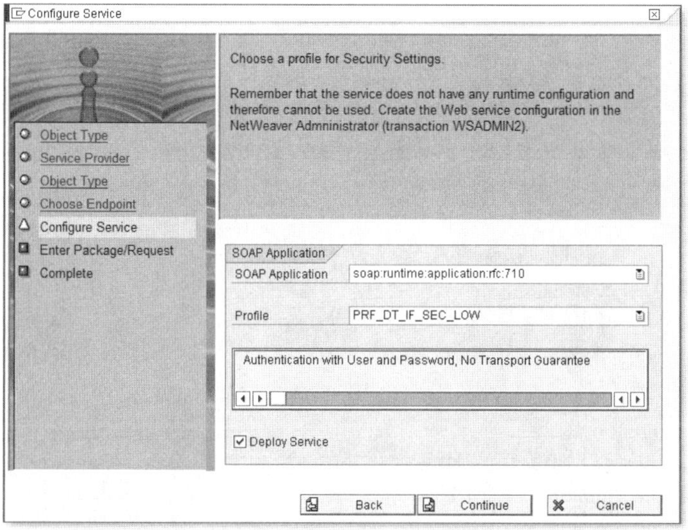


**Figure 10.9** Creating a Service Definition — Part 5

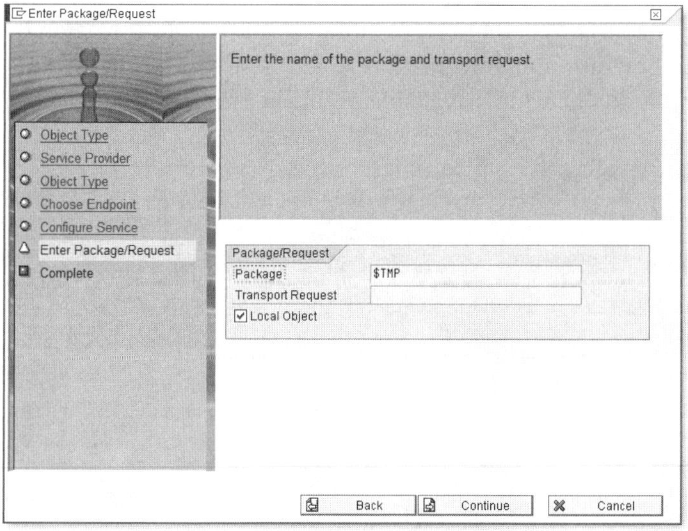


**Figure 10.10** Creating a Service Definition — Part 6

8. Finally, you can complete the service definition by clicking on the Complete button shown in Figure 10.11. At this point, the Service Wizard generates the service provider object.

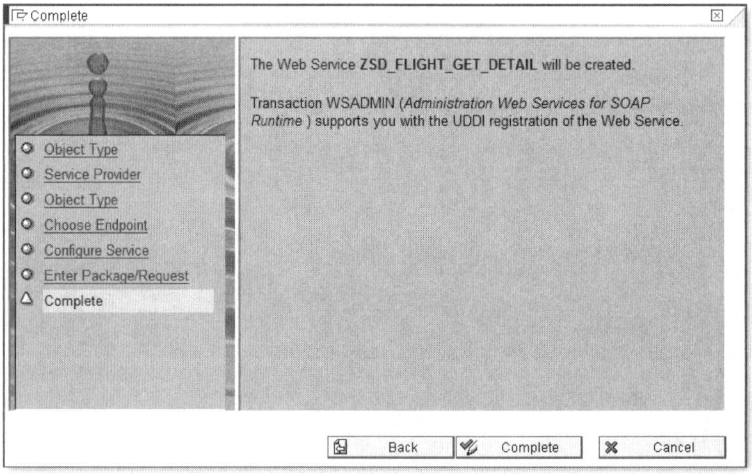


**Figure 10.11** Creating a Service Definition — Part 7

Figure 10.12 shows the completed service definition in the Service Definition editor integrated into the Object Navigator. In this editor perspective, you have the option of changing the names of parameters, defining default values for parameters, and so on. You can find out more information about these features in the SAP Library help for ABAP Workbench Tools available online at *http://help.sap.com*.

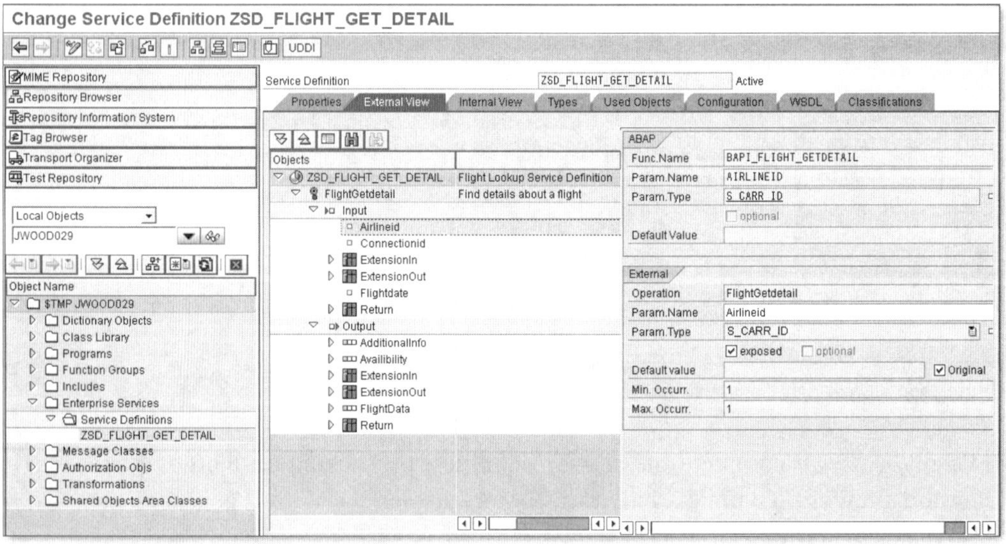


**Figure 10.12** Editing Service Definitions in Transaction SE80

### 10.2.2 Configuring Runtime Settings

As you learned in Section 10.2.1, Creating Service Definitions, service definitions are initially configured with some basic default runtime values by the Service Wizard whenever they are initially created. In most cases, you want to override these default settings in non-test environments. For this task, you must use Transaction SOAMANAGER. Unlike most ABAP Workbench transactions, this transaction opens up a browser window with a Web Dynpro for ABAP based editor. To maintain runtime settings for a service definition, open Transaction SOAMANAGER, and perform the following steps:

1. On the initial SOA Management screen, select the Business Administration tab, and click on the link entitled Web Service Administration (see Figure 10.13).

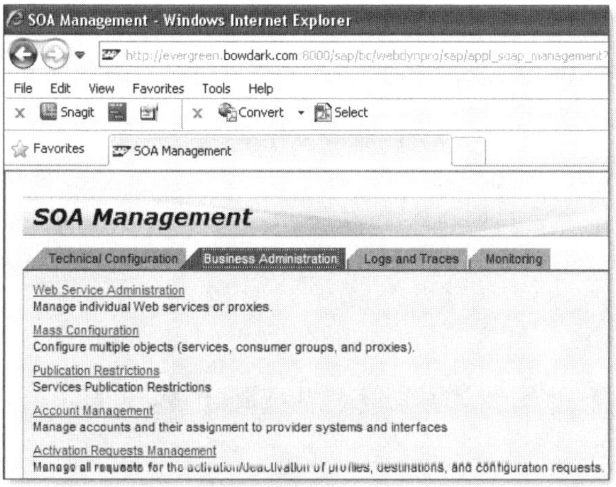


**Figure 10.13** Managing Web Services in Transaction SOAMANAGER

2. This brings you to a screen in which you can search for your service definition (see Figure 10.14). After you've found your service definition, you can click on the Apply Selection button to open the Service Configuration editor.
3. When you open a service definition in the Service Configuration editor, you're initially routed to an overview screen that provides some basic information about the service. Here, you can open the WSDL document for the service by clicking on the Open WSDL Document for Selected Binding link (see Figure 10.15). Figure 10.16 shows the generated WSDL document in an Internet Explorer browser window. For a text-based representation of the WSDL, you can select the View • Source menu option in Internet Explorer and save the XML file to a directory on your local machine.

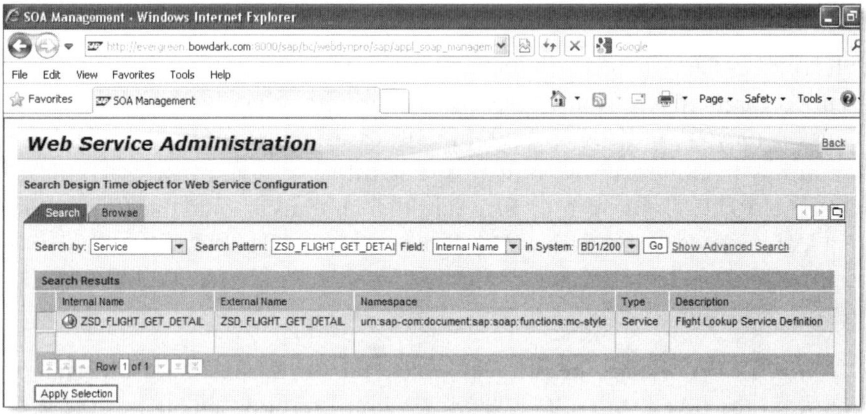


**Figure 10.14** Selecting the Appropriate Service Definition

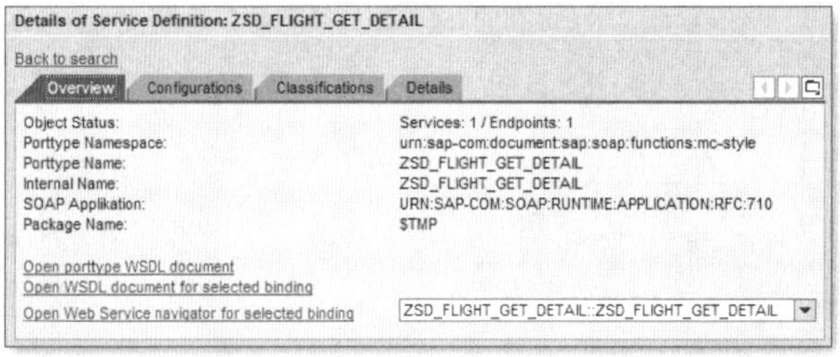


**Figure 10.15** Viewing the Details of a Service Definition

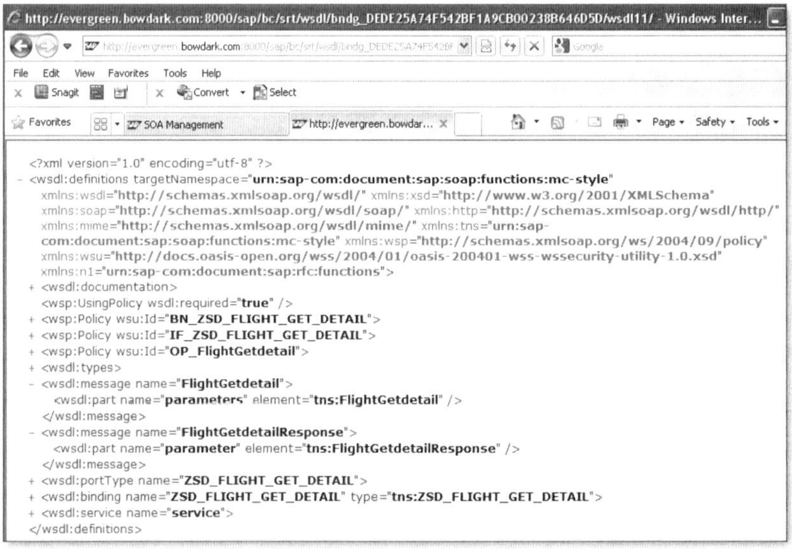


**Figure 10.16** Viewing the WSDL Document for the Service Definition

4. In addition to viewing basic settings, you can also edit an endpoint on the Configurations tab. To do so, simply select the service and click on the Edit button (see Figure 10.17).

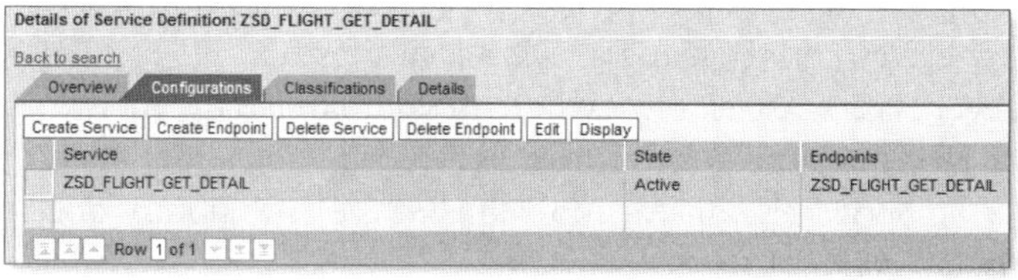


**Figure 10.17** Editing an Endpoint — Part 1

5. This brings you to an editor screen in which you can configure settings related to transport guarantee, authentication, and so on (see Figure 10.18). When you're finished with your configuration tasks, you can confirm your changes by clicking on the Save button.

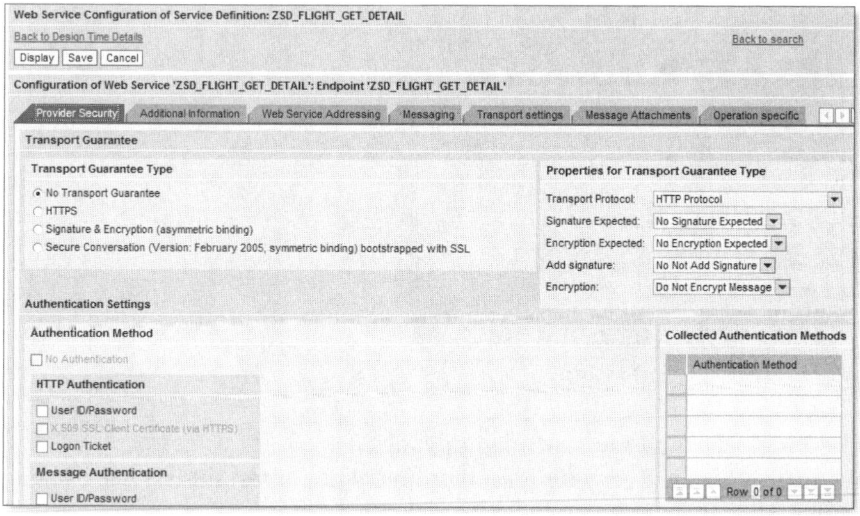


**Figure 10.18** Editing an Endpoint — Part 2

As you can see in Figure 10.18, there are quite a few settings that you can configure for your service endpoints. For simple service scenarios, you probably won't have to worry about most of these settings. However, it's always nice to know they're there if you need them. And when you do, you can consult the SAP Library help documentation available online at *http://help.sap.com* to find out more information about how specific settings work.

### 10.2.3 Testing Service Providers

Before you publish your Web service for others to use, it's always a good idea to test it out and make sure that the underlying service provider is working as it should be. While you could write a simple ABAP test program to test the service, it's much easier to test the Web service using a Web service test tool. If you have access to a SAP NetWeaver AS Java stack somewhere in your landscape, then you can use the Web Service Navigator tool for this task. For information about how to configure and use the Web Service Navigator tool, consult the SAP Library documentation at *http://help.sap.com*.

In addition to the Web Service Navigator tool, there are many other Web service test tools available in the market today; many of which are free. One popular freeware test tool is called soapUI, and it's available for download at *www.soapui.org*.

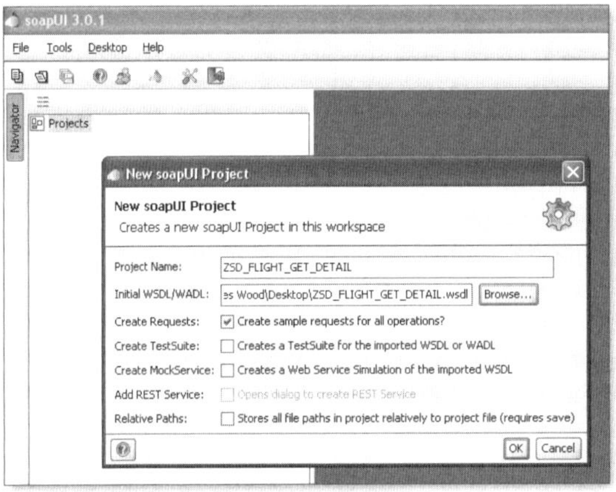


**Figure 10.19** Creating a Project in soapUI

Let's take a look at how to test our flight detail Web service using soapUI. After you have soapUI installed on your local machine, you can test this service by performing the following steps:

1. First, open up the soapUI tool, and create a new project using the FILE • NEW SOAPUI PROJECT menu option.
2. In the resultant dialog box, you can browse to the WSDL file that you want to test with in the Initial WSDL/WADL input field. For example, in Figure 10.19, we've selected the WSDL file that was generated for the `ZSD_FLIGHT_GET_DETAIL` service definition in Transaction SOAMANAGER. Click on the OK button to load the WSDL file.

3. To test the Web service, you must build a SOAP request. You can do this by clicking on the SOAP request in the Projects navigator (see Figure 10.20). Here, as you can see, you can edit the SOAP request XML with the parameters you want to test with.

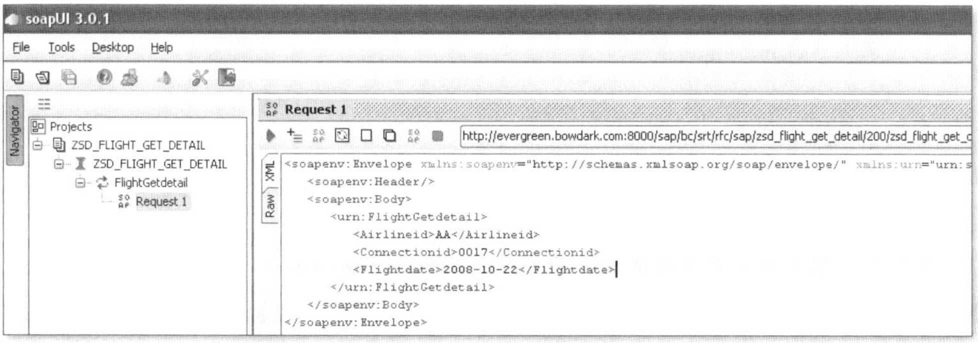

Figure 10.20 Building a SOAP Request in soapUI

4. Because the SOAP runtime component of the ABAP Web Service Framework is implemented in the form of an ICF service, some form of authentication is required to test the Web service. Normally, most services use basic authentication, which can be configured on the Aut tab in the request editor (see Figure 10.21).

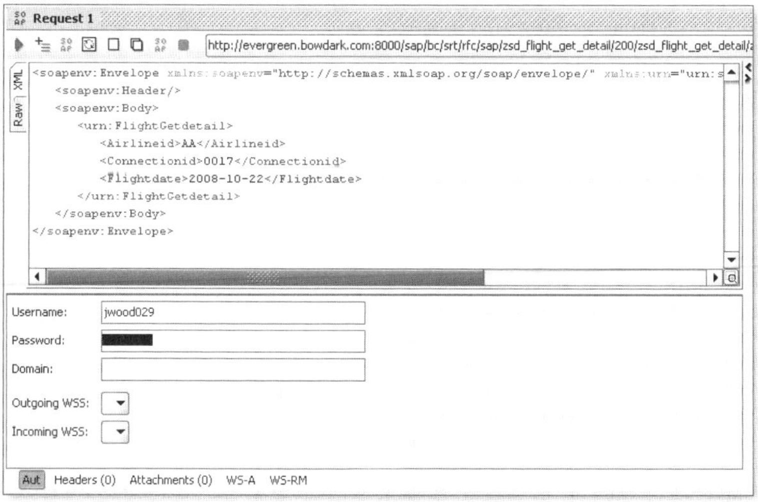

Figure 10.21 Configuring Basic Authentication in soapUI

5. To invoke the Web service, you simply click on the green triangle button in the toolbar above the SOAP request editor (see Figure 10.22).

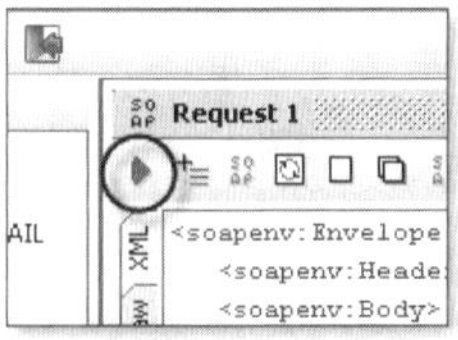

**Figure 10.22** Executing a Test in soapUI

6. Assuming everything is working correctly, you should be able to see a SOAP response message in the response message pane shown in Figure 10.23.

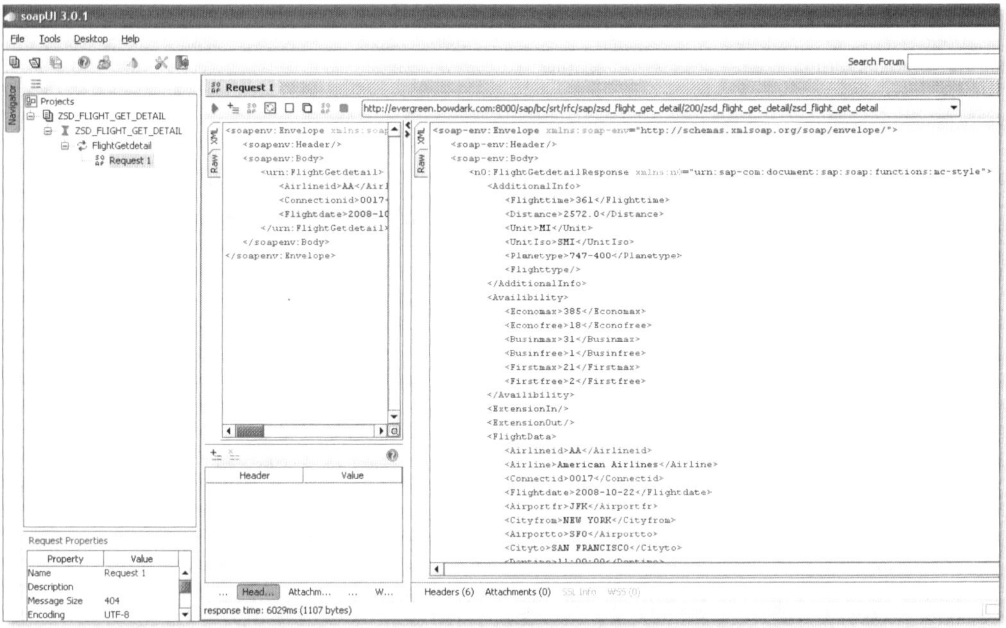

**Figure 10.23** Viewing the Test Results in soapUI

## 10.3 Consuming Web Services

Now that you know how to provide Web services in ABAP, let's take a look at how you consume a Web service using the ABAP Web Service Framework. This process begins with the development of a service consumer in the ABAP Workbench. After this service consumer is created, you can invoke its defined Web service methods just as you would call a normal method in an ABAP Objects class.

In this section, we'll demonstrate how to use ABAP service consumers to access Web services. As a basis for our discussion, we'll consider how to create a service consumer that can be used to invoke the flight search service developed in Section 10.2, Providing Web Services. Then, after the service consumer is created, we'll show you how to use it to access the flight search service in an ABAP program.

### 10.3.1 Creating a Service Consumer

To create a service consumer, we must once again call upon the Service Wizard built into the Object Navigator. Here, you must perform the following steps:

1. First, open up the Object Navigator, and select the appropriate package in which you want to create the Web service consumer object. Then, right-click the package name, and select the CREATE • ENTERPRISE SERVICE context menu option (see Figure 10.24).

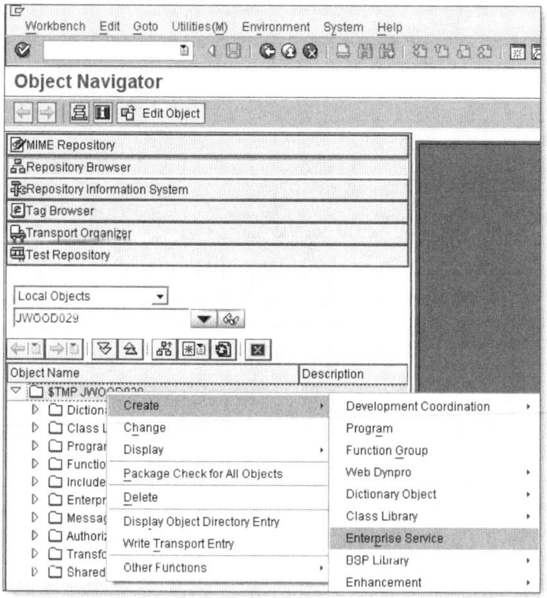


**Figure 10.24** Accessing the Service Wizard in the Object Navigator

2. In the Object Type screen shown in Figure 10.25, select the Service Consumer radio button.

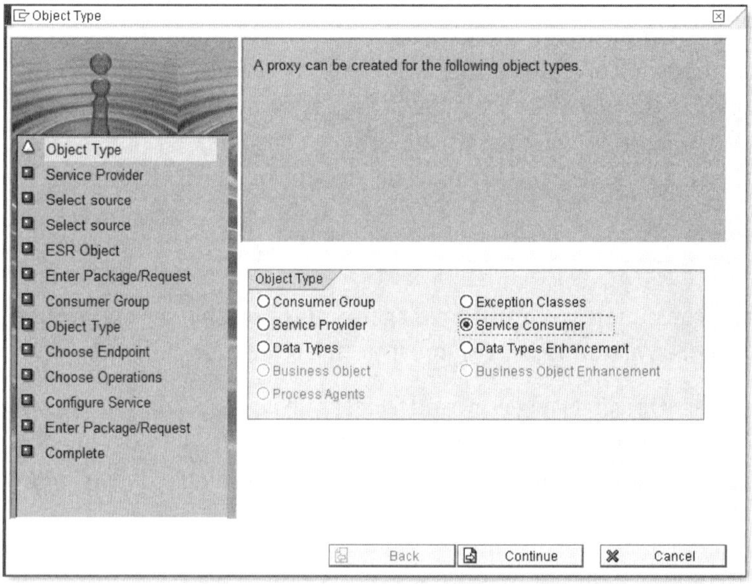


**Figure 10.25** Creating a Web Service Consumer — Part 1

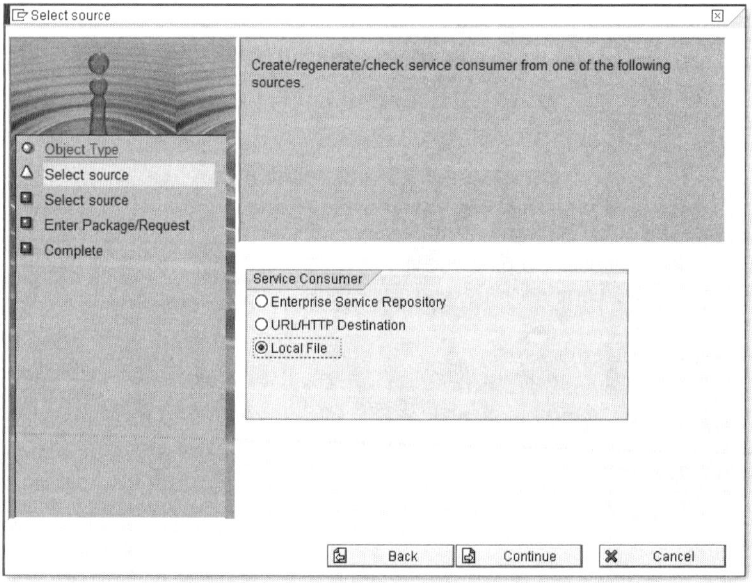


**Figure 10.26** Creating a Web Service Consumer — Part 2

3. The next screen, shown in Figure 10.26, allows you to choose the source of the WSDL file that is being used to generate the service consumer. Here, you can select a WSDL file in the ES Repository, browse to a WSDL file via some external URL, or upload a WSDL file on your local machine.
4. Depending on the type of WSDL source that you select, you're next prompted with an input mask that allows you to specify the source of the WSDL file (see Figure 10.27).

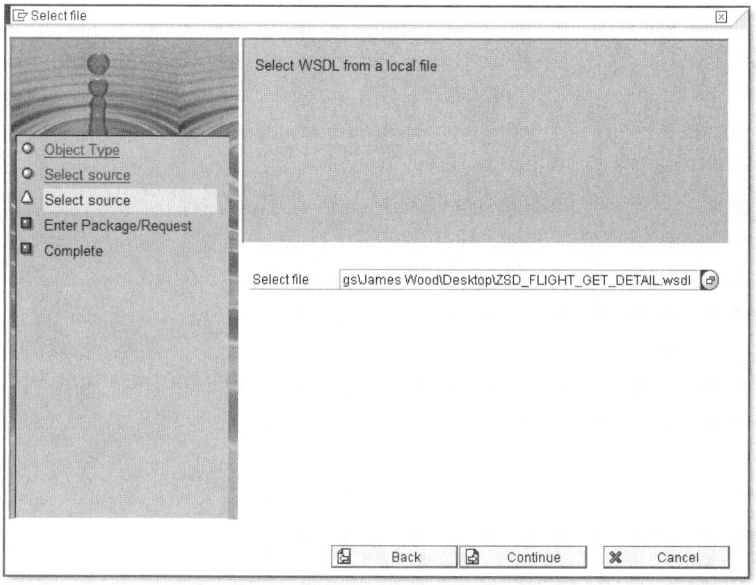


Figure 10.27 Creating a Web Service Consumer — Part 3

5. Before you can complete the definition of the service consumer, you must assign it to a package and a transport request. You must also define a *prefix* that is used by the Service Wizard to generate all of the relevant ABAP Dictionary objects, and so on needed to model the service. As you can see in Figure 10.28, we've simply selected the normal customer namespace prefix Z for the purposes of this example.

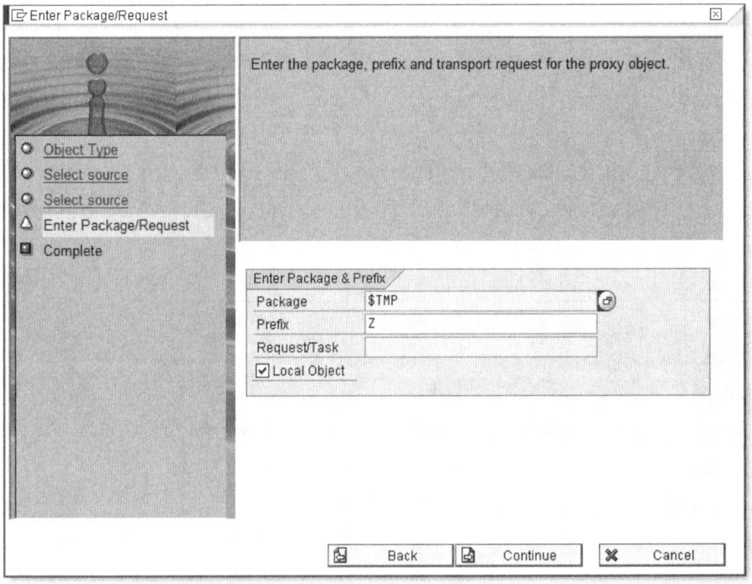


**Figure 10.28** Creating a Web Service Consumer — Part 4

6. After you're satisfied with all of your selections, you can click on the Complete button to generate the service consumer (see Figure 10.29).

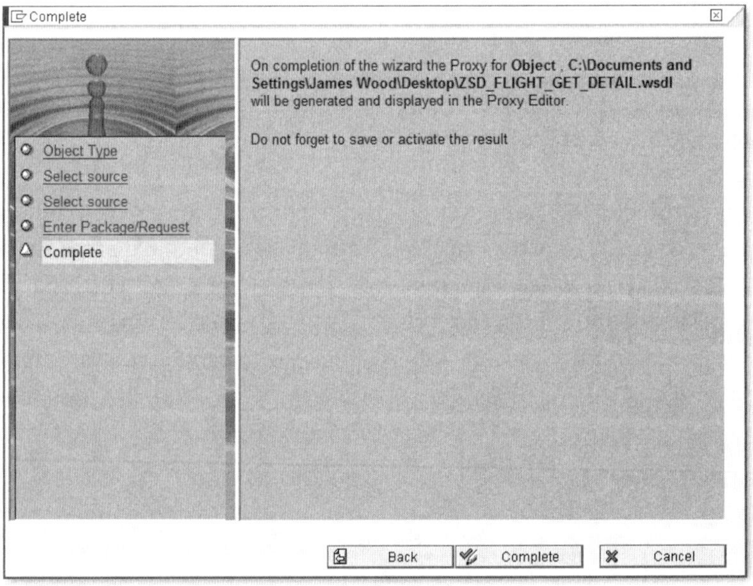


**Figure 10.29** Creating a Web Service Consumer — Part 5

**What If the Service Wizard Looks Different on My System?**

Web service standards, like a lot of standards for cutting-edge technologies, are a moving target. So, while SAP has been bolstering its support for Web services over the past few years, new developments have come along that have impacted how service consumers are configured. Consequently, depending on the support pack level of the SAP NetWeaver system you're working on, you may find that your Service Wizard screens differ from those depicted throughout the course of this section. In this case, we recommend that you refer to the SAP Library help for your particular SAP NetWeaver release online at *http://help.sap.com*.

Assuming all goes well with the proxy generation process, you should see the resultant service consumer in the service consumer perspective of the Object Navigator (see Figure 10.30). Here, you can see the name of the generated ABAP proxy class, its defined operations, and so on.

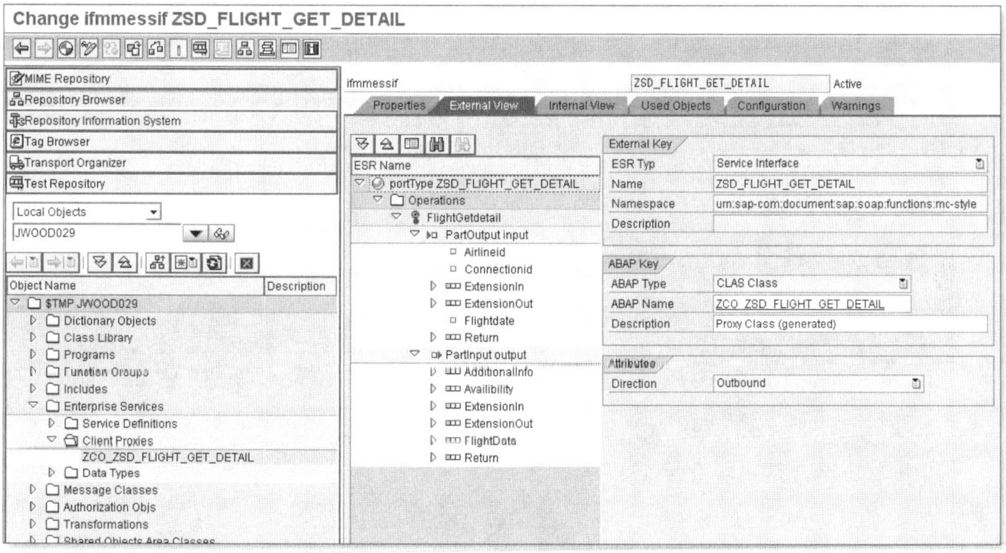


**Figure 10.30** Editing Service Consumers in the Object Navigator

## 10.3.2 Defining a Logical Port

The service consumer that we created in Section 10.3.1, Creating a Service Consumer, is a *design-time* repository object. In other words, while it implements the interface of a particular Web service, it doesn't maintain information internally about concrete service details, such as the target endpoint URL, authentication parameters, and so on. This is by design because such details are *configuration-time* parameters that usually need to be adjusted in different environments. Otherwise, you could run into situations where code in production calls a Web service hosted in a development environment, or vice versa.

Within the context of the ABAP Web Service Framework, the configuration-time details of a service consumer object are defined externally in the form of a *logical port*. In the past, logical ports were maintained in Transaction LPCONFIG. However, beginning with support pack 12 of SAP NetWeaver 7.0, logical ports can now be maintained in Transaction SOAMANAGER.

The steps required to create a logical port in Transaction SOAMANAGER are as follows:

1. First, you must open the transaction and select the Web Service Administration link on the Business Administration tab (see Figure 10.13). Here, search for your service consumer using the Consumer Proxy list option shown in Figure 10.31. After you locate your service consumer, select the entry, and click on the Apply Selection button.

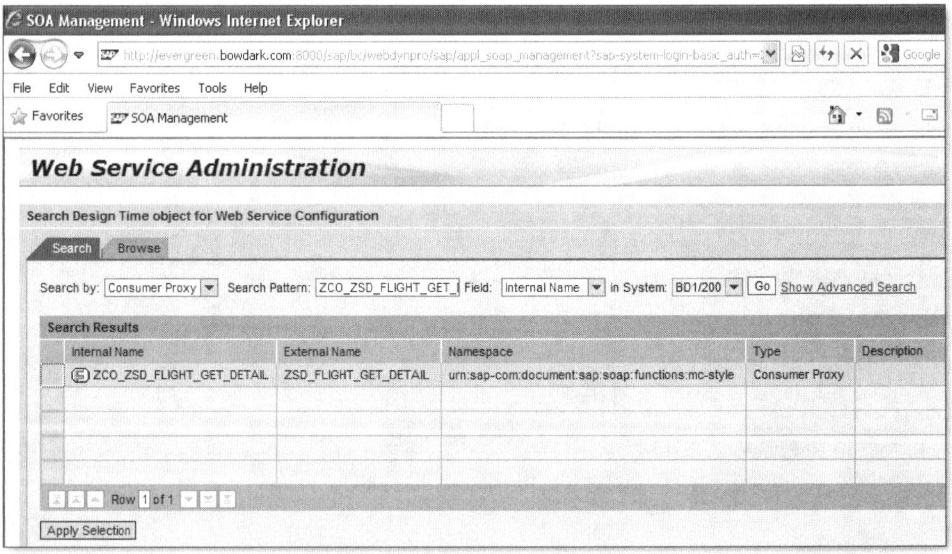


**Figure 10.31** Locating a Service Consumer in SOAMANAGER

2. After the service consumer is selected, the details of the proxy definition are displayed in the lower portion of the screen. To create a new logical port, select the Configurations tab for your proxy definition, and then click on the Create Logical Port button (see Figure 10.32).

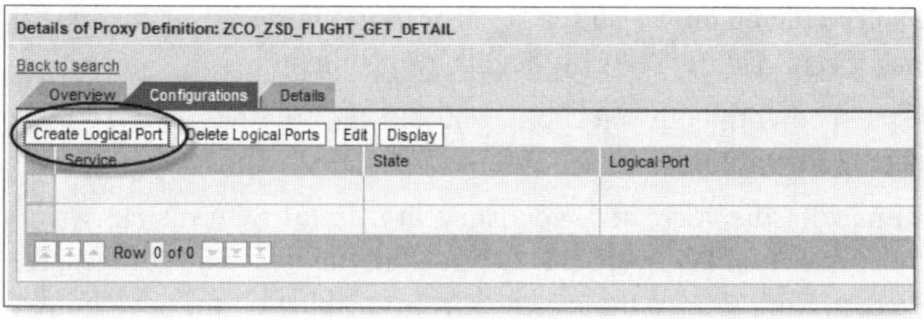


**Figure 10.32** Creating a Logical Port in SOAMANAGER — Part 1

3. In the SOA Management popup screen shown in Figure 10.33, you must define a new service name and logical port name. You also have the option of determining whether or not the logical port is the *default* logical port within the SOAP runtime environment. While most environments only have a single logical port definition for a given service, there are certain scenarios where you might have more than one port for a given service consumer.

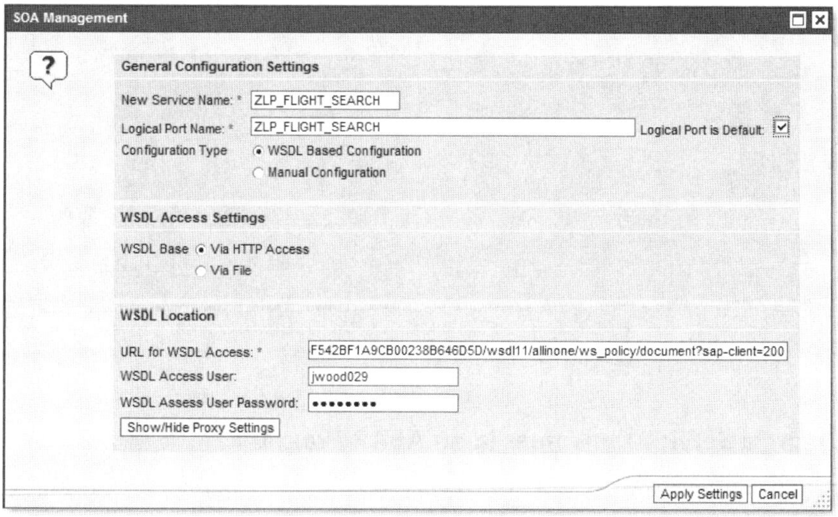


**Figure 10.33** Creating a Logical Port in SOAMANAGER — Part 2

4. In addition to the general configuration settings shown in Figure 10.33, you also need to select the configuration type for the logical port. Most of the time, you should select WSDL Based Communication here because the WSDL document should contain most of the proper settings already. However, if you prefer, you can choose Manual Configuration to define the logical port settings manually. In Figure 10.33, we've selected the WSDL Based Configuration option. When

this option is selected, you must also specify a location for the WSDL file so that the SOA manager can load the relevant details into context.

5. When you're satisfied with your selections, you can click on the Apply Settings button to create the logical port.
6. After a logical port has been created, you can edit it in the SOA manager configuration screen shown in Figure 10.34. When all of the relevant settings have been configured, be sure to save the logical port by clicking on the Save button (see Figure 10.34).

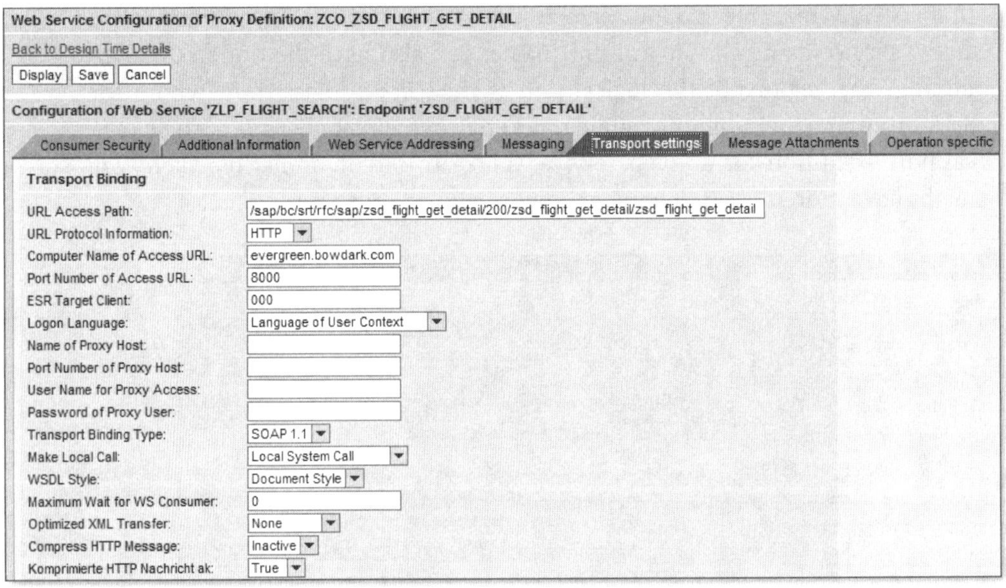


**Figure 10.34** Editing a Logical Port in SOAMANAGER

### 10.3.3 Using a Service Consumer in an ABAP Program

After a service consumer is created, it's very easy to use it to invoke Web services in an ABAP program. For the most part, a Web service call using a service consumer looks like any normal call to a method in an ABAP Objects class. Of course, there is a lot of framework code behind the scenes required to actually transmit the call, but fortunately all of this is abstracted from a client's perspective.

Let's take a look at the code required to invoke the flight search service using the ZCO_ZSD_FLIGHT_GET_DETAIL service consumer created in Section 10.3.1, Creating a Service Consumer. To demonstrate this, we've created a simple report program called ZWSCLIENT_DEMO. Before we look at this code in detail, let's examine how the ABAP Web Service Framework tools can be used to simplify the service call.

In Figure 10.35, you can see that we have a subroutine called GET_FLIGHT_DETAILS that we want to use to invoke the Web service. Rather than coding the service call from hand, you can simply place your cursor on the line in which you want to call the service and drag-and-drop the service consumer object from the Repository Browser on the left side of the screen onto the ABAP editor. Figure 10.36 shows the generated template code provided by the ABAP Web Service Framework. You can then tweak this template code to adhere to project naming conventions, and so on.

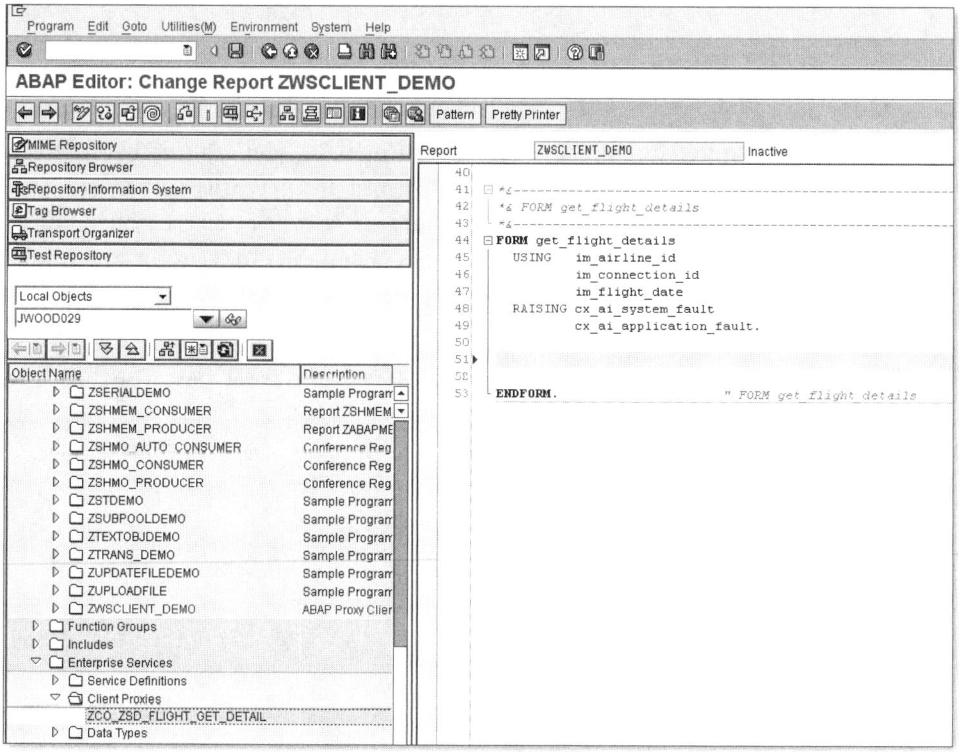


**Figure 10.35** Creating a Service Call in the ABAP Workbench — Part 1

```
*&---------------------------------------------------------------------*
*& FORM get_flight_details                                             *
*&---------------------------------------------------------------------*
FORM get_flight_details
  USING   im_airline_id
          im_connection_id
          im_flight_date
  RAISING cx_ai_system_fault
          cx_ai_application_fault.

DATA: XXXXXXXX TYPE REF TO ZCO_ZSD_FLIGHT_GET_DETAIL .
TRY.
    CREATE OBJECT XXXXXXXX
*  EXPORTING
*    LOGICAL_PORT_NAME  =
        .
  CATCH CX_AI_SYSTEM_FAULT .
ENDTRY.
*   data: OUTPUT type ZFLIGHT_GETDETAIL_RESPONSE .
*   data: INPUT type ZFLIGHT_GETDETAIL .
*TRY.
CALL METHOD XXXXXXXX->FLIGHT_GETDETAIL
  EXPORTING
    INPUT  =
*  IMPORTING
*    OUTPUT =
    .
* CATCH CX_AI_SYSTEM_FAULT .
* CATCH CX_AI_APPLICATION_FAULT .
*ENDTRY.


ENDFORM.                    " FORM get_flight_details
```

**Figure 10.36** Creating a Service Call in the ABAP Workbench — Part 2

Looking at the generated template code in Figure 10.36, you can see that it refers to an ABAP Objects class called ZCO_ZSD_FLIGHT_GET_DETAIL. This class is an ABAP proxy class that is generated behind the scenes whenever a service consumer is created. You can see the name of the generated class in the Proxy group box on the Properties tab of the Service Consumer editor perspective in the ABAP Workbench (see Figure 10.37).

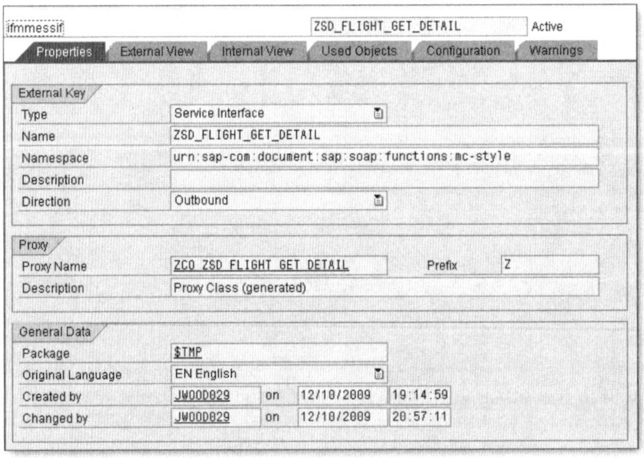


**Figure 10.37** Accessing the ABAP Proxy Class of a Service Consumer

If you double-click on the proxy class name, the ABAP Workbench opens the class in the Class Editor (see Figure 10.38). Here, you can see that the Service Wizard has defined methods based on the WSDL operation details, as well as some framework methods that support more advanced Web service scenarios involving reliable messaging, transaction processing, and so on.

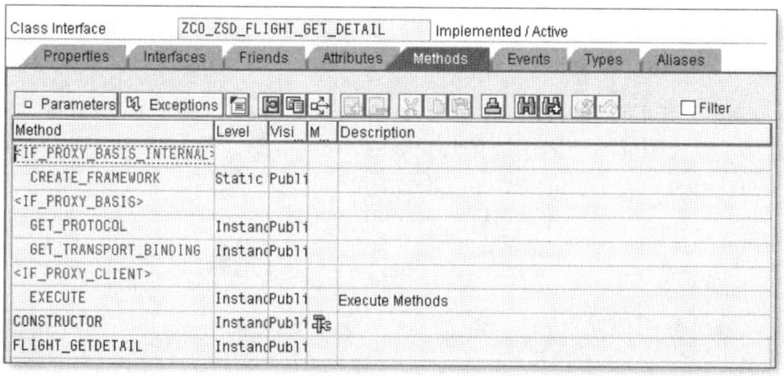


**Figure 10.38** Viewing an ABAP Proxy Class in the Class Editor

Listing 10.1 contains the completed code for the ZWSCLIENT_DEMO report program. This simple report provides a basic selection screen in which users can search for a particular flight connection. As you can see in the GET_FLIGHT_DETAILS subroutine, if you didn't know that class ZCO_ZSD_FLIGHT_GET_DETAIL was an ABAP proxy class, you probably couldn't tell that a Web service was being called when method FLIGHT_GETDETAIL() was invoked. This is of course by design, demonstrating the power of the ABAP Web Service Framework.

```
REPORT zwsclient_demo.
CLASS lcl_flight_service DEFINITION.
  PUBLIC SECTION.
    CLASS-METHODS:
      get_flight_details
        IMPORTING im_airline_id    TYPE s_carr_id
                  im_connection_id TYPE s_conn_id
                  im_flight_date   TYPE s_date.
ENDCLASS.

CLASS lcl_flight_service IMPLEMENTATION.
  METHOD get_flight_details.
*   Method-Local Data Declarations:
    DATA: lo_ws_proxy TYPE REF TO
            zco_zsd_flight_get_detail,
          ls_input    TYPE
```

```
            zflight_getdetail,
          ls_output   TYPE
            zflight_getdetail_response.

*   Lookup the requested flight details:
    TRY.
*     Create an instance of the Web service proxy:
      CREATE OBJECT lo_ws_proxy.

*     Fill in the required parameters:
      ls_input-airlineid    = im_airline_id.
      ls_input-connectionid = im_connection_id.
      ls_input-flightdate   = im_flight_date.

*     Execute the Web service method:
      CALL METHOD lo_ws_proxy->flight_getdetail
        EXPORTING
         input  = ls_input
        IMPORTING
          output = ls_output.

*     Display the results:
      WRITE: / 'Flight', ls_output-flight_data-connectid,
               'from', ls_output-flight_data-airportfr,
               'to', ls_output-flight_data-airportto,
               'departing on',
               ls_output-flight_data-flightdate
               MM/DD/YYYY.
    CATCH cx_root.
      "Exception handling goes here...
    ENDTRY.
  ENDMETHOD.                  " METHOD get_flight_details
ENDCLASS.

PARAMETERS:
  p_carr TYPE s_carr_id,      "Carrier
  p_conn TYPE s_conn_id,      "Flight Number
  p_date TYPE s_date.         "Flight Date

START-OF-SELECTION.
  CALL METHOD lcl_flight_service=>get_flight_details
    EXPORTING
      im_airline_id    = p_carr
```

```
    im_connection_id = p_conn
    im_flight_date   = p_date.
```

**Listing 10.1** Report Program ZWSCLIENT_DEMO

## 10.4 Next Steps

While we hope that this whirlwind introduction to Web services helped answer a few questions, we recognize that it probably raised quite a few more. Realistically, the topic of Web services is so broad that we could write several books and still not cover everything. If you're looking for a more comprehensive description of Web service technology, we highly recommend *Web Services: Principles and Technology* (Pearson Education Limited, 2008).

There is also a wealth of Web service information available on the SAP Developer Network at *www.sdn.sap.com*. In particular, Thomas Jung has provided an excellent video blog that demonstrates some of the more advanced features of the ABAP Web Service Framework, such as reliable messaging and new features available in SAP NetWeaver 7.1. You can access this video blog at *www.sdn.sap.com/irj/scn/weblogs?blog=/pub/wlg/8086*.

## 10.5 Summary

This chapter provided a whirlwind introduction to SOA and SOAP-based Web services. For a more detailed treatment of these topics, we highly recommend *Developing Enterprise Services for SAP* (SAP PRESS, 2009). In addition to comprehensive coverage of the Web Service Framework, this book also provides invaluable knowledge related to SOA modeling and design. In the next chapter, we look at another popular application hosted on the Internet: email.

*When working in a kitchen, instant communication among chefs is key to the success of a meal. For people working out of the same kitchen, this communication is simply verbal; but for other industries, more technological solutions are required. In this chapter, we show you how to send and receive email using ABAP.*

# 11 Email Programming

Normally, whenever we talk about interface programming in ABAP, we're talking about application-to-application (A2A) or business-to-business (B2B) integration scenarios in which two systems exchange *structured messages* (i.e., IDocs, SOAP messages, etc.) that are machine-readable. However, we often need to communicate with end users both inside and outside of the system. For instance, if an error occurs within a critical process, someone needs to be notified immediately. Or, if sales orders are received over the Internet, customers need to be notified of milestones in the order fulfillment process. Most users prefer to receive these kinds of messages via email.

In this chapter, we show you how to send and receive email messages using ABAP. Along the way, we introduce you to the *Business Communication Services* (BCS) API that provides a common interface for transmitting messages via SMTP, fax, SMS, and so on. We conclude our discussion by showing you how email technology can be used to implement some other types of interesting messaging scenarios.

## 11.1 Introduction to BCS

Beginning with release 6.10 of SAP NetWeaver AS ABAP, SAP unified the way that you send and receive email messages within a new object-oriented framework called *Business Communication Services* (BCS). Figure 11.1 shows a UML diagram that highlights the core classes and interfaces that make up the BCS framework.

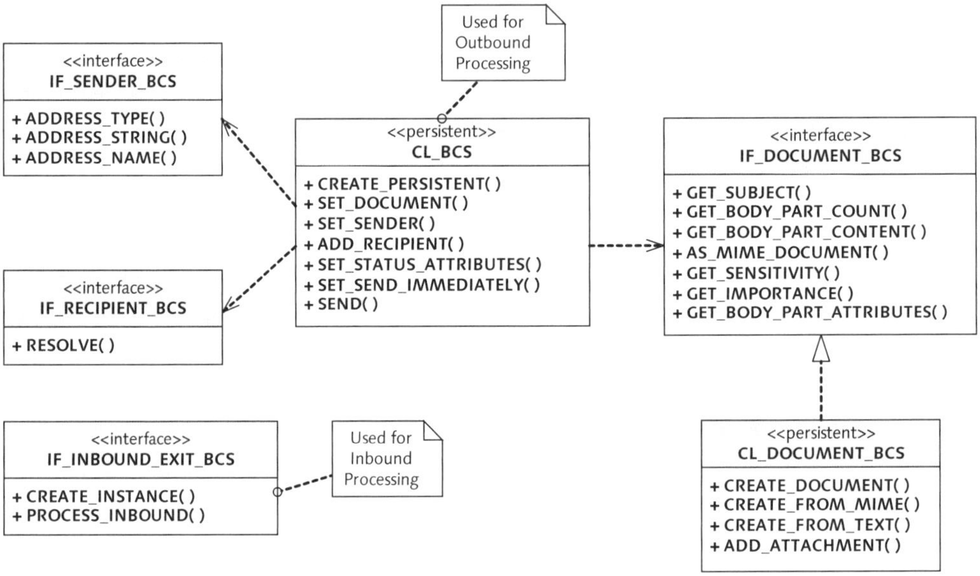


**Figure 11.1** UML Class Diagram for the BCS Framework

One of the beauties of the BCS framework is that it makes heavy use of interfaces. For instance, the `SET_SENDER()` method of class `CL_BCS` expects a sender object that implements the `IF_SENDER_BCS` interface. Out of the box, SAP provides many concrete classes that implement the `IF_SENDER_BCS` interface to make it easy to create a sender using an SAP user name, business partner, or even an address in *Business Address Services* (BAS). SAP provides default implementations for the other interfaces depicted in Figure 11.1 as well. Of course, you can also extend the framework further by developing your own concrete subclasses.

In the upcoming sections, we show you how to use the BCS framework to send and receive email messages. If you're interested in trying out the example code as you go along, you'll need to make sure that the relevant configuration settings have been made to the SMTP plug-in in your local SAP NetWeaver AS ABAP system. You can find a step-by-step guide for configuring these settings in SAP Note 455140.

## 11.2 Sending Email Messages

To understand how to use BCS to send an email message, it's useful to think about its positioning in relation to your preferred email client (i.e., Microsoft Outlook, etc.). Whenever you compose a new email message in your client, you're presented with an editor that allows you to fill in the following information:

- The subject of the message
- A list of recipients who should receive the message
- The body of the message (in various formats)
- An optional set of attachment files

After you fill in all of the pertinent information, you simply click a button to transmit the message. This process works so well that we rarely stop to think about what happens after we click the button. However, from a programmer's perspective, we're very interested in what happens behind the scenes.

### 11.2.1 Understanding the Simple Mail Transfer Protocol

The FMC block diagram shown in Figure 11.2 illustrates the messaging components associated with the transmission of an email message. Whenever you transmit a message using an email client, the client program forwards the message to the mail server configured for your email account using SMTP. SMTP stands for *Simple Mail Transfer Protocol*, which is a simple text-based protocol used to negotiate the exchange of email messages over an IP network such as the Internet. As you can see in Figure 11.2, SMTP isn't only used to transmit the email message from the sender client to its mail server but also to forward messages on to the recipient's mail server. After the message is received by the recipient's mail server, the recipient's mail client can retrieve the message using the POP (*Post Office Protocol*) or IMAP (*Internet Message Access Protocol*).

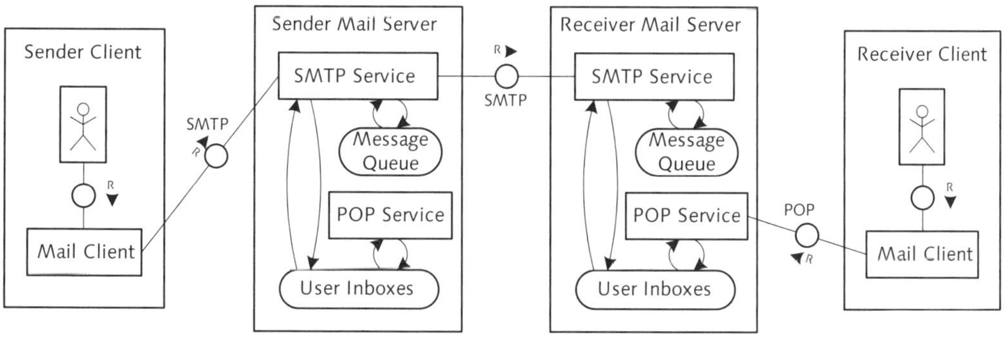


**Figure 11.2** FMC Block Diagram of Email Messaging Components

The asynchronous nature of email messaging implies that each of the messaging components depicted in Figure 11.2 must implement a persistence layer to ensure that messages are delivered reliably. For instance, if the sender mail server (i.e., your corporate Microsoft Exchange server, etc.) is unavailable, then your mail client should store outgoing messages in an *outbox* so that they can be redelivered when the sender mail server comes back online. Similarly, if the recipient's mail server is unavailable, the sender mail server must hang onto the message and try to redeliver it later.

From a programming perspective, the BCS framework takes care of integrating with the SMTP provider (via the SMTP plug-in and SAPconnect) and also provides the persistence layer that all mail clients must implement. If you look carefully at the UML class diagram shown previously in Figure 11.1, you can see that the `CL_BCS` class used to encapsulate a send request is actually a persistent class.

By taking care of the low-level messaging details, BCS lets you focus your efforts on composing messages. In the next few sections, we show you how to use the API to transmit various types of messages.

### 11.2.2 Sending a Plain Text Message

The process flow for creating an email message using the BCS API consists of the following steps:

1. First, you create an instance of the `CL_BCS` persistent class to encapsulate the message being sent using the `CREATE_PERSISTENT()` factory method.

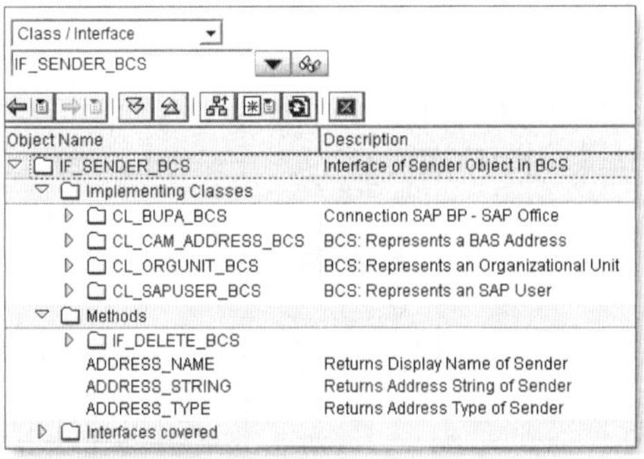


**Figure 11.3** Implementing Classes of Interface IF_SENDER_BCS

2. Next, you can (optionally) specify the user that will be sending the message using the SET_SENDER( ) method of class CL_BCS. Figure 11.3 shows the SAP standard classes that implement the IF_SENDER_BCS interface. These classes allow you to build a sender instance using an SAP user, business partner, and so on.

3. To add recipients to the message, you call the ADD_RECIPIENT( ) method of class CL_BCS. This method expects to receive an instance of a class that implements the IF_RECIPIENT_BCS interface. Figure 11.4 shows the SAP standard classes that implement the IF_RECIPIENT_BCS interface. These classes can generate recipients using SAP user accounts, organizational model constructs, and so on. Also, the CL_DISTRIBUTIONLIST_BCS class can be used to add an entire distribution list to the recipient list. You can maintain distribution lists in the Business Workplace (Transaction SBWP) by clicking on the Distribution Lists button (see Figure 11.5).

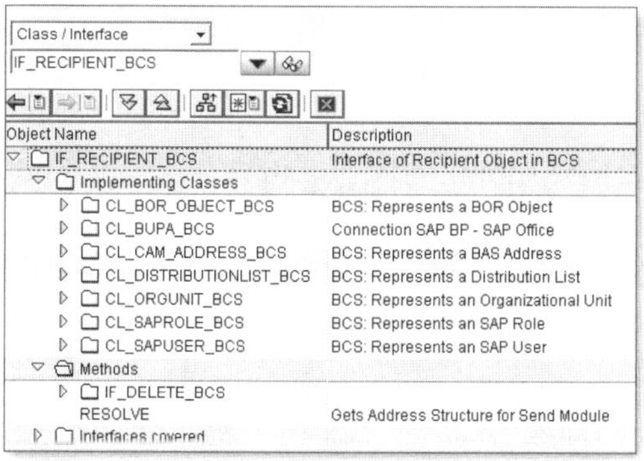


**Figure 11.4** Implementing Classes of the Interface IF_RECIPIENT_BCS

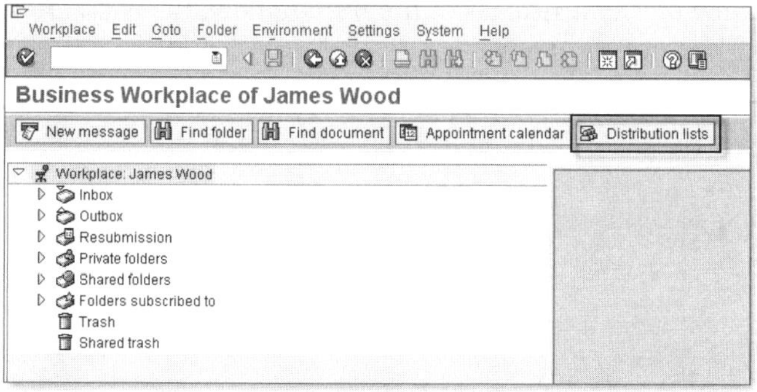


**Figure 11.5** Maintaining Distribution Lists in the Business Workplace

4. After the sender/receivers are set, you need to build the message body. The message body is represented by an instance of a class that implements the IF_DOCUMENT_BCS interface. Figure 11.6 shows the SAP standard classes that implement the IF_DOCUMENT_BCS interface. Most of the time, you'll work with the CL_DOCUMENT_BCS class to construct the message body. After the document has been created, it can be attached to the message by calling the SET_DOCUMENT() method of class CL_BCS.

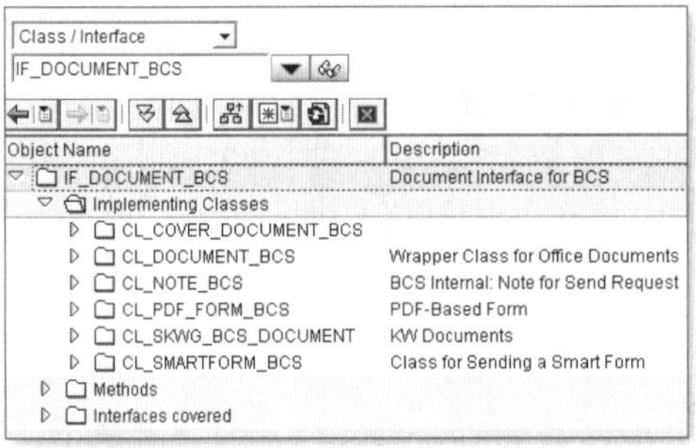


**Figure 11.6** Implementing Classes of Interface IF_DOCUMENT_BCS

5. Finally, after the message is built, it can be submitted using the SEND() method of class CL_BCS. Here, you must follow up the call to SEND() with a COMMIT WORK statement so that the Persistence Service will enqueue the message in the queue of messages waiting to be submitted via SAPconnect. Alternatively, you can manage the transaction using the Transaction Service described in Chapter 7, Transactional Programming.

To demonstrate how all this works, let's consider an example program. The ZMAIL_DEMO1 report program shown in Listing 11.1 defines a local class called LCL_MAIL_CLIENT that encapsulates some of the intricacies of the BCS framework. We'll look at the API methods of this class in a moment.

```
REPORT zmail_demo1.
CLASS lcl_mail_client DEFINITION.
  PUBLIC SECTION.
    CLASS-METHODS:
      send_test_message.

    METHODS:
      create_message RAISING cx_bcs,
      add_recipient IMPORTING im_email_address
                          TYPE ad_smtpadr
```

```
                  RAISING cx_bcs,
      build_payload RAISING cx_bcs,
      send_message RAISING cx_bcs.

  PRIVATE SECTION.
    DATA: message TYPE REF TO cl_bcs.
ENDCLASS.

CLASS lcl_mail_client IMPLEMENTATION.
  METHOD send_test_message.
    "Method-Local Data Declarations:
    DATA: lo_mail_client TYPE REF TO lcl_mail_client.

    "Send an email message:
    TRY.
      "Create a new message:
      CREATE OBJECT lo_mail_client.
      lo_mail_client->create_message( ).

      "Add a recipient to the message:
      lo_mail_client->add_recipient(
        'james.wood@bowdarkconsulting.com' ).

      "Build the message payload:
      lo_mail_client->build_payload( ).

      "Send the message:
      lo_mail_client->send_message( ).
    CATCH cx_bcs.
      "Exception handling goes here...
    ENDTRY.
  ENDMETHOD.                  " METHOD send_test_message

  METHOD create_message.
    "Method-Local Data Declarations:
    DATA: lo_sender TYPE REF TO if_sender_bcs.

    "Create a new send request:
    message = cl_bcs=>create_persistent( ).

    "Create the sender using the current user:
    lo_sender =
      cl_sapuser_bcs=>create( sy-uname ).
```

```
    message->set_sender( lo_sender ).
  ENDMETHOD.                    " METHOD create_message

  METHOD add_recipient.
    "Method-Local Data Declarations:
    DATA: lo_recipient TYPE REF TO if_recipient_bcs.

    "Create a recipient using the provided email address:
    CALL METHOD cl_cam_address_bcs=>create_internet_address
      EXPORTING
        i_address_string = im_email_address
      RECEIVING
        result           = lo_recipient.

    "Add the recipient to the message:
    CALL METHOD message->add_recipient
      EXPORTING
        i_recipient = lo_recipient.
  ENDMETHOD.                    " METHOD add_recipient

  METHOD build_payload.
    "Method-Local Data Declarations:
    DATA: lo_document TYPE REF TO if_document_bcs,
          lt_payload  TYPE bcsy_text.
    FIELD-SYMBOLS:
      <lfs_line> LIKE LINE OF lt_payload.

    "Create a simple text document payload:
    APPEND INITIAL LINE TO lt_payload ASSIGNING <lfs_line>.
    <lfs_line>-line = 'Test Message from BCS'.

    lo_document =
      cl_document_bcs=>create_from_text(
        i_text    = lt_payload
        i_subject = 'BCS Test Message' ).

    "Append the document to the message body:
    message->set_document( lo_document ).
  ENDMETHOD.                    " METHOD build_payload
```

```
  METHOD send_message.
    "Method-Local Data Declarations:
    DATA: lv_req_status  TYPE bcs_rqst VALUE 'N',
          lv_status_mail TYPE bcs_stml VALUE 'N'.

    "Turn off status messages for the request:
    CALL METHOD message->set_status_attributes
      EXPORTING
        i_requested_status = lv_req_status
        i_status_mail      = lv_status_mail.

    "Toggle the flag to send the message immediately:
    message->set_send_immediately( 'X' ).

    "Send the message:
    CALL METHOD message->send( ).

    "Have to commit the changes to enqueue the message:
    COMMIT WORK.
  ENDMETHOD.                   " METHOD send_message
ENDCLASS.

START-OF-SELECTION.
  "Send a simple test message:
  lcl_mail_client=>send_test_message( ).
```

**Listing 11.1** Sending a Plain Text Email Message Using BCS

Now that you've had a chance to peruse the code, let's consider the functionality of each API method in turn:

1. In the CREATE_MESSAGE( ) method, we create an instance of the CL_BCS class and then assign a sender to it via the SET_SENDER( ) method. Here, notice that we're using the CL_SAPUSER_BCS class to create a sender object using the user account that executed the program. Behind the scenes, this class looks at the user master record of the provided user to determine that user's email address. A user's email address is maintained on the Address tab in Transaction SU01 (see Figure 11.7).

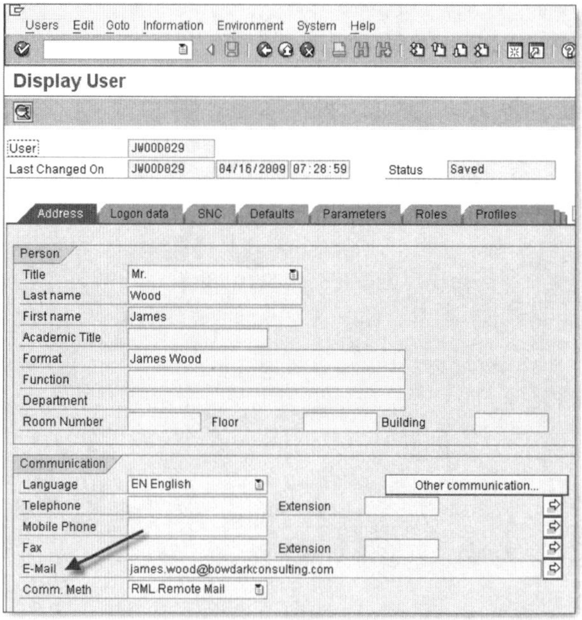

**Figure 11.7** Deriving the Sender Email Address

2. The ADD_RECIPIENT() method enables you to add a recipient to the message using an Internet email address. Here, we're deriving the IF_RECIPIENT_BCS instance using the CREATE_INTERNET_ADDRESS() factory method of class CL_CAM_ADDRESS_BCS. The derived recipient is added to the CL_BCS instance via its ADD_RECIPIENT() method.
3. Because we're only interested in building a plain-text email message, we're using the CREATE_FROM_TEXT() factory method of class CL_DOCUMENT_BCS to create the message body in the BUILD_PAYLOAD() method. We can then append the body to the message by calling the SET_DOCUMENT() method of class CL_BCS.
4. As you would expect, the SEND_MESSAGE() method invokes the SEND() method of class CL_BCS to transmit the message. However, before doing so, it configures a couple of settings on the message. First, it calls the SET_STATUS_ATTRIBUTES() method to notify the BCS framework that we aren't interested in receiving status messages. Secondly, it calls the SET_SEND_IMMEDIATELY() method to inform the BCS framework that the message should be sent immediately. Otherwise, the message is dispatched via a batch send job configured for SAPconnect. Finally, after the SEND() method is called, we must execute the COMMIT WORK statement to cause the message to be persisted to the outbound message queue.

### 11.2.3 Working with Attachments

Simple email messages like the one generated in Section 11.2.2, Sending a Plain Text Message, are often sufficient for sending out status notifications, and so on. However, there are times when you may want to send more than just plain text email. For example, you might want to attach an interactive PDF form, a Microsoft Excel spreadsheet, and so on. Let's now explore how to create attachments to messages.

On the surface, the process of attaching a document to a message is remarkably straightforward: You simply call the ADD_ATTACHMENT() method of class CL_DOCUMENT_BCS. Of course, there's slightly more work involved in preparing the attachment itself. To demonstrate how all of these pieces fit together, let's consider the ZMAIL_DEMO2 report program contained in Listing 11.2.

```
REPORT zmail_demo2.
CLASS lcl_mail_client DEFINITION.
  PUBLIC SECTION.
    CLASS-METHODS:
      send_test_message
        IMPORTING im_attach_file TYPE string,
      get_frontend_file CHANGING ch_file TYPE string.

    METHODS:
      create_message RAISING cx_bcs,
      add_recipient IMPORTING im_email_address
                              TYPE ad_smtpadr
                    RAISING cx_bcs,
      build_payload IMPORTING im_attach_file TYPE string
                    RAISING cx_bcs,
      send_message RAISING cx_bcs.

  PRIVATE SECTION.
    DATA: message  TYPE REF TO cl_bcs,
          document TYPE REF TO cl_document_bcs.

    METHODS: add_attachment IMPORTING im_attach_file
                                        TYPE string
                                RAISING cx_bcs.
ENDCLASS.

CLASS lcl_mail_client IMPLEMENTATION.
  METHOD send_test_message.
```

```
    "Method-Local Data Declarations:
    DATA: lo_mail_client TYPE REF TO lcl_mail_client.

    "Send an email message:
    TRY.
      "Create a new message:
      CREATE OBJECT lo_mail_client.
      lo_mail_client->create_message( ).

      "Add a recipient to the message:
      lo_mail_client->add_recipient(
        'james.wood@bowdarkconsulting.com' ).

      "Build the message payload:
      lo_mail_client->build_payload( im_attach_file ).

      "Send the message:
      lo_mail_client->send_message( ).
    CATCH cx_bcs.
      "Exception handling goes here...
    ENDTRY.
  ENDMETHOD.                    " METHOD send_test_message

  METHOD get_frontend_file.
    ...
  ENDMETHOD.                    " METHOD get_frontend_file

  METHOD create_message.
    ...
  ENDMETHOD.                    " METHOD create_message

  METHOD add_recipient.
    ...
  ENDMETHOD.                    " METHOD add_recipient

  METHOD build_payload.
    "Method-Local Data Declarations:
    DATA: lt_payload  TYPE bcsy_text.
    FIELD-SYMBOLS:
      <lfs_line> LIKE LINE OF lt_payload.

    "Create a simple text document payload:
    APPEND INITIAL LINE TO lt_payload ASSIGNING <lfs_line>.
```

```
  <lfs_line>-line =
    'Test Message from BCS with Attachment'.

  document =
    cl_document_bcs=>create_from_text(
      i_text    = lt_payload
      i_subject = 'BCS Test Message with Attachment' ).

  "Add an attachment to the document:
  add_attachment( im_attach_file ).

  "Append the document to the message body:
  message->set_document( document ).
ENDMETHOD.                  " METHOD build_payload

METHOD add_attachment.
  "Method-Local Data Declarations:
  DATA: lt_attach_raw     TYPE TABLE OF x255,
        lv_attach_raw     TYPE xstring,
        lv_attach_len     TYPE i,
        lt_attachment     TYPE solix_tab,
        lo_attach_path    TYPE REF TO /bowdk/cl_string,
        lv_file_index     TYPE i,
        lo_attach_file    TYPE REF TO /bowdk/cl_string,
        lt_file_tokens    TYPE string_table,
        lv_attach_size    TYPE so_obj_len,
        lv_attach_type    TYPE so_obj_tp,
        lv_attach_subject TYPE so_obj_des.

  "Upload the attachment from the frontend:
  CALL METHOD cl_gui_frontend_services=>gui_upload
    EXPORTING
      filetype                = 'BIN'
      filename                = im_attach_file
    IMPORTING
      filelength              = lv_attach_len
    CHANGING
      data_tab                = lt_attach_raw
    EXCEPTIONS
      file_open_error         = 1
      file_read_error         = 2
      no_batch                = 3
      gui_refuse_filetransfer = 4
```

```
      invalid_type            = 5
      no_authority            = 6
      unknown_error           = 7
      bad_data_format         = 8
      header_not_allowed      = 9
      separator_not_allowed   = 10
      header_too_long         = 11
      unknown_dp_error        = 12
      access_denied           = 13
      dp_out_of_memory        = 14
      disk_full               = 15
      dp_timeout              = 16
      not_supported_by_gui    = 17
      error_no_gui            = 18
      others                  = 19.

  "Check the results:
  IF sy-subrc EQ 0.
    "Convert the raw attachment payload into a
    "binary string:
    CALL FUNCTION 'SCMS_BINARY_TO_XSTRING'
      EXPORTING
        input_length = lv_attach_len
      IMPORTING
        buffer       = lv_attach_raw
      TABLES
        binary_tab   = lt_attach_raw
      EXCEPTIONS
        failed       = 1
        others       = 2.

    "Then, convert the binary string into SOLIX form:
    lt_attachment =
      cl_document_bcs=>xstring_to_solix( lv_attach_raw ).
  ELSE.
    RAISE EXCEPTION TYPE cx_document_bcs.
  ENDIF.

  "Extract metadata about the attachment file:
  CREATE OBJECT lo_attach_path
    EXPORTING
      im_value = im_attach_file.
```

```
    lv_file_index =
      lo_attach_path->get_last_index_of( '\' ) + 1.

    lo_attach_file =
      lo_attach_path->substring(
        im_start_index = lv_file_index ).

    lt_file_tokens = lo_attach_file->split_at( '.' ).
    READ TABLE lt_file_tokens INTO lv_attach_subject
         INDEX 1.
    READ TABLE lt_file_tokens INTO lv_attach_type
         INDEX 2.

    lv_attach_size = xstrlen( lv_attach_raw ).

    "Add the attachment to the document:
    CALL METHOD document->add_attachment
      EXPORTING
        i_attachment_type     = lv_attach_type
        i_attachment_subject  = lv_attach_subject
        i_attachment_size     = lv_attach_size
        i_attachment_language = sy-langu
        i_att_content_hex     = lt_attachment.
  ENDMETHOD.                   " METHOD add_attachment

  METHOD send_message.
    ...
  ENDMETHOD.                   " METHOD send_message
ENDCLASS.

PARAMETERS:
  p_attach TYPE string LOWER CASE OBLIGATORY.

AT SELECTION-SCREEN ON VALUE-REQUEST FOR p_attach.
  "Show a dialog box to allow the user to select a file:
  CALL METHOD lcl_mail_client=>get_frontend_file
    CHANGING
      ch_file = p_attach.

START-OF-SELECTION.
  "Create a test message with an attachment:
  lcl_mail_client=>send_test_message( p_attach ).
```

**Listing 11.2** Sending an Email with an Attachment

The ZMAIL_DEMO2 program shown in Listing 11.2 extends the ZMAIL_DEMO1 program from Listing 11.1 to support the creation of an attachment. To keep things simple, we're simply uploading an attachment file from the SAP GUI frontend using class CL_GUI_FRONTEND_SERVICES as demonstrated in Chapter 5, Working with Files. For brevity's sake, we've also omitted the implementations of the CREATE_MESSAGE(), ADD_RECIPIENT(), and SEND_MESSAGE() methods because they are identical to the ones shown in Listing 11.1.

To see how to build an attachment, let's look closely at the implementation of the ADD_ATTACHMENT() method:

1. This method begins by uploading the attachment file selected in the selection screen parameter P_ATTACH in binary mode. To work with attachments using BCS, we must convert this binary payload into a format compatible with the SAPoffice document API. Because class CL_DOCUMENT_BCS provides a convenient static method called XSTRING_TO_SOLIX() for this purpose, we're converting the raw binary payload into an XSTRING using the standard function SCMS_BINARY_TO_XSTRING. Then, we call XSTRING_TO_SOLIX() to generate the attachment payload.
2. In addition to the payload itself, we're also deriving various other metadata about the attachment, including its type, size, and name. For this task, we're using the /BOWDK/CL_STRING class introduced in Chapter 1, String Processing Techniques.
3. Finally, after all of the attachment metadata has been compiled, we can add the attachment to the CL_DOCUMENT_BCS instance using its ADD_ATTACHMENT() instance method. From this point forward, we can proceed with sending the email message as we usually do.

Technically speaking, there aren't any hard-and-fast rules that specify how many attachments you can add to a message. However, you'll want to be careful about how large your attachment payload becomes — especially if you're sending the message out over the Internet. Therefore, it's always a good idea to monitor the size of attachments when generating email messages.

### 11.2.4 Formatting Email Messages with HTML

Plain text email messages like the one generated in Section 11.2.2, Sending a Plain Text Message, are usually sufficient for implementing email messaging requirements within a corporate setting. However, if you have a requirement for sending a message to an external customer or vendor, then you may need to compose a message with a little more style. In these situations, you can use HTML to create rich text email messages.

Technically speaking, an HTML email is nothing more than a plain text email, except that it contains markup in addition to the plain text content. Given this, you could build the HTML content on the fly in an internal table. However, this process is tedious and error prone. Fortunately, there's a better option.

Most modern email clients support the XHTML standard. XHTML(Extensible Hypertext Markup Language) is an XML-based markup language that extends HTML to provide more structure around Web-based content. As you learned in Chapter 8, XML Processing in ABAP, the Simple Transformation language is highly adept at interspersing the values of ABAP data objects with static XML content to generate an XML document. Consequently, Simple Transformation is a natural fit for composing HTML-based email messages.

To simplify the process of generating HTML-based email messages, we've created a factory class named `/BOWDK/CL_HTML_DOCUMENT_BCS` that defines a method called `CREATE_HTML_DOCUMENT()`. Figure 11.8 shows the signature of this method. As you can see, this method accepts three importing parameters:

- The `IM_TRANSFORMATION` parameter refers to the name of the Simple Transformation program that we want to use to generate the HTML payload.
- The `IM_PARAMETERS` parameter can contain a data object of any type that supplies the transformation program with the parameters it needs to dynamically build an XHTML document. Here, you might pass in a structure containing information that you want to merge into a static XHTML form, for example.
- The `IM_SUBJECT` parameter passes the subject of the document being created. This value shows up in the subject line of the email message in the recipient's mail client.

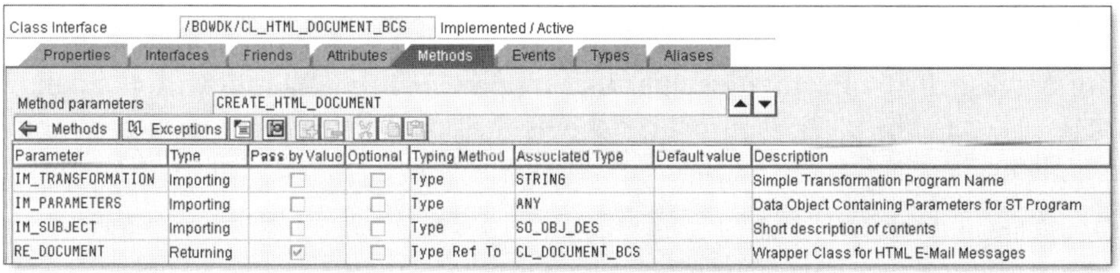


| Parameter | Type | Pass by Value | Optional | Typing Method | Associated Type | Default value | Description |
|---|---|---|---|---|---|---|---|
| IM_TRANSFORMATION | Importing | ☐ | ☐ | Type | STRING | | Simple Transformation Program Name |
| IM_PARAMETERS | Importing | ☐ | ☐ | Type | ANY | | Data Object Containing Parameters for ST Program |
| IM_SUBJECT | Importing | ☐ | ☐ | Type | SO_OBJ_DES | | Short description of contents |
| RE_DOCUMENT | Returning | ☑ | ☐ | Type Ref To | CL_DOCUMENT_BCS | | Wrapper Class for HTML E-Mail Messages |

**Figure 11.8** Signature of Method CREATE_HTML_DOCUMENT()

Listing 11.3 shows the implementation of the `CREATE_HTML_DOCUMENT()` method. As you can see, the `CALL TRANSFORMATION` statement does most of the heavy lifting. After the payload is constructed, we're using the `CREATE_DOCUMENT()` method of class `CL_DOCUMENT_BCS`, per usual.

```
METHOD create_html_document.
  "Method-Local Data Declarations:
  DATA: lv_content_length TYPE so_obj_len,
        lv_language       TYPE so_obj_la,
        lt_html_payload   TYPE soli_tab.

  "Invoke the selected Simple Transformation program to
  "generate the HTML payload:
  CALL TRANSFORMATION (im_transformation)
    SOURCE param = im_parameters
    RESULT XML lt_html_payload.

  "Create the BCS document instance:
  lv_language = sy-langu.

  CALL METHOD cl_document_bcs=>create_document
    EXPORTING
      i_type     = co_document_type
      i_subject  = im_subject
      i_length   = lv_content_length
      i_language = lv_language
      i_text     = lt_html_payload
    RECEIVING
      result     = re_document.
ENDMETHOD.
```

**Listing 11.3** Implementation of CREATE_HTML_DOCUMENT()

Listing 11.4 contains a sample Simple Transformation program that is used to generate a dynamic XHTML message body. Notice how we've highlighted the data root `PARAM` in boldface font; in this case, the name of the data root is important because the framework assumes that it's passing in a data root with the name `PARAM` (see Listing 11.3). Figure 11.9 shows the email message generated by this template.

```
<?sap.transform simple?>
<tt:transform template="Main"
  xmlns:tt="http://www.sap.com/transformation-templates">
<tt:root name="PARAM"/>
```

```
<tt:template name="Main">
<html>
  <head>
    <title>BCS HTML Email Demonstration</title>
  </head>

  <body>
    <h1>
      Hello <tt:value ref="PARAM.FIRST_NAME" />!
    </h1>
    <p>Welcome to Business Communication Services.</p>
    </body>
  </html>
</tt:template>
</tt:transform>
```

**Listing 11.4** Simple Transformation for an HTML Message

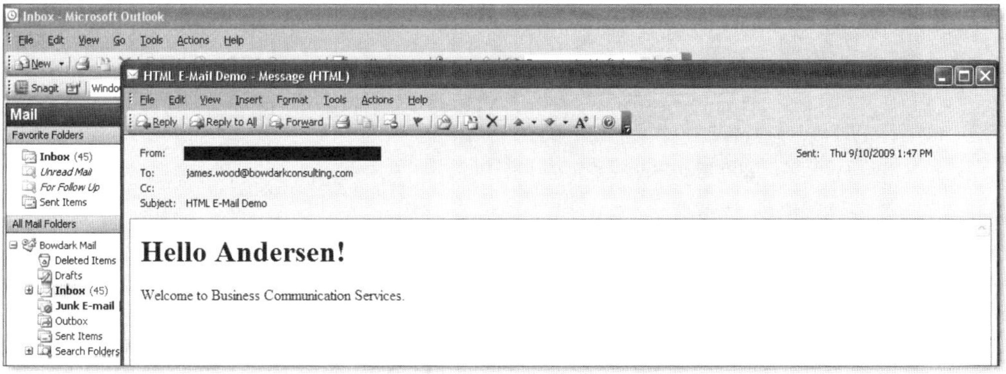


**Figure 11.9** Sample HTML Email Generated by the Framework

## 11.3 Receiving Email Messages

While the SMTP plug-in on SAP NetWeaver AS ABAP is normally used to send messages, it can also be set up to receive messages. Now, you may be wondering why you would want to process inbound email messages using ABAP. After all, SAP NetWeaver AS ABAP isn't going to take the place of a mail client. However, as it turns out, there are some interesting applications that you can develop using this functionality. In this section, we show you how to process inbound message requests using ABAP.

### 11.3.1 Configuring Inbound Processing Rules

The previously mentioned SAP Note 455140 describes the various technical settings required to set up the SMTP plug-in to receive emails. For the purposes of our discussion, we assume that these settings have already been configured. After the inbound processing infrastructure is in place, you can configure inbound processing rules in Transaction SCOT. Here, you select the SETTINGS • INBOUND PROCESSING menu option to open up the exit rules editor (see Figure 11.10).

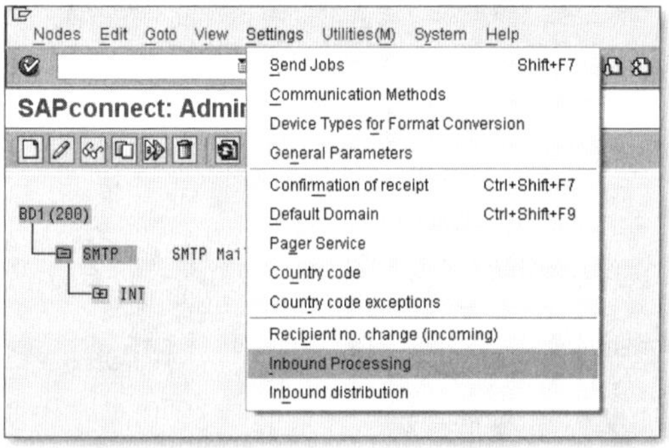


**Figure 11.10** Configuring Inbound Processing Rules

Figure 11.11 shows the exit rule editor perspective of Transaction SCOT. As you might expect given the connotation of the phrase "exit rule," these rules define *user exits* for a particular recipient address or document class. For instance, in Figure 11.11, we're defining a user exit for inbound messages directed at the recipient address *webservices@bowdarkconsulting.com.* In the Exit Name column, we've proposed a class called ZCL_SOAP_MAIL_HANDLER. The only requirement for this class is that it must implement the IF_INBOUND_EXIT_BCS interface (see Figure 11.1). After you've completed your changes, click the Save button to activate the inbound processing rule.

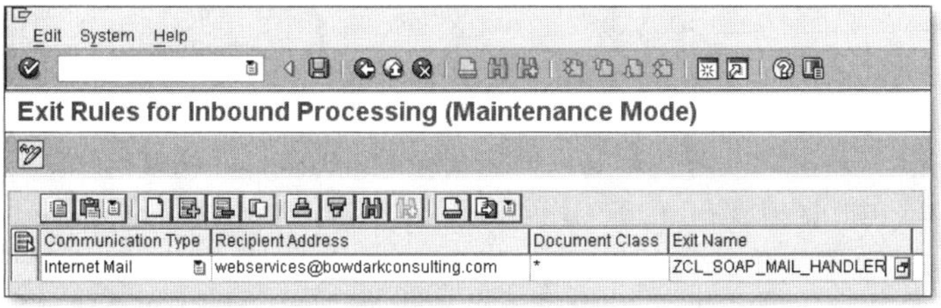


**Figure 11.11** Defining Exit Rules for Inbound Processing

## 11.3.2 Processing Inbound Requests

Now that you understand how exit rules for inbound processing are configured, let's take a deeper look at the inner workings of the IF_INBOUND_EXIT_BCS interface. Looking back at Figure 11.1, you can see that this interface defines two methods: CREATE_INSTANCE() and PROCESS_INBOUND(). Classes that implement the IF_INBOUND_EXIT_BCS interface are intended to be patterned as *singletons*. As such, the framework uses the CREATE_INSTANCE() method to obtain an instance of the inbound mail handler class. The inbound request is then processed by the PROCESS_INBOUND() method.

Figure 11.12 shows the signature of the PROCESS_INBOUND() method. As you can see, this method defines three importing parameters:

- The IO_SREQ parameter contains an instance of the CL_SEND_REQUEST_BCS class that encapsulates the send request. This class can be used to get information about the request such as the sender, the message body, and so on.
- The IT_RECIPIENTS parameter contains a list of the recipients that received this message.
- The IT_DOCTYPES parameter contains a list of the document classes (i.e., document types) contained in the request.

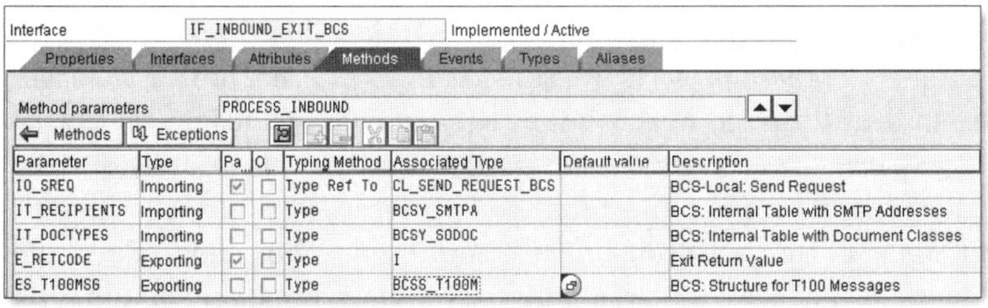


**Figure 11.12** Signature of Method PROCESS_INBOUND()

Within the PROCESS_INBOUND() method, you're free to process the message in any way that you like. To see an example of this, consider the standard class CL_ALERT_CONFIRM_BY_MAIL that is delivered as part of the *Alert Management service* (ALM). The ALM service defines a common framework in SAP NetWeaver AS ABAP for triggering and dealing with alerts. Here, for instance, an alert might be triggered to notify particular users of a critical problem in the system.

The ALM framework allows you to categorize alerts into particular categories. End users can then *subscribe* to receive alerts from these categories based on their business role, and so on. Frequently, the alerts are propagated to users via email. Because the same alert could be received by multiple users, it's important that users have a way to *confirm* alerts so that other users know that someone is working the issue. The CL_ALERT_CONFIRM_BY_MAIL class makes it possible for users to confirm an alert by simply replying to the original alert message. When the confirmation email is received, the BCS framework invokes the PROCESS_INBOUND() method of CL_ALERT_CONFIRM_BY_EMAIL. This method confirms the alert and notifies the other subscribers about the status of the alert via an email response message.

### 11.3.3 Potential Use Cases of Inbound Processing Rules

Earlier, you saw how inbound processing modules can be used to enable ALM alert confirmations via email. This kind of solution can be applied to many types of workflow scenarios in which external users need to interact with some kind of process flow. However, the capabilities of inbound processing modules aren't limited to workflow processing. Next we consider some other potential use cases for inbound processing modules.

#### Using Emails to Trigger System Events

With all of the sophisticated workflow, messaging, and job scheduling functionality built into SAP NetWeaver AS ABAP, you might not ever think about using email to trigger events in the system. Nevertheless, in some cases, it might make sense. For example, imagine that you're participating in a project that is preparing to go live on SAP. Frequently, these projects use some kind of external project management software to coordinate go-live activities between various teams. When it's time to execute a particular task, these tools send an email to the responsible parties advising them that it's time to run a job. If the project scope is small, then it's probably not that big of a deal for someone to monitor his inbox and perform the task when requested. However, for large projects, a certain amount of automation might be desirable.

This automation can be realized in the form of an inbound processing module. In this case, the message handler can interpret the message and execute a task automatically. The results of the task can then be sent back via an email response message.

### Processing SAP Interactive Forms

The SAP Interactive Forms software by Adobe has made it possible to bring sophisticated input forms directly to users, making it easy and convenient for users to interact in processes without ever logging onto SAP. Normally, these forms are passed around using email. In this case, the process flow proceeds as follows:

1. The form is sent to a user's inbox.
2. The user opens up the form, saves a local copy, and begins filling in the data.
3. When finished, the user replies back to the original email and attaches the updated form.

As you might have guessed, the data from the updated form can be extracted and posted to the system using an inbound processing module. If you're interested in learning more about how this works, Jeff Gebo of the SAP RIG has posted an excellent step-by-step tutorial entitled "Send, Receive, and Process Interactive Forms via Email in AS ABAP" online at *www.sdn.sap.com*.

### Processing SOAP Messages

Most of the time, whenever we talk about Web services, we're talking about self-contained software modules that can be accessed using HTTP. However, while this architecture is certainly the norm, it isn't the only way to implement a Web service. Recently, developers have been looking at ways of implementing SOAP messaging over different protocols, such as SMTP. The primary advantage here is that there is a significant email infrastructure from which to leverage — especially when it comes to reliable messaging.

So, you may be wondering, how exactly does this work? Well, the answer is fairly straightforward. Rather than embedding the SOAP envelope in an HTTP request entity, we simply attach it to the message body of the email. Of course, to do this on a large scale, we need a common inbound processing rule that implements the functionality of a SOAP toolkit. This simplifies the deployment process, allowing you to create Web service endpoints quickly and painlessly.

Even though SOAP over SMTP is in its infancy, you can find many resource implementations available online for Java and .NET. These implementations can be used as a guide for developing an ABAP-based solution.

#### Implementing an Asynchronous Query Tool

Due to the asynchronous nature of SMTP, it isn't possible to develop synchronous services using the SMTP plug-in. This implies that the SOAP-based services described in the previous section can only process messages asynchronously. Of course, this doesn't mean that the message handler can't generate a reply message in response to a given request. Rather, it just means that the process that submitted the request isn't blocked waiting for a response.

Despite this fundamental limitation, it's still possible to implement request-reply services using email. For example, let's imagine that you want to check on the status of a workflow process using your PDA. Because most SAP systems sit behind a corporate firewall, it would be expensive to try and deploy a traditional Web-based tool to access the status over HTTP. However, because it's likely that the corporate email server already has a robust security infrastructure built up around it, it would not be that difficult to set up a routing rule to transfer status requests to the backend SAP system. Here, an inbound handler module can intercept the request, determine the status of the workflow process, and send a response back to the sender's email address.

## 11.4 Summary

In this chapter, you learned how to send and receive emails from an ABAP context using the Business Communication Services API. While such capabilities might have been considered a "nice-to-have" in the past, they are increasingly becoming part of a core set of tools that every ABAP developer needs to have in their toolbox. After all, users accustomed to having the world at their fingertips will expect nothing less from their SAP experience. In the next chapter, we shift gears and consider the various aspects of security-based development in ABAP.

# PART IV
# Side Dishes

*Cooking involves high temperatures and can be dangerous if basic safety guidelines aren't followed. Safety is also important in ABAP programming but in a very different way. These days, companies count information stored in enterprise information systems such as SAP among their most valuable assets. Consequently, as ABAP developers, we must do everything that we can to make sure that this information remains safe and secure.*

# 12 Security Programming

In a perfect world, ABAP developers would be able to focus on implementing business logic without concern for security issues. Unfortunately, in the real world, this is seldom the case. It seems that almost every day, there is a report of information being compromised or systems being brought to their knees by malicious users. Given these real and dangerous threats, it's important that software be designed from the ground up with security in mind.

In this chapter, we explore ways of programming for security in ABAP. We begin our discussion by introducing you to the SAP NetWeaver AS ABAP authorization concept, a core component of the overall SAP security model. Next, we look at ways of encrypting data and performing virus scans in ABAP. Finally, we conclude by showing you how to protect your Web content using CAPTCHA.

## 12.1 Developing a Security Model

If nothing else, hackers are certainly creative when it comes to discovering new ways to break into a system. As such, the process of trying to secure a system can seem daunting from a development perspective. Unfortunately, the sad reality is that it's next to impossible to guard against every kind of attack that could be launched against the system. Nevertheless, there are several measures that you can take to protect valuable system resources.

Experience teaches that the first step in addressing security concerns is to turn the problem upside down. Rather than trying to guard against each and every type of attack that you can think of, implement your design from the ground up with the mindset that no one has access to anything unless they are explicitly granted it. After all, it's much easier to grant access than to take it away.

In this section, we consider some of the key elements that make up a holistic security model. As we progress through this discussion, think about how you would apply these concepts to your own programs. This will help put you in the right frame of mind for security programming. Here are the important questions you should begin asking yourself:

- Which users should have access to a particular resource?
- What actions should a user be allowed to perform on a resource?
- Are the lines of communication secured?
- What is the minimum amount of access required to complete a given operation?

### 12.1.1 Authenticating Users

A useful metaphor for thinking about security models is to imagine that the system is like a house. A house contains doors that can be secured with locks. To gain access to a locked house, you must either have a key or be granted access by someone on the inside. In the latter case, you might ring the doorbell or knock on the door to express the fact that you wish to enter. Normally, someone on the inside will come to the door and ask "who is it?" If they recognize your voice when you answer (and you're not the big bad wolf), they will likely open the door and let you in. In technical terms, this process is referred to as *authentication*.

Authentication is all about confirming whether or not user principals are in fact who they say they are. Normally, users are forced to authenticate *before* they can obtain access to the system. Here, if users provide valid user names and passwords, the system assumes that they are legitimate and grants them access. In some cases, this challenge/response system is taken up a notch, requiring users to provide multiple forms of identification. Such measures eliminate the chances that a rogue user might be impersonating a real user after having stolen his password, and so on.

### 12.1.2 Checking User Authorizations

Authentication allows users to get through the front door of the system, but it doesn't say anything about what they are allowed to do after they get there. Unlike homeowners, computer systems don't necessarily have to be hospitable to their users. Systems should not allow users to *make themselves at home*. Rather, they should follow them around and force them to ask whether or not they can perform a particular action. Whether or not the system allows the activity depends upon the *authorizations* granted to that user.

You can think of an authorization as a type of rule that can be defined in the system to grant a user access to a particular resource. To simplify user administration, related authorizations are normally consolidated into *roles* that are closely aligned with the various use cases supported by the system. For example, in a purchasing system, a role might be defined to grant a purchaser the ability to create a purchase order.

### 12.1.3 Securing the Lines of Communication

In the not-so-distant past, SAP software lived on an island in which there wasn't a lot of direct communication with the outside world. However, these days, external communication is commonplace. Therefore, it's vitally important that the lines of communication remain secure from external tampering. This can be achieved using *encryption technologies*.

The term "encryption" implies that we're converting human-readable text into an incomprehensible code that can only be decrypted using a key (or *cipher*). Sometimes this key is shared between communicating parties; sometimes it's not. Regardless of the approach, encryption ensures that even if someone were to intercept an encrypted message as it's transmitted over the network, he would not be able to read it.

Over the years, hackers have occasionally discovered ways to crack encryption algorithms. Consequently, the sophistication of encryption technology has had to improve to stay ahead of would-be hackers. Most modern systems (including SAP) provide useful abstractions that simplify the way that developers interact with complex encryption technologies. For instance, in Chapter 10, Web Services, we saw how ABAP-based Web services could be configured with a transport guarantee based on the Secured Sockets Layer (or SSL) protocol. SSL is used to encrypt data transmitted over the Internet. Similarly, it's also possible to configure encryption for RFC destinations using the *Secure Network Communications* framework (SNC).

### 12.1.4 Programming for Security

The three security measures discussed so far in this section represent the front lines of security for a system. Though these methods can be powerful deterrents for malicious users, they aren't fail safe. Therefore, as a developer, you can't allow yourself to neglect good defensive programming practices by assuming that problems will be handled upstream.

For any software module that you write, it's a good idea to apply a defensive design from the outset. Here, you need to ask yourself questions such as the following:

- What preconditions must exist before a module can be called?
- What happens if a module is called incorrectly? For example, what if certain parameters are supplied with invalid values?
- What kind of exceptions could occur as a result of a particular process?
- How should the system recover from a particular type of exception?

Though defensive programming techniques usually require a little more work upfront, you'll find that the effort is well worth it. This is because defensively programmed modules can be used with the confidence that comes from knowing that they will perform their tasks consistently and reliably. And, at the end of the day, such modules represent one less thing you have to worry about when programming for security.

Perhaps the most important thing to keep in mind when programming for security is to keep things simple. The more complex a piece of code is, the more likely it is that there might be holes in it somewhere. One way to fill in these gaps is to apply the principle of *least privilege*. Here, you only want to give users access to the resources that are absolutely necessary to perform a task. Sticking to this principle reduces scope, making it much easier to track down vulnerabilities within the system.

## 12.2 The SAP NetWeaver AS ABAP Authorization Concept

Before you can ever log onto an SAP NetWeaver AS ABAP system, you must be assigned a user master record. In addition to storing basic information about the user (i.e., the user's contact information, password, etc.), user master records also contain *role assignments*. These role assignments define the actions that a user can perform within the system.

To understand how role-based security works in an SAP NetWeaver AS ABAP system, you need to understand the AS SAP NetWeaver ABAP authorization concept. As we proceed through our discussion, we peel back some of the layers of the authorization concept to see how everything fits together. This insight will help you understand how to integrate your own custom authorization checks into the overall authorization concept.

### 12.2.1 Overview

Before we begin investigating the mechanics of the SAP NetWeaver AS ABAP authorization concept, it's helpful to first see how it is organized. Figure 12.1 shows the relationships between the various elements that make up the concept. Starting from the bottom up, these elements include the following:

- **Authorization object**
  An authorization object represents a particular set of actions that can be performed within the system. Authorization objects can consist of up to 10 authorization fields that are used to define specific authorizations (or permissions). We'll learn more about authorization objects in Section 12.2.2, Developing Authorization Objects.
- **Authorization**
  An authorization is an instance of a particular authorization object. Here, we're not talking about an instance in the object-oriented sense; rather, we're talking about a particular configuration of authorization field values for an authorization object.
- **Authorization profile**
  When a role is generated, the system also generates an authorization profile. An authorization profile aggregates related authorizations together.
- **Roles**
  As you learned earlier, a role defines the actions that a user can perform within the system. Underneath the hood, these authorizations are realized in the form of a generated authorization profile. After a role is created, it can be assigned to users in Transaction SU01.

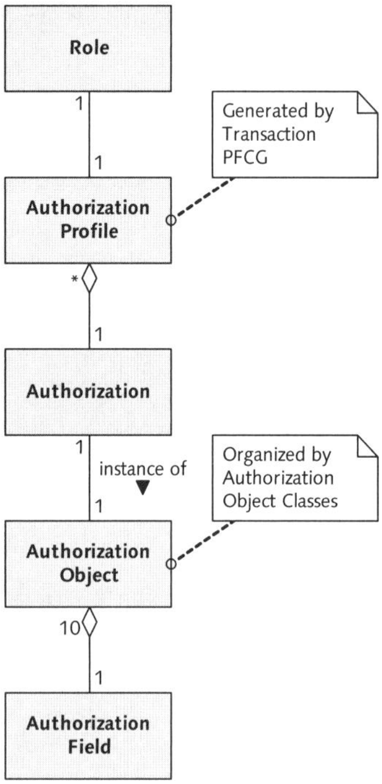


**Figure 12.1** Overview of Elements in SAP NetWeaver AS ABAP Authorization Concept

In Section 12.2.3, Configuring Authorizations, we explain how all of the elements of the SAP NetWeaver AS ABAP authorization concept fit together within the system from a configuration perspective. However, before we do so, we need to see how authorization objects are defined.

### 12.2.2 Developing Authorization Objects

As you learned in Section 12.2.1, Overview, authorization objects represent the basis of the SAP NetWeaver AS ABAP authorization concept. From a conceptual point of view, an authorization object is analogous to a class in the object-oriented programming paradigm. In other words, authorization objects are a type of abstraction that can define up to 10 distinguishing attributes (i.e., authorization fields). Within the scope of the authorization concept, you don't work with authorization objects directly; rather, you work with *instances* of authorization objects (i.e., *authorizations*). An authorization is an instance of an authorization object that defines specific values for the authorization object's authorization fields.

### Case Study: An ABAP Workbench Authorization Object

Sometimes, abstract concepts such as authorization objects are easier to understand after you've seen an example. Therefore, let's look at an actual authorization object in the system: the S_TCODE authorization object. This authorization object is checked by the system whenever a user tries to execute a transaction.

Authorization objects are ABAP Workbench objects that are maintained in Transaction SU21. Figure 12.2 shows the initial screen of this transaction. As you can see, authorization objects are organized into authorization object classes. For instance, as you can see in Figure 12.2, the S_DEVELOP authorization object is assigned to the BC_C authorization object class.

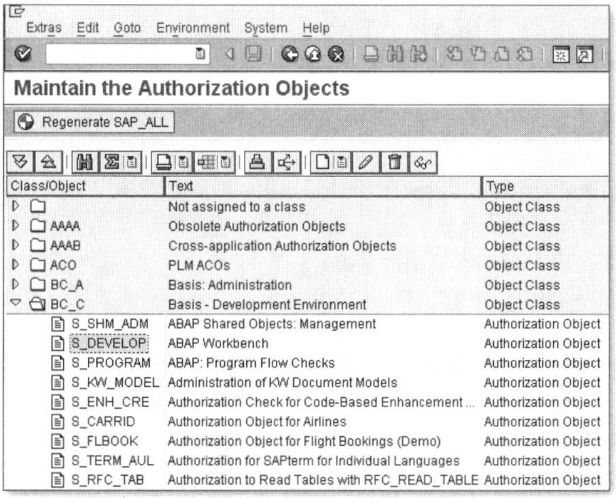


**Figure 12.2** Maintaining Authorization Objects in Transaction SU21

Because we don't know the name of the authorization object class that the S_TCODE authorization object is assigned to, we must search for it. Fortunately, Transaction SU21 makes this easy by providing a search tool. To access this feature, click on the Find button, and enter the name of the authorization object you want to search for. When a match is found, the transaction scrolls down to the matching object and highlights it (see Figure 12.2). From here, you can view the details of the authorization object by double-clicking on it (see Figure 12.3).

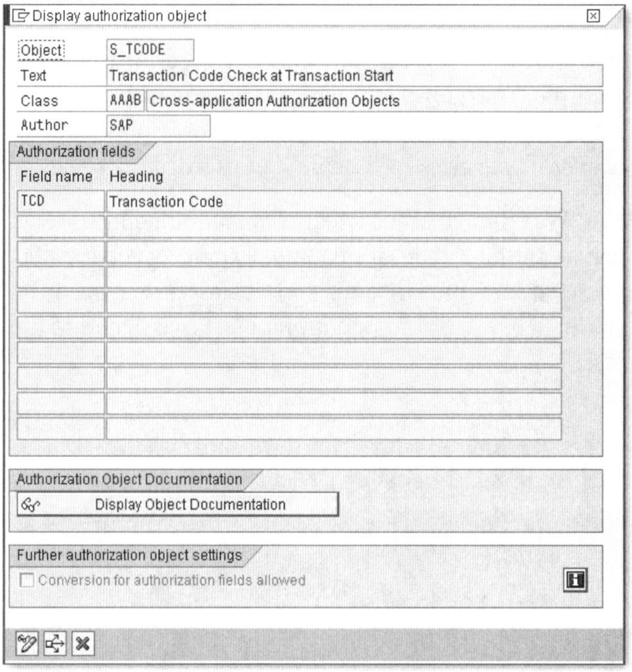


**Figure 12.3** The S_TCODE Authorization Object

As you can see in Figure 12.3, the S_TCODE authorization object only contains a single authorization field called TCD that represents the transaction code a user is trying to access. Therefore, an authorization based upon the S_TCODE authorization object contains a specific transaction code assignment in the TCD authorization field. In this case, the TCD field is sufficient for defining a user's authorization to a particular transaction code. Other authorization scenarios might require additional authorization fields to define a specific authorization.

Authorization fields are maintained in Transaction SU20. Figure 12.4 displays the definition of the TCD authorization field in this transaction. Here, you need only specify a name for the authorization field, as well as a data element that defines the field's characteristics. In the case of the TCD authorization field, the corresponding data element TCODE happens to be defined with a domain (also called TCODE) that has a check table assigned to it. Despite what you might think, the values supplied for an authorization field at runtime aren't checked against this table; rather they are used as a value help when defining authorizations.

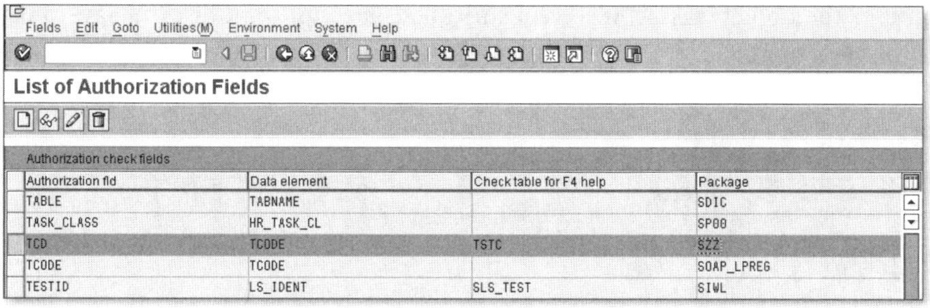


**Figure 12.4** Maintaining Authorization Fields in Transaction SU20

### Case Study: Creating a Custom Authorization Object

Now that you've seen a concrete example of an authorization object, let's think about how we would create a custom one. As a basis for our example, let's imagine that you're developing an administrative console for the online bookstore application introduced in Chapter 6, Database Programming. Among other things, administrative users should be able to use this console to maintain the store's book catalog. However, rather than opening this function up to everyone, you want to control access so that certain users can modify the catalog while others can only view it.

If this console were developed as a Dynpro-based application, the simplest way to control this kind of access would be to configure a series of transaction codes that could be checked against the S_TCODE authorization object. This convention is commonly used by SAP. For example, customer master records can be created in Transaction XD01, changed in Transaction XD02, and displayed in Transaction XD03. Each of these transactions refers to the same program behind the scenes, yet the selected transaction code defines the *mode* of the application. For the purposes of our example though, let's assume that we're building the console as a Web application (perhaps using Web Dynpro for ABAP). Because there is no transaction code here, we need to develop our own custom authorization object to control access to the catalog.

To create our custom authorization object, we must perform the following steps:

1. First, we need to create an authorization object class to organize our custom authorization objects. Authorization object classes are maintained in Transaction SU21. To create an authorization object class, select the Object Class menu option on the drop-down menu tied to the Create button (see Figure 12.5). This brings up the dialog window shown in Figure 12.6. Here, you must provide a

name for the object class as well as a short text description. Click the Save button to save your changes.

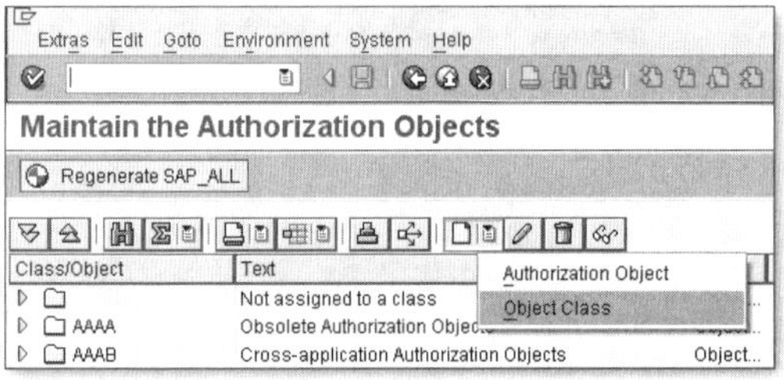


**Figure 12.5** Creating an Authorization Object Class — Part 1

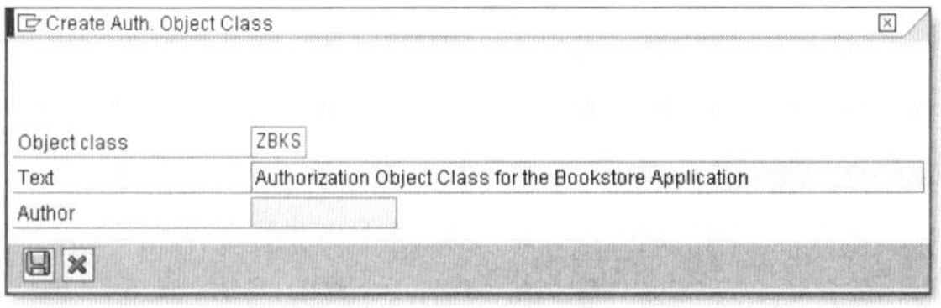


**Figure 12.6** Creating an Authorization Object Class — Part 2

2. After the authorization object class is created, you can right-click it to create new authorization objects (see Figure 12.7).

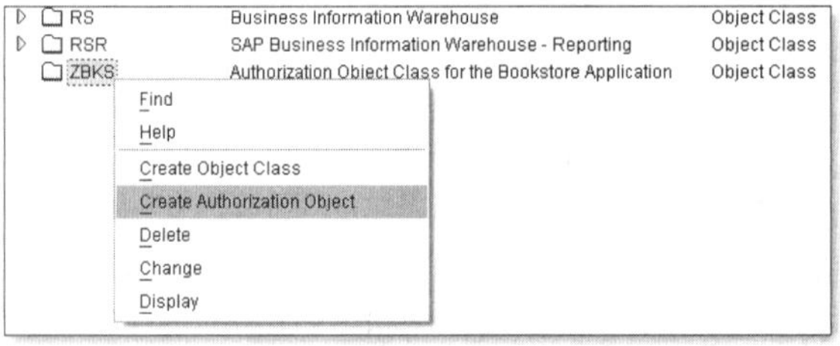


**Figure 12.7** Creating an Authorization Object — Part 1

3. In the Create Authorization Object dialog box shown in Figure 12.8, you must specify the name of the authorization object (in this case, `Z_BOOK`) as well as a short text description of the object. You must also identify the authorization fields that are used to define instances of this authorization object (i.e., authorizations). For the `Z_BOOK` authorization object, we're using the `ACTVT` authorization field predelivered by SAP. Click the Save button to save your changes.

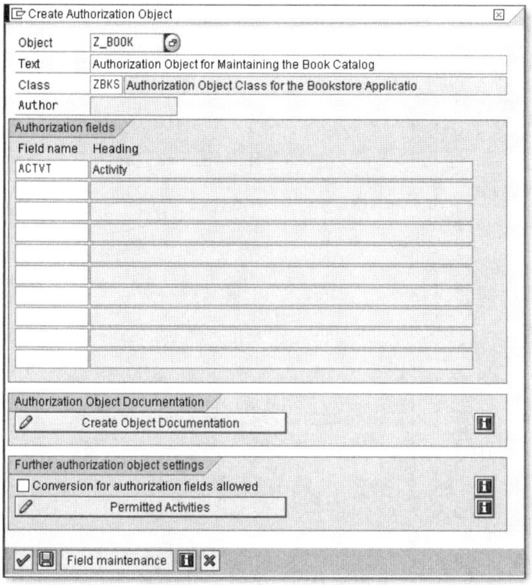


**Figure 12.8** Creating an Authorization Object — Part 2

4. When you click on the Save button, you're prompted to create an object directory entry as usual. Also, because we selected the ACTVT authorization field, we're prompted to maintain the permitted activities for the authorization object (see Figure 12.9). Press the Enter key to proceed.

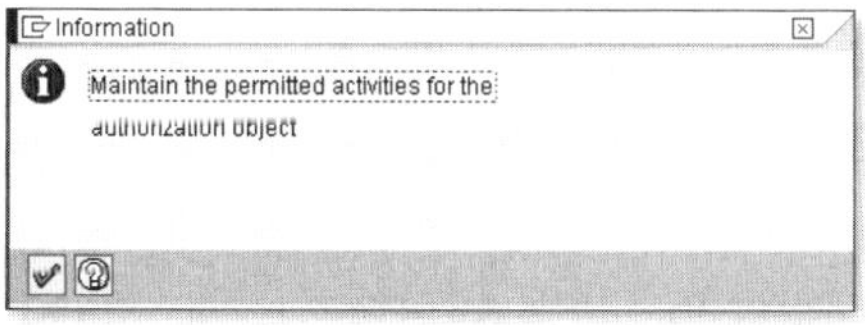


**Figure 12.9** Creating an Authorization Object — Part 3

5. To maintain the permitted activities for the authorization object, click on the Permitted Activities button on the Create Authorization Object dialog screen (refer to Figure 12.8). On the Define Values dialog box shown in Figure 12.10, you can select the types of activities that you want to define authorizations for. Here, we've selected the Create, Change, Display, and Delete checkboxes. When you're satisfied with your selections, click on the Save button to confirm your changes.

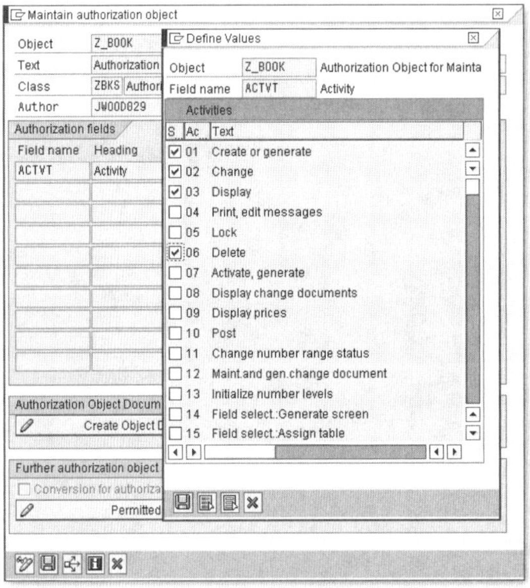


**Figure 12.10** Creating an Authorization Object — Part 4

We explain how to put this authorization object to work in Section 12.2.4, Performing Authorization Checks in ABAP. However, before we do, we need to take a step back and see how authorization objects are used to assign authorizations to users.

### 12.2.3 Configuring Authorizations

As you learned in Section 12.2.2, Developing Authorization Objects, an authorization object is a type of template that can be used to define authorizations. From a maintenance perspective, authorizations are aggregated into roles that are assigned to user master records. While role maintenance is a task that is normally performed by security administrators, it's useful to see how roles are constructed so that you can understand how all of the pieces fit together behind the scenes. With that in mind, let's take a look at a standard role delivered in every SAP NetWeaver AS ABAP system: the `SAP_BC_DWB_ABAPDEVELOPER` role. This role encompasses the standard ABAP Development Workbench transactions used by ABAP developers.

Role maintenance is performed in Transaction PFCG. Figure 12.11 shows the initial screen of this transaction with the `SAP_BC_DWB_ABAPDEVELOPER` role selected. To view this role, click on the Display button.

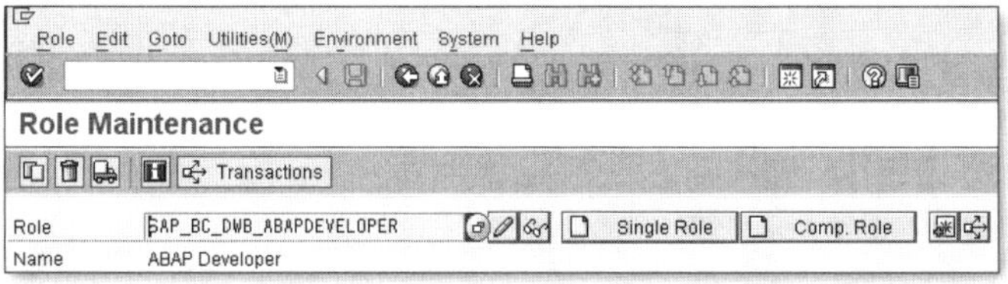


**Figure 12.11** Maintaining Roles in Transaction PFCG

Figure 12.12 shows the maintenance screen that security administrators use to edit roles. As you can see, administrators can assign access to transactions and various other functions on the Menu tab. These functions can be organized into a role menu that is compartmentalized by folders.

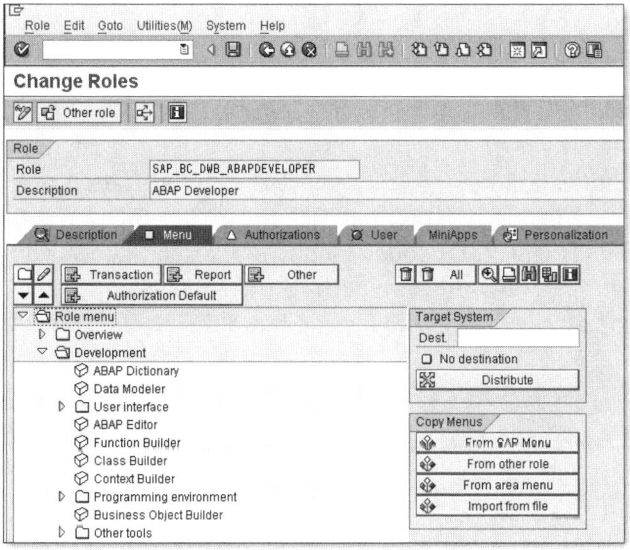


**Figure 12.12** Maintaining Roles in Transaction PFCG

Behind the scenes, the role maintenance transaction keeps a running tab of the authorizations required to access the selected transactions/functions. You can see this information on the Authorizations tab. For instance, in Figure 12.13, you can see that the SAP_BC_DWB_ABAPDEVELOPER role is assigned the authorization profile T_BA800053. This authorization profile can be viewed by clicking on the Display Authorization Data button.

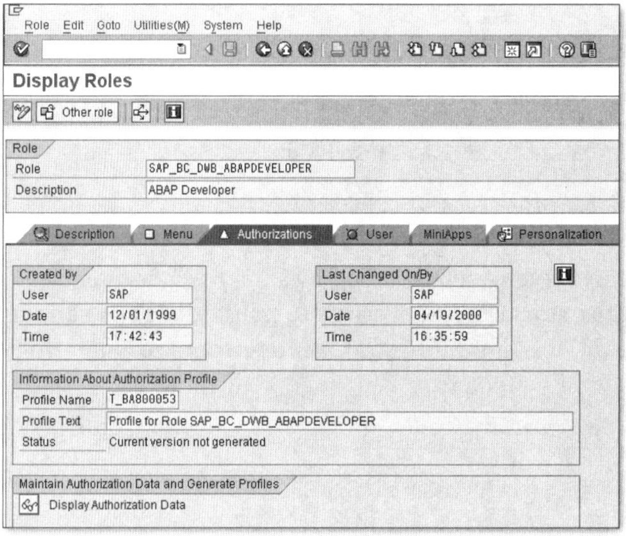

**Figure 12.13** Viewing Authorization Profiles in Transaction PFCG — Part 1

Figure 12.14 shows the authorization data for the T_BA800053 authorization profile. Here, we've selected the menu option UTILITIES • TECHNICAL NAMES ON so that we could see the technical details. This color-coded hierarchical display allows you to drill into authorizations and see how they are put together. You can obtain an overview of the color scheme by clicking on the Legend button.

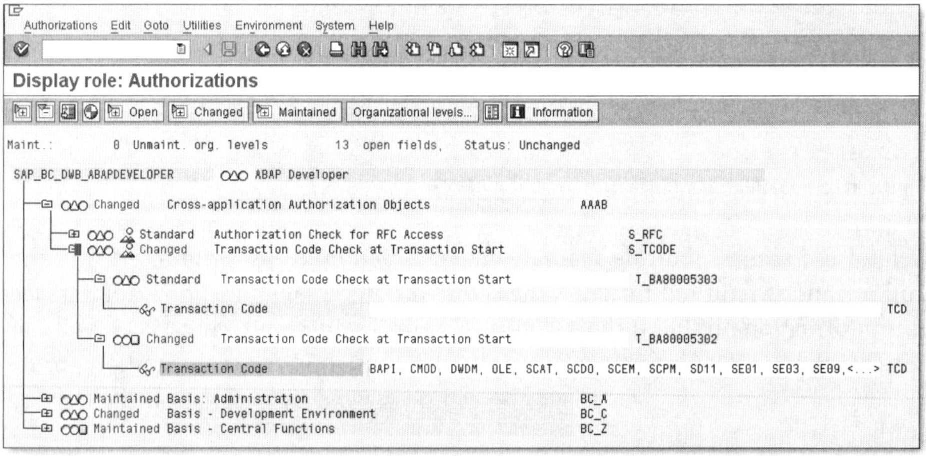

**Figure 12.14** Viewing Authorization Profiles in Transaction PFCG — Part 2

Looking closely at the authorization data in Figure 12.14, you can see that the SAP_BC_DWB_ABAPDEVELOPER role contains an authorization named T_BA80005302 that defines access to Transactions BAPI, CMOD, and so on. This authorization is based on the authorization object S_TCODE described earlier. Administrators can adjust these auto-generated authorizations or even create new ones within this perspective.

After all of the relevant authorizations are defined, the role can be saved and then assigned to user accounts in Transaction SU01. Figure 12.15 shows how the SAP_BC_DWB_ABAPDEVELOPER role is assigned to the user master record for user JWOOD029. This assignment ensures that user JWOOD029 can access Transaction BAPI, and so on. We explain how these authorization checks work in Section 12.2.4, Performing Authorization Checks in ABAP.

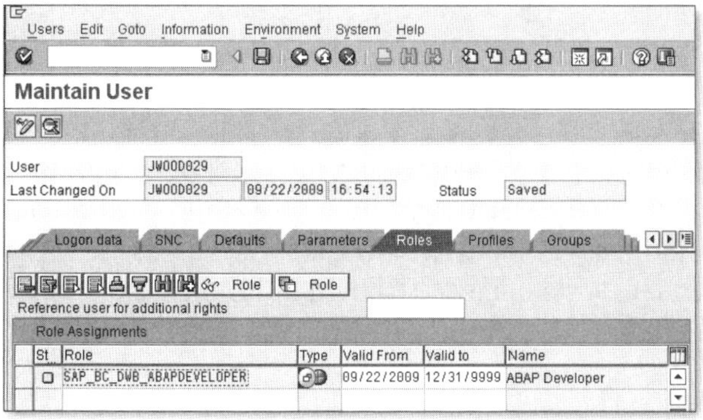


**Figure 12.15** Assigning Roles to Users in Transaction SU01

### 12.2.4 Performing Authorization Checks in ABAP

After security authorizations have been assigned to a user account, the actual process of checking those authorizations in an ABAP program is very straightforward. Authorization checks are performed using the AUTHORITY-CHECK statement. Listing 12.1 shows the syntax diagram for the AUTHORITY-CHECK statement. Here, the authorization object is selected via the OBJECT addition, and specific authorization fields can be checked using the ID additions.

```
AUTHORITY-CHECK OBJECT auth_obj [FOR USER user]
                       ID id1 {FIELD val1}|DUMMY
                      [ID id2 {FIELD val2}|DUMMY]
                          ...
                      [ID id10 {FIELD val10}|DUMMY].
```

**Listing 12.1** Syntax Diagram for the AUTHORITY-CHECK Statement

Getting back to our bookstore catalog example from Section 12.2.2, Developing Authorization Objects, let's see how we can perform an authorization check to determine whether or not a user can add an entry to the catalog. The code excerpt in Listing 12.2 shows how we could use the AUTHORITY-CHECK statement to perform this check. Whenever this code is executed, the system checks to see if the current user has an authorization in his user master record that refers to an instance of the Z_BOOK authorization object. Specifically, it checks for an authorization where the ACTVT authorization field has the value '01'. If the check is successful, SY-SUBRC has the value 0; for a list of possible error code values, consult the ABAP Keyword Documentation.

```
AUTHORITY-CHECK OBJECT 'Z_BOOK'
                    ID 'ACTVT' FIELD '01'.
IF sy-subrc NE 0.
  "Error handling goes here...
ENDIF.
```

**Listing 12.2** Performing an Authorization Check in ABAP

By default, an authorization check is performed against the account of the user who is executing the program. In certain situations, you may want to perform an authorization check for a different user account. In this case, you can use the FOR USER addition of the AUTHORITY-CHECK statement, as shown in Listing 12.3.

```
AUTHORITY-CHECK OBJECT 'Z_BOOK' FOR USER 'pwood'
                    ID 'ACTVT' FIELD '01'.
IF sy-subrc NE 0.
  "Error handling goes here...
ENDIF.
```

**Listing 12.3** Performing Authorization Checks for Specific Users

### 12.2.5 Authorization Concept Review

Like many flexible frameworks, the SAP NetWeaver AS ABAP authorization concept has a lot of moving parts. Throughout the course of this section, we've described the constituent elements of the authorization concept along with their relationships. However, now that you've had a chance to digest all of this, a bit of review is in order.

- From a conceptual perspective, authorizations are aggregated together inside of a role that is maintained in Transaction PFCG. The individual authorizations defined within a specific role are instances of authorization objects. Here, the term "instance" refers to a specific configuration of values for the authorization fields in the authorization object.

- After a role is created, it can be assigned to a user master record in Transaction SU01. At this point, the underlying authorizations become part of that user's profile.
- At runtime, whenever a user attempts to perform specific actions within the system, those actions are checked using the `AUTHORITY-CHECK` statement.
- Custom authorizations can be implemented by creating new authorization objects. Such authorizations are integrated into the framework in the exact same way that standard authorizations are delivered by SAP.

## 12.3 Encrypting Data with ABAP

The term *cryptography*, taken from the Greek, literally means "secret writing." In the context of computer programming, cryptography is used to make sure that sensitive information doesn't make its way into the wrong hands. Normally, whenever we talk about encryption in computer programming, we're talking about encrypting data that is transmitted over the network. As we stated earlier, SAP provides excellent built-in support for encrypting network traffic. However, there are certain situations where you may want to encrypt sensitive data internally. In this section, we show you how to encrypt data using ABAP library functions.

One of the most common use cases for encrypting data internally is the storage of sensitive data such as passwords. You don't want to store this sensitive data in a format that could be read by other users who have access to the database. A common workaround for this is to generate a *message digest* (or hash code) that represents a *fingerprint* of the password.

Figure 12.16 demonstrates how message digest algorithms work. In this case, we've passed the literal text "password" into the algorithm, and it has generated a 32-character hash code encoded in hexadecimal notation. Message digest algorithms are deterministic, which means that the same input sequence generates the same output sequence each time. Consequently, another use of message digest algorithms is to generate a kind of checksum for files that are downloaded off the Internet. Because a given checksum can only be generated by a particular input sequence, you can verify that a file hasn't been tampered with by ensuring that its checksum matches the one originally published by the host.

**Figure 12.16** Generating a Message Digest

Perhaps the most popular of message digest algorithms is the MD5 algorithm developed by Ron Rivest of RSA Security, Inc.. SAP provides an implementation of this algorithm with the `MD5_CALCULATE_HASH_FOR_CHAR` function module. This function, like all message digest functions, is a one-way function. In other words, there is no way to decrypt the generated hash code. Given this, you might be wondering how message digest functions could be used to store passwords. After all, if you can't decrypt the hash code, what good is it?

As it turns out, the one-way nature of message digest functions is very advantageous when it comes to working with passwords. Initially, when a password is created, it's hashed and stored in the database. Because it can't be decrypted, the password hash code can be seen by other users in the system without compromising security. When a user logs on to the system, he is presented with a form to enter his password. To enable a comparison, the proposed plain text password is hashed using the same message digest algorithm. A match only occurs if the proposed password matches the originally created password verbatim. In this way, the system never has to know the actual password to implement authentication.

Listing 12.4 demonstrates how to call the `MD5_CALCULATE_HASH_FOR_CHAR`. As you can see, the call signature is very straightforward, matching the flow depicted in Figure 12.16.

```
DATA: hash TYPE md5_fields-hash,
      password TYPE string VALUE 'itsasecret'.

CALL FUNCTION 'MD5_CALCULATE_HASH_FOR_CHAR'
  EXPORTING
    data           = password
  IMPORTING
    hash           = hash
  EXCEPTIONS
    no_data        = 1
    internal_error = 2
    others         = 3.
```

**Listing 12.4** Calculating an MD5 Hash Code

There are many examples of useful applications of message digest algorithms. In addition to the basic authentication example described in this section, message digests can also be used to perform other worthwhile tasks including the following:

- Single Sign-On (SSO)
- Intelligent message routing based on hash codes of document numbers
- Check-summing to determine if cached objects are still valid

You can find out more about the `MD5_CALCULATE_HASH_FOR_CHAR` function and other hash functions by looking at the documentation for the functions in the standard function group `SECH`. Here, among other things, you'll find another function called `MD5_CALCULATE_HASH_FOR_RAW` that can be used to calculate a hash code for binary data streams.

## 12.4 Performing Virus Scans

Sometimes we get so caught up with firewalls and network security that we fail to pay attention to the real threats associated with external messages coming into the system. For example, consider a web-based application that allows users to upload files to a document management system. Here, it's very possible that these files contain viruses. Ideally, we want to perform a virus scan before trusting these files within the system. Luckily, SAP makes it possible to perform these scans using the *Virus Scan Interface*.

The Virus Scan Interface (VSI) allows you to integrate popular enterprise virus scan solutions into a common infrastructure.[1] Once configured, you can use the VSI to perform virus scans in your ABAP programs using the `CL_VSI` class library. The code excerpt in Listing 12.5 shows how this works.

```
DATA: lo_vsi      TYPE REF TO cl_vsi,
      lv_profile TYPE vscan_profile VALUE 'my_profile',
      lv_payload TYPE xstring,
      lv_retcode TYPE vscan_scanrc.
```

1 You can learn more about the configuration of the VSI in the SAP Library available online at *http://help.sap.com*. Under the SAP NetWeaver section, perform a search using the phrase "Configuration of the Virus Scan Interface."

```
"Obtain a reference to the virus scan interface:
CALL METHOD cl_vsi=>get_instance
  EXPORTING
    if_profile          = lv_profile
  IMPORTING
    eo_instance         = lo_vsi
  EXCEPTIONS
    configuration_error = 1
    profile_not_active  = 2
    internal_error      = 3
    others              = 4.

"Scan a binary payload:
CALL METHOD lo_vsi->scan_bytes
  EXPORTING
    if_data             = lv_payload
  IMPORTING
    ef_scanrc           = lv_retcode
  EXCEPTIONS
    not_available       = 1
    configuration_error = 2
    internal_error      = 3
    others              = 4.
```

**Listing 12.5** Performing a Virus Scan Using the VSI in ABAP

## 12.5 Protecting Web Content with CAPTCHA

Throughout the course of this chapter, we've approached the concept of authentication from the perspective of users. Here, we've been trying to determine whether or not users are who they say they are. One way malicious users try to get around this type of authentication is to launch a *brute force attack* using an Internet robot (or bot). A brute force attack is a type of attack in which every possible password permutation is tried repeatedly until a match is found.

One way to guard against bots is to apply another authentication layer that can be used to ascertain whether or not an authentication request came from a human user. In this section, we show you how to perform these tests in your Web-based programs using a custom CAPTCHA component developed using the Adobe Flex framework.

### 12.5.1 What Is CAPTCHA?

CAPTCHA stands for *Completely Automated Public Turing Test to Tell Computers and Humans Apart*. CAPTCHA programs were invented by Luis von Ahn, Manuel Blum, Nicholas Hopper, and John Langford of Carnegie Mellon University in 2000. Normally, the Turning test is administered by displaying an image that contains a randomized text phrase that the user must verify in a form input field. Figure 12.17 shows an example of a registration form that requires a user to key in the security code depicted in an image.

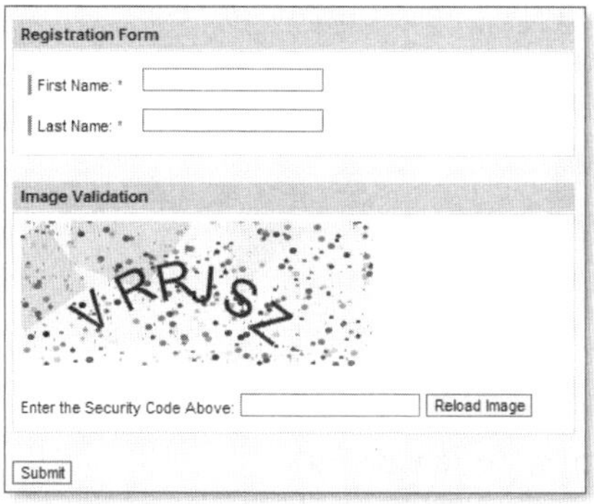


**Figure 12.17** Example of a CAPTCHA Test

As you can see in Figure 12.17, the CAPTCHA image is distorted so that sophisticated bots have a difficult time recognizing the characters. The more obscure the image, the less likely that a non-human could pass the test. In addition to brute force attacks, CAPTCHA is also used to prevent various other types of vandalism such as spam, automated posting to forums, and so on.

### 12.5.2 Developing a CAPTCHA Component with Adobe Flex

Although ABAP can do just about anything, from building a financial statement to managing production operations, one thing it can't do is provide you with a mechanism for generating dynamic images. Therefore, we must look outside the world of ABAP to find a platform that we can use to build our custom CAPTCHA program. For the purposes of this example, we develop our CAPTCHA component using the Adobe Flex framework.

The Adobe Flex framework uses a combination of declarative XML called MXML, and a proprietary language called ActionScript to develop rich Internet applications (RIAs). When deployed to the Web, Flex content is compiled into an intermediate byte code that can be executed using the Adobe Flash Player. The primary advantage here is the fact that the Flash Player is a cross-platform runtime environment that is reportedly installed on up to 99% of the machines connected to the Internet around the world.

Figure 12.18 shows the custom CAPTCHA component that we've created. Here, the randomized text string is stretched across a Bezier curve to make it more difficult to scan. In addition, randomized dots and polygons have been added to further obscure the image. Although the details of Flex-based development are outside the scope of this book, you can find all of the source code/project files used to build our custom CAPTCHA component with the source code bundle for this book available online.

**Figure 12.18** Generated CAPTCHA Component in Adobe Flash Player

### 12.5.3 Integrating the CAPTCHA Component with BSPs

To simplify integration of the CAPTCHA component with Business Server Pages (BSPs), you can use the custom `captchaInclude` and `captcha` elements of the `/BOWDK/BOWDARK` BSP extension provided as part of this book's source code bundle. These extension elements link in all of the necessary MIME objects for embedding the CAPTCHA component inside of a BSP. Listing 12.6 contains a skeleton of a BSP that integrates the CAPTCHA component. You can see an example of a fully functional page in the `/BOWDK/CAPTCHA_TEST` BSP application available as part of this book's source code bundle.

```
<%@page language="abap"%>
<%@extension name="htmlb" prefix="htmlb"%>
<%@extension name="phtmlb" prefix="phtmlb"%>
<%@extension name="/bowdk/bowdark" prefix="bowdk"%>

<htmlb:content design="design2003">
  <htmlb:document>
    <htmlb:documentHead title="CAPTCHA Example">
      <htmlb:headInclude />
      <bowdk:captchaInclude />
    </htmlb:documentHead>
```

```
    <htmlb:documentBody>
      <htmlb:form id="registrationForm" method="post">
        <!-- Form layout & content go here... -->
        <bowdk:captcha />
        <!-- Form layout & content go here... -->
      </htmlb:form>
    </htmlb:documentBody>
  </htmlb:document>
</htmlb:content>
```

**Listing 12.6** Including the CAPTCHA Component in a BSP

The code excerpt shown in Listing 12.6 embeds the CAPTCHA component on a BSP, but to communicate with it, you need to write some JavaScript code. Most of the time, there are two JavaScript functions that you'll want to integrate into your BSP: one to validate a user's security code entry against the security code embedded inside the CAPTCHA component, and the other to allow users to reload the image in the event that it's not legible.

The JavaScript code shown in Listing 12.7 demonstrates how you can trigger the reloading of the CAPTCHA image via JavaScript. This communication is made possible via the `ExternalInterface` ActionScript class that allows you to register JavaScript callback functions inside of a Flex component. In this case, we're invoking the `reloadImage()` function of the custom CAPTCHA component.

```
<script type="text/javascript">
  function reloadImage()
  {
    // Derive the browser container reference:
    var container;
    var captchaSwf = "flexCaptcha";

    if (navigator.appName.indexOf("Microsoft") >= 0)
      container = document;
    else
      container = window;

    container[captchaSwf].reloadImage();
  } // -- function reloadImage() -- //
</script>
```

**Listing 12.7** Reloading the CAPTCHA Image with JavaScript

The JavaScript code required to perform the CAPTCHA test is similar in nature to the code demonstrated in Listing 12.7. As you can see in Listing 12.8, you can check the security code entry using the `checkSecurityCode()` callback function provided with the CAPTCHA component. In this case, we're using the HTMLB eventing mechanism to control whether or not a form gets submitted. For more information about HTMLB, we highly recommend *Advanced BSP Programming* (SAP PRESS, 2006).

```
<script type="text/javascript">
  function checkForm(htmlbevent)
  {
    // Make sure the user entered a valid security code;
    // Derive the browser container reference:
    var container;
    var swf = "flexCaptcha";

    if (navigator.appName.indexOf("Microsoft") >= 0)
      container = document;
    else
      container = window;

    var securityCode =
      document.getElementById("inpSecurityCode").value;
    if (! container[swf].checkSecurityCode(securityCode))
    {
      alert("You entered an invalid security code!");
      htmlbevent.cancelSubmit = true;
    }
  } // -- End of function checkForm() -- //
</script>
```

**Listing 12.8** Performing the CAPTCHA Test with JavaScript

For the most part, you should be able to deploy the CAPTCHA component with your BSPs using the instructions outlined in this section. Of course, because HTML/JavaScript standards are moving targets from browser implementation to browser implementation, you may find that certain tweaks are required to get the component to work. This is particularly the case for obscure browsers that aren't supported by the *SAP Product Availability Matrix* (PAM). To see if your browser is supported in the PAM, navigate to *https://service.sap.com/pam*.

### 12.5.4 Integrating the CAPTCHA Component with Web Dynpro

Beginning with the release of SAP NetWeaver 7.0, EHP 1, it's now possible to embed Adobe Flex components into Web Dynpro for ABAP (WDA) applications. This functionality is driven by a new RIA integration framework called the *Web Dynpro Islands Framework*. The Web Dynpro Islands Framework makes it possible for Web Dynpro components to communicate with Flex components and vice versa.

Realistically speaking, a detailed treatment of Web Dynpro for ABAP and the Web Dynpro Islands Framework is beyond the scope of this book. Nevertheless, we've provided a fully functional WDA application called `ZWDCAPTCHATEST` in the source code bundle available online that you can use as a reference for integrating the CAPTCHA component in your own WDA applications. Figure 12.19 shows an example of the custom `ZWDCAPTCHATEST` application.

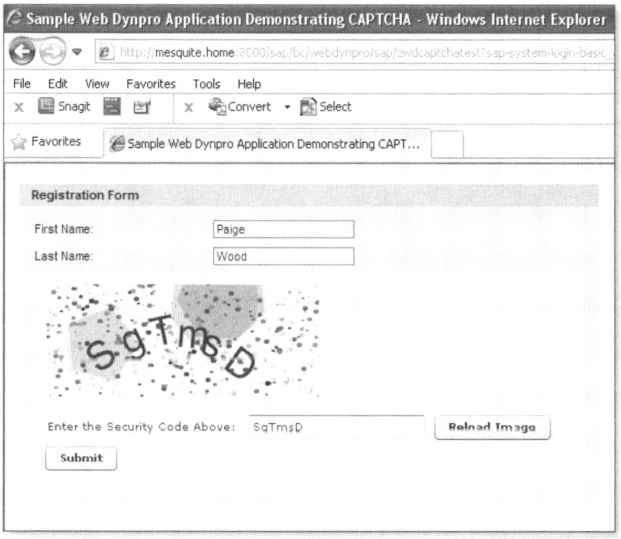


**Figure 12.19** Integrating the CAPTCHA Component in Web Dynpro

If you're new to Web Dynpro and are looking for a good reference book, we highly recommend *Web Dynpro for ABAP* (SAP PRESS, 2006). For more information about the Web Dynpro Islands Framework, check out the SAP Rich Islands wiki page available online at *http://wiki.sdn.sap.com/wiki/display/EmTech/SAP+Rich+Islands+for+Adobe+Flash*. Among other things, this wiki contains detailed examples that show you how to incorporate various kinds of Flex components into WDA applications.

## 12.6 Summary

In this chapter, you learned how to apply the SAP NetWeaver AS ABAP authorization concept toward the development of secure applications in ABAP. This concept, when integrated from the outset, simplifies the development process by reducing potential security holes. In the next chapter, we look at another important aspect of secure programming: logging and tracing.

*Bugs in food are no better than bugs in programs. However, despite our best efforts to eliminate program defects, it seems that there are often elusive bugs that lurk out there on the periphery, waiting to manifest themselves at the most inopportune times. When these errors occur, it's important to have as much information about the error as possible to perform a root-cause analysis. One of the most common ways of storing this information is to put it in an application log.*

# 13 Logging and Tracing

During the early stages of program development, many developers test their programs using the ABAP Debugger tool. Among other things, this tool allows developers to interactively step through their program logic while evaluating the contents of variables that change along the way. Most of the time, the ABAP Debugger tool will help you identify any glaring holes in a program. Then, unit, string, and integration test cycles should squash any remaining bugs in the program logic. Of course, if this method were 100% fail safe, there would never be any errors in productive systems.

Generally speaking, the types of errors that manifest themselves in a production environment are the ones that are erratic and hard to troubleshoot. Given this unpredictability, it can be difficult to set up a debugging session to pinpoint the problem. Rather than trying to guess when an error is going to take place, it's more convenient to turn on a program trace and output relevant messages to a persistent log. Then, whenever an error occurs, the log can be recalled to examine the source of the error.

In this chapter, we introduce you to the *Business Application Log* (BAL) framework provided out of the box with SAP NetWeaver AS ABAP. This framework can be used to implement logging and tracing requirements for ABAP programs. Along the way, we show you how to use a custom class-based API that simplifies the way that you work with the logging framework.

## 13.1 Introducing the Business Application Log

The BAL framework is a comprehensive logging framework that can be used to generate persistent logs. Unlike other logging frameworks that use a file-based persistence mechanism, the BAL framework stores log messages in the SAP NetWeaver AS ABAP system database. This approach makes it possible to update, search, filter, and display logs quickly and easily.

In this section, we introduce you to the BAL and show you how to configure and interact with it using the standard API. We'll then use this information as a springboard for designing a custom logging framework in Section 13.2, Developing a Custom Logging Framework.

### 13.1.1 Configuring Log Objects

BALs are organized by application log objects and sub-objects. These objects, along with a uniquely generated log number and various other metadata, make up a log header record in table `BALHDR`. Log header records give the BAL structure, allowing you to perform searches for logs within a given application area, date range, and so on.

Application log objects are created in Transaction SLG0. When you initially open this transaction, you're prompted with a warning indicating that application log objects are cross-client objects. Figure 13.1 shows the initial screen of Transaction SLG0. As you can see, an application log object consists of an object name and an optional short text description.

To demonstrate how the BAL framework works, let's create a custom application log object and sub-object for the online bookstore application introduced in Chapter 6, Database Programming. To create a new application log object, perform the following steps:

1. In Transaction SLG0, click the New Entries button to open the New Entries: Overview of Added Entries perspective shown in Figure 13.2.
2. In the Object and Object Text columns, enter a name and short text description for the application log object. When you name your log objects, you'll want to keep the name pretty generic. For instance, one of the standard entries provided by SAP is called `ALE`. This log object encompasses all logging related to the Application Link and Enabling framework. For the purposes of our bookstore

example, we've chosen to create a log object called ZBOOK. Here, notice the use of the customer namespace prefix Z. Though Transaction SLG0 only offers a warning if you attempt to use a disallowed namespace, it's always a good idea to create application log objects in a customer namespace to avoid potential collisions down the road. After you've selected your name, press the Enter key to confirm your entry.

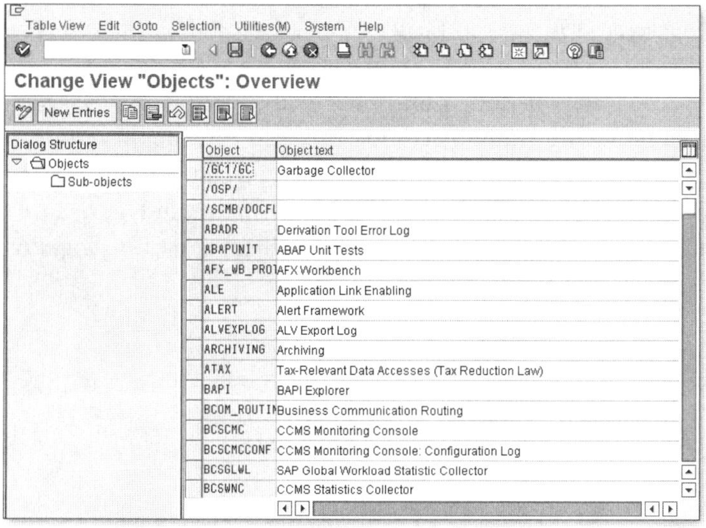


**Figure 13.1** Editing Application Log Objects in Transaction SLG0

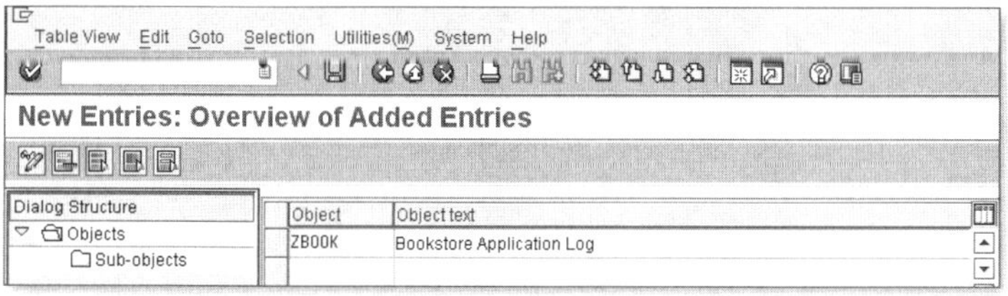


**Figure 13.2** Creating an Application Log Object — Part 1

3. After you've confirmed the log object name, select the record in the table and double-click the Sub-Objects node in the Dialog Structure on the left side of the screen. This brings up the Change View "Sub-Objects": Overview screen shown in Figure 13.3.

4. To create a sub-object, click on the New Entries button.

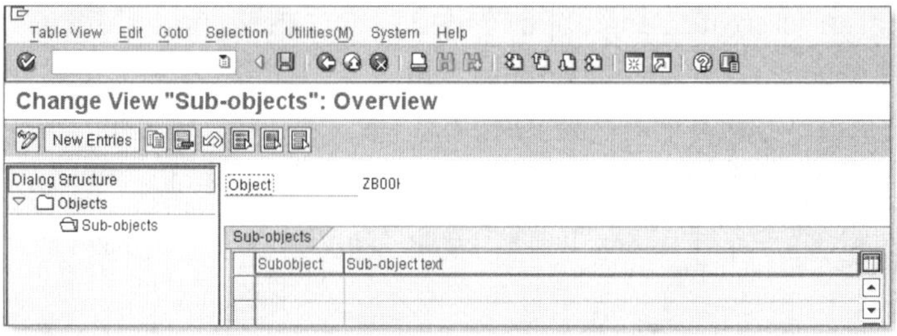


**Figure 13.3** Creating an Application Log Object — Part 2

5. In the New Entries: Overview of Added Entries screen shown in Figure 13.4, you must select a name for the sub-object. You can also provide an optional short text description for the sub-object. At this level, you can get much more specific about the type of logs you want to create. For instance, in Figure 13.4, we've created a sub-object called ZCATALOG. This sub-object is used to log any activity related to catalog maintenance for the bookstore.

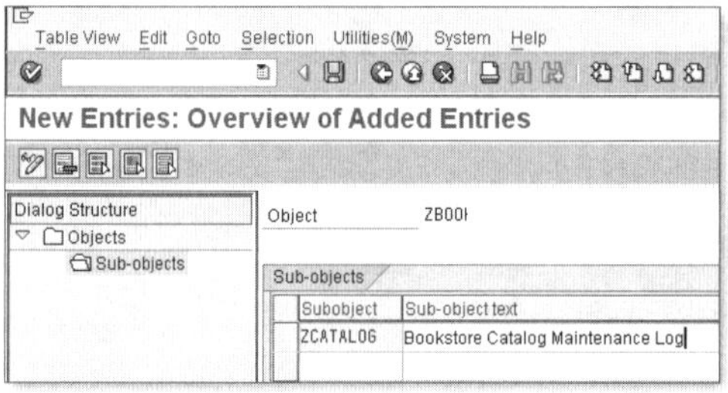


**Figure 13.4** Creating an Application Log Object — Part 3

6. After you've configured your log objects, click the Save button to save your changes. At this point, you're prompted to select a transport request to track the configuration changes.

### 13.1.2 Displaying Logs

Sometimes the easiest way to understand how a software framework such as the BAL works is to look at the results it produces. You can analyze application logs in Transaction SLG1. Figure 13.5 shows the initial screen of this transaction. As you can see, there are many options available to search for a particular application log instance. For example, in Figure 13.5, we're using the ZBOOK and ZCATALOG log objects to search for logs created on 9/29/2009.

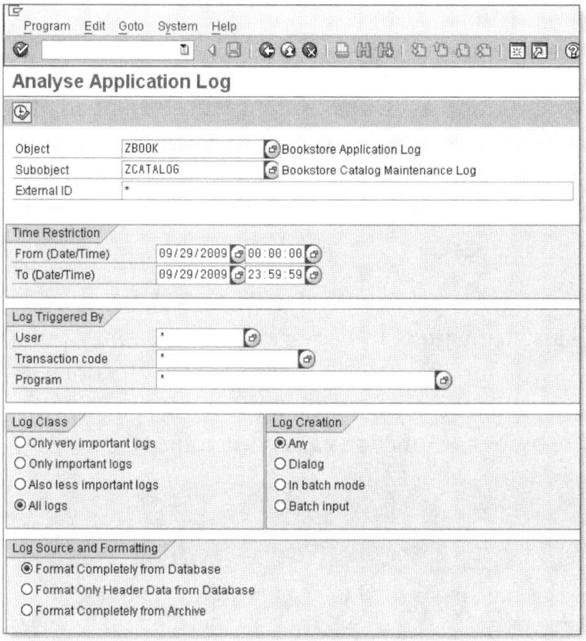

Figure 13.5 Selection Screen of Transaction SLG1

Figure 13.6 shows the log entry that matches the selection criteria proposed in Figure 13.5. As you can see, this log contains various messages with different levels of severity. Here, you can sort the messages, filter by severity, or even output the messages to a local file. In the upcoming sections, we explain how to produce these messages using the BAL API.

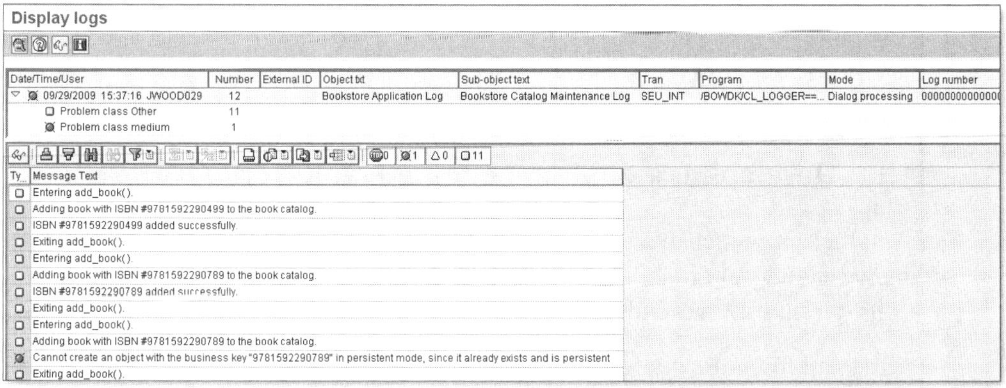

Figure 13.6 Viewing an Application Log in Transaction SLG1

### 13.1.3 Organization of the BAL API

One of the primary goals of any logging framework is to maintain a small footprint and stay out of the way of more important tasks. Therefore, to implement an efficient database-driven logging framework, SAP had to be smart. Rather than incur a database hit each time a message is logged, the API functions of the BAL give you the option of collecting these messages in memory so that they can be written to the database together using the update task.

Table 13.1 highlights some of the API functions provided with the BAL framework; you can find a comprehensive list of functions in package SZAL. The entry point into the log framework is the function module BAL_LOG_CREATE. This function creates a new log instance in memory and associates it with a unique *log handle*. This log handle is the key that binds subsequent function calls with your particular log instance.

| Function Name | Description |
|---|---|
| BAL_LOG_CREATE | This function is used to create a new log instance in memory. |
| BAL_LOG_MSG_ADD | This function is used to add a T100-style message to the log. |
| BAL_LOG_MSG_ADD_FREE_TEXT | This function is used to add a free-form text message to the log. |
| BAL_LOG_EXCEPTION_ADD | This function is used to log a class-based exception message. |
| BAL_DB_SAVE | This function is used to save the log to the database. Here, you have the option of saving the log directly or in the update task. |

**Table 13.1** API Functions of the BAL Framework

## 13.2 Developing a Custom Logging Framework

Given the comprehensive nature of the BAL framework, you might be wondering why we would want to build a custom logging framework on top of it. The answer to this question is two-fold:

1. First and foremost, the custom logging framework employs an object-oriented design that encapsulates various complexities of the BAL framework to sim-

plify your interaction with it. Here, a class-based approach keeps track of the log handle, reduces the amount of code required to invoke BAL API functions, and so on.

2. Secondly, the custom framework makes it possible to implement additional configurability for log objects.

In this section, we demonstrate how this class-based logging framework is implemented. We also show you how to configure log severities that affect the runtime behavior of the framework.

### 13.2.1 Organization of the Class-Based API

Figure 13.7 contains a UML class diagram depicting the core log framework class /BOWDK/CL_LOGGER. This class defines various methods for logging and tracing within a program. As you can see, the names of most of these methods are pretty intuitive. For instance, the DEBUG() method is used to output a free-form debugging message to the log. Each of the free-form log methods such as DEBUG() also have a counterpart method that can be used to log a T100-style message to the log (e.g., DEBUG_MESSAGE(), etc.).

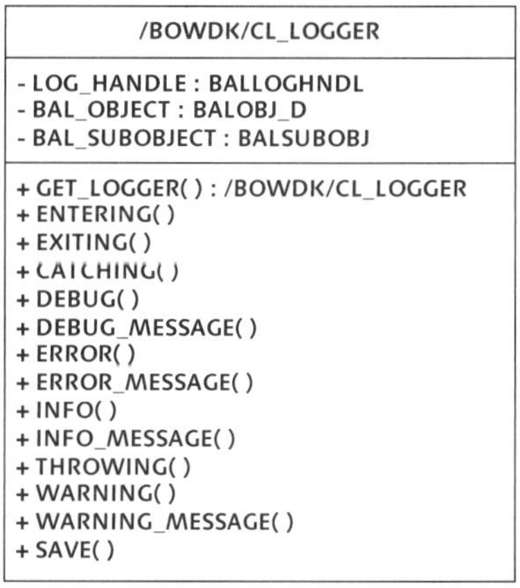


**Figure 13.7** UML Class Diagram of Class /BOWDK/CL_LOGGER

In addition to the typical logging methods, class /BOWDK/CL_LOGGER also defines trace methods such as CATCHING() and THROWING() to trace class-based exceptions and ENTERING() and EXITING() to track call sequences. As you would expect, the SAVE() method is used to save the log to the database.

Another method that you might have noticed is the static `GET_LOGGER()` method. Rather than allowing you to create a log instance directly via the `CREATE OBJECT` statement, class `/BOWDK/CL_LOGGER` routes instance requests through the `GET_LOGGER()` method so it can keep track of instances in context. This makes it possible to share a log instance between modules that are executing within the same program context (i.e., the same internal session).

You can find additional documentation for the methods of class `/BOWDK/CL_LOGGER` in the class documentation available in the Class Builder. This documentation describes the purpose of method parameters, exceptions that can be raised by the framework at runtime, and so on.

### 13.2.2 Configuring Log Severities

In addition to encapsulating log administration tasks, the `/BOWDK/CL_LOGGER` class also assigns a *severity level* to a log instance behind the scenes. This severity level determines whether or not the logger should output messages of a given type. For example, if you were to configure the log framework with a severity level of "Error," the framework would discard all requests to output debugging messages, information messages, and so on. In this way, you can turn the logging level up or down depending upon your needs. For instance, normally logging is turned way down in productive systems.

You can configure the log severity level for a log object by executing Transaction /BOWDK/LOG_CONF. Figure 13.8 shows the maintenance screen for this configuration table. As you can see, the table is keyed by the BAL application object and sub-object described in Section 13.1.1, Configuring Log Objects. For a given log object, you can then select from the Log Severity drop-down list to choose a severity level. After this severity level is set, all subsequent log instances use this severity level to filter out log messages as needed.

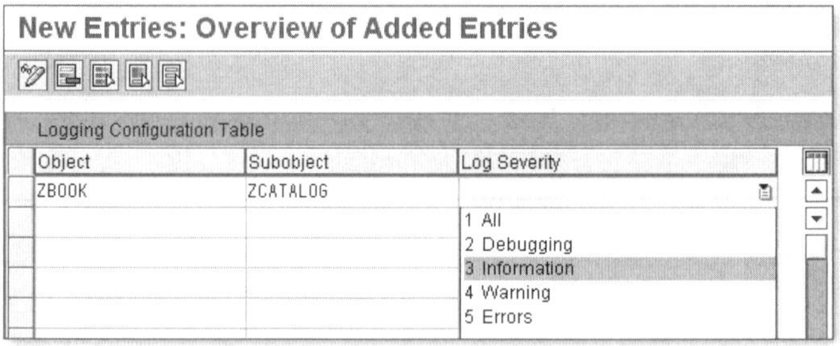


**Figure 13.8** Configuring Log Severities

## 13.3 Case Study: Tracing an Application Program

Like many programming tasks, log development requires you to think about the kinds of information that you need to capture for various stakeholders. For example, as a developer, you're probably interested in capturing a program trace. Administrative types, on the other hand, are probably only interested in looking at technical errors. In some cases, you may want to split a log into multiple sub-objects so that particular sub-objects are intended for different audiences.

Irrespective of the target audience, you'll find that the way that you interact with the logging framework from a technical perspective is always the same. To demonstrate this, let's look at how the log framework can be used to trace through an ABAP program.

### 13.3.1 Integrating the Logging Framework into an ABAP Program

The report program `ZBOOKLOG` shown in Listing 13.1 uses the logging framework to log various milestone events that occur during its execution. This contrived example program uses the `ZBOOK/ZCATALOG` log objects defined in Section 13.1.1, Configuring Log Objects, to output various tracing information as it updates the bookstore catalog. The heavy lifting for this report is carried out by the local `LCL_CATALOG_BUILDER` class.

As you can see in Listing 13.1, class `LCL_CATALOG_BUILDER` obtains an instance to the logger in its `CONSTRUCTOR()` method. This logger instance is then used to output logging and tracing messages inside method `ADD_BOOK()`. Here, we're tracing the entry and exit points of the method using the `ENTERING()` and `EXITING()` methods, outputting debugging and informational messages using the `DEBUG_MESSAGE()` and `INFO_MESSAGE()` methods, and logging exceptions of type `CX_OS_OBJECT_EXISTING`.

```
REPORT zbooklog.
CLASS lcl_catalog_builder DEFINITION.
  PUBLIC SECTION.
    CLASS-METHODS:
      main.

    METHODS:
      constructor RAISING /bowdk/cx_log_exception,
      add_book
        IMPORTING im_isbn TYPE zde_isbn
```

```
                  im_title TYPE zde_title
                  im_publication_date TYPE zde_publish_date,
      log_results.

  PRIVATE SECTION.
    CONSTANTS:
      co_object TYPE balobj_d  VALUE 'ZBOOK',
      co_subobj TYPE balsubobj VALUE 'ZCATALOG',
      co_msgid  TYPE symsgid VALUE 'ZCA_BOOKSTORE'.

    DATA: logger TYPE REF TO /bowdk/cl_logger.
ENDCLASS.

CLASS lcl_catalog_builder IMPLEMENTATION.
  METHOD main.
    "Method-Local Data Declarations:
    DATA: lo_catalog TYPE REF TO lcl_catalog_builder,
          lo_log_ex  TYPE REF TO /bowdk/cx_log_exception.

    "Execute the program:
    TRY.
      "Create an instance of the catalog application:
      CREATE OBJECT lo_catalog.

      "Add some books to the catalog:
      CALL METHOD lo_catalog->add_book
        EXPORTING
          im_isbn             = '9781592290499'
          im_publication_date = '20060301'
          im_title            = 'Advanced BSP Programming'.

      "Notice the duplicate entries...
      CALL METHOD lo_catalog->add_book
        EXPORTING
          im_isbn             = '9781592290789'
          im_publication_date = '20060815'
          im_title            = 'Web Dynpro for ABAP'.

      CALL METHOD lo_catalog->add_book
        EXPORTING
          im_isbn             = '9781592290789'
          im_publication_date = '20060815'
          im_title            = 'Web Dynpro for ABAP'.
```

```
    "Persist the log session:
    lo_catalog->log_results( ).
  CATCH /bowdk/cx_log_exception INTO lo_log_ex.
    MESSAGE lo_log_ex TYPE 'I'.
    RETURN.
  CLEANUP.
    "Persist the log session:
    lo_catalog->log_results( ).
  ENDTRY.
ENDMETHOD.                    " METHOD main

METHOD constructor.
  "Create an instance of the logger for this application:
  CALL METHOD /bowdk/cl_logger=>get_logger
    EXPORTING
      im_object    = co_object
      im_subobject = co_subobj
    RECEIVING
      re_logger    = logger.
ENDMETHOD.                    " METHOD constructor

METHOD add_book.
  "Method-Local Data Declarations:
  DATA: lo_os_ex TYPE REF TO cx_os_object_existing.

  logger->entering( 'add_book( )' ).

  "Create a book persistent object:
  TRY.
    logger->debug_message( im_msg_id = co_msgid
                           im_msg_no = '002'
                           im_msg_v1 = im_isbn ).

    CALL METHOD zca_book=>agent->create_persistent
      EXPORTING
        i_isbn             = im_isbn
        i_publication_date = im_publication_date
        i_title            = im_title.

    logger->info_message( im_msg_id = co_msgid
                          im_msg_no = '003'
                          im_msg_v1 = im_isbn ).
```

```
    CATCH cx_os_object_existing INTO lo_os_ex.
      logger->catching( lo_os_ex ).
    ENDTRY.

    logger->exiting( 'add_book( )' ).
  ENDMETHOD.                    " METHOD add_book

  METHOD log_results.
    TRY.
      logger->save( ).
      COMMIT WORK.
    CATCH /bowdk/cx_log_exception.
    ENDTRY.
  ENDMETHOD.                    " METHOD log_results
ENDCLASS.

START-OF-SELECTION.
  "Execute the catalog load program:
  lcl_catalog_builder=>main( ).
```

**Listing 13.1** Tracing Through an ABAP Program

To save the log to the database, you must call method SAVE() of class /BOWDK/CL_LOGGER. This call, along with the subsequent COMMIT WORK statement, is wrapped up inside the LOG_RESULTS() method of class LCL_CATALOG_BUILDER.

As a rule, you want trap runtime exceptions inside of a TRY statement so that you can ensure that the log is saved in a CLEANUP block. However, be careful when committing the changes because you only want to commit the log entries — not a transaction that might have failed. If in doubt, you may want to refer to Chapter 7, Transactional Programming, to see how you can organize your transactions so that these two concerns can vary independently.

### 13.3.2 Viewing Log Instances in Transaction SLG1

Figure 13.9 shows the log generated for the ZBOOKLOG program in Transaction SLG1 when the log severity is configured to "All." At this level of severity, you can trace the steps of the program up to the point that an error occurred. To view the details of this error, select the message and click on the Technical Info button. This brings up the dialog window shown in Figure 13.10. Here, you can see that an exception of type CX_OS_OBJECT_EXISTING was raised (purposefully, in this demonstration).

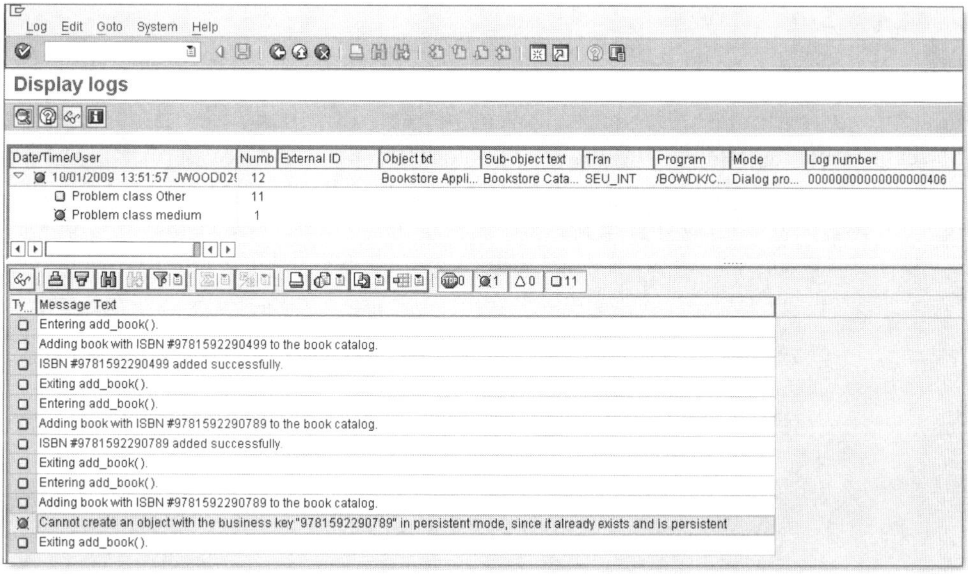


**Figure 13.9** Viewing the Log Results in SLG1

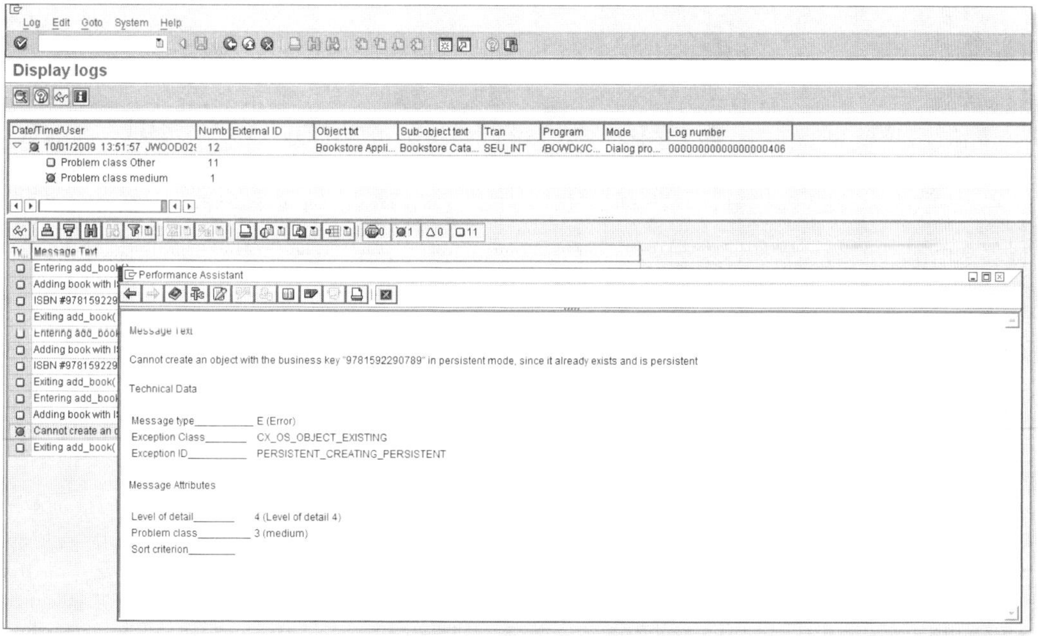


**Figure 13.10** Viewing the Details of a Log Message in SLG1

## 13.4 Summary

In this chapter, you learned how to incorporate the BAL logging infrastructure into your own custom developments. As you've seen, this framework can be used to seamlessly integrate logging and tracing requirements into ABAP applications. The retained information can prove vital in debugging elusive bugs, tracking security breaches, or even identifying performance issues. In the next chapter, we look at how you can interact with the operating system from an ABAP context.

*A chef can't do all of his work alone, so he often relies on a sous-chef for help. Similarly, the ABAP programming language is equipped to do many things, but performing low-level system tasks isn't one of its strong points. Fortunately, ABAP provides a convenient interface for executing operating system commands and scripts to handle these requirements.*

# 14 Interacting with the Operating System

SAP NetWeaver AS ABAP does such a good job of abstracting its surrounding environment that we rarely take the features of its host operating system into account. Perhaps one of the reasons that we cast these details aside is that we want our solutions to be *portable*. While this is certainly a worthy goal, it can sometimes cloud our judgment when it comes to good program design. The reality is that ABAP isn't particularly good at solving certain problems. Rather than trying to reinvent the wheel with convoluted solutions, it's best to solve these problems with the right tool. And sometimes, that tool is sitting on the operating system just waiting to be leveraged.

In this chapter, we show you how to interact with the host operating system of SAP NetWeaver AS ABAP. In particular, we introduce you to a framework that SAP provides as part of the standard distribution to define external commands in a highly portable manner. After we explain the basics of this framework, we develop a case study that demonstrates how to define your own external command and execute it in an ABAP program.

## 14.1 Programming with External Commands

In this section, we show you the basics of programming with external commands in ABAP. Unlike other programming interfaces provided in ABAP, there is no built-in language statement that you can use to execute external commands. Instead, you must define these commands within the system so that they can be executed via standard API functions. In the upcoming subsections, we show you how to configure external commands in the system and leverage those commands in ABAP.

### 14.1.1 Maintaining External Commands

External commands are maintained in Transaction SM69. Figure 14.1 shows the initial screen of this transaction. As you can see, quite a few commands are predelivered by SAP in every NetWeaver system; consequently, it's always a good idea to see if SAP has already configured the command you're looking to execute rather than creating a new command definition from scratch.

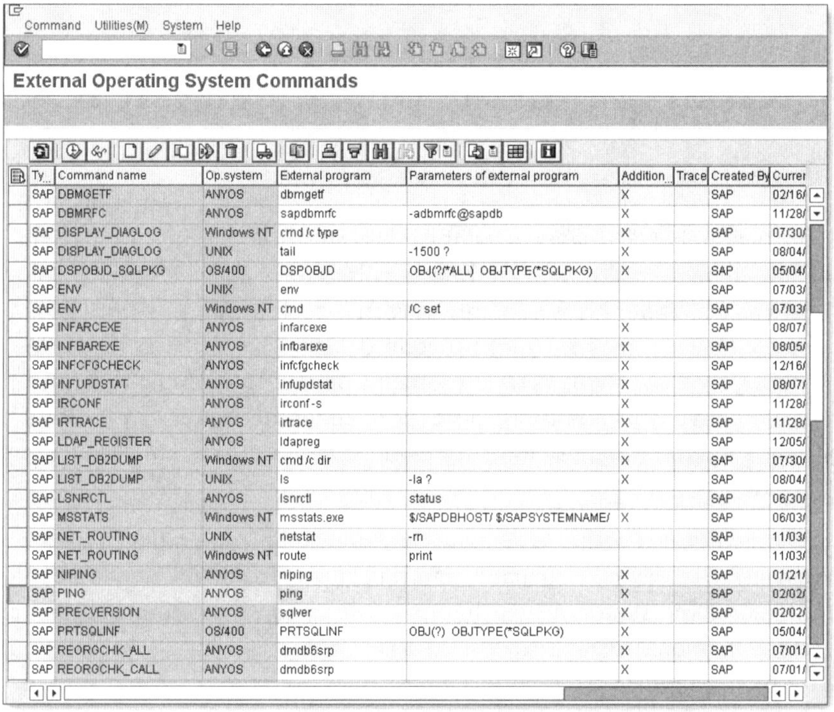


| Ty... | Command name | Op.system | External program | Parameters of external program | Addition... | Trace | Created By | Currer |
|---|---|---|---|---|---|---|---|---|
| SAP | DBMGETF | ANYOS | dbmgetf | | X | | SAP | 02/16/ |
| SAP | DBMRFC | ANYOS | sapdbmrfc | -adbmrfc@sapdb | X | | SAP | 11/28/ |
| SAP | DISPLAY_DIAGLOG | Windows NT | cmd /c type | | X | | SAP | 07/30/ |
| SAP | DISPLAY_DIAGLOG | UNIX | tail | -1500 ? | X | | SAP | 08/04/ |
| SAP | DSPOBJD_SQLPKG | OS/400 | DSPOBJD | OBJ(?/*ALL) OBJTYPE(*SQLPKG) | X | | SAP | 05/04/ |
| SAP | ENV | UNIX | env | | | | SAP | 07/03/ |
| SAP | ENV | Windows NT | cmd | /C set | | | SAP | 07/03/ |
| SAP | INFARCEXE | ANYOS | infarcexe | | X | | SAP | 08/07/ |
| SAP | INFBAREXE | ANYOS | infbarexe | | X | | SAP | 08/05/ |
| SAP | INFCFGCHECK | ANYOS | infcfgcheck | | X | | SAP | 12/16/ |
| SAP | INFUPDSTAT | ANYOS | infupdstat | | X | | SAP | 08/07/ |
| SAP | IRCONF | ANYOS | irconf -s | | X | | SAP | 11/28/ |
| SAP | IRTRACE | ANYOS | irtrace | | X | | SAP | 11/28/ |
| SAP | LDAP_REGISTER | ANYOS | ldapreg | | X | | SAP | 12/05/ |
| SAP | LIST_DB2DUMP | Windows NT | cmd /c dir | | X | | SAP | 07/30/ |
| SAP | LIST_DB2DUMP | UNIX | ls | -la ? | X | | SAP | 08/04/ |
| SAP | LSNRCTL | ANYOS | lsnrctl | status | | | SAP | 06/30/ |
| SAP | MSSTATS | Windows NT | msstats.exe | $/SAPDBHOST/ $/SAPSYSTEMNAME/ | X | | SAP | 06/03/ |
| SAP | NET_ROUTING | UNIX | netstat | -rn | | | SAP | 11/03/ |
| SAP | NET_ROUTING | Windows NT | route | print | | | SAP | 11/03/ |
| SAP | NIPING | ANYOS | niping | | X | | SAP | 01/21/ |
| SAP | PING | ANYOS | ping | | X | | SAP | 02/02/ |
| SAP | PRECVERSION | ANYOS | sqlver | | X | | SAP | 02/02/ |
| SAP | PRTSQLINF | OS/400 | PRTSQLINF | OBJ(?) OBJTYPE(*SQLPKG) | X | | SAP | 05/04/ |
| SAP | REORGCHK_ALL | ANYOS | dmdb6srp | | X | | SAP | 07/01/ |
| SAP | REORGCHK_CALL | ANYOS | dmdb6srp | | X | | SAP | 07/01/ |

**Figure 14.1** Maintaining External Commands in Transaction SM69

To see how OS commands are configured, let's look at a common command available on any SAP NetWeaver AS ABAP host: the `PING` command. If you aren't familiar with the `PING` command, it's a tool that network administrators use to determine whether or not the system can access a particular host over an IP network. Figure 14.2 shows how the `PING` command is configured inside Transaction SM69. You can get to this perspective by selecting a command in the table view shown in Figure 14.1, and then clicking on the Display button in the toolbar. As you can see in Figure 14.2, the definition of an external command is broken up into two distinct parts. In the Command group box, you must configure the following:

- In the Command name field, you must assign a unique name to the command. This name must be defined in the proper namespace (i.e., prefixed with a `Y` or `Z` for the customer namespace, etc.).
- The Operating System field defines the operating system or systems that support this command. In the case of the `PING` command, the generic `ANYOS` value was assigned to indicate that the `PING` command can be run on any host operating system. However, because some external commands are OS-specific, the qualification is necessary.
- The Type field refers to whether or not the command was defined by SAP or a customer.

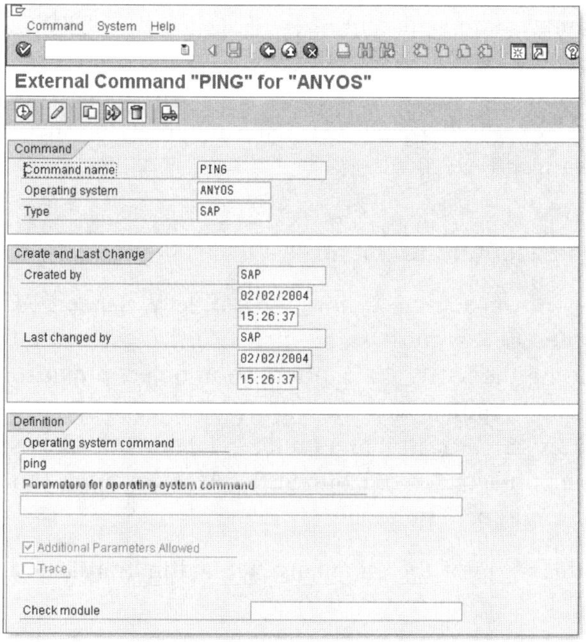


**Figure 14.2** Definition of the PING Command

The actual definition of the command occurs within the Definition group box. Here, you can configure the following:

- In the Operating System Command field, define the command to be executed. This can be a built-in OS command, a path to an executable on the host system, and so on. Essentially, most anything that you can execute from the command line of the OS is fair game here.

- In the Parameters for Operating System Command field, you can define parameters to be passed to the OS command at runtime. Here, keep in mind that these parameters are *static parameters* that will always be passed to the command.
- If you want to allow *dynamic parameters* to be passed into the command, you need to select the Additional Parameters Allowed checkbox. These parameters are passed to the command at runtime using the API functions.
- The Trace checkbox determines whether or not you want the framework to turn on a trace when the command is being executed.
- In the Check Module input field, you can plug in a function module that is called by the framework to validate the external command before executing it. This function module must match the signature of the `SXPG_DUMMY_COMMAND_CHECK` function module provided with the system. Inside this module, you have an opportunity to check dynamic parameters, and so on to determine whether or not the command should be executed. If an exception is raised by the check module, the external command isn't executed.

### 14.1.2 Restricting Access to External Commands

External commands can be very powerful and, if not used correctly, dangerous. Therefore, it's important to protect access to these resources so that they aren't abused. This can be achieved using the `S_LOG_COM` authorization object provided out of the box by SAP. If you aren't familiar with authorization objects, you can learn more about them in Chapter 12, Security Programming. Figure 14.3 shows the definition of this authorization object in Transaction SU21. As you can see, this authorization object defines three authorization fields:

- The `COMMAND` field refers to the name of the command defined in Transaction SM69.
- The `OPSYSTEM` field refers to the operating system assigned to the command in Transaction SM69.
- The `HOST` field refers to the names of the application server hosts that can be used to execute the external command. Normally, this field will be configured with `*` to allow access to all of the application server hosts within the cluster.

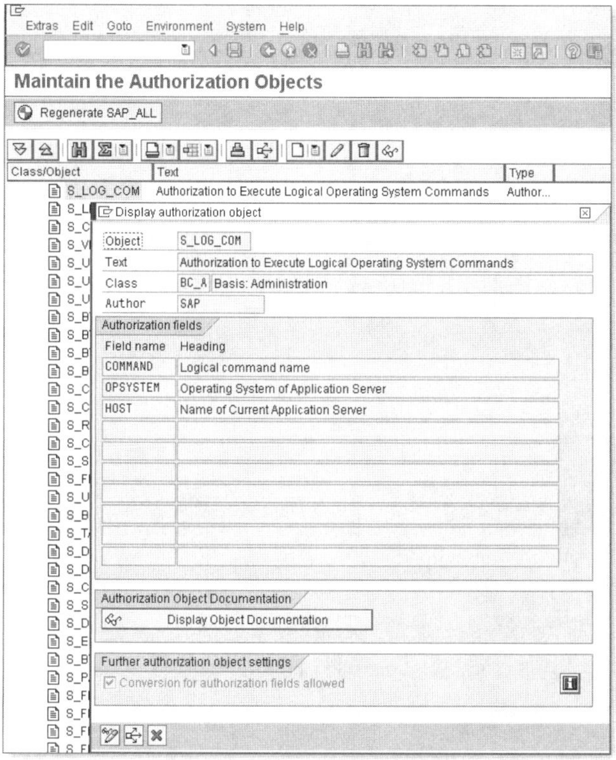


**Figure 14.3** Definition of Authorization Object S_LOG_COM

The `S_LOG_COM` authorization object is checked by the API functions whenever you try to execute an external command. Therefore, without the proper authorizations, you won't be able to execute any external commands.

### 14.1.3 Testing External Commands

After an external command is configured, you can test it out in Transaction SM69. To test an external command, select the command and click on the Execute button in the toolbar (refer to Figure 14.1). Figure 14.4 shows the test screen for the `PING` command. Here, you have the option of plugging in test parameters in the Additional Parameters field. You can also select an execution target to test the command on other application server hosts.

When you click on the Execute button, the external command is executed, and you're navigated to the results screen shown in Figure 14.5. Here, you can see the return code of the command, as well as the generated output.

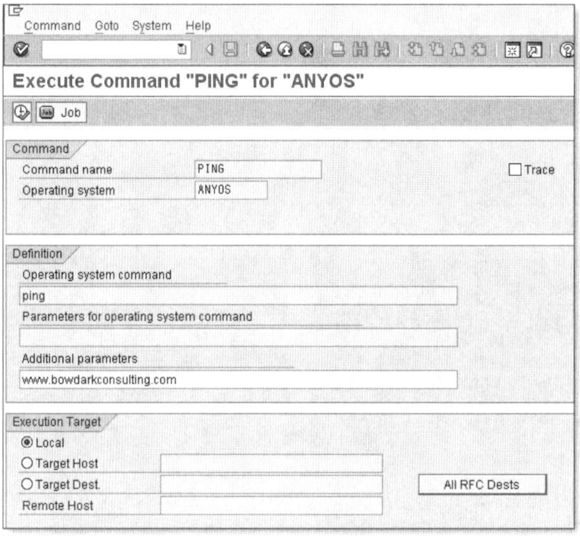


**Figure 14.4** Testing the PING Command in Transaction SM69

**Figure 14.5** Results Screen for Test of the PING Command

It's always a good idea to test out your external commands in Transaction SM69 before implementing the calls in an ABAP program. This is especially true when you're executing the external commands within a batch process running in the background.

### 14.1.4 Executing External Commands in an ABAP Program

To execute external commands within an ABAP program, you can use the standard function module `SXPG_COMMAND_EXECUTE`. To demonstrate how this works, consider the `ZEXTCOMMAND_DEMO` report program shown in Listing 14.1. This program accepts a host name as a parameter and uses it as an argument to the `PING` command. The `PING` command is executed via a call to the standard API function `SXPG_COMMAND_EXECUTE`.

```
REPORT zextcommand_demo.
CLASS lcl_command_interface DEFINITION.
  PUBLIC SECTION.
    CLASS-METHODS:
      execute_command IMPORTING im_command_name
                           TYPE sxpgcolist-name
                                im_param_string
                           TYPE btcxpgpar.
ENDCLASS.

CLASS lcl_command_interface IMPLEMENTATION.
  METHOD execute_command.
    "Method-Local Data Declarations:
    DATA: lv_status  TYPE extcmdexex-status,
          lv_retcode TYPE extcmdexex-exitcode,
          lt_output  TYPE STANDARD TABLE OF btcxpm.
    FIELD-SYMBOLS:
      <lfs_output> LIKE LINE OF lt_output.

    "Execute the selected command:
    CALL FUNCTION 'SXPG_COMMAND_EXECUTE'
      EXPORTING
        commandname                = im_command_name
        additional_parameters      = im_param_string
        operatingsystem            = 'ANYOS'
      IMPORTING
        status                     = lv_status
        exitcode                   = lv_retcode
```

```
      TABLES
        exec_protocol                  = lt_output
      EXCEPTIONS
        no_permission                  = 1
        command_not_found              = 2
        parameters_too_long            = 3
        security_risk                  = 4
        wrong_check_call_interface     = 5
        program_start_error            = 6
        program_termination_error      = 7
        x_error                        = 8
        parameter_expected             = 9
        too_many_parameters            = 10
        illegal_command                = 11
        wrong_asynchronous_parameters = 12
        cant_enq_tbtco_entry           = 13
        jobcount_generation_error      = 14
        others                         = 15.

    "Display the results of the command:
    LOOP AT lt_output ASSIGNING <lfs_output>.
      WRITE: / <lfs_output>-message.
    ENDLOOP.
  ENDMETHOD.                    " METHOD execute_command
ENDCLASS.

PARAMETERS:
  p_host TYPE btcxpgpar LOWER CASE OBLIGATORY.

START-OF-SELECTION.
  "Execute the 'PING' command:
  lcl_command_interface=>execute_command(
    im_command_name = 'PING'
    im_param_string = p_host ).
```

**Listing 14.1** Executing External Commands in ABAP

Figure 14.6 shows the selection screen of the ZEXTCOMMAND_DEMO program. When this program is executed, the selected host name is pinged from the OS level of the SAP NetWeaver AS ABAP host, and the results are displayed in the standard list (see Figure 14.7).

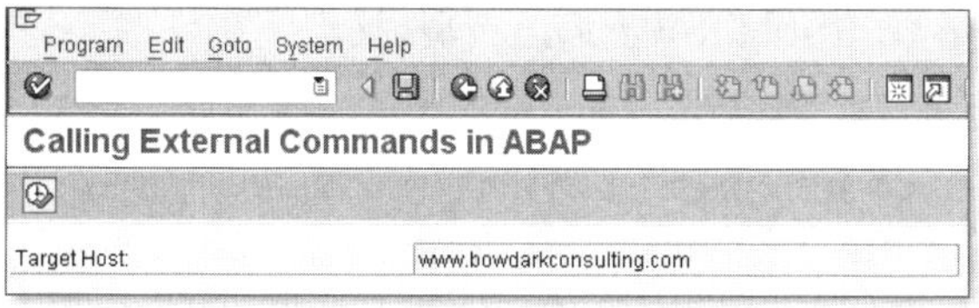


**Figure 14.6** Calling an External Command from ABAP — Part 1

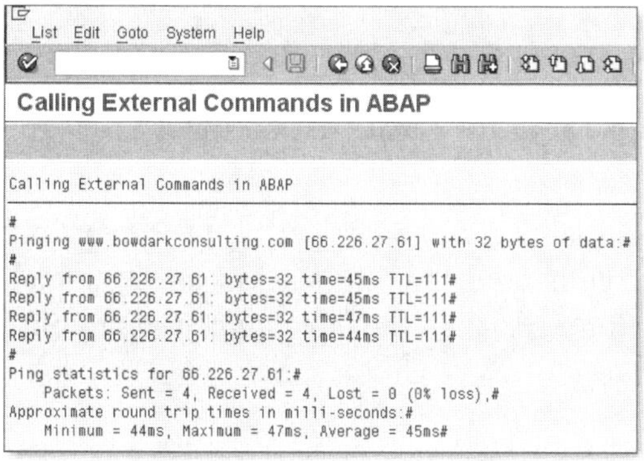


**Figure 14.7** Calling an External Command from ABAP — Part 2

## 14.2 Case Study: Executing a Custom Perl Script

Now that you have a feel for how external commands are configured and executed from an ABAP context, let's see how to create a custom command and put it to work in your landscape. So far, our focus has been on executing standard OS commands such as the `PING` command. However, technically speaking, we can execute just about anything that we can normally execute from the command line. Among other things, this allows us to tap into rich scripting environments that can make it possible to automate some very complex maintenance tasks.

One of the most popular languages used for automating system tasks is Perl. In this section, we show you how to harness the power of Perl in your own developments. Because the details of Perl programming are outside the scope of this book, we keep the script simple. As we progress through this example, keep in mind that the concepts described aren't limited to Perl; you can easily substitute Python or any other scripting language if you prefer.

### 14.2.1 Defining the Command to Run the Perl Interpreter

Before you can begin executing Perl scripts via ABAP, you must first define an external command to execute the Perl interpreter.[1] In many ways, the Perl interpreter is analogous to the ABAP runtime environment. However, unlike ABAP, there is no intermediate compilation step in Perl. Rather, you simply define your Perl script and pass it to the interpreter in source form. The interpreter then transforms the Perl code into an executable format and executes the code on the fly.

To create the external command for the Perl interpreter, perform the following steps:

1. First, open Transaction SM69, and click on the Create button (refer to Figure 14.1).
2. Figure 14.8 shows the Create an External Command perspective of Transaction SM69. Here, you must assign the command a name (Z_PERL in this example) and also define the path to the Perl interpreter in the Operating System Command field.

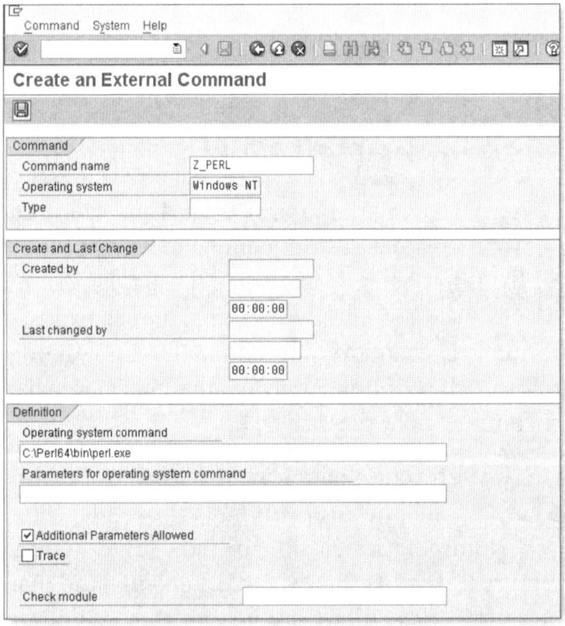


**Figure 14.8** Creating an External Command for the Perl Interpreter

1 Note: This step assumes that the Perl interpreter is already installed in your environment. If your application server host is based on some flavor of UNIX, then you probably already have a copy of Perl lying around. If not, you can find out where to obtain a distribution at *www.perl.org*.

3. Because we're passing in the target Perl script to execute dynamically, make sure the Additional Parameters Allowed checkbox is selected.
4. Finally, you can save the Perl command by clicking on the Save button.

### 14.2.2 Executing Perl Scripts

After the external command is defined for the Perl interpreter, you can execute Perl scripts in much the same way that we executed the PING command in Listing 14.1. For the purposes of this example, let's consider a Perl script that can be used to calculate the total size of a given directory on the application server host. You might use a script like this to determine whether or not an archive job needs to be executed, for example.

Listing 14.2 contains an example of a Perl script that calculates the size of a given directory that is passed in via the command-line arguments. The actual calculation is performed by a recursive subroutine called get_directory_size. After the directory size is calculated, the results are written to the standard output — you'll see the importance of this in a moment.

```
#!/usr/bin/perl
# Used to patch up file names in a system-agnostic way:
use File::Spec;

# Obtain the target directory to scan from the command line
# parameters:
my $target_directory = shift @ARGV;

# Calculate the directory size:
my $size = &get_directory_size($target_directory);

# Output the calculated value to standard output:
print "$size\n";

sub get_directory_size
{
  # Local Data Declarations:
  my($dir)  = @_;
  my($size) = 0;
  my($fd);

  # Try to open the provided directory:
```

```
  opendir($fd, $dir)
       or die "Cannot read from $dir: $!";

  # Iterate (recursively) over each of the files in the
  # directory:
  foreach my $file ( readdir($fd) )
  {
    # Skip over the "dot" files:
    next if ( $file =~ /^\.\.?$/ );

    # Patch up the path:
    my($path) = File::Spec->catfile($dir, $file);

    # Accumulate the directory size:
    $size += ((-d $path) ?
      get_directory_size($path) :
      (-f $path ? (stat($path))[7] : 0));
  }

  # Close the directory handle:
  closedir($fd);

  # Return the size of the directory:
  return($size);
}
```

**Listing 14.2** A Perl Script to Calculate the Size of a Directory

As we mentioned earlier, Perl scripts don't have to be compiled. Therefore, the only prerequisite for executing the Perl script shown in Listing 14.2 is to place the source code in a directory that is accessible on the application server host. After this is in place, you can execute the script using the additional parameters shown in Figure 14.9. Here, the first parameter refers to the path of the Perl script; the second refers to the directory whose size we want to calculate. Figure 14.10 shows the execution results of the script in Transaction SM69. The number in the results section is the size of the *E:\sapdb* directory in bytes.

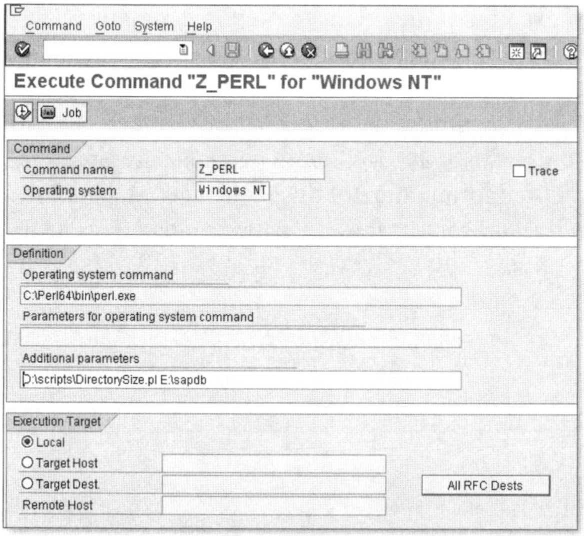


Figure 14.9 Executing the Directory Size Script — Part 1

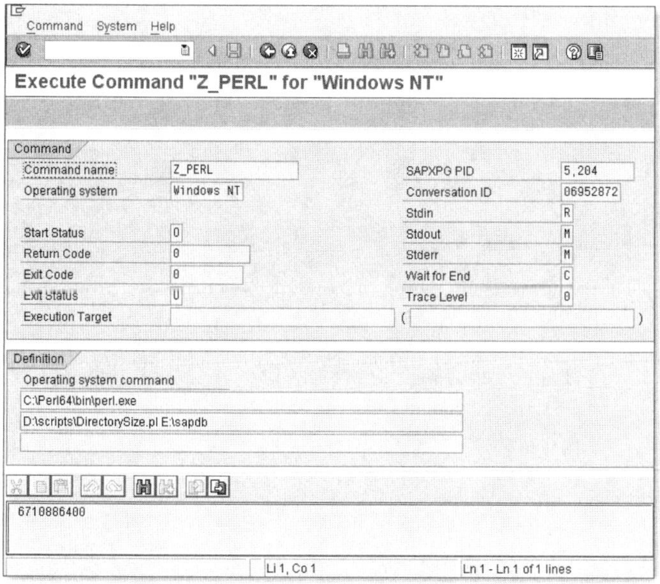


Figure 14.10 Executing the Directory Size Script — Part 2

To execute the Perl script via ABAP, you must use the SXPG_COMMAND_EXECUTE function demonstrated in Section 14.1.4, Executing External Commands in an ABAP

Program. Listing 14.3 shows an example of this with the report program ZPERL_DEMO. For the most part, this code is pretty much the same as that demonstrated earlier in Listing 14.1. However, notice how we're extracting the directory size. Because the Perl script in Listing 14.2 outputs the directory size to the standard output, we can read this data in the EXEC_PROTOCOL table parameter returned by SXPG_COMMAND_EXECUTE. Given the free-form nature of this table, you can pass back many kinds of information from the Perl context into the ABAP context (e.g., XML, etc.).

```
REPORT zperl_demo.
REPORT zperl_demo.

CLASS lcl_perl_utils DEFINITION.
  PUBLIC SECTION.
    CLASS-METHODS:
      get_directory_size IMPORTING im_directory
                                   TYPE string
                         RETURNING VALUE(re_size) TYPE i.

  PRIVATE SECTION.
    CONSTANTS:
      CO_COMMAND_NAME TYPE sxpgcolist-name VALUE 'Z_PERL',
      CO_SCRIPT_NAME TYPE string
                   VALUE 'D:\scripts\DirectorySize.pl'.
ENDCLASS.

CLASS lcl_perl_utils IMPLEMENTATION.
  METHOD get_directory_size.
    "Method-Local Data Declarations:
    DATA: lv_param_string TYPE sxpgcolist-parameters,
          lv_status       TYPE extcmdexex-status,
          lv_retcode      TYPE extcmdexex-exitcode,
          lt_output       TYPE STANDARD TABLE OF btcxpm.
    FIELD-SYMBOLS:
      <lfs_output> LIKE LINE OF lt_output.

    "Derive the Perl script parameter string:
    CONCATENATE CO_SCRIPT_NAME im_directory
           INTO lv_param_string SEPARATED BY SPACE.

    "Execute the Perl script:
    CALL FUNCTION 'SXPG_COMMAND_EXECUTE'
```

```
      EXPORTING
        commandname                   = CO_COMMAND_NAME
        additional_parameters         = lv_param_string
      IMPORTING
        status                        = lv_status
        exitcode                      = lv_retcode
      TABLES
        exec_protocol                 = lt_output
      EXCEPTIONS
        no_permission                 = 1
        command_not_found             = 2
        parameters_too_long           = 3
        security_risk                 = 4
        wrong_check_call_interface    = 5
        program_start_error           = 6
        program_termination_error     = 7
        x_error                       = 8
        parameter_expected            = 9
        too_many_parameters           = 10
        illegal_command               = 11
        wrong_asynchronous_parameters = 12
        cant_enq_tbtco_entry          = 13
        jobcount_generation_error     = 14
        others                        = 15.

    "Display the results of the command:
    READ TABLE lt_output INDEX 1 ASSIGNING <lfs_output>.
    IF sy-subrc EQ 0.
      re_size = <lfs_output>-message.
    ELSE.
      re_size = 0.
    ENDIF.
  ENDMETHOD.                    " METHOD get_directory_size
ENDCLASS.

CLASS lcl_perl_test DEFINITION   "#AU Risk_Level Harmless
                    FOR TESTING. "#AU Duration Short
  PRIVATE SECTION.
    METHODS:
      test_get_dir_size FOR TESTING.
ENDCLASS.

CLASS lcl_perl_test IMPLEMENTATION.
```

```
  METHOD test_get_dir_size.
    "Method-Local Data Declarations:
    DATA: lv_dir      TYPE string,
          lv_dir_size TYPE i.

    "Define a test directory to scan:
    lv_dir = 'E:\sapdb'.

    "Test the directory size calculation routine:
    lv_dir_size =
      lcl_perl_utils=>get_directory_size( lv_dir ).

    CALL METHOD cl_aunit_assert=>assert_not_initial
      EXPORTING
        act = lv_dir_size
        msg = 'Directory size calculated incorrectly.'.
  ENDMETHOD.
ENDCLASS.
```

**Listing 14.3** Executing a Perl Script in an ABAP Program

## 14.3 Summary

This chapter demonstrated how you can interact with the underlying operating system of the SAP NetWeaver AS ABAP host. This functionality can prove quite useful in circumstances where you need to automate certain external tasks. In the next chapter, we look at ways of implementing interprocess communication in ABAP.

*There is always a lot happening at once in a kitchen, so chefs must have the ability to work together and communicate to perform well. In software programming, ever-increasing performance demands are addressed by parallel programming. One of the fundamental prerequisites for implementing parallel solutions is the ability for parallel processes to communicate with one another. In this chapter, we'll look at ways of implementing interprocess communication (IPC) in ABAP.*

# 15 Interprocess Communication

The rapid growth of the IT industry in recent years has sent software researchers scrambling in search of better ways to tackle complex problems. Though there is no general consensus about how to go about solving these problems, one thing most researchers can agree on is that centralized solutions can't possibly scale to meet the demands of an ever-growing landscape. In their book *Swarm Intelligence: From Natural to Artificial Systems* (Oxford University Press, 1999), Eric Bonabeau, et al. describe how artificial intelligence offers an "...alternative way of designing 'intelligent' systems, in which autonomy, emergence, and distributed functioning replace control, preprogramming, and centralization." The basic point here is that it's unrealistic to build "God-like" programs that are overburdened with too many responsibilities. It's better to spread the load across individual agents that are adept at solving smaller problems. Sometimes these agents can execute their tasks in parallel, maximizing system resources and improving overall execution time.

In Chapter 16, Parallel and Distributed Processing with RFCs, we look at ways of distributing the load in ABAP. However, before we do so, we first need to consider how those separate processes communicate with one another. After all, these tasks often need to be synchronized. Therefore, in this chapter, we show you how to access and work with the shared memory segment of SAP NetWeaver SAP NetWeaver AS ABAP.

## 15.1 SAP NetWeaver AS ABAP Memory Organization

Before we begin exploring techniques for working with shared memory in ABAP, it's useful to take a step back and see how memory is organized within SAP NetWeaver AS ABAP. This knowledge will help you make informed decisions when it comes to applying one data sharing technique versus another.

Figure 15.1 depicts the basic memory organization of an SAP NetWeaver AS ABAP instance. As you can see, SAP NetWeaver AS ABAP carves out two slices of data within the virtual memory of the host operating system: local memory and shared memory. As an ABAP developer, you may be somewhat familiar with the local memory segment because this is where much of the data associated with your running programs resides. Looking carefully at Figure 15.1, you can see that each work process has a section of local memory associated with it. These memory areas can be expanded to a certain degree via the heap space available in the local memory and the extended memory buffer in shared memory.

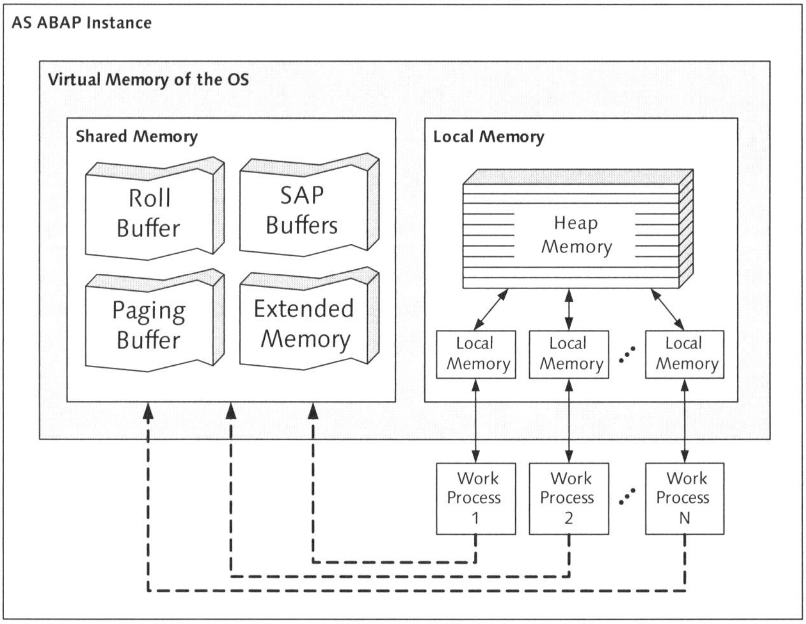


**Figure 15.1** Memory Organization of an SAP NetWeaver AS ABAP Instance

In addition to the local memory associated with individual work processes, an SAP NetWeaver AS ABAP instance also allocates various buffers within a segment of memory collectively referred to as *shared memory*. Table 15.1 describes the buffer types allocated within shared memory.

| Buffer Type | Description |
|---|---|
| Roll buffer | The roll buffer keeps track of *user contexts*. A user context contains basic information about a logged-on user such as personal settings, authorizations, and the programs the user is currently running. |
| SAP buffer | The SAP buffer area contains system-specific objects such as generated ABAP code and buffered table data. |
| Paging buffer | The SAP paging buffer contains ABAP objects such as extract datasets as well as data clusters and shared memory objects. |
| Extended memory buffer | The extended memory buffer contains data/objects associated with users and their currently running programs. In particular, extended memory is used to store dynamic data objects such as internal tables, instances of ABAP Objects classes, and so on. |

**Table 15.1** Description of Buffers Maintained in Shared Memory

For the most part, ABAP developers interact with two of the buffer types listed in Table 15.1: the extended memory buffer and the paging buffer. As described in Table 15.1, the extended memory buffer contains dynamic data objects such as internal tables or instances of ABAP Objects classes. You can think of extended memory as a large heap of memory that is allocated on a first-come, first-serve basis. However, despite the fact that dynamic data objects are stored in an area of shared memory, they can't be shared between programs running in different contexts. If you want to share data objects with other programs, you must store them in the paging buffer. In the next two sections, we show you how to access the paging buffer from an ABAP context.

## 15.2 Data Clusters

Prior to release 6.40 of SAP NetWeaver AS ABAP, the only way you could store data objects in the paging buffer in shared memory was to store them in a *data cluster*. A data cluster is a special type of object that aggregates data objects together so that they can be stored in certain types of storage media. In this section, we show you how to work with data clusters from an ABAP context.

### 15.2.1 Working with Data Clusters

Data clusters can only be processed from an ABAP context using a special syntax. To create a data cluster in ABAP, you use the EXPORT statement whose syntax is shown in Listing 15.1. Here, you have several syntax variants to choose from, depending upon the type of data that you want to store in the cluster, as well as the type of storage media that you want to work with.

```
EXPORT parameterlist TO medium [COMPRESSION { ON | OFF }].
```

**Listing 15.1** Syntax Diagram of the EXPORT Statement

After a data cluster is created, you can access it using the IMPORT statement. Listing 15.2 shows the basic syntax of the IMPORT statement.

```
IMPORT parameterlist FROM medium [conversion_options].
```

**Listing 15.2** Syntax Diagram of the IMPORT Statement

To delete a data cluster from a storage medium, you use the DELETE statement, as shown in Listing 15.3.

```
DELETE FROM
  { MEMORY ID id } |
  { DATABASE dbtab(ar) [CLIENT cl] ID id } |
  { SHARED MEMORY dbtab(ar) [CLIENT cl] ID id } |
  { SHARED BUFFER dbtab(ar) [CLIENT cl] ID id }.
```

**Listing 15.3** Syntax Diagram for the DELETE Statement

In the upcoming sections, we show you how to use these statements to share data between ABAP programs. Because this chapter is about interprocess communication (IPC), we concentrate our focus on the syntax variants that relate to the ABAP and cross-program memory areas. For a complete description of available syntax options, perform a keyword search on the EXPORT, IMPORT, and DELETE statements in the ABAP Keyword Documentation.

### 15.2.2 Storage Media Types

Table 15.2 describes the storage media types that you can choose from when working with data clusters. For the purposes of this chapter, we focus our attention on the ABAP memory and shared memory buffer storage media types.

| Storage Media | Description |
|---|---|
| Byte string | When this storage medium is used, the data cluster is written out to an internal program variable of type XSTRING. |
| Internal table | This storage media type refers to a standard internal table that contains two columns:<br>The first column must be of type S (short integer) and contains the length of the second column in bytes.<br>The second column must be of type X and contains the actual contents of the data cluster.<br>Depending on the size of the second column, the data cluster may be distributed over multiple rows of the internal table. |
| ABAP memory | This storage media type refers to a special memory area within the internal session of the currently executing ABAP program and any programs called from it using the CALL TRANSACTION or SUBMIT statements. In other words, this memory can be used (with some restrictions) across a program call stack. |
| Database table | This media type allows you to write a data cluster out to a database table that adheres to a particular structure. You can see an example of this structure with the standard INDX table in the ABAP Dictionary. |
| Shared memory buffer | This media type refers to the shared memory segment described in Section 15.1, SAP NetWeaver AS ABAP Memory Organization. Unlike ABAP memory, this media type can be shared across all programs running on the same SAP NetWeaver AS ABAP instance. |

**Table 15.2** Storage Media Types for Data Clusters

### 15.2.3 Sharing Data Objects Using ABAP Memory

Frequently, you may encounter a situation where you need to share data objects between two or more programs within the same call stack. For instance, let's imagine that you've written a program that calls a BAPI to create some kind of master data. Now, let's further suppose that this master data object has been customized to include certain customer-specific data fields. While some BAPIs provide *extension* table parameters to allow you to pass in these fields and process them using a Business Add-In (BAdI), let's assume that this BAPI doesn't afford us this luxury. Given these constraints, how can we pass in the custom data fields to the BAPI?

One option is to store the data object(s) in the ABAP memory prior to calling the BAPI module. This special memory area can be read by modules within the same call stack (or program hierarchy), which means you can pass data from the following:

- An executing program to another program that has been called using the SUBMIT statement.
- One dialog module to another.
- An executing program to a function module.

The syntax diagram contained in Listing 15.4 demonstrates the expanded syntax of the EXPORT statement when it's used to store data objects in the ABAP memory. As you can see, you have some options for how you want to represent the data objects. The first two syntax variants accomplish the same thing; they allow you to bind data objects to parameter names of your choosing. The only caveat here is that the parameter names can't exceed 255 characters in length. The (ptab) option allows you to define these data object bindings inside of an index table that uses name/value semantics. You can learn more about this option in the ABAP Keyword Documentation for the EXPORT statement.

```
EXPORT {p1 = dobj1 p2 = dobj2 ...} |
       {p1 FROM dobj1 p2 FROM dobj2 ...} |
       (ptab)
    TO MEMORY ID id.
```

**Listing 15.4** Syntax for the EXPORT Statement Using ABAP Memory

The second part of the syntax described in Listing 15.4 is the designation of the ABAP memory storage medium. Here, you use the TO MEMORY ID addition of the EXPORT statement to indicate that you want to export the cluster to ABAP memory. The id field refers to a flat character object that can't exceed 60 characters in length. When defining an ID, give it a meaningful name, but keep in mind that the namespace of this memory ID is limited in scope to the current program's call stack rather than the system as a whole.

To demonstrate how ABAP memory works, let's take a look at the ZABAPMEM_PRODUCER program shown in Listing 15.5. In this contrived example, we're calling the GUID_CREATE function module to simulate the creation of a business document. The generated GUID value is then wrapped up in a data cluster and written to the ABAP memory under the memory ID MYDOCNO. After the GUID is stored in memory, ZABAPMEM_PRODUCER then calls another report program called

ZABAPMEM_CONSUMER using the SUBMIT statement. We look at what happens after this call in a moment.

```
REPORT zabapmem_producer.
DATA: guid TYPE guid_16.

START-OF-SELECTION.
* Simulate the creation of a business document by
* generating a GUID value:
  CALL FUNCTION 'GUID_CREATE'
    IMPORTING
      ev_guid_16 = guid.

* Output the generated document number:
  WRITE: / 'Generated GUID is:', guid.

* Create a data cluster to store the GUID in ABAP Memory:
  EXPORT docnum = guid TO MEMORY ID 'MYDOCNO'.

* Call a consumer program to further process the document:
  SUBMIT zabapmem_consumer AND RETURN.

* Try to read from the data cluster stored at the
* memory ID called "MYDOCNO"; Should fail since the
* consumer program deletes the data cluster:
  CLEAR guid.
  IMPORT docnum = guid FROM MEMORY ID 'MYDOCNO'.
  WRITE: / 'Retrieved GUID is:', guid.
```

**Listing 15.5** Sharing Data Objects Using ABAP Memory — Part 1

Listing 15.6 shows how the ZABAPMEM_CONSUMER report program is constructed. First, it imports the GUID from the MYDOCNO memory ID using the IMPORT statement and writes it to the standard list output. Then, after the GUID is imported, it deletes the data cluster stored in the MYDOCNO memory ID using the DELETE statement.

```
REPORT zabapmem_consumer.
DATA: guid TYPE guid_16.

START-OF-SELECTION.
* Read from the data cluster stored at the
* memory ID called "MYDOCNO":
  IMPORT docnum = guid FROM MEMORY ID 'MYDOCNO'.
```

```
  WRITE: / 'Imported document number is:', guid.

* Delete the data cluster from the ABAP memory:
  DELETE FROM MEMORY ID 'MYDOCNO'.
```

**Listing 15.6** Sharing Data Objects Using ABAP Memory — Part 2

Because the ZABAPMEM_PRODUCER program called the ZABAPMEM_CONSUMER program using the AND RETURN addition of the SUBMIT statement, execution in ZABAPMEM_PRODUCER continues after ZABAPMEM_CONSUMER is finished running. Looking back at Listing 15.5, you can see that ZABAPMEM_PRODUCER attempts to re-read the GUID from the MYDOCNO memory ID. However, because ZABAPMEM_CONSUMER deleted the data cluster at this memory ID, the IMPORT statement doesn't find anything there. You can see evidence of this if you execute the ZABAPMEM_PRODUCER program. Figure 15.2 shows the list output from the ZABAPMEM_CONSUMER program. Here, you can see that it did indeed find the generated GUID in the ABAP memory. If you press the F3 key, you'll see the list output of the ZABAPMEM_PRODUCER program. In this case, notice that no GUID was retrieved via the IMPORT statement (refer to Figure 15.3).

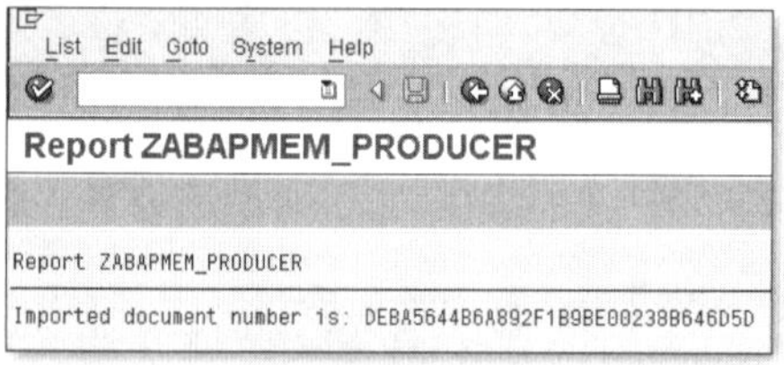


**Figure 15.2** Executing the ZABAPMEM_PRODUCER Program — Part 1

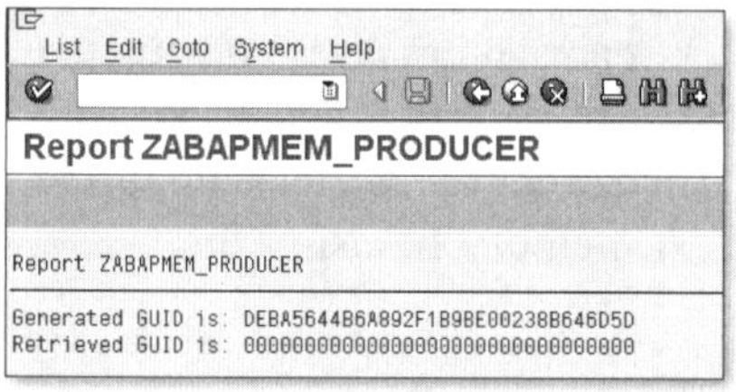


**Figure 15.3** Executing the ZABAPMEM_PRODUCER Program — Part 2

### 15.2.4 Sharing Data Objects Using the Shared Memory Buffer

The data sharing technique described in Section 15.2.3, Sharing Data Objects Using ABAP Memory, is effective when you want to share data between programs within the same call stack. However, sometimes you may need to share data between programs that aren't in the same program hierarchy. In this case, instead of storing the data objects in the ABAP memory, you can store them in the cross-transaction application buffers of the shared memory.

The syntax diagram contained in Listing 15.7 demonstrates the syntax of the `EXPORT` statement when shared memory is used as the storage medium. At first, the syntax may look a little bit strange because there are seemingly two options that refer to the same thing: `SHARED MEMORY` and `SHARED BUFFER`. Technically speaking, both of these options refer to the same shared memory buffer described in Section 15.1, SAP NetWeaver AS ABAP Memory Organization. However, internally, they refer to separate areas of the shared memory buffer that are managed differently. These subtle differences are evident when you start to run out of buffer space. In the case of the buffer referred to by the `SHARED MEMORY` option, the ABAP runtime environment restricts you from writing to a full buffer until you explicitly clean up some space using the `DELETE FROM SHARED MEMORY` statement. Conversely, if the buffer referred to by the `SHARED BUFFER` option becomes full, the system automatically cleans up data objects that are infrequently used. As you can imagine, this kind of behavior can lead to some unexpected occurrences if you're not careful. You can configure the size of these buffer areas using the profile parameters `rsdb/esm/buffersize_kb` and `rsdb/obj/buffersize`, respectively.

```
EXPORT {p1 = dobj1 p2 = dobj2 ...} |
       {p1 FROM dobj1 p2 FROM dobj2 ...} |
       (ptab)
    TO { SHARED MEMORY dbtab(ar) [FROM wa]
                                 [CLIENT cl] ID id } |
       { SHARED BUFFER dbtab(ar) [FROM wa]
                                 [CLIENT cl] ID id }.
```

**Listing 15.7** Syntax for EXPORT Statement Using Shared Memory

Now that you understand the differences between the shared memory buffer types, let's take a look at the rest of the syntax shown in Listing 15.7:

- The `dbtab` specification refers to an ABAP Dictionary table that defines the *structure* of the memory table to be created in the shared memory buffer. Here, the ABAP Dictionary table is used for reference purposes only; no data is actually stored in the table at runtime when this variant of the `EXPORT` statement is used. The table in question must follow the rules outlined in the ABAP Keyword Documentation for the `EXPORT` statement. Rather than define a custom table, many developers simply work with the default `INDX` table provided by SAP.

- After the dbtab specification, you must select a two-character line area identifier (i.e., the (ar) specification in Listing 15.7) that effectively partitions the memory table much like the MANDT field organizes client-specific tables in the ABAP Dictionary.
- After you define the structure and organization of the memory table, you have the option of including a work area whose structure mirrors that of the database table specified with the dbtab option. Here, you can define various types of metadata (i.e., date/timestamps, user name, program, etc.) that other programs can read during the import process.
- You also have the option of specifying a client using the CLIENT addition. If you bypass this option, the system implicitly selects the current client for you behind the scenes.
- Lastly, the ID option allows you to specify an identifier for the data cluster in shared memory. One thing to keep in mind here is that, unlike the identifiers used to tag data clusters in ABAP memory, these identifiers have a global scope within the application server instance. Therefore, you must make sure that you choose your identifiers carefully.

If you're still confused about the syntax outlined in Listing 15.7, perhaps an example will help clear things up. The report program ZSHMEM_PRODUCER shown in Listing 15.8 generates a GUID using the GUID_CREATE function module, and outputs the GUID to shared memory using the EXPORT statement. In the process, it also fills out various metadata in a work area of type INDX. Here, we're specifying the name of the user that created the data cluster, the executing program, and the date the data cluster was created.

```
REPORT zshmem_producer.
DATA: guid TYPE guid_16,
      wa   TYPE indx.

START-OF-SELECTION.
* Simulate the creation of a business document by
* generating a GUID value:
  CALL FUNCTION 'GUID_CREATE'
    IMPORTING
      ev_guid_16 = guid.

* Output the generated document number:
  WRITE: / 'Generated GUID is:', guid.

* Create a data cluster to store the GUID in ABAP Memory:
```

```
  wa-aedat = sy-datum.
  wa-usera = sy-uname.
  wa-pgmid = sy-repid.

  EXPORT docnum = guid
      TO SHARED MEMORY indx(st)
    FROM wa
      ID 'MYDOCNO'.
```

**Listing 15.8** Exporting a Data Cluster to Shared Memory

The ZSHMEM_CONSUMER report program shown in Listing 15.9 demonstrates how another program in a different work process can come along and read from that shared memory area using the IMPORT statement. Figure 15.4 shows the output of the ZSHMEM_CONSUMER report. Here, notice how the metadata created by the ZSHMEM_PRODUCER report is read into the wa work area by the IMPORT statement.

```
REPORT zshmem_consumer.
DATA: guid TYPE guid_16,
      wa   TYPE indx.

START-OF-SELECTION.
* Read from the data cluster stored at the
* memory ID called "MYDOCNO":
  IMPORT docnum = guid
    FROM SHARED MEMORY indx(st)
      TO wa
      ID 'MYDOCNO'.

  WRITE: / 'Created by:', wa-usera.
  WRITE: / 'Created on:', wa-aedat MM/DD/YYYY.
  WRITE: / 'Source Program:', wa-pgmid.
  WRITE: / 'Imported document number is:', guid.
```

**Listing 15.9** Importing a Data Cluster from Shared Memory

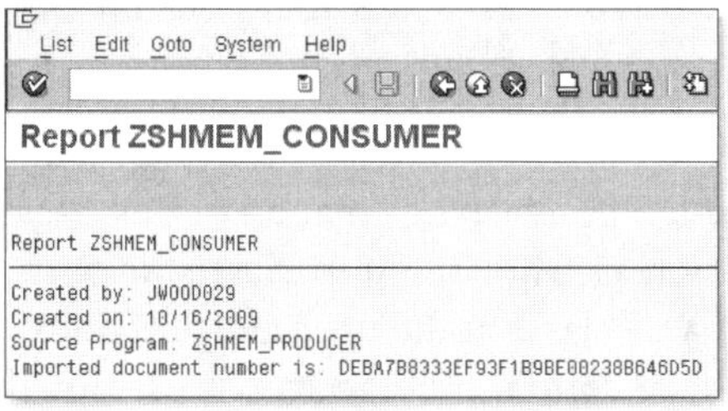


**Figure 15.4** List Output of the ZSHMEM_CONSUMER Report

## 15.3 Working with Shared Memory Objects

In Section 15.2, Data Clusters, we showed you how to share data objects between ABAP programs using data clusters. Though data clusters are powerful, they aren't without certain limitations:

- Data clusters don't support the use of reference types (i.e., instances of ABAP Objects classes and data references).
- There are no locking mechanisms for data clusters. This implies that if multiple programs try to access the same data cluster, the results are unpredictable.
- There is no support for encapsulating the data objects stored in the data cluster to control external access. Ideally, we want to surround these data objects with business logic that performs authorization checks, validations, and so on before updating or reading the data objects stored in a data cluster.

SAP addressed all of these issues and more when it introduced shared memory objects in release 6.40 of SAP NetWeaver AS ABAP. In this section, we show you how to harness the power of shared memory objects in your own custom developments.

### 15.3.1 Architectural Overview

Shared memory objects are instances of ABAP Objects classes that can be stored in a special section of the shared memory buffer whose size is configured using the `abap/shared_objects_size_MB` profile parameter. In some respects, the architecture of shared memory objects is similar to that of data clusters in the sense that the object instances are stored in a special container called a *shared memory area*. However, as you'll soon see, shared memory areas are quite a bit more sophisticated than data clusters.

Shared memory objects are created and manipulated in much the same way that you interact with normal ABAP Objects classes. Figure 15.5 contains a UML class diagram that highlights the base components of the shared memory objects API. From a developer's perspective, there are two types of classes that you interact with when working with shared objects: an *area class* and an *area root class*.

The area class is a generated class that gets created when you define a shared memory area in Transaction SHMA. You'll see how to influence the creation of this class in Section 15.3.2, Defining Shared Memory Areas. The `ZCL_AREA` class shown in Figure 15.5 illustrates the API of a generated area class. In the upcoming sections, you'll see how many of these methods work in common usage scenarios. However, before we move on from area classes, it's important to understand exactly what they represent.

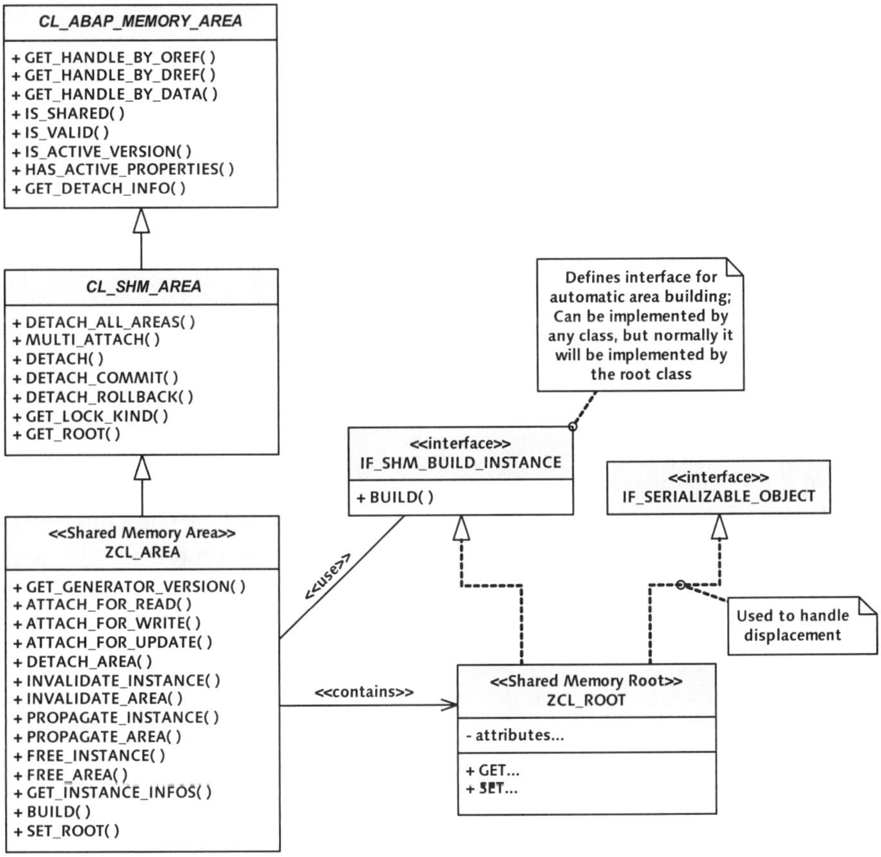


**Figure 15.5** UML Class Diagram for Shared Memory Objects

As we mentioned earlier, shared memory objects are stored inside of a special container in the shared memory buffer called a *shared memory area*. Instances of a shared memory area are assigned a name and can optionally maintain several *versions* internally. The term *instance* here should not be confused with an instance in the object-oriented context. Instead, you should simply think of an area instance as a self-contained section of the shared memory buffer where shared memory objects can be stored. To access an area instance version from an ABAP context, you must obtain an *area handle*. This handle *binds* the current program (or more accurately, its internal session) with an area instance version. From a programming perspective, the area class defines the structure of this area handle. Figure 15.6

illustrates the relationship between an area handle and an area instance version. You can obtain an instance of an area handle by calling the static `ATTACH_FOR_...` methods of the area class.

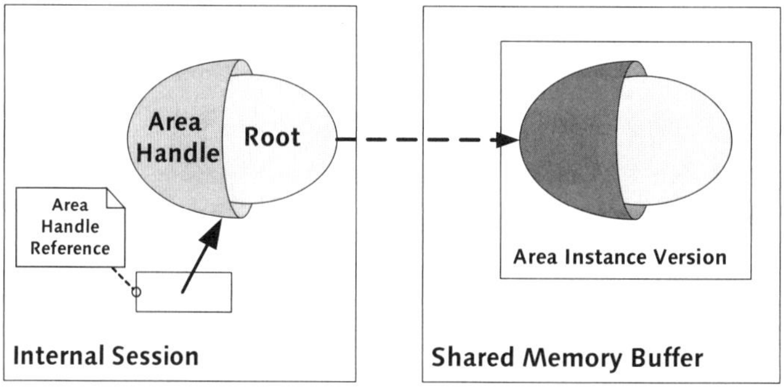


**Figure 15.6** Relationship Between an Area Handle and an Area Instance

After you've obtained an area handle instance, you can use this handle to store instances of shared memory objects in shared memory. Each shared memory area is associated with an *area root class*. The term "root" here connotes that you can build complex data structures within an area instance version — starting from the root class and branching outward from its internally defined instance attributes. The only prerequisite for defining an area root class is that it must have the Shared Memory-Enabled checkbox selected on the Properties tab of the Class Builder (see Figure 15.7). Otherwise, a root class is basically just like any other ABAP Objects class.

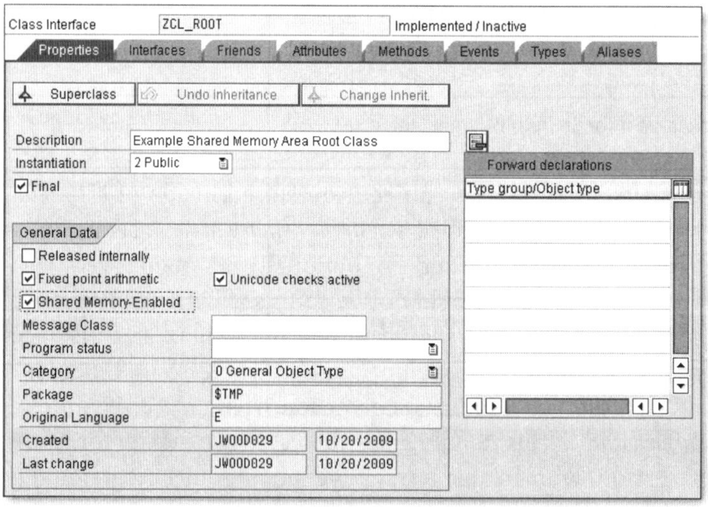


**Figure 15.7** Defining Shared Memory-Enabled Classes

The ZCL_ROOT class depicted earlier in Figure 15.5 illustrates the positioning of an area root class within the shared memory objects framework. As you can see, there's a close relationship between an area class and its assigned area root class. The signature of the SET_ROOT() method of the area class is customized to receive instances of the area root class.

The UML class diagram in Figure 15.5 also depicts two optional relationships that you can define for area root classes: namely the implementation of the IF_SHM_BUILD_INSTANCE and IF_SERIALIZABLE_OBJECT interfaces. We'll look at when and why you might want to implement these interfaces in the next section.

### 15.3.2 Defining Shared Memory Areas

Before we can begin storing objects in the shared memory buffer, we must first configure a shared memory area in Transaction SHMA. Shared memory areas are repository objects that define a *template* for what a shared memory area instance will look like inside the shared memory buffer. As you'll soon see, you have many options to choose from when configuring shared memory areas. Therefore, to better understand the implications of each of these settings, we'll consider the configuration of a shared memory area in the context of an example. Here, let's imagine that we're creating a conference registration application, and we want to cache frequently accessed static information, such as conference rooms.

Figure 15.8 shows the initial screen of Transaction SHMA. To define a new shared memory area, enter an area name in the Area Name input field, and click on the Create button. As you can see in Figure 15.8, we've named the shared memory area for our "room" entity object ZCL_ROOM_AREA. Here, we're using the familiar "CL_" ABAP Objects class name prefix for the area because the system will be generating an area class with the same name behind the scenes when we save our changes.

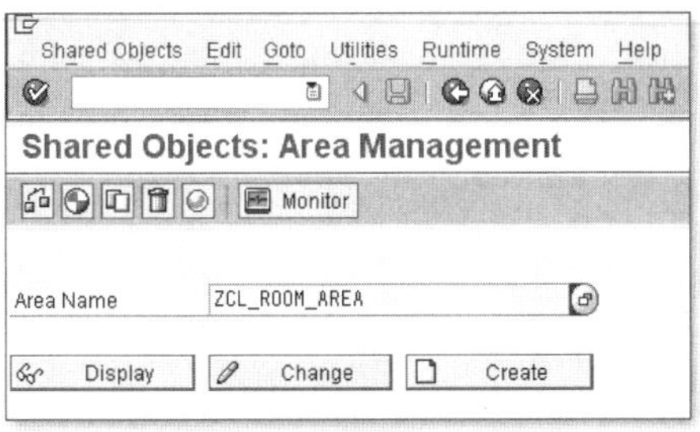


**Figure 15.8** Initial Screen of Transaction SHMA

Figure 15.9 shows the configuration screen of Transaction SHMA for the ZCL_ROOM_AREA area. Table 15.1 describes each of the various properties shown in Figure 15.9 in more detail. As you'll see, some of these properties are statically defined while others can be overridden dynamically at runtime.

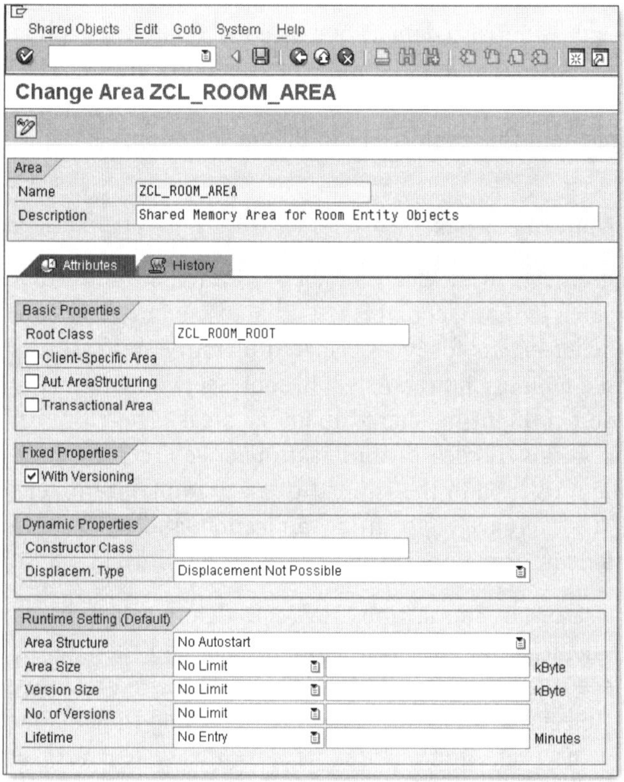


**Figure 15.9** Configuring a Shared Memory Area

### Basic Properties

The properties defined in the Basic Properties group box shown in Figure 15.9 directly influence the way that the underlying area class is generated behind the scenes. As such, these properties are configured statically by developers at build time. Table 15.3 describes each of these settings in detail.

| Property | Description |
|---|---|
| Root Class | Associates the shared memory area with an area root class. Here, the only prerequisite is that the area root class has the Shared Memory-Enabled checkbox selected in the Class Builder (refer to Figure 15.7). In the ZCL_ROOM_AREA shown in Figure 15.9, we've proposed a root class called ZCL_ROOM_ROOT. |
| Client-Specific Area | Because shared memory is allocated at the application server level, shared memory areas are client-independent by default. However, if the Client-Specific Area checkbox is selected, the API methods of the area class are enhanced to include a CLIENT importing parameter that can be used to logically partition the memory area into client-specific silos. |
| Automatic AreaStructuring | Normally, an area instance is only created when an ABAP program explicitly creates one. However, if the Automatic Area Structuring checkbox is turned on, the system automatically builds an area instance before it is accessed via a read operation, and so on. For this to work, you must specify a class that implements the IF_SHM_BUILD_INSTANCE interface in the Constructor Class input field in the Dynamic Properties group box (see Figure 15.9). |
| Transactional Area | If you're using a shared memory area as a buffer for some records stored in a database table, it's important that these two data stores stay in sync. One way to achieve this kind of synchronization is to select the Transactional Area checkbox. In this case, whenever a change is made to an area instance, the change doesn't go into effect until a database commit occurs. |

**Table 15.3** Basic Properties of a Shared Memory Area

After you've defined the basic properties of a shared memory area, you can save your changes by clicking on the Save button (refer to Figure 15.9). Behind the scenes, an area class with the same name is generated. Figure 15.10 shows the generated area class for the ZCL_ROOM_AREA that we've been exploring in this section.

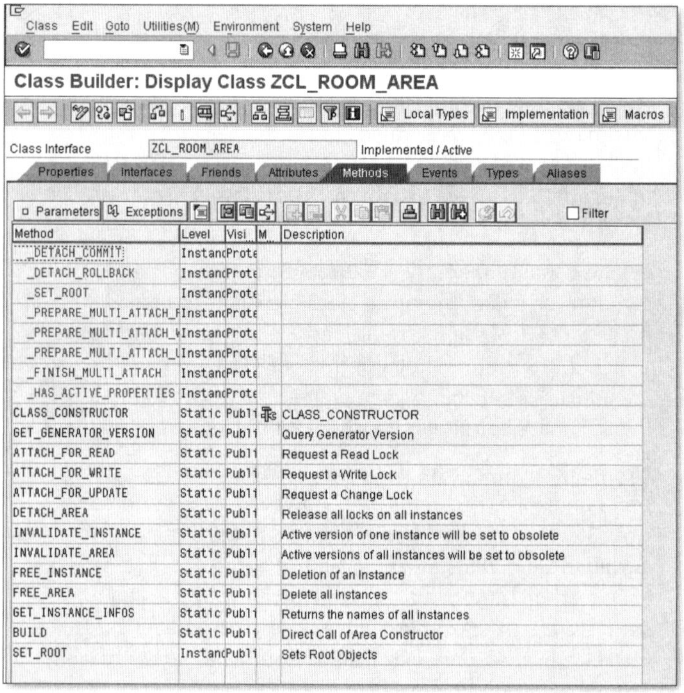


**Figure 15.10** Viewing the Generated Area Class in the Class Builder

After an area class is generated, keep in mind that any changes you make to the basic properties of an area cause a change to the underlying area class; you receive a prompt like the one shown in Figure 15.11 if you attempt to change the basic properties of a shared memory area in Transaction SHMA after the area class has been generated. This warning is particularly important because any existing area instance versions are *invalidated* whenever the changes to the area are activated. Suffice it to say that such changes should be well coordinated to avoid any unpleasant side effects. We'll look at ways to assess the potential impacts of such changes in Section 15.3.6, Monitoring Techniques.

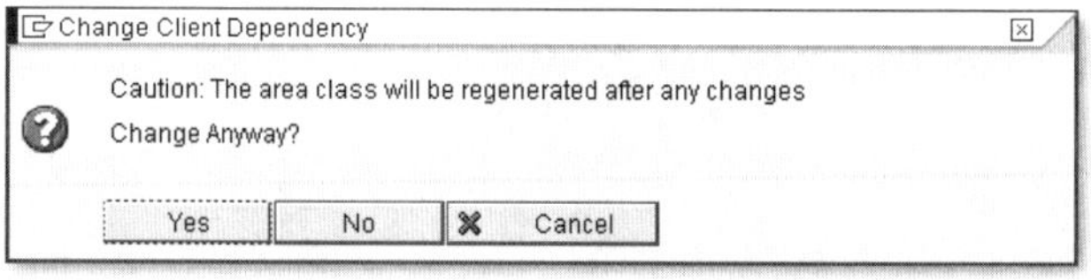


**Figure 15.11** Warning Message for Changes to Basic Properties

### Fixed Properties

The lone property to configure in the Fixed Properties group box is the With Versioning checkbox shown earlier in Figure 15.9. Normally, area instances only maintain one version internally: the active version. However, when versioning is turned on, the default behavior changes, and you can have multiple versions maintained within a given area instance. You'll learn more about the effects of selecting this option in Section 15.3.5, Area Instance Versioning.

Fixed properties, much like basic properties, are defined statically by developers. However, when changes are made to fixed properties, the underlying area class doesn't have to be regenerated. Such changes should be made with care, however, because preexisting area instances are invalidated whenever the changes are saved in Transaction SHMA.

### Dynamic Properties

The properties in the Dynamic Properties group box shown earlier in Figure 15.9 influence the lifecycle of the area instance. As we mentioned before, the Constructor Class input field works in conjunction with the Automatic Area Structuring property to enable the runtime environment to automatically create a default area instance on demand. This feature comes in handy whenever an ABAP program tries to access an area instance that doesn't yet exist.

You can plug in any ABAP Objects class in the Constructor Class input field as long as it implements the `IF_SHM_BUILD_INSTANCE` interface. However, most developers prefer to implement this interface in the root class because it makes logical sense that this class would know how to initialize itself (and thus, the surrounding area). Looking back at the UML class diagram in Figure 15.5, you can see that the `IF_SHM_BUILD_INSTANCE` interface defines a single method called `BUILD()` that can be used to initialize an area instance. You can think of this method like a factory or default constructor method. If you prefer to invoke this functionality directly, you can do so by calling the static `BUILD()` method in the generated area class.

The Displacement Type property determines whether or not area instances can be displaced in situations where there isn't enough space in the shared memory buffer. If the Displacement Possible option is selected, then the runtime environment has the option to evict area instances that aren't being used to recuperate additional space. A less severe alternative here is to select the Displacement Possible with Backup and Recovery option. In this case, the shared objects inside the area instance can be restored as long as the root class implements the `IF_SERIALIZABLE_OBJECT` interface. Consequently, it's a good idea to always implement the `IF_SERIALIZABLE_OBJECT` tag interface when defining root classes.

### Runtime Settings

Until now, all of the properties we've considered refer to settings that must be configured at *build time*. However, when we deploy these shared memory areas on a physical SAP NetWeaver AS ABAP instance, there are certain runtime settings that we must consider at *deployment time*. Table 15.4 describes the runtime settings that can be configured for a shared memory area.

| Property | Description |
|---|---|
| Area Structure | This property works in conjunction with the Automatic Area Structuring property defined in the Basic Properties group box. Depending on the value of this setting, you can choose from the following three configuration options to define the proper behavior at runtime:<br>**No Autostart:** When this setting is selected, the Automatic Area Structuring property must not be selected. In this case, area instances aren't created dynamically under any circumstances.<br>**Autostart for Read Request:** When automatic area structuring is turned on, this setting instructs the runtime environment to create an area instance whenever a read request is made against an area instance that doesn't exist.<br>**Autostart for Read Request and Every Invalidation:** This setting instructs the runtime environment to create an area instance whenever a read request is made against an area that doesn't exist. Area instances are also automatically regenerated whenever they are invalidated by the system. You'll learn more about invalidation in Section 15.3.5, Area Instance Versioning. |
| Area Size | This property defines the maximum size of an area in the shared memory in kilobytes. Whenever a maximum size is defined, the sum total size of all area instances of this type can't exceed the configured value. |
| Version Size | This property defines the maximum size of an area instance version in kilobytes. |
| No. of Versions | This property defines the total number of allowed versions for a given area instance of this type. |
| Lifetime | This setting can be used to control the lifetime of an area instance. For more information about this setting, consult the SAP Library documentation. |

**Table 15.4** Runtime Settings for Shared Memory Areas

By default, the initially configured runtime settings are transported with the shared memory area whenever it's promoted to other environments. However because runtime settings are dynamic, they can be overridden in a given environment by opening Transaction SHMA and selecting the RUNTIME • CHANGE RUNTIME ATTRIBUTES menu option (see Figure 15.12). Figure 15.13 shows the Change Runtime Settings screen of Transaction SHMA. This screen varies depending on whether or not the shared memory area is defined as a client-specific area. In this case, the settings can be configured on a client-by-client basis.

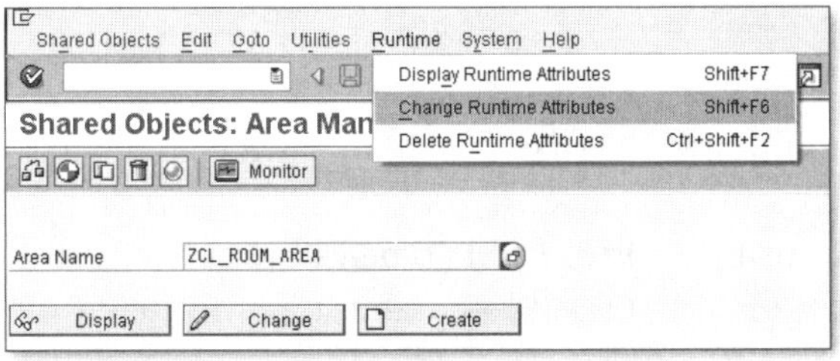


**Figure 15.12** Changing Runtime Attributes — Part 1

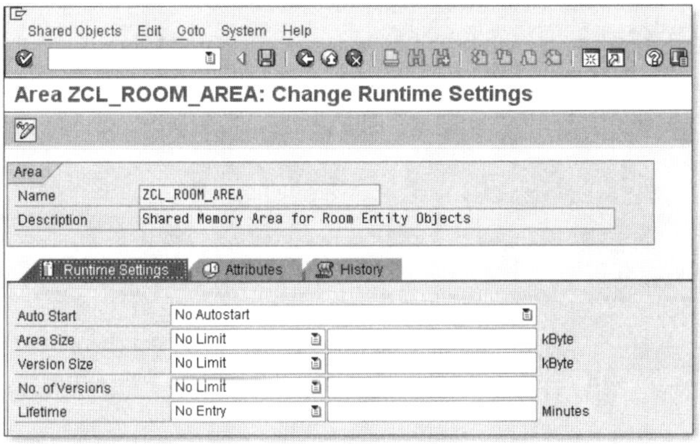


**Figure 15.13** Changing Runtime Attributes — Part 2

## 15.3.3 Accessing Shared Objects

Now that you understand how shared memory areas are configured, let's learn how to interact with them using the generated API methods of the area class. As a basis for our discussion, we work with the `ZCL_ROOM_AREA` area class and the `ZCL_ROOM_ROOT` area root class introduced in Section 15.3.2, Defining Shared Memory Areas.

As we mentioned previously, a typical use case for shared memory objects is to implement some kind of shared buffer or cache within the system. In the case of our conference registration application, we want to cache information about conference rooms that can be booked for individual sessions. By caching this information in shared memory, we can improve performance by avoiding unnecessary database hits. Of course, this approach doesn't work in all cases. For example, it wouldn't make sense to buffer information about individual sessions in the conference because the times/locations of those sessions would likely change quite a bit during the registration process.

### Structuring the Shared Memory Object

To implement our conference room buffer in shared memory, we've defined a private instance attribute called ROOMS in the ZCL_ROOM_ROOT class, as shown in Figure 15.14. This attribute is defined using a custom table type called ZTTCA_ROOMS. Figure 15.15 shows the definition of the ZTTCA_ROOMS table type in the ABAP Dictionary.

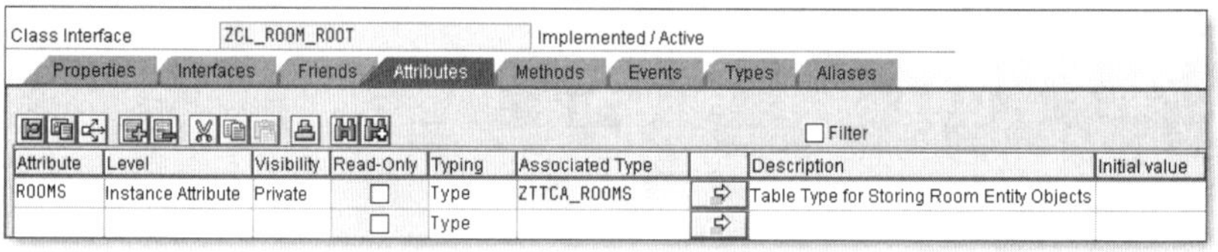


**Figure 15.14** Caching Information in the Area Root Class

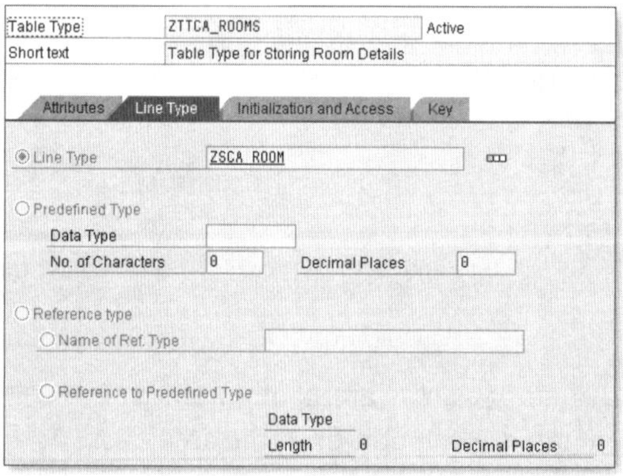


**Figure 15.15** Definition of Table Type ZTTCA_ROOMS

Normally, the buffered data would come from some kind of persistence store such as a database table. However, for the purposes of this contrived example, we simply define some arbitrary room data inside the constructor method of class ZCL_ROOM_ROOT. Here, we use the structure type ZSCA_ROOM, as shown in Figure 15.16.

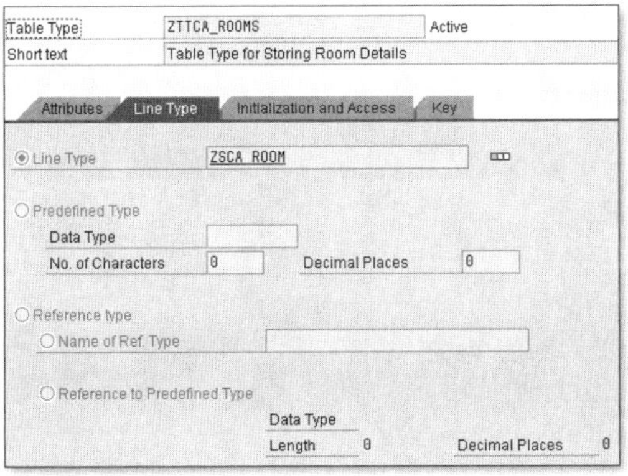


**Figure 15.16** Definition of Structure Type ZSCA_ROOM

## Building the Shared Memory Cache

Now that you know how the conference room buffer is structured in memory, let's see how to build the room cache in an ABAP program. The ZSHMO_PRODUCER report program shown in Listing 15.10 demonstrates how the API methods of the area class can be used to build this cache. The cache is built in four steps:

1. First, we obtain an area handle by calling the static ATTACH_FOR_WRITE() method defined in the ZCL_ROOM_AREA area class. Here, we're passing in an explicit instance name (i.e., 'CONF_ROOMS') to identify the target area instance. The ATTACH_FOR_WRITE() method generates an area handle pointing to this area instance, and also creates a *write lock* that allows our program exclusive write access to the shared memory area. We investigate locks further in Section 15.3.4, Locking Concepts.
2. Next, we create an instance of the ZCL_ROOM_ROOT area root class using the familiar CREATE OBJECT statement. However, notice how we're using the AREA HANDLE addition to associate the area root class with a particular area instance (i.e., the one created in the previous step).
3. After the area root instance is created, we can bind it to the area instance using the SET_ROOT() instance method of the area handle.

4. Finally, we can store the shared memory object in shared memory using the `DETACH_COMMIT()` method of the area handle. If we had decided that we didn't want to go through with the changes, we could have called the `DETACH_ROLLBACK()` method to discard the changes and remove the write lock.

```
REPORT zshmo_producer.
CLASS lcl_registration_service DEFINITION.
  PUBLIC SECTION.
    CLASS-METHODS:
      cache_rooms.
ENDCLASS.

CLASS lcl_registration_service IMPLEMENTATION.
  METHOD cache_rooms.
    "Method-Local Data Declarations:
    DATA: lo_handle TYPE REF TO zcl_room_area,
          lo_root   TYPE REF TO zcl_room_root,
          lo_ex     TYPE REF TO cx_root.

    "Build a default area instance:
    TRY.
      "Obtain an area handle in write mode:
      lo_handle =
        zcl_room_area=>attach_for_write( 'CONF_ROOMS' ).

      "Create the default root object & bind it to the
      "area handle:
      CREATE OBJECT lo_root AREA HANDLE lo_handle.
      lo_handle->set_root( lo_root ).

      "Commit the changes:
      lo_handle->detach_commit( ).
    CATCH cx_shm_error INTO lo_ex.
      "Exception handling goes here...
    ENDTRY.
  ENDMETHOD.                    " METHOD cache_rooms
ENDCLASS.

START-OF-SELECTION.
  "Cache room information in shared memory:
  lcl_registration_service=>cache_rooms( ).
```

**Listing 15.10** Storing Room Information in Shared Memory

After you run the ZSHMO_PRODUCER program, an area instance called CONF_ROOMS exists in shared memory, containing a shared object that implements our conference room buffer. In this contrived example, we're simply creating some arbitrary room data in the constructor method of the ZCL_ROOMS_ROOT area root class (see Listing 15.11). In a real-world environment, this data would likely be loaded from some database table.

```
METHOD constructor.
* Method-Local Data Declarations:
  FIELD-SYMBOLS:
    <lfs_room> LIKE LINE OF rooms.

* Create a few room records and store them in context:
  APPEND INITIAL LINE TO me->rooms
              ASSIGNING <lfs_room>.
  <lfs_room>-room_no = 100.
  <lfs_room>-description = 'Main Conference Room'.
  <lfs_room>-max_occupants = 100.

  APPEND INITIAL LINE TO me->rooms
              ASSIGNING <lfs_room>.
  <lfs_room>-room_no = 200.
  <lfs_room>-description = 'Testing Room'.
  <lfs_room>-max_occupants = 10.

  APPEND INITIAL LINE TO me->rooms
              ASSIGNING <lfs_room>.
  <lfs_room>-room_no = 300.
  <lfs_room>-description = 'Programming Lab'.
  <lfs_room>-max_occupants = 25.
ENDMETHOD.
```

**Listing 15.11** Initializing the Conference Room Buffer

### Reading from the Shared Memory Cache

After the conference room buffer is built, other programs can come along and access that shared buffer using API methods defined in the area class. This approach is evidenced by the ZSHMO_CONSUMER report program shown in Listing 15.12. This program provides a selection screen parameter called P_SEATS that allows users to search for conference rooms that can accommodate a given number of attendees.

```
REPORT zshmo_consumer.
CLASS lcl_registration_service DEFINITION.
```

```
  PUBLIC SECTION.
    CLASS-METHODS:
      find_room IMPORTING im_seats TYPE i.
ENDCLASS.

CLASS lcl_registration_service IMPLEMENTATION.
  METHOD find_room.
*   Method-Local Data Declarations:
    DATA: lo_handle  TYPE REF TO zcl_room_area,
          lt_rooms   TYPE zttca_rooms,
          lo_ex      TYPE REF TO cx_root,
          lv_message TYPE string.
    FIELD-SYMBOLS:
      <lfs_room> LIKE LINE OF lt_rooms.

    "Try to locate a conference room:
    TRY.
      "Obtain an area handle in read mode:
      lo_handle =
        zcl_room_area=>attach_for_read( 'CONF_ROOMS' ).

      "Search for rooms that meet the given criteria:
      lt_rooms =
        lo_handle->root->get_rooms_by_size( im_seats ).

      "Release the area handle:
      lo_handle->detach( ).

      "Output the results:
      LOOP AT lt_rooms ASSIGNING <lfs_room>.
        WRITE: / 'Room', <lfs_room>-room_no,
                 'seats', <lfs_room>-max_occupants,
                 'people.'.
      ENDLOOP.
    CATCH cx_shm_error INTO lo_ex.
      lv_message = lo_ex->get_text( ).
      MESSAGE lv_message TYPE 'I'.
    ENDTRY.
  ENDMETHOD.                    " METHOD find_room
ENDCLASS.

PARAMETERS:
  p_seats TYPE i OBLIGATORY.
```

```
START-OF-SELECTION.
  "Look in shared memory to find a conference room:
  lcl_registration_service=>find_room( p_seats ).
```

**Listing 15.12** Reading Room Information from Shared Memory

As you can see in Listing 15.12, we're accessing the CONF_ROOMS area instance via an area handle. Because we're only reading from the buffer, we're obtaining this handle via a call to the static ATTACH_FOR_READ() method. We're implementing our room search via a call to the GET_ROOMS_BY_SIZE() instance method defined in the ZCL_ROOMS_ROOT area root class. Here, notice that we can use the public ROOT instance attribute on the area handle to access the shared memory object. The implementation of the GET_ROOMS_BY_SIZE() method is shown in Listing 15.13.

```
METHOD get_rooms_by_size.
* Method-Local Data Declarations:
  FIELD-SYMBOLS:
    <lfs_room> LIKE LINE OF rooms.

* Retrieve the set of rooms that are big enough
* to accommodate the requested size:
  LOOP AT me->rooms ASSIGNING <lfs_room>.
    IF <lfs_room>-max_occupants GE im_room_size.
      APPEND <lfs_room> TO re_rooms.
    ENDIF.
  ENDLOOP.
ENDMETHOD.
```

**Listing 15.13** Implementing Method GET_ROOMS_BY_SIZE()

Figure 15.17 shows the selection screen of the ZSHMO_CONSUMER program. Here, you can see that we're searching for a room that can accommodate 12 attendees. In the results screen shown in Figure 15.18, you can see that the GET_ROOMS_BY_SIZE() method found two rooms that could hold that many people.

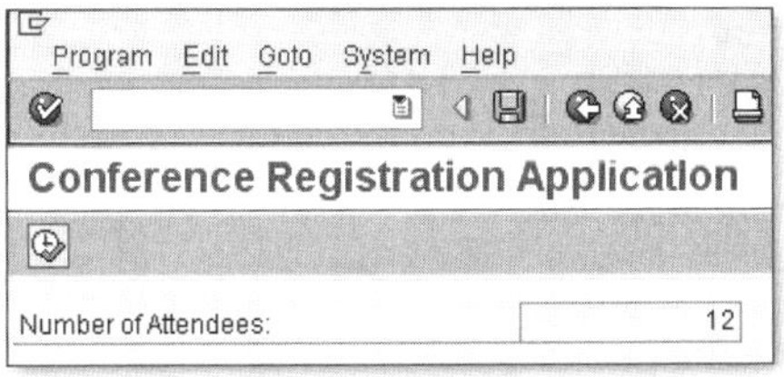


**Figure 15.17** Searching the Room Buffer for Conference Rooms — Part 1

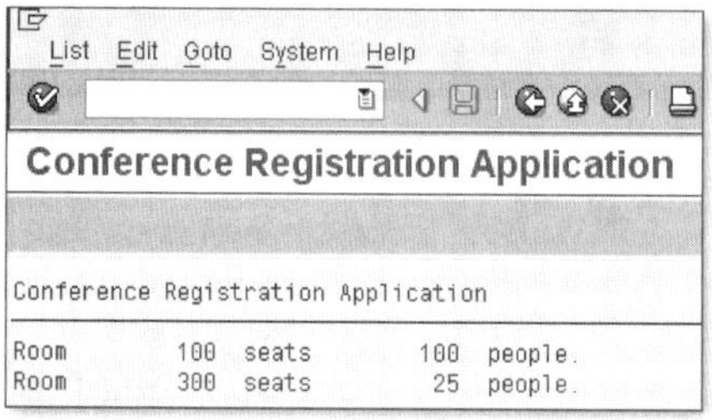


**Figure 15.18** Searching the Room Buffer for Conference Rooms — Part 2

### Implementing Automatic Area Structuring

Now that you've seen a fully functional example demonstrating the use of shared objects, let's take a step back and look at how we could improve on our design. One of the limitations of the current approach is that the producer must create the buffer *before* the consumer tries to access it; otherwise, a runtime error occurs. Ideally, we want to initialize our buffer on demand using lazy initialization techniques. Fortunately, SAP provides exactly what we're looking for with the Automatic Area Structuring property described in Section 15.3.2, Defining Shared Memory Areas.

Figure 15.19 shows the changes we must make to our `ZCL_ROOM_AREA` to enable automatic area structuring. We've turned on automatic area structuring for read requests and every area instance invalidation. Rather than define the constructor class elsewhere, we've simply implemented the `IF_SHM_BUILD_INSTANCE` interface in the `ZCL_ROOM_ROOT` root class.

Listing 15.14 shows the implementation of the `IF_SHM_BUILD_INSTANCE~BUILD()` method in class `ZCL_ROOM_ROOT`. As you can see, the code is almost identical to that of the `ZSHMO_PRODUCER` example from Listing 15.10. The only differences lie in the way that we deal with exceptions and handle transactional areas.

```
METHOD if_shm_build_instance~build.
* Method-Local Data Declarations:
  DATA: lo_handle TYPE REF TO zcl_room_area,
        lo_root   TYPE REF TO zcl_room_root,
        lo_ex     TYPE REF TO cx_root.

* Build a default area instance:
  TRY.
*   Obtain an area handle in write mode:
    lo_handle =
      zcl_room_area=>attach_for_write( inst_name ).
```

```
*   Create the default root object & bind it to the
*   area handle:
    CREATE OBJECT lo_root AREA HANDLE lo_handle.
    lo_handle->set_root( lo_root ).

*   Commit the changes:
    lo_handle->detach_commit( ).

*   Also trigger a database commit for transactional areas:
    IF invocation_mode EQ
         cl_shm_area=>invocation_mode_auto_build.
      CALL FUNCTION 'DB_COMMIT'.
    ENDIF.
  CATCH cx_shm_error INTO lo_ex.
     RAISE EXCEPTION TYPE cx_shm_build_failed
                EXPORTING previous = lo_ex.
  ENDTRY.
ENDMETHOD.
```

**Listing 15.14** Implementing Automatic Area Structuring

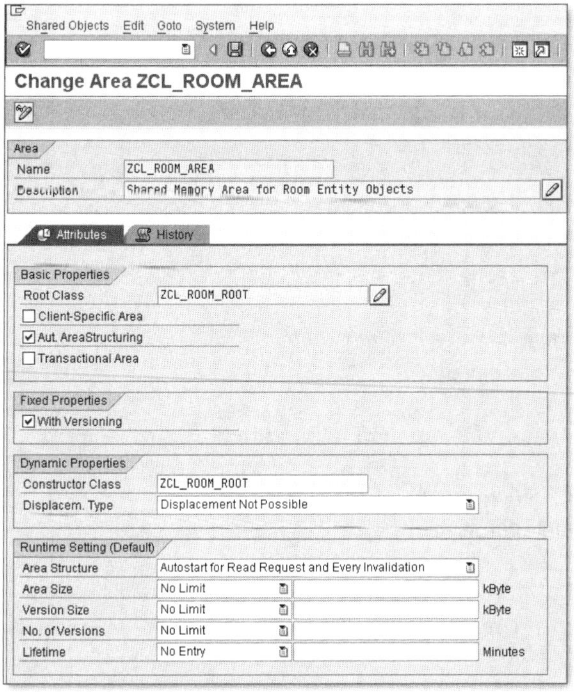


**Figure 15.19** Configuring Automatic Area Structuring

After all of the necessary changes are in place, we can begin to access our conference room buffer on demand. However, there is one wrinkle to all of this that we have to account for. Whenever the system discovers that an area instance needs to be created, it creates that area instance in a separate task. Consequently, the very first call to `ATTACH_FOR_READ()` will fail because this method doesn't wait for the area instance to be built before returning. The workaround here is to place the handle request logic inside of a loop statement that gives the system a little bit of time to go off and initialize the area instance. You can see an example of this kind of approach in the `ZSHMO_AUTO_CONSUMER` report program listed in Listing 15.15.

```
REPORT zshmo_auto_consumer.
CLASS lcl_registration_service DEFINITION.
  PUBLIC SECTION.
    CLASS-METHODS:
      find_room IMPORTING im_seats TYPE i.
ENDCLASS.

CLASS lcl_registration_service IMPLEMENTATION.
  METHOD find_room.
    "Method-Local Data Declarations:
    DATA: lo_handle  TYPE REF TO zcl_room_area,
          lt_rooms   TYPE zttca_rooms,
          lo_ex      TYPE REF TO cx_root,
          lv_message TYPE string.
    FIELD-SYMBOLS:
      <lfs_room> LIKE LINE OF lt_rooms.

    "Try to locate a conference room:
    TRY.
      "Obtain an area handle in read mode:
      WHILE lo_handle IS NOT BOUND.
        "Raise an exception if a handle is not bound
        "after three tries:
        IF sy-index GT 3.
          RAISE EXCEPTION TYPE cx_shm_no_active_version
            EXPORTING
              area_name = 'ZCL_ROOM_AREA'
              inst_name = 'CONF_ROOMS'.
        ENDIF.

        "Create a "read" handle for the shared memory area:
        TRY.
```

```
          lo_handle =
            zcl_room_area=>attach_for_read( 'CONF_ROOMS' ).
        CATCH cx_shm_error.
          WAIT UP TO 1 SECONDS.
        ENDTRY.
      ENDWHILE.

      "Search for rooms that meet the given criteria:
      lt_rooms =
        lo_handle->root->get_rooms_by_size( im_seats ).

      "Release the area handle:
      lo_handle->detach( ).

      "Output the results:
      LOOP AT lt_rooms ASSIGNING <lfs_room>.
        WRITE: / 'Room', <lfs_room>-room_no,
                 'seats', <lfs_room>-max_occupants,
                 'people.'.
      ENDLOOP.
    CATCH cx_shm_error INTO lo_ex.
      lv_message = lo_ex->get_text( ).
      MESSAGE lv_message TYPE 'I'.
    ENDTRY.
  ENDMETHOD.                    " METHOD find_room
ENDCLASS.

PARAMETERS:
  p_seats TYPE i OBLIGATORY.

START-OF-SELECTION.
  "Look in shared memory to find a conference room:
  lcl_registration_service=>find_room( p_seats ).
```

**Listing 15.15** Accessing Area Instances On Demand

### Abstracting the Shared Memory API Calls

The example programs described throughout the course of this section are for demonstrative purposes only. As a rule, you'll want to encapsulate access to shared memory objects inside of a more generic business object. This shields the complexities of the shared memory objects API from end users.

In fact, we highly recommend that you abstract *all* of your entity objects inside of a business object wrapper class. General use of this approach gives you lots of flexibility to tweak low-level details and in some cases swap out persistence layers. For instance, imagine that you have a business object that is providing read-only access to a database table. Depending on the nature of the data, you might be able to improve performance by substituting shared memory objects for the database-level access.

### 15.3.4 Locking Concepts

So far, we've side-stepped locking issues when it comes to shared memory areas. However, now that you understand how to access shared memory areas, it's time to take a look at the underlying locking mechanisms that govern concurrent access to shared memory areas. There are three types of locks that can be set on a shared memory area:

- **Read lock**
  A read lock is set when an area handle is bound to an area instance via a call to the `ATTACH_FOR_READ()` method of the area class. Many read locks can be created against an area instance. However, only one read lock can be set within a particular internal session. After a read lock is set, you can read from the bound area instance until the lock is either explicitly removed via a call to the `DETACH()` method of the area class or implicitly removed when the program ends. When one or more read locks are in place, no other program can come along and change the contents of the area instance because all change lock requests will be denied. Thus, you can rest assured that any data you're reading is up to date and valid.
- **Write lock**
  A write lock is set whenever an area handle is bound to an area instance via a call to the `ATTACH_FOR_WRITE()` method of the area class. A write lock is an exclusive lock; there can't be any other read or change locks against an area instance whenever a write lock is in place. After a write lock is set, you can read/write to the bound area instance until the lock is removed. Write locks can be removed by calling the `DETACH_COMMIT()` or `DETACH_ROLLBACK()` methods of the area class. These methods either commit or roll back the changes to the area instance, respectively. If a program ends without an explicit write lock removal, the system implicitly calls the `DETACH_ROLLBACK()` method of the area class.
- **Update lock**
  An update lock is set whenever an area handle is bound to an area instance via

a call to the ATTACH_FOR_UPDATE() method. Like write locks, update locks are exclusive locks; there can't be any other read or change locks against an area instance when an update lock is in place. After an update lock is set, you can read from or update the bound area instance until the lock is removed. Update locks are removed via the DETACH_COMMIT() or DETACH_ROLLBACK() methods of the area class. These methods either commit or roll back the changes to the area instance, respectively. If a program ends without an explicit update lock removal, the system implicitly calls the DETACH_ROLLBACK() method of the area class.

As we mentioned earlier, locks make the process of working with shared memory objects much more predictable. In particular, locks help you avoid phantom reads, non-repeatable reads, and dirty reads against an area instance. As you program access to area instances, you should be mindful that locks might be in place when you attempt to access an area instance. You can deal with these exceptions by surrounding your attachment method calls within a TRY statement. You can see the types of exceptions that can be triggered by looking at the signature of the "ATTACH_FOR_" methods of the area class.

### 15.3.5 Area Instance Versioning

In Section 15.3.4, Locking Concepts, we introduced you to locking concepts for shared memory areas. Though we generically described how locks were set against an area instance, we were not being 100% accurate. To be precise, locks are technically set against an *area instance version*. We've avoided this intricacy until now because the area instances we've described have only maintained a single version internally. However, as you learned in Section 15.3.2, Defining Shared Memory Areas, it's technically possible for an area instance to maintain multiple versions internally using *area instance versioning*.

When area instance versioning is turned on, the rules for locks change. For instance, you might recall from Section 15.3.4, Locking Concepts, that it's not possible to set a change lock on an area instance that currently has one or more read locks against it. With versioning, the change lock is allowed but with a twist. Read locks always access the *active version* of the area instance. When a request comes along to create a change lock, a copy of the active version is created, and the change lock is applied to the new version. While that version is being updated, other read requests work off of the active version. As soon as the changes to the new version are committed via a call to the DETACH_COMMIT() method of the area handle, that version replaces the current active version, and any new read locks are bound against the new version.

To put versioning into perspective, let's take a look at the lifecycle of an area instance version, starting with the very first version created. The UML state machine diagram shown in Figure 15.20 depicts this lifecycle. As you can see, while an area instance version is being created, it's initialized with the *Building* status. After the changes are committed using the `DETACH_COMMIT()` method, the status of the area instance version changes to *Active*. At this point, all incoming read locks are associated with this active version. During this time, let's imagine that a program comes along and wants to make an update to the area instance. With versioning turned on, this change lock request is granted, and a new version is created and initialized with the *Building* status. When these changes are committed, the first area instance version is marked with the *Obsolete* status. In this case, any preexisting read locks remain associated with the first area instance version, while any new read lock requests are associated with the second (or *active*) area instance version. After the last read lock is removed on the first area instance version, its status changes to *Expired*. At this point, the runtime environment can delete the area instance version and reclaim its used resources.

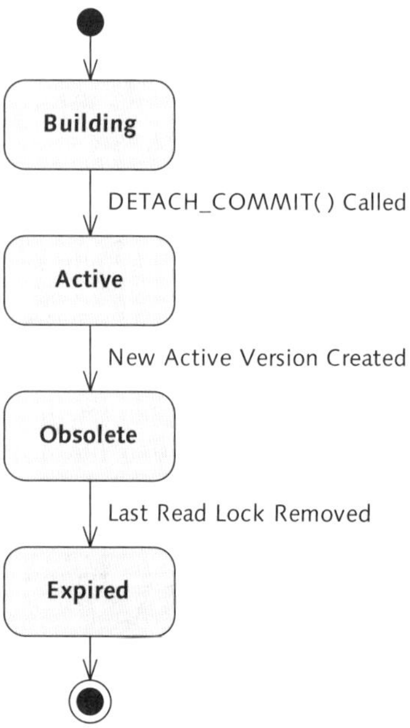


**Figure 15.20** UML State Machine Diagram of an Area Instance Version

Area instance versioning makes it possible to implement more generalized shared memory programming techniques in which a given area instance is changed frequently. In spite of this, you should be careful because non-coordinated access could lead to unpredictable results. Generally speaking, SAP recommends that you use shared memory objects as a type of shared buffer whose contents are relatively static in nature. Nevertheless, it's nice to know the capabilities are there if you need them.

### 15.3.6 Monitoring Techniques

Normally, whenever we talk about the organization of memory segments, we speak in very abstract terms. In other words, we can draw pictures like the one shown earlier in Figure 15.1, but we can't really see what's going on at runtime. However, when it comes to shared memory areas, we can.

You can see how resources are allocated for shared memory areas in Transaction SHMM. Figure 15.21 shows the initial screen of this transaction. Here, you can see our ZCL_ROOM_AREA shared memory area selected on the Areas tab. In this overview display, you can see the number of instances/versions in memory, as well as information such as total allocated size, version statuses, and the current number of read/change locks. You can also narrow your focus in the View drop-down list to look at lock allocation, user assignments, and so on.

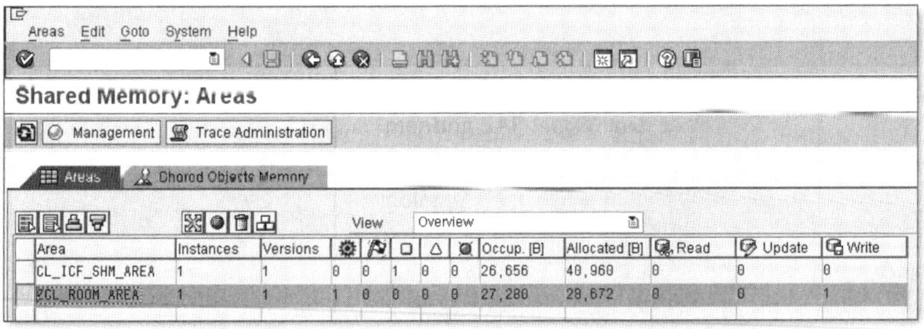


**Figure 15.21** Viewing Shared Memory Areas in Transaction SHMM

To look at allocations on an instance-by-instance basis, double-click on the shared memory area in the areas table depicted in Figure 15.21. This brings up the detailed screen shown in Figure 15.22. From here, you can drill in further to see detailed information about a particular instance. For example, Figure 15.23 shows detailed lock information about the CONF_ROOMS area instance created by the ZSHMO_PRODUCER program demonstrated earlier in Listing 15.10.

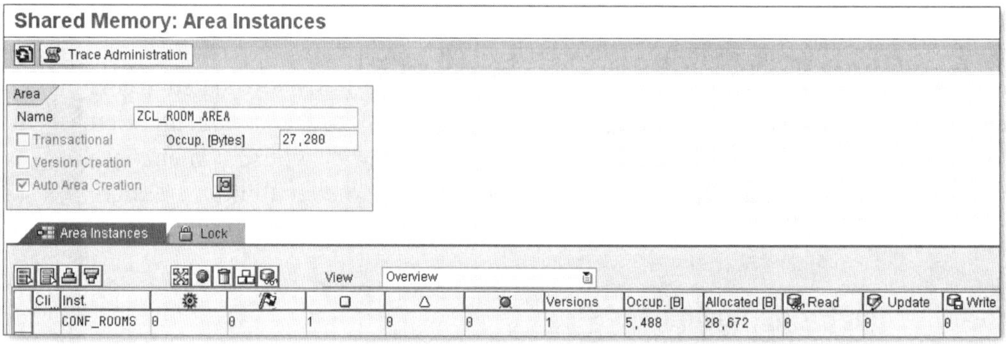


**Figure 15.22** Viewing Shared Memory Areas by Instances

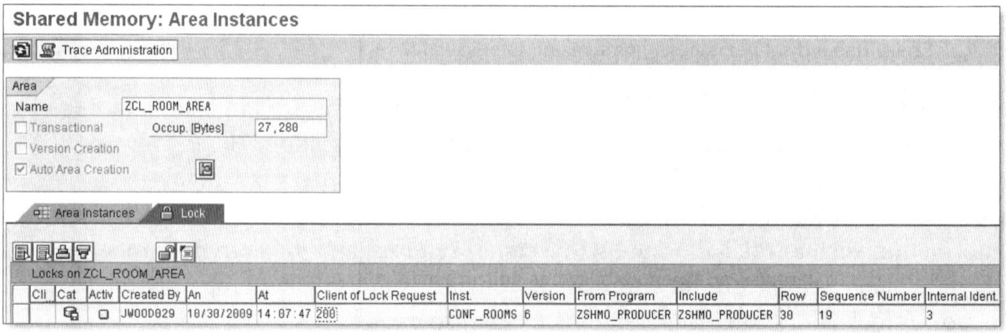


**Figure 15.23** Viewing Detailed Information for an Area Instance

For the most part, the interface of Transaction SHMM is fairly intuitive if you're familiar with shared memory objects. If you want to learn more about specific features of this transaction, you can find detailed information in the SAP Library available online at *http://help.sap.com*.

## 15.4 Summary

In this chapter, you learned how to use the shared memory segment of SAP NetWeaver AS ABAP to enable interprocess communication between ABAP programs. While these techniques are often used to pass data to and from user exit contexts, and so on, they also make it possible to implement sophisticated parallelized solutions. In the next chapter, we explore options for parallelization in ABAP.

*Usually, whenever chefs try to multitask in the kitchen, the results are disastrous. However, computers excel at multitasking, making it possible to achieve exponential performance improvements with just a few tweaks to the recipe. In this chapter, we show you how to implement parallel and distributed processing in ABAP.*

# 16 Parallel and Distributed Processing with RFCs

In 1965, Intel Corporation co-founder Gordon E. Moore published an article entitled "Cramming More Components onto Integrated Circuits" in which he postulated that the number of components that could be placed on a computer chip would double every two years. Over time, history has shown this theory to be remarkably accurate when it comes to projecting improvements in hardware capacity. In fact, hardware capabilities have advanced to the point that most software is unable to take advantage of all of the additional processing power.

Unfortunately, there is no magic button that you can press to optimize your ABAP code to exploit the untapped potential of the system. Instead, you have to design your programs from the ground up to use these resources in a sensible manner. Beyond basic performance-tuning techniques, this process often involves the implementation of *parallelized algorithms*.

Parallelization and distributed processing are very advanced topics in computer science; topics that many developers prefer to shy away from. However, when used properly, parallelization and distributed processing can greatly improve the performance of certain types of tasks. In this chapter, we show you how the RFC interface can be used to implement parallelization and distributed processing in ABAP.

## 16.1 RFC Overview

If you've been around ABAP for a while, you've likely interacted with the *remote function call* (RFC) interface at some point along the way. For many years, the only way to interface directly with an SAP system was through the RFC interface. In this section, we introduce you to the RFC interface and its use within SAP NetWeaver AS ABAP. However, because this chapter is concerned with parallelization and distributed processing, we don't spend much time describing how the RFC interface can be used to enable communication between SAP systems and the outside world. For more information about these topics, check out *SAP Interface Programming* (SAP PRESS, 2009).

### 16.1.1 Understanding the Different Variants of RFC

Before we delve too far into the details of RFC programming in ABAP, it's useful to first take a look at the various flavors of RFC that are supported by SAP. Table 16.1 describes the RFC variants provided with release 7.0 of SAP NetWeaver AS ABAP. Understanding how these variants work will help you figure out how to select the right tool for the job.

| RFC Variant | Description |
|---|---|
| Synchronous RFC (sRFC) | As the name suggests, sRFC is used to invoke a remote-enabled function module *synchronously*. This implies that the host system must be available at the time of invocation for the call to work.<br>An example of sRFC usage is a client program calling a BAPI function on another system. |
| Asynchronous RFC (aRFC) | The use of the term *asynchronous* here is somewhat misleading. An aRFC still requires that the receiver system be available to process the request. However, the difference is that the client doesn't block while the function is executing. Instead, it can proceed with other tasks while the function module executes in a separate task (session).<br>The aRFC protocol can be used to implement parallelization in ABAP programs. We explain how to exploit this functionality in Section 16.2, Parallel Processing with aRFC. |

**Table 16.1** Description of RFC Variants

| RFC Variant | Description |
|---|---|
| Transactional RFC (tRFC) | As opposed to aRFC, tRFC implements true asynchronous processing. In fact, tRFC semantics guarantee that a function is executed *exactly once* in the receiver system, even if the receiver system is unavailable at the time of invocation. In this case, the system buffers the LUW in the system database so that it can be reprocessed later.<br>The tRFC protocol is most commonly used to transmit and receive Intermediate Document (IDoc) messages. |
| Queued RFC (qRFC) | While the tRFC protocol guarantees that a given LUW is executed exactly once in a receiver system, it doesn't provide any guarantees about the order in which the LUWs are processed. To achieve a quality of service of *exactly once in order*, you must use the qRFC protocol.<br>The qRFC protocol implements a queuing mechanism on top of the tRFC protocol to ensure that LUWs are processed serially.<br>qRFC is used extensively by the SAP NetWeaver PI and BI usage types to throttle messaging. It's also used to implement point-to-point middleware among the SAP ERP, SAP CRM, and SAP SCM Business Suite solutions. |
| Background RFC (bgRFC) | The bgRFC protocol was introduced with release 7.0 of SAP NetWeaver AS ABAP as an eventual replacement to the tRFC and qRFC protocols. Among other things, bgRFC offers improved scalability and performance. |
| Local Data Queue (LDQ) | Each of the RFC variants described thus far are implemented in terms of the *push principle*. With the LDQ variant, data is stored and extracted on demand by clients using the *pull principle*.<br>The LDQ variant is optimized for mobile clients that periodically need to synchronize with the server, and so on. |

**Table 16.1** Description of RFC Variants (Cont.)

### 16.1.2 Developing RFC-Enabled Function Modules

Each of the RFC variants described in Table 16.1 is based on the invocation of an RFC-enabled function module. For the most part, there's not much difference between a remote-enabled function module and a regular function module. The most pronounced difference is the configuration of the function's *processing type*.

Figure 16.1 shows the configuration of standard BAPI module BAPI_FLIGHT_GETDETAIL in the Function Builder (Transaction SE37). As you can see on the Attributes tab, this module is configured with the Remote-Enabled Module processing type.

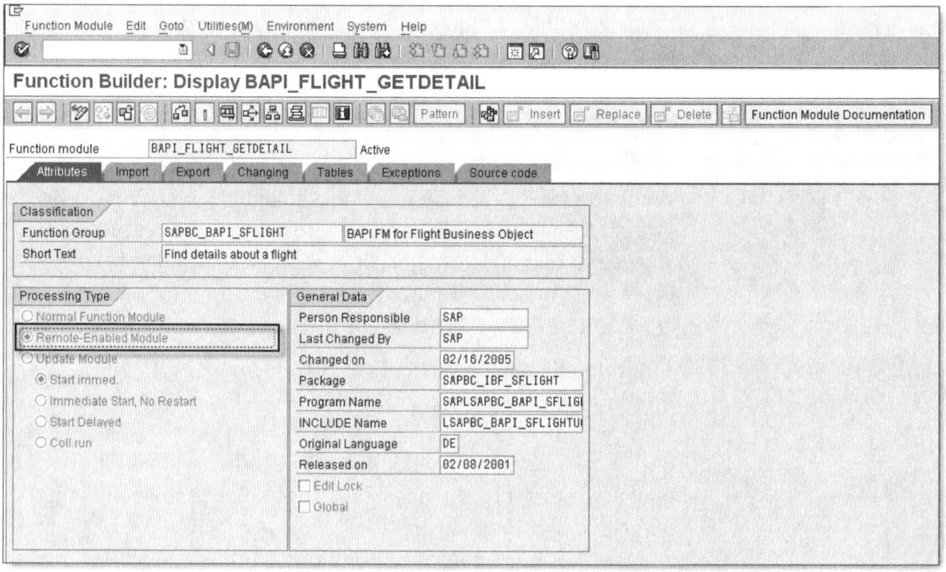

Figure 16.1 Defining Remote-Enabled Functions

In addition to the configuration of the remote-enabled processing type, there are some additional rules that must be adhered to in order to define an RFC function. At a high level, these rules are related to the fact that the function may or may not be called from an ABAP context. Therefore, it doesn't make sense to pass parameters using reference semantics. Instead, parameters for RFC modules are always passed by value. If this seems confusing, don't worry; the syntax check lets you know if you go astray.

Each SAP system comes predelivered with many useful RFC-enabled function modules out of the box, including BAPIs. To search for RFC-enabled function modules in your system, you can choose the RFC Modules radio button in the Additional Selections group box of the function module search help in the Repository Info System (see Figure 16.2).

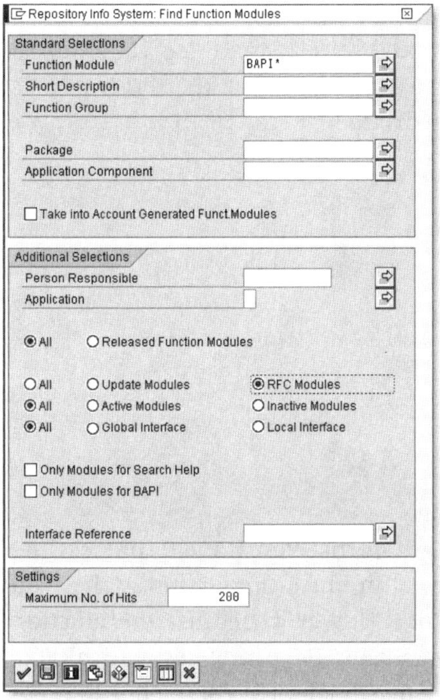


**Figure 16.2** Searching for RFC-Enabled Function Modules

## 16.2 Parallel Processing with aRFC

Now that you've had a chance to familiarize yourself with the RFC interface, it's time to learn how to put it to work to solve the problem at hand: implementing parallel processing. In this section, we show you how to implement parallelized algorithms in ABAP.

### 16.2.1 Syntax Overview

Before we begin looking at how to implement parallel solutions in ABAP, we need to take a look at the syntax of a few statements that are used to handle asynchronous processing.

#### Calling an RFC Function Asynchronously

To call an RFC function asynchronously, you must use the `STARTING NEW TASK` addition to the `CALL FUNCTION` statement. This addition causes the function module to execute in a separate task whose name is defined by the `task` identifier. The `IN GROUP` addition shown in Listing 16.1 allows you to specify an RFC server group in which to execute the function module. You'll learn more about RFC server groups in Section 16.2.2, Configuring an RFC Server Group.

```
CALL FUNCTION func STARTING NEW TASK task
           IN GROUP {group|DEFAULT}
      parameter_list
      [{PERFORMING subr}|{CALLING meth} ON END OF TASK]
   EXCEPTIONS
     communication_failure = 1 {MESSAGE msg}
     system_failure        = 2 {MESSAGE msg}
     resource_failure      = 3
     others                = 4.
```

**Listing 16.1** Syntax Diagram for an aRFC Function Call

After you specify the task and RFC server group that you want to process the function with, you can provide a parameter list in much the same way that you normally pass parameters to function modules. However, because the function call is asynchronous, you aren't allowed to use `IMPORTING` parameters with aRFCs. Instead, these values must be retrieved after the function is complete using the `RECEIVE` statement, which we cover in a moment. `CHANGING` and `TABLES` parameters are allowed, but they only support the passing of data into the function module in this context.

To collect the results of the aRFC, you must specify a callback subroutine/method using the `PERFORMING/CALLING...ON END OF TASK` addition shown in Listing 16.1. Within these modules, you can use the `RECEIVE` statement to obtain the results of the function call.

Like any function call, aRFCs can trigger various types of exceptions. In addition to the standard `COMMUNICATION_FAILURE` and `SYSTEM_FAILURE` exceptions triggered by the system when there is a system-level error, aRFCs can also raise an exception called `RESOURCE_FAILURE`. A `RESOURCE_FAILURE` exception occurs when there aren't enough resources available to process the request. In Section 16.2.4, Case Study: Processing Messages in Parallel, we look at ways of dealing with these exceptions in a logical manner.

### Implementing Synchronization with the WAIT UNTIL Statement

In an ideal world, there would be enough work processes available to process every LUW independently. Unfortunately, that is rarely the case. Therefore, when implementing parallel solutions in ABAP, it's important to try and throttle the aRFC traffic in accordance with the resources available in the system. From a code perspective, this implies that we may have to *wait* for the system to catch up from time to time. We can implement this wait step using the `WAIT UNTIL` statement whose syntax is shown in Listing 16.2.

```
WAIT UNTIL log_exp [UP TO sec SECONDS].
```

**Listing 16.2** Syntax Diagram of the WAIT UNTIL Statement

As you can see in Listing 16.2, the syntax of the `WAIT UNTIL` statement is fairly straightforward. Essentially, it allows the calling program to wait until a given logical expression becomes true. You also have the option of defining a timeout for the wait operation using the `UP TO sec SECONDS` addition.

In Section 16.2.4, Case Study: Processing Messages in Parallel, we see how the `WAIT UNTIL` statement can be used to throttle aRFCs and also determine when the parallel processes are complete.

### Retrieving Results from an aRFC Function Call

As you saw earlier in the syntax diagram of an aRFC function call shown in Listing 16.1, the results from an aRFC are retrieved asynchronously *after* the function is finished processing. In this case, the system invokes the callback handler routine specified in the original aRFC function call. Within this routine, you can obtain the results of the function call using the `RECEIVE` statement whose syntax is shown in Listing 16.3.

```
RECEIVE RESULTS FROM FUNCTION func
  IMPORTING
    ...
  CHANGING
    ...
  TABLES
    ...
  EXCEPTIONS
    communication_failure = 1
    system_failure        = 2
    others                = 3.
  [KEEPING TASK].
```

**Listing 16.3** Syntax Diagram of RECEIVE Statement

The code excerpt contained in Listing 16.4 demonstrates how the RECEIVE statement is positioned within a callback routine that is registered with thc CALL FUNCTION statement. Here, notice that the RECEIVE statement doesn't need to specify anything else besides the name of the function module it's retrieving the results from; the system takes care of the binding of the parameter list to the actual result values. After you retrieve the results, you can associate them with the original function call using the taskname identifier provided in the interface of the callback module.

```
FORM on_function_complete USING taskname.
* Retrieve the results of the aRFC call:
  RECEIVE RESULTS FROM FUNCTION 'SOME_FUNCTION'
    IMPORTING
      ...
    CHANGING
      ...
    TABLES
      ...
    EXCEPTIONS
      communication_failure = 1
      system_failure        = 2
      others                = 3.

* Associate the results with the given task name:
  IF sy-subrc EQ 0.
    ...
  ENDIF.
ENDFORM.
```

**Listing 16.4** Using the RECEIVE Statement in a Callback Routine

In addition to the typical parameter list specification, the RECEIVE statement also allows you to hang on to the context of the called function module after the callback routine is finished. In this way, you can leverage the global data in the called function's function group in subsequent calls that use the same task name.

### 16.2.2 Configuring an RFC Server Group

By definition, parallelized algorithms are designed to be resource-intensive. In other words, instead of executing the tasks of a program step by step in a single work process, we want to distribute the load across multiple work processes. However, we need to be careful here because we don't want to take hold of every available resource in the system and bring the system to its knees. Realistically, we need to strike a balance between the amount of resources we want to have and the resources available within the system at the time our program is going to run.

To set some boundaries for parallel processing, you must configure an *RFC server group*. RFC server groups define resource-allocation rules, allowing you to apportion work processes from one or more SAP NetWeaver AS ABAP application server instances. Of course, there are no guarantees that these work processes will be available at runtime. Rather, the RFC server group sets an upper bound on the number of processes that can be used by parallelized programs.

RFC server groups are maintained in Transaction RZ12. Figure 16.3 shows the overview screen of Transaction RZ12. Here, you can create server groups, assign server instances, delete assignments, and so on.

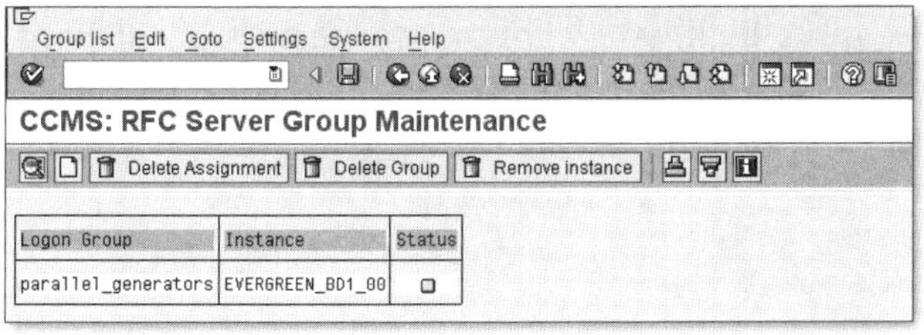


**Figure 16.3** Maintaining RFC Server Groups in Transaction RZ12

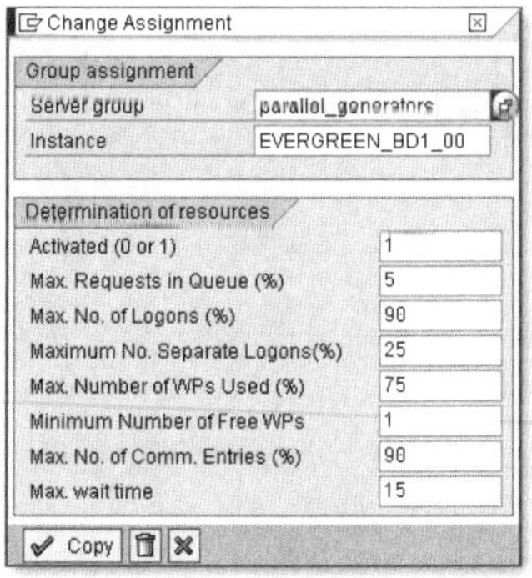


**Figure 16.4** Defining an RFC Server Group in Transaction RZ12

By default, each SAP NetWeaver AS ABAP instance comes pre-installed with an RFC server group called `parallel_generators`. Figure 16.4 shows an example configuration of this server group. Normally, RFC server groups are maintained by Basis administration staff. However, if you're curious to know more about how they are configured, perform a keyword search on the phrase "RFC Server Group" in the SAP Library documentation available online at *http://help.sap.com*.

### 16.2.3 Defining Parallel Algorithms

Given the distributed nature of parallelized solutions, it's important to have a plan in place before you start programming. In particular, it's crucial that roles and responsibilities are assigned correctly, and that you understand how the aRFC interface operates conceptually. In this section, we show you how to organize your code to support parallelization.

In many respects, the flow of a parallelized program in ABAP isn't all that different from a typical report program. To put all this into perspective, let's consider an example. Imagine that you want to develop an extract program to transmit a series of sales order messages to some external system. Because the number of sales order messages could be quite high, you want to implement a parallelized solution to improve throughput. The UML sequence diagram in Figure 16.5 illustrates the basic flow of this extract program.

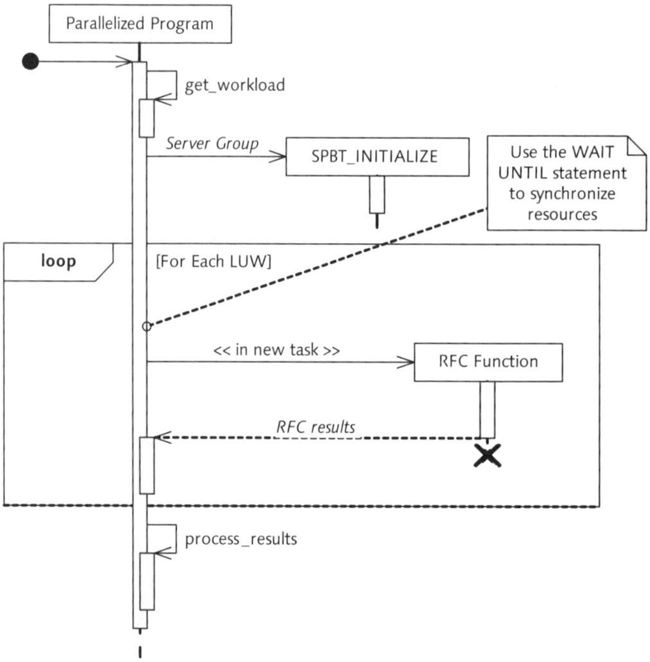


**Figure 16.5** UML Sequence Diagram of a Parallelized ABAP Program

Looking at the UML sequence diagram in Figure 16.5, let's consider the steps required to implement the extract program:

1. First, the program calculates its workload using a routine called GET_WORKLOAD. Here, the program would likely have selection screen parameters that are used to define a query to select the relevant sales order numbers to be extracted.
2. After the extract data set is defined, we're ready to process and distribute the sales orders in parallel. However, before we do so, we need to initialize the *parallel background task* (PBT) environment using the standard function module SPBT_INITIALIZE. This function binds the program with a particular RFC server group, provides you with information about the number of free work processes, and so on.
3. After the PBT environment is initialized, we can begin dispatching the sales orders. This task is performed in an RFC-enabled function module whose job is to extract the relevant sales order information, construct an IDoc, and dispatch the IDoc using standard function MASTER_IDOC_DISTRIBUTE.
4. Because each RFC is executed asynchronously, the controlling program doesn't block and wait for the results of the distribution process. Instead, it defines a callback subroutine in the RFC that the system uses to transmit the results from the asynchronous call back to the calling program. Here, the calling program can use the RECEIVE statement to obtain the EXPORTING, CHANGING, and TABLES parameters from the RFC.
5. Within the looping process, it's likely that there will be times when there aren't enough resources available to process a request. Therefore, we must implement logic to throttle the requests. This can be implemented using the WAIT UNTIL statement.
6. Finally, after all of the aRFCs have been implemented and we break out of our loop, we must once again wait for all of the remaining RFC functions to finish processing before we output the results of the job. For this task, we must use the WAIT UNTIL statement.

For the most part, implementing parallelized algorithms in ABAP is as simple as the flow depicted previously in Figure 16.5. However, before you start developing your own programs, there are a few design points that you should be mindful of:

- By definition, parallel processing implies that each LUW must be able to execute independently. While the IPC features described in Chapter 15, Interprocess Communication, can be used to synchronize tasks to a certain degree, they add a level of complexity to the solution that might not be manageable. As a rule, it's better to avoid parallel processing if there are dependencies between the LUWs.

- There are no guarantees that the LUWs are processed in the order that they were called. This is particularly the case with RFC server groups that are distributed across multiple application servers. Here, one server might be running more slowly than the others, and so on.
- Due to limitations of the aRFC interface, the called RFC module must not include a function call using the destination `BACK`.
- Similarly, the calling program must not change to a new internal session (e.g., using the `SUBMIT` or `CALL TRANSACTION` statements) after making an aRFC.

### 16.2.4 Case Study: Processing Messages in Parallel

In Section 16.2.3, Defining Parallel Algorithms, you learned the basics of defining parallel algorithms in ABAP. Next we show you how to actually implement these solutions in an ABAP report program called `ZPARALLEL_DEMO`, which is based on the sales order extract example described in that section. For brevity's sake, we don't include the source code of this program in its entirety. However, a complete version is available in the source code bundle available for this book online.

#### Defining the Remote-Enabled Function Module

Before we begin developing the `ZPARALLEL_DEMO` program, we need to define an RFC-enabled function module to process sales orders. To keep things simple, we simply create a remote-enabled function module called `Z_RFC_CREATE_MESSAGE` to simulate this functionality. As you can see in Listing 16.5, this function module is simply generating a document number using the standard `GUID_CREATE` function.

```
FUNCTION Z_RFC_CREATE_MESSAGE.
*"----------------------------------------------------------
*"*"Local Interface:
*"  EXPORTING
*"     VALUE(EX_MESSAGE_NUMBER) TYPE  GUID_16
*"     VALUE(EX_PROCESSED_TIME) TYPE  SY-UZEIT
*"----------------------------------------------------------
* Simulate the creation of a sales order:
  CALL FUNCTION 'GUID_CREATE'
    IMPORTING
      ev_guid_16 = ex_message_number.
```

```
  ex_processed_time = sy-uzeit.
ENDFUNCTION.
```

**Listing 16.5** Implementation of Z_RFC_CREATE_MESSAGE

### Initializing the PBT Environment

After the RFC function has been created, we're ready to begin developing the parallelized solution. This process begins with the call to standard function SPBT_INITIALIZE. However, in an effort to simplify interaction with the PBT framework, we've provided a utilities class called /BOWDK/CL_PBT_UTILITIES that will perform this task (and others) on our behalf. Listing 16.6 shows how to create an instance of the PBT utilities service. Here, as you can see, this utility receives two importing parameters: the RFC server group and a *task prefix*. This task prefix is used to simplify the creation of task names for individual aRFCs. We'll see how this works in a moment.

```
METHOD execute.
  TRY.
    "Initialize the PBT utilities service:
    CREATE OBJECT pbt_service
      EXPORTING
        im_server_group = im_group
        im_task_prefix  = im_prefix.

    "Dispatch the selected number of messages:
    dispatch_messages( im_msgs ).
  CATCH /bowdk/cx_pbt_init_error.
    "Exception handling goes here...
  ENDTRY.
ENDMETHOD.                    " METHOD execute
```

**Listing 16.6** Initializing the PBT Environment

As you can see in Listing 16.6, the CONSTRUCTOR() method of class /BOWDK/CL_PBT_UTILITIES may raise an exception of type /BOWDK/CX_PBT_INIT_ERROR. This exception class consolidates various exceptions that might be triggered by function SPBT_INITIALIZE. If this exception is triggered, then the PBT environment isn't ready to process messages, and the program can't proceed.

### Dispatching the Messages

After the PBT environment has been initialized, we can begin the dispatch process that parcels out the work to the RFC server group resources. Listing 16.7 shows how we're dispatching messages using the aRFC interface. Because we aren't working with live data, the program uses a parameter called `P_MSGS` to define how many messages we want to run the simulation with. This parameter is used to control a `WHILE` loop that dispatches the requested number of messages. Inside of the `WHILE` loop, we perform the following steps:

1. First, we're using the `WAIT UNTIL` statement to make sure that we don't overwhelm the RFC server group by dispatching too many requests at once. This logic is driven by a counter variable called `BUSY_PROCESSES` that gets incremented when an aRFC is made and decremented when it completes. The logical expression in the `WAIT UNTIL` statement says that we should wait to proceed until the number of active processes is less than the number of free work processes available in the RFC server group. Unfortunately, this number of free work processes isn't 100% accurate because it's calculated when the PBT environment is initialized in the call to `SPBT_INITIALIZE`. Nevertheless, it does give us a pretty good metric in which to attempt to throttle the aRFC requests.
2. Next, we use the instance method `GET_NEXT_TASK_NAME()` of class `/BOWDK/CL_PBT_UTILITIES` to derive a unique task name to associate with our aRFC.
3. After we determine the task name, we can invoke the `Z_RFC_CREATE_MESSAGE` function asynchronously using the `CALL FUNCTION` statement variant outlined earlier in Listing 16.1. Here, we define the callback method `ON_MESSAGE_CREATED` to collect the results of each function call.
4. After we call the RFC function, we need to check the results:
   - If the call was successful, then we want to log some information about the task in an internal table attribute called `TASK_LIST`. We also want to increment a couple of counters: one to keep track of the number of executing processes, and the other to keep tabs on the number of messages submitted.
   - If an exception of type `COMMUNICATION_FAILURE` or `RESOURCE_FAILURE` is raised, we need to deal with the possibility that one of the application server nodes in the RFC server group is unresponsive. In this case, we can use the `GET_DESTINATION_FOR_TASK()` and `BLOCK_SERVER()` instance methods defined in class `/BOWDK/CL_PBT_UTILITIES` to remove the server from the resource

pool. In situations where you're dealing with live data, you need to make sure that the failed message gets reprocessed.

- If an exception of type RESOURCE_FAILURE is triggered, there simply aren't enough resources to process the request at the moment. In this case, we want to wait for some of the aRFC functions to catch up using the WAIT UNTIL statement.

5. Finally, after all of the messages have been submitted, we break out of the WHILE statement. However, just because all of the requests have been submitted doesn't mean that the RFC functions are finished processing. Therefore, at this point, we need to execute another WAIT UNTIL statement to wait until all of the messages have been submitted.

```
METHOD dispatch_messages.
  "Local Data Declarations:
  DATA: lv_task    TYPE char8,
        lv_dest    TYPE rfcdest,
        lv_message TYPE char80.
  FIELD-SYMBOLS:
    <lfs_task> LIKE LINE OF task_list.

  "Send the requested number of messages:
  WHILE requested_msg LT im_msgs.
    "Try to keep the throughput in check:
    WAIT UNTIL busy_processes
      LT pbt_service->get_free_work_processes( ).

    "Derive the next task name:
    lv_task =
      pbt_service->get_next_task_name( ).

    "Call the RFC module asynchronously to simulate
    "the creation of a message:
    CALL FUNCTION 'Z_RFC_CREATE_MESSAGE'
         STARTING NEW TASK lv_task
         DESTINATION IN GROUP pbt_service->server_group
         CALLING lcl_parallelizer=>on_message_created
           ON END OF TASK
      EXCEPTIONS
        communication_failure = 1 MESSAGE lv_message
        system_failure        = 2 MESSAGE lv_message
        resource_failure      = 3.
```

```
"Check the results:
CASE sy-subrc.
  WHEN 0.
    "If the call is successful, go ahead log the
    "message:
    APPEND INITIAL LINE TO task_list
                 ASSIGNING <lfs_task>.
    <lfs_task>-task_name = lv_task.
    <lfs_task>-destination =
      pbt_service->get_destination_for_task( ).
    <lfs_task>-requested_time = sy-uzeit.

    "Keep track of the running work processes:
    ADD 1 TO busy_processes.

    "Also increment the message counter:
    ADD 1 TO requested_msg.
  WHEN 1 OR 2.
    "If we get to here, then there has been some
    "kind of system-level error.
    WRITE: / lv_message.

    "Remove the given destination from the pool
    "of PBT resources:
    lv_dest =
      pbt_service->get_destination_for_task( ).

    pbt_service->block_server( lv_dest ).

    "Check to see if there are resources still
    "available:
    IF pbt_service->has_resources( ) NE abap_true.
      MESSAGE
        'There are no more PBT resources available!'
         TYPE 'I'.
      RETURN.
    ENDIF.
  WHEN 3.
    "If we get to this point, then all the processes
    "are busy. Thus, we wait until something becomes
    "available:
    WRITE: / 'No resources available...sleeping.'.
```

```
        WAIT UNTIL processed_msg GE requested_msg
          UP TO '1' SECONDS.
        CONTINUE.
    ENDCASE.
  ENDWHILE.

  "Wait until the job(s) are completed before returning:
  WAIT UNTIL processed_msg
    GE requested_msg.
ENDMETHOD.                    " METHOD dispatch_messages
```

**Listing 16.7** Dispatching Messages in Parallel

### Collecting the Results of the Function Calls

In the `CALL FUNCTION` statement contained in Listing 16.7, we defined a callback method called `ON_MESSAGE_CREATED` that gets executed whenever an RFC function completes. The implementation of this method is contained in Listing 16.8. Here, we perform three steps:

1. First, we decrement our `BUSY_PROCESSES` counter attribute because one of the RFC functions has finished running.
2. Next, we use the provided `P_TASK` parameter as a key to look up the corresponding task list record. We can then update this record with the results of the `Z_RFC_CREATE_MESSAGE` function using the `RECEIVE` statement.
3. Lastly, we increment the `PROCESSED_MSG` counter attribute to keep track of the total number of processed messages.

```
METHOD on_message_created.
  "Method-Local Data Declarations:
  FIELD-SYMBOLS:
    <lfs_task> LIKE LINE OF task_list.

  "Decrement the running process counter:
  SUBTRACT 1 FROM busy_processes.

  "Update the task list with the results of the message
  "creation process:
  LOOP AT task_list ASSIGNING <lfs_task>
    WHERE task_name EQ p_task.

    RECEIVE RESULTS FROM FUNCTION 'Z_RFC_CREATE_MESSAGE'
```

```
      IMPORTING
        ex_message_number      = <lfs_task>-document_number
        ex_processed_time      = <lfs_task>-processed_time
      EXCEPTIONS
        communication_failure = 1
        system_failure        = 2.
  ENDLOOP.

  "Increment the message counter:
  ADD 1 TO processed_msg.
ENDMETHOD.                    " METHOD on_message_created
```

**Listing 16.8** Collecting the Results of the aRFC Functions

### Executing the Simulation Program

Now that you understand how all of the pieces fit together, let's try to run the ZPARALLEL_DEMO program and see what happens. Figure 16.6 shows the selection screen of this program. Here, we've selected the default RFC server group parallel_generators to run the job. We've also created a task name prefix called IDOC. At runtime, each of the aRFCs are executed with a task name of IDOC0001, IDOC0002, and so on. Finally, we've proposed a message count of 25. Of course, you can adjust this up and down to see how the system responds.

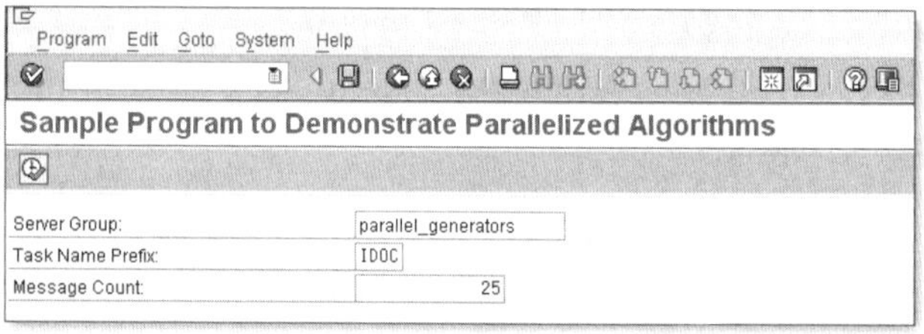


**Figure 16.6** Executing the Simulation Program — Part 1

Figure 16.7 shows the results of the simulation for 25 messages. As you can see, there were a couple of times where there were not enough resources available to dispatch the aRFC request. If you run the simulation again for 50 or 100 messages, you may see more occurrences of this in the output.

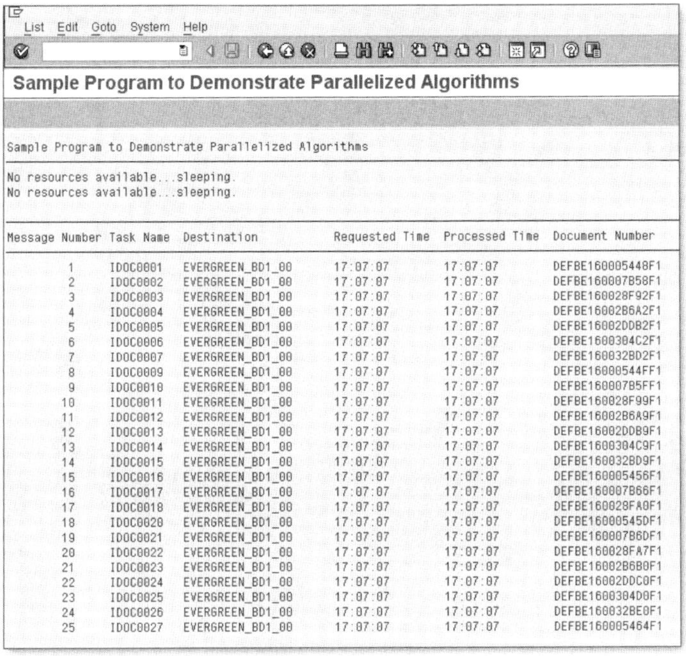

**Sample Program to Demonstrate Parallelized Algorithms**

Sample Program to Demonstrate Parallelized Algorithms

No resources available...sleeping.
No resources available...sleeping.

| Message Number | Task Name | Destination | Requested Time | Processed Time | Document Number |
|---|---|---|---|---|---|
| 1 | IDOC0001 | EVERGREEN_BD1_00 | 17:07:07 | 17:07:07 | DEFBE160005448F1 |
| 2 | IDOC0002 | EVERGREEN_BD1_00 | 17:07:07 | 17:07:07 | DEFBE160007B58F1 |
| 3 | IDOC0003 | EVERGREEN_BD1_00 | 17:07:07 | 17:07:07 | DEFBE160028F92F1 |
| 4 | IDOC0004 | EVERGREEN_BD1_00 | 17:07:07 | 17:07:07 | DEFBE16002B6A2F1 |
| 5 | IDOC0005 | EVERGREEN_BD1_00 | 17:07:07 | 17:07:07 | DEFBE16002DDB2F1 |
| 6 | IDOC0006 | EVERGREEN_BD1_00 | 17:07:07 | 17:07:07 | DEFBE1600304C2F1 |
| 7 | IDOC0007 | EVERGREEN_BD1_00 | 17:07:07 | 17:07:07 | DEFBE160032BD2F1 |
| 8 | IDOC0009 | EVERGREEN_BD1_00 | 17:07:07 | 17:07:07 | DEFBE16000544FF1 |
| 9 | IDOC0010 | EVERGREEN_BD1_00 | 17:07:07 | 17:07:07 | DEFBE160007B5FF1 |
| 10 | IDOC0011 | EVERGREEN_BD1_00 | 17:07:07 | 17:07:07 | DEFBE160028F99F1 |
| 11 | IDOC0012 | EVERGREEN_BD1_00 | 17:07:07 | 17:07:07 | DEFBE16002B6A9F1 |
| 12 | IDOC0013 | EVERGREEN_BD1_00 | 17:07:07 | 17:07:07 | DEFBE16002DDB9F1 |
| 13 | IDOC0014 | EVERGREEN_BD1_00 | 17:07:07 | 17:07:07 | DEFBE1600304C9F1 |
| 14 | IDOC0015 | EVERGREEN_BD1_00 | 17:07:07 | 17:07:07 | DEFBE160032BD9F1 |
| 15 | IDOC0016 | EVERGREEN_BD1_00 | 17:07:07 | 17:07:07 | DEFBE160005456F1 |
| 16 | IDOC0017 | EVERGREEN_BD1_00 | 17:07:07 | 17:07:07 | DEFBE160007B66F1 |
| 17 | IDOC0018 | EVERGREEN_BD1_00 | 17:07:07 | 17:07:07 | DEFBE160028FA0F1 |
| 18 | IDOC0020 | EVERGREEN_BD1_00 | 17:07:07 | 17:07:07 | DEFBE16000545DF1 |
| 19 | IDOC0021 | EVERGREEN_BD1_00 | 17:07:07 | 17:07:07 | DEFBE160007B6DF1 |
| 20 | IDOC0022 | EVERGREEN_BD1_00 | 17:07:07 | 17:07:07 | DEFBE160028FA7F1 |
| 21 | IDOC0023 | EVERGREEN_BD1_00 | 17:07:07 | 17:07:07 | DEFBE16002B6B0F1 |
| 22 | IDOC0024 | EVERGREEN_BD1_00 | 17:07:07 | 17:07:07 | DEFBE16002DDC0F1 |
| 23 | IDOC0025 | EVERGREEN_BD1_00 | 17:07:07 | 17:07:07 | DEFBE1600304D0F1 |
| 24 | IDOC0026 | EVERGREEN_BD1_00 | 17:07:07 | 17:07:07 | DEFBE160032BE0F1 |
| 25 | IDOC0027 | EVERGREEN_BD1_00 | 17:07:07 | 17:07:07 | DEFBE160005464F1 |

**Figure 16.7** Executing the Simulation Program — Part 2

## 16.3 Summary

This chapter demonstrated ways of implementing parallelized solutions in ABAP.

We hope that you've enjoyed the sampling of recipes provided in this cookbook, and trust that you'll be able to use, enhance, and combine them in your own development tasks.

# The Author

**James Wood** is the founder and principal consultant of Bowdark Consulting, Inc., an SAP NetWeaver consulting and training organization. With almost 10 years of experience as a software engineer, James specializes in custom development in the areas of ABAP Objects, Java/J2EE, SAP Process Integration, and the SAP Enterprise Portal.

Before starting Bowdark Consulting, Inc. in 2006, James was an SAP NetWeaver consultant for SAP America, Inc. and IBM Corporation, where he was involved in multiple SAP implementations. He holds a master's degree in software engineering from Texas Tech University. He is also the author of *Object-Oriented Programming with ABAP Objects* (SAP PRESS, 2009). To learn more about James and the book, please check out his website at *www.bowdarkconsulting.com*.

# Index

## A

## B

## C

## D

## E

## J



## K



## L



## M

## S

## V



## W



## X

## Y



## Z

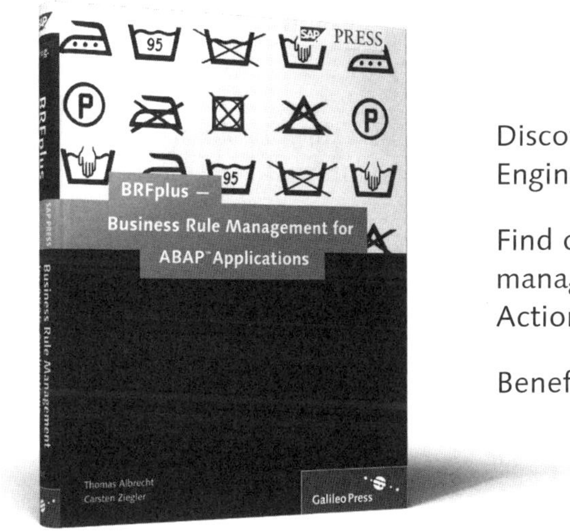


Discover the brand-new ABAP Rules Engine

Find out about functionality, content management, and Expression and Action Types

Benefit from extensive code tutorials

Thomas Albrecht, Carsten Ziegler et al.

## BRFplus – Business Rule Management for ABAP Applications

In modern architectures, business rules are modeled and maintained in central engines. But how can you modify existing rules or develop your own? How can these rules be integrated into the applications? BRFplus is the tool of choice for developing business rules in ABAP.
This book introduces BRFplus in all its aspects. It explains the tool's architecture and how its rules are structured. You will learn how to modify and develop rules, how to incorporate them into your own landscape, and how to extend BRFplus. Including extensive examples and tutorials, this book is a one-stop resource for developers as well as business analysts.

approx. 320 pp., 69,95 Euro / US$ 69.95
ISBN 978-1-59229-293-6, Nov 2010

SAP PRESS